Extraordinary Circumstances

Extraordinary Circumstances

The Seven Days Battles

Brian K. Burton

Indiana University Press / Bloomington and Indianapolis

The book is a publication of

Indiana University Press
601 North Morton Street
Bloomington, Indiana 47404-3797 USA

www.iupress.indiana.edu

Telephone orders 800-842-6796
Fax orders 812-855-7931
Orders by e-mail iuporder@indiana.edu

First paperback edition 2011

∞ The paper used in this publicaiton meets the minimum requirements of the American National Standard for Information Sciences—Permanence of Paper for Printed Library Materials, ANSI Z39.48-1992.

Manufactured in the United States of America

The Library of Congress cataloged the original edition as follows:

Burton, Brian K., [date]
Extraordinary circumstances : the Seven Days Battles / Brian K. Burton.
p. cm.
Includes bibliographical references (p.) and index.
ISBN 0-253-33963-4 (alk. paper)
1. Seven Days' Battles, 1862. I. Title.
E473.68 .B87 2001
973.7'32—dc21

2001000532

ISBN 978-0-253-33963-8 (cl.) ISBN 978-0-253-22277-0 (pbk.)

2 3 4 5 6 16 15 14 13 12 11

CONTENTS

MAPS

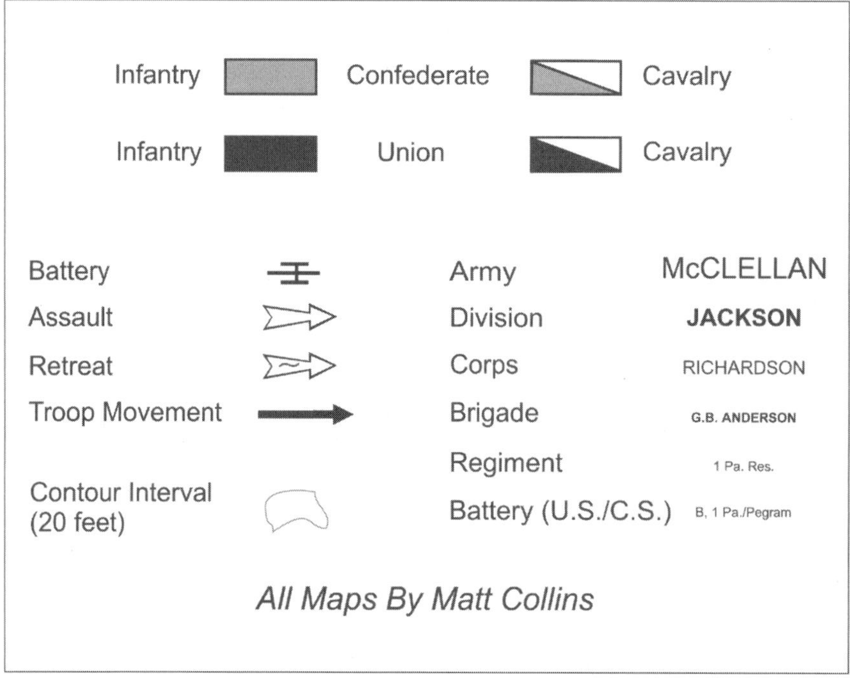
Infantry
Confederate
Cavalry
Infantry
Union
Cavalry
Battery
Assault
Retreat
Troop Movement
Contour Interval
(20 feet)
Army
McCLELLAN
Division
JACKSON
Corps
RICHARDSON
Brigade
G.B. ANDERSON
Regiment
1 Pa. Res.
Battery (U.S./C.S.)
B, 1 Pa./Pegram
All Maps By Matt Collins

ACKNOWLEDGMENTS

In 1984, WHEN I FIRST HAD the idea of writing what became *Extraordinary Circumstances*, I was a journalist and MBA student. Now, sixteen years later, I am an associate professor specializing in business ethics and the director of an MBA program. Obviously, much has changed in those sixteen years. One thing that has not changed, however, is my motivation for writing this book. I distinctly remember looking at a book that listed good studies of various Civil War campaigns and being astonished that none were listed for the Seven Days Battles. I had just finished J. F. C. Fuller's *Military History of the Western World*, in which the Seven Days were listed as one of the decisive campaigns in Western history. How could such an important campaign have lacked story-tellers? I resolved to tell the story.

This book is the product of that resolution. However, its style has changed over the years. At the beginning I was influenced by such general histories as Fuller's and Kenneth P. Williams's *Lincoln Finds a General*, which focused on command decisions and critiques. In the process of writing the book, however, I read more campaign histories—in particular John J. Hennessy's *Return to Bull Run*. These books showed me that a true history of a campaign must include not only the command decisions and critiques I had focused on, but also the stories of the people those decisions affected: the soldiers themselves. So the story has changed to fit my new purpose.

Many people have crossed my path as I have worked on this story. Almost all of them have had a hand in this book in one way or another. To tell how would be to write an autobiography, not a brief acknowledgments section. Many people who deserve inclusion here will thus be left unmentioned, but you know who you are, and I thank you.

Many others must be mentioned because their contributions have been substantial. Of my professional colleagues, Harvey C. Bunke and W. Harvey Hegarty, my mentors, have given great encouragement in many ways. David McCalman and Jonathan Johnson, my fellow doctoral students at Indiana University, pushed me to work on the manuscript. Dr. McCalman read and commented on drafts of the earlier chapters. Peter Haug, Mark Springer, and Bruce Wonder in Western Washington University's Department of Management have supported this endeavor for the last five years, Peter and Mark as fellow members of the department's military history section. Peter, whose interest in the Seven Days is as keen as mine, made many helpful comments and accompanied me on my last prepublication trip to Richmond.

The librarians, archivists, and members of the Civil War community I have met in the course of my research have been unfailingly helpful and encouraging. I wish I had space to list all the people in various libraries around the country who worked to fulfill my wishes, many of which probably seemed excessive. I must mention Dr. Richard Sommers, David Keough, and Pamela Cheney at the U.S. Army Military History Institute at Carlisle Barracks, Pennsylvania. My two weeks spent there were very enjoyable because of their help. The encouragement I received from Dr. Sommers was particularly helpful. Also of great help was Donald C. Pfanz at the Fredericksburg and Spotsylvania National Military Park, who graciously helped with some last-minute long-distance research.

Richard A. Sauers spent some of his precious time compiling a list of articles pertaining to the Seven Days from the *National Tribune*. Mark Davis, Vesta Lee Gordon, Helen Milliken, Kimberly Morris, Charlotte Ray, Anne Rodda, Jordan Ross, Robert N. Smith, Floyd Weatherbee Jr., Patti Woolery-Price, and Karan Zucal all helped gather material in places I could not reach easily from Ferndale, Washington. Stephanie Yuhl, now at Valparaiso University, was particularly diligent in finding material I would have overlooked. Agnes Gish was a godsend, especially in her willingness to travel from Richmond to Fredericksburg on a moment's notice. David Lambert was very helpful in finding material in the Boston area. Ronald L. Waddell spent more time, I am sure, than he desired in copying material from rare books in the U.S. Army Military History Institute's library.

At Richmond National Military Park, Michael Andrus conducted me around the battlefields on a rainy afternoon in 1990, when this book was little more than a pipe dream and some pages. Robert E. L. Krick is an acquaintance of more recent vintage, but his help in pinpointing sites and maps and his overall interest in the project have been greatly appreciated.

Members of the Indiana University Press staff have been very helpful and encouraging ever since I submitted an early draft of the manuscript. Collectively they have shown patience regarding my inability to meet self-imposed deadlines and support for the idea of this book. They and the reviewers of earlier drafts have made many helpful suggestions that allow the final product to be much better than it would have been.

Dale Wilson, a freelance copy editor contracted by the press, has made substantial contributions. He has taken a manuscript written over fifteen years in various styles and turned it into something consistent. At the same time, he has made many valuable substantive suggestions and caught many errors in the manuscript. Any that remain, of course, are my responsibility.

Matt Collins, the cartographer for this project, put up with my predilections as well as those of others who examined his handiwork. We were able to work closely together and still become friends, something that is not always possible. The maps are the result of his labors, but any problems with them remain my responsibility.

On a more personal level, several people deserve more thanks than I can give them. Without Anna Poiree, this book never would have seen the light of day. Her willingness to spend two days a week for two summers watching a toddler so that the toddler's father could sequester himself in his den and work was worth more than I can say. My family has been very supportive, although I am sure some of them wondered why I was doing this. My mother, Kathryn Burton, sister Lynne, and grandmother Georgia have given me great encouragement, particularly when the project seemed overwhelming (as it often has in the last three years). My father, Joseph Burton, started my interest in the Civil War more than thirty-five years ago. He then took two trips with me to Richmond to walk the ground. More recently, he read the entire manuscript twice and caught many mistakes. Those that are left are my fault, not his. His interest and encouragement have been of incalculable value.

Two people stand out above the others. One cannot even read these words yet. My son Andrew was born four days before I received Indiana University Press's letter expressing interest in the manuscript, and he has been with me for all the pain and pleasure of making the book into what it is now. His presence has been inspirational, and his smile has helped keep me going. I hope that when he is old enough to read this he will enjoy it.

The other is my wife, Lori. This book and our relationship began at about the same time, and I am very happy that the book project is coming to a close and our relationship is continuing. Lori does not have a great interest in the Civil War herself, and the battlefield trips have been trying for her, but she never let me drop the project, even when it seemed the best thing to do. Her support, her encouragement, but most of all her love have seen me through these sixteen years, and because of that this book is lovingly dedicated to her.

BRIAN K. BURTON
Ferndale, Washington
September, 2000

Extraordinary Circumstances

CHAPTER ONE

"The Nation Has Been Making Progress"

In May of 1862, the Civil War was just over a year old. The North was closing in on victory; on almost every front the Federals had an advantage over the Confederates. The first four months of 1862 in the western theater had been decisive ones. Brigadier General George H. Thomas had turned away a Confederate invasion of Kentucky at Mill Springs in January. In early February Brig. Gen. Ulysses S. Grant took Fort Henry on the Tennessee River and Fort Donelson on the Cumberland River, opening both vital arteries to the Union. Nashville was taken soon after. Marching down the Tennessee, Grant had stopped at Pittsburg Landing in southern Tennessee, where Confederates under Gen. Albert Sidney Johnston attacked him in early April. But Johnston was killed, and Grant, reinforced by Brig. Gen. Don Carlos Buell, repulsed the rebels, forcing them to retreat to Corinth, Mississippi. Major General Henry W. Halleck, the overall Union commander in the western theater, then combined Grant's and Buell's forces to move on Corinth, a strategic rail center.

The Mississippi River divided the Confederacy, and its importance to Midwest business and agriculture as well as its strategic importance demanded Federal attention. In late February Brig. Gen. John Pope advanced against New Madrid, Missouri, located on the river. By early April—actually, on the same day as the conclusion of the battle of Pittsburg Landing (also known as Shiloh)—Pope had taken both New Madrid and Island No. 10. This dual success opened the river to Yankee navigation nearly to Memphis. Moving inland from the south, Rear Adm. David G. Farragut ran his ships past the forts guarding the river's mouth and forced the surrender of New Orleans in late April.

The city was occupied by troops under Maj. Gen. Benjamin F. Butler. Fort Pillow, north of Memphis, and Vicksburg, Mississippi, where high bluffs contained rebel cannon, were the only real obstacles keeping the Yankees from regaining complete control of the river.

If the North controlled the Mississippi, the Confederate states of Arkansas, Louisiana, and Texas would be isolated from the rest of the South, and Missouri would be securely in the Union. The Yankees also had success in that theater. The battle of Pea Ridge, or Elkhorn Tavern, fought in northwest Arkansas in March, gave the North control of Missouri for the moment and opened Arkansas and Texas to invasion. In the Southwest, an engagement at Glorieta, in the New Mexico Territory, ended a Southern invasion.

Along the Gulf Coast, several harbors that could shelter ships attempting to pass through the Yankee blockade had been captured. Included were (besides New Orleans) Pensacola and Apalachicola, Florida. On Florida's Atlantic coast, Saint Augustine and Jacksonville had fallen. Fort Pulaski, a supposedly impregnable work guarding the harbor at Savannah, Georgia, was taken by Brig. Gen. Quincy A. Gillmore on April 11—one day shy of the first anniversary of the firing on Fort Sumter. The forts at Port Royal, South Carolina, had fallen the previous November. Brigadier General Ambrose E. Burnside took Roanoke Island, at the northern end of North Carolina's Outer Banks, in February and New Bern, on the mainland behind the Outer Banks, in March. When Fort Macon at the southern end of the Outer Banks fell in April the Northerners had complete control of the Outer Banks.

A ray of hope for the Southerners came from the Shenandoah Valley in Virginia. Major General Thomas J. "Stonewall" Jackson attacked a Federal force at Kernstown in March. The battle did not go Jackson's way, but it got the Northerners' attention. He aimed to keep that attention and won a battle at McDowell in early May. The Union forces in the Valley were scattered, and Jackson moved toward each in turn, winning two more engagements in late May. President Abraham Lincoln then attempted to concentrate his forces there and deal Jackson's relatively small command a death blow.[1]

The worst news for the Confederates came in the East, which most people considered the war's most important theater. The main Union army, the Army of the Potomac, had landed in Virginia and was moving inexorably up the Peninsula between the York and James Rivers—a strip of land that aimed straight at Richmond, the Confederate capital. The advance had been slow in coming. Major General George B. McClellan, brought from western Virginia to Washington after the debacle at Bull Run in July 1861, had drilled the raw soldiers into a well-disciplined army. McClellan was born in Philadelphia on December 3, 1826. His parents took advantage of the educational advantages that city offered, and he attended the University of Pennsylvania before entering West Point at age sixteen. He graduated from the academy in 1846 ranked second in his class and joined the Corps of Engineers. He was not yet twenty years old when he went to Mexico as a member of Maj. Gen. Winfield Scott's staff. McClellan was recognized for gallantry in the ensuing campaign.

After the war, McClellan taught at West Point, supervised the construction of a fort, and served in various parts of the country. In 1855 he and two other officers traveled to Europe to observe the Crimean War. McClellan visited many European military facilities and on his return wrote a report entitled *Armies of Europe*. He also designed a saddle that the army promptly adopted. It was the last saddle the army approved. McClellan resigned his commission in 1857 and became the chief engineer of the Illinois Central Railroad. He then switched to the new Ohio and Mississippi Railroad, where he became vice president and then president of the company. In 1860 he married Ellen Marcy, the daughter of Randolph B. Marcy.

When civil war broke out, McClellan offered his services to the Union. By May 4, 1861, he was a major general in command of the Department of Ohio. He crossed the Ohio River in late May, and in June troops under his overall command defeated Confederates at several places in western Virginia. McClellan had a small part in these successes, most of the credit belonging to Brig. Gen. William S. Rosecrans. Nevertheless, McClellan's troops had won the first Federal victory, and he was a hero in the eyes of the people. He was the natural choice to restore order to the Army of the Potomac after Bull Run.[2]

His accomplishment in restoring order should not be diminished. Soldiers in the Civil War based much of their behavior on their generals. McClellan won the admiration, almost the reverence of his men; soldier after soldier praised "Little Mac," as they adoringly called him. One, Alfred N. Ayres of the 72nd New York, said, "The Army of the Potomac almost worship their General." Another, George Kenney of the 71st Pennsylvania, wrote, "He is beloved by his army as ever Washington was." McClellan succeeded even beyond expectations in the task, becoming general in chief of all the Union armies in the process.

But the North wanted action, and "On to Richmond" was the cry. Through a combination of circumstances, McClellan had not moved south by early February 1862, so Lincoln ordered all Union armies to advance on Washington's birthday. In response, McClellan revealed his plan to land at Urbanna, located on the Rappahannock River near where that watercourse empties into the Potomac. This move would flank the Confederate lines at Manassas Junction, the site of the Bull Run battle, which McClellan considered too strong to attack.

Early in March, before McClellan could move, Gen. Joseph E. Johnston pulled his rebel army back from those fortified lines to behind the Rappahannock. This move made a landing at Urbanna useless. Any force landing there still would be more distant from Richmond than Johnston in his new lines—

exactly what the Urbanna operation was designed to prevent. McClellan decided to shift the landing from Urbanna to the Peninsula. Like the Urbanna plan, it was good strategy. Both rivers, especially the James, would make good supply lines, and the Peninsula was anchored by Fort Monroe, a strong fortress.

At about the same time as Johnston's withdrawal from Manassas, the Confederates unveiled the CSS *Virginia,* a type of ship the Americas had never seen. Built on the hull of the scuttled Federal ship *Merrimack,* but with iron covering it above the waterline, the *Virginia* decimated the Northern blockading force at Hampton Roads on March 8. Nothing built of wood could stand a face-to-face fight with the ironclad, so it was able to prevent Union transports and supply ships from entering the James and York Rivers. Fortunately for both McClellan and the Union navy, another iron ship the likes of which no one had ever seen showed up the evening of the *Virginia's* triumph. This vessel, the USS *Monitor,* was even stranger than its Southern counterpart—and just as invulnerable. The epic battle of the ironclads the next day showed the *Virginia* could be neutralized, and by April 1 McClellan was at Fort Monroe.

Not all of his army was with him, however. When Lincoln agreed to the Peninsula plan he ordered McClellan to leave Washington adequately protected. McClellan and his corps commanders met in council and decided a force of about fifty-five thousand men would be sufficient for that purpose. However, in reaching that number, McClellan counted the forces in the Shenandoah Valley opposing Jackson, as well as new regiments still in Pennsylvania. Besides that, he double counted the force defending Washington, which had no field artillery and thus was of little fighting value. Whether or not Lincoln's stipulation was good military judgment, McClellan did not comply with it. When the adjutant general, Brig. Gen. Lorenzo Thomas, and Maj. Gen. Ethan A. Hitchcock, Lincoln's military adviser, confirmed that judgment, the president ordered one of McClellan's corps to remain near Washington to achieve the required number of defenders. The corps most easily detained was Maj. Gen. Irvin McDowell's I Corps, the second largest in the army at thirty-three thousand effectives. McClellan also lost the title of general in chief. On March 11 Lincoln relieved McClellan of those duties because he had "personally taken the field at the head of the Army of the Potomac." McClellan, who had avoided Lincoln's messenger, former Ohio governor William Dennison, learned of the move when he read about it in a newspaper report. Lincoln then took steps to assure Little Mac of his trust and promised McClellan command of the Army of the Potomac, easing some of the tension between the two men.

McClellan got to the Peninsula before Johnston. The Confederate commander there, Maj. Gen. John B. Magruder, had fewer than twenty thousand men, but the fortifications near Yorktown were strong, and he marched and countermarched his men to make the force seem larger. Plagued by terrible weather throughout April, and convinced that the rebel force was far stronger

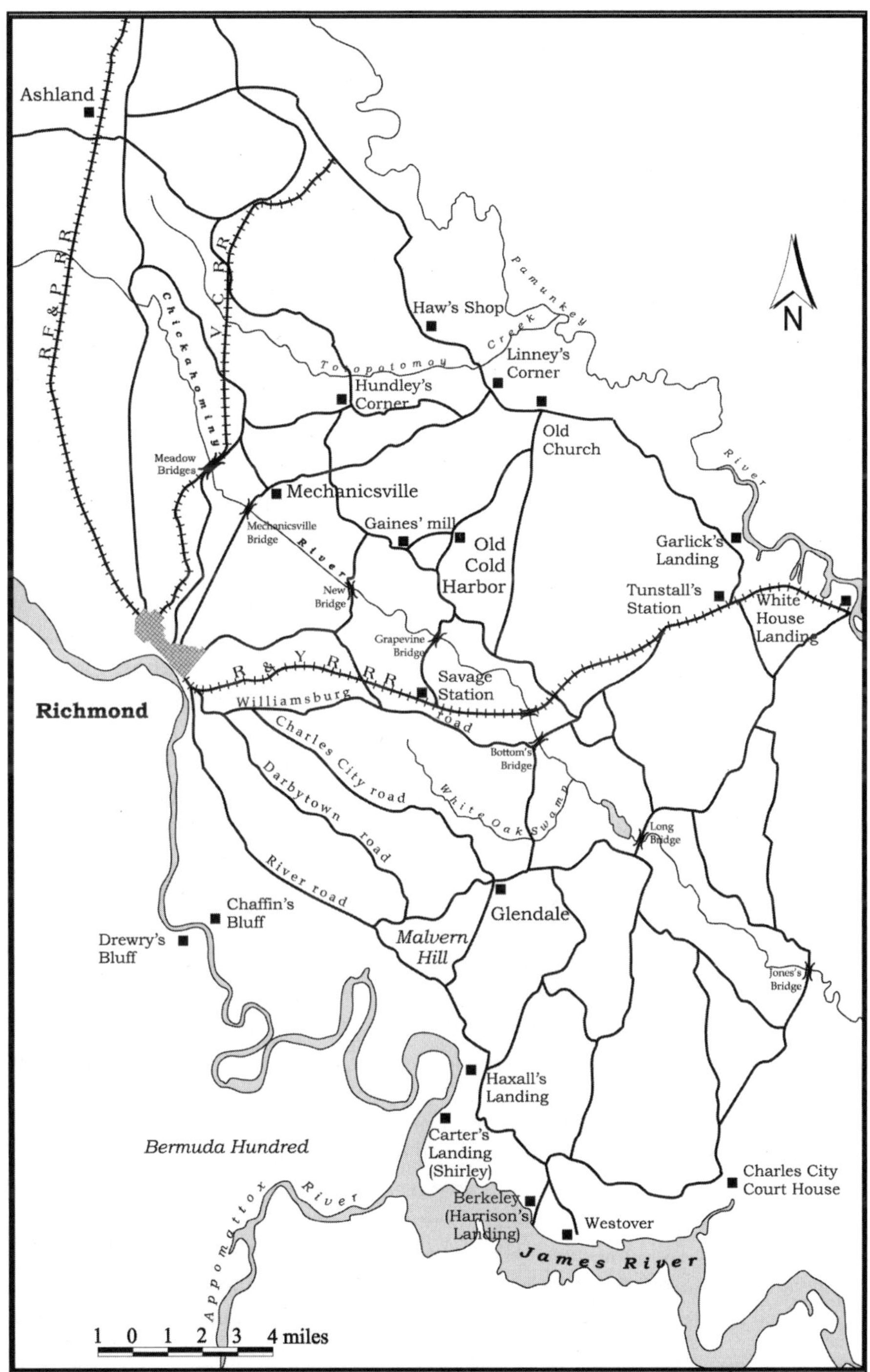

The area of the Seven Days campaign

than it really was, McClellan settled down opposite Magruder's trenches into a siege that lasted a month. It was a situation that prompted Johnston to tell Gen. Robert E. Lee, Confederate president Jefferson Davis's military adviser, "No one but McClellan could have hesitated to attack." McClellan was ready to attack by the first week of May, but Johnston pulled back the night before the scheduled Union assault, leaving a detachment to fight a rear-guard action at Williamsburg. A few days later the Southerners abandoned Norfolk, and the *Virginia* was destroyed so the Federals would not capture it. By the middle of May, with improving weather, the rebel army had backed up about as far as it could go, to the settlements just east and southeast of Richmond.[3]

The cascade of bad news in the first half of 1862 depressed many Southerners. The news from Shiloh had been "dispiriting and saddening," one visitor remembered. Albert Sidney Johnston's death saddened even those who saw the battle as glorious. The fall of Island No. 10 was "a terrible blow," a Richmond lady noted. Then came the loss of New Orleans, which the same lady called "as unexpected as mortifying and discouraging." It caused a lack of confidence in the government, and no one talked of anything else in early May.

The talk quickly turned to events closer to home after Yorktown and Norfolk were abandoned and the *Virginia* was destroyed. These blows were felt strongly, capping a month of reverses. The Richmond townspeople's spirits, which had risen on seeing Johnston's army march through on its way to Yorktown, sank again. Confederate cavalry colonel Williams Wickham wrote to Confederate congressman William C. Rives: "Our unhappy country appears to be completely ruined. I was in Richmond yesterday & it is almost the universal opinion that the city will be in possession of the Yankees in a few days." Another of Rives's correspondents called the *Virginia*'s destruction "a cruel and disgraceful suicide." A Richmond tavern keeper remembered the residents' attending church every night to pray for the city's deliverance. John B. Jones, a clerk in the War Department, noted in his diary on May 9, "No one, scarcely, supposes that Richmond will be defended." Confederate secretary of war Stephen R. Mallory wrote in his journal, "The hour is dark & gloomy for our beloved South."

The Confederate Congress and President Davis did not help that attitude. Congress adjourned hastily and left Richmond in late April, sent on its way with scorn but leaving the city in despair. Davis sent his family to Raleigh on May 10, perhaps revealing his judgment that Richmond soon would be under attack. Many Richmonders followed these examples, and those who stayed kept their trunks packed. Business was suspended, and some bankers refused deposits while preparing for departure. Rural residents entered the city hoping for protection.

Many politicians and newspaper editors blamed Davis for these events, although others came to his defense. Some called for more action, but Davis already had stretched the Confederate theory of limited government by suspending the writ of habeas corpus and instituting conscription. Others, such as Southern radical Edmund Ruffin, thought Davis unequal to the current crisis. Some were willing to credit Davis for the effort the South had put forth, even as they criticized politicians in general. But the public worried more about the Unionists than Davis's actions and wanted assurance that Richmond would not be left to the Yankees. That desire was incorporated into a resolution by the Virginia legislature.[4]

Despite their gloom, Richmond's citizens were determined to defend their city. The "wonderful composure" noted by one correspondent might have stemmed from the people's collective decision to see the city destroyed rather than surrendered. Ruffin, himself despondent but determined to see the struggle through, saw no public display of depression. Instead, the people were ready to sacrifice all. They were prepared to put the town to the torch. "Better death than subjugation," wrote one man.

Spirits rose after May 15, when the Southern determination and ability to defend Richmond was tested for the first time. Union gunboats, including the *Monitor*, attacked the newly constructed Confederate artillery position at Drewry's Bluff. This position, high above the south bank of the James River, was in some ways the key to Richmond. If it fell, the Northern navy could steam all the way to the Southern capital, and the city would be in serious jeopardy. Farmers, seeing the warships, ran into Richmond with the news that the Yankees would arrive in a few hours. Richmond civilians heard the sound of guns for the first time in the war, and excitement and anticipation were the prevailing emotions. But the rebel gunners, including some from the *Virginia*, repulsed the gunboats, and all of Richmond reacted joyfully or with "wordless thankfulness." Breaths came easily for the first time in a while, and more normal activities resumed.

Even before Drewry's Bluff, some saw what most did not. Virginia politician James A. Seddon wrote on May 10, "The last month or two has been a period of many reverses and great gloom in our public affairs, but gleams of light and hope are already streaking the Horizon and give augury of a glorious day of Triumph to ensue."[5]

Meanwhile, the Confederate army retreated even farther. After stopping east of the Chickahominy River on May 9, Johnston resumed his westward movement on the fifteenth so as to be in position to defend the city against attack from the south as well as the west. By the seventeenth the army was in position west of the Chickahominy just a few miles from Richmond. This, along with the rest of the news in the spring, caused attitudes in the North to be upbeat, even joyous. Every success increased hope of an early end to the conflict. The war was progressing well, and the seceding states might be brought quickly back into the fold. After all, by early May the Yankees had retaken two state capitals, the South's largest city, fifty thousand square miles of land, and captured thirty thousand Confederate soldiers. New York lawyer George Templeton Strong wrote in his diary after hearing of the fall of New Orleans, "The nation has been making progress." Later in May he recorded the city's rejoicing at the news that the *Virginia* had been destroyed and Norfolk taken.

This sense of optimism manifested itself in at least two actions. Lincoln's secretary of state, William H. Seward, had imprisoned many people he suspected of disloyalty. But by the spring of 1862 Lincoln and his new secretary of war, Edwin M. Stanton, decided, unlike Davis, that most of these political prisoners could be released. Stanton also ordered all recruiting offices closed in early April, at least partially because they were inefficient but also because they might not be needed.

Lincoln had framed Federal war aims in terms of preserving the Union. He made no public pronouncements linking the war with the end of slavery, the institution whose existence in the South had been a major cause of the conflict. Lincoln knew that as long as the war's primary goal was to restore the Union he would have overwhelming support in the North. Including the abolition of slavery as a war aim would substantially lessen that support. It now looked as though the war could be won and the states reunited without slavery being an issue. Perhaps then the South would listen to reason and not demand the right to expand slavery into new territories. In exchange, the North would cease calling for the abolition of slavery where it already existed. Lincoln underlined his intent by revoking Maj. Gen. David Hunter's orders to free slaves in Union-controlled areas in Georgia, Florida, and South Carolina. He knew he could play what later generations would call the race card, but he wanted to keep control of that card for as long as he could.

Not everyone shared Lincoln's goal of restoring the Union above all. Many Republicans went beyond their party's stated platform by demanding the complete abolition of slavery. In their view, Lincoln was not prosecuting the war aggressively enough or making it the revolutionary experience they desired. Members of the Democratic Party, on the other hand, approved the limited goals Lincoln stated publicly but worried that he might—because of either his own inclination or pressure from his party—turn the war into just the revolutionary struggle the Republicans wanted. In the middle were the War Democrats, who wanted an aggressive war and had split from their Democratic brethren without completely joining the Republicans.

Lincoln shared with his Republican colleagues some dissatisfaction in the progress of the war; more notably, he worried about its outcome. In early May he responded to McClellan's request for Parrott guns, rifled artillery pieces with much greater range and accuracy than smoothbore cannons, by expressing fear that providing them might mean "indefinite procrastination" and asked Little Mac, "Is anything to be done?" When Lincoln telegraphed Halleck in early May to advise him of the good news along the James he added, "Be very sure to sustain no reverse in your Department." He was not ready to relax until he knew the Union would be restored.[6]

The war's progress also interested European countries, particularly Great Britain and France. In Great Britain, public sentiment favored the South. The upper classes were strongly pro-Confederate, and many in the working classes also hoped for Southern success. The economic impact of cotton was a factor among those working in the textile industry, but Britain also thought the Southern slaves would benefit from Confederate independence, as the Southern view that slaves were treated kindly had gained credence there. Much argument was made in the British and French press concerning mediation between the two sides, but Europeans did not understand that the North viewed their calls for mediation as support for the South. Mediation, Northerners thought, could accomplish nothing toward the restoration of the Union. George Templeton Strong wrote, "[I]t will be a weary while before England can be to us what she was a year ago."

The fall of New Orleans dismayed the British. In the South it was reported that Richard Bickerton Pemell, Lord Lyons, the British minister to the United States, had sailed to London to tell the government the South would soon succumb. But General Butler's proclamation that women in New Orleans who were disrespectful toward Union officers would be treated as common prostitutes turned many against the Yankees, eroding the goodwill Northern victories had gained. In both Britain and France the calls for mediation became louder, and some in the British press called the official policy of neutrality wrong. The British government, however, was not interested in mediating the dispute despite Parliament's strong pro-Southern leanings. Napoleon III of France was more inclined toward mediation but would not act alone. So the two powers stayed out of the fray, watching the military situation closely for an indication of the ultimate outcome.[7]

That military situation worsened for the South in late May as McClellan continued to pressure Richmond. Despite the destruction of the *Virginia*, McClellan based his army at White House, the home of one of Robert E. Lee's sons, on the Pamunkey, instead of the James. This was in part because McDowell's corps, now based in Fredericksburg about fifty miles north of Richmond, would soon be moving straight south by land to join McClellan. Lincoln had released McDowell's corps to rejoin the Army of the Potomac on May 17.

"The daily news from Richmond keeps us almost breathless with anxiety," wrote a North Carolina woman in her diary. But in Richmond itself, cheering news came from the Shenandoah and Stonewall Jackson. His moves in late

May scattered the Federal forces in the lower Valley. On May 24 Lincoln ordered McDowell to send twenty thousand men (two divisions) in an attempt to trap Jackson. McDowell's third division, under Brig. Gen. George A. McCall, stayed at Fredericksburg. None went to McClellan. When informed of this he responded: "Telegram of 4 p.m. received. I will make my calculations accordingly." Those calculations included an advance to the Richmond, Fredericksburg, and Potomac Railroad north of the Chickahominy River by Brig. Gen. Fitz John Porter's V Corps. They won an engagement at Hanover Court House along the way, then destroyed bridges and track before returning to their camps, also north of the Chickahominy.

The news from the Valley affected both North and South. On May 25 George Templeton Strong wrote, "These are critical hours." One day later, John B. Jones noted, "We are now so strong that no one fears the result when the great battle takes place." Edmund Ruffin, in Richmond at the time, saw the same sentiment throughout the city: "[A]ll of our army & citizens are eager for a general & fair battle." Meanwhile, Joseph Johnston was planning for that battle. He knew that McClellan's dispositions left the Federals vulnerable to an assault. To protect the White House base, and to ease the junction with McDowell, McClellan had just over half his army north of the Chickahominy River, the largest of a multitude of streams that cut the Peninsula into pieces. It could be crossed only at bridges by large armed forces. Johnston realized that both parts of the Union army were susceptible to attack, and heavy rain fell on seven days between May 20 and May 30, endangering the bridges. The rain was especially heavy on May 30, and Johnston attacked on May 31.

Unfortunately for Johnston, the same rains that had seemed to isolate the Union force on the south bank of the Chickahominy delayed his own troops. The Confederate staff was not up to the occasion, and some of the Confederate commanders (Maj. Gens. James Longstreet, Gustavus W. Smith, and Benjamin Huger) did not function well. Despite these problems, the rebels had initial success against elements of Brig. Gen. Erasmus D. Keyes's IV Corps. But Brig. Gen. Edwin V. Sumner pushed his II Corps across the Chickahominy just before the bridges failed, and the Union line stabilized with the help of units from Brig. Gen. Samuel P. Heintzelman's III Corps. June 1 saw more fighting but little change, and the battle of Seven Pines was over.

The North did not see this "grim fight" as a defeat. Lincoln thanked McClellan for the news that the Yankees had held their own. The South, on the other hand, saw it as a "glorious victory" yet wished for more results. The ladies of Richmond, having prepared before the battle, cared for the many wounded. Women of all ages toiled in the hospitals while the funerals continued day and night.

Of the more than eleven thousand casualties suffered in this battle, however, none was more important than Joe Johnston himself who, late on the thirty-first, was severely wounded by a shell fragment. Gustavus Smith took command of the army, but he was not the long-term solution. Jefferson Davis needed a general of high rank and stature to command the army defending the country's capital. Of the five full generals the Confederacy had commissioned in 1861, however, four were disqualified for one reason or another. Samuel Cooper, the adjutant general, was invaluable in his position. Joe Johnston could not resume command until he recovered from his wounds. Albert Sidney Johnston had been lost at Shiloh, and P. G. T. Beauregard was ill and out of favor with Davis. That left Robert E. Lee. Davis may have been unsure of Lee's capabilities as an army commander, though he had no doubts of Lee's brilliance as a military planner. Davis feared that Lee might possess an intellectual's hesitancy, leading to excessive caution, but he had no real choice and on June 1 appointed Lee to the post.[8]

Robert Lee was fifty-five years old in the summer of 1862. His father, Henry, the "Light Horse Harry" Lee of Revolutionary War fame, had been an excellent cavalry commander but a largely absentee father. His ancestors had held important positions in Virginia government for almost two hundred years, and two of his cousins signed the Declaration of Independence. His mother was Ann Hill Carter, of the famous Peninsula family.

Most of Lee's education came from his mother and the schools in Alexandria, where they lived. Robert learned of the greatness of his father's Revolutionary commander, George Washington. It was Henry who first uttered the phrase, "First in war, first in peace, and first in the hearts of his countrymen," about Washington. The Washington connection was enhanced by Lee's marriage to Mary Custis, the great-granddaughter of Martha Washington. He thus became guardian of the Washington tradition and the Custis estates.

Lee graduated with distinction from the United States Military Academy and joined the Corps of Engineers. When the Mexican War erupted in 1846 he joined Winfield Scott's headquarters staff. His performance in Mexico was so outstanding that Scott said Lee was the finest soldier he had ever seen in the field. During Scott's campaign from Veracruz to Mexico City Lee formed his rules of command and his strategic thoughts, based on observations of Scott's system. Also while in Mexico he was in the company of many other officers who would gain fame later, including George McClellan, Thomas Jackson, and Ulysses "Sam" Grant.

Service in Mexico was brief, and Lee came back to the United States recognized by his peers but not the country. He served as superintendent of West Point and then transferred to the cavalry on the western frontier. After a few years he asked for a desk job in Washington so he could repair his father-in-law's tangled affairs. When John Brown seized the arsenal at Harper's Ferry, Lee headed the troops who forced Brown to surrender.

Lee was not a fire-breathing Southern radical. Yet he thought secession was a right given to the states, and while he would not consciously fight for slavery, he would also not fight against what he considered to be his native land, Virginia. So when Abraham Lincoln, acting on Scott's recommendation, offered Lee the command of the chief Union army, Lee waited until Virginia decided what it would do. The day after Virginia seceded, Lee resigned his commission in the U.S. Army and accepted a commission from Virginia. Soon after that the Confederacy took over all Virginia troops, and Lee became a full general. He first commanded troops in West Virginia, then moved to South Carolina, failing in each case to accomplish much in positions from which accomplishing anything was close to impossible.

In March 1862, Jefferson Davis called Lee from South Carolina to be his military adviser, a man who could suggest but not direct. For most men this would have been an impossible assignment. Davis—a West Point graduate, a colonel in the Mexican War, and a former U.S. secretary of war—thought highly of his own military ability and firmly exercised his constitutional power as commander in chief. "[A]t the first tidings of the sound of a gun, anywhere within reach of Richmond, he was in the saddle and off for the spot," one Richmond woman said of Davis, who may have believed he would have to take command in the field himself.

Whatever Davis's opinion of Lee as a commander, he had respect for Lee as a man and as a military thinker. Lee thus became a sort of chief of staff, as well as a liaison between Davis and his army commanders, particularly Johnston. Lee also conceived and guided the execution of Jackson's Valley campaign. The moves, of course, were Jackson's, but the strategic concept, that of keeping reinforcements from the Union army on the Peninsula, was Lee's.[9]

Upon taking command at Richmond, Lee wrote to Charlotte, the wife of his son Col. William H. F. "Rooney" Lee, that he wished the task of commanding his new army had "fallen upon an abler man, or that I were able to drive our enemies back to their homes. I have no ambition and no desire but for the attainment of this object, and, therefore, only wish for its accomplishment by him that can do it most speedily and thoroughly." Others seconded Lee's wish for an abler man. One Southern woman wrote in her diary, "His nickname last summer was '*old-stick-in-the-mud*,'" and noted the accusation that Lee was the primary reason the Confederates had retreated to Richmond. Others saw Lee's appointment in a better light. John B. Jones called it "the harbinger of bright fortune." Stephen Mallory thought Lee inspired confidence, but said Joe Johnston in the field "would be worth ten thousand men to us." The consensus on Lee seemed to settle on his undoubted ability as a staff officer and untried nature as an army commander.

Lee first had to shape up his army, which had been named the Army of Northern Virginia. Johnston had left it with no small lack of either supplies or discipline. Lee improved the quartermaster's service, provided food and clothing, tightened discipline, and reduced favoritism. A Northern newspaper correspondent remarked at the time, "A more marked change for the better never was made in any body of men than that wrought in his army by the sensible actions of General Lee." He also reorganized his artillery reserve into five battalions; later in the month he placed artillery customarily attached to brigades under the command of divisional chiefs of artillery, who thus gained some control.[10]

Men in the Army of Northern Virginia, not knowing of the plan Lee had conceived, did not appreciate their new commander's ideas about keeping them busy. Digging ditches, they reasoned, was work for slaves, not whites, and they called Lee the "King of Spades" after what seemed to be his favorite weapon—they had not yet begun to call him "Marse Robert," which would become their favorite name for him. Lee noted: "Our people are opposed to work. Our troops officers community & press. All ridicule & resist it."

In part that was because the soldiers knew attack was necessary. For example, Thomas Pitts of the 3rd South Carolina wrote: "McClellan should not be allowed to entrench and make all his preparations for a decisive move while we lie quietly on our oars. He should be attacked before this can be done." But in part their grumbling came from a lack of confidence in Lee himself, mirroring that of the civilian population. One soldier, on learning that Lee had taken command, cried: "Beautiful state of affairs! This army after Johnston has gotten it in shape to whip the enemy, now to be given to a failure!" Another said, "No one can supply the place of Johnston." Others were willing to give Lee a chance, however. J. E. Whitehorne of the 12th Virginia wrote home, "I hope he will do better than Johnston," while Pitts expressed the belief that Lee would implement the policy Pitts advocated.[11]

McClellan had passed judgment on his fellow West Point engineer two months earlier. In a letter to Lincoln, Little Mac wrote, "I prefer Lee to Johnston—the former is *too* cautious & weak under grave responsibility—personally brave & energetic to a fault, he yet is wanting in moral firmness when pressed by heavy responsibility & is likely to be timid & irresolute in action." Meanwhile, others were passing judgment on McClellan. Radical Republicans had decided early that McClellan was not their man. They and their press allies gave McClellan little credit for anything and agitated for a change of commanders, thinking Little Mac too slow. McClellan had reorganized his army from four corps to six and put two of his favorite subordinates, Fitz John Porter and Brig. Gen. William B. Franklin, in command of the new corps. Republicans raised such a protest that Lincoln felt compelled to ask whether McClellan felt "strong enough, even with my help" to prevail over the politicians.

Other Northerners besides Radical Republicans wanted military movement, so many were dissatisfied with McClellan. George Templeton Strong noted twice in the first two weeks of June that people were grumbling about McClellan's lack of action. But Little Mac did have his defenders, both in the press and among the public. Some, such as Strong, thought him hamstrung by intrigue in Washington, and Democrats who worried that freeing the slaves would become a war aim supported McClellan, who was a proponent of limited war aims.

Lincoln was among those becoming frustrated with McClellan. At one point during the crisis caused by Jackson's Valley campaign, the president wrote Little Mac, "I think the time is near when you must either attack Richmond or give up the job and come to the defence of Washington." But he had not quite given up on McClellan, either, and he continued to respond with moderation to McClellan's complaints and requests. This attitude probably was part of the reason antislavery politicians thought Lincoln also was too slow.[12]

McClellan, though perhaps slow, did plan to move forward. The weather, however, frustrated those plans. He once said he would move as soon as the weather and ground permitted. On another occasion he promised to fight as soon as Providence approved. It rained five of the first six days of June, however—nine inches according to one measurement—ruining the roads even further after the heavy rains in late May. The Chickahominy normally was fordable (at least for infantry) almost everywhere, being less than 20 feet wide and only a few feet deep. Yet it was fringed with underbrush and trees and surrounded by bottomland up to a mile wide that flooded easily. Lee wrote to Davis on June 5, "You have seen nothing like the roads on the Chick—y bottom." Brigadier General William Nelson Pendleton, Lee's artillery chief, wrote his daughter on June 6: "More water on the earth I have hardly ever seen than now. . . . Horses and riders are often in danger of becoming involved in some slough beyond extraction in the field and swamps all around the city. . . . Artillery is with difficulty moved at all, and by no possibility can it be manoeuvered to any extent on a battle-field anywhere near." By June 7 McClellan had reported to Washington that the entire Chickahominy flood plain held between three and four feet of water. On June 8 Col. William Averell of the 3rd Pennsylvania Cavalry told his father that a four-mule team had drowned on a major road.

It rained only a couple of days more in the two weeks after June 6, but it took time for the dirt roads to dry. Brigadier General John G. Barnard, the Army of the Potomac's chief engineer, wrote that by June 20 artillery could operate easily, although corduroy roads of logs had to be laid half a mile on either side of the river to allow the guns to cross the bottomland. About that time, McClellan began making moves preparatory to an attack. Apparently Providence was getting ready to cooperate. McClellan may have told Lincoln and Stanton what they wanted to hear, but his messages to his wife are quite similar.[13]

In planning an attack, McClellan had one major obstacle to overcome—Lee's army. And he had magnified that obstacle beyond reason. His intelligence chief, Allan Pinkerton, was and would continue to be a good detective, but he seemed to have a problem with military intelligence. His reports consistently credited the Confederacy with having a force that, when considered logically, it simply could not have had. As one writer put it, "Language is scarcely strong enough to condemn in appropriate terms the inefficient administration of the service of information whereby so gross a miscalculation should have been evolved, and especially since the two armies, with the exception of Jackson's corps, had been within close contact for more than a month." By June 26 Pinkerton estimated the Army of Northern Virginia's strength at 180,000. He reported that the rebels had thirty-nine more infantry regiments, two more cavalry regiments, thirty-three more artillery batteries and battalions, and seven more units of other types than Lee listed in his official order of battle. Uriah H. Painter, a correspondent for the *Philadelphia Inquirer*, estimated the Confederate force at about 100,000, of whom 20,000 to 30,000 were raw and undisciplined—an estimate close to the actual figure of about 90,000 effectives. Painter based his estimate on discussions with prisoners, contrabands, and deserters, as well as an examination of muster rolls. All of these sources of information were available to Pinkerton, yet his estimates were almost double those of the newspaper reporter.

There are several possible explanations for Pinkerton's colossal errors in reporting. Perhaps he was in awe of McClellan, and, knowing that Little Mac was reporting exaggerated figures to Washington, instructed his agents to render reports that would support McClellan's numbers. Or McClellan could have deliberately altered the numbers on both sides to strengthen his argument that he needed reinforcements.[14]

As for the first possibility, Pinkerton's early May estimate of the Confederate army at Yorktown was extremely accurate in terms of the number of regiments, brigades, and other units present. However, earlier estimates and his June 26 estimate were far off the mark. Thus, if he had instructed his men to report information that would support McClellan, his men followed those instructions only sporadically. As for the second possibility, it would be easy for McClellan to alter the strengths. Many types of numbers can be used to measure the size of an army, and McClellan used several of them. For instance, his June 20 report showed that just slightly fewer than 146,000 men should have been with the Army of the Potomac. But the total number present for duty and properly equipped was only 114,691, of whom about 16,000 were noncombatants or stationed at other locations. McClellan was missing about 40,000 men, or about 28 percent of his paper strength, and had only about 98,000 frontline soldiers on June 20. Because some of those soldiers would not fight in a battle, the Unionists' effective fighting strength was about 91,000 men on June 20.

Many of the 40,000 missing were ill. More than 12,000 men were reported to be either sick or under arrest, and the vast majority of them probably were sick. Some of the more than 29,000 reported absent in that report undoubtedly also were sick. James Lee Graham, a steward in the division hospital from the 62nd Pennsylvania, thought 25 percent of the army was sick on June 16. Brigadier General Philip Kearny, who commanded a division in the Union III Corps, believed the army was losing 1,500 men a day through sickness and picket fighting (of which there was relatively little). William C. Wiley of the 70th New York put it this way: "If General McClellan does not hurry up the heat and water will so use up his Army that he will have no one to do the fighting."[15]

But Little Mac was not reporting estimates of Confederate numbers in the same way he reported his own. He either innocently reported the numbers Pinkerton gave him or knowingly inflated Pinkerton's numbers by considering them to be the rebels' effective strength and adding a certain percentage to reach a paper strength. For instance, knowing the incidence of sickness in his own army, McClellan could have used a similar percentage for the Confederate army and added an amount to account for those men. In fact, there was sickness in the Army of Northern Virginia, as David Winn of the 4th Georgia noted, much of it caused by drinking fouled water. Major General Daniel Harvey Hill said that 30,000 were missing from the army. But he intimated that these were not sick but dodgers.

To arrive at Pinkerton's estimate of 180,000, however, we must add much more, almost 100 percent to the Southerners' true effective strength and 15 percent to the highest non-Pinkerton estimate of Confederate numbers.[16] Almost 100 percent over actual figures is a common figure with the reports submitted by Pinkerton and credited by McClellan. Even in October 1861 the Union estimate of Confederate strength was close to double the actual strength.

One officer in the Army of the Potomac wrote that the detective's reports were "the principal cause of the failure of as pure a man and as popular a soldier as the century had seen." But the responsibility for the overestimates belongs to McClellan. The first substantial overestimate of Confederate numbers occurred in early August 1861 and was McClellan's alone. Pinkerton's first strength report, while an overestimate, was not as high as McClellan's, and Little Mac then told Pinkerton to make his estimates high. McClellan had other estimates, but he chose to report higher numbers. Moreover, as Pinkerton improved his estimates of the number of rebel regiments—to the point where he was only 20 percent or so off—he stopped using regiments to estimate strength and instead resorted to irrational methods.

The best analysis is that McClellan believed his own numbers, there was no attempt to deceive people in Washington, and Pinkerton was sycophantic enough to change his method to fit McClellan's estimates. If this analysis is correct, it is hard not to criticize McClellan for what seems to be an obvious overestimation. Walter Taylor, one of Lee's aides, noted that McClellan's knowledge of Joe Johnston and his contact with the Confederates during the move up the Peninsula should have given him enough information to doubt Pinkerton. Also, one has to wonder how McClellan could have envisioned success given these odds.[17] Nevertheless, he did envision success, and he seems to have believed the reports. Their content dictated caution.

Lee's situation, on the other hand, dictated action. He did not have much time. McClellan, though slow, was moving toward his objective. He was almost close enough to Richmond to lay siege to the capital. That was a no-win scenario for the Confederates. Lee needed to devise a plan to avoid a siege and move McClellan away from the city, giving himself room to maneuver and forcing the Yankees into the open where Lee might be able not only to gain a victory but also to annihilate the enemy.

D. H. Hill, at the head of one of Lee's divisions, was not sure the new army commander was up to the task. "General Lee is so slow and cautious," he wrote his wife in mid-June. One of Jefferson Davis's staff officers, Col. Joseph C. Ives, had a different read on the man. To a question from Lt. Col. E. Porter Alexander, the army's ordnance chief, Ives answered: "Alexander, if there is one man in either army, Confederate or Federal, head and shoulders above every other in audacity, it is General Lee! His name might be Audacity." Lee's plan was strong evidence for Ives's view. He instructed Maj. Walter H. Stevens, the army's chief engineer, to dig trenches and construct earthworks around Richmond until just a few troops could stop an attack by many opponents. Once those defensive positions were complete, Lee would attack with as many men as could be spared. Lee wrote to Jefferson Davis shortly after taking command that his opponent would "make this a battle of Posts. He will take position from position, under cover of heavy guns, & we cannot get at him without storming his works, which with our new troops is extremely hazardous." An aide remembered Lee saying, "If we leave this line because they can shell us, we shall have to leave the next for the same reason, and I don't see how we can stop this side of Richmond."[18]

Lee also would reinforce his army. He would do it at the last minute and with the most famous soldiers in the Confederacy: Stonewall Jackson and his Valley army, bringing his total force to about equal with McClellan's ninety-one thousand effectives. Jefferson Davis and Lee had formed a plan before Seven Pines that called for Maj. Gen. Ambrose P. Hill's division to turn the Union right flank. Lee held a council of war on June 3, and after the council was over Davis headed toward the front. Lee caught up with president and asked for his advice. Davis suggested using the same plan they had earlier discussed, but instead bring Jackson from the Valley to hit the Union right rather than use Hill.

On June 6, even before the Valley campaign ended gloriously at Cross Keys and Port Republic, Lee asked Jackson where reinforcements would best be sent. Lee's intent probably was to allow Jackson to invade the north, but his note crossed with one from Jackson that reinforced Davis's ideas. On the eighth, Lee told Jackson to be ready to come to Richmond. Less than a week later, on June 11, Maj. Gen. William H. C. Whiting took brigades commanded by Brig. Gen. John B. Hood and Col. Evander M. Law toward the Valley, and Brig. Gen. Alexander R. Lawton's brigade of Georgians also headed that way. The men marched through Richmond with flags waving and bands playing. They were instructed to talk about a northward movement so Union spies could hear of it and pass the information along. Whiting carried orders instructing Jackson to send his best units to Richmond as quickly as possible to assist in the attack. Lee told Jackson to "move rapidly to Ashland . . . and sweep down between the Chickahominy and Pamunkey, cutting up the enemy's communications, &c., while this army attacks General McClellan in front."[19]

Before Lee wrote Jackson, however, he made plans to find the exact situation on the Federal right. On June 10 he sat down with a young man he knew well. Just twenty-nine years old, James Ewell Brown Stuart was, like Lee, a Virginian and a West Point graduate. Stuart, known as "Jeb," had spent most of his military service with the cavalry on the frontier. While there he invented a device that would secure a cavalryman's saber to his belt and brought it back east to show the War Department. While Stuart was in Washington, John Brown attacked the Federal arsenal at Harper's Ferry. Lee, given the task of capturing Brown, chose Stuart as an aide. It was not the first time the two had met: Lee had been superintendent at West Point when Stuart was a cadet. Stuart followed his state into the Confederacy and rose rapidly in rank. He was a colonel in the cavalry before First Manassas, and a brigadier general after that battle.

Lee told Stuart, who commanded all of the Army of Northern Virginia's cavalry forces, to lead most of his men in a raid north of the Chickahominy to get information on McClellan's right flank and the road network between the Chickahominy and Pamunkey Rivers. Stuart told Lee he could ride all the way around McClellan's army and return safely. Lee, a gambler but no showman, wrote detailed instructions to his young subordinate the next day that included the phrase, "[B]e content to accomplish all the good you can without feeling it necessary to obtain all that might be desired."

Stuart secretly picked twelve hundred men for his expedition, including Lee's son Rooney (who owned the home McClellan was using for his base) and nephew Fitzhugh. He visited Edmund Ruffin in Richmond to procure a guide, as one of Ruffin's farms was in the area. Then, on June 12, Jeb roused his staff at 2 A.M. with the announcement, "Gentlemen, in ten minutes every man must be in his saddle!" That first day Stuart tried to make his ride look like a trip to reinforce Jackson, heading north and camping on the South Anna River twenty-two miles above Richmond. According to one trooper, little occurred during the day. That night, however, Stuart narrowly missed capture at the nearby home of Col. Williams Wickham, who was recuperating from a wound.

By the next day the entire command knew what it was up to. John Mosby, a member of Stuart's staff, figured it out when Stuart asked him to go to Hanover Court House with a few men. Hanover was east of their current location, and nobody going to Jackson would care much about it. But Mosby had scouted the area for Stuart earlier and knew it was in the rear of the Union forces, parallel to the Pamunkey. Mosby found a few Yankee cavalry at Hanover. Fitz Lee tried to cut the Federals off, but as soon as the Northerners caught sight of Mosby and his scouts they fled toward Haw's Shop, farther down the road. Mosby called the pursuit a "fox chase" for a mile or two. The rebels found little resistance, and captured a number of Federals. Some of the Yankee prisoners belonged to Fitz Lee's old Regular Army cavalry company, provoking some rueful laughter.[20]

Meanwhile, the Northerners started to respond to the reports of Stuart's advance. Brigadier General Philip St. George Cooke, Stuart's father-in-law, commanded a division of the Army of the Potomac's cavalry. Cooke turned fifty-three the second day of his son-in-law's expedition. A Virginia native and West Point graduate, he was a veteran of many years' service on the frontier and in Mexico, and the author of a work on cavalry tactics. His family was a classic example of the tensions caused by secession: he and one son-in-law fought for the Union, while Stuart, another son-in-law, and Cooke's own son served the Confederacy. When Cooke heard of rebel cavalry in his rear he ordered six squadrons from the 5th U.S. Cavalry to reinforce his pickets, who occupied a position between Haw's Shop and Totopotomoy Creek about a mile from the shop. The 9th Virginia Cavalry scattered the Yankees, and Stuart crossed the creek.

The rebels next came to Linney's Grove, one mile south of the creek. More Northerners under Capt. William B. Royall were there, but Royall's force was too small to affect Stuart, and after artillery failed to move the Yankees, two companies of the 9th Virginia Cavalry dislodged them. It was here that the Confederate force lost its only man killed during the whole expedition—Capt. William Latane, the squadron commander, who led the initial charge and died in a saber-and-pistol duel with Royall. The Union officer himself was wounded in five places.[21]

Stuart pressed on past Old Church, which he thought might be heavily guarded. It was not, and the appearance of the gray-clad horsemen caused the Yankees there to flee. Quite a few supplies were left, however, and the men grabbed boots, guns, and other material (including liquor), then set the tents on fire. They did not stay long, however, for a rumor spread that one of the tents contained powder.

Stuart then had a decision to make: Should he continue around McClellan's army and cross the Chickahominy east of the Yankees, or should he retrace his steps? The Unionists, now alerted to Stuart's presence, could resist him almost anywhere, but resistance was more likely to come where he had already been. Crossing the Pamunkey and returning by a more northerly route would be impossible, for the bridges had been destroyed and the river was high. Glory and possible targets on McClellan's supply line lay ahead of him. However, Stuart already had the information Lee sought, and he probably could go back the way he had come before the Yankees could trap him. By going on, he risked falling into a Northern trap either north or south of the Chickahominy. Stuart reflected on all this, then turned to Lt. John Esten Cooke of his staff and said, "Tell Fitz Lee to come along, I'm going to move on with my column." Cooke, understanding the meaning of the words, replied, "I think the quicker we move the better," laughing as he said it. Stuart agreed. "Right," he said, "tell the column to move on at a trot." He had decided to go around the Union army.

The column continued to Tunstall's Station on the Richmond and York River Railroad. Stuart sent two squadrons to destroy Garlick's Landing on the Pamunkey. The detachment captured a number of Yankees and burned wagons and two Union schooners (a third got away). Because Tunstall's might be guarded, the artillery was hurried to the head of the main column. On the way, however, the guns became mired in a mud hole. The artillerymen waded into the knee-deep mud and rescued them, receiving a keg of Union whiskey as a reward.

As the rebels neared the station, Capt. Richard Frayser and some men advanced ahead of the column and met up with an enemy squadron. The Union commander asked Frayser to which unit he belonged. Knowing the 8th Illinois Cavalry was on station in the area, Frayser replied that he was from that unit. Just then Stuart appeared at the head of the main body. The Unionists turned to flee, but their commander had enough time to tell Frayser to go to hell with his 8th Illinois. Lieutenant W. T. Robins and part of the 9th Virginia Cavalry charged and captured the small infantry force guarding Tunstall's as well as the stores there. Mosby said the guards at the station carried unloaded rifles.

Tunstall's was on McClellan's main supply line, and while Stuart's men were destroying the place, they heard a train coming. Robins tried to turn a switch but could not, so his men placed obstructions on the tracks as Rooney Lee set an ambush with a squadron. The train's engineer, approaching the station slowly, saw the trap and suddenly put on a burst of speed, rushing through the fusillade of fire. Some soldiers (and perhaps civilians) riding on flatcars jumped off to escape the fire; others hugged the cars. Captain William D. Farley of Stuart's staff rode after the train and shot the engineer, but the train got away safely. Officers from the train warned the 93rd New York, a regiment stationed about a mile away, to form in line.[22]

Stuart now had another important decision to make. White House Landing, McClellan's base, was only four miles away. If Stuart could destroy that, McClellan would be forced to retreat. Jeb later told Lieutenant Cooke that the temptation was great. However, the risks also were great, and maybe Stuart remembered Lee's note. He turned from that chance and headed for the Chickahominy.

The Yankees were behind him. Philip Cooke had sent a message to Brig. Gen. George Sykes, in command of a V Corps division, asking for help. Sykes responded by sending Col. Gouverneur K. Warren's brigade to join the pursuit. The 1st U.S. Cavalry, with Cooke accompanying it, and four squadrons of the 6th Pennsylvania Cavalry also looked for Stuart. Brigadier General John F. Reynolds's brigade of the Pennsylvania Reserves, just arrived on the Peninsula, moved from Dispatch Station near the Chickahominy northeast toward Tunstall's.

None of the Northern units found Stuart's men, however, for the tired Southern troopers reached the Chickahominy without further incident at dawn on June 14. All along the route to the river the Confederates captured wagons and sutler's stores. The troopers, who had been in their saddles for nearly twenty-four hours and had fought three small engagements, were exhausted. Stuart fell asleep in the saddle, one knee over the pommel, with his arms folded. Lieutenant Cooke held him up so he would not fall off, and Stuart's horse kept going without guidance. Everyone looked forward to an easy crossing of Jones's Bridge (also called Forge Bridge), south of New Kent Court House, or a ford near the bridge. But the recent rains had caused the river to rise, making the ford unusable (Rooney Lee almost drowned testing it), and the bridge was heavily damaged. After dragging himself from the river, Lee told Cooke, "Well, Lieutenant, I think we are caught." When Cooke suggested a few days later that they might have been forced to surrender, Stuart said one other possibility remained: "To die game."

Quickly, for no one knew when Federals might appear behind them, the rebels worked on the bridge. Stuart lay on the bank in what Mosby termed "the gayest humor I ever saw." The men finished repairing the bridge in a few hours and were on their way again, their Yankee prisoners crossing first. Riding steadily, the prisoners and their captors reached Richmond on June 16. They had just accomplished something very few horse soldiers ever have: they had ridden completely around an enemy army.

Their escape was relatively close. The temporary bridge was still burning when eight men from the 6th Pennsylvania Cavalry, commanded by Maj. Robert Morris, reached it. The five Confederates on the other side left at a rifle shot, but the bridge was unusable. Colonel Richard H. Rush of the 6th Pennsylvania Cavalry went back to his camp "looking as cross as a savage."[23]

Stuart arrived a day earlier than his men, having ridden to report to Lee with only Frayser and a courier for company and with only two hours' sleep. A few days after hearing that report Lee wrote in a letter, "The General deals in the flowering style, as you will perceive if you ever see his report in detail; but he is a good soldier." Stuart certainly could turn a phrase. After the raid, he said he had left one general behind: "General Consternation." Jeb probably gave Lee all sorts of descriptions of the adventures he had on the ride. But the news Stuart brought was far more important: he had gleaned much information on the roads and terrain between the rivers, and had discovered that the Federals seemed content to supply their army from White House Landing. The mere fact of his being able to ride completely around McClellan showed that the Union army's right flank rested on nothing more than the ground the soldiers walked on. Jackson's route to the Federal rear was open.

This news more than compensated for the risks Stuart had taken. The raid had an undeniable psychological and moral impact. The men were greeted warmly everywhere they turned. The ladies called out: "Hurrah for Stuart's cavalry! God bless you boys, you have covered yourselves all over with glory." Southern spirits rose at the news, whereas Northerners considered it a "bad sign." But Stuart's information set the stage for the whole campaign. With the Chickahominy bottomland a morass, the Union army's right flank could be rolled up before the left flank, on the south side of the river, could give any assistance. Also, the Federals' supply route did not sound well protected. A substantial force—say, Stonewall Jackson's Valley army—might be able to sever it completely, forcing McClellan to give up on laying siege to Richmond.

Lee did not waste any time. He had received a letter from Jackson in which Stonewall said he would rather not move north in the Valley until he could hold the territory. Lee could not spare the men for that, and if Jackson could not attack where he was, Lee wanted him in Richmond. Stuart's report gave Lee the information he needed to direct Jackson to the proper place. In a June 16 letter, Lee ordered Stonewall and his army to march from the Shenandoah to Richmond, "at the proper time suddenly descending upon the Pamunkey. To be efficacious, the movement must be secret." His plans were still evolving, but one part was already written in ink: Jackson would sweep from the northwest down the Pamunkey River to flank the Union right. If McClellan should get a little too much wind of this, he might take away the opportunity dangling in Lee's face.[24]

Stuart's raid was a humiliating experience for the Federals. Jeb showed that his father-in-law was not his match and that McClellan's rear was poorly guarded. One Union soldier wrote that the raid had been accomplished "under McClellan's nose." A Union diarist thought there was "[a] screw loose somewhere no doubt." Fitz John Porter ordered an investigation into Cooke's conduct during his pursuit of Stuart.

McClellan may have unwittingly instigated the raid and helped its success. Robert E. Lee's wife was at White House Landing before the Yankees arrived and moved several times to try to leave the Federal lines, eventually ending up near Old Church. She finally decided she should relocate inside the Confederate lines, and McClellan passed her through on June 10. Rumors flew that she had given her husband information Stuart then used on his ride. One rebel officer, Col. Thomas R. R. Cobb of Georgia's Cobb Legion, told his wife the rumors were true, and the fact that Lee met with Stuart on the eleventh is suspicious. But Lee would have needed intelligence anyway, and he did not order Stuart to ride around the army. At most, Mrs. Lee could have given information about outposts near her, as it is doubtful she or anyone else had unlimited freedom to move.[25]

Whether the humiliation and rumors bothered McClellan or not, he was in an upbeat mood. He wrote to his wife, Lincoln, and Stanton of beginning his advance toward Richmond "on Tuesday or Wednesday," or "within a couple of days," or "day after tomorrow." But as it has been put, the "Day after tomorrow was slow in coming." Allan Pinkerton kept sending reports indicating that at least 150,000 rebels were in Richmond, with more on the way. A contemporary account had observations of up to 20,000 Confederates coming from northern and northwestern Virginia early in the month, and others—between 50,000 and 100,000—coming in by railroad beginning the fifteenth. The roads had to be dry enough to permit his heavy artillery to move into place so he could capture Richmond with as little loss of life as possible. A pro-McClellan account written at the time of the campaign stated that the delays in the campaign—which it termed "great"—were caused by McClellan's preference to fight a "war of intrenchments." Most of his men knew of this preference. Solomon Beals of the 18th Massachusetts, for example, wrote to his brother, "I understand Genl. McClellan says he will plow up every inch of ground between here and the city before he will have his men cut up by musket." They liked it for an easily understood reason, even if it meant that taking Richmond would be later rather than sooner. "Who is it that will not justify his delay, when every day's delay may be the saving of a hundred lives," asked the 96th Pennsylvania's Lewis J. Martin.[26]

Stuart's ride probably did make McClellan think seriously about changing his base from White House Landing to somewhere on the James River. Alexander S. Webb, an aide to McClellan during the campaign, wrote that Little Mac "was induced to make this latter move by Stewart's [*sic*] cavalry raid on the 11th [*sic*] rather than with any intention of changing his line of attack or transferring his army to that point." Webb further noted that "McClellan's base of supplies at the White House had become a source of anxiety, since he seemed to doubt his ability to keep his connection with it secure, and because the rain and mud had rendered the roads almost impassable for wagons." The raid had put others to thinking. Frederick Wead, an aide to Brig. Gen. Henry W. Slocum (who commanded one of Franklin's divisions), wrote on the sixteenth that he thought McClellan would change his base to the James. Wead called it "a delicate and difficult undertaking."[27]

McClellan had mentioned using the James River as a base in early May. In response to a telegram from Stanton reporting a Federal attack on Norfolk, McClellan said, "Should Norfolk be taken and the Merrimac destroyed, I can change my line to the James River and dispense with the railroad." The date of the dispatch was May 10, and the *Virginia* was destroyed the same night. But McClellan did not change his base. Why, if Little Mac considered moving his base to the James in early May, did he not do it until after he was under attack?

The James would be the better river to use as a line of communication. It was wider and deeper, Union gunboats could sail up it and cooperate with the army, and it provided a solid flank, which the York and Pamunkey did not. The Army of the Potomac could have swept up any rebels on the river's north bank as it moved up the Peninsula, and the gunboats could protect shipping moving up the river.

McClellan said he kept White House Landing as a base because Lincoln's order to McDowell restricted that force's movements to keep it between Richmond and Washington. But that order was not given until May 17. If McClellan had begun to change his base before May 17, his argument might make sense, for Lincoln also required McDowell to be supplied from West Point—the eastern terminus of the Richmond and York River Railroad, McClellan's primary supply line. But McClellan did not change his base before May 17, when it would have been easy for him to do so. The Confederates were retreating up the Peninsula, the Army of the Potomac was following them, the two armies were not in close contact, and a shift of supplies would have been a large but relatively straightforward task. McClellan might have been concerned about the York River line but unaware of the safety of the James. However, communication with the navy could have illuminated him. The navy's failure to destroy Drewry's Bluff had shown that it could take warships that far up the James, so the river must have been safe to transports for quite a distance. After McDowell was diverted to the Shenandoah Valley on May 24,

McClellan had only the lame excuse that he was waiting for McDowell to return. But his reply to the telegram notifying him of McDowell's change of orders suggests he did not expect that that force would be his to use any time soon.[28]

McClellan's calculations in May convinced him that his best course of action was to remain where he was. His analysis was flawed, however. With one day's preparation, McClellan could have constructed fairly extensive field fortifications. A few more days' effort could have produced nearly impregnable works from the Chickahominy to south of White Oak Swamp. With the Union advantages in river transport and such works, McClellan could have operated two bases at once while crossing his other units, either at Bottom's Bridge (where the first two corps crossed) or below that point, without fear of a serious reverse.

A more interesting option would have been to transfer his supply line to the Richmond, Fredericksburg, and Potomac Railroad. This would have the great advantage of covering Washington with the entire Army of the Potomac, thus freeing more troops from Washington's defense once Jackson's threat ended. However, this line was vulnerable to flank attacks and enemy raids, and its lack of naval support gave up a large Union advantage in a campaign based on the Peninsula.

Whether McClellan's base was on the James or at White House Landing, he needed to keep a substantial force north of the Chickahominy. McCall's division joined McClellan by water, and perhaps the rest of McDowell's corps would follow by water as McClellan desired, but Stanton and Lincoln still were concerned about leaving Washington uncovered. There is no indication that the supplies for McDowell still would have to come from West Point, so there may have been no reason for the Federals' supplies to continue to come by the York River. McClellan could have asked Lincoln to approve a change of base, but he needed to protect the Richmond and York River Railroad for another reason. Since he thought the Confederates outnumbered him by a large margin, he needed to besiege them, fixing them in place, so he could use his heavy siege guns, which he considered his great equalizer. As Lee told Davis, "The enemy cannot move his heavy guns except on the R.R." The only railroad on that part of the Peninsula was the Richmond and York River line. If it had to be used for the siege guns, it might make sense to use it for supplies as well—if it could be protected.

By late June, Fitz John Porter's V Corps was protecting the railroad by itself. Sumner's II Corps stayed south of the river after Seven Pines. Brigadier General William F. Smith's VI Corps division had crossed to the south bank on the fifth. McClellan's plans for a siege required the possession of the area around Old Tavern (of which only a chimney remained). This was at the point where the Nine Mile road coming northeast from Richmond turned southeast toward Seven Pines and another road headed north to New Bridge across the Chickahominy. Little Mac wanted Franklin to attack Old Tavern with both Smith's and Henry Slocum's divisions, so Slocum came south of the river on the eighteenth. McCall, recently arrived on the Peninsula, placed two brigades in the area just east of Mechanicsville vacated by Franklin's men. These movements meant that four of five corps were south of a river that could rise quickly—as it had during the last week of May. Moreover, only one corps, albeit one that, augmented by McCall's division, was the strongest in the army, stood between the rebel host and McClellan's base.

Little Mac knew his force dispositions were faulty, as did others. Philip Kearny said they could only have been caused by treason. But keeping the army split more evenly while still attacking south of the river was not an option for McClellan. Little Mac might have decided to entice Lee to attack north of the Chickahominy, forcing a change of base. Less deviously, it could have been the most obvious manifestation of his decision to change base if attacked. Porter and McClellan discussed a change of base in June and decided it would be too dangerous against Lee (suggesting that McClellan's opinion of Lee had changed since April). Only necessity, in the form of an attack on the poorly protected supply line, would trigger the change.[29]

Little Mac thus kept his base on the York and continued to wait for dry weather and hard roads. Soldiers, politicians, and civilians on two continents also waited for McClellan to move on Richmond and force the decisive battle all knew was coming.

CHAPTER TWO

"How Are We to Get at Those People?"

SOME SOLDIERS WERE NOT IDLE during the month of June. McClellan ordered several reconnaissances, and minor skirmishing occurred often. Artillery would fire at opposing infantry, in turn drawing fire from opposing guns. One battery expended 630 rounds during one such incident. Other, more consequential fighting occurred as well. Such skirmishes were inevitable since the two armies were within a mile of each other in most places. One observer called the events "most ludicrous," which they would have been had people not been killed as a result. They certainly did not accomplish anything.

Picket duty was commonplace for soldiers on both sides, of course—surprise had to be avoided—and it was not an easy task. One writer called this time his brigade's "most harassing and critical period" in its history because of such duty. Nevertheless, the men found ways to make it easier. The soldiers on both sides became familiar with each other, and informal truces sprang up—in some cases, even more than that. On the twenty-first John Tilley of the 15th Georgia went to the Yankee lines for a chat. He and a Federal picket exchanged pipes and pleasantries, but the Unionists would not exchange papers. When the get-together broke up, both sides tipped their caps. On at least one part of the line pickets could pick cherries in the open without worry. In some places, however, too much of this fraternizing was frowned upon. Brigadier General William T. H. Brooks told his father that "but for the most stringent orders the men would assemble in crowds and pass the day gossiping with the opposite party."

On the north side of the river Federal soldiers took care of Southern civilians.

Fanny Gaines Tinsley was living with her parents inside Porter's lines while her husband worked in the Confederate Treasury Department. The officers brought the family newspapers, guards stood watch at each door and at the vegetable garden to prevent mischief, and soldiers would drive the family's cows into the yard so they could be milked. The Yankees paid twenty-five cents for a quart of milk.

Some men wanted to fight. In the 3rd South Carolina, someone suggested crossing to the north side of the Chickahominy to capture a Union battery. A call was made for a hundred volunteers, and that number was speedily reached, including at least twenty-five lieutenants and captains. The next day, having been drilled, the volunteers formed up as darkness fell, when an order came down canceling the mission. Some of the men were happy, but others were disappointed—at least one man because he missed a chance to find clothes and shoes.

Most of the contacts between Unionists and Confederates involved good-natured bantering. John Everett of the 11th Georgia went to the Federal lines to exchange newspapers and got into a debate with his foes. The Yankees were actually friendly, Everett told his mother in a letter. The men agreed not to shoot at each other, and the Yankees told Everett the rebels they had thus far encountered also were friendly. Everett said all they wanted was their rights and they would get them. The Unionists demurred, saying that they would take Richmond soon and then there would be peace. "I told [them] that if peace was never made till they got Richmond that it would never be made for they could not take Richmond with all of their forces right here in a pile and then they would have to kill every one of our men before they took it."[1]

One of the contacts between Northerner and Southerner had more serious consequences. Captain Thomas M. Key of McClellan's staff met with Brig. Gen. Howell Cobb, who commanded a brigade in Lee's army, on June 15 for the purpose of discussing an exchange of prisoners. Key apparently suggested to McClellan that he also bring up the possibility of an end to hostilities, and Little Mac agreed. Key and Cobb met on the Mechanicsville Bridge at 11 A.M. and moved to a hut built by Union pickets for their meeting. Colonel James H. Simpson of the 4th New Jersey, who was the field officer of the day, was unsure of this location and of Key's credentials. Simpson actually requested some documents before he allowed the meeting to continue.

The prisoner exchange issue was discussed, but the greater part of the meeting was spent in an exchange of views. Speaking as individuals and not representatives of their respective nations, they debated several points regarding the ability and desire of the South to continue the struggle. Key said he thought the war could be ended by Confederate submission and Lincoln's offer of amnesty to the South. Cobb replied that such an act on the rebels' part would be impossible, and that he thought the South would win the war.

Apparently Key had thought the Confederates might not actually fight when push came to shove. He said as much to Simpson after the meeting. Why anyone, Union or Confederate, would believe either side lacked the will to fight by that point in the war is incomprehensible. More interesting, however, are the comments Key made in a letter to Stanton describing the meeting. His impression was that Confederate leaders could not control the masses in their own land, reconstruction was impossible before the complete defeat of all rebel armies, and it might be necessary to end slavery to end the rebellion. Coming from a trusted McClellan aide, these are startling sentiments indeed. McClellan forwarded Key's letter to Stanton with the request that it remain confidential. Stanton replied that he did not think it appropriate for officers meeting to discuss prisoner exchanges to bring up other subjects, including peace.

McClellan had supplies made ready to be sent from White House Landing to the James River and ordered some cavalry and topographical engineers to study the ground between his supply line and the James.[2] Lee, meanwhile, was finalizing a plan that would make those preparations necessary. On June 16, after he told Stonewall Jackson to bring the Valley veterans to Richmond, he rode to the Chickahominy River with his military secretary, Col. Armistead L. Long. Lee, looking over the northern bank of the river, mused, "Now, Colonel Long, how are we to get at those people?" Long kept quiet, for he knew Lee well enough to know that the question was rhetorical. Obviously the Federal right flank was the weak point, even if that flank consisted (as it did at that time) of two corps, the V and VI. Stuart once had proposed an attack on McClellan's left flank from the direction of the James River, but the Union defenses there were regarded as too strong.[3] The only question was whether the rebels would attack on both sides of the Chickahominy, or whether part of the Army of Northern Virginia would stand on the defensive while the rest joined Jackson on the north bank of the river.

Lee, back at his headquarters, was still debating this point with himself when Maj. Gen. James Longstreet, one of Lee's division commanders, arrived. Longstreet suggested that Lee move Jackson from the Valley to Richmond to help attack McClellan's right. Lee told his subordinate that the very same order had gone with General Whiting when that officer's division was sent to Jackson, and revealed his tentative plan for Jackson to move on McClellan's line of communications while the rest of the army made a frontal assault. Longstreet replied that the Federals had probably destroyed the Pamunkey River bridges Jackson might need if he met a reverse. He also voiced the opinion that a frontal attack against most of a larger army was risky.

Lee agreed. The two men discussed possibilities and came up with a whopper. Six of the army's ten divisions would concentrate north of the Chickahominy to attack the Federals (leaving only John Magruder's three small divisions and Maj. Gen. Benjamin Huger's division opposing four Union corps). Jackson would get behind the Unionists, forcing them out of their entrenchments. At the same time, Longstreet, D. H. Hill, and A. P. Hill would lead their divisions against the Federals on the north bank. Caught between the hammer and the anvil, McClellan's forces there would disintegrate and the Northern supply line would be unprotected, forcing the rest of the army to retreat under the threat of further attack.

Longstreet had long considered this plan. Before Seven Pines he had suggested to Joe Johnston that the Union line at Beaver Dam Creek, a stream less than two miles east of Mechanicsville and the westernmost Yankee position, could be turned. Apparently he made the same suggestion to Lee the day after the commander's first council of war. Whether Longstreet should get credit for planting the idea in Lee's mind is an open question, but the Confederates really had only one option, and both Lee and Longstreet were good enough soldiers to see it.[4]

The plan hinged on three assumptions. One was that the Confederate command could coordinate its movements to have Jackson on the Army of the Potomac's right flank or in its rear before Longstreet and the two Hills launched their attacks. The second was that once McClellan was attacked, he would not seize the initiative and assault the weakened rebel defense line in front of Richmond. The third was that the attacks, even if they failed to annihilate the Yankees, would push them far enough down the Chickahominy that Lee could link his forces.

Lee's plan—splitting his force to gain an advantage at the critical point—was right out of Napoleonic warfare, which he had studied for decades. But even Bonaparte might have been reluctant to separate a numerically inferior force by a river fewer than ten miles from his nation's capital unless he had no other choice. Lee's aide-de-camp, Col. Charles Marshall, said that was exactly the case. Lee could not attack the Union right without crossing the river, he could not safely attack the larger Union force on the south bank, and he could not just sit and wait for McClellan to do something.[5]

President Davis saw a weak point in the plan, however. Davis thought highly of McClellan and had appointed him to the Crimea observation team. The president told Lee that if McClellan was as good as he thought, then the Union commander would immediately move on Richmond. If Little Mac should revert to his training and behave like an engineer, however, the plan would work because McClellan would move to protect his line of communications. Lee had an answer to Davis's objections: "If you will hold him as long as you can at the intrenchment, and then fall back on the detached works around the city, I will be upon the enemy's heels before he gets there." Davis thought that answer over for a day, and gave Lee the go-ahead.[6]

Davis's point deserves consideration. Lee knew from Northern newspapers that McClellan thought himself heavily outnumbered, but he could not be absolutely sure that the Federal commander would take no aggressive action.

What could Lee have done if McClellan had attacked? New Bridge, six miles northeast of Richmond, would link up the two wings of the Confederate army. However, the Yankees' north-bank force might retreat to it if McClellan did attack, and in any case it would not allow Lee's north-bank force to quickly cross the river. Joseph Johnston thought Lee was making the same mistake that McClellan had made before Seven Pines. Johnston was so sure McClellan would attack and take Richmond that he had ordered an extra train to take him out of harm's way while he recovered from his wounds.

Lee's plan was obvious to at least one Union commander. Phil Kearny wrote in a June 22 letter that the Confederates' "next act of the drama" would likely be an attack on the Army of the Potomac's communications. The rebels would fail if they attacked directly, Kearny thought, but they might leave some men in front of the Northerners on the south bank of the Chickahominy, cross to the north bank with the rest of their force, and cut off the Federals' communications. McClellan also considered the possibility of Lee's attacking north of the river. On June 23, the day Lee's plans solidified, McClellan's chief of staff (and father-in law), Brig. Gen. Randolph B. Marcy wrote Porter: "The troops on this side (of the river) will be held ready either to support you directly or to attack the enemy in their front. If the force attacking you is large the general would prefer the latter course, counting upon your skill and the admirable troops under your command to hold their own against superior numbers long enough for him to make the decisive movement which will determine the fate of Richmond." McClellan's idea apparently was to allow as many Confederates as possible to cross to the river's north bank, then make a sudden charge along the Richmond and York River Railroad and the paralleling Williamsburg road into Richmond.[7]

McClellan did not follow through when the event actually occurred, of course, but that he thought about an attack at all shows just how dangerous Lee's plan could have been. It thus must have been founded on the gravity of the situation and possibly on understanding of McClellan's character. After all, if Lee just sat there, McClellan eventually would bring up the siege guns and blow him out of his trenches. Moreover, Lee's strategy, while risky, would give his army numerical superiority at the point of attack.

One other aspect of Lee's plan deserves attention. The first assumption, that close cooperation would occur among the officers carrying out the plan, might be wondered at since they were working with a new commander. None of them had worked with Jackson at this level of command, and the staff and couriers necessary to ensure coordination would labor in unfamiliar territory seeking men they did not know in uncertain locations.[8]

Meanwhile, Jackson and his men had left the Valley. On June 17 they headed for Ashland, a station on the Richmond, Fredericksburg, and Potomac Railroad about seventeen miles northwest of Porter's position. Jackson had arranged for some captured Northern surgeons to hear him giving Col. Thomas T. Munford of the cavalry orders that spoke of northward movements. Then the prisoners were sent north themselves. But Confederates got no news, factual or otherwise. Of course there was speculation. J. William Jones, a chaplain serving with Jackson, expected to turn north through Greene County when he got to Charlottesville. Instead, the force headed east to Gordonsville. Arriving there, Jones was told by a Presbyterian minister with whom Jackson had stayed that the men would move on Culpeper, directly north of Gordonsville. Instead, they went southeast to Louisa Court House. They thought from there that the rebels would march northeast through Spotsylvania Court House to go after McDowell at Fredericksburg. Whiting had it figured out early. He told his wife he presumed that he and the rest of Jackson's force would attack McClellan's right and rear, which he called "a hazardous but if successful a glorious blow." Shepherd Pryor of the 12th Georgia in Ewell's division wrote on the nineteenth that he thought they were headed to Richmond. A man in Lawton's brigade told his sister, "General Jackson don't tell his business to any body, our officers don't know what or where we are going to do."

Colonel Bradley T. Johnson, commander of the Maryland Line, met up with Jackson on a street at the beginning of the march. Jackson asked Johnson if he had received the order. Johnson replied that he had not. "Want you to march," Jackson said. Johnson asked when. Jackson said, "Now." When Johnson asked which direction, Jackson said, "Get in the [railroad] cars, go with [Brig. Gen. Alexander] Lawton." Johnson, somewhat puzzled, said, "How must I send my train, and the battery?" Jackson answered, "By the road." Johnson, whose confusion was growing by the second, finally noted, "Well General, I hate to ask questions; but it is impossible to send my wagons off without knowing which road to send them." Jackson merely said, "Oh! Send them by the road the others go."[9]

Stonewall had ordered Whiting's force to Mount Crawford, a few miles northwest of Port Republic and Jackson's camp at nearby Mount Meridian, when it arrived in the Valley. But then Jackson moved Whiting to Staunton, southwest of Port Republic. Once outside of Jackson's earshot, Whiting started complaining. The thirty-eight-year-old Mississipian graduated from West Point in 1845, a year before Jackson and with the highest marks achieved at the academy until that time, and spent his prewar career in the coveted Corps of Engineers. It was probably natural for a soldier considered one of the elite in the prewar army to look down upon Stonewall, who achieved only middling success as a cadet. "I believe Jackson hasn't any more sense than my horse," he snorted. The next morning Whiting received an order to move to Gordonsville, northeast of Charlottesville on the railroad. "Didn't I tell you he was a fool, and doesn't this prove it?" he snarled. "Why, I just came through Gordonsville day before yesterday." To his wife he wrote, "I only hope that all will turn out for the best."[10]

Despite the secrecy, Jackson at first made good time. On the eighteenth his leading elements marched about twenty-five miles and camped near Charlottesville. Others made as few as twelve miles and were still near Waynesboro. The next two days, using both trains and roads, some units got as far as Frederickshall east of Gordonsville. But others, bogged down by wagons, dust, and weariness, got only a few miles beyond Charlottesville. The Valley army and its reinforcements thus were strung out over forty miles of Virginia countryside.

While going through the mountains they were tempted by the many stills in the area, and Hood started a rumor of a smallpox outbreak to keep the men moving. He came upon a drunk soldier and ordered the man back to his unit, but the soldier could not stand up. A few more sober soldiers came along, and Hood told them to help the drunk. Just then the soldier said, "Don't you fellers that ain't been vaccinated come near me—I've got the small-pox—tha's wha's the masser with me." Through his laughter, Hood told the other soldiers to let the poor man be.[11]

Jackson told Rev. Robert L. Dabney, his chief of staff, that the force was headed to Richmond, to keep that fact secret, and to direct the march while Stonewall went to meet with Lee in the capital. Before he climbed aboard the train that was to take him there, he shook hands with his staff as if he were off to Europe. One staff member said, "What the devil is he up to now?" Someone else asked Jackson: "General, where are you going?" Stonewall looked at the man, said, "Can you keep a secret? Yes? Ah, so can I," and boarded the train.

Later that day, Dabney ate with Maj. Gen. Richard S. Ewell, Jackson's senior division commander. Ewell liked Jackson, but he was irritated with the worse-than-usual secrecy that kept even him in the dark. "Here, now," he complained to Dabney, "the General has gone off on the railroad without intrusting to me, his senior Major General, any order, or any hint whither we are going; but [Maj. John A.] Harman, his Quartermaster, enjoys his full confidence, I suppose, for I hear he is telling the troops that we are going to Richmond to fight McClellan." Dabney could only answer, "You may be certain, General Ewell, that you stand higher in General Jackson's confidence than any one else, as your rank and services entitle you to. As for Major Harman, he has not heard a word more than others. If he thinks that we are going to Richmond, it is only his surmise, which I suppose every intelligent private is now making."

At least for some of the men it was a pleasant march. Jacob Barger of the 52nd Virginia wrote home that the Virginia piedmont was "a nice country." At one settlement the citizens begged to be allowed to serve the men food they had prepared, and Ewell agreed to let each regiment halt for a short time. The women did the serving, of course, and Maj. Campbell Brown of Ewell's staff noticed one tall soldier get a glass of buttermilk, then stoop low to get a second, and then put on a disguise to get a third. It is not clear whether he was more interested in the female company or the buttermilk.[12]

Jackson's road to Richmond was longer than he had planned. Hearing a false rumor of a Federal advance from the Rappahannock, he got off the train at Gordonsville and waited for his men. By Saturday the twenty-first, even the rear unit—the Stonewall Brigade—had made it as far as Gordonsville. At Frederickshall, the 2nd Mississippi drew two days' rations and tried to cook them—no easy task considering the lack of wood in the area. In more than four days of marching, some of Stonewall's men had covered about eighty miles, a pretty good rate of advance, while others had gone about sixty miles. Much of the column rested on the twenty-second, although trains transported some of the trailing units to Louisa Court House. It was Sunday, and Jackson disliked any sort of action on the Sabbath unless it was militarily necessary. Moreover, Lee's letters had mentioned nothing about a specific date on which Jackson was expected to arrive. Besides, the men had marched for four days straight. He therefore gave most of them a rest, which was in line with his thought that it was better for a man to rest one day in seven (Sunday, the Biblically appointed one) than to march all seven. In this instance it was the right move.[13]

Meanwhile, Stonewall left his troops that night for a meeting with Lee on June 23. He might have left earlier on the twenty-second, giving himself a chance to get some rest as well, but it is not likely that he realized he would need that rest—and any absence during the day would have been noticed and commented on by his men. A Mrs. Harris, with whom Jackson was staying, asked Stonewall to eat breakfast with her the morning of the twenty-third. Jackson thanked her and said that if he were able, he would. When morning came, Mrs. Harris sent word to Jackson's room. The only person there was Jackson's servant, Jim, who said, "Lor, you surely didn't spec to find the General here at dis hour, did you? You don't know him, den. Why, he left here at 1 o'clock dis morning, and I spec he is whipping de Yankees in de Valley agin by now."

In reality, he was headed to Richmond. Stopping at the home of Matthew Hope, a landowner in lower Louisa County, Jackson asked Hope for two good saddle horses as he had very important business at Richmond and their horses were exhausted. Jackson promised to send them back. Hope did not recognize the most famous soldier in the Confederacy, and refused to give horses to what he believed were two straggling cavalrymen. Jackson, not revealing his identity, said he had to have the horses and that Hope might as well saddle them. Hope, probably indignant by this point, said he had servants to saddle horses. He did not saddle horses for himself and he certainly would not for them. If you are to take the horses, Hope finally said, you must saddle them yourselves. Jackson and his staff officer did so and rode away. Several days later the horses came back with General Jackson's compliments. Hope said, "Why did he not tell me that he was General Jackson, I would have let him have every horse on the place, and saddled them myself." With fresh horses, Jackson showed up at Lee's headquarters early on the afternoon of the twenty-third. The Confederate commander had also summoned Longstreet and the two Hills to his headquarters at the Dabbs house.[14]

Jackson, after his Valley campaign, was quite possibly the most famous soldier in the world. Certainly he was the one most feared by the Yankees. Born in Virginia in 1824, Jackson was raised by his uncle after his parents died in poverty. Although he had little formal education, he was able to gain entrance to West Point and graduated in 1846, just in time to be assigned to Mexico and Maj. Gen. Winfield Scott's brilliant campaign. After the end of the Mexican War he became a professor at the Virginia Military Institute in Lexington. When Virginia seceded, Jackson became a colonel, then a brigadier general, and finally a major general after First Manassas, in which he earned his enduring nickname of "Stonewall." Then, in early 1862, came the Valley campaign that elevated him almost to Great Captain status around the world.

Jackson's eccentricities—particularly his religious fanaticism, his habit of sucking on lemons, and his stern discipline—made troops look upon him with a mixture of disgust and humor in the beginning. After the early part of the Valley campaign, however, they were convinced that he could do no wrong. Much of the Confederacy and most of the Union generals were also convinced, and the mere possibility of his move to Richmond excited Washington.

James Longstreet was a South Carolinian born in 1821. His father died when he was twelve and the family moved to Alabama, from where he went to West Point. Spending time with schoolmates, including Sam Grant, Longstreet joined many future comrades and enemies in Winfield Scott's Mexican War army. He too had fought at First Manassas and was given a key assignment at Seven Pines. However, he used the wrong road the first day and attacked too weakly on the second, contributing heavily to the Confederate failure there.

Daniel Harvey Hill was born in the same year and the same state as Longstreet, and he graduated from West Point in the same year—1842. After his service in the Mexican War he taught at several colleges in Virginia and North Carolina. Hill won the Civil War's first land battle, if anyone could be said to have won it, at Big Bethel, Virginia. After that he joined Joe Johnston's army as a division commander and took part in all the previous battles of the Peninsular campaign. Hill was brave, almost too brave, and typically not afraid to speak his mind. He was also Stonewall Jackson's brother-in-law, having married a sister of Jackson's second wife.

The other Hill, Ambrose Powell, was the youngest of the five men gathered on June 23. Born in Virginia in 1825, he graduated from West Point just in time to see service in Mexico. After secession he eventually gained command of a brigade, which he handled so well during the rear-guard action at Williamsburg that he was promoted to major general and command of a division. Word spread through both armies that Hill and George McClellan had competed for the hand of Ellen Marcy, with McClellan winning. Union soldiers maintained that A. P. Hill always fought hard when he knew McClellan was on the other side.

Lee explained the general situation as he saw it to his subordinates. That situation had changed in the week since Lee had ridden along the Chickahominy. All of Franklin's corps was now south of the river and Porter's corps, reinforced with McCall's division, had spread itself to cover the area. Pickets covered the Chickahominy crossings at Meadow Bridges, nearly due west of Mechanicsville, and the Mechanicsville Turnpike. Two brigades of McCall's division were in a strong position behind Beaver Dam Creek. The rest of the corps was camped on or near the Gaines farm, about three miles from the Beaver Dam Creek line near New Bridge. Including McCall, Porter had about twenty-six thousand officers and men present and equipped.[15]

The road network between the Chickahominy and Pamunkey rivers gave Jackson only two possible routes to turn the Beaver Dam Creek line. One was to head to Old Church, an area that Stuart had scouted during his ride. At Old Church, Stonewall would be within ten miles of White House Landing. But he also would be about seven miles from Porter's right flank, and at least that far from any Confederate troops. If Porter could hold the Beaver Dam Creek line with at most one division, he could throw two fresh divisions at Jackson's three smaller, more fatigued divisions. Even if Porter did not attack, Jackson would not be in a position to threaten the Beaver Dam Creek line at Old Church.

The second route led to Pole Green Church, which Lee thought was about a mile and a half north of Beaver Dam Creek and a little farther than that north of the road from Mechanicsville to Old Church. At Pole Green Church, Jackson would be much closer to the rest of Lee's army and more menacing to Yankees behind the creek, even if he might not be completely on their flank. Porter could still extend his line to meet Stonewall, but Jackson would be in less danger. He also would have his choice of several roads to take to march the six or so miles to Old Cold Harbor, a crossroads a couple of miles northeast of Porter's main force at the Gaines farm.

If Jackson forced Porter to retreat from Beaver Dam Creek, the rest of Lee's troops could advance down the road from Mechanicsville to Old Cold Harbor, passing the Gaines farm and mill and the settlement of New Cold Harbor along the way. This would be Porter's retreat route to reach the complex of bridges commonly called Grapevine Bridge, across which Sumner had crossed with his corps during the battle of Seven Pines. Lee knew of one more creek—Powhite Creek—that provided a defensive position for Porter along this road, but Jackson at Old Cold Harbor would flank any force there. If Stonewall could reach Old Cold Harbor, Lee could keep the Yankees from preparing defensive positions and perhaps force a battle in the open. Finally, a road from Old Cold Harbor led fairly directly to the Richmond and York River Railroad, McClellan's supply line. Lee would thus have the option of sending Stonewall to the railroad, cutting McClellan off completely from his base.

Lee chose the second route. Jackson would bring his force from Ashland to Pole Green Church to turn Porter's right flank, with one of A. P. Hill's brigades guarding his flank and flushing any Yankee pickets along the Chickahominy. The rest of A. P. Hill's division would cross the river at Meadow Bridges, one and one-half miles west of Mechanicsville and three miles west of Porter's position. As A. P. Hill moved east he would uncover the bridge carrying the Mechanicsville Turnpike over the river. Longstreet and D. H. Hill would cross there, D. H. Hill moving to support Jackson and Longstreet supporting A. P. Hill. The combined force would then drive at Porter, forcing him behind New Bridge, and then press toward the Richmond and York River Railroad via Old Cold Harbor to cut McClellan's supply line.

This was a bold stroke. A staff officer later remembered reading the written order, General Orders no. 75, and sitting in silence for some time: "Here, thought I, is the most momentous act of war ever revealed to me." It also was somewhat confusing. It seemed to give Jackson two tasks: to turn the Beaver Dam Creek line by getting on Porter's flank or in his rear, and to help with the attack itself. Lee's June 11 letter to Jackson makes clear that Jackson's task was to cut Porter's communications and turn him out of his lines. But this was to be paired with a frontal attack on McClellan's entire army. Lee's June 16 letter to Jackson gives no evidence that this plan had been discarded, as indeed it had not been at that point. Lastly, General Orders no. 75 did not give positive directions one way or another. After the war, Charles Marshall wrote that Lee did not want Jackson or anyone else to fight at Beaver Dam Creek. Lee's idea was to compel McClellan to come out of his trenches. "General Lee . . . told me that he did not anticipate battle at Mechanicsville or Beaver Dam," Marshall recalled. "He thought that Jackson's march turning Beaver Dam would lead to the immediate withdrawal of the force stationed there, and did not intend that a direct attack should be made on that formidable position."[16]

After Lee sketched out his ideas he left the room and his lieutenants worked on the details. Longstreet asked Jackson when he could have his force in position. "The morning of the 25th," Stonewall answered. Longstreet wrote that he "expressed doubt of his [Jackson's] meeting that hour." The doubt was justified, for on the afternoon of the twenty-third some of Jackson's units were still fifty miles from Ashland. Jackson agreed, and the four men set the twenty-sixth as the date. Lee returned and was informed of his subordinates' decisions.

At least that is the story that has come down to us from Longstreet and D. H.

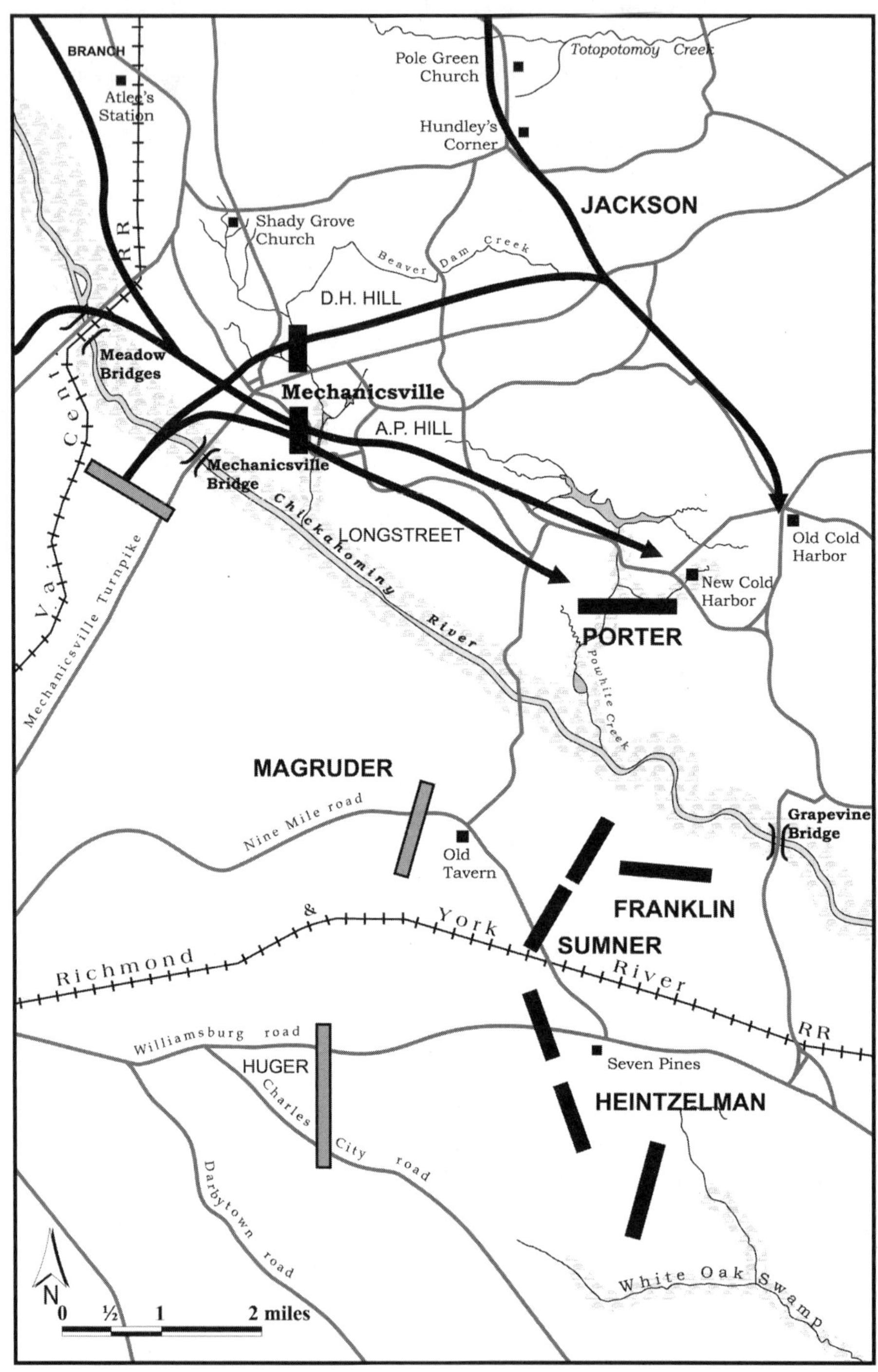

Lee's plan as given in General Orders no. 75

Hill (with minor differences). After the war, however, Lee remembered that he, not Longstreet, had questioned Jackson's ability to arrive on the twenty-fifth and had insisted that Jackson give himself one more day to get into position. Lee could not have known of Longstreet's claim or Hill's story, since both were made public well after his death. It is probable, though not certain, that the two subordinates would not have known about their commander's tale.[17]

At the end of the meeting, Lee gave his lieutenants verbal instructions that were put in writing the next day. The generals went back to their commands, Jackson riding all night (his second sleepless night in a row) to reach his troops. Lee spent the twenty-fourth writing orders, planning, and perhaps considering what Providence might have in store for him in his first decisive battle as commander. The day before the conference, he had written to a relative: "Our enemy is quietly working within his lines, and collecting additional forces to drive us from our Capital. I hope we shall be able yet to disappoint him, and drive him back to his own country." He probably thought that he had done what he could, and he was ready to place that hope in the blessings of his God. One of his commanders, Brig. Gen. Robert A. Toombs of Georgia, felt that God would be with the army. "If McClellan is unwise enough to fight us here," Toombs wrote his wife, "we shall whip and drive him out of Virginia."

Some Confederates agreed with Toombs. One soldier told his wife and sister that he thought it would take only a couple of hard fights before peace would come.[18]

Southern civilians also were confident of the results of the upcoming battle. John B. Jones wrote of his fellow Richmonders, "They regard victory as a matter of course." Some of this confidence was due to Jackson's Valley campaign, which was universally regarded as brilliant and marred only by the death of Stonewall's cavalry officer, Turner Ashby. The confidence also might have come from the rebel army's position, which, as Stephen Mallory explained, allowed for retreat to a line of entrenchments in case of defeat. In case of victory, Mallory thought, the Yankees would be routed. Many Southerners worried that no battle would occur. "McClellan advances, entrenching as he comes," one woman wrote. "Why do we allow it?" And Jones noted that people actually feared there would be no fighting, for they knew that without battle McClellan would besiege the city.

Many Northern civilians also were confident and eagerly awaited the taking of Richmond, which might mean the end of the war. Part of the reason for this confidence was that newspaper accounts were upbeat. The reporters were under tight restrictions. Randolph Marcy was both the main information source and chief censor, ensuring that only positive news came from the front. Some still worried, however. The taking of Corinth by Halleck's army in late May, the Confederate evacuation of Fort Pillow on the Mississippi in early June, and the resulting surrender of Memphis were more than offset by Jackson's

Valley campaign, Stuart's ride, and a failed assault near Charleston, South Carolina, at Secessionville. On June 20 George Templeton Strong wrote, "Perhaps we are a shade less blue than three days ago, but still very blue indeed." Three days later, Strong felt "as if heavy disaster might be at our doors." Lincoln worried about many fronts. When the rains were turning the Chickahominy bottomland into a morass he reminded McClellan of his line of communication. To a positive report from Halleck he responded with a question about the upper Mississippi. He had to deal with the aftermath of the Valley campaign. On June 23 Lincoln visited the retired Winfield Scott at West Point to ask for advice.

Most Union soldiers were confident because of their faith in McClellan. William Barker, a gunner with Battery A, 1st Rhode Island Light Artillery, said, "If there is a battle to take place I do not care how soon it comes if Little Mac is all ready." Others figured that, as Theodore Dodge of the 101st New York put it, getting into Richmond would only be accomplished through "a bloody day." Still others, like John H. Burrill of the 2nd New Hampshire, were not even sure that they could defeat the Southerners.

In late June, Richmond resident Sallie A. Putnam stood on the roof of the Virginia capitol. Using field glasses, she could see encampments everywhere and knew the soldiers were waiting for battle. She was confident the South would triumph in that battle, but the price in human blood to be paid for that victory was depressing.[19] Many of the soldiers Putnam saw were new at the game of war. Nearly one-fourth of Lee's regiments had yet to experience a major battle. Lee could not know how they would react to their first sight of combat. Nor could he know how his army—newly organized and with a history of a lack of coordination among its elements—would function as a unit.

McClellan's army was more experienced, with more than three-quarters of his regiments veterans of at least one major battle. But in Porter's corps, the most exposed part of the army, McCall's division was green, and many of the Regular Army units in Sykes's division were composed of recruits with no experience. These units included about half of Porter's men. Little Mac's organization and commanders had been tested, particularly at Seven Pines, but McClellan himself faced the ultimate test. He was readying an attack on Richmond. Could he succeed in taking the capital? So much depended on the result. A Union victory, even if it did not end the war, would signal that the end was near. The war could remain one of limited aims, as McClellan saw it. The ending would preserve, not revolutionize, the government. Great Britain and France would know the eventual outcome, and thus would not grant the Confederacy recognition. A Union defeat, however, would prolong the war indefinitely and might tilt the balance toward foreign recognition of the South. In that case, the war indeed might become the revolutionary struggle the radicals wanted. Only one thing was sure: the battle would be decisive.

CHAPTER THREE

"The Responsibility Cannot Be Thrown on My Shoulders"

George McClellan had a plan to succeed in this decisive battle. He thought his army had been poorly supported and he was sure the rebels outnumbered him, but he had the big siege guns that would equalize matters. All he needed was a place to put them. Others were thinking along the same lines. On June 24 Brig. Gen. William F. Smith asked McClellan to come to his VI Corps division's front, which was next to the south bank of the Chickahominy at a place called Golding's Farm. Smith had turned thirty-eight earlier in the year. The Vermont native graduated fourth in the West Point class of 1845 (the same class that produced the Confederate Whiting) and, like all high-ranking graduates, had chosen the engineers. After a prewar career at West Point and other places, he had been a staff officer at Bull Run and became a brigade commander shortly after that battle. Smith was called "Baldy" in the army, although his head was not completely clear of hair.

The two generals went forward to the Federal picket line, where Smith pointed out to McClellan the Old Tavern site, "the key of the position" because it was at the intersection of the road to New Bridge and the Nine Mile road. McClellan knew the importance of the Old Tavern area. He wrote his wife on June 15 that the next battle would be fought there. After that date John Barnard, McClellan's chief engineer, received almost daily reports from Lt. Cyrus B. Comstock on Confederate activity between Union positions and Old Tavern.

If McClellan attacked and took a position at Old Tavern he would accomplish several things. He would shorten the line of communication with Fitz John Porter's corps north of the river. New Bridge was almost five miles closer to Porter's lines than was Grapevine Bridge and two miles closer than Woodbury's Bridge. If McClellan advanced on a broad enough front, he would flank the northern part of the Confederate line, which would allow him to bring his big guns closer to Richmond because the rebel line would be forced back. McClellan told his wife that once he gained possession of Old Tavern he would force the rebels into their works, shell the city with his heavy guns, and then carry it by assault.

Smith said he could capture the tavern area as long as he was supported by the force on his left. McClellan agreed but wanted the Union reserve artillery to get some glory, so he asked Smith to dig gun emplacements on Garnett's Hill, the next hill to the west in an area full of ravines, by daylight on the twenty-fifth. Although the area of digging was within thirty paces of the rebel pickets, engineer colonel Barton S. Alexander had the work done so quietly that the Confederates did not know of it until daylight.

By then, however, McClellan had changed his mind about exactly how the attack should commence. His new plan, fitting for a man of extreme caution, did not call for accomplishing everything at once. First the troops around Seven Pines, southeast of Fair Oaks Station, must push their lines westward, past a swamp and some woods that separated them from the Confederates. With their support, Smith's division and the artillery could attack and take the Old Tavern position. Then, with the rail line secured, the big guns could come up. He notified Smith on the evening of the twenty-fourth not to move the guns up to their new positions until the next night.[1]

McClellan had decided to attack. This was a rarity; nonetheless, the evidence is there. Samuel Heintzelman's III Corps would make the assault. A Pennsylvanian, Heintzelman was one of the oldest generals in either army—a few months shy of fifty-seven. He graduated from West Point in 1826, when Robert Lee was a plebe. A lifetime soldier, he was brevetted for bravery in the Mexican War. His division had broken at Bull Run despite his efforts, and at Seven Pines he had again failed to rally a broken line. Heintzelman had advised McClellan not to attack the Confederate lines at Yorktown.

Heintzelman's division commanders, Brig. Gens. Joseph Hooker and Phil Kearny, had not shown any reluctance to attack. The forty-seven-year-old Hooker had served as a staff officer in the Mexican War and had a record equal to that of any other first lieutenant who served there. He resigned from the army in 1853, and the outbreak of war gave Hooker a chance to redeem his fortunes after hard times in civilian life. Given a division command, he fought his troops hard during the advance up the Peninsula. He did not, however, surpass Kearny in fighting spirit or ability. Kearny was the object of Winfield Scott's admiring comment, "the bravest man I ever knew, and a perfect soldier." Born in 1815 to a military family—his uncle, Stephen Kearny, was a Mexican War hero—Philip became a second lieutenant in his uncle's regiment. He then went abroad and served with the French in Algiers, fought in Mexico (where his left arm was wounded so severely it had to be amputated), and later joined French emperor Napoleon III's Imperial Guard. When war broke out he came home to fight, and he too distinguished himself in the advance up the Peninsula.

On the evening of June 24, Little Mac ordered the advance, telling Heintzelman, "If it is a possible thing, take advantage of the weakness of the enemy and push your pickets at least to the edge of the next clearing." McClellan actually thought the rebels might be weak somewhere. "I have been all over the right to-day and will open with heavy guns to-morrow. To-morrow night I hope to gain possession of the Garnett field, and by another day of the Old Tavern and some ground in advance. It will be chiefly an artillery and engineer affair." Here McClellan showed his true feelings on the nature of battle. He wanted to move up his guns, and he knew he needed to take territory to do so. Yet he wanted the effort to take the territory to be an engineering operation, without the rivers of blood seen at Shiloh. On the twenty-third he wrote his wife, "Every poor fellow that is killed or wounded almost haunts me."

The order was issued at 6:30 P.M. on the twenty-fourth, and Heintzelman passed it along to Hooker and Kearny that night. Hooker, however, did not give the order to his brigade commanders until the next morning. The attack began at 8 A.M. in a rain shower, with Hooker's division leading, Kearny's division supporting his left, and Brig. Gen. Israel B. Richardson's division from Sumner's corps available if needed on the right.

The ground as described by Hooker did not seem worth the price to be paid. Heavy woods covered the half-mile in front of his position, and through those woods was a swath of swampy ground that was often waist deep. On either side of the swamp was undergrowth. Once the Union troops got past these obstacles they came upon an open field that extended a little more than half a mile, with Confederates on the other side. To the right of the field was the Williamsburg road; Brig. Gen. Daniel Sickles's Excelsior Brigade of New York troops marched along it. On Sickles's left, between the Williamsburg and Charles City roads, was Brig. Gen. Cuvier Grover's brigade—composed of Massachusetts, New Hampshire, and Pennsylvania regiments. Colonel Joseph B. Carr's brigade of New Jersey and New York volunteers formed the reserve.[2]

Sickles, then forty-four, was a native of New York, an attorney, and a nationally known political figure. While a member of Congress in 1859 he shot his wife's lover and was the first man acquitted through the use of the temporary insanity defense (devised by Edwin Stanton, Sickles's lead counsel). When war broke out, Sickles helped recruit and was named commander of the Excelsior Brigade.

Grover, by contrast, was a thirty-three-year-old Maine-born West Point graduate with ten years of service in the West behind him. Although still a captain in the Regular Army, he was serving as a brigadier general of volunteers.

Hooker's third brigade commander, Joseph Carr, was also thirty-three, a child of Irish immigrants from Albany, New York, and engaged in the retail tobacco business. A colonel in the militia in 1861, he helped organize the 2nd New York.

On Grover's front, the 1st and 11th Massachusetts regiments (the 11th on the left) met increasing resistance as they moved toward the main Confederate position. The resistance became stout enough that Grover ordered six companies of the 2nd New Hampshire to support the middle of the line, the other four New Hampshire companies to support the right, and five companies of the 16th Massachusetts to assist on the left. This move was forced on Grover because the Excelsior Brigade was having problems. The New Yorkers "went in with a cheer," but they had trouble getting through abatis, a swamp, dense undergrowth, and heavy timber. The distance between Grover's right and Sickles's left kept increasing, and Grover had to shift seven companies from the 26th Pennsylvania to his right flank to attempt to maintain the Union line's continuity. Hooker sent the 8th New Jersey of Carr's brigade to support the advance.[3]

Major General Benjamin Huger, a veteran of thirty-seven years in the military, commanded the men all these Yankees were moving toward. Born a few months after Heintzelman in Charleston, South Carolina, Huger graduated from West Point a year ahead of Heintzelman and posted a distinguished record in the U.S. Army, holding several staff positions. In Mexico he received three brevets for his work as Winfield Scott's ordnance chief. After Fort Sumter surrendered he resigned to join the South. It was Huger who had abandoned Norfolk, and thus the *Virginia*, in May. He had commanded his division at Seven Pines without spectacular results (he was not given a major part in the battle).

Ambrose R. Wright's Alabamians, Georgians, and Louisianans held the area around the Williamsburg road on the north. Wright, a thirty-six-year-old politically prominent Georgian, had studied law under his future brother-in-law, Herschel Johnson (a Georgia governor and U.S. Senator). It was probably because of his political connections that he became colonel of the 3rd Georgia one month after Fort Sumter. Promoted to brigadier general in early June, he came to Virginia to take command of his mostly Georgia brigade.

Brigadier General William Mahone's Virginia brigade held the lines covering the Charles City road. Mahone was the son of a Virginia tavern keeper. He graduated from the Virginia Military Institute in 1847, and was five months shy of his thirty-sixth birthday as the Seven Days began. He studied engineering while teaching at a military school, and later became president and superintendent of the Norfolk and Petersburg Railroad. Joining the Confederate army as colonel of the 6th Virginia, he had helped capture the Norfolk Navy Yard and erect the Drewry's Bluff defenses before coming to the north side of the James with Huger.

Wright's supporting force on the left was Brig. Gen. Lewis A. Armistead's Virginia brigade, while Brig. Gen. Robert Ransom's North Carolina brigade, just arrived from Petersburg and temporarily under Huger's command, was in Wright's rear. Supporting these forces was Brig. Gen. Samuel Garland's brigade of D. H. Hill's division.

Wright's picket force on the south side of the Williamsburg road, the 4th Georgia, was struck early. The courier Col. George P. Doles of the 4th Georgia sent back to warn Wright of the impending attack had fled from the field without delivering the message, so the first the brigade commander heard of the attack was when his pickets started coming out of the woods. Wright immediately brought up two regiments, the 1st Louisiana and 22nd Georgia, to support the 4th Georgia. He later said they drove the enemy back more than a quarter of a mile along the Williamsburg road through a cornfield before the Yankee defense stiffened in a patch of trees. Wright indicated that he thought the enemy brigade was Sickles's, but it seems obvious from the description that it was Grover's. Of course, Grover reported no such retreat. Instead, he claimed that none of the rebel charges was able to break his line. In any event, that part of the line stabilized. As one Confederate remembered, "We fought, skirmished, retreated, and put up as big a bluff as possible."[4]

As the action settled down on Grover's front, Sickles came alive. Having worked his way through most of the obstacles in front of him, Sickles was attempting to clear the rest of the woods of rebel pickets when Wright's 3rd Georgia and Ransom's 25th North Carolina began moving toward him. Ransom sent the Tar Heels in response to Wright's request for help, and they led the attack. It was a hot fight for a while, and one man from the 25th North Carolina was hit and headed to the rear for treatment. Ransom saw the man and asked if he were badly hurt. The soldier replied, "No; it's nothing but a scratch; just enough to fool the doctor." Ransom thought the answer gave him some indication of the man's feelings, but he asked how the soldier liked fighting. The man said, "O, General, it's fine sport, but a leetle dangerous."

The worst of this attack seems to have fallen on the Excelsior Brigade's right flank, just north of the Williamsburg road. Someone in the left wing of the right-flank regiment, the 71st New York, thought rebels were on the flank and let everyone know it. The rest of the brigade, seeing its flank support melt, started backward. Sickles, along with Maj. Herbert von Hammerstein of McClellan's staff, got the men organized and moving forward again. Another of Carr's regiments, the 7th New Jersey, supported by the 19th Massachusetts from Brig. Gen. Napoleon J. T. Dana's brigade in Brig. Gen. John Sedgwick's II Corps division, moved forward. The 7th New Jersey had to wade through waste-deep water to get to the front, but once there the regiment drove the Confederates back through the woods. Or perhaps it did not, as Wright wrote that after the rebel charge, the lines remained where they had been in the morning.[5]

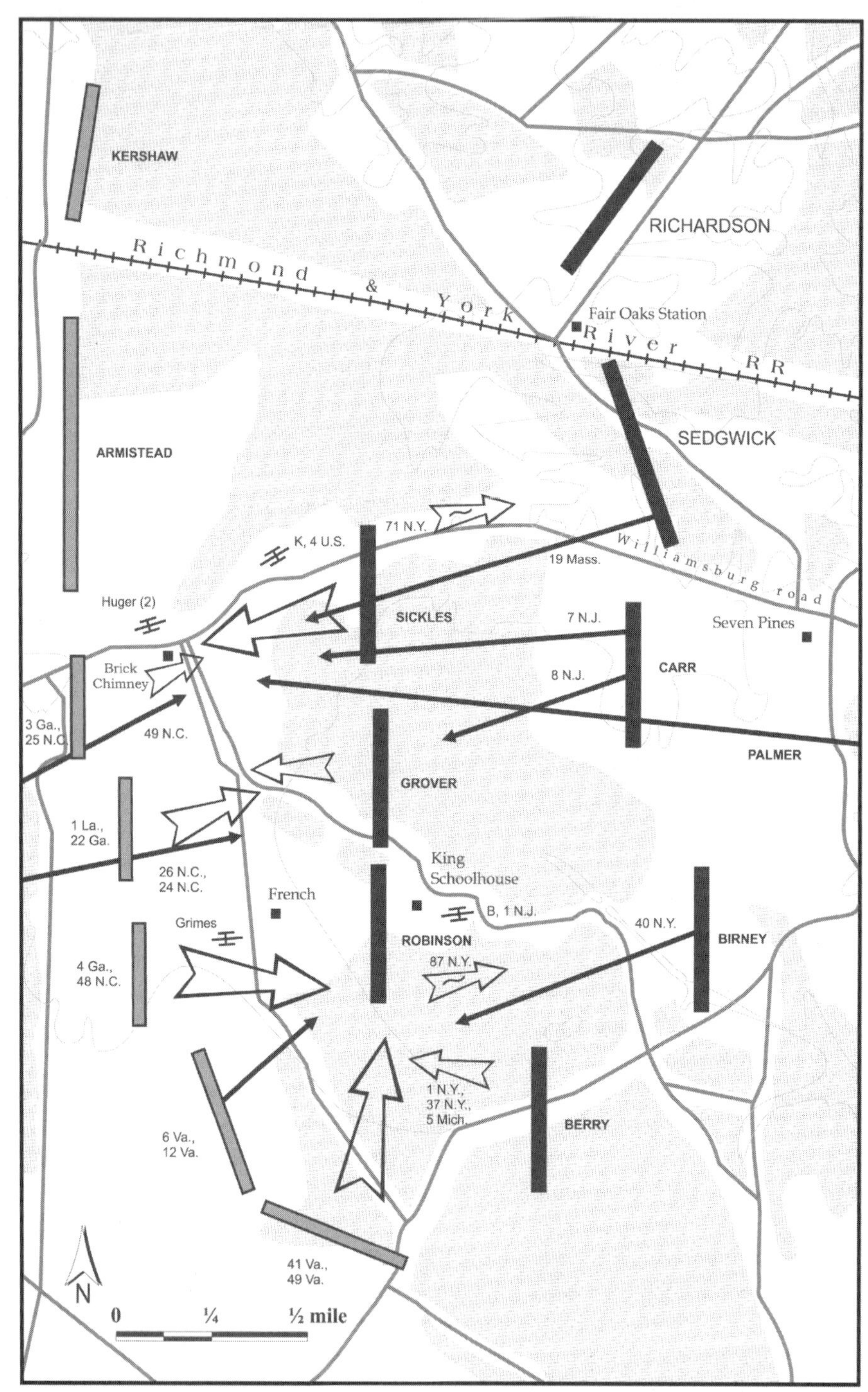

Oak Grove, June 25, 1862

Meanwhile, Heintzelman had ordered Brig. Gen. David B. Birney's brigade from Kearny's division to support Hooker. Birney had just reported to Hooker at about 11 A.M. when the division commander received orders from Randolph Marcy to withdraw. Birney returned his men to their camps, and Sickles's men retreated over the ground they had taken earlier—although not before Sickles protested through an aide that he was driving the Confederates back. One regiment, the 73rd New York, had made it as far as a place called the Brick Chimney before it was recalled. Grover either never got the order or found he was too engaged to obey it and stayed where he was.

The order originated with Heintzelman, who had been receiving Hooker's requests for reinforcements. "Fighting Joe" thought he was outnumbered three to one (which was in no sense true—Huger's whole division, not all of which confronted Hooker, plus Ransom's brigade had barely nine thousand men, whereas Hooker's division alone had nearly that many), and Heintzelman telegraphed that "fact" to McClellan's headquarters. Faced with that alarming news, McClellan decided to rethink the idea of attacking. Heintzelman later testified that the order to stop the movement at Oak Grove was a mistake, but since he had brought the order about himself, he was to blame for it.

With the order came information that McClellan was headed to the front, and a later order told Heintzelman not to move back another inch until the army commander got there. Everything pretty much stopped until 1 P.M., when Little Mac arrived. By then the morning rain had ended, and McClellan took off his coat and climbed a tree so he could see the Confederate position better. Notwithstanding the bullets directed at him, he took some notes and climbed back down. He had no problem seeing a Union advantage and ordered the advance to resume.[6]

At about the same time Sickles began his advance to retake the ground from which he had just withdrawn, another of Ransom's regiments, the 49th North Carolina, moved up to support Wright. The Federals found the going slow once more—it was "the hardest fighting of the day," one man said—as the swamp, undergrowth, and Confederates again took their toll. The 73rd New York got back to the Brick Chimney, which the rebels had reoccupied, and drove their opponents off a second time. Two brigades from Brig. Gen. Darius N. Couch's IV Corps division were ordered to support Hooker's attack, and Brig. Gen. Innis N. Palmer's Massachusetts, New York, and Rhode Island regiments went to help Sickles.

Palmer had just turned thirty-eight in the spring. The New Yorker graduated from West Point in the class of 1846 along with Couch, McClellan, and many other prominent generals, and had served well in the Mexican War and in the 2nd U.S. Cavalry—Robert E. Lee's regiment. His men took their positions in front of the Excelsior Brigade. Couch went along as a volunteer, apparently peeved that someone else was ordering one of his brigades around. Captain

Thomas W. Osborn's Battery D, 1st New York Light Artillery, began firing over the heads of the Unionists to hit the woods beyond. At the same time, Heintzelman ordered Capt. Gustavus A. De Russy, his artillery chief, to support Hooker with a section of guns. A section of Battery K, 4th U.S. Artillery, commanded by Lt. Tome Henderson posted itself on the Williamsburg road and opened with good effect. Wright ordered a section of Capt. Frank Huger's Company D, Virginia Light Artillery, to respond. Huger got his two guns within eight hundred yards of Henderson's section before opening up. The Union guns ran out of ammunition and got more before the rebels opened fire, but soon after the gun battle started it ended with Henderson pulling out. Captain Huger kept banging away for a while, hurting the 2nd Rhode Island quite a bit but other regiments very little. The Confederates finally stopped about sundown.[7]

Not all the action was on the northern end of the Union line. Farther south, Brig. Gen. John C. Robinson's brigade of Indiana, Pennsylvania, and New York infantry formed the right of Kearny's line, and Robinson advanced his men to stay even with Hooker. Brigadier General Hiram G. Berry's Michigan and New York regiments did the same on Robinson's left, with Berry's men covering an approach to the Union lines from the Charles City road. "This is the hour for which we have been longing," Kearny called out to his men. "We'll see you in Richmond, General Phil!" a soldier shouted back. "That's the spirit," Kearny replied. As the 20th Indiana advanced a man caught sight of a dead Confederate with a heavy gold ring. The Hoosier tried to pull the ring off the Southerner's finger but the flesh slipped off instead, so the ring stayed where it was.

Robinson's advance, along with Grover's, was made in full view of Billy Mahone. Seeing the fighting north of him, Mahone readied his men to move to Wright's support but was too late to help in the morning. After the Union advance stopped, however, Mahone moved to the cover of some woods to support Wright's right flank, bringing with him two guns from Capt. Carey F. Grimes's Virginia battery.

Artillery began the heavy combat on the south end of the line. Robinson's advance, though contested enough to force him to bring up his reserve regiment, the 87th New York, had passed King's Schoolhouse and brought his left near an orchard, driving Confederates out of three nearby buildings. The 63rd Pennsylvania kept going until it was half a mile nearer Richmond than any other troops from Kearny's division. It stayed there for an hour before being withdrawn. While out there, one of the Pennyslvanians, Will Davison, was picking a huckleberry when a bullet cut off his right forefinger. Davison looked at his hand, said, "Well, they can just keep their damned berries," and headed for the rear.

Mahone saw the advance and ordered Grimes's guns into action. Rebel sharpshooters also were annoying the Yankees from the French home, a two-story frame house. Robinson noticed and sent word to Kearny that he could use some artillery of his own. A section of Battery B, 1st New Jersey Artillery, under Lt. A. Judson Clark soon appeared, and the 37th New York of Berry's brigade also came forward. One of Clark's guns gave the house four ten-pound shots, rendering it useless. Grimes responded, and the Union guns retired.[8]

Robinson was forty-five years old in June 1862. The New York native had been dismissed from West Point but later was directly commissioned in the Regular Army and became a career soldier. He was commander of Fort McHenry in Baltimore at the outbreak of hostilities. The man called "the hairiest general . . . in a much-bearded army" saw his main action on June 25 late in the day. The 4th Georgia from Wright's brigade, after its encounter with Hooker's men in the morning, had been moved to Wright's extreme right flank. Ransom's 48th North Carolina had been ordered twice to support the Georgians—once in the morning, and then again in the afternoon after moving back to some field works. At about 6 P.M., Wright ordered these two regiments to attack the Federals in front of them, the 87th New York. Robinson moved the 20th Indiana up on the New Yorkers' right, and the battle raged. The 48th North Carolina wavered, and Mahone ordered the 12th Virginia and part of the 6th Virginia to support the Tar Heels. Then he ordered the 41st and 49th Virginia to flank the Unionists. The 41st Virginia got caught up in some woods, but the 49th kept going. The Virginians hit the 87th New York in the flank, and the Federals broke.

Colonel Alexander Hays of the 63rd Pennsylvania was posted just to the right of the 20th Indiana. He said of this action, "It would have been a funny sight to an uninterested observer to have witnessed both sides on a *regular go*, but the rebels found out the game first, and turned after ours." Despite the efforts of their commander, Lt. Col. Richard A. Bachia, the New Yorkers were through for the day. The 20th Indiana also had to break. The Hoosiers rallied to Robinson, who told them, "Get out of this or you will all be captured." The Confederates stood "exulting over the glorious victory," one man wrote.

But part of Birney's command came to the Unionists' rescue. Earlier in the afternoon, Kearny had ordered Birney to relieve Grover. David Birney, just turned thirty-seven and the son of antislavery leader James G. Birney, was a Philadelphia lawyer. He had taken the 40th New York, 4th Maine, and part of the 101st New York to Hooker's position in response to that order. Once he got there he was ordered to charge a group of rebels who proved not to exist. Changing front a couple of times, Birney took some fire and wound up somehow with his left flank connected to Berry's 1st New York. He thus was behind Robinson, not Grover. Finally, at about 6:30, Birney—probably thoroughly confused by this time, and having just survived a court-martial for disobeying orders—asked Kearny whether he was actually supposed to relieve Grover. Kearny said not until Birney had received orders from him, and then detached the 40th New York. That regiment, with Kearny himself in the ranks, came to Robinson's assistance. The brigade commander and an aide attempted to lead the reinforcements through the woods, but instead they met up with a battalion of Confederates who shot their horses. Undaunted, the 40th New York and 20th Indiana counterattacked to stop the Confederate rush. Berry's 1st New York and 5th Michigan also helped repair the breech in the Union line. In the 12th Virginia, a man called, "Look to the left! The Yankees are flanking us!" The Virginians did the prudent thing and fell back as fresh troops arrived.[9]

While the battle was joined in the south, Wright also ordered the 1st Louisiana and 22nd Georgia to regain ground in the center of Wright's line. The 49th North Carolina of Ransom's brigade had been supporting Wright's men, but it was relieved by Ransom's 24th North Carolina, which joined the Louisianans and Georgians. C. S. Powell "came near getting wobbly" as the 24th entered battle for the first time. Bill Scott, marching near Powell, was shot, fell, and said, "Boys, I am killed." He was the first member of the 24th to die in battle.

By then Grover had lost his only reserve, seven companies from the 16th Massachusetts, which had been ordered to support Robinson. However, the 8th New Jersey, which had previously supported his right, moved to his left flank. Grover received the Confederate attack, and this part of the battle was "awful" according to a Federal participant. Lieutenant Colonel Henry K. Burgwyn of the 26th North Carolina, which relieved the 24th on Lee's direct order, said the fire was "as awful as I could desire." Either Grover beat off the attack and then withdrew the brigade voluntarily or Wright's men forced him back, depending upon which report is to be believed. Jeremiah Downes of the 11th Massachusetts told his mother that "they found we were too heavy for them," so perhaps this time Grover was more accurate. It was dark by the end of this fight. Birney's brigade, minus the 40th New York, finally relieved Grover's regiments, and Birney himself was withdrawn before dawn on the twenty-sixth.[10]

The night was not quiet, however. Nervous pickets and various orders caused what Heintzelman called "several picket stampedes." The 96th Pennsylvania from Slocum's division—which had not even been involved in the battle—got called into line at 11 P.M. The 26th North Carolina, ordered to go on picket, separated into two sections, neither of which knew where the other was; perhaps one section fired into the other. Confederate fire stampeded pickets from the 101st New York, and routed some New Yorkers who were throwing up breastworks. Even though the 10th Massachusetts was not under fire, its men scattered everywhere when it received the order to fall back. The sounds of the wounded crying out "were harrowing in the extreme," one member of the 20th Indiana recalled.[11]

This first battle of the Seven Days is commonly called Oak Grove but also was known as King's Schoolhouse, French's Field, or the Orchard. More than seventeen thousand Federals, not all of whom engaged in the fighting, had advanced against about seven thousand rebels, although the fighting in most sectors was relatively light. The cost on the Union side was 67 killed, 504 wounded, and 55 missing, mostly in Hooker's division—although the 20th Indiana from Robinson's brigade lost 125 men, including 32 missing. The Confederates lost 66 killed, 362 wounded, and 13 missing, most of them from Wright's brigade. The 1st Louisiana suffered 135 casualties, the 22nd Georgia 89, and the 48th North Carolina 88. Nobody seems to agree on who accomplished what. Heintzelman considered that his object had been accomplished. McClellan, who had watched the afternoon's engagement from a redoubt, reported to Stanton that the troops had "behaved splendidly." Wright, on the other hand, maintained that he held the same line in the evening that he had in the morning. The question that remains unresolved concerns who was responsible for the Union withdrawal. Did Heintzelman pull his troops back voluntarily, allowing Wright to move forward once again, or did Confederate attacks push the Federals back? In the end, which side is right makes little difference, for Oak Grove was not only the first but the least significant of any major fight in the Seven Days. It has been called the "Battle of Casualties" because that was its only real importance.[12]

The sounds of battle worried Lee. McClellan might have made a crucial first move, taking the initiative away from Marse Robert, or perhaps Little Mac had learned of Lee's plans. Some artillery fire coming from the north bank of the Chickahominy may have increased Lee's concerns, as Porter was using the heavy guns to shell positions that were to be attacked on the twenty-sixth. This shelling kept up until after 5 P.M. Lee wrote to Davis that Oak Grove had given him some anxious moments, but after seeing the field in the late afternoon and hearing the reports of the action he decided to not change his plans. Lee was not happy with Huger's part in the action, however. He received word that Huger had not been at his post that morning and sent the division commander, upon whom a lot would rest if McClellan moved forward, a sharply worded note telling him to get to the front with his troops and stay there.[13]

Lee's other subordinates kept moving toward their appointed positions. D. H. Hill functioned as Huger's reserve during Oak Grove—one of his brigades received some artillery fire—but that night he moved his force to the Mechanicsville Bridge. A. P. Hill concentrated his division at Meadow Bridges after a march that one artilleryman remembered as "a luxury" because the men moved under a clear sky on dry roads. Longstreet prepared his command to move early the next morning for the Mechanicsville Turnpike. They moved with faith in Lee and his plans, according to Brig. Gen. William Dorsey

Pender, who commanded a brigade in A. P. Hill's division. "Our Generals who have access to General Lee are beginning to gain a great deal of confidence in him," Pender wrote in a letter to his wife. Pender also said that fighting was near, and that Stonewall Jackson would be involved in it. "Jackson is undoubtedly near but no one knows where he is or when he came. Our Major Generals know nothing of his whereabouts, only we all feel convinced that he will be about when the battle comes off which must be in a very few days."[14]

While Jackson was in Richmond on the twenty-third, his leading units managed to move only from Frederickshall to just east of Beaver Dam Station, a little more than ten miles, despite the fact that at least some units used every road they could find and even marched through the fields and trees. Stops were frequent, including a two-hour wait at Beaver Dam Station for the 2nd Mississippi before it marched a couple miles east of the station. The Stonewall Brigade made it only to a couple of miles east of Louisa Court House, so the front and back of the column were still separated by nearly twenty miles.

Apparently neither Dabney, nor the rest of Jackson's staff, nor the generals in charge of the units themselves could get the men to move very well. Dabney, who was suffering from an intestinal problem, had been driven to bed. The roads were terrible, so the wagons were slowed, stretching out the column even more. Dabney believed that inexperienced subordinates helped delay the march, and he derided members of the young staff, who he called "julep-drinking officers," for their carelessness on the march. Douglas believed that Dabney was incapable of handling the position into which Jackson had placed him—a modern historian has called the minister "wholly unsuited" to these particular duties—and Douglas noted as well that the army was tired. For whatever reason, the twenty-third was not a good day.[15]

Jackson met his men at Beaver Dam Station on the morning of the twenty-fourth. When Douglas reached Jackson that afternoon, Stonewall presented quite a sight. "The General must have been on a rollicking frolic," Douglas reported. "His wet and muddy uniform was being dried by the fire and the appearance of his ponderous boots indicated that he might have been wading all night through mud and mire." At that point Jackson was asleep, having tried to relax through the reading of a novel and given up the attempt. Meanwhile, his leading units moved not quite fifteen miles to within five miles of Ashland Station on the Richmond, Fredericksburg, and Potomac Railroad. The rear units, riding on rail cars part of the way, made it to about four miles past Beaver Dam Station, cutting the separation to less than ten miles. Again the day had not been what it could have been. At one point guide Lincoln Sydnor lost his way because of all the new roads that had been cut, and Ewell threatened to hang him. Two rainstorms, one in the morning and another in the evening, made the roads slippery and the men miserable.[16]

On the twenty-fifth Jackson received the services of Maj. Jasper Whiting, who knew the area of the march and whose services proved "invaluable" according to Douglas. Combined with Dabney's brother C. W., who also knew the area, Stonewall now had people who could guide him toward Richmond. He also had his objective. During the night he had received his copy of General Orders no. 75. Nevertheless, there were some differences between the orders and a memorandum Jackson had of the discussions at the Dabbs house meeting. The memorandum had Stonewall reaching the Mechanicsville Turnpike behind the Union lines using the second road east of the Chickahominy. Several roads could have qualified, but the most likely route was the one leading from the Ashcake road by Pole Green Church to Hundley's Corner. From that point, a couple of roads would lead to the Mechanicsville Turnpike. General Orders no. 75 specified the road to Pole Green Church but had Jackson merely bearing toward Cold Harbor (whether Old or New was not specified) and turning the Beaver Dam Creek line. The orders also gave Stonewall a broader area to choose from for his starting point on the twenty-sixth—merely some convenient point west of the Virginia Central Railroad on the way from Ashland to the Slash Church (Lebanon Church, probably), along the Ashcake road. The memorandum's description seemed to indicate a campsite around the Slash Church.[17]

However, in most respects the documents were similar. Neither mentioned the possibility of Jackson's fighting at Beaver Dam Creek, both had Jackson supported by D. H. Hill bearing toward Cold Harbor (the orders told Stonewall to bear well to his left), and both mentioned Jackson's ultimate goal as the Richmond and York River Railroad.

The march on the twenty-fifth did not begin well in the morning rain. Dabney, blaming the young staff for not having the wagons in place, said that the troops were not ready to move before an hour past sunrise, which would have been early just a few days after the summer solstice. But some regiments in Ewell's division still had not left their camps by late morning. The roads were messy because of the rain, and bridges were out—because of either rain-swollen creeks or Union cavalry activity. Lieutenant Colonel Will T. Martin, now commanding both the Jeff Davis Legion and the 4th Virginia Cavalry, drove a company from the 8th Illinois Cavalry out of the area. Martin's command suffered two men wounded; the Federals lost one killed and one wounded. Stonewall's leading units reached Ashland that afternoon and camped a mile or so east. The Stonewall Brigade made it a couple miles past the South Anna River and stopped about a mile west of Ashland. Jackson's army was finally together.[18]

Given the late sunset at that time of year, it is possible that Jackson could have pushed the men to get at least the leading units nearer to the railroad, but he did not, despite at least two obvious displays of concern regarding his failure to fulfill his orders. When Winder met with his commander that evening, Jackson said to him, "You must have your men cook their rations and be ready to start tomorrow morning at dawn." Winder complained, "That is impossible, because of the position of my baggage-train." Presumably the train was at the rear of the line. Jackson did not care. "General Winder, it must be done," he snapped. Dabney related that Stonewall was "scarcely courteous" in his tone. The second evidence of Jackson's concern was in his order for the following day: that the men move at 2 A.M., well before sunrise and an hour earlier than the start time called for in General Orders no. 75.

However, the extra hour would not make up for the five miles between Ashland and the Virginia Central Railroad. As a result, Stonewall sent Lee a message notifying the army commander that he would be late and giving the reasons. He also received a message from Lee to the effect that two roads would be available to Jackson for the next day's advance. The column on the more westerly road, which basically paralleled the railroad and met the road coming from Meadow Bridges, would unite with Brig. Gen. Lawrence O'B. Branch's brigade of A. P. Hill's division coming from Half Sink Farm, while the rest of the force used the road leading to Pole Green Church. This could help make up some time. Finally, Jeb Stuart appeared at Jackson's headquarters; Stuart would cover Stonewall's left and was ready to give him any information he might want.

That night, Ewell and Whiting came to Jackson with the suggestion that the command move by two parallel roads instead of on one road only. Jackson listened to them and then, despite Lee's message, asked that they wait until the morning for his decision. After the division commanders left Jackson's tent, one said to the other, "Do you know why General Jackson would not decide upon our suggestion at once? It was because he has to pray over it, before he makes up his mind." Just after that, the other commander realized that he had left his sword in Jackson's tent and went back to get it. Sure enough, when he entered he saw Stonewall on his knees.[19]

Jackson may or may not have slept on the night of the twenty-fifth. If he did, it was precious little, particularly following the events of the previous three days. He had ridden all night on the twenty-second, attended Lee's conference on the twenty-third, ridden again all that night, gotten some sleep during the day on the twenty-fourth, and probably slept some but not fully that night. Thus, on the morning of the twenty-sixth, Jackson was going to war having slept no more than six or seven hours in the preceding four days. Douglas once wrote, "He could sleep anywhere and in any position," and reported that Jackson used time others may have given to socializing to sleep. But Douglas also reported that Jackson typically slept "a great deal," and he almost certainly would have been feeling the effects of his lack of sleep by the twenty-fifth or twenty-sixth.[20]

Stonewall might have found some energy, from either joy or fury, if he had known of an incident that had occurred the day before. A man named Charles

Rean wandered into Union pickets near Hanover Court House and was sent to Fitz John Porter's headquarters, where Porter talked with him. Rean stated that he was an escaped prisoner of Jackson's; Porter sent him on to the provost marshal with the request that he be made to tell the truth. Apparently, however, Rean was believed and let go. Porter found that out and had him arrested again, making sure that McClellan talked with Rean. Pinkerton interrogated him as well. Under pressure from Pinkerton and McClellan, Rean finally said that he was from Jackson's command, which was headed straight for the Union rear. The junction of that force with Lee's army would occur on the twenty-eighth, and Jackson had fifteen brigades, including Ewell's and Whiting's divisions, according to Rean. Stonewall actually had nine brigades.

McClellan wasted little time getting the report to Stanton, telegraphing him at midnight on the twenty-fourth and asking for any reports Washington may have heard as to Stonewall's whereabouts. Stanton did not know, and said so. He told McClellan what he had heard, and concluded by saying, "I think, therefore, that while the warning of the deserter to you may also be a blind, it could not safely be disregarded." Stanton at least was learning of Jackson's penchant for ruses, and the Confederate may have deceived everyone so much that the truth suddenly stood out. Pinkerton, who was so far off base in his estimates of Confederate forces, also thought Rean was a plant: "My own impression is that he has been sent within our lines for the purpose of conveying to us the precise information which he has thus conveyed."[21]

McClellan's visit to the front on the twenty-fifth, and in his view the success of the day, had put him in good spirits. His telegrams of the afternoon of the twenty-fifth show that he was not down about Jackson's appearance, if Stonewall was indeed there. At the same time the last of three reports McClellan sent from the front went over the wires, Little Mac received a message from Porter that greatly disturbed him and caused him to return to his headquarters. Porter said contrabands had reported that Jackson was at Hanover Court House (he was not even close and was not going there in any event), and that P. G. T. Beauregard and reinforcements were in Richmond (they were in Mississippi). Although McClellan later testified that he did not regard this report as fully authentic information, he did not act that way at the time. The rebels had done what he wanted the Union to do: concentrate force. He expected Jackson to attack his right and rear, but he could not move other forces to support Porter because he estimated the total Confederate force at two hundred thousand; if he moved too many people, the rest of the Southern host would tear his left to bits. At 6:15 he sent another telegram to Stanton reporting the news:

> I regret my great inferiority in numbers but feel that I am in no way responsible for it as I have not failed to represent repeatedly the necessity of reinforcements, that this was the decisive point, & that all the available means of the Govt should be concentrated here. I will do all that a General can do

with the splendid Army I have the honor to command & if it is destroyed by overwhelming numbers can at least die with it & share its fate.

But if the result of the action which will probably occur tomorrow or within a short time is a disaster the responsibility cannot be thrown on my shoulders—it must rest where it belongs. . . .

I feel that there is no use in my again asking for reinforcements.

McClellan's analysis will not stand. He should have known he was not greatly inferior in numbers to Lee. Brigadier General George G. Meade, in command of a brigade of the Pennsylvania Reserves only since the middle of June, had read the report of Jackson's arrival on the right. It, plus the great show in front of him, "leads me to doubt whether their army is as strong as reported and whether they do actually outnumber us as some believe," he wrote to his wife. If Meade could reach that conclusion in a few days, McClellan should have been able to do the same.

Little Mac also should have understood the importance, particularly in Lincoln's mind, of defending Washington against even a minor threat. He should have known that any reinforcements Lincoln was willing to send, other than McDowell's men near Fredericksburg, would not be as well trained as McClellan's men and might not respond well to a battlefield situation. McClellan should have remembered that a division's worth of troops at Fort Monroe could have come to the front lines at any time.

The responsibility for any defeat would fall where it should, at least as far as Lincoln was concerned. The president was not one to disclaim responsibility, and if McClellan's defeat were truly caused by a lack of reinforcement, Lincoln would acknowledge the fact. It was partly frustration at what Little Mac thought was a criminal lack of support by the Lincoln administration that boiled over in this telegram. It must have taken all of Lincoln's tact and understanding to reply as mildly as he did: "I give you all I can, and act on the presumption that you will do the best you can with what you have, while you continue, ungenerously I think, to assume that I could give you more if I would. I have omitted and shall omit no opportunity to send you reinforcements whenever I possibly can."[22]

On the night of the twenty-fifth, Lee found himself in a tight situation, but he had devised a good strategy to attempt to change that. In fact, Porter Alexander thought Lee's chance for success was the greatest ever given a Confederate general. McClellan, on the other hand, was in a relatively good position—he had advanced between half a mile and a mile since Seven Pines—and had found a plan to keep improving it. Yet he was haunted by Jackson and by the overestimates of Lee's force that he accepted. He had waited just long enough to give Lee time. One Confederate put it this way: "[I]t now began to dawn on him that Lee was about to attack him, and the question now was not whether he could capture Richmond, but whether he could successfully retreat." Now that Lee had taken the initiative, McClellan, with his doubts and fears, would let him have it.

McClellan's mercurial nature rose again shortly after he had unburdened himself. Possibly it was that he had work to do; he expected an attack the next day. He ordered Sumner and Heintzelman to prepare defensive lines behind which to fight if attacked (members of the 10th Massachusetts from Palmer's brigade, in fulfilling this order, hit a rebel mass grave and stopped their work in that area immediately). Smith was notified to do nothing that might bring on a general engagement. McClellan also ordered Brig. Gen. Ambrose Burnside, in command of Union forces on the North Carolina coast, to cut the railroad over which Beauregard must travel with those of his forces not already in Richmond. To White House Landing went the order that no civilian was to be allowed to come to the front.

McClellan visited Porter's corps that night and found it ready to receive the Confederate attack. McCall's division was charged with the forward defense. The brigades of Brig. Gens. John Reynolds and Truman Seymour were moved to positions behind Beaver Dam Creek after McClellan heard the captured Confederate Rean's story. Meade's brigade, along with most of Porter's other two divisions at the Gaines farm, was ready to move at the first alarm. Colonel Robert C. Buchanan's brigade of Brig. Gen. George Sykes's division had moved out in the morning toward Hanover Court House and, accompanied by the 6th U.S. Cavalry, camped near Totopotomoy Creek that night.

Whatever the reason for McClellan's shift in mood, at 10:40 P.M. he telegraphed Stanton, "If I had another good Division I could laugh at Jackson. . . . Nothing but overwhelming forces can defeat us." Of course, as he had already stated that two hundred thousand Confederates were ready to attack him, the overwhelming forces must have seemed close at hand. After another telegram got ammunition moving to the front lines, McClellan left Porter for his own headquarters. After getting a little sleep, he toured the lines south of the Chickahominy. By 9 A.M., suffering from neuralgia but over a bout with malaria and probably running on adrenaline, he telegraphed Stanton, "There is no doubt in my mind now that Jackson is coming upon us, and with such great odds against us we shall have our hands full."[23]

CHAPTER FOUR

"Charging Batteries Is Highly Dangerous"

June 26 was to have been the big day for McClellan, the day of the attack on Old Tavern. There was no reason not to go ahead except the ones in his mind: Jackson's dominant reputation, the erroneous and exaggerated information he received, and the effects that information had on a temperament at once cautious and persecuted. Confident in himself and in his army, yet mortally afraid of failure, he could not bring himself to see the truth for what it was. Porter Alexander put the situation aptly when he wrote of McClellan, "He had come within arm's length, but allowed the initiative to Lee."

As the morning of a beautiful June day passed and nothing happened, he had ample opportunity to order the attack. He did not. The only action taken by Union units was the shelling of Confederate artillery around New Bridge, ordered by Fitz John Porter and conducted by the same siege guns used the day before. By the same token, McClellan had ample opportunity to move units to the north bank to help Porter against Jackson. He did not. By noon, still on the south bank of the Chickahominy, he was to the point that he even worried about silence in a telegraph to Stanton: "All things very quiet on this bank. . . . I would prefer more noise." He could have had the noise anytime he wanted; he just could not bring himself to order any.

McClellan was not the only person near Richmond wondering about the quiet along the Chickahominy. Theodore Fogel, in the 2nd Georgia's lines south of the river, wrote: "not a gun has been heard on our lines today, the stillness is awful, the pickets have even ceased firing at each other."[1]

Robert E. Lee also looked for tidings as the quiet continued. Stonewall Jackson and his foot cavalry should have left their camps at 2 A.M. on their way to flanking the Union left, but nothing had been heard. A. P. Hill was by Meadow Bridges, D. H. Hill by Mechanicsville Bridge, and Longstreet behind D. H. Hill. Longstreet and D. H. Hill were on the Mechanicsville Turnpike by 8 A.M., and Lee arrived soon after. A short time after that, Jefferson Davis and his staff joined the gathering on the bluffs south of the Chickahominy.

Lawrence Branch had moved his North Carolinians a half-mile into the woods at Half Sink after finding out that his original position, nearer to the river, was exposed to enemy pickets. He had waited for Jackson to send notice of his approach, as Hill had ordered that morning. Stonewall sent Branch a note at 9 A.M. advising him that his vanguard was crossing the Virginia Central Railroad. This meant that Jackson was already six hours behind the schedule set in General Orders no. 75. If Branch had communicated that fact to A. P. Hill, "Little Powell" might not have launched what was to prove a suicidal attack later in the day. Although Branch, a forty-one-year-old North Carolinian, had been tutored by Secretary of the Treasury Salmon P. Chase, had graduated from Princeton and studied law, and had served in Congress before the war, he had never studied military matters before joining the Confederate army. Branch merely crossed the Chickahominy as soon as he received Jackson's note, a few minutes before 10 A.M.

Lee wrote to Jefferson Davis that morning, "I fear from the operations of the enemy yesterday [Oak Grove] that our plan of operations has been discovered to them." If Marse Robert was considering that possibility after apparently dismissing it the day before, his anxiety must have been growing steadily. A messenger bringing word that all was quiet south of the Chickahominy described Lee's appearance in his memoirs: the commander's tie had slipped around until the bow rested under an ear, and one pants leg was "notably displaced."[2]

Jackson, Branch, and their commands were running into constant, if minor, harassment from Union cavalry posted at intersections along their lines of march. Despite his orders, Stonewall had not started his march until after sunrise that morning. Winder had been up at 1:15, but he received orders not to move until the men got rations. That postponed his march until six. The men were short on water, searching the country for wells so they could fill their canteens. Shortly after crossing the Virginia Central Railroad, as Lee had suggested, Jackson split Ewell's division from the rest of his force. Stonewall headed east to Taliaferro's mill and then south to Hundley's Corner, near the Pole Green Church—a spot that would put him square on the flank of the Union troops behind Beaver Dam Creek. On the way he passed the birthplace of Henry Clay and pointed it out to his staff and made a few comments about Clay as well.

Stonewall marched down the road he called the Ashcake road with skirmishers deployed—a slow way of moving, although necessary since he was moving

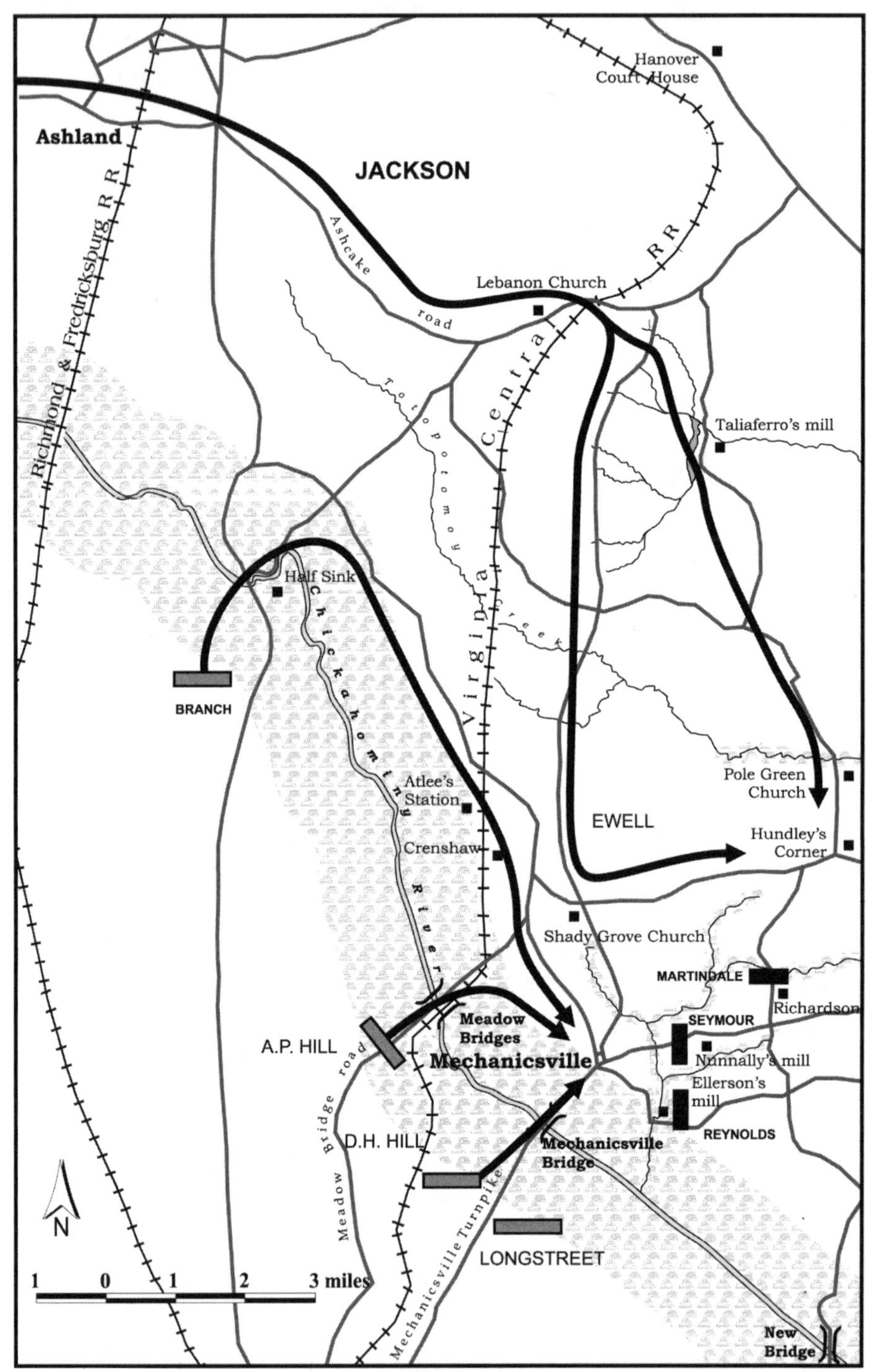

Confederate movements, June 26, 1862

through enemy-occupied territory. His men ran into some obstructions in the road, Yankee pickets along the way, and more substantial trouble at the bridge over the Totopotomoy Creek. There, a company of the 8th Illinois Cavalry had partially destroyed the bridge and felled trees across the road south of the bridge. Skirmishers from John B. Hood's Texas Brigade crossed the creek to drive off the troopers, and Capt. James Reilly's North Carolina battery shelled the opposite bank as well. In getting into position, Reilly moved into a field behind a man sitting on a fence yelling encouragement to the troops. When the guns opened fire, the man fell off the fence, got up cursing the rebels, rounded up his slaves who were working in the field, and took shelter in a nearby house. Reilly's fire and Hood's advance had an immediate effect. The Union cavalry fled so fast that some troopers left their axes still in the trees. Whiting's division got the bridge repaired, but from then on cavalry dogged the march.[3]

Ewell took the road south to Shady Grove Church, less than two miles from Mechanicsville, from which he could either join with Branch and the rest of A. P. Hill's division to complete the line or move east to rejoin Jackson. One of the few Civil War generals to be born in the District of Columbia, Ewell was forty-five years old. A West Pointer—class of 1840—he spent his entire prewar career in the Southwest and Mexico before resigning in 1861. "Old Bald Head" distinguished himself in Jackson's Valley campaign, commanding one of Stonewall's two divisions and fighting the battle of Cross Keys himself. On this day he and his men dealt with the same delaying tactics as did Jackson. Early in the afternoon, the men of the 1st Maryland saw the cavalry screen in front of them stop. Immediately the shout rang out, "Look out boys, fight on hand! Cavalry videtting to the rear." Two companies of the 1st Maryland drove the Northerners off. During this skirmish the men saw heavy columns to their right. That was Branch, marching down a parallel road. The North Carolinians could see Ewell's column as well, and they cheered the news of Jackson's arrival at Richmond.

Branch had experienced an almost continuous skirmish between his leading elements and Union cavalry until he ran into two hundred horsemen from the 8th Illinois Cavalry blocking the road at Atlee's Station, five miles north of Mechanicsville. One officer called their stand "determined," but the 7th North Carolina drove the troopers back and captured their battle flag. The Yankees made their last stand in front of a large, white house on the east side of the railroad, but one round from a section of Capt. Marmaduke Johnson's Virginia battery scattered them. The residents of the house, quite grateful at being delivered from the Northerners, shared their food with the soldiers, to whom it seemed like nectar of the gods. After Branch brushed these troopers aside, Union resistance consistently slowed his march. He and Ewell met about one mile north of Shady Grove Church near Crenshaw's at 3 P.M. There the roads the two commands were using were a quarter mile apart. However, since Branch had no orders or news, Ewell decided to move east to Hundley's Corner, where Jackson would be.[4]

The news of Jackson's advance probably reached McClellan before it reached Lee. The Union commander had notified Washington at noon that someone, probably Jackson, had forced his advanced cavalry pickets from their positions. He expected his communications to be cut off, but he was not despairing: "Do not believe reports of disaster & do not be discouraged if you learn that my communications are cut & even Yorktown in possession of the enemy." He added a plaintive request for confidence from Stanton: "Hope for the best & I will not deceive the hopes you formerly placed in me."

There were several possible responses to the Confederate thrust. One almost certain response, however, was a change of base to the James River. The change of base would be necessary if McClellan's communications were indeed cut, and McClellan was ready for the move. On June 23 his quartermaster, Brig. Gen. Stewart Van Vliet, had notified navy flag officer Louis M. Goldsborough that transports loaded with supplies would be headed from White House to the James River in "a day or two" and asked that they be guarded by gunboats. Goldsborough had taken offense to the tone of Van Vliet's request, and by the time McClellan himself wrote to Goldsborough on the afternoon of the twenty-sixth, he felt the transfer was vital to his army's safety.

McClellan must have realized that big siege guns would be of no further use; the battles to be fought would not be matters of artillery and engineering but of bullets and blood. Without the need for the Richmond and York River Railroad to move his guns, he could transfer his base to the strategically superior James. Yet he was not committed to the move. Supplies on transports could be moved back to White House easily if an opening presented itself. McClellan on the afternoon of the twenty-sixth was in a very flexible position.

He seems to have known this. A flurry of dispatches went out from his headquarters that afternoon. To the corps commanders on the south bank went the instruction to be ready to move in any direction. To Porter went the command to send baggage and heavy guns to the south bank of the Chickahominy so he could move more quickly. The trains crossed the river all afternoon and evening. To White House Landing went the order to send as many supplies to the front as possible and get the rest ready to move if necessary. All these dispatches have the feel of an army ready to do something.[5]

Two offensive actions were possible. First, McClellan could hold the Confederates on the north bank of the Chickahominy with Porter's corps and march with the rest of his army through the rebel positions and into Richmond. Major Joseph L. Brent of Magruder's staff wrote: "it is self evident that our position was so inherently weak that McClellan could have easily broken our lines." There is evidence that McClellan thought of it. Baldy Smith wrote after the war that McClellan consulted Franklin and himself about an attack. The two subordinates had encouraged Little Mac. A note from McClellan to Porter at 3:15 asked, "Tell me whether position of affairs is such that an attack on Old Tavern by Franklin would aid you." He had not given up the idea of attacking yet. At 4:30, he wrote his wife: "I think the enemy are making a great mistake, if so they will be terribly punished. . . . I give you my word that I believe we will surely win & that the enemy is falling into a trap. I shall allow the enemy to cut off our communications in order to ensure success."

The other possible offensive action was to strengthen Porter and fight a winner-take-all battle north of the Chickahominy. To that end, McClellan asked Keyes, Heintzelman, and Sumner how many men they could spare for a move across the river and still hold their lines. Keyes could not volunteer any, but Heintzelman was willing to give up two brigades—one-third of his force—and Sumner decided he could do with half his present force. That would have given Porter some twelve thousand more troops, increasing his total to about thirty-eight thousand. Compared with McClellan's exaggerated estimates of Confederate forces this was a small number, but it would have been much closer to the actual number of Southerners on the north bank.[6]

McClellan chose neither of these two options. Since he expected to have his communications cut, to attack and suffer a crushing defeat would mean the loss of his trains and no supplies for his army. Even if he won the battle and took Richmond, he would have lost communication with his supplies, and keeping open communications with supply bases was considered essential. Finally, given McClellan's overestimate of Lee's numbers, attacking did seem out of the question.[7]

Little Mac's caution was reinforced by happenings south of the river. Lee thought that some demonstrations there would be enough to keep reinforcements from going to Porter. He counted on their psychological effect on McClellan to be enough to prevent a Union attack. John Magruder repeated his Yorktown performance, and this time Benjamin Huger joined him. The two divisions kept up a constant fire with patrols and frequent artillery barrages. They were to press the Yankees if possible, and defend themselves if necessary.

Many Federals were deceived. Horton Keith of the 6th Vermont in Baldy Smith's division wrote that he and his comrades were "expecting every moment to be attacked ourselves." And Theodore Dodge of the 101st New York noted in his journal, "The Rebels are in too great force in front to admit of an attack by us." More important, McClellan believed this. With Pinkerton's estimates of two hundred thousand men (including Beauregard as well as Lee) opposing him, Little Mac thought that not only was Jackson coming down on his right, but also forces at least as strong would strike his left. Writing of events on the twenty-seventh, he said: "The operations of this day proved the numerical superiority of the enemy, and made it evident that while he had a large army on the left [north] bank of the Chickahominy, . . . he was also in large force between our army and Richmond." Lee's gamble had worked.[8]

But his strategy was not working quite as well. The troops who were to turn Porter's flank were still struggling through the countryside northeast of Richmond. As the day got longer and word came of no Union activities south of the river, Lee's anxiety for that area probably waned. But his anxiety about the delay in the battle caused by Jackson's tardiness probably increased. With every passing hour the chance for surprise and enough light to force the Federals out of their trenches and attack them in the open was fading.

A. P. Hill's anxiety was also increasing. Little Powell was not one to let the grass grow under his feet. His orders were to cross the river as soon as Branch cleared the opposite bank and then sweep the area from Meadow Bridges to Mechanicsville of Federals, clearing the way for Longstreet and D. H. Hill. But he was to wait for Branch, who in turn was to stay abreast of Jackson. As Jackson was late, so was Branch, and Hill became impatient with the delay, knowing as Lee did that delay could be more than dangerous. In his report of the battle he wrote, "Three o'clock having arrived, and no intelligence from Jackson or Branch, I determined to cross at once rather than hazard the failure of the whole plan by longer deferring it."

It is likely that Lee, if consulted, would have approved this move. But Hill did not check with his commander first, which is inexcusable. Also, Little Powell did not attempt to communicate with either Branch or Jackson. Why Hill did not send couriers to other commanders or confer with Lee before crossing, when the commander-in-chief was less than two miles away, is unknown. But Hill was not censured—by Lee at the time, or by any of the Southern writers after the war—either for his lack of communication or for crossing the river. It is possible that Hill may have misunderstood Lee's orders and thought that Lee intended that there be fighting at Mechanicsville. A misunderstanding is not necessary, however. Hill could have understood perfectly that Lee did not want to fight Union troops at Beaver Dam Creek yet felt that any delay would give the Yankees more time to figure out what Lee was doing. He also may have wanted to ensure that all Confederate troops got across the river that day.[9]

Lee also could have tried to get information. Yet historians have agreed that there is no record that he either moved from his observation site on Chickahominy Bluff, south of the river, or sent couriers to any of the commanders responsible for beginning the action. But some evidence has been consistently ignored. Major Brent of Magruder's staff wrote after the war that he had been sent by his commander to find out what was going on north of the river and to report that matters on his front were quiet. Brent found Lee on the Mechanicsville road about 3 P.M. Lee said he was happy to see Brent and asked about the state of affairs with Magruder. Brent filled him in. Lee then said: "I suppose you have come to find out the cause of our delay, as Genl. Magruder must be anxious. We have been waiting for Genl. Jackson, from whom I have not heard, but I cannot wait longer, and have just sent orders to Genl. Hill to cross at Meadow Bridge." Brent's postwar account is supported by a letter from Thomas Goree, one of Longstreet's aides, written a few weeks after the battle. If these two accounts are to be credited, then Lee and Hill decided at the same point that the time had come, Jackson or no Jackson. It clears up the mystery of Lee's not censuring Hill for crossing the river. It also allows Lee to have a little more credit (or blame) for control of the day's events than he has been given—although if Hill's report is to be believed, he made the decision before he heard from Lee. However, Lee was still less active than he should have been. He probably heard twice from Maj. Charles Richardson, commanding the 2nd Battalion of the army's artillery corps and posted just south of the river along the turnpike, that the Yankees were gone from the works on the other side of the river. But other than moving to Richardson's position, Lee did nothing.[10]

More blame for the fog on the Confederate side can be laid at Branch's door. That officer, more than Jackson, was in a position to communicate with the rest of the army, and any communication could have moved Lee to modify his plan. No one knew that at 3 P.M. Branch was three miles from Mechanicsville, or that Jackson, his forces split, was even farther away. They could have known if Branch had taken a few minutes to send a courier with the tidings of the march. But he did not send a message, and Hill knew nothing about happenings on the north side of the Chickahominy as he moved his troops across Meadow Bridges. The crossing was simple, as only three companies of the 13th Pennsylvania Reserves stood guard and the Confederates were concealed from Union sight by the lay of the land. The rest of the day, although Hill did not know it, would not be quite as simple, at least partially because of the man commanding the Northern forces.

That man was Fitz John Porter, a native of New Hampshire and an army man in a navy family. Porter's uncle, David, had been a commodore, and his cousin David Dixon Porter was less than a year from earning fame on the western rivers. Born in 1822, Fitz John had attended West Point and fought with great distinction in the Mexican War. After the war he returned to West Point as an artillery instructor and then served as Albert Sidney Johnston's adjutant during the 1857 Utah expedition. At the outbreak of civil war he became colonel of the 15th U.S. Infantry and soon a brigadier general of volunteers. After service as chief of staff to Robert Patterson in the Shenandoah, he went to Washington at McClellan's request to help train the Army of the Potomac. A division commander in III Corps at the beginning of the Peninsular campaign, he was promoted to command of the V Corps during it. That promotion no doubt was the result of both his record and his unswerving loyalty to McClellan. Little Mac relied upon Porter more than anyone else as a sounding board and as a commander; that is undoubtedly why Porter's corps was the one standing alone on the north bank of the Chickahominy.

Porter (and McClellan, who had joined him early in the afternoon) heard a single cannon shot fired from his troops guarding the crossings at 2 P.M. That was the signal that the rebels were beginning to cross. He had seen dust clouds to his north and west all day, and he had surmised that Jackson was headed that way. Now it seemed that Lee was ready to attack him directly. Porter thus ordered Meade's brigade to support its Pennsylvania brethren along Beaver Dam Creek. Three batteries of artillery—Battery B of the 1st Pennsylvania Light and batteries C and K of the 5th U.S.—were in place along the line. In the morning, Brig. Gen. John H. Martindale's Maine, Massachusetts, Michigan, and New York troops of Brig. Gen. George W. Morell's division moved along the creek northeast of the main position to protect against any flanking moves. Martindale stopped his men just south of the creek at a Colonel Richardson's house and sent a reconnaissance party north along the road to Hanover Court House. Sykes's men (including Buchanan, who had rejoined the division that morning) had been ready to cross the Chickahominy, but those orders were countermanded and the Regulars stayed on the north bank of the river. Another brigade of Morell's division, New Yorkers, Michiganders, and Pennsylvanians commanded by Brig. Gen. Daniel Butterfield, moved toward Old Church by Old Cold Harbor to protect the rear. However, shortly after Butterfield began the move he received orders to find a strong position and stop there. He then received orders to move toward Mechanicsville, and the brigade finally settled down in Sykes's rear, marching quite a few miles and losing some men with what John Berry of the 16th Michigan called sunstroke. Nevertheless, they fought no Confederates that day.

The Northern troops who would fight on the twenty-sixth had a good position from which to do so. Both Lee and Porter described the position as a very strong one; Lee's judgment was one reason he did not want to attack there. Beaver Dam Creek's banks rose sixty to seventy feet in a steep slope, preventing the crossing of artillery and greatly impeding the progress of infantry. Two bridges crossed the creek, one for the Mechanicsville Turnpike and the other on the road to Gaines's mill. Another mill, Ellerson's, stood just east of the creek on the latter road. The Federals, of course, destroyed the bridges. They also felled trees on the banks to increase the difficulty of climbing. To the west of the creek were open meadows, giving the Union artillery clear fields of fire. The creek was impassable from the Chickahominy north to where the road to Gaines's mill crossed it, and Jedediah Hotchkiss, Jackson's mapmaker, thought the "highest engineering skill in the Federal army" had been at work behind it.[11]

A. P. Hill moved toward this position down the north bank, with fifes playing and drums beating as if on parade, forcing the Federals back as he went. Not that there were many Federals: the 5th Pennsylvania Reserves guarded the Mechanicsville Turnpike bridge, three companies from the 13th Pennsylvania Reserves covered the road from Meadow Bridges, and four companies of the 1st Pennsylvania Reserves were in Mechanicsville itself. Three other companies from the 13th Pennsylvania Reserves supported the cavalry pickets.

Mechanicsville, located a half-mile from the Chickahominy, was a village of half a dozen houses, two or three stores, as many blacksmith and carpenter shops, and some beer shops (including a beer garden that had been used as a Northern camp). The settlement itself had not been treated well by the armies. Yankee shells earlier in the campaign had riddled most buildings. The only house that remained relatively unscathed would be used as a hospital before the day was done.

When Lt. W. F. Dement of the 1st Virginia Artillery fired the first shot of the battle at the Yankees, they fell back rapidly to their positions across Beaver Dam Creek. This allowed D. H. Hill's leading brigade, Georgians and North Carolinians under Brig. Gen. Roswell S. Ripley, to begin crossing at the Mechanicsville Bridge about 4 P.M. The crossing was difficult because the Unionists had broken the bridge before retreating.[12]

At least one company of Federal skirmishers fought too long around Meadow Bridges. Captain Edward Irvin's company of the 13th Pennsylvania Reserves of Reynolds's brigade (also known as the 1st Rifles or the Bucktails) was one of the companies sent out to support the cavalry. It held its ground because Irvin would not take a messenger's word that the order to withdraw had been given; he wanted orders from Maj. Roy Stone, the regimental commander. Irvin and his men were almost immediately surrounded by the Confederate advance and took to the swamp, where they stayed for four days. They finally surrendered, but not before they buried their rifles in the swamp. Captain John Jewett's company almost suffered the same fate, but it managed to get back to the Union lines.

As Porter saw the number of Confederates headed toward him increasing, he ordered Morell's third brigade, consisting of one regiment each from Massachusetts, Michigan, New York, and Pennsylvania under Brig. Gen. Charles Griffin, and Col. Hiram Berdan's 1st U.S. Sharpshooters to take positions behind the front line. That line was held by two brigades of the Pennsylvania Reserves commanded by John Reynolds, who was looking forward to his forty-second birthday in September. The Pennsylvanian graduated from West Point in 1841 and after nineteen years in the army (including service in Mexico) was named Commandant of Cadets at West Point in 1860. Reynolds's brigade—consisting of the 1st, 2nd, 5th, 8th, and 13th Pennsylvania Reserves—was on the right, covering the extension of the Mechanicsville Turnpike. The 9th, 10th, and 12th Pennsylvania Reserves of Truman Seymour's brigade covered the road that crossed Beaver Dam Creek at Ellerson's mill. Battery B, 1st Pennsylvania Light Artillery, and Battery K, 5th U.S. Artillery, covered the northern part of the line, while Battery C, 5th U.S. Artillery, covered the middle of the line. Batteries A and G of the 1st Pennsylvania Light Artillery were moving toward the line. Porter also moved Sykes's division a little closer to Reynolds's position.[13]

The Confederates were also moving closer to that position. Brigadier General Charles W. Field's Virginians of A. P. Hill's division marched through Mechanicsville, and the fourteen Union guns in line across Beaver Dam Creek opened fire. Field called it "the most destructive cannonading I have yet known." As Hill had sent one battery of his divisional artillery to support each brigade while keeping the rest south of the Chickahominy, he could not mass the guns necessary to counter this fire. Captain William J. Pegram's Virginia battery, attached to Field's brigade, set up once and retired because of the heavy fire, then set up again and took fire from three separate batteries, losing four of its six guns disabled. Pegram himself sat "motionless in the saddle, no more concerned at the shells which were ploughing up the dust about him than if he had been lounging on the porch in Franklin Street." One member of the battery remembered that the guns were almost red hot at the end of the day.

Captain R. Snowden Andrews's Maryland battery was moving with Pender's brigade, and one of its sections entered the contest after ten or fifteen minutes' rest in a grove of trees. The fire kept the air vibrating continuously. Two men working one of the guns had agreed to switch between loading and ramming the piece when one got tired. The switch had just occurred when one of them was hit in the chest by a round of solid shot and killed. Soon enough the other man, John Hatton, was wounded, but he was ashamed after crying "Ouch!" and kept to his work. Andrews himself was hit in the leg and hopped to the rear.

Even those not in the fight felt the sting of the Federal guns. Captain William G. Crenshaw's battery of Virginians, attached to Brig. Gen. Maxcy Gregg's reserve brigade, did not return fire at all that day. Nevertheless, the shot and shell came "in a too dangerously close proximity to make us in the least comfortable" according to William E. Jones. The fire was "the most terrific" Jones had yet heard.[14]

Lee, south of the Chickahominy, almost certainly could have seen this shelling and its effect. He is reported to have sent a courier with orders to Hill not to press the assault. This order is part of a quite confusing story told by Thomas W. Sydnor, a local man and a lieutenant in the 4th Virginia Cavalry. Sydnor, in a much-quoted letter written many years after the war to Jedediah Hotchkiss, said that on the night of the twenty-fifth he warned Lee of quicksand in the area south of the road to Old Church, the northernmost of the two roads crossing Beaver Dam Creek. This area is where Field's troops were headed.

Lee had sent Sydnor to Hill on the afternoon of the twenty-sixth with an order not to launch a general attack. After the battle, Lee—in Sydnor's presence—asked Hill if he had received the order, and Hill responded that he had.

Sydnor's account is called into question by a number of factors. First, if Sydnor warned Lee on the night of the twenty-fifth about the quicksand, why did Lee wait until after Hill crossed the Chickahominy to order him not to launch a general assault? Second, there was no general assault at Mechanicsville. The movements on the Confederate left, where the quicksand supposedly was, were in response to Union artillery fire and were by no means a general assault ordered by Hill. The movements on the Confederate right constituted an assault, but that assault was ordered by, among others, Lee himself. Third, there is no record, either official or unofficial, of Lee's censure of A. P. Hill.[15]

Order or no order, the men on Hill's left could not stay where they were. Their only hope was to get close enough to the Union lines so that the artillery would not be able to fire on them for fear of hitting friendly troops. Thus, Field's men and the Alabamans, Georgians, and Tennesseans led by Brig. Gen. James J. Archer moved through about a mile of open field to the edge of the creek, where trees would shelter them. At the same time, Brig. Gen. Joseph R. Anderson got one of his artillery units, Capt. David G. McIntosh's South Carolina battery, to open on the Union batteries while Anderson took his brigade of Georgia and Louisiana troops to the north to capture the Yankee guns from the flank. McIntosh found some small earthworks the Federals had made and set up in them, allowing his guns to keep firing all afternoon and evening.

At this point the Confederates began to suffer from a lack of staff work, in particular a problem with maps. Brigadier General Richard Taylor, one of Jackson's brigade commanders, said, "The Confederate commanders knew no more about the topography of the country than they did about Central Africa." Lee's army was going into battle with inadequate maps of the country less than ten miles from its capital, and Anderson's brigade suffered from this problem. The forty-nine-year-old Anderson, a Virginia native and West Pointer, had managed the Tredegar Iron Works in Richmond—one of the young Confederacy's most important assets. When war came, he decided he would rather command soldiers than workers. Anderson had lived in the capital for years, but he and his men did not know exactly where they were going, and they wound up north of guns and sharpshooters but in range and view of them. One of his regiments, the 35th Georgia, crossed the creek—which had been turned into a lake by a Northern-made dam—and drove back Reynolds's 1st Pennsylvania Reserves. The 14th Georgia and 3rd Louisiana Battalion moved troops across to support the 35th Georgia and reached some Yankee breastworks. But the 22nd Massachusetts and 13th New York of Martindale's brigade came up on the right and the 2nd and 3rd Pennsylvania Reserves with four guns of Battery G, 1st Pennsylvania Light Artillery, on the left. After some hand-to-hand combat at the breastworks and double-canister charges from the Pennsylvania gunners, the rebels fell back a little and the assault turned into a firefight. McIntosh kept his guns working fast—at times they became so warm he had to stop firing to let them cool. Captain Carter M. Braxton's Fredericksburg (Virginia) battery joined the South Carolina gunners, but they could not help Anderson's troops advance across a ravine into the fire of four enemy regiments, so he fell back after dark.[16]

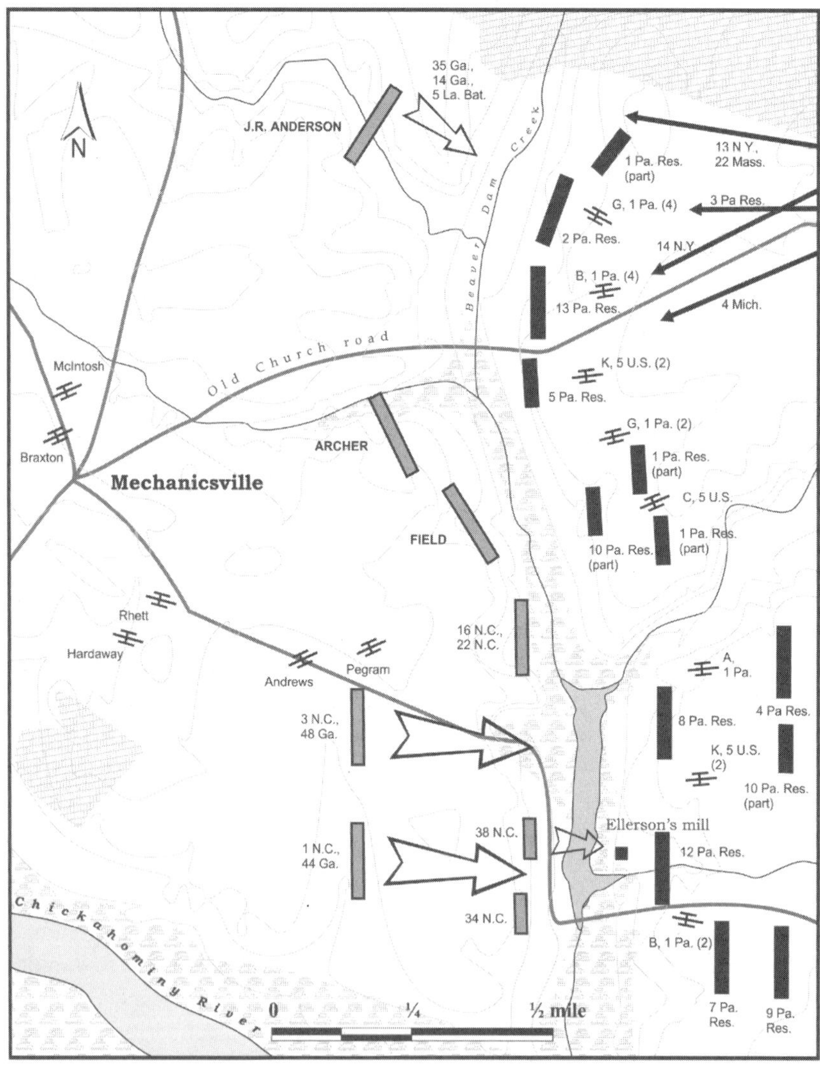

Mechanicsville, June 26, 1862

Unlike Anderson, Field and Archer knew where they were, but like him they knew it was impossible for them to advance beyond the west bank of Beaver Dam Creek. The horse of the 19th Georgia's Lt. Col. Thomas Johnson knew even more quickly, realizing after two rounds of grapeshot that Beaver Dam Creek was no place to be and refusing to go forward another step. The two brigades engaged the 13th, 5th, and parts of the 1st and 10th Pennsylvania Reserves from the time of their arrival at around 4 P.M. until it became dark five hours later. The 4th Michigan and 14th New York from Griffin's brigade and cannon from two sections of Battery B, 1st Pennsylvania Light Artillery, one section of Battery K, 5th U.S. Artillery, and one section of Battery G, 1st Pennsylvania Light Artillery, also entered the contest. Archer's men fought under many disadvantages. Particularly troublesome were the trees felled by the Northerners, which could only be traversed with great difficulty under heavy fire, and a millpond that made it impossible to cross the creek without swimming. Once, the artillerymen let the Confederates approach within forty yards before firing triple charges at them. A Union gunner said that the combination of musket and cannon fire "left them laying sweltering in their own blood," while Benjamin Roher, the surgeon of the 10th Pennsylvania Reserves, wrote his wife that his soldiers "literally mowed down the enemy as they approached our front." Johnson was killed, the brigade's flag was riddled with ten bullet holes, and a splinter was torn from its staff. Fortunately no one ordered these rebels to actually storm the position.[17]

Not so fortunate were Ripley's and Pender's brigades. Ripley crossed the Chickahominy by 4 P.M., just before Lee himself. In his first pitched battle as army commander, Lee got as close as practical to the front lines. He soon discovered that President Davis had the same idea, having also crossed the river with Secretary of War George W. Randolph and some staff officers. Lee was not in exactly a safe place—there was no safe place from Union artillery in the fields around Mechanicsville—so Davis was not safe, either. General Lee met Davis with a frigid glare, glanced at the people with him, and asked, "Who are all this army of people, and what are they doing here?" Davis, who usually brooked no such obvious tone of disapproval, of course understood that Lee was saying this was no place for the president of a country. He paused before replying, "It is not my army, General." Lee, not to be denied, said, "It certainly is not my army, Mr. President, and this is no place for it." Perhaps only Lee could get away with this sort of talk. Davis, seeing that Lee was adamant, finished the conversation with, "Well, General, if I withdraw, perhaps they will follow." He did turn toward the bridge, but as soon as he was out of Lee's sight he found another observation point and stayed there throughout the battle.

Lee had other things besides the safety of Jefferson Davis on his mind by that time. He had probably learned that A. P. Hill's advance was not caused by his own order or any news of Jackson's approach. He now had three brigades engaged with the enemy at a place where he did not want to fight. He had no idea if Jackson was on Porter's flank, but the stiffness of the Federal resistance showed that Stonewall probably was not where he should have been. Lee did not know that McClellan was watching the same battle, but he knew time was running short. If Lee did not force Porter out of the Beaver Dam line, the Union army could attack south of the river the next day with eight larger divisions against four smaller ones. Disappointed by Jackson's failure to show, and understanding his precarious position, Lee was, as he put it, "obliged to do *something*."

Lee did not worry about an attack south of the river so much as McClellan's moving a substantial force that would both cover the Union right flank and threaten any troops Lee could send to support Jackson. It would be difficult to find troops to hit the Yankee right in any event. D. H. Hill and Longstreet were having trouble crossing the Chickahominy because of the broken bridge. Maxcy Gregg's brigade of A. P. Hill's division was just approaching Mechanicsville from the west, while Branch's brigade was still moving toward the village from the northwest.[18]

Porter's left flank was conveniently available. Beaver Dam Creek was a formidable obstacle there, but an admittedly failed assault provided some hope for success. Pender's brigade of Arkansans, North Carolinians, and Virginians, moving to Field's right, saw D. H. Hill's men crossing the river on the Mechanicsville Bridge. Fearing they might be mistaken for Yankees, Lt. John Hinsdale, one of Pender's aides, had a battle flag waved. The 16th and 22nd North Carolina got lost (again because of the lack of accurate maps) and mingled with Field's soldiers. However, the rest of the brigade moved south of the road from Mechanicsville to Old Cold Harbor. By this time the roar of cannon was almost continuous, and Pender, noticing one section each of Battery B, 1st Pennsylvania Light Artillery, and Battery K, 5th U.S. Artillery, had directed the 34th and 38th North Carolina to get to the right of the guns and eliminate them. The 34th got sidetracked, but the 38th made "a desperate charge" and got as close as 150 yards from the guns. Then the 12th Pennsylvania Reserves of Seymour's brigade and the 7th Pennsylvania Reserves of Meade's brigade opened up. The 7th had prepared for an inspection by McClellan that morning, but he did not make it. Hearing the firing to the west, however, they had moved to the 12th's support.

Despite the fire, and the fact that the Tar Heels had to contend with the creek and the mill dam as well as Northern bullets, the 38th charged down the hill on the west side of the creek to some downed trees and stumps a hundred yards from the Union position. Having been cut up badly, and figuring the various difficulties "could not be overcome by my regiment," Col. William J.

Hoke pulled his men back. The order to retreat could not be heard in the heat of battle, so the word was passed along the line. On the way back, Hoke was wounded in the leg and took shelter in a rifle pit, enduring at least a hundred rounds of shot and shell going over his head before Christian Miller and Smith Powell of the 1st North Carolina got him out safely. Meanwhile, the men had been scattered—Lt. Col. R. F. Armfield of the 38th North Carolina at first could rally only thirty-five men.[19]

More force might lead to more success. Below what seemed to be the south end of the Union lines the ground leveled out. The attackers would need to go through woods and swamps, but there were no steep slopes to impede their effort to get around the flank. It would be a difficult, but not impossible, move. Roswell Ripley's brigade was in a perfect position to make it. Ripley, born in Ohio in 1823 and a West Point graduate at twenty, was both a soldier in and historian of the Mexican War. He had married into the prominent Middleton family in South Carolina and resigned from the army; when war broke out he chose his wife's region and occupied Fort Sumter after its surrender. Ripley was replaced at Charleston by John Pemberton and put in his current command. He moved his men to the right on Lee's order so they could turn the Yankee line. Davis, still on the field, sent D. H. Hill a message to that effect without bothering to tell Lee, and A. P. Hill asked Ripley to make the same move.[20]

At about the same time D. H. Hill met Pender—eleven years younger than Ripley but also a West Point graduate at twenty and a veteran of skirmishes against the Indians on the West Coast. Pender was new to brigade command (having been rewarded with the promotion for his gallantry at Seven Pines) and perhaps too enthusiastic. He said that although his brigade had been hurt he could turn the Union left if two of Ripley's regiments supported him while the other two attacked in front. Hill ordered Ripley to carry out this plan. Hill's son later asserted that Hill had not sent Ripley forward until after a second order from Lee that was confirmed by Davis. Major A. C. Avery, a member of Hill's staff, said that the charge was neither planned by Hill nor executed under his direction. But he must have meant merely that the orders came from Lee and Davis, for Hill was involved in the chain of command and had discussed the idea with Pender. Also, Hill did not attempt to communicate with Lee, which he should have done if he thought the assault was doomed from the beginning. The assault reflected the effects of confusion and the inexperience of all involved.[21]

The plan as concocted by Hill and Pender was different from what Lee had in mind. Lee wanted a turning movement, but under the plan Pender proposed and Hill agreed to, some of the Confederates would again be crossing open ground and attacking Federals in prepared positions. Part of Hill's artillery supported their infantry brethren, but it would not matter. As the enemy guns got the range, one member of the 1st North Carolina remembered, a shell burst close to a bluebird, making it "foolish." The next one barely missed Ripley's head. The 44th Georgia went toward the creek, with the 1st North Carolina following. "A more hopeless charge was never entered upon," said Porter Alexander. The Georgians got as far as the creek and stood in it exchanging shots with the well-protected Federals until their ammunition ran out, which was just before the men ran out. The regiment lost 335 men killed or wounded—including its colonel, lieutenant colonel, two captains, and ten lieutenants—out of 514 who entered the battle (more than 65 percent of its strength). The 1st North Carolina, which stopped about halfway down the hill to fire and stayed there through three orders to retreat, lost its colonel, lieutenant colonel, major, six captains and lieutenants, and 133 men killed or wounded. The Northern gunners had let some rebels come within forty feet before blasting them with canister. A Union officer said that the Confederate casualties looked "like flies in a bowl of sugar." Colonel Montford Stokes of the 1st North Carolina said as he was carried off the field that his troops "have shown themselves to be men."

The 3rd North Carolina and 48th Georgia, heading straight across the creek north of Ellerson's mill, also got to the mill race but no further, taking shelter there and not suffering as much as the brigade's other two regiments. Captain A. Burnet Rhett's South Carolina battery, Capt. P. H. Clark's Virginia battery, Capt. Jefferson Peyton's Orange (Virginia) Artillery, Capt. J. W. Bondurant's Jeff Davis (Alabama) Artillery battery, and Capt. R. A. Hardaway's Alabama battery, all of which had been forced to wait while the bridges across the Chickahominy were repaired enough to allow the limbers to cross, arrived. The gunners' fire eased some of the pressure on the rebel infantry.[22]

The 7th and 12th Pennsylvania Reserves, defending this area, had inflicted the damage to that infantry with a cost to themselves of 40 men killed, wounded, or missing. Batteries L and M, 3rd U.S. Artillery, arrived about sundown, but the guns were not needed. Porter telegraphed his wife that night, "We are victorious today against great odds." In reality, the odds were the other way around. As one Confederate wounded in the charge told his wife, "Charging batteries is highly dangerous." The total losses at Mechanicsville, a battle no one wanted, were about 1400 Confederates out of close to 10,000 engaged, and 361 Federals of about 14,000 nominally engaged. Of those, McCall's division lost 298 out of some 8,000 effectives, and 75 of the 298 came from the 13th Pennsylvania Reserves. The final attack by Ripley was unnecessary. Longstreet's division, the final division to cross the river, finished its movement after dark, and he could have accomplished it without the final assault. D. H. Hill wrote twenty years later: "The attacks on the Beaver Dam intrenchments, on the heights of Malvern Hill, at Gettysburg, etc., were all grand, but of exactly the kind of grandeur which the South could not afford." Of course, Hill had contributed to the grandeur by following Pender's badly misguided suggestion.[23]

By 9 P.M. the fighting had deteriorated to an artillery duel, and Lee met with his division commanders. No one had heard from Jackson; only Branch had seen Ewell. Nothing but smoke had been seen to the north, and little gunplay had been heard. Nothing could help Magruder and Huger in the event of an attack south of the Chickahominy the next day, but Lee sent notes ordering them to hold the line at all hazards. As the firing died down, brigades that had seen hard service were relieved by D. H. Hill's and Longstreet's men.[24]

That night, many men watched the artillery fire in amazement. Benjamin Roher and his fellow surgeons stopped work at dark and "sat enjoying the scene, there was a perfect blaze of lightning from the continuous discharge of cannon." On the other side of Beaver Dam Creek, one Confederate said the beauty almost made him forget the danger he was in. Others were not caught up in the martial spirit, and one Northern artilleryman found the scene "truly appalling." One Yankee soldier wrote his cousin that "it was awful the rebels in front of our cannon that were wounded blended with the cry of our own dying and wounded some would cry for some one to come and kill them so they would be out of pain." Charles Becker of the 9th Pennsylvania Reserves remembered how the moon lit up "thousands of ghastly faces" of both sides. John McAnerney of the 3rd Alabama lost all hope of survival, figuring he would be among those sent toward the creek in the morning.

Many men had no blanket. Eugene Blackford of the 5th Alabama saw one covering an apparently sleeping man. He thought that using part of it to sleep on, thus avoiding the dew that would soak him by morning, would do no harm. When he awoke the next morning and noticed the other man was still asleep, he shook him and discovered he was dead. Blackford noted that "it made small impression upon me."

There was some joy in the Confederate camps, however. About sundown, as Longstreet's division was waiting to cross the Chickahominy, an officer rode down the 19th Virginia's line and reported that they had joined with Stonewall Jackson's men. The Virginians shouted and waved their hats at the news.[25]

Unfortunately, no real junction with Jackson had been made, although the distance between the two forces was less than four miles in a straight line. Stonewall, after crossing Totopotomoy Creek, moved toward Hundley's Corner. Ewell must have reached Shady Grove Church, less than two miles from Mechanicsville, before 5 P.M. Brigadier General Isaac R. Trimble, commanding a brigade in Ewell's division, reported hearing guns at 4 P.M., and one artilleryman said that the roar "exceeded anything I ever heard during the war." J. William Jones wrote later that cheers rang up and down the column when the firing was heard, and that the men moved "with the eagerness of veterans" to reach the field. Having no orders to join the fight, Ewell turned east to reunite with Jackson without even bothering to send a courier south to find out what was going on.

Stonewall's vanguard reached Hundley's Corner somewhere around 5 P.M., and Ewell arrived on his right a short time later. The sound of firing to the south was clear from that point also, either on the march or shortly after arrival. This forced Jackson to decide whether or not to march his troops, who had been on the road all day, to the sound of the guns. What and where were the guns, anyway? Would the road south lead him to the enemy's rear or to a strongly held position? Had his approach already forced the Federals back? An aide described Stonewall at Hundley's Corner as bearing an "anxious and perplexed countenance," but no amount of thought would answer the questions. Jackson did know Lee's order, though. He was to bear "well to his left, turning Beaver Dam Creek and taking the direction toward Cold Harbor." Which Cold Harbor is not mentioned—probably Old Cold Harbor was meant—but clearly Lee wanted to keep Stonewall away from the Beaver Dam line. Lee did not want Jackson to fight at Beaver Dam; he did not want anyone to fight there. The big question Jackson needed to answer was whether anything had changed Lee's desire. He had not heard from the army commander, and after talking with Ewell—who had talked with Branch that afternoon—he knew little more than before. Branch could not have known when he met Ewell what was occurring on the Chickahominy.

Moreover, Jackson apparently had no one to send off to find out the true situation. Dabney had six men under him—two assistant adjutant generals, two men from the engineers, and two clerks—and Jackson had been forced to find his own guide for the day's march, having no good map of the area. But Stonewall had a man with intimate knowledge of the area and plenty of people to use as couriers just to his left. Jeb Stuart, who had scouted the ground during his ride around the Union army, was protecting Jackson's flank. The two generals met during the march, and Jackson could have asked Stuart or sent to him later for a guide and a courier, but he apparently never did. And it might not have been in Jeb's character to question the actions of a superior officer, so he probably did not suggest using a trooper as a courier.[26]

By the time Jackson and Ewell reached Hundley's Corner, it was probably too late to do anything, despite Trimble's view that "we should have marched to the support of General Hill that evening." A march of perhaps two miles would have put their leading elements on Beaver Dam Creek by 6:30, but the rest of the Valley army was strung out on the road and would not have made it to the field until after dark. Porter could have held Jackson off until then and then slipped away. Besides, it is likely that Jackson thought the firing he heard was nothing more than the guns supporting the Chickahominy crossing. He thus contented himself with keeping the Unionists to his immediate front from bothering him. Hearing gunplay a little closer than Mechanicsville, Stonewall asked Bradley Johnson, commanding the Maryland Line, "What's that firing, Colonel?" Johnson answered that it was enemy skirmishers in a thicket. When Jackson asked why they had not been stopped, Johnson explained that he could not do it without charging or shelling them. "Well, sir," Jackson responded, "you must stop that firing; make them keep quiet!" Johnson ordered the Baltimore Artillery to fire at the skirmishers, and after two shells the Yankees fell back.

That night, Stonewall's pickets had orders to shoot anything that moved in front of them. About midnight in Richard Taylor's brigade of Ewell's division an unearthly cry was heard. The men tumbled out of their sleeping bags and blankets and were trying to form up when they saw a crazed mule running through camp. It turned out that two officers' horses began fighting, screaming as they did so, and the commotion scared the mule—along with many men. Members of the 31st Georgia from Alexander Lawton's brigade were in the road waiting for someone to tell them where to sleep when something flew over them. Panic-stricken, they headed into a field next to the road. No one knew what had gone over them, but it caused at least one sergeant mortification at his men's conduct.[27]

Jackson did what he thought Lee wanted him to do; he was too good a soldier to do otherwise. He should not be criticized for not going to A. P. Hill's aid; he could have done nothing after arriving at Hundley's Corner. His mission was to get to the Pole Green Church area as quickly as he could and turn the Beaver Dam Creek position. This seems obvious from the written record, and Jackson's actions indicate he understood that this was what was expected of him.

A discrepancy between what was discussed at Lee's council of war and what was contained in the written orders, as well as a possible misunderstanding of the road network, might have led to problems. The memorandum Jackson had in his possession after the council contained the phrase "Jackson will endeavor to come into the Mechanicsville Turnpike in rear of Mechanicsville." According to the orders, however, Jackson was only supposed to head toward Pole Green Church and Hundley's Corner, then head for Cold Harbor. Stonewall would have operated on orders, not memoranda, so, given the late hour, he stopped. As for the road network, the road Jackson took to get to Hundley's Corner dead-ended there, possibly causing confusion over which road he should take to get to Cold Harbor. However, this is unlikely, for Ewell marched right by a road heading south just west of Hundley's Corner. It seems clear that Jackson was correctly following orders.

He also has been criticized for his tardiness. Yet he seemingly moved as fast as conditions allowed, and he acted in accordance with Lee's orders. The root cause of the timing problem was the date Lee picked: it was too early. Jackson had his input into that selection, as we have seen, but questions from Lee or the other generals concerning his forces' whereabouts would certainly have caused a further postponement.[28]

Jackson could have ensured that the columns kept in contact, and, what is more, he did not keep in contact with the rest of the army on his march. Of course, this criticism goes both ways: if Jackson did not communicate, neither did Lee. The various staffs were inefficient. It was not only the lack of maps. They needed to find guides and couriers who knew the country, suggest courses of action, and ensure that necessary actions were taken. None of these happened.[29]

Lee himself was inefficient as well. He had been on Winfield Scott's staff in Mexico, but Scott's army was much smaller than Lee's, and Scott's staff was relatively larger than Lee's, so the lessons Lee undoubtedly learned would not translate. Any lessons from West Point would not have translated, either. Lee needed a larger staff as well as more competence in the people he had. Branch, Ewell, both Hills, Pender, Ripley, even Jefferson Davis, all contributed to the carnage on Beaver Dam Creek. The soldiers, some of them new, had behaved well, but the officers and staff had failed them.

Competence reigned on the other side of creek. Porter had done everything he needed to do, and Reynolds and Seymour handled themselves well. Seymour reported that much of the credit for the battle's success belonged to Reynolds, whose "study of the ground and ample preparations, even to the smallest detail, justify his high reputation as a soldier." Seymour, meanwhile, gave the soldiers reason to appreciate him. A forty-seven-year-old Vermont native, he was in the celebrated West Point class of 1846, fought in Mexico, and helped defend Fort Sumter. In the spring of 1862 he had taken Brig. Gen. Edward O. C. Ord's place in the Reserves. The men initially did not take to the newcomer, but his performance at Mechanicsville was the sort to justify confidence. McCall's men had an advantageous position in their first fight, but they defended like veterans. The artillery was handled flawlessly, as were most Union artillery units during the Seven Days.

McClellan had stayed at Porter's headquarters throughout the battle, and at 9 P.M. he sent two telegrams. One went to Randolph Marcy reporting that not a single foot of ground was lost. The other went to Stanton: "The firing has nearly ceased. I have nearly everything in the way of impediments on the other side of Chickahominy & hope to be ready for anything tomorrow. . . . Victory of today complete & against great odds. I almost begin to think we are invincible." The victory was certainly complete, but as had Porter, Little Mac got the odds wrong. No assault against a prepared position succeeded in the Civil War with anything approaching equal forces for the defender, and in this case the defender had superior numbers.

Union soldiers' reactions to the battle were initially strong. On the south bank of the river, men eagerly listened to every rumor during the day and evening. Men in the 1st Minnesota, a II Corps regiment, thought Franklin's men would join them in an assault that day—pretty close to McClellan's earlier plan. But nothing happened, and other rumors raged until the cannons at Beaver Dam Creek began firing. Finally, Marcy sent word that McClellan had beaten the rebels badly. At the news, cheers rang in every camp for hours. Horses at headquarters reared at the sound. Bands that had not played in weeks broke out their instruments, swinging into "Dixie" and "Yankee Doodle." One officer thought that the bands' playing "must have astonished the rebels even more than it did us." But the rebel bands were playing, too, and their soldiers were cheering, which puzzled some of the Northerners. Not all were able to get into the spirit, however. As one man put it, "We had been deceived so much that we all said 'wait and see.'"[30]

The citizens of Richmond were in no mood for waiting, however. During the day many had congregated on rooftops and hills. The women gathered in groups to listen together, gaining strength from their numbers to face what they knew would come with the battle. The men not in the army also listened to the firing, which came from the northeast. John B. Jones was sure it was Jackson. The smoke and bursting shells were visible well into the night. By then the wounded had begun to enter Richmond. The women asked them for tidings and heard of Jackson's arrival. The railroad station was converted into a temporary hospital, and bandages and rags were in short supply. Many people could not sleep as they worried about their friends and family members in the army. In New York, newsboys called out, "Great battle at Richmond and defeat of McClellan" as they sold their extra editions. In Washington, Stanton and Lincoln started arranging to move five thousand men to reinforce McClellan. They knew from his telegrams that a battle had been fought and won, but nothing else.[31]

While McClellan was at Porter's headquarters, many reports came in confirming the appearance of Jackson's force on the right flank. Something needed to be done or Porter's corps could be swallowed whole. McClellan then would be cut off from his base and in great danger. After the afternoon of the twenty-sixth, Little Mac apparently never considered an offensive. Porter wanted McClellan to either bring the entire army across the river to face Lee (an impossibility) or strengthen the north-bank force slightly while the rest of the army attacked south of the river. Fitz John must have seen what McClellan did not: that Lee was risking everything on the attack north of the river. The Beaver Dam line was not the place to make a stand, considering Jackson's position, but there were other creeks that would serve just as well. McClellan ignored the advice, however, and Porter, ever loyal, made no mention of the incident in his public writings on the campaign.

Baldy Smith and William Franklin proposed a variant of this move. Bring the V Corps troops south of the river, they said, and destroy the bridges. Porter's men could watch the river while the fresh troops on the south side attacked in force, beating the portion of Lee's army facing them before the rest of the Confederates could cross at Mechanicsville. But this choice would expose either supply route—to the York or to the James—to attack. The York River line would have to be given up. Porter might be able to watch the Chickahominy to keep Lee from crossing in the immediate vicinity, but whether or not he could move quickly enough to keep Confederates from crossing at some point farther downstream and cutting the army off from the James is an open question. Moreover, it must be remembered that McClellan thought there were at least 180,000 Confederates, some of them ready to attack his communications while others defended Richmond. He testified before the Joint Committee on the Conduct of the War that at the time he thought the rebels had enough force south of the river to stop such a concentration. Attacking may have been the correct move in reality, but in McClellan's world it was not one he could consider.[32]

With offensive action ruled out, McClellan was left with three choices—but really only two, as Porter would probably need to be reinforced whatever decision was made. A retreat down the Peninsula was possible. In fact, Lee thought it most probable, and Maj. Gen. Erasmus D. Keyes, the IV Corps commander, sent McClellan a note saying that it would be the best course of action. But Jackson's presence and the difficulty of getting Porter's right flank secure made such a move hazardous. The fact that McClellan's line of communication laid in almost the same direction as Porter's front made it very hard to cover the whole line. Also hazardous, but the best choice in the presumed circumstances, was the change of base. If Porter could hold off Lee's force on the north bank for another day McClellan could organize affairs on the south bank, possibly getting the base established before the rebels could do anything about it. Porter suggested this move to McClellan as well. Finally, McClellan was relatively unencumbered because of the slowness of his advance, as the big siege guns had not been brought up from White House Landing yet and so did not need to be saved.[33]

McClellan decided to go with changing his supply base and told Porter that he would decide whether to hold the Beaver Dam line or retreat to a new one at his own headquarters. As he left Porter he said: "Now, Fitz, you understand my views and the absolute necessity of holding the ground, until arrangements over the river can be completed. Whichever of the two positions you take, *hold* it." Porter responded, "Give yourself no uneasiness, I shall hold it to the last extremity." Fitz John later remembered that he thought McClellan meant he would move on Richmond, even if it meant that the V Corps would be destroyed.

This, of course, was a mistaken impression. When Little Mac got to the Trent house, he made the only possible decision. He moved Porter's troops back to another suitable defense line, one that would protect Woodbury's, Alexander's, and Grapevine Bridges (the rest had been destroyed) so he could cross the next night. The new line would give Porter enough cover to enable him to hold the Confederates at bay. Chief engineer John Barnard helped Porter select a line behind Boatswain's Swamp near Gaines's mill. Then Barnard returned to McClellan's headquarters to remind him of the necessity of reinforcing Porter with Henry Slocum's division and also to obtain axes for Porter's troops to improve the already strong defensive position. Barnard later wrote that 30,000 to 40,000 men should have been sent to Porter if he were to stay on the north bank. But the Boatswain's Swamp line was a strong one even without 40,000 reinforcements.

Technically, McClellan's move was not a change of base but the abandonment of a base, as he had no other base established. But the base on the James could be set up easily, with supplies loaded on ships waiting to be moved and the navy controlling the river nearly to Drewry's Bluff. The movement would be a retreat and hazardous, but it was not necessarily subjecting the army to isolation from any source of supply as long as the move was competently handled. The appearance of Jackson on Porter's right flank had made the abandonment of White House Landing imperative, a fact that was obvious on June 26.[34]

At White House Landing itself, rumors about Jackson's arrival had caused alarms among the sutlers and civilians at the landing. Ships were moving toward the mouth of the Pamunkey, and officers put their private and official effects on board steamers so they could get away instantly. Marcy told Brig. Gen. Silas Casey not to abandon the depot without the certainty that a superior force was upon him, but some of the soldiers had already been told that they were leaving as soon as possible. At least at White House Landing, then, people knew what was in store. Such preparations implied that the army would change its base, and a change in base would necessitate the withdrawal of the army—or an attack toward Richmond, which was not in the cards.

After giving a few more orders, McClellan retired for a few hours' sleep. The next day would possibly be the most important of his career. Meanwhile, Porter's corps began its retrograde movement. The Pennsylvania Reserves spent half the night getting more ammunition and cleaning their rifles; then the order to retire reached them, and the preparations for the move lasted the rest of the night—keeping the men from getting away without noise in the dark. The heavy artillery was moved to the south bank of the river, although there was not enough time to move a regimental hospital. At least some trains did not cross the Chickahominy until 4 A.M.[35] Six infantry brigades also began moving during the night. For many, it would be their last march.

CHAPTER FIVE

"Little Powell Will Do His Full Duty To-day"

Troops on the west side of Beaver Dam Creek also spent the night of June 26 in motion while the army commander snatched a few hours' sleep. General Lee shifted brigades so fresh forces would be able to attack at dawn, keeping the pressure on McClellan. Otherwise, Lee later commented, "Disaster was to be apprehended." He had done all he could to help his right, ordering Benjamin Huger to hold his lines at bayonet point and telling him to call for reinforcements from Drewry's Bluff and the defenses of Richmond if he needed them. This order prompted a series of exchanges between Huger, Secretary of War Randolph, and Maj. Gen. Theophilus H. Holmes at Petersburg, who thought Federals were landing on Bermuda Hundred. Nothing of the sort was happening, although the Union navy did threaten the area, and most of Brig. Gen. John G. Walker's brigade came from Drewry's Bluff to reinforce Huger.[1]

Overnight, Porter had extricated most of the Pennsylvania Reserves. However, because of the late start, part of Seymour's brigade, the 13th Pennsylvania Reserves of Reynolds's brigade, and some artillery still held the lines. Reynolds was retreating along a road that led by two mills, Nunnally's and Gaines's, to the new position. Once the brigade finished clearing the area around Nunnally's mill, Reynolds ordered the rear guard to retreat, but two companies of the 13th Pennsylvania Reserves did not get the order. The 9th Pennsylvania Reserves of Seymour's brigade had relieved the 12th Pennsylvania Reserves, but about twenty men from the 12th did not hear the order. The rest of Seymour's men, along with Meade's brigade, moved southeast along a road that paralleled Reynolds's route but was closer to the Chickahominy.[2]

A. P. Hill put his division under arms when the Unionists began shelling the Confederate positions. In fact, the shelling awakened Hill in an unpleasant way: a shell passed through the room in which he was sleeping. John Hinsdale watched the smoke from the guns settling over the valley "like a white pall." One man called the fire "murderous." Brigadier General Winfield S. Featherston's men, at the head of Longstreet's division, had gone to sleep the night before not at all concerned about any Federals, but the fire of the infantry supports awakened them. Confederate rifles and cannon responded, and the shelling lasted more than an hour. At length, D. H. Hill ordered two of his brigades, commanded by Brig. Gens. Samuel Garland Jr., and George B. Anderson, to flank the Union right. Pender had put some artillery into position to answer the Federals and lined up his brigade to charge, but soon found that no Federals were left to charge. Maxcy Gregg's 1st and 12th South Carolina had moved ahead and cleared the 9th Pennsylvania Reserves from the lines behind Beaver Dam Creek. The twenty men of the 12th Reserves who remained behind were all either killed or captured in the Confederate attack. Another company of the 12th Reserves, commanded by Capt. Richard Gustin, held its position at Ellerson's mill for nearly an hour before withdrawing with a loss of only three men wounded. The two companies of the 13th Reserves that had not received Reynolds's order to withdraw were also captured. By 9 A.M. the rebels had repaired the bridges over the creek and were pursuing the Federals, with A. P. Hill's men following Reynolds's route and Longstreet on Little Powell's right.[3]

Stonewall Jackson's men were also moving—if later than some might have wanted, still fairly early in the day. The Stonewall Brigade began moving about 5 A.M., and it was next to last in line. Lieutenant Colonel R. H. Cunningham Jr., commanding Jackson's second brigade, reported being awakened soon after daylight by cannon fire, and that soon thereafter his brigade, in the extreme rear of the army, was on the march. Captain Melhorn of the 10th Virginia put the first booming of the guns forty-five minutes before sunrise, and he marched about half a mile before 7 A.M. Even Watkins Kearns of the Stonewall Brigade, who was relatively cynical about his marches, noted that he was up and marching early.[4]

As Jackson marched down to the Walnut Grove Church intersection, he saw some skirmishers approaching. Stonewall signaled to the troops, but when he received no reply he ordered artillery to fire and disperse the skirmishers, who turned out to be Maxcy Gregg's South Carolinians. The fire wounded two skirmishers. When Jackson reached the church, he met A. P. Hill, whose troops were moving to the right of the Bethesda Church road. Lee rode up while the two generals were talking.[5]

This was probably the first public meeting of the famous Valley leader and his new commander. Hill quickly excused himself to lead his troops on the pursuit, and Lee sat on a cedar stump to discuss the day's plan with Stonewall. No one recorded that conversation, although Dabney could not help trying to eavesdrop. Lee no doubt sketched out his plan calling for Jackson to attempt to turn the Federal right flank resting (as he thought) on the east bank of Powhite Creek. To do that, Jackson would need to reach Old Cold Harbor, a small crossroads named for a tavern less than two miles east of Dr. Gaines's mill on Powhite Creek. But he would need to march his men much farther than that, more than four miles, as the most direct route from Walnut Grove Church to Old Cold Harbor ran right past Gaines's mill. Jackson's route would be east-northeast from the church to Richardson's Crossroads near Bethesda Church and then southeast past Beulah Church to Old Cold Harbor. With D. H. Hill in support, Jackson would have overwhelming force behind Porter's right flank. Soon Jackson took his leave of Lee and resumed his flanking march.[6]

A. P. Hill's march also continued. He headed toward New Cold Harbor, a settlement about one mile west of Old Cold Harbor. To get to New Cold Harbor, however, the troops had to cross Powhite Creek. Little Powell had direct orders to attack the Federals as soon as he found them, unlike the day before. Maxcy Gregg, a forty-seven-year-old South Carolina lawyer and states-right advocate who had fought in the Mexican War, led his advance troops. Gregg had signed up after secession, commanded a regiment at Charleston Harbor, and became a brigadier general the previous December. As he passed Selwyn (the Hogan house and Lee's field headquarters during the march), he and Lee discussed the attack Gregg's troops were to make. Presumably, Lee said that the defense at Powhite Creek would be strong. Longstreet and Gregg then conferred on the roads to be taken to the Union position.

Gregg's brigade and the rest of Hill's and Longstreet's divisions marched through the abandoned, burning Union camps. They found large piles of burning supplies and all kinds of knapsacks and personal equipment, and they could see blazes and columns of smoke everywhere. One soldier noted that "our ardor prevented us from pillaging as freely as we learned subsequently to do," but others were not so bashful. Crenshaw's battery got to a camp that was already being stripped, and the gunners joined in. One man got a hat and a memo book that he used as a diary. Another picked up a rubber blanket, a highly prized item on the Peninsula. Others picked up coffee and sugar that had not been torched.[7]

The 1st and 12th South Carolina, Gregg's leading regiments, made contact with the Federals at Powhite Creek around noon or shortly thereafter. The 9th Massachusetts, part of Charles Griffin's brigade of Morell's division, was in position at Gaines's mill. The South Carolinians first engaged the Bay Staters from behind abandoned boxes and barrels, then moved the Yankees away from the mill with a charge and help from Andrews's battery. Gregg's men took advantage of some food and liquor left at the mill by the retreating Federals,

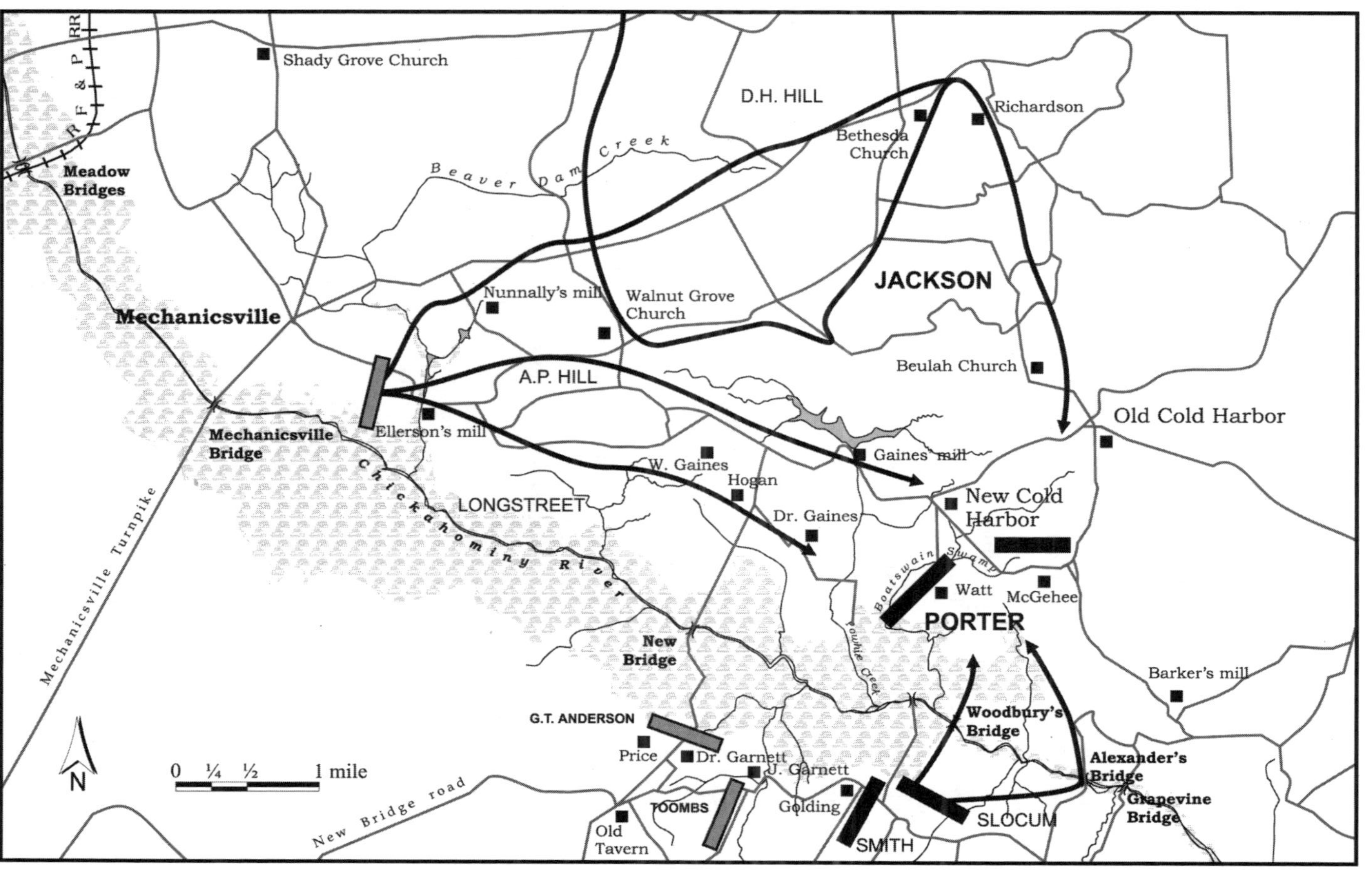

Troop movements, June 27, 1862

including some brandy from a surgeon's tent that a captain said would stimulate the men after a hard run. Afterward, they repaired a bridge and crossed the creek. However, they did not search the mill, and they heard later that one of A. P. Hill's staff officers captured twenty-five Yankees hiding there.

The crossing of Powhite Creek had been too easy—it took only two regiments to force what was supposed to be Porter's main position. Something obviously was not right, and it must have been the information Lee had gained—which had come from his reserve artillery commander, William Pendleton, on the south bank of the Chickahominy. Gregg, forming his brigade between Gaines's mill and New Cold Harbor, kept moving southeast. A. P. Hill, in his official report, called this advance "the handsomest charge in line I have seen during the war." Several Union skirmishers began retreating from a belt of pine trees through a wheat field, and the Confederates shot at them. One fell wounded but got up to attempt to reach his lines. As all the Yankees who had not been shot had passed out of sight, the whole line fired at this one poor soldier, with minié balls kicking up dust around his feet. The rebels were yelling, "Kill him!" "Shoot him!" and "Down with the fellow!" among other things, but none of the bullets hit him. They later found him exhausted by his ordeal and loss of blood.

As Gregg's troops began to cross the wheat field themselves, they came under heavy rifle and artillery fire. Here, it seemed, was the main Union force. It was positioned on the east bank of Boatswain's Swamp, several lines deep, with artillery on a plateau more than fifty feet above the stream in back of the infantry. Gregg's force had to cross about a quarter-mile of open ground, crest the top of a rise, descend fifty feet or more to a swamp surrounded by underbrush, and then face the Federals on the other side. The southern end of the line, where Boatswain's Swamp turned south into the Chickahominy, looked to be impassable. The northeastern end of the line was not visible from Gregg's position.

This was an obviously strong position, perhaps as strong as the one at Beaver Dam Creek. Worse yet, Jackson's march would not flank the position unless the line was short. Lee could put pressure on the entire line, but he could not force Porter out of it without a major battle. Why had this mishap occurred? Boatswain's Swamp was not on Lee's map, but that is really no excuse. They were on Confederate soil, so the maps should have been accurate. Anyone who knew about Powhite Creek should also have known about Boatswain's Swamp. Anyone in the neighborhood, if asked, could have told Lee about the second watercourse. Again, the culprit seems to be poor staff work.[8]

Porter had used the time he had gained through his withdrawal well. He had selected the final positions himself as he and engineer John Barnard reconnoitered the ground, and he had used good judgment in placing his forces. Morell and Sykes were on the front line. Morell was on the left behind Boatswain's

Swamp with Butterfield, Martindale, and Griffin from left to right. Griffin's men straddled the road from New Cold Harbor to the Watt house, Porter's headquarters. Sykes, a thirty-nine-year-old Delaware native and West Pointer who had earned command of all the Regular Army infantry in the Army of the Potomac after a stellar performance at Bull Run, was on the right along a ridge covering the road from Old Cold Harbor to Grapevine Bridge. Gouverneur Warren's New Yorkers and Col. Robert C. Buchanan's regulars lined up from left to right, with Buchanan's right just west of the road to Grapevine Bridge around the McGehee house. Sykes's other brigade—commanded by Maj. Charles S. Lovell of the 10th U.S. Infantry, as its assigned commander, Col. William Chapman, was ill—was in reserve. The Grapevine Bridge area was key to Porter, for it and the nearby Alexander's and Woodbury's Bridges were necessary for any Yankee crossing of the Chickahominy.

Artillery batteries were scattered along the line. On the left, only two two-gun sections—one from Capt. William B. Weeden's Battery C, 1st Rhode Island Light Artillery, and one from Lt. John B. Hyde's Battery E, Massachusetts Light Artillery—were able to get in line; the other guns set up behind the line. On the right, where the terrain was less favorable, Capt. Stephen H. Weed set up his Battery I, 5th U.S. Artillery, on the right of the line, while Capt. John Edwards put the three sections of Batteries L and M, 3rd U.S. Artillery, in various positions along the line itself. McCall's division formed the reserve, with Meade on the left near the Chickahominy, Reynolds on the right covering some roads in that direction, and Seymour in reserve behind the second line of Yankees. Cooke's cavalry force was placed on the extreme left with orders to strike the Confederates in the wheat field if the opportunity presented itself. One soldier wrote that the only problem with the line was that it was too long for the number of men available.

By midmorning, all of Porter's forces were in their assigned positions, some even fortified with coffee—the servants of one company in the 14th New York were brewing some as the soldiers came back from a night in the woods. The men strengthened their new positions as best they could with field fortifications, abatis, and other obstacles. The infantry had to borrow tools from the artillery because Porter's requested axes had not arrived and they had thrown some of the few axes they carried aside during the retreat. Rails, logs, bricks, and even knapsacks were used. A little more time and effort might have made the position impregnable. One Confederate wrote that it was still "so formidable that a commander of less nerve than Lee would have hesitated to attack." Despite their hard work, the men of the V Corps had some time for personal matters. Mail arrived and was distributed, and some were allowed to take cigars from the Regulars' sutler before the sutler's supplies were destroyed.[9]

Across the river, troops in the Union VI Corps—who had cheered the evening before when hearing of the results of Mechanicsville—were astonished to see their V Corps brethren retreating through the open fields. They were equally disappointed to see the Confederates advancing through those same fields. Others heard rumors that Porter had retreated, with some even saying that he had been "whipped all to pieces." Men on the north side of the river were also wondering what was happening. In the 11th U.S. Infantry they were asking themselves, "Why the dickens were we retreating? The enemy had not whipped us, had he? Impossible, we regulars had not got a slap at him yet."[10]

By the time Porter had gained his new line, McClellan had awakened from his few hours' sleep. That sleep, however needed, had been unfortunate, for when Barnard returned from Porter's headquarters to report to McClellan—and give him Porter's requests for reinforcements and axes—Barnard did not wake him. The army's chief engineer, just turned forty-seven, had graduated second in his West Point class at age eighteen and spent the next twenty-nine years in the army despite some deafness. One would think that all those years in the army would have taught Barnard the importance of delivering messages promptly and the fact that sleep must sometimes be sacrificed. Instead, he met some of Slocum's men heading to Porter's aid and apparently did not understand exactly what he was to do regarding the axes, so he went to his tent until afternoon. Thus, McClellan's first intimation that Porter thought he might need help was when he received Porter's early morning telegram that said: "I hope to do without aid, though I request that Franklin or some other command be held ready to reinforce me. The enemy are so close that I expect to be hard pressed in front." At 9 A.M. McClellan countermanded an earlier order that had sent Slocum's division across the Chickahominy to support Porter (and incidentally into Barnard's path), because the firing on Porter's front had stopped. At 10 A.M. he telegraphed Stanton that "the whole army [is] so concentrated that it can take advantage of the first mistake made by the enemy."

By noon, McClellan had his first report of contact—probably a combination of the fighting withdrawal conducted by Seymour and some artillery fire reported by Sykes. He magnified it in a dispatch to Stanton, calling it a heavy attack by three divisions, including Jackson's. Before that he had received reports from Sumner and Franklin of a threatened attack, and from Heintzelman of a column of Confederates marching on his front. By early afternoon, McClellan was so worried that he sent a brooding telegram to Stanton: "We are contending at several points against superior numbers. . . . Thus far we have been successful, but I think the most severe struggle is to come. . . . This may be the last dispatch I send you for some time. . . . Goodby, and present my respects to the President." McClellan's reliance on Pinkerton's reports and his own caution again had taken hold of him, and he was worried that he might not survive the campaign.[11]

Once again John Magruder had deceived McClellan. Called "Prince John" by his fellow West Point graduates, Magruder was fifty-five years old. Brevetted three times for gallantry as an artillery officer in the Mexican War, he had spent his entire adult life in the Regular Army. Magruder was known in the army for organizing amateur theatrical productions, and many at the time attributed his success at deceiving McClellan at Yorktown to those experiences. Magruder had been ordered to demonstrate against the enemy on the south bank of the Chickahominy to find out what the Federals were doing and deceive them about his strength. In executing this order, Magruder attacked Union pickets, shelled Union lines, and in general made a lot of noise. Armistead Long of Lee's staff said that Magruder seemed to become paralyzed when someone else was in charge, but that the sounds of battle on the twenty-seventh got his blood going, whereupon he made such a demonstration that McClellan was convinced. Huger, told to hold his line "at all hazards," presumably conducted operations similar to Magruder's with similar success.

It may be said in hindsight that these actions should not have fooled anyone. But McClellan was not the only one deceived. The results of the Confederates' operations on other Yankees can be seen not only in the responses of the Union corps commanders, but also in the report of Thaddeus Lowe, an aeronaut who had convinced Abraham Lincoln and then McClellan of the usefulness of aerial reconnaissance. Lowe had been going aloft in a balloon throughout McClellan's campaign to observe the Confederates. When one Confederate saw a balloon go up, he told his officer, who called it a star instead. "Star, hell!" the soldier replied. "I tell you it's a balloon. Are the Yankees smart enough to catch the stars?" Confederates tried often to shoot down the balloons, which created commotion not only in Lowe's camp but also sometimes in the nearby infantry camps. On one occasion, *New York Herald* correspondent George Townsend was with Lowe in the air when the rebel artillery opened fire. Lowe told his men on the ground to pull him down, and Townsend fainted before they landed. Some rebels thought their opponents got a lot of information from the balloon flights, but Alexander Webb of McClellan's staff informed his family that they should not believe the stories of Lowe's exploits. This time Lowe hurt the cause by sending word at 9:20 A.M. that the Southerners on the south bank of the Chickahominy seemed ready to attack at any time.

One Northern picket heard a discussion between two rebels. "Uncle Robert," one said, "is goin' to gobble up the Yankee army and bring 'em to Richmond." The other replied, "Well, we uns'll have a right smart lot of 'em to feed; and what are we uns goin' to do with 'em when we uns catch 'em?" The first soldier answered, "Oh, every one of we uns will have a Yank to tote our traps!"

A Massachusetts private, Warren Lee Goss, recalled that one of his comrades heard orders of the kind usually given to large bodies of troops coming from the Confederate lines. Goss and his friends were puzzled, however, because they could not hear the tramping of feet that always accompanied such orders. Another Unionist told his mother that his line felt attacks all day, "although these attacks were not very violent."[12]

These operations probably also had their effect on McClellan's activity, or lack of it, that day. Little Mac stayed on the south bank of the Chickahominy, at his headquarters at the Trent house. Given the reality of the situation, he should have been with Porter if he had no intention of attacking south of the river. However, given McClellan's thoughts—either of Union attacks on the south side or of overwhelming Confederate force and rebel attacks on both sides of the river—he would have been right to stay at a central, known location so as to be able to conduct the affairs on both sides.[13] He was wrong about the attacks on the south bank, but he had received erroneous reports from his subordinates. He could have seen for himself, but he had to stay in communication with Porter. He could have joined Porter, but he had great confidence in that general and less in those on the south bank. All in all, his staying put does not seem unpardonable, and it is certainly less liable to censure than other actions he took that day.

For instance, the order to halt Slocum's movement was wrong. The excuse that no fighting was occurring on Porter's front is lame. Porter and others in the high command thought he was facing 80,000 rebels. If Porter were beaten too early in the day, McClellan himself—if he really faced 200,000 Confederates—would be facing massive enemy forces on two sides. Slocum's 8400 men, in position sometime in the morning of June 27, would have increased Porter's chances of surviving any fighting. Moreover, McClellan had to have known there would be fighting north of the river that day.

When Porter again asked for reinforcements, after realizing that McClellan was not going to attack south of the river and after the first Confederate blows started to fall, McClellan was prompt in sending Slocum. He also sent two brigades from Sumner's corps in response to a 5 P.M. telegraph message from Porter saying that he was hard pressed and might not be able to hold his line. These two brigades made up Sumner's entire reserve. Franklin, having given up one division, did not feel comfortable sending over any more men. McClellan asked Keyes to send one brigade to headquarters at 5:50 P.M., but that was far too late to help Porter. Heintzelman was only asked to prepare a reserve. Perhaps his response of the day before, when he said that the two brigades he could spare were worn out and would not be able to fight, was enough for McClellan, or perhaps the III Corps was too far away to be able to reinforce Porter in time. At least McClellan asked for reinforcements, and he had to rely on his corps commanders' answers. It also must be remembered that the corps south of the Chickahominy had only two divisions each, so nearly one-quarter of McClellan's strength south of the river actually headed to Porter's help on the twenty-seventh. Given McClellan's ideas of Lee's strength, he must have been nervous removing that many men from his lines on the south bank, and he must also have felt Porter's desperation.[14]

One possible reason why McClellan was slow to react, at least before Porter's messages started sounding ominous, was that he apparently could not hear the sounds of battle. Brigadier General Andrew A. Humphreys, McClellan's chief topographical engineer during the campaign, said afterward that not a sound of musketry could be heard at headquarters, which was about two miles from the field. They could see the bursting of artillery shells, of course, but no more. Franklin, on the front lines about two miles from the left of Porter's line, did not hear a single gun—rifle or cannon—all day. A Confederate staff officer with Magruder and Davis at dinner, one mile from Longstreet's lines across the river, could see the final assault but could hear only indistinct noise. Yet people throughout Richmond could hear the sounds of battle, and residents climbed hills, went to their roofs, or traveled to the suburbs to see the smoke from the muskets and cannon. Two decades after the war, John B. DeMotte, a professor at DePauw University in Indiana, wrote that differing densities of air masses probably caused the aural anomaly as varying amounts of water vapor and varying air temperatures may act to block sound waves.[15]

Lee, coming up to Boatswain's Swamp with his forces, certainly could hear the firing. He needed to improvise a plan to deal with the actual tactical situation. A. P. Hill and Longstreet had their forces in place behind Powhite Creek. As far as Lee knew, Jackson and D. H. Hill also should have been in position. Lee apparently thought that Jackson's position at Old Cold Harbor would extend the Confederate line to the east of Porter's position, thus forcing the Yankees to extend their own line, weakening it somewhere. As would anyone, Lee had to conclude that Porter would take troops from the most advantageous ground, that directly opposite Longstreet and A. P. Hill. Unfortunately for Marse Robert, his initial assumption was wrong: Porter's line already extended as far as Jackson's position.

Gregg, meanwhile, had asked Hill for permission to attack the main Union line, but the division commander decided to wait for Longstreet to come up on his right. Now that Longstreet was in position to protect his flank, Hill was once again ready to do battle. Earlier, as Hill had been watching troops move from Mechanicsville, he had seen his old regiment, the 13th Virginia in Ewell's division. He took time from his duties to shake hands with a private and ask about "the boys of the old 13th." As Hill rode off, the soldier turned to a friend and said, "Little Powell will do his full duty to-day."[16]

There is some uncertainty about when Hill ordered the attack (he wrote 2:30, whereas Gregg wrote 4 P.M.), but there is no uncertainty about its lack of success. Gregg got Johnson's and Crenshaw's batteries set up. Johnson's battery was waiting to fire when a well-known Richmond lawyer rode up, saying he wanted to see a great battle. Johnson told him to leave, but the lawyer would not listen. Finally, Johnson told the man to move to a hill about a quarter of a mile in front of the battery and opposite the Union guns. The lawyer did so and raised a green silk umbrella, pushing his silk hat from his forehead. At about that time, Crenshaw's battery set up just in front of the lawyer in an open field. Artillery in an open field is bound to draw fire, and this case was no exception. The lawyer hurriedly packed up and left, saying he had seen as much of a battle as he cared to see. The rebels returned fire, kicking up dirt all around the horse of Lt. Col. Hiram Duryee of the 5th New York, the famous Duryee Zouaves of Warren's brigade, which was manning that part of Porter's line. Duryee yelled out, "Boys, the horse stands it well." A man in the ranks called back, "Yes and by God so does the rider," and the regiment cheered up and down the line.

The 1st and 12th South Carolina made the initial assault to the east of the road leading from New Cold Harbor to the McGehee house. The 12th, on the left of the assault, overlapped the left wing of the 1st, causing confusion within the Confederate force. Advancing through thickets of young pine trees up the slope from Boatswain's Swamp, they were met by the 5th New York along with Edwards's guns on the infantry's right. Duryee told his men, "Fire low and don't waste a cartridge." They advanced to the top of a hill and let loose a volley.

Berry Benson of the 1st South Carolina remembered, "What we had seen before was child's play." Color Sergeant James Taylor of the 1st South Carolina fell at once. His blood could still be seen on the regimental flag as late as 1889. What happened next is uncertain: either Col. D. H. Hamilton picked up the colors and gave them to Cpl. Shubrick Hayne of Company L, or Hayne got the colors himself. In either event, Hayne was soon mortally wounded, and Alfred Pinckney of Company L seized them. He was killed immediately. Perhaps Philip Gadsden Holmes of Company L took up the task, or perhaps he was merely just behind the flag. However, if he held the flag at all it was not for long, as he fell with three mortal wounds. Dominick Spellman of Company K, the Irish company, finally raised the flag and kept it the rest of the day. Hamilton immediately promoted Spellman to color bearer as a reward for his gallantry. Considering what happened to those who came before him, it seems a dubious honor.[17]

One Yankee remembered that the cannon fire from both sides made the ground tremble. Gregg was so galled by the fire of two of the Union guns that he sent the 1st South Carolina Rifles to capture them. This regiment, also known as Orr's Rifles, had feasted on Union food west of Gaines's mill. The Yankees gave them a different meal when the South Carolinians arrived on the field. Sykes had moved the artillery that had offended Gregg to the rear, and the 5th New York had been withdrawn to a cut in the road to get out of the bothersome Confederate artillery fire. When the Gamecocks entered the woods where the guns had been they were fired upon from their left by the 12th U.S. Infantry of Buchanan's brigade, supported by the 14th U.S. Infantry of the same brigade and the 10th and 17th U.S. Infantry from Lovell's brigade. Warren's 10th New York kept up its fire on the rebels' right. Captain William Partridge led his company of Duryee's Zouaves out as skirmishers, and when the riflemen came too close he shouted for the men to retreat, but he was shot through the heart. More than ten of his men took aim at the shooter, and it was heard later that the man fell with eight bullets in him. The rebels forced the regulars back to their reserve lines, but the 5th New York came out of the cut and hit hard—making what one rebel remembered as "the most desperate charge I ever witnessed in the war." A retreat was ordered, but more than half the regiment did not hear the order. Lieutenant William W. Higgins and thirty riflemen held off the New Yorkers for a moment, but finally the Confederates retreated.

Warren later wrote his wife, "Nothing you ever saw in the pictures of battles excelled it," but Pvt. John W. Urban of the 1st Pennsylvania Reserves, sent to support the 5th New York, had a different view. Urban called the fight "as terrible as human beings can make it." He described the battle as one of rifle butts and bayonets, and remembered how disorganized the New Yorkers had been—even in victory. It was understandable, according to Urban. After all, he said, they had lost three hundred dead or wounded (the reported casualties were 162). The Yankees captured a wounded member of Orr's Rifles and asked him some questions but did not try to move him. In fact, they treated him well, except for one Federal who demanded his cartridge box at bayonet point.[18]

Meanwhile, the 1st South Carolina Infantry had been so badly cut up—including losing its second in command, Lt. Col. Augustus M. Smith, in one man's opinion the most severe loss in the brigade—that Gregg pulled it back north of the swamp. Not everyone got the order in the confusion, however, and Capt. W. J. Haskell of Company H finally had to retreat on his own. The regiment became demoralized and scattered during the retreat over the swampy, wooded ground. Haskell and about twenty of his men wound up joining three other regiments in charges during the battle.[19]

The 13th South Carolina Infantry supported the 12th on its left, while Gregg's other regiment, the 14th South Carolina Infantry, arrived from picket duty just in time. Gouverneur Warren, a thirty-two-year-old New Yorker, had graduated from West Point second in his class and spent his prewar days in the engineers before becoming lieutenant colonel and then colonel of the 5th New York. He attacked with his own brigade. The 12th and 14th U.S. Infantry from Buchanan's brigade also moved forward, with the 2nd, 10th, and 17th U.S. Infantry from Lovell's brigade and Buchanan's 3rd U.S. Infantry in support. The 14th South Carolina, sent into the center of Gregg's line, blunted the charge on its front and prevented the Yankees from setting up a battery (probably Edwards's) on the brow of the hill. Firing took the place of charging on both sides.

During the fight, Lee and some of his staff rode near the lines. Fire was reaching the general, and the men were trying to get him to retire. Just then, some of Gregg's men ran panic-stricken out of the woods. Lee turned to the men around him and cried, "Gentlemen, we must rally those men." As usual, what Lee wanted, he got. The soldiers did rally and were taken back into the fight by Gregg and Capt. A. C. Haskell, Gregg's assistant adjutant-general.

Johnson's battery fought on until twenty men and ten horses had been killed or wounded. By that point, the entire battery had been disabled. Crenshaw's battery was under fire from three Union batteries for two hours and was unable to move much due to the narrowness of the opening in the trees in front of it. After having five men and eleven horses shot, the battery moved back about two hundred yards. Less than an hour later—about enough time to replace the ammunition used in the first action—it moved forward again and continued dueling with the Yankee guns for about an hour. By then, two guns were disabled and the other two were too hot to fire. One gunner wrote in his diary, "Words are inadequate to describe it," but he did note that an Englishman in the battery said "it was the hottest place this side of 'ell." One section of McIntosh's Pee Dee Artillery battery moved into line to replace Johnson, but the men could not tell friend from foe in the smoky afternoon and were withdrawn. McIntosh's horse, for which he paid $750, was killed under him.

After the battles, Colonel Hamilton of the 1st South Carolina was talking with Adjutant General Cooper and Secretary of War Randolph. During that conversation the name of Maj. Edward McCrady Jr. of the same regiment was brought up, and Hamilton gave a somewhat discouraging report of McCrady's behavior at Gaines's Mill. Gregg was quick to correct the story. McCrady had been ill in Richmond but came out to the battlefield wishing to help in any way he could, even though he did not feel well enough to join the regiment. Gregg agreed to use him as a staff officer and eventually requested that McCrady rally some troops. The major did so until his strength gave out, then attempted to rejoin his own regiment but fell out of his saddle exhausted. He finally made his way back to Richmond in a carriage. Hamilton remained in command while ill later in the campaign, but Gregg said it was not right for the colonel to apply his own standards to other men, especially those who had been sick for a month.[20]

Branch took his brigade in to the right of Gregg along the same road. The 7th North Carolina advanced to a rail fence in front of a wood to engage the 10th New York from Warren's brigade and the 6th U.S. Infantry from Lovell's brigade, along with Berdan's 1st U.S. Sharpshooters, and fell back when the 28th North Carolina did not keep pace. The 6th U.S. received fire from its own comrades in blue and struggled to hold its position for a time. It was not helped when the 9th Massachusetts of Griffin's brigade, positioned on the regiment's left, broke not once but twice. The 14th New York, just left of the 9th Massachusetts, also received fire from the rear as well as the front, but the Federals finally started to fire on the rebels.

The sharpshooters had been deployed as skirmishers along with the 9th Massachusetts in front of Griffin's position. Volunteers selected for their skill, the sharpshooters were trained to fire at officers and color bearers as well as artillerymen. They fired and fell back, dodging from tree to tree to gain time to load and aim, making every shot count. A few of the men failed to hear the bugle call for their return to the main line, however, and were caught in the open with rebels hot on their heels. One man was struck a glancing blow on the forehead by a ball. The wound bled heavily, and the stunned man jumped crazily four or five feet in the air. Just as he landed the order to fire came over the din. The tardy sharpshooters ducked just in time to miss the volley. As one of them put it, "I had a most sincere desire to be somewhere else."

The fire and a bayonet charge was enough to stop the 7th North Carolina, in which some of the men had already broken and run. When the regiment fell back, Union fire reached the 37th North Carolina, which was in any case troubled by the swamp and undergrowth. The fire staggered the 37th's right flank, and some of the 28th (which had retreated when the 7th did, then advanced with the 37th) fell back. Three of the companies eventually rallied and fought with other regiments. The 7th and what was left of the 28th again advanced, but they were stopped. The 7th North Carolina lost its commander, Col. Reuben P. Campbell, who fell while holding his regiment's colors. As he went down, the flag covered his body "as perfectly as if it had been placed there by deft and designing hands." Branch said Campbell could be "classed among 'the bravest of the brave'." The colors had already been deadly to Cpl. Henry T. Fight and Cpl. James A. Harris during the charge. After Campbell went down, Lt. Duncan C. Haywood grabbed the flag, and he too was killed. The flag had been hit by thirty-two bullets and was "literally shot to pieces."

Branch was forced to bring in his other three regiments, the 18th and 33rd North Carolina along with the 37th, on the west side of the road. They could not advance against the 9th Massachusetts, which had stiffened, along with the 14th New York and 62nd Pennsylvania of Griffin's brigade. Timothy Vedder of the 14th New York reported home, "We stood it and give it to them as fast as they give it to us," which was pretty fast—in one 14th New York company eighteen men fell in twenty minutes. In fact, without reinforcements, Branch might not have held his position against the Northerners. One of his regimental commanders, Col. Robert H. Cowan of the 18th North Carolina, wrote, "Nothing but the thickness of the woods saved us from total destruction in our first unassisted efforts upon the enemy's position."[21]

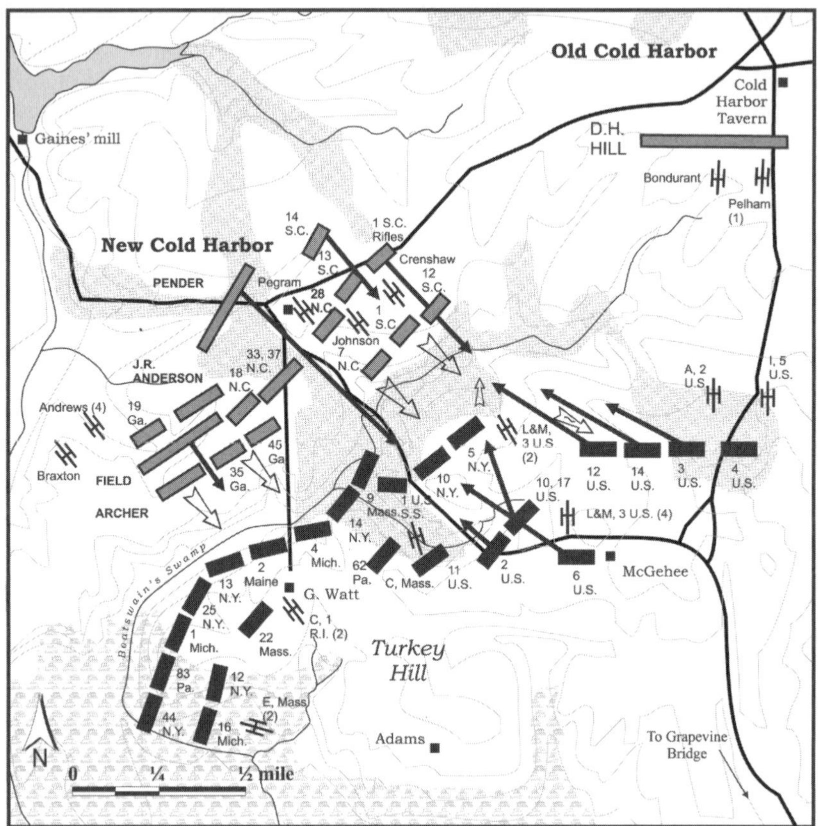

A. P. Hill's attacks, Gaines's Mill, June 27, 1862

The reinforcements Branch got came from Pender's brigade. After scattering a few infantry left at Gaines's mill (perhaps those left in the mill by Gregg's men), Pender got part of Andrews's battery in line north of Boatswain's Swamp. The guns fired for a while without effect, and then the infantry went forward to Branch's support. These rebels charged into the Unionists and actually through them for a time after some heavy fighting. Two regiments, the 16th and 22nd North Carolina, reached the crest of the hill before being thrown back by flanking fire. Colonel James Connor of the 22nd was wounded, and Lt. Col. R. H. Gray took his place, later telling his father that "no description of a battle I have ever seen approached to anything like the reality." As the 16th and 22nd fell back they took the rest of the brigade with them, and while the Tar Heels rallied and tried again, the Union fire was too much for them. The 22nd's flag was only relatively better off than the 7th's, having fourteen holes in it.[22]

Joseph Anderson's brigade came up on Branch's right, traversing a hill before beginning the descent to Boatswain's Swamp. Anderson had his five regiments arrayed in a line of battle, but he wanted some artillery. McIntosh's battery was unavailable, and Anderson asked for Capt. Greenlee Davidson's Letcher Artillery battery. But Davidson was still on the south bank of the Chickahominy, and did not make it by the time Anderson was ordered into the battle. Without any artillery support, Anderson charged three times toward the segment of the Federal line manned by the 4th Michigan and part of the 14th New York of Griffin's brigade and the 2nd Maine from Martindale's brigade. The men of the 2nd Maine had taken advantage of a rail fence to their front, using dirt, their knapsacks, tents, and blankets to make a barricade. Some men in the 4th Michigan found hay bales and covered them with dirt so they would not catch fire from the muskets' discharge.

Anderson, in only his second fight, did what he could, but he never came close to a breakthrough. During the first charge, some of Anderson's troops broke, causing some consternation among the 55th and 60th Virginia of Field's brigade, which were attacking with the Georgians. Anderson, attempting to rally his men, grabbed one regiment's colors and planted it near the crest of a hill. Only the more intrepid of his men gathered around him, however. After the third charge failed, he ordered his men to lie down north of the swamp, pulling back the 35th and 45th Georgia, which had advanced somewhat farther on either flank than did the center.[23]

Archer's brigade moved in on Anderson's right as Braxton's battery began shelling the Union line. The three Tennessee regiments and the 5th Alabama Battalion got into line, with the 19th Georgia in reserve. These men found Yankees behind a triple line of earthworks with logs on top. The forty-four-year-old Archer was not a West Point graduate, but he nevertheless had joined the Regular Army twice as an officer—once during the Mexican War and then seven years later after practicing law. He was new to the brigade, having been colonel of the 5th Texas until early June. Taking his new command down a deep cut road for about four hundred yards, Archer formed his line and headed toward an apple orchard about two hundreds yards in front of him. Reaching that place, the troops lay down and waited for about an hour. Then a courier came and talked with Archer, who ordered the charge.

The rebels raised their famous yell and charged across an open plain, through an old field, and over deep gullies for about six hundred yards. When they got within 150 yards of the Union position they fired, but the line began to waver in the face of the Federals' return fire. When Archer yelled, "Follow me!" and waved his sword, the men again moved forward. Lieutenant James J. Crittenden of Archer's staff moved behind the 5th Alabama Battalion saying, "My brave Alabamians, I know I may depend on you; keep cool; remember your state," and similar statements. The brigade listened, and the colors got within twenty paces of the 2nd Maine, but the fire was too heavy. In fact, the 5th Alabama Battalion lost its colors to the 2nd Maine when its color bearer, M. T. Ledbetter, was wounded in the hip.[24]

Martindale, the Union brigade commander in this sector, was the son of a New York congressman. He had graduated third in the West Point class of 1835—not good enough to get into the Corps of Engineers—and so had resigned to become a lawyer. When war broke out he reentered the service. He had already made his presence felt—with his superiors, if not with the men he commanded. When he reached his assigned position behind Boatswain's Swamp, Martindale decided he wanted the defensive line advanced so the first position would be between that stream and Powhite Creek, just underneath the crest of a hill.

Martindale's immediate superior was George Morell. By a strange coincidence, Morell was two months older than Martindale, born in the same state, and graduated in the same West Point class. But Morell was at the top of the class and got an engineering appointment. After two years he resigned to enter the railroad construction business and then practiced law. Completing the strange link between the two, he became a brigadier general on the same day as Martindale. When Morell pointed out that Porter had chosen the position, Martindale changed his tune. He decided he instead wanted artillery on the crest of the hill along with the second line of troops. He asked Morell twice and finally received the answer that Porter was in charge of the artillery. As Porter at that time was only a few hundred yards away, Martindale went to corps headquarters. While there he ran into Charles Griffin, a thirty-six-year-old Ohioan who had taught artillery tactics at West Point after trying them out himself in the Mexican War and had just been elevated from battery to brigade command. Griffin agreed with Martindale's assessment, but the agreement did little good. Only two pieces of artillery from Weeden's battery, commanded by Lt. William W. Buckley, came forward. The infantry cleared fields of fire through the woods for the guns. Martindale felt after the battle that had twenty guns instead of only two been employed, "we might have done much greater execution."

But even with a position that may not have been optimal and only two guns, Martindale made the going tough for the attacking Confederates. Colonel Elisha Marshall told the 13th New York, "Wait till you see their shins, then give 'em hell." Half an hour after Archer's first attack failed he tried again, this time with the 19th Georgia also on the front lines. Archer and a few of his men, not more than a hundred according to him, made it somewhat farther than the rest during this charge, but still did not reach the Union line. The 1st Tennessee fought the 13th New York from fifty feet away, the Tennesseans bowing their heads and slouching as if walking into hail.[25]

The final brigade from A. P. Hill's division to see action was Field's, which had been ordered to support Anderson's attack. Field was a Kentucky native and a lifelong soldier. He graduated from West Point in 1849 at the age of twenty-one and stayed in the army until he resigned in 1861. He had moved from the rebel cavalry to command of a brigade in March, and his men got within a hundred yards of the Union line in their first attempt (with Anderson). Trying again when Archer did, they suffered the same result. The 47th Virginia's commander, Col. Robert M. Mayo, reported receiving fire from the second line of Confederates. Pegram's battery had regrouped despite losing four guns and forty-six men at Mechanicsville and was helping cover the rebel line in this area, changing places from east of the road along which Hill's men had been charging to the garden at New Cold Harbor when matters turned sour. Union skirmishers probably opposed this movement. In any case, the Yankees moved out to stop some rebel artillery from setting up. Hill, no doubt getting desperate by this time, turned to Capt. Gilbert Wright, at the head of a company of Cobb Legion cavalry and Little Powell's escort, and told him to charge the skirmishers. The horse soldiers made it back with only one man wounded, although several horses were killed or wounded—an amazing result considering Wright's estimate that three or four regiments fired on them.

Pegram's battery did get going, and it had "terrible effect" on the Yankees according to one account, but it drew fire in return. One of the shells intended for the battery instead burst not far from an intersection where Lee and his staff, Powell Hill and his staff, Pender, and Pender's aide Hinsdale were observing the action. No one was hurt, but none of them lingered either. Other shots, particularly from sharpshooters, had more effect on the battery. It lost five more horses killed, making it seventeen horses killed in two days of fighting. Nor did the guns help the infantry much; the rebel dead and wounded were everywhere in front of the 2nd Maine's breastworks.[26]

Thus ended the first attack at Gaines's Mill. It had been wholly borne by A. P. Hill, and it was a total failure. Hill's orders were to find and engage a fleeing enemy. Instead (through no fault of his own) he attacked a prepared position exactly where Porter wanted the rebels to strike. The results were staggering. Gregg's brigade, which went into battle with no more than 2,500 men, lost 854 killed or wounded. The 1st South Carolina Rifles reported 76 killed, 221 wounded, and 58 missing, the worst losses of any Confederate unit in the battle. Archer, who reported having only 1,228 men before Mechanicsville and had lost 214 men there, lost another 321 at Gaines's Mill. While other brigades did not break down their losses by battle, Hill reported having 14,000 men, including artillery, before the campaign started, and he had lost about 810 men at Mechanicsville. Therefore, Little Powell had at most 13,200 men at Gaines's Mill. He probably lost more than 2,000 of them—half his losses for the campaign—during the afternoon.[27] Hill indeed had done his full duty, but more would need to be done to secure Lee's first battlefield victory.

CHAPTER SIX

"We're Holding Them, but It's Getting Hotter and Hotter"

THE LONGER LEE WAS forced to wait, the worse his situation became. He had uncovered New Bridge, and it was rebuilt on the twenty-seventh after the Federals tore it down the day before. Lee thus had direct contact with Magruder and Huger, but it was tenuous. He needed to maintain pressure to keep McClellan blind as to the true situation, and the only force he had close at hand for that purpose was James Longstreet's division.

Longstreet was in reserve that day and had settled his brigades on the west side of Powhite Creek. Brigadier Generals Cadmus M. Wilcox's, Roger A. Pryor's, and Winfield S. Featherston's brigades were in the front, with Brig. Gen. George E. Pickett's brigade in support, and the brigades of Brig. Gens. James L. Kemper and Richard H. Anderson bringing up the rear. Old Pete was facing Porter's left on Turkey Hill, which was crowned with batteries. Union guns south of the river could easily enfilade Longstreet's lines. Longstreet said he was "in the position from which the enemy wished us to attack him."

Longstreet would not have the luxury of refusing the offer to attack, however, as few Confederates north of the Chickahominy would be kept out of the battle. In Old Pete's case, the summons came after A. P. Hill's attack had failed. Longstreet put the time at about 5 P.M., when he received an order from Lee to create a diversion on the Union left. Captain Benjamin Smith's 3rd Company, Richmond Howitzers, and Capt. Victor Maurin's Donaldsonville (Louisiana) Artillery battery had already attempted to counter the Union guns on both sides of the river, but the range was too great for Maurin's guns and the three twelve-pound howitzers from Smith's battery. Only Smith's Parrott rifle could engage the guns on the south bank of the river. Infantry was needed, and Longstreet ordered Wilcox to take the three leading brigades and advance against the Federal left flank—not to enter the open, merely to harass the Union line from the edge of the woods east of Powhite Creek. Crossing Powhite Creek in its current state meant using a bridge for artillery. But Unionists had destroyed the bridge in Wilcox's area, so the Southerners used debris from the old bridge and from the abandoned Union encampments to rebuild it. As the 9th Alabama charged across a ravine, Thomas W. Atkins and Sam Crews, good friends in Company F, fell into a hidden ditch. Atkins got up, but Crews seemed to be more seriously hurt. He drank some water from Atkins's canteen but died a few minutes later. It turned out he had been shot in the heart as he fell. Crews was the first—but not the last—man in his company to be killed.

By the time the bridge was rebuilt, Pickett's Virginians on the left of Wilcox's force had also engaged the Federals. Pickett, thirty-seven, had been born in the city he was now defending. He was another member of the West Point class of 1846 and a veteran of the Mexican War, but he had entered this battle somewhat concerned. He had felt "the spirit of my dear mother" the previous night, and took the feeling to mean some message was being sent to him, perhaps a warning of what might happen during the next day's battle. Nonetheless, he led his men into the fight and advanced to within seventy-five yards of the enemy line at the top of a hill. The men stopped charging and started to shoot from prone positions in response to a mistaken order given by Col. Robert E. Withers of the 18th Virginia, who was trying to get other troops to rally. The Virginians fired fairly well, but the return fire was much heavier. They stayed where they were, suffering heavy losses.

The fire that cut them down came from Butterfield's brigade at the left end of the Union line. Butterfield was a thirty-year-old New York lawyer. He had been the colonel of the 12th New York, the first Union regiment to enter Virginia after that state seceded, before becoming a brigadier general. His men were feeling good despite the retreat because they thought McClellan was drawing Lee into a trap. They were ready for their work. "[O]ur fire was too much for them and back they went," recalled one member of the 44th New York. Having moved up some artillery when he saw the Confederate movement, Butterfield felt so comfortable that he sent the 12th New York and 16th Michigan to help Martindale on his right. They saw no action, however, as it turned out that Martindale did not need them.[1]

Longstreet concluded that the Northerners were in such force that a diversion would do no good. He approached Richard Anderson and said, "My part of this work has not been accomplished, and I have nobody to do it with but you." Anderson was a South Carolinian a few months shy of his forty-first birthday. An 1842 West Point graduate, he had fought in Mexico and had watched Fort Sumter fall. Early in 1862, after he succeeded Beauregard in command at Charleston, he was given command of a brigade. "Well, General," Anderson inquired, "what is it you want done?" Longstreet said, "The enemy must come off that hill before night." Anderson responded, "If any one brigade in the army can do it, mine can."

Longstreet ordered Anderson to send part of his brigade to support Pickett and part to guard Wilcox's right flank. He also ordered Kemper's brigade to move up to support the division's attack, which was being launched in response to a note from Lee saying that unless he could do something, all would be lost. Just as Longstreet was preparing for the assault, he saw Whiting burst from the woods to the north with his division, which was part of Jackson's command.

D. H. Hill had joined Jackson's troops in their attempt to get on Porter's flank. Jackson had procured a guide, Pvt. John Henry Timberlake from the 4th Virginia Cavalry, and started off with Ewell's division in the lead followed by Whiting's division and Jackson's own division, commanded by Brig. Gen. Charles S. Winder. D. H. Hill took the Mechanicsville Turnpike straight to Bethesda Church, from where he would turn right.

After the shelling of his fellow Confederates near Beaver Dam Creek, things were progressing relatively smoothly for Stonewall until he took a right turn before he reached Bethesda Church. Jackson seemed to be in a bad mood during the march; one man said it was the only time he ever saw the general out of humor. He gave sharp, crisp orders. As the march continued, the sounds of firing kept getting closer. Some of the men saw Branch's brigade moving in column across an open field. Stonewall finally turned to Timberlake and asked where the firing was coming from. The cavalryman answered that it came from the direction of Gaines's mill. "Does this road lead there?" Jackson asked. Timberlake responded in the affirmative. "But I do not wish to go to Gaines's mill," Jackson explained. "I wish to go to Cold Harbor, leaving that place to the right." Timberlake told Stonewall he should have told him that beforehand. In all, Dabney estimated that about an hour was lost as a result of the wrong turn. Several halts were caused by Federal obstructions on the route. On one of them the 4th Alabama was lying along both sides of the road when a Union wagon, its driver out foraging for Porter's mess, came along. The Alabamians captured the wagon and driver and the lucky among them got some free food.[2]

Jackson could have kept going and wound up in the same place that some of his men did later. Ewell eventually attacked barely more than a mile from where Jackson turned around. However, such a movement by Jackson merely would have given Lee more men at one of the most easily defended parts of the Union line instead of putting pressure on more of that line. Not only that, but it was not Lee's original plan, and at that early hour Jackson could not have known that the situation had changed dramatically.[3]

Once Stonewall got on the road he wanted, he saw another column moving at right angles to his line of march. Whiting, riding ahead, reported that it was the enemy. Jackson looked for a minute and then told the lead regiment to continue. Further investigation showed it to be D. H. Hill. J. W. Jones reported that Jackson "was almost rude" to Whiting as he got his force moving again. The men in both columns were surprised at seeing each other, and Hill—who had known Dabney before the war—expressed astonishment at seeing the clergyman in uniform. Hill then told Dabney to halt the Valley troops, as he was supposed to go first. Jackson fell in behind. Around noon, Stonewall passed the head of Hood's brigade, whose commander was tired of marching and wanted to fight some Yankees. "General Jackson, the enemy keeps well out of my way—what shall I do?" Hood asked. "Press on, sir, press on," replied Jackson.

When Hill reached Old Cold Harbor he gathered in a few wagons, including ambulances, and prisoners left there by the Federals. Some men heard that the camp was McClellan's headquarters and that he had just left. Hill kept moving south of Old Cold Harbor until he found the Yankees—Sykes's division—posted south of what he called Powhite Swamp (but what surely was Boatswain's Swamp). Hill ordered the Jeff Davis Artillery to shell the Union position, which consisted of Buchanan's brigade west of the road from Old Cold Harbor to Grapevine Bridge and Weed's battery on a knoll east of the road that Weed called "a beautiful one for artillery." The Alabama gunners set up at a distance Weed estimated at not over a thousand yards and which one rebel called "too near the enemy." Bondurant bravely stayed on his horse during the shelling, but bravery was no match for artillery. Rhett's battery came up in support, but it could not fire because Southern troops were in the way, and the Union battery forced Bondurant to withdraw in about half an hour. While doing so, his battery scattered Jackson, Hill, and their staffs, who had gotten a little too close to the Federal guns.

Another Union battery—Light Battery A of the 2nd U.S. Artillery, commanded by Capt. John C. Tidball—then reinforced Weed's guns, while Capt. P. H. Clark's Virginia battery and Lt. C. W. Fry's Orange (Virginia) Artillery battery took position near Rhett. Stuart and his cavalry had also come up after having skirmished with the 6th Pennsylvania Cavalry. Captain John Pelham, the commander of Stuart's artillery (such as it was), opened fire with his two guns, a Blakely rifle and a Napoleon smoothbore. The Blakely was soon disabled, but Pelham kept a solitary fire going with his Napoleon.

Instead of coming in on the Union flank as Lee had thought, Jackson had run head on into the right of the Union line. General Orders no. 75 was still operative, and Jackson again probably assumed that he was to get into a flanking position and then hit the Northerners as they retreated. But he was not in a flanking position, and by Dabney's watch it was 2 P.M., hardly the best time to start looking for a place from which to flank the enemy. Jackson ordered Hill to move back to the edge of the woods running along the east side of the road on which they had advanced. From there Jackson expected to be able to cut off Porter's retreat. Meanwhile, Stonewall sent Capt. J. K. Boswell, his chief engineer, to tell Lee the situation.[4]

Jackson himself wrote that he was unacquainted with the ground and worried about casualties from friendly fire (as well he might worry after firing into A. P. Hill that morning). He also thought that A. P. Hill and Longstreet could drive the Federals into him. This reasoning was unimaginative. Porter most likely would have retreated to the south or southeast no matter what McClellan's plans were. Hill's men were northeast of the Union right, so a retreat would move the Northerners farther away from Hill's men. Moreover, taking Hill's troops out of a possible direct confrontation gave Sykes a chance to meet and drive back Gregg's attacks without having to worry about his right.[5]

While Hill was moving into his new position, Ewell and the rest of Jackson's command took a different road from Beulah Church, which was less than a mile north of Old Cold Harbor. Jackson probably meant to spread his forces to form a line, and it appears he used the second road from Beulah Church for that purpose. Stonewall must have received Lee's message to attack from Boswell, and he told Ewell to go in to the right of Hill. Ewell got his men in line and started off. Jackson warned Ewell that the trees ahead of his men were probably full of Yankees and ordered him to send out a strong skirmish line. Ewell soon met Maj. Walter Taylor, Lee's adjutant general. Taylor was looking for Jackson's column, and the staff officer told Ewell to march to A. P. Hill's aid.

Ewell sent Brig. Gen. Arnold Elzey with his Virginians and Georgians to the right into some woods on the east side of the road from New Cold Harbor to the McGehee house. As Elzey's troops moved into position, one of them saw Lee and other officers talking underneath a tree. Just then, a staff officer brought the Confederate commander a message, and he mounted and rode away with his staff, looking to the soldier "beyond question the finest horseman and grandest looking man I had ever seen." These men found none of the enemy in the woods, and Ewell sent his aide, Maj. Campbell Brown, back to get orders from Jackson.

While Ewell was waiting for Stonewall's instructions, he received some from Lee. Marse Robert told Ewell to put his other two brigades—Trimble's and Taylor's—on the west side of the New Cold Harbor road. As soon as Brown got back from seeing Jackson—with the acknowledgment that Stonewall had been misled as to where the Yankees were and giving Ewell the same order as Lee did—the aide was sent back on Lee's order to summon Whiting and Jackson's own division.

Meanwhile, Elzey moved his brigade into position to support Gregg. The forty-five-year-old Elzey was originally born Arnold Jones but dropped his last name in favor of his middle name (Elzey) when he went from Maryland to West Point. He dispatched three of his regiments—the 12th Georgia and 25th and 52nd Virginia—to guard batteries, while the 13th, 31st, 44th, and 58th Virginia moved to the front. After clearing the woods, these regiments quickly found the Unionists beyond the trees and became engaged in a heavy firefight with Sykes's Northerners. Samuel Buck of the 13th Virginia later remembered that he could barely hold his gun because the barrel was so hot. At one point Buck looked up to see a Unionist headed straight toward him. Buck was helpless, being in the process of capping his gun, but a South Carolinian shot the

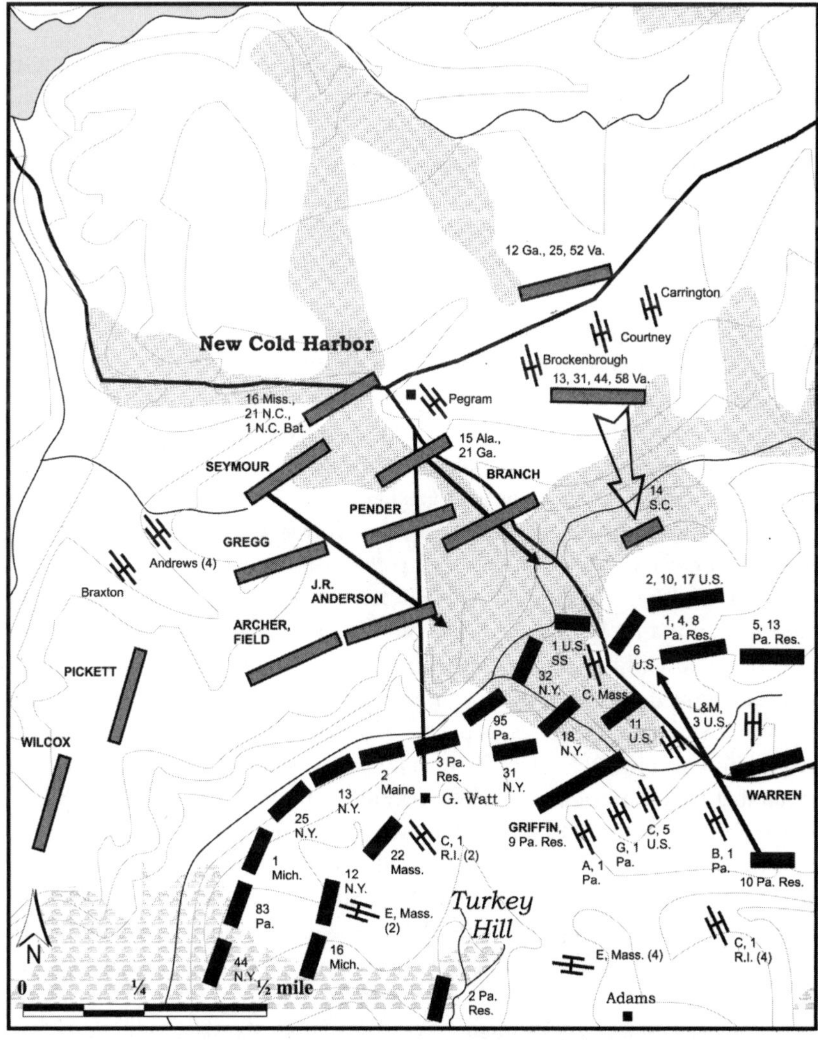

Ewell's attacks, Gaines's Mill, June 27, 1862

Yankee. Elzey went down with a severe wound to the head—"a horrible sight" according to a member of the 3rd Alabama—that would keep him from active service for some time.

The 13th Virginia lost five color-bearers and a total of 112 killed or wounded out of about 250 engaged, including several members of the Trice family, from which five brothers had enlisted. One was killed at Fort Donelson in Tennessee earlier in 1862. Two more were killed in this action with the 13th Virginia, while another was wounded five times. The fifth brother, unhurt while fighting with the 13th, took some prisoners to the rear, joined the 56th Virginia of Pickett's brigade, and was severely wounded while fighting with that unit.[6]

Meanwhile, Gregg, as a result of a mix-up among the troops of the 13th South Carolina, wound up with several of that regiment's companies marching toward the rear. The 13th's commander, Col. O. E. Edwards, wanted to change his position slightly, as he was under fire from his right. Unfortunately, some of his right-hand companies did not hear the order when he shouted it out in the din of battle and became separated from the rest of the regiment. They wound up moving to the rear under Maj. T. S. Farrow. Gregg formed a reserve with Farrow's soldiers and some remnants of the 1st South Carolina Infantry under Colonel Hamilton of the latter regiment. A. P. Hill then ordered this force to support Anderson's and Field's cut up brigades.

Trimble's brigade—composed of regiments from Alabama, Georgia, Mississippi, and North Carolina—went into action on Elzey's right, marching down the road from New Cold Harbor to the McGehee house—in the wrong direction, going south instead of southeast as Lee wanted. The sixty-year-old Trimble, one of the few officers in the Army of Northern Virginia older than its commander, was a West Pointer who left the army and became a railroad engineer. A hard fighter, Trimble had "a talent for mistakes," and Brown (who must have put a lot of mileage on his horse that day) went to straighten him out. Before anything could be done, however, heavy fire hit Trimble's men, and they moved farther to their right to shelter themselves. At that point Lt. C. Wood McDonald, Elzey's inspector general, came to Trimble to beg for help. Trimble told McDonald he would give assistance, but in his own way, protecting his men from fire. That apparently failed to satisfy McDonald, for he rode away yelling at Trimble—and was shot dead at the edge of the road.

As the 15th Alabama and 21st Georgia advanced—the 21st Georgia under its major, as the colonel had fallen into a drunken stupor and could not be wakened—the 16th Mississippi and 21st North Carolina became separated from the rest of the brigade by retreating Confederates. Trimble noted that the rebels falling back were in such good order that they must not have done much fighting, but he was using an excessively high standard. The retreating troops may have been Branch's or Pender's, who had indeed fought hard and been roughly repulsed by Griffin's Federals, or from Brig. Gen. Richard Taylor's brigade (whose story is still to be told). If they were marching back in good order, it should be taken as a compliment to their discipline and not a reflection of their lack of fighting spirit.

In any event, Trimble's leading two regiments moved forward to the assault. Private Gus McClendon of the 15th Alabama got a shoe stuck in the mud around the swamp. He was going to leave it there until Trimble saw him and said kindly, "Soldier, get your shoe." Body armor would have been better, as the Confederates headed into what Trimble called "a perfect sheet of fire" laid down by troops from Warren's brigade; the 2nd, 6th, 10th, and 17th U.S. Infantry regiments from Lovell's brigade; and Berdan's sharpshooters. Trimble's men could not break the line, but they held on to what ground they could, supported by a Virginia regiment. The yelling and sound from guns was so great that McClendon could only tell when he had fired by the kick of his musket. He and his mates had to change guns throughout the afternoon as theirs would get too hot to fire.[7]

Trimble's men had a more difficult time holding ground than they might have if matters had gone differently on their right, where Richard Taylor's brigade was to attack. Taylor was not with his men; he had been taken ill on the night of the twenty-fifth and had remained at Ashland while Jackson's command marched to Hundley's Corner. Although Taylor heard artillery on the twenty-seventh and made his way in an ambulance to the scene of fighting, Col. I. G. Seymour of the 6th Louisiana commanded the brigade. The 1st Louisiana Special Battalion, the famous "Louisiana Tigers" commanded by Maj. C. Roberdeau Wheat, was in this brigade. The Tigers were a hard-living, hard-fighting bunch, and they and their commander had earned Stonewall's respect—which was returned in greater measure by Wheat and his men—even though Henry Kyd Douglas said, "No two men could be more unlike" than the general and the major.

Wheat was concerned for Jackson that day and told Stonewall: "General, we are about to get into a hot fight and it is likely many of us may be killed. I want to ask you for myself and my Louisianans not to expose yourself so unnecessarily as you often do. What will become of us, down here in these swamps, if anything happens to you, and what will become of the country! General, let us do the fighting. Just let me tell them that you promised me not to expose yourself and then they'll fight like—er—ah—Tigers!" Jackson shook Wheat's hand and replied, "Much obliged to you, Major. I will try not to go into danger, unnecessarily. But Major, you will be in greater danger than I, and I hope you will not get hurt. Each of us has his duty to perform, without regard to consequences; we must perform it and trust in Providence." After Wheat rode away to his battalion, Jackson remarked: "Just like Major Wheat. He thinks of the safety of others, too brave ever to think of himself." Earlier that morning

Wheat had gathered his officers together, taken out a devotional book, and read a prayer for a "Joyful Resurrection." He thought the prayer particularly appropriate for a day on which thousands would risk their lives.[8]

As Seymour, Wheat, and the rest of the Louisianans moved down the New Cold Harbor road, Porter ordered fresh troops into action. George Meade, forty-six years old and born in Spain of American parents, was a civil engineer despite a relatively low (nineteenth of fifty-six) standing at West Point. He reentered the army before the Mexican War and stayed in it until he became commander of a brigade in the Pennsylvania Reserves. Most of that brigade was sent from the left of McCall's line toward the Union center. The 4th Pennsylvania Reserves marched to the support of Warren's force and the 3rd Pennsylvania Reserves relieved the 4th Michigan from Griffin's brigade. The 7th Pennsylvania Reserves headed toward the left of the line to support Butterfield's men. Seymour's brigade, forming a general reserve, was sent to the right of Sykes's line, but the 9th and 10th Pennsylvania Reserves moved to Warren's rear as the battle progressed. The 9th Reserves wound up supporting Griffin's 9th Massachusetts and 62nd Pennsylvania, countercharging as many as four times with parts of Griffin's regiments. Colonel Samuel Black of the 62nd Pennsylvania was killed instantly by a bullet between the eyes during one of those charges (two men of the regiment almost were captured the next morning trying to retrieve Black's body). Some of Reynolds's brigade, which was located on the right, moved to the area where Morell's and Sykes's lines joined—in particular the 5th and 13th Reserves, which ended up supporting Sykes. The 1st and 8th Pennsylvania Reserves moved to the support of Warren, while the 2nd Pennsylvania Reserves supported Martindale.

Slocum had also come up by this time. At thirty-four he was the youngest division commander in the army. The West Pointer resigned from the army after seeing some action in Florida and returned to his native New York to practice law. Perhaps because of his youth, Slocum had literally worried himself sick over the Northern situation. He wrote his wife that he "was taken with a fit of vomiting" on the twenty-seventh and had to get off his horse and go to some shade to recover. In fact, he apparently left the field due to his illness. His men were in position just south of the Chickahominy near Alexander's and Woodbury's Bridges, just west of Grapevine Bridge and about two miles from the front lines.

Brigadier General John Newton's brigade began its movement at 2 P.M. when the order was received. Newton, a thirty-nine-year-old Virginia native and West Point-trained engineer, apparently crossed at Alexander's Bridge. His brigade arrived at the Watt house between 3:30 and 4 P.M., just as the last of Porter's reserve units had been put into the fight. As they marched up the hill, they passed ambulances and wounded men walking past. The wounded could only agree on one thing about the battle: "there was hot work over the hill yonder."[9]

Captain William Biddle of McClellan's staff reached Porter just before Slocum did and asked the V Corps commander if he had any message for McClellan. "You can see for yourself, Captain," Porter said. "We're holding them, but it's getting hotter and hotter." Just then, the head of Newton's brigade made its appearance, accompanied by Lt. Emory Upton's Battery D, 2nd U.S. Artillery. After the brigade waited for half an hour for orders, Porter split it up. Two regiments, the 31st New York and 95th Pennsylvania under Newton's command, headed off in a northwesterly direction, while the 18th and 32nd New York, commanded by Col. Roderick Matheson of the 32nd, followed a more northerly route toward Warren's and Lovell's men. Griffin in turn pulled his force out of the line, and Upton's guns were placed still farther to the right.

Meanwhile, Seymour ran into the 95th Pennsylvania as it was moving into the line at the double-quick, and paid the ultimate price: he was shot from his horse and died within a few minutes. Command of his brigade fell to Col. Leroy A. Stafford of the 9th Louisiana. Wheat also was shot. According to some, he asked about Jackson with nearly his last breath, whereas others said he was killed instantly. One man reported that four men were killed and four others severely wounded within ten steps of Wheat in just fifteen minutes. The brigade could not stand Newton's fire—especially as the Federals were fighting from behind breastworks on the other side of the crest of the ridge and so were invisible to the attacking rebels. One man, asked why he was retreating, yelled, "They have killed the old Major (Wheat) and I am going home. I wouldn't fight for Jesus Christ now!"[10]

This endangered the 15th Alabama and the 21st Georgia, as Newton was continuing the advance with the 31st New York and could possibly reach their flank. Not only that, but Trimble was not at the front to help rally his troops, having gone to the rear to bring up the remainder of his brigade. Ewell, however, was on the field, and worked feverishly to keep his men in line. His favorite horse was killed under him, and a bullet passed through his bootleg and slightly bruised his ankle. Others helped the line hold. Lieutenant Colonel John F. Trentlen of the 15th Alabama, temporarily in command because Col. James Cantey and two companies had gotten separated from the regiment, kept men in line who in some cases had no ammunition and no supporting troops. Another man, who most of the Confederates thought was an officer on horseback, rode up and down the line shouting encouragement to the troops who stayed in line and rallying those who appeared ready to break. In reality the man was a private—Frank Campion of Company F, 15th Alabama—who had grabbed a riderless horse and performed what may have seemed a miracle. Campbell Brown came upon some of Seymour's men and the 15th Alabama's

Colonel Cantey with his two companies and worked to get them into a supporting position.

Ewell had also tried to get his artillery into a supporting position behind Elzey's line. Brockenbrough's battery, joined by the Charlottesville (Virginia) Artillery and Capt. A. R. Courtney's Virginia guns, actually unlimbered, but the Charlottesville battery at least fired very little—perhaps out of fear of hitting rebel infantry. One of the Charlottesville gunners, Wilbur F. Davis, thought the musketry at Gaines's Mill was the most continuous and prolonged he heard throughout the war.[11]

By 5 P.M., Ewell's entire division, except for the Maryland Line, had seen heavy fighting. One brigade had been forced back and had lost many of its officers. The other two were barely holding onto their positions. But Whiting was coming up, after a period in the afternoon when apparently confusing orders had caused him to halt. After giving Ewell his orders, Jackson told Dabney to go to Whiting, Winder, and the other brigadiers in Jackson's own division, with orders to move *en echelon* from left to right, find the enemy, and fight him—going to the sound of the heaviest firing if they could not follow orders. Just as Dabney was ready to leave, Jackson caught sight of his quartermaster, Maj. John Harman. Knowing that Dabney had been ill, Stonewall sent Harman instead (over Dabney's protests). Harman reached Whiting, but the quartermaster was no master of military terms, and Whiting could not understand anything except to await further orders. Dabney wrote long after the war that Whiting had been drinking. Yet in light of subsequent events, it is safe to say that Harman was the problem. Whether Winder and the other brigade commanders understood is not known, but since Whiting was ahead of them they could not move anyway. Thus, two divisions awaited orders that had already been given to them.

Fortunately for Jackson, Dabney was not sure that Harman would deliver the instructions accurately. Jackson could have put the orders in writing, clearing up everything, but apparently he did not do so. Dabney followed Harman, probably after noting that Whiting was not moving. Once Dabney found Whiting, he asked whether Harman had delivered the orders. Whiting said that he had, but that he had been unable to understand a word he said. Dabney explained what Jackson wanted and, after arguing with Dabney a little, Whiting moved forward. The division, with Evander Law's Alabamians, Mississippians, and North Carolinians on the right and John Hood's Texans and Georgians with the Hampton Legion from South Carolina on the left, angled to the west through the area around Gaines's mill and past Taylor's brigade. Whiting reported receiving requests for support from several different generals' aides, who reported that both Hills were hard pressed (although Ewell was probably meant instead of D. H. Hill).

It seemed to Whiting that the whole front was in need of support, so he kept moving. One member of Hood's brigade later remembered that the men had heard the firing before setting off and saw wounded men relatively early in the march. The numbers of wounded increased as they got closer to the front. When they arrived in the rear of A. P. Hill's division they reportedly saw not merely individual stragglers but whole regiments out of control (something of an exaggeration, but Hill's well-used men would have looked disorganized by that point). Some of the men said they might be too late to do any good, but Hood and Whiting urged them to move forward as quickly as they could.

Whiting kept looking for the proper place to go in until he found Lee. The army commander probably had found it difficult to maintain any semblance of control on that confusing, deadly day, but he knew where he wanted Whiting's troops and sent them on farther to the right of the rebel line. It was there that Whiting and Longstreet met just as Longstreet was preparing to advance.[12]

At about 5 P.M., there was a sort of lull in the battle along Boatswain's Swamp. When Porter earlier reported that he had beaten back the Confederate attacks, McClellan responded, "If the enemy are retiring and you are a chasseur, pitch in." Later, McClellan told Porter, "Try to drive the rascals and take some prisoners and guns." But at 5 P.M. Porter sent a telegram describing his men as "pressed hard, very hard" and begged for reinforcements so he could hold his line. Brigadier Generals Thomas F. Meagher's and William H. French's brigades from Israel Richardson's II Corps division moved by Alexander's and Grapevine Bridges in response. Little Mac told Porter of the move and added, "You must hold your own until dark." Later that hour the commander in chief wired Porter, "You must beat them if I move the whole Army to do it & transfer all on this side." This had to have been an attempt to buck up Porter, for even if McClellan had the inclination to move the entire army north of the Chickahominy, he could not have accomplished that feat in the daylight left. He might have thought about doing it the next day if Porter was successful, but that was not the meaning of his message.

Until Richardson's brigades arrived, Porter had all the men he would get. Almost all of the Pennsylvania Reserves were in the fight. The 5th and 13th Reserves, in support of Sykes's line, worked so hard that the gun barrels blistered the men's hands. The 1st, 4th, and 8th Reserves allowed Warren to retire with his well-fought men. At one point, the 4th Reserves were pushed hard enough to make them retreat, but the rest of the line held, and the 4th moved to support the 3rd Reserves in Griffin's old lines. Company B of the 1st Reserves found itself without a commissioned officer. Lieutenant Joseph Stewart of Company H was selected to take charge of the company by Col. R. Biddle Roberts. Upon hearing the news, Stewart smiled, saluted, ran to the company, and at the instant of assuming command fell dead with a bullet in his head. The 10th Reserves, supporting batteries on Sykes's part of the line for a while, moved to the center and came under heavy attack for two hours. When the 7th Reserves got to Butterfield's line, the men began to lie down as usual, but Butterfield told them, "Boys, don't lie down; we can whip the rascals standing up." Eventually even he decided that the fire was too much, however, and the Pennsylvanians were permitted to assume a more comfortable and safer position.[13]

Porter also had all of Slocum's division up by this time. Brigadier General George W. Taylor's New Jersey brigade, the second of Slocum's units to cross the Chickahominy, moved into position near the center of Porter's line. The 3rd and 4th New Jersey were in front with the 1st and 2nd New Jersey in support. Captain William Hexamer's Battery A, New Jersey Light Artillery, accompanied them. Taylor was almost twenty years older than Slocum and had served in both the navy and army before returning to New Jersey to manufacture iron and engage in mining. He was given a brigade command when Phil Kearny took over a division, and that promotion seemed reasonable considering Taylor's foresight on June 27: he had sent Lt. E. B. Grubb of his staff across the river to sketch the Union line.

When the order first came to support Porter, Lt. Col. Robert McAllister of the 1st New Jersey was writing a letter to his wife. He told her he did not think the division would make it to the front line in time to do any good. Some of the men did not know where they were going until they crossed the river, when they began to hear the roar and see the wounded; then the order to move out at the double-quick came. The brigade occupied a position in a field of clover five hundreds yards from the front line, which proved to be close enough to get hit by bullets, so the men were ordered to lie down. Soon the two lead regiments advanced. The 3rd New Jersey went in on the right of Newton's line while the 4th New Jersey moved in a different direction. As Taylor began to move forward, an officer rode up and began speaking rapidly in French. Taylor, not familiar with the language, turned to Grubb and said, "Who the devil is this, and what is he talking about?" Grubb, who knew the man, said, "This is the Comte de Paris [or perhaps the Duc de Chartres] serving on General McClellan's staff, and he has come to you by General Porter's orders under which you are to give him one of our regiments." Taylor asked, "Do you know him?" Grubb replied that he did, and Taylor said, "Very well, then give him the Fourth Regiment and go and see where he put it and come back and report." The 4th New Jersey went to where the 11th Pennsylvania Reserves of Meade's brigade was waiting, and the two regiments moved to support Meade's 3rd Pennsylvania Reserves on Newton's left. Soon the 4th New Jersey relieved the Pennsylvanians, whose guns were overheated and fouled and whose ammunition had run out after holding off the enemy for two hours. The 1st New Jersey and the four companies of the 2nd New Jersey that crossed the river were held in reserve.[14]

Colonel Joseph J. Bartlett's brigade of Maine, New York, and Pennsylvania regiments was the last of Slocum's units to reach the field, along with Capt. Josiah Porter's 1st Battery, Massachusetts Light Artillery. Some of Bartlett's men thought they were headed back to camp until they turned left toward the river. Once they crossed, they were ordered to the left of the line to support Butterfield's men. Bartlett, who was unusual for both his age (twenty-seven) and his lack of West Point training or military experience (he was a lawyer in his native New York), saw that the Union left was protected by cavalry while some troops to his immediate front were wavering, so he started the 16th New York forward. At that point, one of Porter's aides directed Bartlett to move to support Sykes. Bartlett's men thus marched about a mile to the extreme right of Porter's line. The brigade then stopped to rest, and Clement Potts in the 96th Pennsylvania volunteered to fill his company's canteens. Before Potts could get back with the water, Bartlett moved the brigade forward and to the left to support Buchanan's brigade, Edwards's battery, and Lt. Henry W. Kingsbury's Battery D, 5th U.S. Artillery, around the McGehee house. Porter's battery, lacking any position from which it could fire effectively, was placed in reserve.[15]

D. H. Hill, meanwhile, was readying an advance against this position. During the afternoon, as he and his staff rode by the 12th Alabama of Brig. Gen. Robert E. Rodes's brigade, a Yankee shell burst and a piece of it went under Hill's arm, tearing away part of his uniform and leaving some flesh exposed. Hill's expression never changed. Captain Jule L'Etondal of Company A, 12th Alabama, who weighed at least 250 pounds, carried an umbrella with him. While the company was exposed to heavy fire and marching toward the enemy, L'Etondal kept the umbrella open, using it to shade himself from the hot sun. The men of Company A kept saying, "Put down that umbrella, you are attracting the enemy's fire to us." L'Etondal responded, "I won't, it is much too hot," and kept using the umbrella.

The 5th Alabama had been under the Yankee shelling for some time when someone discovered that the house the regiment was next to was actually an intact sutler's store. The men quickly made off with its contents and a soldier gave an officer a bottle of claret. Not so pleasant was the sight of Lt. M. S. Ramsay having his head taken off by a shell.

By 5 P.M. Hill was ready to advance in response to Jackson's order. Garland's brigade held the left, with Anderson, Rodes, Col. Alexander Colquitt's Alabamians and Georgians, and Ripley to the right in that order. Hill also had all seven of his batteries in position to support the assault. He had to get across the remains of Boatswain's Swamp and then cross about four hundred yards of open field to get to the position held by Buchanan's men just north of the road from New Cold Harbor to the McGehee house.

Buchanan was old army. He had turned fifty-one in the spring, and was one of the few Union soldiers to have fought in both the Black Hawk and Mexican Wars. His right flank now extended just across the road from Old Cold Harbor to Grapevine Bridge. The 4th U.S. Infantry was east of the road supporting Weed's battery, the 3rd U.S. Infantry was just west of the road, and the 12th and 14th U.S. Infantry were in line on the edge of the field to the west of the 3rd U.S.

The men of the 14th U.S. were downhearted after the sutler's stores and supplies in their old camp were put to the torch. When the regiment finally reached its assigned spot, there was no shade. At about noon, Capt. John O'Connell, the regimental commander, gave the order to load and told his men to fire low and keep from getting too excited. The Confederates began shelling, and their second shot hit a log cabin in back of the soldiers, scattering several civilians who had taken shelter there. One shell just missed Capt. Jonathan Hager and landed at the foot of the color corporal but did not explode. Sergeants Patrick Kerens and Morris Reed volunteered to find the enemy position. They saw the advance on the 5th New York, and Reed was ready to shoot a rebel officer when other Confederates tried to shoot him. He and Kerens ran through a fence and met their comrades as they moved into position.

Confusion reigned for a while in the 4th U.S. After the regiment took its position its commander, Maj. Delozier Davidson, left the field to look for reinforcements. Unable to find any, Davidson returned and directed Capt. Joseph B. Collins to move a short distance to the right. Davidson then headed to the rear, leaving his horse on the field with his orderly, and disappeared, putting Collins in effective command. Stuart's cavalry captured Davidson, who was still wandering around north of the Chickahominy, the next morning.

Hospital units behind the lines were already at work. Wounded soldiers who could walk headed for the hospitals' red flags, guided by a steady stream of stretcher bearers. The surgeons and stewards treated the wounds as best they could. One steward stationed behind the regulars noticed many stragglers leaving the lines as far as he could see, with no one there to stop them.[16]

The Confederate advance against those still in line was jumbled as the brigades slogged through the swamp and its accompanying undergrowth. The left wheel that put D. H. Hill's division into proper position had to be shortened, throwing some regiments to the rear of others and effectively putting them out of the fight. Others were mixed up with different brigades, so some command control was lost. The 3rd and 6th Alabama from Rodes's brigade got ahead of their brethren when the other three regiments ran into Anderson's men. The 3rd Alabama then found more Confederates in its front and stopped, leaving the 6th Alabama advancing with no support. Colonel John B. Gordon, finding his men exposed to flanking fire from other rebels and frontal fire from the Federals, moved back to the southern edge of the swamp.

Anderson's brigade drove some Union skirmishers from the swamp and also stopped on the edge of the woods.

At about this time Hill noticed Winder's and Lawton's brigades of Jackson's old division approaching on his right. Winder, a Maryland native and at one time the youngest captain in the U.S. Army, was, at thirty-one, one of the Confederacy's youngest generals. After commanding artillery in the bombardment of Fort Sumter, he had commanded the 6th South Carolina until taking command of the Stonewall Brigade, Jackson's original command. He was supposed to have taken his brigade and the others from Jackson's division to the right of Whiting's division. When he began his movement, however, he lost track of the force ahead of him and instead headed toward the nearest firing, which he noted in his diary was "terrific—never heard such." Encountering A. P. Hill, Winder asked him for orders. Hill told Winder to stay where he was, and then ordered him to move two regiments (the 2nd and 5th Virginia) to support Pegram's battery.

About a half-hour later Hill ordered Winder forward, and as the brigade made its way through the brush it picked up several other units, including the Hampton Legion, the 1st Maryland, 12th Alabama, 52nd Virginia, and 38th Georgia. A staff officer gave Winder's command to the various regimental commanders, and one said he would not move until ordered to do so by his own brigade commander. The staff officer decided he did not have time to waste on the man and kept on riding.

Lawton followed Winder, moving somewhat to the right of Winder's main body in his march. He told the men to trot instead of walk. The men threw away excess equipment, and some fell out of the ranks with heat exhaustion. Lawton was a forty-three-year-old South Carolinian. He graduated from both West Point and the Harvard Law School and then became president of a railroad and a state legislator before the war, which he helped cause by taking Fort Pulaski. Seeing that the frontline rebels needed assistance, and not finding Jackson, he moved his brigade toward his immediate front, running into Ewell in the midst of the forest. The brigade, advancing with 3,500 men in line of battle, must have made a distinct impression on Ewell, who waved his sword and cried out, "Hurrah for Georgia!" Lawton's movements made the Confederate left more or less one solid line.

Two other rebel brigades were on the north bank of the Chickahominy—Brig. Gen. John R. Jones's Virginians (temporarily commanded by Lt. Col. R. H. Cunningham of the 21st Virginia due to Jones's illness) and Col. E. V. Fulkerson's Virginians, both of Jackson's division. These two brigades, ahead of Winder in the marching order, followed Whiting's force. Cunningham wound up all the way on the right of the line supporting Wilcox, while Fulkerson moved through bogs and swamps dodging incoming shot, shells, and balls to support Whiting.[17]

On the Union side, Bartlett's brigade had formed a second line behind Buchanan's and Warren's men in a ravine. Although firing was constant along the lines, it must have been clear to all that the crisis of the battle was near. Lee met Jackson on the road from Beulah Church that Ewell, Whiting, and Winder had used with the greeting, "Ah, General, I am very glad to see you. I had hoped to be with you before." Jackson, no doubt perturbed by the day's problems, nodded and mumbled a reply. "That fire is very heavy; do you think your men can stand it?" Lee asked. "They can stand almost anything! They can stand that," Stonewall replied.

Jackson later received a message to the effect that the Yankees were not retreating as they should have been. "Tell them if they stand at sunset to press them with the bayonet!" Stonewall responded. Jeb Stuart, who was with Jackson, commented, "You had better send a second messenger, General, this one may be shot." Not thinking of the first courier's reaction on hearing this somewhat off-the-cuff discussion of his fate, Jackson agreed and told a mounted man to go along with the messenger. However, Capt. A. S. "Sandy" Pendleton, one of his aides, volunteered instead. "Tell them this thing has hung in suspense too long," Jackson told Pendleton, "sweep the field with the bayonet." One eyewitness reported that Jackson was more excited at this point than he had ever seen him and wanted Stuart to charge the Yankees with his cavalry. Jeb declined, saying there were too many cannon, but pointed out to Stonewall that some of his own artillery was idle. Jackson sent orders to all his batteries.

After Lee left Jackson he found A. P. Hill and ordered him to advance and communicate the same order to all the other commanders.[18] Longstreet, on the right, and D. H. Hill, on the left, were already advancing in response to earlier orders, so the effect was one gigantic charge, bearing down on a tired but reinforced Union line behind Boatswain's Swamp. The crisis of the battle for Lee and Porter, for Federal and rebel, had come.

CHAPTER SEVEN

"I Have a Regiment That Can Take It"

THE FINAL DESPERATE CONFEDERATE effort at Gaines's Mill was an aggregation of small events, each person in each area thinking that his was the most important. It is important to remember, however, that all these events took place at very close to the same time.

On the Confederate left, D. H. Hill found Sam Garland and George B. Anderson talking "with great enthusiasm"—some described the conversation as "contention"—about the possibility of taking Buchanan's line in flank and the concern about some Yankee guns (Lt. Horace Hayden's section of Edwards's battery). The two were each thirty-one years old and newly promoted brigadiers. Garland was a Virginia lawyer who graduated from the Virginia Military Institute, using his off time to organize the Lynchburg Home Guard (later part of the 11th Virginia) before attaining brigade command in late May. Anderson was a Tar Heel and a West Point-trained cavalryman who had switched to infantry at the outbreak of hostilities and got his brigade in early June.

Hill asked both young officers whether the artillery would affect their movement. "I don't think it can do much harm, and I am willing to risk it," Garland answered. Anderson agreed, so Hill ordered the entire division to advance. Still concerned about the guns, though, he also ordered five regiments to attempt to capture them. Two regiments from Arnold Elzey's brigade that had been separated (probably the 25th and 52nd Virginia, although the 12th Georgia is also a possibility) moved to the batteries' rear led by Hill's volunteer guide, Thomas W. Sydnor.

Meanwhile, the 1st and 3rd North Carolina of Roswell Ripley's brigade and the 20th North Carolina of Garland's brigade were ordered to attack in front. Only the 20th North Carolina actually assaulted, however. At least some of the men in Ripley's regiments thought they were in reserve. As the 20th North Carolina advanced, an exploding shell and minié balls hit Sgt. Kiah Harris of Company A at the same time, causing nine different mortal wounds. Colonel Alfred Iverson was also seriously wounded, but the regiment captured the guns. The men turned one gun around to fire on the Yankees, but no ammunition was available. Hill believed the 20th North Carolina's charge turned the tide of the whole battle in the Confederates' favor.

The rest of Anderson's brigade also charged. Captain Thomas Blount, the quartermaster of the 4th North Carolina, grabbed the 30th North Carolina's flag, riding ahead with it. The 30th followed Blount with a yell, but the quartermaster soon paid for his ardor as he was shot dead from the saddle. The men kept going and carried the Union position. "It was the most exciting scene I ever witnessed," wrote Capt. William E. Ardrey of the 30th.

General Rodes probably should not have been on this field. The thirty-three-year-old VMI graduate and civil engineer had been badly wounded at Seven Pines and still was not ready for field duty. Whether that affected his brigade or not, two of his regiments did not move with the rest. When some troops on his left broke, Rodes thought the whole division was in trouble and went looking for supporting troops. Finding Colquitt's brigade and the 3rd and 6th Alabama of his own brigade, he told Colquitt to help on the left and ordered his own troops forward again. Three of Colquitt's regiments never got into the battle. But the 5th Alabama, supported by the 26th Alabama, captured some Union guns despite the loss of its commander, Col. C. C. Pegues—who after being hit told his second in command, Maj. E. L. Hobson, it was his last wish that the 5th Alabama should allow no regiment to pass it. Captain Eugene Blackford took his colonel's wish to heart. After the charge he spied some artillery left on the field and rushed down the slope. At the bottom he found just his own company, about thirteen men, still with him as some Yankees from the 2nd New Jersey of Taylor's brigade headed toward him. He told them to surrender and they did so on the spot. The rest of the regiment wheeled to the left to help Garland's and Anderson's men.[1]

Ripley's brigade on the right of Hill's line was even more confused. Some of it was not even on the field, as the 44th Georgia and part of the 1st North Carolina (the two regiments cut up at Mechanicsville) were left to guard the Mechanicsville Turnpike Bridge on Lee's order. The 48th Georgia moved to help rebels to its right but never got into position. And, as mentioned earlier, the rest of the 1st and 3rd North Carolina watched the 20th North Carolina charge.

Colonel Bradley T. Johnson and the 1st Maryland had spent the day supporting Brockenbrough's battery. At one point a civilian visitor, George Kyle, rode

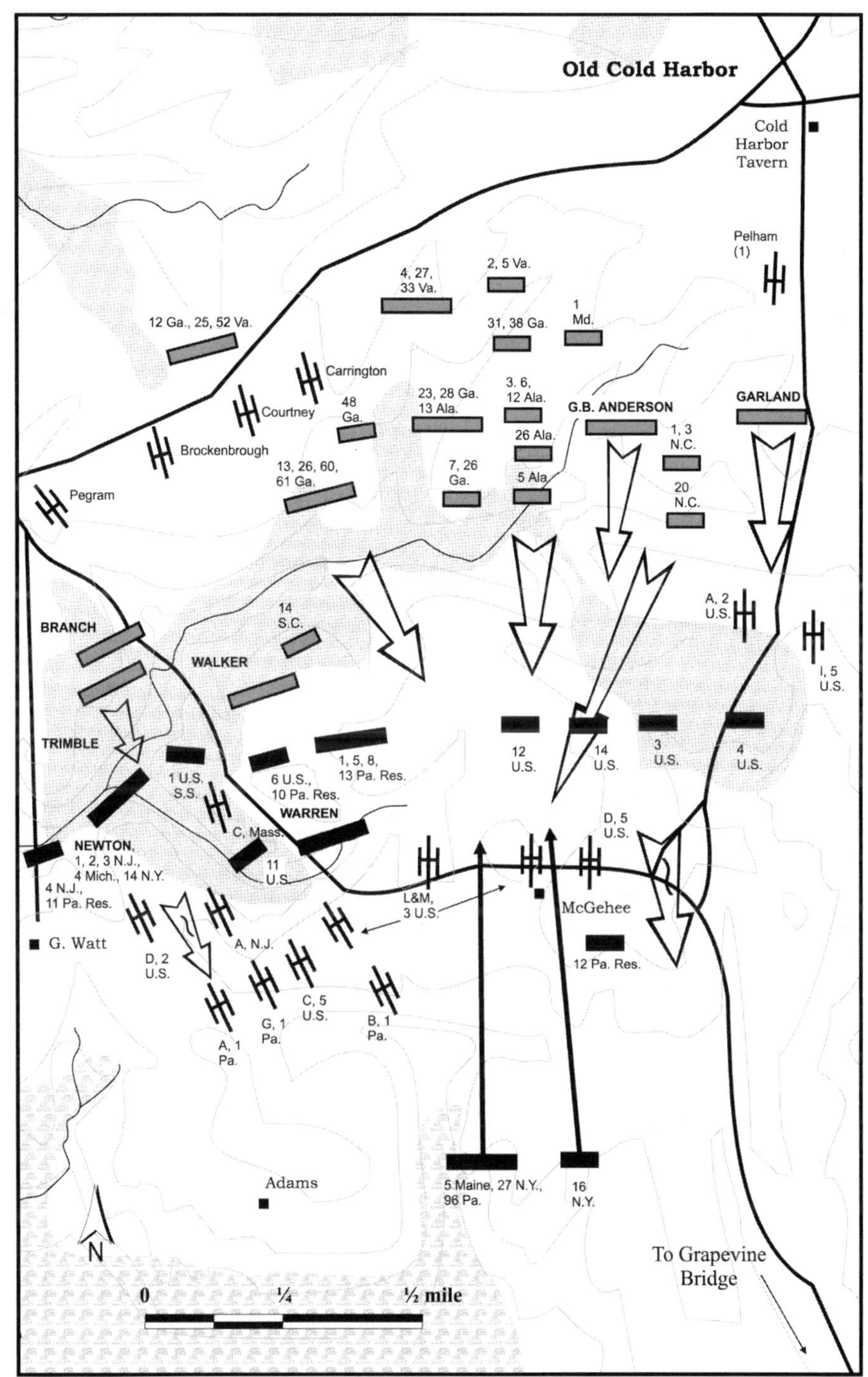

Final assaults on Sykes's line, Gaines's Mill, June 27, 1862

up to the regiment with some letters. "As they may be the last you will ever receive, I would advise you to lose no time in reading them," he said. The men, in the midst of battle, stopped to read the missives from their friends across the border.

Eventually Johnson spied Jackson and went to him, saying, "Good evening, General!" "Good evening, Colonel," was Stonewall's response. "If you want me, I am here," replied Johnson. "Very good, sir," said Jackson. His teeth were clenched, his lips clamped, and his eyes blazed with excitement as he listened to the sounds of battle. At that moment, horsemen appeared in the field where the two men were. Jackson turned his horse straight toward them, jerked upright, and raised his right forearm to form an L. Johnson, thinking Jackson wanted the horsemen to come over, said, "I'll bring them to you," but got no response. He then realized Jackson was praying.

Stonewall finally told Johnson to charge with all available infantry except for a hundred to guard each battery. Johnson protested that no infantry would be left. Jackson then said, "I shall support the batteries with cavalry, and, Johnson, make your men shoot like they are shooting at a mark, slow and low, hit them *here* and *here*." He thrust a hand at Johnson's waist. Johnson remembered later that this was the only time he ever heard Jackson use someone's name.

Johnson got his thirty-two-year-old Maryland blood going and yelled, "Men, I have offered to lead forward the line that never yet broke—never can be broken. Forward, quick march, guide center!" As the regiment moved forward, Johnson called a halt just short of the crest of a small rise and had the men lie down while he went forward to reconnoiter. At that moment, two Alabama regiments and the 5th North Carolina from Garland's brigade fell back in disorder (perhaps the breaking that Rodes saw). Johnson helped the regimental officers rally their men, appealing to their state loyalty.

More disordered troops appeared after the 1st Maryland passed the crest, and Johnson had his men perform the manual of arms to keep them steady. Finally, the rebels hit the Union line and overran it. But the battery they had been trying to capture, Kingsbury's, had limbered up and departed.[2]

Winder led his diverse force forward. Jackson, watching the battle, wanted his old brigade in the fighting to turn the tide decisively and said, "Where is the 1st brigade?" "In the woods, yonder, General" came the reply. "Order it to advance!" Stonewall hollered. It did, shouting, "Jackson! Jackson!" As the brigade passed the 1st Maryland, Lt. McHenry Howard, one of Winder's aides, yelled at some Marylanders, "Are you going to remain here like cowards while the Stonewall Brigade is charging past?" A soldier aimed his musket at Howard, but an officer knocked his gun into the air and the man charged with the rest of the Confederates. The Valley veterans headed through woodland so dense that one remembered, "a man ten yards in front could not be seen." They passed many dead soldiers. The Union artillery was firing so fast that it sounded to Lieutenant Howard like "the roar of falling water or rising and falling like the groaning of heavy machinery in motion in an old building. . . . It was the only field I had seen on which the smoke of battle rested, through which the setting sun shone red and dim"—an observation shared by a Union staff officer.

The 2nd and 5th Virginia, moving in advance of the rest of the line, were halted by Union fire. One man wrote, "It was the awfullest time that I ever saw." The 2nd Virginia lost Col. J. W. Allen killed and Maj. F. B. Jones mortally wounded at about the same time, but the regiments held on until the rest of Winder's force caught up. The 33rd Virginia was held up because it had to go around a Georgia unit and through a swamp before getting into action. Colonel William S. H. Baylor of the 5th Virginia, noticing some space between his men and the 2nd Virginia, saw a regiment in between and somewhat to the rear of both. When he found out it was the 38th Georgia of Alexander Lawton's brigade, he asked to see its colonel. All the field officers had been wounded, and Capt. Edward P. Lawton, General Lawton's adjutant general, was leading it. The Georgians had run out of ammunition, but they still had bayonets, and Baylor asked Captain Lawton if he would fill the space between the two regiments. Lawton said he would. The two regiments charged, and as they drew within seventy-five yards of the Yankee infantry and battery, the Northerners retired slowly, leaving their cannon behind. The rest of the brigade, perhaps after seeing Ewell at the top of the hill south of Boatswain's Swamp, pushed the Federals three hundred yards beyond the McGehee house. There, according to one account, a man found a copy of Lee's General Orders no. 75 addressed to D. H. Hill.[3]

Buchanan, on the extreme right, retreated partially because of the Confederate charge and partially because he believed the Union left had given way, judging from the cheering and firing. Major Nathan Rossell, commanding the 3rd U.S. Infantry, was mortally wounded and his regiment almost surrounded at one point, but Capt. Thomas W. Walker got the men out of trouble. That retreat caused the 14th U.S. Infantry, on the left of the 3rd U.S., to pull back after it had fought for almost two hours with hardly an interruption. After a brief respite, the 14th U.S. was surprised by more fire, and Captain O'Connell ordered a fighting withdrawal. Major Henry B. Clitz of the 12th U.S. did the same, calling, "Step now, men, if you ever stepped." However, he was wounded twice while guiding his men and fainted. He was subsequently taken to the McGehee house and then captured. About 9 P.M. Clitz was taken in to see Hill, and the Southern general called for a surgeon to dress his old friend's wounds.[4]

The rebels then fell heavily on Joseph Bartlett's brigade. The 16th New York and 96th Pennsylvania moved to hold off the Southerners. Bartlett noted that many of the company-level officers in the 96th Pennsylvania were not enthusiastic about the movement, so he moved the 5th Maine into line and then the 27th New York. Finally, the 96th Pennsylvania was ready and moved to the front line, where the Pennsylvanians got to a fence and held their ground. "I for one always hooted at the idea of 'lead and iron hail' but I saw and heard on that day what I have no longer any curiosity to hear and see," wrote Maj. Lewis Martin. The 5th Maine stopped shooting because the men thought they were firing on friends. A captain looked through his field glass and said, "They are rebels; boys, give it to them."

The 16th New York charged from a different fence toward the 20th North Carolina and retook Hayden's guns, despite Col. Joseph Howland being severely wounded in the left leg. The fighting was severe: the 20th North Carolina lost 70 killed and 202 wounded, while the 16th New York suffered 32 killed and 162 wounded. Lieutenant Colonel Franklin J. Faison, who took over command of the 20th North Carolina after Iverson fell, was mortally wounded himself while turning one of the guns on the charging Federals. The man who shot him was killed almost immediately. Twenty-seven bullets hit the Tar Heels' flag. The men of the 16th New York went into the battle wearing white straw hats given them by Howland's wife earlier in the month. They were pleasant, helping the men in the heat before the battle started. But the hats only drew extra attention from Southern marksmen—perhaps making the rebels shoot high—and many were gone before the battle ended. The 27th New York moved to help the 16th, entering "some of the most desperate firing I ever saw" in the words of one soldier. A couple of companies of the 5th Maine lost their way and joined the 27th to fight. The Confederate onslaught—the fire "was more than flesh and blood could resist," one veteran remembered—and lack of ammunition finally forced Bartlett to retire. According to Cyrus Stone of the 16th New York, Bartlett's was the last brigade off the field, but it left Hayden's section behind and almost left a regimental flag before Bartlett called, "Boys don't leave your colors." Howland, who had stayed mounted despite his wound, dismounted weakly after the contest and fell asleep under a tree. He awoke in the dark to find his horse nuzzling him. Howland "cried like a child" as he embraced the horse's neck and got to his lines in safety. One of Bartlett's aides wrote, "How anyone escaped is a mystery to me."[5]

One reason Bartlett retired, moving back regiment by regiment, was that he was flanked on the left by Lawton's brigade. Before the charge, some of Lawton's units were confused, thinking they were firing on fellow Southerners. Colonel Clement A. Evans of the 31st Georgia had read a passage from the Bible before ordering his men to charge a Union battery. Sensing an advantage given to them by their buck-and-ball cartridges, they began to run toward the guns. Evans thought his regiment would be cut to pieces without any support, and he ordered a halt—threatening the men with his sword and finally stopping the color company. The regiment then began a firefight with the Unionists, losing many more men than it might have, according to one veteran. The 31st finally ran out of ammunition and other units took the battery.

Lawton was nominally headed toward Buchanan's left, where Maj. Charles Lovell, a fifty-one-year-old Regular Army veteran from Massachusetts, had moved with most of his brigade. Lovell's three frontline units, the 2nd, 10th, and 17th U.S. Infantry, had run out of ammunition. By the time he reached division headquarters, the Confederates had forced the Union line back. George McCall's units on this part of the line, the 1st, 5th, 8th, and 13th Pennsylvania Reserves, also reported running out of ammunition. What checked Lawton most was the problem of telling friend from foe in the confusion and fading light. At one point the Georgians could see the Union and Confederate lines, and both sides fired on Lawton's men at the same time. Lawton finally grew so cautious that he pulled back a few hundred yards to where he knew there were rebels. Soon he heard of the order to charge and the need for his support, so he again advanced, but he had only returned to his furthest advance point when he heard the cheering. The 2nd U.S. Infantry, having reformed, attempted a charge but was thrown back. At that point the battle on the Union right largely stopped, and the Southerners prepared for a possible Union counterattack as night fell.

Gouverneur Warren's brigade and Lovell's 6th U.S. Infantry, to the west of the 2nd U.S., were not heavily engaged in opposing the charge, and part of McCall's division was just as fortunate. These regiments went through heavy fighting—the 10th Pennsylvania Reserves ran out of ammunition in this area—but the main thrusts of the Confederate assaults swept to the southwest and east of them. Warren and that part of John Reynolds's brigade between George Sykes's and George Morell's line held their ground throughout the assaults, only retiring to support batteries or because of lack of ammunition. Lovell's 11th U.S. Infantry, to Warren's left, had watched the action all day without being involved. The regulars saw Capt. Augustus Martin's Battery C, Massachusetts Light Artillery, make the woods in front "a hell on earth" and watched men going into the fight and coming out wounded and on stretchers. Straggling occurred, and Capt. John W. Ames, thinking it was beginning to look a little like Bull Run, worked to get the men back in line. When Lovell's men finally moved back, Martin brought his horses up to remove the guns. The 11th U.S. moved up to the front and fired five times at the advancing rebels, probably Lawton's men. That, along with Martin's blasts of canister, allowed both the artillery and infantry to get off the field.[6]

To the left of the 11th U.S., John Newton's men and the 1st and 3rd New Jersey of George Taylor's brigade held their lines for more than two hours. The 1st New Jersey had gone in about half an hour after the 3rd, marching through a waist-deep swamp to get into position. Lieutenant Colonel McAllister, commanding the regiment due to the illness of Col. Alfred T. Torbert, ordered a charge, but the undergrowth was too thick to permit it. So the men endured the fire from Elzey's brigade, now commanded by Col. James A. Walker, and the 16th Mississippi, 21st North Carolina, and 1st North Carolina Battalion of Isaac Trimble's brigade. Trimble's men had advanced through two regiments who were retiring. "You need not go in," the retreating rebels cried, "we are whipped; you can't do anything!" The Valley veterans yelled back, "Get out of our way; we will show you how to do it!" As they advanced, a colonel stopped Trimble and asked where his troops were going. When Trimble replied that they were to drive the Federals off, the colonel said: "You cannot do it. Four attempts have been made by four different regiments and each has failed." "We can and we will drive them," responded Trimble, "Forward, boys, and give them the bayonet!" Collecting bits and pieces of other regiments, Trimble advanced, and his men swept up the slope through "a perfect shower of balls," not firing until they had crossed the swamp.

The 31st New York and 95th Pennsylvania had to retreat when the Confederates threatened to surround them. Colonel J. M. Gosline and Maj. William B. Hubbs of the 95th Pennsylvania both were mortally wounded during the withdrawal. This threatened Newton's other regiments, the 18th and 32nd New York, and they engaged in a "race for our lives," escaping capture by not more than a minute according to one estimate. McAllister saw troops give way on his right and left. That allowed a cross fire to hit his men, and it also put them in danger of being captured. He barely ordered a retreat in time; as he put it, "three minutes more and we would all have been captured." At least some of Slocum's men left "in *not very good order.*" Captain William Hexamer, whose battery was in back of these lines, waited until after the infantry had cleared his guns and then fired case and canister, but he had to retreat, losing one gun when its horses were shot. His men won the admiration of the Prince de Joinville, who said he had never seen soldiers so cool in the face of attack as the men in that battery. Other troops in this area, including the 4th Michigan and 14th New York of Charles Griffin's brigade, and Taylor's 2nd New Jersey, retired when the troops on their left collapsed. They were joined by Emory Upton's battery, which fell back after firing a barrage of double canister.[7]

Parts of the 15th Alabama and 21st Georgia attacked Capt. Hezekiah Easton's Battery A, 1st Pennsylvania Light Artillery. Easton stopped one charge, but the 2nd Pennsylvania Reserves broke, and he lost his support. Easton shouted that the rebels would not take his guns except over his body. The concussion from one shell blew a man six feet into the air, giving him time to do a complete somersault before he landed on all fours. But it was not enough. Easton was killed and the Alabamians and Georgians, followed quickly by the 5th Texas and part of the 18th Georgia from William Whiting's division, took the guns.

Captain Henry DeHart's Battery C, 5th U.S. Artillery, got into line to Easton's right a little before the final assault, but he was flanked by Confederates hidden by smoke and lost three of his six guns. Captain Mark Kerns of Battery G, 1st Pennsylvania Light Artillery, who had been wounded in the leg, remained on the field and fired guns himself until his battery was about to be overrun. He managed to retire with four of his six guns. The other two had to be abandoned because no horses were left to pull them. Captain James Cooper's Battery B, 1st Pennsylvania Light Artillery, was in line behind the others and became the Confederates' focus. The Pennsylvanians responded by giving "them the best we had," using spherical case shot with "frightful effect." Finally, a colonel called out, "For God's sake, Captain Cooper, get your battery off or it will be taken in five minutes." The Pennsylvanians left without loss.

Two regiments stood their ground to Newton's left: the 11th Pennsylvania Reserves from George Meade's brigade and Taylor's 4th New Jersey. However, as the lines around them collapsed, Confederates, mainly from the 5th Texas, surrounded them. Trimble said this charge "could not be surpassed for intrepid bravery and high resolve." One man in the 5th Texas who was not so brave cried out, "Boys, don't go in there; you will all be killed." Another soldier growled back, "Shut your mouth, you coward, or I will shoot you."

After reaching the top of the hill, the 5th Texas was fired upon from the rear by the 4th New Jersey. However, most of the Yankees, particularly the officers, apparently thought better of such a hopeless fight, and lowered their flags and raised their hats and handkerchiefs in surrender. Some Unionists forgot to drop their guns or did not hear the orders and got shot at as a result, while some Confederates knocked other men's guns in the air to keep them from hitting anybody. Colonel J. H. Simpson of the 4th New Jersey wrote that although his troops and those of the 11th Pennsylvania Reserves could have fought until they were all killed, "humanity, and, as I think, wisdom, dictated that we should at last yield."

Lieutenant Grubb, having gone along with the 4th New Jersey as Taylor ordered, watched it and the 11th Pennsylvania Reserves move into the trees. Then armed rebels appeared not more than thirty yards from the right of the Union line. Remembering Taylor's order to report back on where the 4th New Jersey went, Grubb lay down on his horse and put spurs to it, heading out of danger. Taylor was with the 3rd New Jersey when Grubb found him. "Where is the Fourth?" the brigade commander asked. "Gone to Richmond, sir," Grubb answered. Taylor was not amused. "Young man, this is no place for levity," he said. "They are captured," explained Grubb, "every man of them" (which was not quite true: eighty-three men had returned to camp by July 4). "My God, My God," Taylor cried, wringing his hands at the news.

The New Jersey officers wanted to surrender to the 5th Texas's Lt. Col. J. C. Upton, who had entered battle that day dressed in an undershirt and carrying a frying pan. The Union officers could not believe at first that Upton was an officer, but they finally raced each other to surrender to him, and he received about twenty swords. A few minutes after this incident, Upton heard a commotion and was told that some of the prisoners were trying to escape. "Let 'em go you infernal fool," he said, "let 'em go! We'd a damned sight rather fight 'em than feed 'em!"

Trimble's men also captured seven weapons called coffee-mill guns. These were crank-operated early versions of a machine gun, capable of firing sixty rounds per minute from a hopper mounted atop a single barrel. Pennsylvania

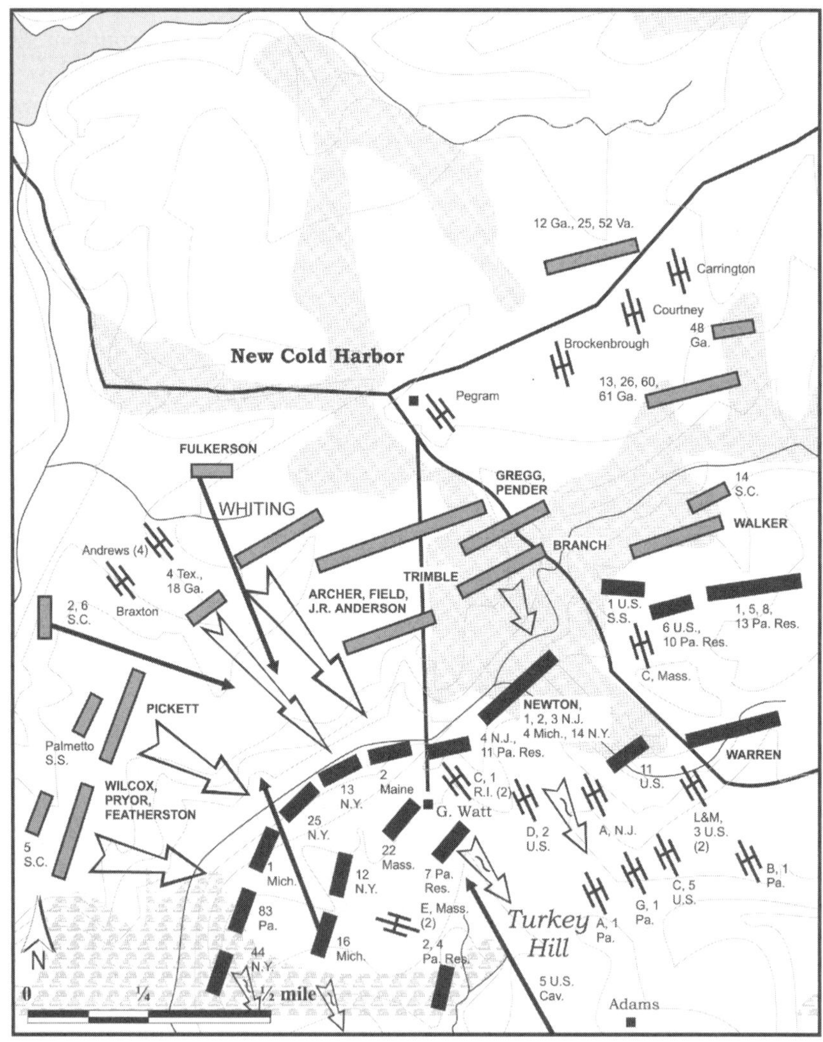

Final assaults on Morell's line, Gaines's Mill, June 27, 1862

governor Andrew Curtin liked them so much that he equipped some Keystone State regiments with them. For part of the battle the guns were given to Taylor's brigade, which apparently used the same type of cartridge—one in which the powder and ball were enclosed in "some inflammable paper" so the soldier did not have to bite the end off the cartridge before loading. All the guns used in the battle were captured.[8]

On the Confederate right, James Longstreet welcomed Whiting's arrival. It allowed Old Pete to keep Kemper's brigade in reserve against a possible Union counterattack. Longstreet motioned for Whiting to move his men in on Pickett's left. Whiting lined his troops up with Evander Law's brigade on the right and John B. Hood's men on the left. Hood, who had just turned thirty-two, attended West Point and served with Robert E. Lee on the frontier. A Kentucky native, he had moved from being colonel of the 4th Texas to brigade command that spring. As his troops were moving into position, Lee rode up to him. The army commander told Hood the Confederates had been unable to break the Union line and then asked, "Can you break his line?" Hood answered that he would try. As Lee rode away, he lifted his hat and cried, "May God be with you!" Whiting pointed to a Union battery and said it must be taken. Hood asked why it had not already been taken, and Whiting replied that the position was too strong, and three brigades from other divisions had failed. "I have a regiment that can take it," Hood said, and rode off.

As the line moved forward, an opening appeared between the right of Law's line and the left of Longstreet's men. This was more open ground and better for an advance, even if it was more exposed to the enemy's fire. Hood seized the opportunity. One soldier in the 4th Texas remembered that as he saw Hood leave the gathering of officers, "I knew what to expect," and he was right. Taking command of the 4th Texas and as much of the 18th Georgia as he could gather, Hood angled them across the field behind Law. Realizing that even this late in the day his troops would have no chance to break the line if they stopped to return the Federal fire, Hood gave the command that no one would fire until he ordered it. Each soldier felt that the crisis of the battle had come.

The 4th Texas's new colonel, John Marshall, was a political appointee, a protégé of Sen. Louis T. Wigfall. He had begun the war as the regiment's lieutenant colonel. The men were not sure that he was up to the task of directing the regiment in battle, although they knew he was brave. They must have felt better with Hood at their head. Moving forward with the Georgians, the Texans passed over dead and wounded men and horses, broken wagons and caissons, and discarded personal gear. They were hit by enfilading fire from the entire left side of the Union line. Unnerved soldiers fled past them. Other troops told the 4th Texas that the position could not be taken. That only added to their determination. Less than two hundred yards from Boatswain's Swamp they encountered a line of rebels hugging the ground while a young lieutenant begged them to advance. Lieutenant Colonel Bradfute Warwick of the 4th Texas took their flag, trying to encourage them, but it had no effect. As Warwick carried the flag forward, the lieutenant dropped his sword, grabbed a rifle, and joined the charge.

Marshall was shot early in the assault, and Warwick took over. As they neared the Yankee line, Warwick gave the order to halt and fire, but Hood quickly countermanded it. The general stayed with the men until they got within a hundred yards of Boatswain's Swamp. Then he ordered the Texans and Georgians to fix bayonets and charge at the double-quick. The rebels continued forward over a rise, then down the hill to the swamp, across the swamp, and into the Union defenses. Suddenly there was no stopping them; Union forces that had been in line all day had taken all they could, and the sight of the Texans and Georgians heading up the hill at them with such grim determination was too much. The two regiments had broken the Federal defense.[9]

Whiting's other brigade also moved forward. Law, a twenty-five-year-old South Carolina Military Academy graduate and teacher, commanded this brigade, and Whiting accompanied it. Members of the 11th Mississippi, from Whiting's home state, heard him say that once the order to charge was given, there would be no retreat order. "I will lead you," he continued, "and I believe you will carry the works." He waved his hat and yelled, "Mississippians, charge!" The rebel yell rang out and the 11th, along with the 4th Alabama and 6th North Carolina of Law's brigade and the rest of Hood's brigade (the 2nd Mississippi moving up in reserve), headed for the Union line. Falling to the ground as they got to the top of a rise north of the swamp, they began to fire back at the Northerners. But Whiting rode down the line yelling, "Charge men, for God's sake charge bayonets." The men got back up and rushed to the swamp. On the way A. L. P. Vairin of the 2nd Mississippi was hit in the pit of the stomach with a ball. Fortunately, the blanket he wore as a scarf was strong enough to stop the bullet. The rest of the brigade made it to the swamp, broke through the breastworks, and scattered the Yankees, who left "like rats from a burning ship" according to one Texan. Jim Harrison of the 4th Alabama was so eager to get to the crest that he fell into a trench filled with Federals. He shot one and the others surrendered.

Major John C. Haskell, an aide to Brig. Gen. David R. Jones of Magruder's command, had been sent north of the Chickahominy to deliver a message. He stayed, and Whiting asked him to rally some men who had been scattered and lead them into the fight. His men lay down also as they got close to the Yankees, and Haskell fought with a color-bearer over a flag, finally winning the argument and hitting the man with his sword. His horse was wounded soon after, but Haskell did not notice it. He put spurs to the animal, which then leapt over the breastworks, was shot dead in the air, and landed with Haskell under him. The men followed, but not before Haskell killed a Union officer who first demanded his surrender and then was about to shoot him when Haskell ran him through with his sword.[10]

On Whiting's right, George Pickett's men joined in the charge. After the men had stopped by mistake, Col. Eppa Hunton of the 8th Virginia (who had been sick in Richmond but went to the front over his doctor's protests) came up to Colonel Withers of the 18th Virginia and asked what should be done to get the men out of the carnage. Withers said, "Push forward, as no troops can live long under such a fire as this." Riding to the color guard, Withers told the color-bearer to walk with him. After they had gone a few steps the brigade got the idea and charged. Richard Anderson then came up with part of his brigade and joined the assault. The combined momentum was enough to get through all three Union lines. Withers was shot through the lungs, and the entire color guard—a sergeant and eight corporals—of Company E, 18th Virginia, was either killed or wounded. When another company's color-bearer was shot a lieutenant picked up the flag but fell almost immediately. The company commander then grabbed the colors and took them over the breastworks.

The 16th Michigan from Dan Butterfield's brigade headed to the breach but was stopped thanks to some quick thinking by Col. Micah Jenkins of the Palmetto (South Carolina) Sharpshooters of Anderson's brigade. One of Jenkins's men who had sprained his ankle during the charge saw the Michiganders marching up. Limping over to Jenkins, he reported what he had seen. Jenkins was skeptical, but said, "I shall see who they are." Stepping forward, he asked the marchers what unit they belonged to. When the answer, "Sixteenth Michigan," came back, Jenkins ordered his men to fire. Captain Thomas Carr fell dead, the first man of the regiment killed. The Yankees and rebels had a back-and-forth battle until enough Confederates joined the fight to force the 16th back and capture its flag. Many of the Federals wound up crossing the river without benefit of a bridge, while their colonel, T. B. W. Stockton, and fifty-two others were captured. One Confederate remembered of Stockton, "His bravery cost him a heavy defeat."

Pickett was wounded in the shoulder during the charge but kept going with his men for a time, his horse following him. As John Haskell was leading his men forward he found Pickett in a hollow. Pickett thought his wound was mortal and, perhaps remembering his feeling of the night before, called for litter bearers. Then Haskell examined the wound, saw that it was slight, and rode off, satisfied that Pickett could take care of himself. Eppa Hunton took command of the brigade after Pickett was wounded, although it was not officially noted.[11]

John Martindale's men, specifically those of the 1st Michigan and 13th and 25th New York, manned the defenses broken by Whiting and Pickett. All these regiments had built breastworks and repulsed several charges—"we fought like tigers," one Michigander wrote home—but the lateness of the day, the weariness of the men, and the impetuosity of the attack forced them back. The 22nd Massachusetts, in reserve, was surprised when the 13th New York came through the smoke, the men calling, "Get up, boys, and give them some!" But the 22nd had to fall back when its flank was threatened. Colonel Jesse A. Gove was killed when he got caught between his men and the enemy. When the regiment's color-bearer was shot, a member of the color guard fired at the nearest rebels and tore the flag out of a Southerner's hand, losing his right arm to a minié ball in the process. Peter Fagan was saved when Owen Hart shot a rebel who had drawn a bead on Fagan. "I saved you that time, Peter!" Hart yelled. Fagan soon found himself alone and ran so fast returning to his company that Capt. Mason Burt said he would run Fagan against any soldier in the Army of the Potomac. The 13th New York's color-bearers were wounded and about to be captured with their flags when they saw an artilleryman. They threw the flags to the gunner, who left with them just before the sergeants were taken prisoner.

The 2nd Maine, on the far right of Martindale's line, was not hit directly but was forced to fall back when the breakthrough occurred. The 7th Pennsylvania Reserves of Meade's brigade was on Butterfield's right behind a ravine full of dead rebels when some live ones came up and forced the regiment back. "For awhile the retreat almost amounted to a rout," one Pennsylvanian admitted. Lieutenant Buckley's two guns kept firing, with three men at each gun, until the broken infantry had passed. By then, however, the horses had been shot or stampeded, and the guns had to be abandoned.[12]

Cadmus Wilcox's, Roger Pryor's, and Winfield Featherston's brigades charged as one unit. A native of North Carolina who grew up in Tennessee, Wilcox graduated with the West Point class of 1846 and, after fighting in Mexico, stayed in the service until the South seceded. He accepted a commission as colonel of the 8th Alabama, then was promoted to command of the brigade in late 1861. It was posted on the right with the 10th and 11th Alabama in front and the 8th and 9th Alabama behind. Pryor, a Virginia lawyer and newspaper editor who resigned from Congress before Virginia seceded and supposedly declined the honor of firing the first shot on Fort Sumter, was less than a month from his thirty-fourth birthday. He moved his brigade to Wilcox's left. Featherston, a forty-one-year-old Tennessean who fought the Creek Indians at age seventeen and became a lawyer in Mississippi, also had been in Congress. His brigade was in a supporting position. Featherston's brigade included the 19th Mississippi, which had a new color-bearer that day. Every previous color-bearer had been killed, and Jim Moser of Company K was reluctant to take on the duty, but he did so after requesting that he be allowed to say good-bye to his company.

Featherston simply said, "Charge them boys," and his small brigade headed forward, at times going through the two in front. The 19th Mississippi lagged behind its flag, and Moser was called back to the regiment. "Bring the line up to the colors," he said. "The colors are going where commanded." Moser fell, but the men kept going. Lieutenant Robert Miller of Pryor's 14th Louisiana had a bullet pass through his scabbard and kill a man beside him. "The bullets came so thick that I felt a desire to see how many I could catch with my open hand stretched out," he later recalled. Major J. H. Williams of the 9th Alabama said it was "a mystery to me how any of us escaped." A man in the ranks wrote, "The whole brigade literally *staggered* backward several paces as though pushed by a tornado." But yelling and running through Boatswain's Swamp, they swarmed Butterfield's men. Colonel J. J. Woodward, the 10th Alabama's commander, was shot in the head and killed, and Lt. Col. S. F. Hale, commanding the 11th Alabama, was wounded in the left arm, shoulder, and leg. Their men wavered but then drove the Northerners from their lines. In the 8th Alabama, Capt. G. W. Hannon had a premonition that he would be killed but led his men anyway. He was shot during the charge and died shortly afterward.[13]

Butterfield had seen the pressure building along Martindale's front. He switched the 83rd Pennsylvania's front to help meet the attack and moved the 12th New York by the flank. Part of the latter regiment broke ranks as a result of the 1st Michigan's retreat. Colonel Stephen W. Stryker and part of the 44th New York also retreated, but Lt. Col. James Rice rallied some of the men. The 44th's skirmishers did not know of the retreat, and as they fell back before Wilcox's charge, they ran into other Southerners in their own trenches and were taken prisoner. One New Yorker wrote home, "I seen our boys drop like sheep not only our Reg't but different ones I didn't expect to get across alive."

The 83rd Pennsylvania, low on ammunition, was heartened when Butterfield yelled out, "Your ammunition is never expended while you have your bayonets, my boys, and use them to the socket," but it also did not get the order to retreat (the messenger having been shot while trying to deliver it). Colonel John W. McLane, the 83rd's commander, was struck down by the 5th South Carolina of Anderson's brigade when the two regiments met in the same way as the 16th Michigan and the Palmetto Sharpshooters. Both sides claimed to have refused surrender demands, and both sides claimed that the other fired treacherously. The Pennsylvanians—helped by Maj. Ernest von Vegesack of Butterfield's staff, who rode up and down the line to maneuver the troops to face the Confederates—stood firm for a while. Oliver Norton had three guns shot up, a ramrod cut in two, and was hit three times by minié balls, one of which went through his canteen. The South Carolinians finally drove him and his surviving mates toward the Chickahominy. "[I]t seemed as though not one of us could live to get to the river," one Pennsylvanian remembered, but whether by swimming or fallen trees, they crossed it and reentered the Union lines on the south bank. Some of the 44th New York and the 4th Pennsylvania

Reserves, sent to help Butterfield's line, also crossed the Chickahominy into the lines of Baldy Smith's VI Corps division to escape capture. Battery E of the Massachusetts Light Artillery, in position to support Butterfield, lost four guns because it lacked horses to bring them off. The Southerners captured one immediately and planted their flag on it, then got three more during the battery's retreat. One gunner wrote, "At one time the retreat came up to Bull Run and though I was yelling with pain from riding so fast it made me laugh to see the tall running some of them was doing." Another artilleryman left his shirt with the guns. After retrieving it, he decided to give the Southerners one more blast. Loading the gun himself, he left the rammer in it, fired, and then ran. He survived but never returned to the battery.[14]

Whiting, after gaining the top of the rise, had asked Longstreet for reinforcements and had received some of Richard Anderson's men. E. V. Fulkerson's brigade also moved up to support Hood, and Fulkerson fell mortally wounded while attempting to survey the situation. The 4th Texas, gathering in an orchard after its exertions, charged again—this time more than four hundred yards through a deep hollow with a gully to get to the Union artillery. Lieutenant Colonel Warwick jumped up to lead his men, ran about a dozen strides, and was mortally wounded by a shell fragment. Hood pulled the regiment back after Warwick fell, then it and the 18th Georgia again charged the guns. Haskell, still at the head of his group, did not make it in time; a round of solid shot tore his right arm off. The 44th New York's surgeon, William Frothingham, who was at a hospital between the two forces, threw all of his instruments and medicines onto a pack mule and headed to the rear surrounded by fleeing soldiers.[15]

One of the most controversial events on the Union side during the Seven Days occurred at this point in the battle. Philip St. George Cooke's cavalry was in position to protect Porter's left flank and under orders to strike the enemy on the plain between Powhite Creek and Boatswain's Swamp if possible. But Cooke was told he would have nothing to do on the hill south and east of the swamp, where the main Union position was.

When Cooke noticed the infantry giving way, however, and three batteries firing at the enemy, he ordered the 1st and 5th U.S. Cavalry to charge when the safety of the artillery required it. He then moved the 6th Pennsylvania Cavalry to the right of Batteries B and L of the 2nd U.S. Artillery, which were unsupported and ready to retire from their position on the left of the line. The Pennsylvania troopers held this position until Confederates threatened their line of retreat, when they moved back about four hundred yards to find part of the 9th Massachusetts Infantry of Griffin's brigade holding steady. The 1st U.S. Cavalry was some distance in its rear, and Cooke ordered the regulars to the left of the infantry. A squadron of the 4th Pennsylvania Cavalry, which had just arrived, moved to the left of the regulars. As the Confederates advanced, a battery behind the cavalry opened fire, hitting Union troops instead of rebels. Cooke then ordered a retreat, as he was told Porter had done. Meanwhile, the 5th U.S. Cavalry charged. As it did, one Confederate "felt the ground begin to tremble like an earthquake and heard a noise like the rumbling of distant thunder." But its mission was as suicidal as that of the famed British Light Brigade, and it failed. The Southerners were waiting and fired a volley that left only a few troopers still willing and able to charge. The rebels followed up the volley with a bayonet charge. A bayonet stuck in the side of a Yankee horse, which galloped off with the rebel's musket. One squadron commander, Capt. William P. Chambliss, was wounded and captured, and Capt. Charles J. Whiting, commanding the regiment, was also captured in the effort. But the batteries the charge was intended to save escaped.

That was Cooke's story. Captains Wesley Merritt and James P. Martin, members of Cooke's staff during the battle and both later to hold high positions in the army, argued that the cavalry charge saved Porter from destruction. The Comte de Paris also agreed with Cooke. Porter saw a much different picture, however. "To this alone [the cavalry charge] is to be attributed our failure to hold the battle-field and to bring off all our guns and wounded," he wrote in his official report. Later, in an article in *Battles and Leaders of the Civil War*, he reiterated this point of view. But Fitz John was wrong. Morell said that the cavalry did carry men and horses off in the charge, but he noted its steadying influence on the infantry nearby. Captain James M. Robertson, commanding Batteries B and L, 2nd U.S. Artillery, reported that the cavalry had covered his retreat. William Weeden, commanding Morell's artillery, attributed the loss of one gun to the cavalry's retreat, saying, "The whole line of artillery was thrown into confusion." Lieutenant John G. Simpson of Easton's battery said that if infantry had charged instead of cavalry, the battery might have been saved—but he did not attribute its loss to the charge. Lieutenant Eben G. Scott of DeHart's battery, also in McCall's division, reported that the battle might not have been lost without the cavalry's charge and the resulting confusion—but he did not lose his guns because of it.

Several Confederate reports mention the cavalry charge, all with the sentiments expressed later by Law: "[T]he diversion by the cavalry . . . did delay their capture for the short period it took to repulse it, and gave time for the artillerists to save some of their guns." This best sums up the matter. The battle had been lost and nothing could change that, least of all a charge by a single cavalry regiment—which merely served to kill and wound a few more men.

The charge reunited Hood with some of his former fellow cavalrymen, however. The 5th U.S. had been the 2nd U.S. Cavalry before the war, and Captain Whiting had been his company commander. Hood treated the captured officer with respect and arranged a transfer to a field hospital for Chambliss, his friend at West Point and in the 2nd Cavalry.[16]

The Union artillery did help stop the Confederates' momentum. Robertson's batteries used their last stores of ammunition after the infantry broke. Weeden's two sections that escaped capture fired about forty rounds each after the infantry retired. And so it went, all across the field. In all, nineteen of Porter's ninety-two guns were captured on the field at Gaines's Mill, strong evidence of the courage of the gunners.

Guns from Union batteries stationed on the south bank of the Chickahominy played a part as well. One Confederate said their fire was the only reason the Southerners did not annihilate the Union army. However, at least some of the shots fell short into Butterfield's skirmishers, and a message was sent to the gunners to let them know.

Not long after the cavalry charge, cheers could be heard coming from the Union rear. The cheering men were from Thomas Meagher's and William French's brigades. Although they were too late to save the line, they arrived in time to keep the defeat from becoming a full-scale rout. As these brigades came up to the Union position they saw men and horses fleeing, some crying that they had been "cut to pieces." The sight was "frightful," according to a Pennsylvanian viewing it from the top of the hill above Grapevine Bridge, with everything that could move running toward the bridge. The 8th Illinois Cavalry tried to stem the tide but was only partially successful, and one trooper called it "heart-sickening."

French, a forty-seven-year-old Marylander who fought the Indians in Florida and in Mexico after graduating from West Point, was senior to Meagher, one of the more colorful characters in the war. The latter was a thirty-nine-year-old native of Ireland and a veteran of the independence movement there. Banished to Tasmania, Meagher escaped and made his way to New York, where he became a leader of the large Irish community. He was a natural to command the "Irish Brigade" he formed in the winter of 1862. As the senior officer, French ordered Meagher to send some of his men forward to control the runaway troops. A company of the 69th New York did stop much of the rout. Porter told French to move the brigades to the crest of the hill behind the Watt house and hold that position, which they did under fire from Confederate artillery. The fire suddenly switched to the right, and Porter ordered Meagher to move that way to relieve Sykes's regulars. French and Meagher helped support a line that "had not been routed" but was on the verge of it after a savage afternoon of fighting. After the war, the Irish Brigade historians and Meagher's biographers liked to tell of a grand charge by their heroes that drove the rebels back at bayonet point. However, there is no mention of such a charge in any reports, and the casualty reports do not support the notion of hard fighting by the men of II Corps. The ten regiments involved reported a total of sixteen casualties. In fact, the only resistance seemingly encountered by French and Meagher was from V Corps stragglers. Benjamin Roher, a surgeon with the 10th Pennsylvania Reserves, was not about to bet much on this outcome, though. He was between the Irish and the Confederates, and he and his fellow workers "concluded to skedaddle."

French and Meagher did help the Yankees. The 9th Massachusetts, also an Irish regiment, was falling back when it encountered Meagher at the head of his brigade. "Colonel Cass, is this you?" Meagher asked when he saw Col. Thomas Cass covered with blood and dirt. "Hello, General Meagher, is this the Irish Brigade?" Cass replied. "Thank God, we are saved."

Taylor's brigade in Henry Slocum's division had just been rallied when Meagher moved into position on its right, helping to stabilize it. The Southerners moved out of the woods, took some pieces of artillery in the field, and stopped. Staff officer Grubb recalled: "There is no question that our brigade and others would have fought on that last line, but I think that it would have been a forlorn hope. The battle was totally lost and every man knew it."

As the 29th Massachusetts stopped with their Irish brethren at the base of the hill, Lt. Thomas Mayo was killed by a solid shot that also took the bayonet off a soldier's rifle. Guns appeared on the crest as the brigade marched up the hill, but they left when they saw the advancing Federals. Soon darkness came and all shooting in the Yankee center stopped.[17]

Confederates had heard the cheering of French's and Meagher's men as well. D. H. Hill prepared for an attack, as did Charles Winder. Winder eventually decided the Federals were not going to attack and wanted to advance, but Hill, supported by Lawton—who had also arrived—did not think entering woods in the dark against an unknown foe was the thing to do. He later admitted that Winder was right; however, Hill's original judgment seems correct. Troops who have marched and fought for an entire day might not behave very well in a night attack. The Confederates probably were almost as disorganized by success as the Unionists were by defeat. The 4th Texas sustained casualties (including Lt. L. P. Lyons of Company F, who was mortally wounded) after all its charges when the 1st Texas fired on it. On the right, Bartlett's Yankees cheered when he told them that the left wing of the army was in Richmond. That drew fire from Southern artillery, one shot of which landed in the middle of the 5th Maine. And so the battle finally came to an end.[18]

What a battle it had been. About ninety-three thousand troops (including French's and Meagher's brigades) had fought in it, making it the second largest battle (after Shiloh) of the war thus far. It had been continuous from 2 P.M., when Gregg first made contact with the Union skirmishers, until darkness fell around 9 P.M. A Captain Wingfield, a veteran of Jackson's campaigns, wrote, "This surpasses any battle for the severity of musketry that I have witnessed." Stonewall Jackson found Jeb Stuart after midnight and lay down next to him.

"Well," said Jackson, "yesterday's was the most terrific fire of musketry I ever heard!" Noble J. Brooks of Cobb's Legion said the sight was "awful and terrible beyond the power of human tongue to tell or pen to describe." Colonel R. Estvan of Stuart's cavalry wrote, "In bygone days I had been on many a battlefield in Italy and Hungary; but I confess that I never witnessed so pitiable a picture of human slaughter and horrible suffering."

Longstreet wrote in his report, "There was more individual gallantry displayed upon this field than any I have ever seen." The Union guns were so fouled from continuous fire that in some cases they could only be loaded by putting the rifles' rammers against trees and hammering. Soldiers of the 9th Massachusetts used up their allotted sixty rounds of ammunition, scavenged among the dead and wounded for more, and fired all they could get their hands on before they were relieved. A. L. Long said that many considered Gaines's Mill the most stubbornly fought battle of the war.[19]

The Confederates, attacking constantly against an extremely strong position, suffered greatly. The separately reported losses—not including most of A. P. Hill's division, or Trimble's, George B. Anderson's, Garland's, Pryor's, or Featherston's brigades—were 4,690. Little Powell probably lost more than 2,000 killed or wounded. Trimble's brigade was engaged again only at Malvern Hill, where it hardly fought, so most of its 400 reported casualties can be traced to Gaines's Mill. Garland's report seems to indicate about 500 casualties at Gaines's Mill. Jackson's estimate of casualties for the campaign would then give Anderson about 350. Pryor discusses great loss at both Gaines's Mill and Glendale, and his total casualties were 862, so about 430 can with caution be assigned to Gaines's Mill. Featherston's brigade seems to have been less severely engaged at Glendale, so of his 666 reported casualties for the campaign, about 400 might have occurred at Gaines's Mill. Probably about 8,700 rebels were killed or wounded out of 57,000 effectives.

The Union casualties were 6,837 out of about 36,000 effectives, of which only 31,000 were really in the fight. Included in the casualties were 2,836 missing. Meade's and Taylor's brigades each lost a regiment captured and more than 1,000 men killed, wounded, or captured. McCall's division, which had lost 298 men the day before at Mechanicsville, lost another 1,651 at Gaines's Mill—almost 25 percent of its effective strength gone in two days of fighting. Sykes's and Morell's divisions lost 20 percent of their effective strength—Sykes's losses amounting to 1,154 and Morell's 1,905. Slocum's division, which got to the field late, lost the most men of all: 1,971, 23 percent of its effective strength. Four of McClellan's eleven divisions suffered staggering losses. Making matters worse, they were in two corps commanded by men he trusted—Porter's V and Franklin's VI. In all, nearly 13,000 men were shot in those seven hours around Boatswain's Swamp.

Some individual regiments took incredible losses. The 9th Massachusetts suffered the highest number of killed or wounded on the Union side: 206, including four captains killed. The 16th New York suffered 194 killed or wounded. Of the forty-eight Federal regiments seriously engaged at Gaines's Mill, fifteen lost at least 100 men killed or wounded.

Losses were even higher on the Confederate side. In addition to the 1st South Carolina Rifles's 297 killed or wounded, the 4th Texas lost 253 men—including its colonel, lieutenant colonel, three captains, and seven lieutenants (although the color-bearer miraculously remained untouched). The 20th North Carolina lost 272 killed or wounded, and the 38th and 31st Georgia 342 between them.

In twenty-six battles the Union had greater numbers of effectives engaged than at Gaines's Mill. Yet in only one one-day battle did a Yankee army inflict more damage relative to its size: the July 22, 1864, battle near Atlanta. Including the captured, on only sixteen occasions did the Federals sustain more casualties in a single battle or campaign, and only two of those—Antietam and Fredericksburg—were one-day battles. In only nine battles for which figures are available did the Confederates suffer greater losses than at Gaines's Mill, and of those, only Antietam was a one-day battle.[20] Gaines's Mill thus was not merely the worst battle of the Seven Days, it was also one of the most costly of the war.

CHAPTER EIGHT

"You Have Done Your Best to Sacrifice This Army"

During the battle of Gaines's Mill, Stonewall Jackson found himself confronted by fifteen or twenty Union pickets. He charged and captured them before they could blink. As they were marched to the rear, one man kept saying, "We had the honor of being captured by Stonewall Jackson himself." Meanwhile, Stuart and his cavalry had little to do all day except endure the Union shelling. As one shell went whizzing over the staff's heads, John Esten Cooke ducked—as did everyone else. But Cooke ducked a little too far and fell off his horse. Stuart yelled over, "Hallo, Cooke! Are you hit?" The lieutenant said, "Oh, no, General; I only dodged a little too far."

After darkness fell, D. H. Hill and Lawton went to examine the Union line. They got within about thirty yards but were not fired upon, probably (Hill thought) because they were mistaken for a party sent out to get water from the well at the McGehee house. The two Confederate commanders met that party on the way back but again escaped unharmed. William H. Osborne of the 29th Massachusetts wrote Hill after that story was published saying that he remembered the incident and added, "I suppose you will not blame me for saying that we all should have esteemed it a great honor if we had made your acquaintance that night."

After the 4th Texas broke the Union line, a lone sniper was still firing at the Texans from a log stable, and Pvt. Jim Stringfield went after him. Stringfield's commander was the normally mild-mannered Lt. L. P. Hughes, who did not use strong language. However, when he saw Stringfield go he yelled, "Go it, Stringfield—go it! Kill him, dod dam it, kill him."

The 4th Texas almost caught a bigger fish after the battle. One man from each company stood picket near the Watt house. They heard horses and the clanking of sabers from their own lines. Asking for the riders' identities, they got the amazing answer, "Major-General McCall, of the Grand Army of the Potomac." The pickets demanded McCall's immediate surrender, but he and his escort put spurs to their horses and escaped down the hill, pursued by some minié balls.

The Confederates, not to be outdone by the Yankess, got a balloon in the air on June 27. Porter Alexander, the lucky officer to go up in it, said it had been made in Savannah by Dr. Edward Cheeves of many patterns of silk varnished with gutta-percha car springs dissolved in naphtha, and had arrived in Richmond June 24. His first day up in it was the twenty-seventh, when the balloon was inflated with illuminating gas from the Richmond Gas Works and taken out about two miles on the Williamsburg road. Alexander saw and reported Henry Slocum's movements, but he did not like the duty much because he had an impulse to jump from the six-hundred-foot-high balloon. The balloon saw more use until July 4, when the boat that accompanied it ran aground in the James River and was captured. The crew, including Alexander, escaped.[1]

For the most part Gaines's Mill was fought with better generalship than was Mechanicsville, although there were some glaring shortcomings. Lee was hamstrung, or hindered himself, by his lack of accurate maps. A map showing Boatswain's Swamp may have made Lee change his plan, as he would have assumed Porter would be behind it and not Powhite Creek. Other than that (of course the *that* is vital), Lee's ideas were sound. His work at Gaines's Mill, while not above reproach, was good. He could not let McClellan take a breath, given his army's disposition. The execution of his ideas for that fight left something to be desired—because of faulty information and poor staff work, and to some extent because of Jackson.[2]

Porter Alexander later wrote that if Jackson had started as early as he was accustomed to, he would have hit Porter's flank during the Union retreat. But Jackson's start was not extremely late, and in itself that delay was not important. Porter was not doing what Lee thought he would do—protect the Yankee supply line—so his flank would never be in a position to be attacked by Jackson during a retreat.

A longer delay was caused by Stonewall's secrecy on the way to Old Cold Harbor and his confusion once he got there. The first was unfortunate, but its effect was in preventing Jackson from reaching Old Cold Harbor and attacking before Sykes was reinforced. Its importance depends on how quickly he perceived the true situation. If Jackson had brought up all his force and attacked early in the afternoon, Porter's right—which was not as well protected by the swamp—might have weakened or broken, despite the fact that Sykes's regulars were the troops there. The ground was not as advantageous for defense, the Yankees were not as numerous as they were later, and more Confederates would have attacked them. Porter would have been in a serious situation in that case. But Jackson should not be censured for caution. Nor can he be censured for not attempting to communicate with Lee to get precise instructions. When it was clear that Jackson was facing not a flank but the front of Union troops, he sought Lee's wishes and got them.[3]

The other Confederate commanders also performed their parts well. A. P. Hill was the quiet star of the day. He showed the ability to execute orders promptly and diligently, he was not impetuous but he hit hard, and his relentless attacks played a major part in the ultimate Confederate victory. One disinterested Confederate veteran wrote, "It was due to the daring and intrepidity of Hill's Light Division at Gaines's Mill, more than to any other, that made it possible for the stirring events and unprecedented results that followed." Longstreet several times remarked on the courage of Hill's men and their effect on the Union troops. Old Pete, D. H. Hill, Whiting, and the brigade commanders all played their parts as well as could be expected, moving fast and hitting hard in the first real display of what would become the Army of Northern Virginia's trademark in battle. Some unit cohesion was lost, but this was because of Lee's converging battle plan and the need to shore up parts of the line, not because the commanders had bad days. The various staffs in the army also functioned well, carrying orders and directing troops to the proper spots.[4]

After the war a controversy arose over who first broke the Union line. A large part of this controversy was played out between veterans of Pickett's and Hood's brigades in the pages of the *Confederate Veteran*, but others also had their say. D. H. Hill always maintained that he had broken through first. Jedediah Hotchkiss said that only after Jackson had crushed the Union right did he send Hood and Law to the center of the Confederate line, a demonstrably false claim. Archer's veterans claimed some credit for being with Hood. Archer himself merely said that he was getting ready to charge with about a hundred men when Hood took the batteries. Longstreet gave equal credit to all commanders on his side of the line, although he did give special notice to Anderson, Pickett, and Hood. Walter Taylor thought the weight of evidence rested with Hood, but in truth it would be impossible to tell who actually broke the line. Everything happened so close it really does not matter. Hood's charge has gained the attention, probably the result of the consensus at the time. In fact, the 4th Texas gained such a reputation from its charge that the men felt compelled to live up to it in every subsequent battle. But all the Confederate troops, veterans and rookies alike, showed their battle prowess at Gaines's Mill.[5]

On the other side, Porter had done all that could be asked. In fact, D. H. Hill called Porter's work "unsurpassed on any field during the war." Outnumbered most of the day, he had used his reserves wisely. Porter had so many fires to fight at once that he wound up committing forces piecemeal to plug gaps, but it is hard to see what else he could have done. To Porter, not losing would have been as good as winning. As long as he kept his force together, McClellan would have all the time he needed to carry out his plans, whatever they might be. Porter would have been withdrawn that night in any event. Phil Kearny took Porter to task for mismanagement of George Taylor's brigade—probably an example of Kearny's caring for his old command—and Slocum actually wrote a letter to Secretary of War Stanton protesting Porter's promotion to major general of volunteers after the battles. Slocum said Porter did not use his artillery well—something Confederates probably would have laughed at—and also criticized him for breaking up his own division and brigades. Strangely, Slocum criticized Porter for offering battle—a decision that he must have known was McClellan's to make.[6]

Porter's troops fought hard in defense. One Confederate wrote after the war that the fact that the smoke from the Yankees' guns hung in the area of the swamp, obscuring the Confederate charges, was all that allowed even the final effort to succeed. Sykes's troops proved their character by not breaking, merely retreating before superior numbers. The other divisions, including Slocum's, held as long as they could, and only an extraordinary effort by the Confederates forced them from their lines. Porter said Slocum did not report to him as he should, but this minor point was seemingly made in response to Slocum's criticism of him. Porter also preferred charges against Martindale for leaving his command, but Martindale was cleared, and, taking Porter's charge at face value, it is hard to see what difference Martindale would have made if he had been at his proper post.[7]

It is difficult to judge McClellan's work. He was plagued by his belief in Confederate numerical superiority and the rebels' demonstrations. It is easy to criticize him for being cautious, not being at the front (wherever that may have been), not sending reinforcements more quickly, and so on. However, given his view of the situation, even McClellan—at least before 8 P.M.—cannot be criticized too harshly. His problems with reinforcements cannot be laid completely at his door. Other moves could be suggested. Yet McClellan's problems were more fundamental, concerning the reality of the situation rather than which tactical move would be the best. It is hard to see that McClellan, from where he sat, could have overruled his corps commanders, especially when Porter was not requesting any assistance.[8]

There was, in fact, more than just a demonstration on the south bank of the Chickahominy. About sundown, Union troops near Fair Oaks Station opened fire on the 53rd Virginia (of Armistead's brigade in Huger's division) with muskets and artillery and then advanced. The Virginians were a little shaky. Three companies (including one without a commander) fell back before the fire. They returned to the lines, however, and the regiment's left wing drove the Federals back.

A larger engagement also took place south of the river. Both sides had been busy around the area of James Garnett's farm, due north of Seven Pines and on the edge of the bluffs running along the Chickahominy. The Union lines ran south from the river on Golding's Plain, more than half a mile east of the Confederate front in the vicinity of the Garnett house. Between them was a steep ravine, a creek, and a hill called Garnett's Hill. The previous night, troops from Brig. Gen. William T. H. Brooks's brigade of Smith's VI Corps division had worked on artillery emplacements on Garnett's Hill. In the morning, Brooks's men were replaced and Brig. Gen. Winfield Scott Hancock's brigade from the same division continued the work. Six batteries of the Union reserve artillery made ready to move into position. While the men were working, Confederates could be seen forming around Garnett's house.

These rebels were from Maj. Gen. David R. Jones's division. Another of the West Point class of 1846, the thirty-seven-year-old South Carolinian had fought in Mexico and stayed in the army until secession. He was at Fort Sumter and lowered the U.S. flag there after its surrender. Jones's men were part of John Magruder's command. Robert Toombs's brigade was on the west side of the ravine (the Union works built the night before included some rifle pits on the east side of the same ravine). Colonel George T. Anderson's brigade was to the northwest along the road to New Bridge near Mrs. Price's house, less than a mile from James Garnett's house. When Jones noticed what the Unionists had done he reported it to Magruder. Prince John had Jones move two guns up from Capt. James Brown's Wise (Virginia) Battery to an overseer's house midway between James Garnett's house and Dr. Garnett's house (just east of Mrs. Price's). Either the 7th or 8th Georgia from Anderson's brigade (the record is unclear) supported Brown's guns. The 1st Georgia Regulars and the 9th Georgia, also of Anderson's brigade, moved to support a pair of howitzers from Col. Stephen D. Lee's artillery from Magruder's division near Mrs. Price's house. The artillery was ordered to fire whenever it could see the enemy.

Smith had prepared to receive a Confederate attack when he received an order to avoid bringing on a general engagement. In response to this, he moved Hancock back a few hundred yards, leaving the rifle pits manned by a strong picket force. Five guns from Maj. Elisha S. Kellogg's 1st Connecticut Artillery, Lt. Adelbert Ames's Battery A, 5th U.S. Artillery, and Capt. J. Howard Carlisle's Battery E, 2nd U.S. Artillery, moved to command Hancock's left flank. Although designed to prevent a fight, the movements drew Confederate notice. Then McClellan and his staff rode along the Union lines, and the men greeted them with loud cheers. This did not escape Confederate attention, and the rebels thought the cheers were the prelude to an attack. The Southern guns opened fire, and the Union guns responded, helping to keep alive the impression that the Southerners were still strong south of the Chickahominy. As Hancock was walking down his line, his orderly asked if they should take shelter. "No; we ain't any better than those men laying there," the general replied, and ordered those men into a ditch for protection. The shelling lasted for about an hour, as the rest of the Wise Battery and Capt. John Lane's Company E of the Sumter (Georgia) Artillery joined the contest on the Southern side and Battery A, 1st Rhode Island Light Artillery, added its guns on the Union side. Colonel Lee eventually withdrew all the Confederate cannon as the fight involved twenty-three well-emplaced Union guns against ten Confederate guns in an open field. One of Lane's men told his wife, "We then was ordered to leave the field, which we did as quick as possible." Gilbert Thompson, an engineer working on some earthworks in the ravine between the lines who was stuck there when the shelling began, wrote, "I never wish to have an enemy in a more hellish place."[9]

Both sides along this part of the front lines then turned some of their guns north of the Chickahominy to support their comrades at Gaines's Mill. Smith, easily able to see the advancing Confederates, used the 1st Connecticut Heavy Artillery to try to stop them. After the war, Smith remembered that the gunners' fire stopped attacks two or three times. Once, Smith himself aimed a gun whose discharge scattered a whole rebel regiment. Jefferson Davis was observing the battle from a farmhouse when he received a note from Lee warning him of possible artillery fire. Davis left the house a few minutes before Yankee shells practically destroyed it. A VI Corps officer later wrote that they "all felt that we ought to attack to make a diversion" for their comrades on the north bank. They were cheered when they saw Slocum's men headed into the fray. "We surely thought the day would be ours," was how one man put it. Some Yankees could not see the action and "were filled with intense anxiety." All they could do was send a man up a tree to observe and report, but this method of gaining information was "far from satisfactory." Men on the Southern side of the lines were equally confident, knowing their comrades' character and beginning to believe in Lee after hearing that Jackson was on the Federals' flank.[10]

However, before the final charges north of the river, things once again began to heat up south of it. Magruder wanted to know more about the Union lines and told Jones in the early afternoon to send Toombs and Anderson to probe them. Prince John later made his ideas explicit. He wanted another regiment from Anderson's brigade (again either the 7th or 8th Georgia) to join the two that had supported the howitzers posted to the northeast of Nine Mile road running from Richmond through Fair Oaks Station to Seven Pines. Firing on the right would signal the beginning of the demonstration. Infantry and artillery on Toombs's right would feel the enemy out with a strong picket force, with the rest of the infantry ready to follow up any advantage gained. Toombs was to make the same arrangements and advance when he saw the units on his right advance.

At about 4 P.M., Maj. Gen. Lafayette McLaws, another of Magruder's division commanders, advanced the 7th and 8th South Carolina of Brig. Gen. Joseph B. Kershaw's brigade, but they withdrew under heavy fire, the 7th South Carolina having lost its first man killed in the movement. Some of Brig. Gen. Richard Griffith's Mississippi troops also moved forward about that time. Lane's battery and the Ashland (Virginia) Artillery battery commanded by Lt. James Woolfolk began to shell the Union lines from about six hundred yards between 6:30 and 7 P.M., perhaps in response to movement in the Union lines. Two companies of the 1st U.S. Sharpshooters had just headed from their rifle pits to get some food. Hancock saw them and said he hoped they would stay a little longer. They had just returned to the rifle pits when Woolfolk opened up. The sharpshooters began their work, and Ames's battery responded as well. A brisk duel developed for about ten minutes before the Confederates withdrew. One of their shells went through the tent of George Selkirk, the adjutant of the 49th New York in Brig. Gen. John W. Davidson's brigade, passing just over his bed.

Shortly after that fire ended, Toombs heard more on his right. It was the beginning of the demonstration. Toombs, less than a week from his fifty-second birthday, was a politically prominent lawyer from Georgia and had almost been chosen Confederate president. Instead he became secretary of state but resigned that position to become a brigadier general. He also was elected to the Confederate Congress. He originally reacted with astonishment to the order to advance and said he would not obey it unless it came in writing, as he doubted the order's authenticity. But when he heard the signal he advanced seven companies of the 2nd Georgia to the ravine just behind his pickets.[11]

Winfield Hancock was a thirty-eight-year-old Pennsylvanian who served in Mexico and California after graduation from West Point. In the fall of 1861 he returned to the East and McClellan made him a brigade commander. Seeing Toombs's movement, he ordered his men to fire. One Yankee skirmisher, Ed Richards of the 6th Maine, got caught between the two lines and had to lie in Garnett's wheat field until the day ended (Hancock's earlier withdrawal had put the wheat field between his men and the Confederates). The wheat field had a small rise in it that sheltered some of the rebels but not all, and the 2nd Georgia kept up the fire—basically one regiment against an entire brigade—for about half an hour. In fact, the regiment got within about forty yards of Hancock's line at about 7:30 P.M.

William Brooks was three years older than Hancock and an Ohio West Pointer who had also served in Mexico and on the frontier before taking command of his Vermont brigade. He brought up the 4th Vermont and the

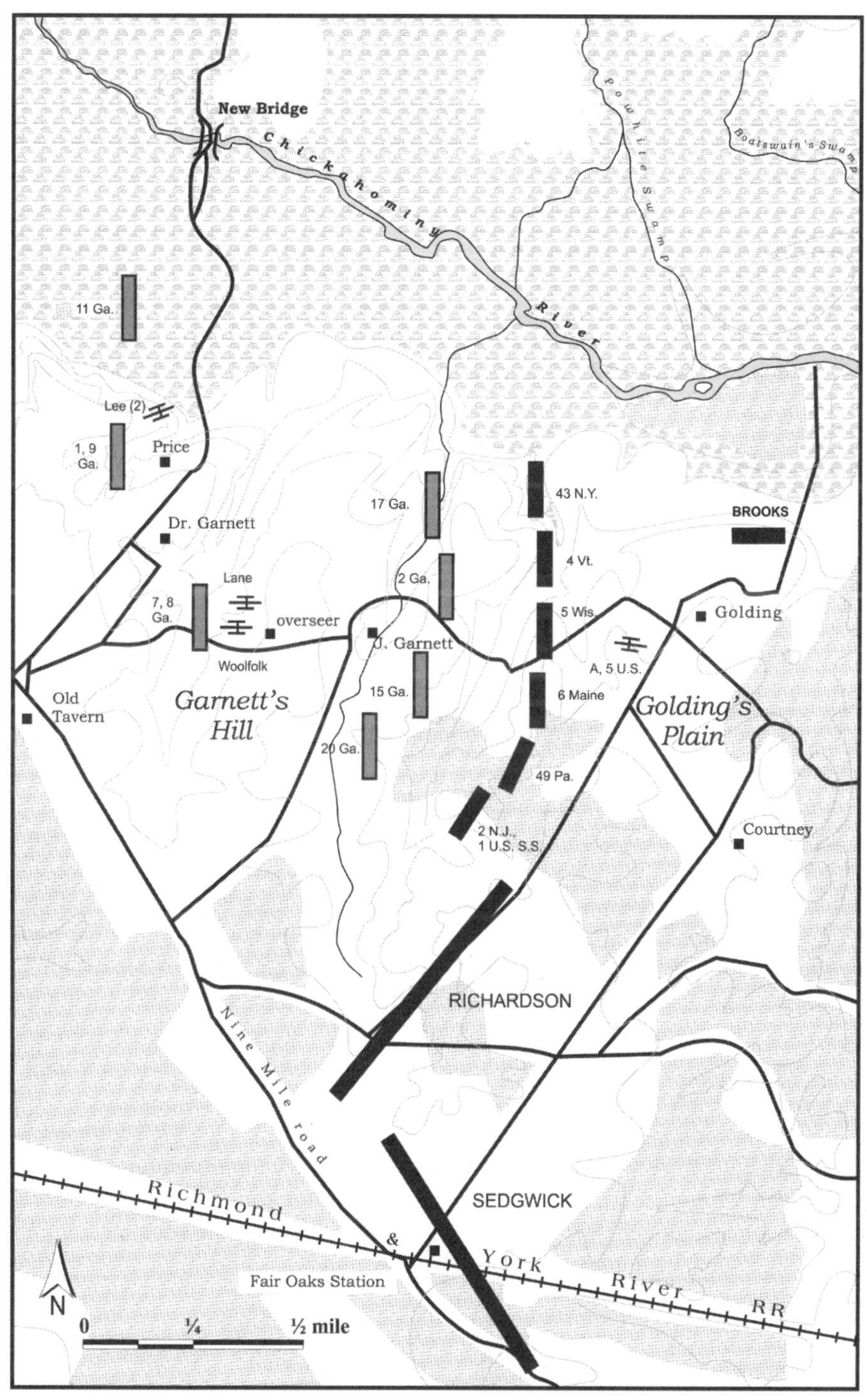

Garnett's Farm, June 27, 1862

remnants of Taylor's 2nd New Jersey from supporting positions. The sharpshooters also got into line. The 15th Massachusetts of John Sedgwick's II Corps division got into rifle pits on Hancock's right, and Edwin Sumner sent Sedgwick's 7th Michigan at the double-quick, but neither regiment was needed. Toombs, seeing the reinforcements moving in, ordered the 15th Georgia to support the 2nd Georgia in the ravine, the 17th Georgia to move to the left flank, and the 20th Georgia to move to the right flank. The Georgians wanted to create enough of a ruckus that no reinforcements could go to the north bank of the Chickahominy, and they went to work with a will. The fire lasted until dark, or about an hour and a half; it was so hot that in the two companies of the 2nd Georgia commanded by Lt. Col. William R. Holmes, only two men could fire their rifles at the end of it. The Yankees "gave them hell," despite the darkness that made many guess at their targets. Some of the men in the 5th Wisconsin ate during the battle, "determined not to die hungry at least."[12]

The 15th Georgia lost its colonel, William M. McIntosh, who fell mortally wounded, and the pressure on it and the 2nd Georgia was intense enough that Toombs called the 7th Georgia to his support, intending to move the 20th Georgia to the center and put the 7th on the right flank. Before that was necessary, however, darkness set in.

Just before dark Kellogg, who had two companies of infantry in support of his guns, overheard an officer ordering two companies to protect a bridge that led from the line back to Hancock's camp. He immediately volunteered for the duty, and remained in position protecting the bridge until 2 A.M., when Hancock relieved him. Later, Hancock was withdrawn to the position he had previously held.

It had been a short, inconsequential, and useless engagement. The Confederates had no chance to accomplish anything of importance, such as forcing the Federals away from the Chickahominy crossings, because of the lateness of the hour and the small number of Confederates involved. And no activity at that hour would affect the number of reinforcements headed to Porter. But it was a sharp skirmish. The 2nd Georgia lost 120 men killed or wounded, and Toombs's brigade as a whole close to 200 out of 1,500 men. On the Union side, 105 were killed or wounded and 13 were missing from Hancock's brigade and the 4th and 6th Vermont of Brooks's brigade, a force of about 3,500 men. For two hours' work and the small forces involved, those losses were quite heavy. In fact, the intensity of the fighting caused Franklin to believe information suggesting that the Confederate attack was made by two full brigades instead of one.[13]

Darkness put an end to all of the fighting on June 27. What Lee had gained was enormous, if at great cost. His army was connected again, with the New Bridge area taken. He had forced Porter out of a position that Lee thought covered McClellan's retreat route to White House. Lee sent a message to Davis thanking God for the victory and saying he would renew the fight in the morning. However, since he had not attacked early enough or succeeded in trapping Porter, he must have been at least somewhat disappointed.

Richmond's citizens were spared Lee's disappointment, however. The wounded kept coming, but they brought news of the victory and Jackson's certain arrival. The ladies again went to work, and some could not help thinking of the wounded beyond their reach. "Think of the poor fellows lying out all this night, bleeding, dying, with no one to minister to or raise them from the ground, whilst we can go peacefully & quietly to bed, to sleep and forget them," wrote one diarist.

Disappointed would not have been the word to describe McClellan's feelings. After he sent French and Meagher to Porter he heard nothing until after the battle. No one else on the south bank heard anything, either, and some men started to cheer when a rumor passed through the ranks that Porter had beaten off the rebels. They wanted to believe it, no matter what else might be happening. Little Mac, his headquarters camp already broken up, sat on a stump waiting for news. He got it first from Humphreys in the observation balloon, then from Col. A. V. Colburn, his assistant adjutant general, then from the volunteer French aides—the Duc de Chartres, the Comte de Paris, and their uncle, the Prince de Joinville—who had been with Porter. The two younger Frenchmen had tried to get Porter to send their uncle to McClellan to ask for reinforcements, and the prince turned to leave but did not actually go. The Comte de Paris then came back to Porter with tears in his eyes and begged Porter to send the prince off. The prince finally left just before the dam broke. His nephews apparently caught up and went with him to McClellan to deliver the news. The prince had not left because the situation did not seem that bad to him.[14]

At 8 P.M. McClellan wrote to Stanton: "Have had a terrible contest. Attacked by greatly superior numbers in all directions on this side; we still hold our own, though a very heavy fire is still kept up on the left bank of the Chickahominy. The odds have been immense. We hold our own very nearly." This message makes no sense. McClellan was at the Trent house when he wrote it, so "this side" can only mean the south side. The left bank would be the north side. But he must have known that the line had broken on the north side, and he cannot have said "We hold our own very nearly" with that news fresh in his mind. He must have been hoping against hope that Porter could pull the fat out of the fire before he needed to telegraph Stanton again.

McClellan saw several options at this point. He could have concentrated his army on the north bank. This would have been wrong, however, for the Confederates had the roads to White House well covered and Porter was penned in a small semicircle near Grapevine Bridge. It would have been impossible to supply the army from White House. But the same was true if the army concentrated on the south bank, as the supply line would still be cut. The base thus had to be changed to the James River. He did not advance toward Richmond because Lee was in his rear. With limited rations, the length of time required to take Richmond—coupled with the possibility that Lee could take his supply wagons from behind—meant he might have to fight his way to the James just to get food. These arguments make sense, except that McClellan had a three-to-one numerical superiority on the south bank. If he had attacked on the twenty-seventh he might have forced Lee into a quick retreat. If he had attacked successfully along the Chickahominy bluffs, admittedly tough going for offensive operations, he might have split the Confederate force in two.

But McClellan had no idea he had such an advantage; he could see only the possibilities of losing his army, not those of gaining the other fellow's army. Given that orientation, a concentration on the south bank to cover a change of base was the only reasonable move. Yet McClellan's army was not large enough to hold a long line including the present front south of the Chickahominy and all the possible crossings. One can call the maneuver a change of base, as McClellan and many others have—even "a deliberately planned movement"—but tactically it would be a substantial retreat.

Once McClellan was sure of the result on the north bank, he notified his corps commanders and later called them together. Porter was disappointed. His work north of the river was being wasted, and he wanted McClellan to attack Richmond. At least one story suggests that Porter was not the only one who felt that way. When Heintzelman passed word of the retreat along to his division commanders, Kearny and Hooker were incensed—even if Hooker as late as 6 P.M. thought the Confederates were still going to advance. They persuaded Heintzelman to accompany them back to the Trent house. Kearny said to McClellan, "The enemy lines around Richmond are thin. They can and must be broken. An order to retreat is wrong! Wrong, sir! I ask permission to attack Magruder at once." McClellan had a one-word answer: "Denied." Hooker, the brigade commanders who had come along, and even Heintzelman, who had not been willing to give up any units to send to Porter, thought Kearny's idea was a good one. Kearny spoke again. "I can go straight into Richmond," he claimed. "A single division can do it, but to play safe use two divisions—Hooker's and mine." The move could have freed prisoners, upset Lee's ideas, shaken the Confederacy's resolve, and perhaps even captured important rebels. "It will be a glorious stroke, a brilliant thrust. I can do it and bring my men out of there."

McClellan was unmoved. "Nothing has changed, General," he said. "The retreat will be made on schedule." Brigadier General Hiram G. Berry, who commanded a brigade in Kearny's division and was there, described what happened next. "Phil unloosed a broadside. He pitched into McClellan with language so strong that all who heard it expected he would be placed under arrest until a general court-martial could be held. I was certain Kearny would be relieved of his command on the spot." McClellan wisely did not discipline Kearny; possibly he knew he would need Kearny's fighting ability during the movement to the James. However, he was right in refusing to order an advance by only one or two divisions.

Although by this account Heintzelman seems to have supported a move on Richmond, other evidence from Heintzelman himself tells a different story. McClellan sent the III Corps commander a telegraph message around 11 P.M. requesting his presence at headquarters. Once Heintzelman got there, McClellan outlined two possible courses of action. One was to move to the James River. The other was to risk battle south of the Chickahominy with all the force on that side of the river. McClellan was inclined to the latter course but thought the whole army would be destroyed by a defeat. Heintzelman impressed upon McClellan the importance of saving the army and recommended the movement to the James. McClellan agreed with Heintzelman but said he was still inclined to risk the battle. Finally, however, he decided on the retreat. These two accounts cannot be wholly reconciled, but they end at the same point—McClellan ordering the move to the James. It is interesting, however, that McClellan (according to Heintzelman) was even at this point considering a winner-take-all battle south of the Chickahominy.[15]

Units received directives to take all necessary supplies they could get in their wagons, destroy everything else, and leave their wounded in the care of doctors and attendants with sufficient medical stores. McClellan knew he was leaving those men to certain capture, but he could not have transported them and still moved quickly. Erasmus Keyes was ordered to move his IV Corps across White Oak Swamp, a watercourse to the south, and take strong positions to cover the passage of the trains and other troops. Earlier, Heintzelman had been ordered to send someone to White Oak Swamp to ensure that bridge building activity there continued to move along as quickly as possible. Captain Ira Spaulding of the 50th New York Engineers, set to destroy bridges across the Chickahominy, was pulled out of that position and sent to White Oak Swamp to build them. He and his men marched all night, arriving at 4 A.M.

The Yankees on the north bank of the Chickahominy began their retreat across the river. French and Meagher covered the V Corps and Slocum's division as they trudged across Grapevine, Alexander's, and Woodbury's Bridges. Once they were across, Slocum returned to his lines and Porter moved his men to the Trent house as best he could. As the II Corps brigades lay on the ground, they could hear Southern officers giving commands to men within two hundred yards of their positions. McCall crossed first. Many of his men had left everything on the field. Then came Sykes's division, ordered to cross at midnight. Finally, at 2 A.M., Morell crossed the river. One of Morell's soldiers recorded in his diary, "Everything is in the greatest confusion, horse foot and artillery are mixed up together with no kind of order." Another soldier wrote, "One of those awful marches, night marches where we move 150 or 100 feet to rest ten minutes or one-half hour." What was left of the 16th Michigan made it to the Trent house about 2 A.M., while the 83rd Pennsylvania and 44th New York spent the night in Baldy Smith's lines. Some of the artillery did not get across until 6 A.M. An engineer waiting to destroy the bridges wrote, "Such a night I hope to never pass again; wounded men, Uh! I cannot tell it all." Later in the night, French and Meagher moved back from their advanced positions, and crossed the river around daylight—but not before some men from the 29th Massachusetts heard several Confederates discussing what had happened and what would happen next.[16]

Those who stayed north of the river suffered in a different way. One wounded man from the 10th Alabama lay with nothing over or under him until midnight, when a couple of comrades found him, gave him something to lie on, and covered him with a blanket. They could not stop the groans and cries of the other wounded, however. Another rebel, writing home on paper taken from a knapsack belonging to a member of the 83rd Pennsylvania, told his mother the groans of the wounded were "truly distressing." He was helping ease the suffering of a couple of mortally wounded men from the Pennsylvania regiment, including Maj. Louis Naghel. Others searched for comrades to help. John Hinsdale of Pender's staff led one such party with torches, the men moving the wounded to a road where they could be picked up for transport. Still others looked for their kin, as did Berry Benson of the 1st South Carolina, who found his wounded brother and stayed with him all night. A number of Federals also were still north of the river. William Westervelt of the 27th New York, having hurt his ankle and foot during the fight, found a hole filled with water and put his foot in it, finally falling asleep after midnight.[17]

At White House Landing, the trees along the banks were cut so gunboats would have clear fields of fire. All that could be moved had been sent down the river to either West Point (where the Pamunkey and Mattapony Rivers formed the York) or Cumberland (between White House and West Point), was in readiness for such a move, or was loaded on trains to go to the front. Later, the sick and wounded arrived on trains. They wanted to leave as quickly as possible, and only soft words persuaded them to go to the hospitals at the landing. Some three thousand fugitive slave women and children were loaded onto canal boats for evacuation. The husbands and fathers of those slaves, who were used as laborers at the landing, were understandably nervous at the prospect of being captured by the rebels, and an army band played at their camp to try to lift their spirits. Lieutenant Colonel Rufus Ingalls of the quartermaster department assured the slaves that they would not be left behind, and their energy level rose. By nightfall, a chaplain who tried to store some baggage at the landing wrote, "all was confusion."[18]

Like much of his army, McClellan too was on the road. The headquarters moved to Savage Station, a little more than a mile southeast of the Trent house, along with Porter's trains. During this time McClellan sent several messages. One went to his wife. Another asked Louis Goldsborough, the flotilla commander, to send gunboats as far up the Chickahominy as he could, and also to have the gunboats on the James cover his left flank as far up that river as possible. Then, at 12:20 A.M. on the twenty-eighth, Little Mac sent another telegram to Stanton.

This is possibly the most infamous telegram sent during the Civil War. It was obviously written by someone depressed and upset at the outcome of the day's battles and at what he perceived as the lack of support he and his army had received. It also seems written by someone not in full possession of his faculties. McClellan again speaks of "several strong attacks" on his side of the river. He says he brought his "last reserves into action" on the north bank. He says that if he had "20,000 or even 10,000 fresh troops to use to-morrow" he could take Richmond (he had that many on the south bank and more). He lost the battle, he says, because he did not have enough men. He expresses heartfelt feelings for every brave man lost—feelings a general cannot afford to have. He says he must have very large reinforcements if he is to retrieve Union fortunes. He says Lincoln is wrong in considering him ungenerous when he says his force is too weak. He cannot be held responsible for the results of the day.

Then come the last three paragraphs. In the first he says that he has "seen too many dead and wounded comrades to feel otherwise than that the Government has not sustained this army. If you do not do so now the game is lost." He might have seen dead and wounded comrades at the Trent house or Savage Station—but not at the front, because he was not there (possibly for good reasons). It is possible that he did not see anyone killed or wounded on the twenty-seventh before he wrote this telegram.

The next paragraph makes McClellan's view a bit more clear: "If I save this army now, I tell you plainly that I owe no thanks to you or to any other persons in Washington"—presumably including Lincoln. Then the final paragraph, really just a single sentence, laying out his view for the world: "You have done your best to sacrifice this army."

McClellan knew the telegram was insubordinate. He thought it might be the last one he ever wrote, so he wanted to set the record straight. Of course, he did not know that the telegraph officer who received the message in Washington was so horrified that he showed it to his immediate superior, Edward S. Sanford, the military telegraph supervisor. McClellan also did not know that

Sanford, equally horrified, deleted the last two paragraphs before sending it to Stanton.

The verdicts on the telegram's contents have tended to fall into two camps: one supporting McClellan and the other criticizing him. There is no doubt that the last two sentences are unbelievable, nor is there much doubt that McClellan should not have sent the telegram at all. Whether one believes what McClellan said in most of it depends on whether one believes in him. The facts certainly do not seem to support him.[19]

McClellan and Lee both rested that night, getting ready for the coming exertions. Each knew the campaign was far from over.

CHAPTER NINE

"His Only Course Seemed to Me Was to Make for James River"

Robert E. Lee had written Jefferson Davis that his forces would "renew the contest in the morning" in his note announcing the victory at Gaines's Mill. However, when the Confederates awoke on the morning of June 28, they had no one to fight north of the Chickahominy. There were plenty of Federal soldiers, but almost all of them were either dead or wounded. The houses in the area were taken over for hospitals. Berry Benson got his wounded brother to one, and he looked into the garden to see amputated limbs lying everywhere.

The Confederates had few hospital stores and only inexperienced surgeons, but Lee ordered that they "treat the whole field alike." A Confederate officer, realizing the rebels' medical corps could not deal with the number of wounded, found some Union ambulances. The first train, sixty wagons filled with two hundred wounded, was ready about midnight. But when it got to Richmond, the first two hospitals the officer tried were full. A tenement that had been used as a tobacco warehouse was converted, although it was "horrible." The wounded waited an hour and a half in the wagons before the building was ready. The officer said, "Never had my vision beheld such a spectacle of human destruction" as the battlefield at Gaines's Mill.

The wounded were filling more than old tenements in Richmond. The existing hospitals were overcrowded and new ones took time to set up, so residents were asked to take one or two wounded men into their homes to care for them. The chief of police wanted every available vehicle put to work transporting the wounded from the battlefield to the city. The mourning began as well. Lucy Munford wrote her sister Jennie of all their acquaintances who had lost a family member, ending by saying, "Nearly all of the families in Richmond have been bereaved but this." Lucy was caring for the wounded along with the other women, who one observer thought had undiminished energy despite their grief. They now understood what a great fight really was, the observer noted. Some men stopped their business dealings to help the women care for the wounded.

Others rejoiced in the victory. John B. Jones exulted in his diary when he heard of Lee's note to Davis. Jones also saw the Yankee prisoners coming into the city, estimating their number at between four thousand and five thousand. Still others thought of what was to come. Stephen Mallory wrote in his journal: "The heaviest of the fighting is yet to come. God grant that it may succeed."[1]

Rebel soldiers walked the battlefield in sickening wonderment. "Never before did I see so many dead men, such a scene of blood and carnage," one wrote. "Men with no arms, some without legs, others with part of their head off, some with their bowels out, and every conceivable sight for humans to be killed."

J. Wood Davidson, a South Carolina soldier, woke from a sleep troubled by the cries of wounded and lights carried by men who were seeking them. No burials had been made, and he saw Federals and Confederates, the Zouaves of the 5th New York and Wheat's Tigers, Hood's Texans, and others. Some were wounded, while others were horribly mangled, and the smell of blood, the "most disgusting horror of a battlefield—to me," was everywhere. Yet in the afternoon he once again walked the field.

Some men got used to the carnage quickly. Jim Branscomb of the 3rd Alabama wrote to his sister, "I think no more of walking over a dead man now than you would a hog." Others were interested in what the Federals had left. In the 30th North Carolina men ate Northern crackers and drank Northern coffee. Afterward, William Ardrey walked over the battlefield, listing what he found in his diary: artillery, horses, guns, knapsacks, clothing, "in fact every thing that is used in war." Later that day he enjoyed butter, beef, and whiskey left behind by the enemy. W. A. Kenyon, writing to his brother on captured paper, told him, "We have been living high."[2]

John Reynolds, the Federal brigade commander, and Capt. Charles Kingsbury (Reynolds's assistant adjutant general) hid themselves in the timber during the night, having gotten entangled in swampy ground while trying to reach the Union rear. Upon awakening on the morning of the twenty-eighth, they found the Union troops gone and the bridge across the river broken down. Reynolds tried to make it to the river but could not get through the Confederate lines. He surrendered to pickets from the 4th Virginia of the Stonewall Brigade, stationed on the rebel left, and by chance was brought before D. H. Hill. The two men had been tentmates in the old army, and Hill reported, "Not an unkind word had ever passed between us." Reynolds, embarrassed at his situation, sat down, put his face into his hands, and finally said, "Hill, we ought not to be enemies." Hill tried to comfort his friend, saying that Reynolds's conduct in Mexico and before the war would protect him from suspicion. The Confederate offered Reynolds rebel money, which the Northerner refused, then sent the prisoner to Richmond in his personal ambulance.

William Westervelt of the 27th New York awakened to the sounds of wounded and stragglers chased by Southern cavalry and running toward a bridge. Despite his swollen ankle he got up and ran as best he could with the other Yankees, but the bridge was gone. Most of the Northerners gave up, but Westervelt found a log and paddled across. When he started moving again the adrenaline wore off and he collapsed in pain. He eventually made his way to the field hospital at Savage Station.[3]

Stonewall Jackson found his way to the area of Hood's charge. Surveying the area, he remarked, "The men who carried this position were soldiers indeed!" Jackson also found a group of Federal wounded. B. J. Coll of the 62nd Pennsylvania was with Lieutenant Patterson of that regiment and two hundred to three hundred other wounded who had not been able to get away on the twenty-seventh. After they were captured they saw a group of rebel officers and Patterson asked who they were. He was told that they were Lee, Longstreet, A. P. Hill, D. H. Hill, and Jackson. Just then Stonewall came over and asked Patterson, "Whose troops were engaged yesterday?" Patterson answered, "General Fitz John Porter's corps." Jackson asked him if that was all and Patterson said yes. Apparently Stonewall did not like that answer (which was not completely true), for he threatened to cut Patterson's ears off with his sword if that lie were repeated. Patterson did not know the details of Slocum's involvement, for he replied: "Notwithstanding the fact that I may lose my ears, I repeat that the only troops engaged yesterday were those of General Porter's corps. Slocum's division came over late in the evening, but was not engaged." One presumes that Jackson did not carry out his threat.

Lee himself searched for his youngest son, Pvt. Robert E. Lee of the Rockbridge (Virginia) Artillery. That unit had not done any fighting at Gaines's Mill, having halted on Winder's orders. General Lee did not know this, however, and he was looking to make sure his son was still alive. Finally, on the left of the line, he found the Rockbridge cannoneers—but not Robert. A search discovered him sleeping soundly under a caisson. Another artilleryman used a sponge staff on young Lee, who finally awoke and was told someone wanted to see him. Half awake, Robert crawled out from under the caisson to find his father and the general's staff looking at him. The two exchanged greetings, then the general rode off. Young Robert later reported that he was somewhat dazed by the freshness of his father and his fellows, but he remembered, "[W]hen I saw my father's loving eyes and smile it become clear to me that he had ridden by to see if I was safe and to ask how I was getting along."[4]

While his troops rested and walked what was for many the first battlefield they had seen, Lee could only wait for information on what McClellan was doing. Alexander and his balloon would have been most helpful on this day, but high winds prevented a Confederate ascension. Lee had sent Longstreet's men forward early to find Yankees. They found no enemy north of the river but plenty in the works south of it, contradicting an earlier report Lee had received. These may have been the rebels who flushed some Union caissons heading toward the river just as one of the bridges was being destroyed. The drivers cut the traces and swam the horses across, while the workers—from the McClellan Dragoons of Little Mac's headquarters detachment—fired their revolvers at the Southerners. Yankee infantry came up and the dragoons finished their work on the bridge.

When Lee heard that the Northerners were still in their positions south of the Chickahominy, his first thought was that McClellan might cross to the north bank of the river farther downstream to attempt to preserve communications with the White House supply base. He therefore sent Ewell's division, with the 9th Virginia Cavalry screening in advance, to take the Richmond and York River Railroad—McClellan's supply route. The railroad crossed the Chickahominy between Grapevine Bridge and Bottom's Bridge, very near to Dispatch Station on the north side of the river. Ewell's troops had seen hard fighting the previous day, as had most of the Confederate forces north of the river, but they were the closest to Dispatch Station and so had the least amount of ground to cover. The rest of Stuart's cavalry supported Ewell, traveling by a road northeast of that used by the infantry.[5]

Lee also ordered Longstreet to gather such guns as could reach the south bank of the river to shell the Federal positions there. Again, the choice of Longstreet seems to have been one of convenience. As Longstreet wrote in his official report, "The range was so great, however, that we could do but little more than annoy him." Longstreet failed even to mention the cannonade in his memoirs. Other rebel guns would have an effect on Northerners on the twenty-eighth, but they came from the south side of the river.

Information began to reach Lee before noon. A courier from Isaac Trimble's column gave Lee the message that Union forces could be seen moving south and Union supplies were being burned. Trimble ascertained this by sending an officer up a tree with a field glass. Lee wrote back that the Federals were still in their lines on the Confederate right and Longstreet's artillery had failed to dislodge them.

This was the first piece of evidence to indicate a Federal retreat. Soon clouds of dust south of the Chickahominy began to obscure the horizon. Surely this was a sign of a Northern retreat, although Whiting had his doubts: He claimed it was all a ruse McClellan was putting on before he would march on Richmond. D. H. Hill, hearing this claim, replied to Whiting, "Don't you think that this *ruse* of McClellan is a leetle expensive?"

Then came another note from Trimble, who was farther south now and could see four distinct fires and infantry, artillery, and wagons moving south. Trimble, always anxious for a fight, wrote to Lee: "the enemy were certainly retreating with great precipitation, as burning stores were a sure indication, and ought to be vigorously pursued."[6]

But Lee first had to figure out where McClellan's troops were headed before he could pursue them. He got more information from Dispatch Station. Stuart and his men had gotten ahead of Ewell's infantry. Cutting back to the southwest to reach the road to Dispatch Station, Jeb put one squadron of Col. Thomas Cobb's Legion of Georgia cavalry at the head of the column. They encountered two companies, E and K, of Col. John F. Farnsworth's seemingly ever-present 8th Illinois Cavalry at the station. Farnsworth had been able to remove the wounded and the medical staff, as well as many supplies, from the hospital there. The Federals then burned the hospital, but they could not stop the Confederates. Major William G. Deloney's squadron of Cobb's Legion put first one Federal company, then the other, to flight, the rebel troopers charging in an "all out style," Deloney reported. The Yankees fired once and ran, but the rebels caught up with some after a second charge. "Sabred several of them and took one prisoner" was how Deloney put it. The Unionists fell back to Bottom's Bridge, a little more than a mile southwest of Dispatch Station. Few casualties were suffered on either side in this engagement. Stuart, arriving a short time later, began tearing up the track and cut the telegraph wires connecting the south bank of the Chickahominy to White House Landing.

Meanwhile, Capt. James Brady, the commander of Battery H, 1st Pennsylvania Light Artillery, and charged with the defense of the railroad bridge across the Chickahominy, saw the smoke from the burning hospital at Dispatch Station. Brigadier General Henry M. Naglee, who commanded a brigade in Brig. Gen. John J. Peck's division of Keyes's IV Corps, had ordered Brady to prepare to burn the bridge after stragglers and wounded came from the station. The smoke from the station indicated that Confederates had reached it, so Brady fired the bridge.

Ewell, whose troops joined Stuart's cavalry in the destruction of the railroad when they reached the station, must have seen the burning bridge, just as Stuart must have. One of the two, probably Stuart, reported the news to Lee and also mentioned that no enemy troops were in sight. That message cleared matters up some for Lee. If McClellan destroyed the railroad bridge, he would not try to protect his supply line by concentrating north of the river that close to Richmond.[7]

Two courses of action then seemed to Lee open to McClellan. He could move his base to some forward point on the James River, enabling his army to stay relatively close to Richmond, or he could retreat back down the Peninsula, basing himself either at some other point on the Pamunkey or York Rivers, farther downstream on the James, or at Fort Monroe on the end of the Peninsula. If McClellan retreated down the Peninsula, Lee would want to keep as many men as possible north of the Chickahominy. That river changes from flowing southeast near the battlefields of the twenty-sixth and twenty-seventh to flowing east for a few miles, but it then turns nearly south. McClellan would have to cross it if he retreated down the Peninsula. By staying north of the river, Lee would avoid having to cross that stream twice more, probably without benefit of bridges and possibly in the face of Union resistance. However, if Little Mac changed his base to some forward point on the James, Lee would need all his men south of the Chickahominy. Otherwise, McClellan could move toward Richmond with a united army against only Magruder and Huger. The change of base and movement of the Army of the Potomac would also leave it vulnerable to attack.

The evidence indicates that Lee thought McClellan would change his base to some relatively forward point on the James. In his report, Lee noted: "from the position it [McClellan's army] occupied the roads which led toward James River would also enable it to reach the lower bridges over the Chickahominy and retreat down the Peninsula." This sounds as though Lee's first guess was that McClellan was staying close to Richmond. A dispatch sent from Lee to Jefferson Davis on the twenty-ninth reads in part: "his [McClellan's] only course seemed to me was to make for James river & thus open communications with his gun boats and fleet." D. H. Hill said that Lee judged his opponent would not withdraw his army straight back down the same Peninsula it had marched up six weeks before. That would be demoralizing to any army, and particularly to McClellan, who was a proud man. Lee's report, of course, could have been written with hindsight and cannot be regarded as conclusive evidence of his thoughts at the time. However, the dispatch he sent on the twenty-ninth can be, and it is obvious from that dispatch that Lee not only thought of the possibility of McClellan's moving to the James, he thought it was the obvious move once the railroad bridge had been destroyed.

But Lee could not rely on sketchy information and knowledge of character to make this decision. He wisely did not take the gamble to act on his belief. If his army went south and McClellan went east, Lee would lose any chance of destroying the Northern army. If his army went east and McClellan went south, Lee would be farther away from Richmond than was his opponent. He could not counter any move until he had more evidence of it.[8]

Lee decided to send Stuart, who could get units to the crossings south of Bottom's Bridge, to bring him that evidence. He sent Stuart a message to that effect, also telling Ewell to move south about three-fourths of a mile to Bottom's

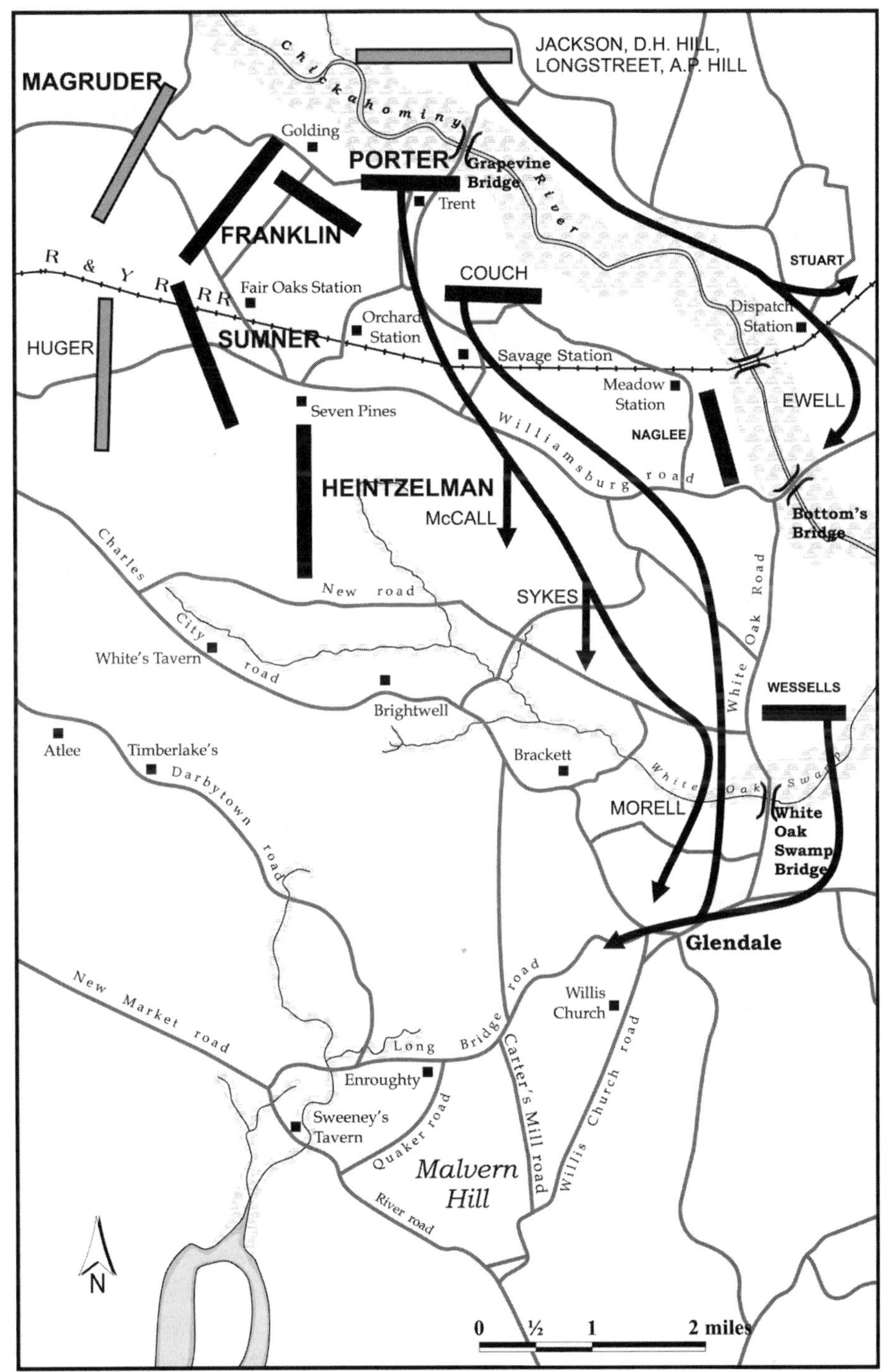

Troop movements, June 28, 1862

Bridge to guard against any attempt by Yankees to cross the river there. Campbell Brown, Ewell's aide, had to work hard to get Trimble to follow the rest of the division as Trimble had taken a road different from the one Ewell wanted and had found a position to his liking. Brown finally convinced Trimble to rejoin the division. The brigade commander was disappointed that he "did not even strike a Yankee picket-post or stray Regim't."

One squad of Yankee horsemen, from the Oneida Cavalry of McClellan's headquarters units or the McClellan Dragoons, chased Ewell as he and his staff were reconnoitering toward the bridge. Ewell told Bradley Johnson to "drive those fellows off who had given him chase." One company went out, followed by Johnson with a larger force. Johnson saw a heavy column of cavalry ready to charge a little distance off. Half a mile from the main body, he wheeled his horse around and yelled to some imaginary Confederates, "Come on my brave men, here we have a whole regiment of them!" The Federals rode off at that. Once the rebels got near Bottom's Bridge, Ewell sent Johnson to a hill overlooking it. Johnson could see that a lot of work had been done on both sides of the river, apparently to prepare for the placement of heavy guns. Ewell ordered some guns from Brockenbrough's battery to open on the Northern position.[9]

The Unionists were ready for an attack at Bottom's Bridge. On the twenty-seventh, two IV Corps generals had reconnoitered the approaches to the bridge. John Peck was a forty-one-year-old New Yorker who, after graduating from West Point in 1843 and fighting in Mexico, had become successful in business. Peck had taken command of one of Keyes's IV Corps divisions after Seven Pines when Brig. Gen. Silas Casey was pushed aside. Henry M. Naglee, one of Peck's brigade commanders, was older than his chief at forty-seven and a native of Philadelphia. A West Pointer who was in civil engineering before the Mexican War and a banker afterward, Naglee resigned his Regular Army commission to become a brigadier general of volunteers. The two found a place for a redoubt capable of holding up to twelve guns and had it built. Naglee's brigade, composed of Maine, New York, and Pennsylvania troops, was stationed between Bottom's Bridge and the railroad bridge. The 85th Pennsylvania from Brig. Gen. Henry W. Wessells's brigade of the same division, as well as Lt. Charles H. Morgan's Battery G, 4th U.S. Artillery, joined it. One of Morgan's guns joined three guns of Battery E, 1st Pennsylvania Light Artillery, commanded by Capt. Theodore Miller and two guns of Brady's Battery H, 1st Pennsylvania Light Artillery, at Bottom's Bridge. One of Miller's guns and two of Brady's were at the railroad bridge, and the other five guns from Morgan's battery were placed about seven hundred yards to the left rear of the Bottom's Bridge position.

Miller had received reports all day on the twenty-eighth of Confederate troops in sight, and he had tested the range. At about 2:30 that afternoon he could see Brockenbrough setting up. The rebel guns did not open fire until about 4 P.M. Miller and the guns near the railroad bridge immediately returned it. The Confederates fired twelve shells before they sought shelter from the Northern guns. "That'll do," Ewell told Johnson, "we've found out what we want." For that brief period, though, the cavalry in the bottomland on the east bank listened to the shells pass. Although nothing came close, the sound was "rather unpleasant," reported one of the horse soldiers.

This inconsequential artillery duel unnerved McClellan enough that he told Porter to send Sykes's division to the bridge and even sent a follow-up message urging speed. But Sykes did not go all the way to the bridge, and Ewell's force did nothing further that day. At least he was in position, though. Stuart had already left Dispatch Station by the time Lee's message got there. Apparently Jeb discussed with Ewell the possibility of further offensive moves, and Ewell decided to stay at the station. Stuart, however, took his cavalry toward White House to see if a Federal force stood in the way. The first enemy he found was a train of forage wagons with a few cavalrymen serving as escorts. Stuart's men captured the train, as well as several sutlers' establishments the rebels found farther down the road. The Confederate cavalry also flushed some Federal pickets, who headed toward White House Landing. Soon smoke could be seen rising from the landing (it also could be seen from the Gaines's Mill battlefield). At some point Stuart sent Lee a message that he had seen some enemy troops in the distance and was headed that way to investigate.[10]

Silas Casey was now in command of the Union forces at White House Landing. Casey was a month shy of his fifty-fifth birthday and a lifelong soldier. His division took the brunt of the Confederate attack at Seven Pines, where his position was overrun. McClellan, believing that Casey had lost his men's confidence, had put the older general in charge at White House and replaced him with Peck on June 23.

Casey had heard early of the presence of Confederates at Dispatch Station. The telegraph stopped working about 9 A.M. after receipt of a message, "Go to Hell, you damned Yankees, we will be there in 20 minutes." He placed Lt. Col. Henry B. McKean's five companies of the 6th Pennsylvania Reserves under the command of Brig. Gen. George Stoneman. A thirty-nine-year-old New York native and member of the West Point class of 1846, Stoneman was the chief of the Army of the Potomac's cavalry. He had two thousand horse soldiers with him, plus the 17th New York from Butterfield's brigade, the 18th Massachusetts from Martindale's brigade, and an artillery battery. These troops, as well as McKean's companies, were stationed at Tunstall's Station, less than four miles from White House and a place Casey called "the key-point of White House Station." Casey also ordered five companies of the 11th Pennsylvania Cavalry, the other five companies of the 6th Pennsylvania Reserves, six companies of the 93rd New York Infantry, and Battery F of the 1st New York Artillery, all at White House Landing, to be ready to support Stoneman.

But Stoneman, despite an earlier discussion with Casey and a train ride to see for himself what was coming, had decided he could not fight the approaching Confederates. Rufus Ingalls sent word to Stoneman of the rebels' telegraph message. Pickets were also bringing in that information. Brigadier General William H. Emory, in command of the cavalry in Stoneman's force, reported that fifty thousand men were on the way. One cavalry officer wrote in his diary, "The absurdity of the statement was apparent," but no one bothered to get a good idea of the actual number of rebels. On July 10, Stuart had only 3,475 men in his entire cavalry force—six regiments, four lesser commands, and one artillery battery. On this journey he had only three regiments, three lesser commands, and the artillery with him.

Despite their numerical superiority, Stoneman, Emory, and Col. Henry S. Lansing of the 17th New York decided that they could not hold off the Confederates. Instead, they would try to cut their way through to Long Bridge and cross the Chickahominy to reach their fellow Unionists. Then Ingalls informed Stoneman that they were the only Federals on that side of the river, that sixty thousand rebels (only a slight exaggeration) were between them and the Army of the Potomac, and that he could transport twelve hundred men. At that news, Stoneman ordered the entire command back to White House.

Ingalls warned Casey that Stoneman wanted to embark the troops on transports. Stoneman apparently had not received Casey's note advising him of the transfer of McKean's force to Stoneman's command, for Casey had to send Lt. E. Walter West, his aide, to get McKean to retreat at the double-quick. As the infantry arrived at White House and stacked arms, word was received that the rebel cavalry was in sight. Stuart had passed Tunstall's Station and was trying to cross Black Creek less than a mile east of Tunstall's. Some of Stoneman's cavalry disputed the crossing, which was made more difficult by the destruction of the bridge over what Stuart called "this difficult stream, whose abrupt banks and miry bed presented a serious obstacle to our progress." Pelham's horse artillery dispersed the Union cavalry, including some dismounted troopers hidden on the banks of the creek. Stuart tried to make the Yankees think he had some infantry and more artillery than merely Pelham with him, but the Northerners had already given up by that point. W. D. Farley led a group of dismounted troopers across the creek to make sure no other Yankees lingered, while W. W. Blackford, the engineer, worked to repair the bridge. Night fell before it was ready, though, so Stuart's command spent the night along Black Creek.[11]

Meanwhile, White House Landing was in flames. The wounded had been loaded onto transports earlier. Once the signal for all others to embark was sounded from a gunboat, soldiers assaulted the sutlers' stores, gathering as much as they could before their officers stopped them. As soon as Stuart was sighted, Casey ordered that the remaining stores be burned at Ingalls's request. In fact, everything combustible was put to the torch: tents, beds, liquor, medicines, utensils, oranges, lemons, baggage, food, clothes, and even a couple of locomotives. Colonel Thomas F. Morris of the 93rd New York supervised the firing, while Casey himself gave it much attention. The 18th Massachusetts and 93rd New York boarded transports, while the 17th New York rode on navy gunboats. Casey got on board the steamer *Knickerbocker* and ordered the transports off about 7 P.M. Waters Braman of the 93rd New York, the last man ashore, set fire to the wharf. Stoneman began his retreat to Yorktown about 9 P.M. The gunboats stayed behind. Colonel Lansing of the 17th New York called the fire "magnificent, but sad; it lighted up the whole country." Benjamin Ashenfelter of the 6th Pennsylvania Reserves said the sight "was one long to be remembered by me."

Casey was already aboard the *Knickerbocker* when he saw the White House itself on fire. He stated in his report that its burning was "against my express orders." Lansing reported that the culprit was a private in the 93rd New York. One man who witnessed the burning wrote, "Few of us grieved when this property of a rebel officer was in flames," whereas some expressed regret because it could have been used as a hospital. Still others were saddened because of its association with Washington, even though the building dated from after the Revolutionary period. One New Yorker wrote, "It was gone, and there was no use in crying over it."[12]

While Stuart went to White House Landing, Lee heard nothing further from him on the twenty-eighth. That was more tragic for the Confederate cause than the burning of the White House. If Stuart had been at Dispatch Station when Lee's order to watch the lower Chickahominy crossings came, he could have split his force in two for reconnaissance purposes. One could have gone to White House Landing to check on the Unionists there and the other could have moved down the north bank of the Chickahominy to watch for any westward Yankee movements. It was about thirteen road miles from Bottom's Bridge to Jones's Bridge, likely the farthest Stuart would need to ride to check on Union intentions. Once he got to Jones's Bridge, it would be about eighteen miles back to Lee. Couriers from Stuart might have reached Lee in time to let Marse Robert move troops on June 28.

The Confederate cavalry also might have crossed the river south of Bottom's Bridge, at a ford or an unguarded bridge. This move could have gained the same information as a move down the north bank, and perhaps even more. Whether that information could have reached Lee in time to make any difference is another question. There was no chance of Stuart's crossing the Chickahominy at Bottom's Bridge or anywhere upstream from there until New

Bridge. All Stuart could have done from New Bridge would have been to move south, below Huger's position, and down the New Market road. It is doubtful that such a move made at the beginning of the day could have gotten Lee information more quickly than a ride down the north bank of the Chickahominy. Once Lee sent Stuart to Dispatch Station, however, moving south along the river was Jeb's only chance at getting information.[13]

Since Stuart did none of these, because he had gone to White House Landing, Lee got no hard information and could make no major moves. A. P. Hill's division, used hard at Beaver Dam Creek and at Gaines's Mill, rested near the mill and buried the dead. D. H. Hill moved toward Grapevine Bridge, which was destroyed early on the twenty-eighth by the 4th U.S. Infantry. Stopping at Turkey Hill overlooking the bridge, Garland's brigade saw Union forces on the opposite bank and formed a line of battle. Several batteries opened up on the Federals. Most of the rest of Jackson's command stayed put, but Whiting followed Hill, stopping after about half a mile and camping at the McGehee house. The 42nd Virginia of Cunningham's brigade reconnoitered toward Grapevine Bridge early in the morning, but it was then ordered back to Barker's mill, about a mile northeast of the bridge. Jackson also began to try to get Grapevine Bridge repaired, but his efforts apparently had little effect. Longstreet's only action was the previously mentioned artillery fire.[14]

Five of the six Confederate divisions north of the river, then, did very little on June 28. They had been fought, and in Jackson's case marched, to the point of exhaustion. They both needed and deserved the rest. And Lee could not very well send them someplace until he was certain of his plans. Nonetheless, every hour Lee waited for information, and every hour the men spent resting, lessened the chance for a decisive victory.

While nearly all was quiet on the north bank of the Chickahominy on June 28, the south bank was the scene of much activity. "The truth is that after Gaines's Mill and Cold Harbor, McClellan was only intent on *saving his army*, as Mr. Lincoln had advised," wrote one Confederate after the war. Much of the activity came as the result of this intention. McClellan wanted Keyes and Porter in position south of White Oak Swamp to cover the trains' movement. It was the first significant task given to Keyes. The Massachusetts native was fifty-two and an 1832 West Point graduate. He subsequently taught there, as well as serving as Winfield Scott's aide and military secretary and in infantry, cavalry, and artillery commands. Keyes was one of the men named by Lincoln to command a corps in McClellan's army. He later remembered that McClellan never asked for his opinion during the first part of the Peninsular campaign—even being left out of councils of war.

Keyes had received McClellan's order at 1 A.M. It required him to get three of his five brigades, together with all their artillery and baggage, across White

Oak Swamp by noon. Henry Wessells's brigade in Peck's division was camped just north of the swamp, which flowed from just behind the southern part of the Union line to the Chickahominy about two miles southeast of Bottom's Bridge. But Peck's other brigade, Naglee's unit, was still needed to protect the Chickahominy crossings against Confederate attacks from the east. Keyes's other division, commanded by Darius Couch, was camped at Savage Station, fully five miles from the bridge over White Oak Swamp via the Williamsburg and White Oak roads.

That bridge, called White Oak Swamp Bridge, had been destroyed by Hooker. After receiving McClellan's order, Keyes examined the bridge and found it "not in a condition to allow the crossing of any wheeled vehicle." It had to be rebuilt —not only to get Keyes across the swamp, but because almost all of McClellan's army needed to use the road from Savage Station to reach the James River. Other bridges also would have to be built. No one bridge could handle the traffic of an entire army needing to make a speedy change of base.

Brigadier General Daniel P. Woodbury, the fifty-one-year old New Hampshire West Pointer who commanded the army's engineer brigade, had joined Spaulding at White Oak Swamp to build two bridges: one at the passage of White Oak road and another about a mile upstream at Brackett's Ford. Woodbury and his men of the 15th and 50th New York Engineers and Capt. James Duane's battalion of U.S. Engineers also repaired the corduroy roads leading through the swamp so wagons could travel through it. The first bridge was completed by 6 A.M., and not long after that the bridge was ready for wheeled traffic. That morning the engineers built the bridge at Brackett's Ford.

Keyes also told Couch to fall back to White Oak Swamp and ordered Peck to cross the swamp the first moment he could do so. Innis Palmer's brigade was Couch's first unit to reach the swamp. Peck took it and Wessells's brigade, together with three batteries of artillery and a squadron of cavalry, across as soon as the first bridge was finished.

Palmer's brigade, moving in the lead, reached its assigned position covering the intersection of the Willis Church (or Quaker), Charles City, and Long Bridge roads, about two miles southwest of White Oak Swamp, before noon. Keyes had found a local farmer when he arrived at White Oak Swamp and ordered him under pain of death of describe all the roads and paths leading to the James River and to Richmond. The farmer did so, and Keyes had a clear picture of the transportation network. The intersection to which he directed Palmer's brigade was called Glendale, and it was important to the Union army because the one road known to McClellan that led from White Oak Swamp to the James River was the Willis Church road. It started at Glendale and crossed over an eminence named Malvern Hill to reach the River road. If Confederates took Glendale while the Northerners were still north of it, the Yankees might have to attack just to get to their new base.

Couch arrived shortly after noon with the rest of his division in tow. For some it had been a hard march. Brigadier General John J. Abercrombie's brigade was the one ordered to help Porter the evening before. It had begun about 2 A.M., and some men fell out of line from exhaustion. Brigadier General Albion P. Howe's brigade made what one man called "a circuitous route of some ten or twelve miles" for a march that should have covered only about five. Couch was in place at Glendale before nightfall, with Peck's men on his right and left. That afternoon, Peck sent Wessells's 96th New York Infantry and the 8th New York Light Artillery from the IV Corps artillery reserve to destroy Long Bridge, which crossed the Chickahominy five miles southeast of Bottom's Bridge and four miles east of White Oak Swamp Bridge. At the same time, a small infantry force and a section of artillery went to Jones's Bridge, a little more than six miles downstream from Long Bridge, to destroy it as well. With these moves, all the bridges across the Chickahominy that the rebels might use to attack the Federal flank or rear were either guarded or destroyed.

Wessells's 85th Pennsylvania was left to guard Brackett's Ford, while the 92nd New York, also of Wessells's brigade, watched White Oak Swamp Bridge. Peck placed a guard on every house within two or three miles of the Union position with orders to stop any person leaving the premises. With that, the IV Corps settled in. Keyes informed the army chief of staff, Randolph Marcy, about the topography around Glendale: "This position is not more easily defended than 10,000 others in a level wooded country; it is not supported on either flank or in the rear." He said that if another corps could get to his position he could move on to protect the trains as they rolled toward the James River.[15]

Porter's exhausted corps was next to move. However, that movement did not commence until the afternoon. Morell's division, the last of the V Corps divisions to cross the Chickahominy, left the Trent house for Savage Station early that afternoon—just a few hours after the 83rd Pennsylvania and 44th New York rejoined their brigade. At the station, Marcy ordered Morell to cross White Oak Swamp, give Woodbury and the engineers all possible help, and support Keyes. The men made it across the swamp before sunset (some as early as 4 P.M.) and camped for the night on the Britton farm on high ground south of the swamp. The division commander detailed five hundred men to help Woodbury in his work.

Unfortunately, the night was not restful for some soldiers. At about 1 A.M. Martindale's brigade was aroused by a false alarm. The men took their arms and repacked the wagons in preparation for a fight. None came, but Maj. Francis A. Schoeffel of the 13th New York reported that his command slept no more that night. Griffin's and Butterfield's brigades apparently got more rest, as neither general mentioned the false alarm and one diarist called the stampede "nothing serious."

The first group of trains left Savage Station at 4 P.M. Captain Alexander Bliss, in charge of the wagons, prescribed a certain order of departure to try to reduce confusion, but to no avail. Bliss left the station at 9 P.M. with the headquarters wagons. After half a mile he found the trains stopped by a minor obstruction that the teamsters had not bothered to remove; they went to sleep instead. Bliss removed that obstruction and many others. Still, it was daylight before he reached White Oak Swamp Bridge—even though he formed two columns of trains when the terrain allowed. Some of the wagons did not move from 9 P.M. to 3 A.M., and those that did found travel was slow. Captain William LeDuc, in charge of the II Corps trains, had to shake one driver ahead of him to wake the man. The wagon had run into something and the driver was too tired to find out what it was. The rain that began to fall only added to the problems.

Sykes's division began its march in the late afternoon after protecting the Chickahominy crossings all day. It headed down the Williamsburg road and then a secondary road for White Oak Swamp after the men got a gill of whiskey each. Some of the more fortunate found their quartermasters among the wagons and retrieved their knapsacks, gladly taking on the extra weight. But all were so tired they could barely get out of the way of the wagons and constantly passing horsemen. They were "spiritless" and took every halt as a chance to sleep. Around midnight, some mules running loose down the road were magnified into a charge of Southern cavalry, and the whole column got off the road until the source of the alarm was discovered.

Sykes finally turned his command off the secondary road and onto the road leading to Brackett's Ford. John Donn of the United States Coast Survey, who was attached to the topographical engineers and had reconnoitered the road that morning, guided the column. Donn took three tries to find the entrance to the road, which was more of a cart track and not often used. The trees looked like huge columns to one soldier, the branches Gothic arches. Finally, Sykes halted the head of the force north of the swamp at 2 A.M. Some of the men did not stop at all during the night, while others got an hour's sleep.

McCall did not get the order to fall back until 8 P.M. By that point, the route from Savage Station to White Oak Swamp must have been a jumble of infantry, horses, artillery, and wagons, and McCall made little headway during the night. He took the artillery reserve with him, and the guns eventually formed a line seven miles long. Regiments were placed throughout the artillery train, and flanking parties moved to the left and right of the column. Some of the units did not begin until after midnight. The exhausted soldiers were on edge. One man's musket discharged accidentally and his mates, who thought he was a Confederate, fired upon him.

In the middle of the night an officer told McCall he was on the wrong road and would have to turn back. The Pennsylvania Reserves' commander had turned sixty in March, and had spent more than half his life in the army. He fought against the Seminoles in Florida, served with Zachary Taylor in Mexico, and was one of two inspectors general before his retirement in 1853. War brought him back to the army as the Pennsylvania unit's first commander. He could tell a bad idea when he saw it and ignored the officer. The same man came back an hour later and told McCall it was McClellan's order to move to another road, but McCall said to tell the commanding general that that would be impossible. Presumably riding ahead of his troops because of this confusion, McCall reached Savage Station around 1 A.M. McClellan greeted him by saying, "Here is General McCall, the hero of Mechanicsville." Little Mac then asked if he should destroy the trains to let the army move faster. McCall responded that he would fight for every inch of ground before he destroyed a single wagon. This no doubt was an exaggeration, but it probably gave McClellan some confidence.

The artillery reserve had been gathered together during the day. Lieutenant Samuel S. Elder's Battery K, 1st U.S. Artillery, stayed behind at the Courtney house, behind the VI Corps positions, when the rest of Lt. Col. George W. Getty's brigade of regular batteries moved to Savage Station. Elder's battery joined them during the early evening. Captain J. Howard Carlisle's brigade of regular batteries had also congregated around the Courtney house. Major Albert Arndt's brigade of New York batteries had been ordered to Savage Station at about 11 P.M., and soon after that he headed toward White Oak Swamp, reaching it about midnight. Lieutenant Colonel William Hays's brigade of regular batteries moved from the Trent house in the evening. Major E. R. Petherbridge's Maryland Light batteries, after being stationed near Woodbury's Bridge over the Chickahominy during the day, left for White Oak Swamp around 11 P.M., making as little noise as they could. Most of these units were on the road all night, as were the V Corps guns. Some of those gunners, completely worn out by their actions of the last two or three days, fell from their horses asleep—giving a moment of hilarity to those still awake. The 1st Connecticut Heavy Artillery began its retreat at about 4 P.M. after destroying an eight-inch howitzer and a rocket battery. It reached its campsite south of White Oak Swamp about midnight.[16]

Other artillery units were in action on the twenty-eighth as part of the largest engagement on a day "like the calm in the eye of a great storm." Longstreet's rifled guns fired their ineffectual rounds in response to a request from David Jones on the south bank of the river. Jones had received information, perhaps because of a note from Lee to Magruder, that the Yankees were about to retreat. Wishing to confirm this information, he looked for himself. What he saw convinced him that the information was accurate, and he went to Magruder's headquarters. Magruder was not there, so Jones sent Capt. Osman Latrobe, his acting adjutant and inspector general, across the river to ask Lee for some artillery support for a possible attack.

Jones did not rely only on Longstreet's guns. At Mrs. Price's house, Jones and Pendleton, the reserve artillery commander, had assembled five long-range guns. These consisted of a two-gun section of Lane's battery, two three-inch rifled guns from Woolfolk's battery, and one gun from Capt. W. J. Dabney's Virginia battery. Jones ordered them to fire on the Union positions near the Golding house, where Toombs had attacked the previous day. Then Jones sent word to Toombs that upon any positive signs of an enemy retreat he should occupy Federal redoubt number six near the Golding farm, a key point in the Union line, and fire on the Yankees. Believing that more artillery would be useful, Jones then ordered James Brown's battery and Capt. George V. Moody's Louisiana battery to positions at the overseer's house on the Garnett farm. They were not to fire, however, until the effect of the long-range guns could be seen.

Having made all his dispositions, Jones then returned to the long-range guns to direct their fire and observe its effect, which may have been magnified by Union movements. Brigadier General William B. Franklin, whose VI Corps held this part of the Northern line, was thirty-nine years old. The Pennsylvanian had graduated first in his West Point class and became an engineer. After serving in the Mexican War he supervised the construction of the Capitol dome and an addition to the treasury building in Washington. McClellan named him, along with Porter, to command one of the provisional corps formed on the Peninsula. Franklin had decided the Confederates were in great force opposite him. He could see the batteries forming and decided to move his men into the woods surrounding the Golding farm. Baldy Smith changed position to face the Chickahominy—leaving his flank open to the enemy—to prepare to act as rear guard for the army during its retreat. To strengthen the position, his men needed to clear a large forest that obstructed their view of the river. The 6th Maine and 5th Wisconsin of Hancock's brigade, being lumbermen, were detailed to the task, along with Brooks's brigade of Vermonters, who all could handle an ax. Smith recalled that they would cut a tree so that when it fell it would take down other trees. He said the falling trees looked like "grass before the mowers." Brigadier General John Davidson's 7th Maine was sent to make obstructions to delay any pursuit.[17]

These movements could be interpreted as a disorderly Federal retreat, and Jones did so. He sent Capt. E. N. Thurston of his staff to tell Toombs that the enemy was retreating and order Brown and Moody to open fire on the Yankees to Toombs's right. All this fire caused some consternation among the intended targets. Members of the 5th Wisconsin found the largest trees around to hide behind, a sight one soldier described as "very amusing for a looker-on." The men fell back about a mile, and George Thomas wrote home, "There was not a knapsack on one of the men in our company." The 96th Pennsylvania of Bartlett's brigade had just pitched tents when word came to pack up again.

Shells started falling as the tents were being struck; the Pennsylvanians also left their knapsacks and had to get them later. A man in the 1st Minnesota of Sedgwick's division, in front of Smith's position by mistake as part of a working party, described it as "a perfect shower of shell." The 6th Vermont, just back from picket duty, was being paid when the guns opened up, and "the way we skedaddled was not slow, I tell you," Vermonter Horton Keith admitted in a letter home.

Despite the panicked running, the artillery play caused little damage. One man was sitting when a solid shot hit the ground under him, lifting him several feet in the air but not hurting him. When Moody began firing, however, he came under fire from Capt. Thaddeus P. Mott's 3rd New York Light Artillery, which was posted between Smith's and Slocum's positions. After a couple of hours Mott's fire caused Moody and Brown to fall back.[18]

Meanwhile, the Southern command structure was breaking down. Jones's actions showed initiative. But an attack, even one contemplated only if the enemy showed signs of retreating, should have been cleared with Magruder. As Magruder could not be found, the next logical step was to check with Lee. He had asked Lee for support for an attack, but he had not asked Lee whether the attack fitted the commanding general's plan before he gave orders to Toombs.

After Thurston's departure Jones headed back to Magruder's headquarters. Thurston rejoined him along the way. Toombs had sent the staff officer to George T. Anderson with instructions for Anderson to attack while Toombs supported him. This was the reverse of what Jones's message had instructed. It was also unfortunate, because Anderson had only the 7th and 8th Georgia ready to attack, and they faced Davidson's brigade of New York and Maine troops. Toombs, on the other hand, faced Smith's now-empty line.

Jones then met Magruder. Prince John later reported that Jones asked him if Magruder had ordered Toombs to attack Golding's farm. If Jones was accurate, however, this question makes little sense. Jones's order itself was for Toombs to move forward if the Union forces showed signs of a positive retreat. Jones thought he had seen the signs and had communicated such to Toombs. It is true that Jones had not literally ordered Toombs to attack, but the implication seems clear enough. Perhaps Jones merely meant to see if Magruder had turned a suggestion into an order.

Magruder was still under orders from Lee to hold his position, make demonstrations to determine enemy operations, and pursue if the Yankees should retire. Jones's orders to Toombs were consistent with these orders, but an attack on an occupied position was not. When Jones told Magruder about Toombs's order to Anderson, Prince John told Jones to countermand it immediately. This resolve was further strengthened by the message from Lee brought by Captain Latrobe. Lee said the Yankees were still in their lines in force and there should be no attacks south of the river unless the commanders were assured of success. Jones sent Capt. James W. Ford of his staff to Toombs with instructions to stop the attack.

Magruder had come down with indigestion, which was perhaps understandable given the pressure he had been under since the evening of the twenty-fifth. Only he and Huger had stood between three-quarters of the Union army—sixty-five thousand men or so—and Richmond. Communication with Lee on the north bank of the Chickahominy was tortuous until the morning of the twenty-eighth, after Gaines's Mill had cleared the Federals off the north bank. Even then, however, New Bridge could be commanded by Union artillery and so was of little use for the crossing of large forces. Now the whole Unionist host was on the south side of the river, and Magruder had more than eighty thousand men to contend with. If Anderson's attack failed, the Northerners might follow it up, punch a hole in the Confederate lines, and head toward Richmond with nothing in their way. Magruder "was the more anxious to have this order countermanded" because of these possibilities.

Shortly after Ford left, Stephen D. Lee, Magruder's artillery chief, reported that the attack had carried the Union works. Magruder sent a messenger to General Lee with word of the success. He must not have been quite sure of himself, though, because he sent Capt. A. G. Dickinson, his assistant adjutant general, to find out what the situation really was. Magruder also headed in that direction.

Before Prince John got to Garnett's farm he met Dickinson, who was on his way back. The aide had the true, sad tale. Dickinson had met Anderson as the latter was withdrawing his men from their advanced positions. Anderson came from Georgia, as did his men. The thirty-eight-year-old Mexican War veteran had been a cavalry officer in the Regular Army despite not attending West Point. He switched to infantry after Georgia seceded and commanded the 11th Georgia and then the brigade. Anderson had moved out with the 7th and 8th Georgia as soon as he received the order to attack from Toombs. The two regiments advanced toward the woods containing the Unionists. The 49th Pennsylvania of Hancock's brigade, as well as the 33rd New York and a detachment of the 77th New York from Davidson's brigade, were on picket duty there, supported by a section of Mott's battery. The 49th Pennsylvania also had two more of the coffee-mill guns. Only about a hundred Pennsylvanians manned the picket line, and they were forced back through several positions by the possibility of flanking maneuvers. One of them, Joe Robbins, must have been a little slow getting away, because some rebels were close enough to yell a surrender demand. Robbins yelled back, "Surrender hell!" The potential captors warned him that they would shoot, and Robbins told them, "Shoot and be damned." They did, but missed. A private in the 77th New York, John Ham, was not as lucky. He had sworn never to retreat before the rebels. Among the few pickets from his regiment defending an advanced redoubt, Ham stood

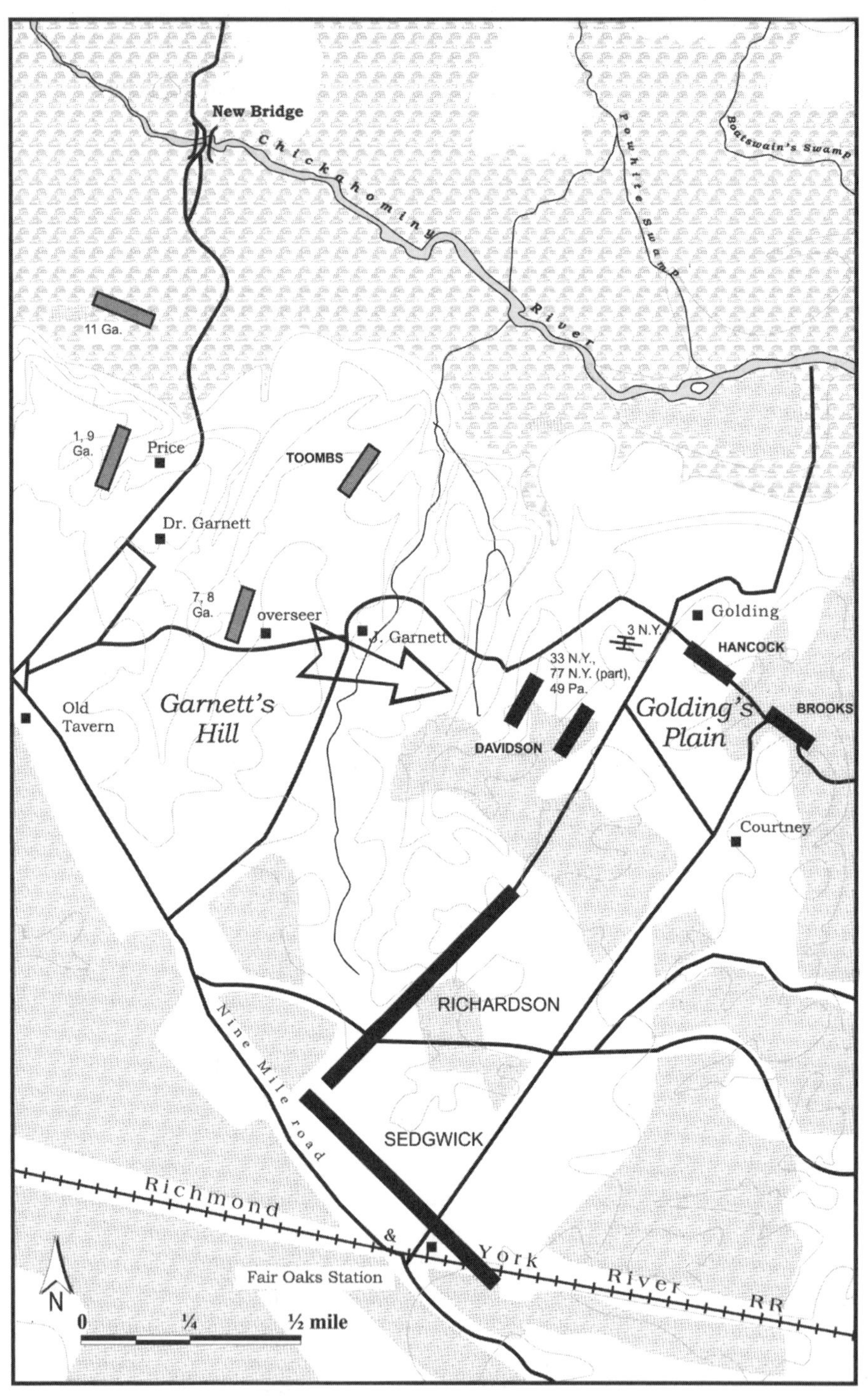

Garnett's or Golding's Farm, June 28, 1862

alone, continuing to load and fire as the Confederates charged. Ham's body was found later riddled with bayonet wounds and bullet holes—a mark of the rebels' "savage brutality" according to one of his mates.

Finally, noticing the Confederate main body coming into view, Capt. James D. Campbell, in command of the pickets, ordered a volley, and the artillery fired grape and canister as well. A bullet struck down Col. L. M. Lamar of the 8th Georgia, who was seriously wounded and captured. Several other field officers of that regiment, which was leading the attack, were also captured. Anderson, seeing the possibility of breaking through the Union line, called on Toombs for support two or three times. Before any support could come, however, Captain Ford arrived with the countermanding order, and the Georgians retired from the field. A detachment from the 49th New York, to the south of the action, got "the satisfaction of soon seeing them run."

Anderson's regiments suffered large losses in what must have been a short engagement, variously called Garnett's or Golding's Farm. The 8th Georgia reported 14 killed, 68 wounded, 6 missing, and 17 taken prisoner—including one officer killed, five wounded, and three captured. The 7th Georgia's casualties included 7 men killed, 62 wounded, and 8 missing. The Confederates thus suffered 182 casualties out of approximately 1,300 men. The only official Union losses were in the 49th Pennsylvania's picket detachments, variously reported as 2 or 3 killed, 2 wounded, and 2 missing. The Federals could not have had more than 500 men engaged. Captain George O. Dawson of the 8th Georgia reported that the attack started about 3:30, and Franklin remembered the engagement beginning in the middle of the afternoon. But most other reports indicate the action as taking place in the late morning.[19]

Magruder had to send another message to Lee informing the army commander of the true situation—which was, as one Southerner put it, "one of the very few instances in which we have failed to accomplish what we have undertaken to do." Lee, no doubt tired of the whole matter, told Magruder to secure a report from Toombs and forward it to the secretary of war. Toombs evidently never made that report. He did, however, tell Confederate vice president Alexander Stephens that the attack was ordered by Magruder and said, "That too [the order] I think he sought to put on D. R. Jones." This is probably evidence of Toombs's animosity toward Magruder, whom he had called an "old ass," and West Pointers in general. Jones certainly was responsible for the attack. Toombs did not have to order Anderson in—he was to go in himself, and it would have been better for the Confederates if he had—but Jones had precipitated this "ill-advised action."

Magruder's lines were quiet the rest of the day, and that night he received a message from Lee to maintain vigilance, have his men sleep on their arms, and be prepared for anything. Pendleton, who had passed a confidential message from Jefferson Davis to Lee, delivered this note on his return trip.

Magruder passed the instructions along to Huger and stayed up all that night making sure they were executed. Huger's lines had been quiet all day, although pickets could hear the sound of Union wagons moving that night. Brigadier General John G. Walker's brigade, just arrived from the Drewry's Bluff defenses south of the James River, crossed to the north bank of the Chickahominy in response to an order of the night before—perhaps to have some fresh troops available to Lee on that side of the river. Along the lines, men were worried that McClellan would move on Richmond.[20]

On the other side of the lines, however, preparations were being made for a move in the opposite direction. Richardson's division struck its tents, packed its wagons, and sent them to Savage Station. After dark most of Meagher's brigade followed the wagons to Savage Station, reaching it at about 2 A.M. and getting a couple hours' rest before moving on to Meadow Station, one mile east. The 69th New York stayed on picket duty at Fair Oaks Station. At about 8:30 P.M. the 15th Massachusetts, of the brigade in Sedgwick's division temporarily commanded by Col. Alfred Sully of the 1st Minnesota, moved to Savage Station, where it camped for the night. It did so "with sad hearts, not knowing the plans of our 'little George,' and, though hopeful still, fearing misfortune." The rest of II Corps remained in position all day. Heintzelman's III Corps did the same. His men struck their tents around 10 P.M. in preparation for movement. Carr's brigade in Hooker's division relieved Grover's brigade of picket duty around 4 P.M.

This does not mean that the camps were quiet, however. Hospitals at the front were closed, and the sick and wounded were moved to Savage Station. They asked Rev. J. J. Marks, in charge of the hospital, "Doctor, we are not to be left here, are we?" All extra clothes and supplies were sent to the rear, along with all the rations and ammunition that could be moved. Anything that could not be taken was destroyed. Others continued to work on fortifications that would no longer be used. Some of Sedgwick's men built traverses inside the works until the middle of the afternoon. A group of men from the 101st New York engaged in the same work just half an hour after returning from picket duty.[21]

Rumors flew through the camps about stores being burned at White House Landing, Porter and everyone else retreating, the army advancing on Richmond, and so forth. One private wrote in his diary that he did not believe any of the bad rumors. However, they must have taken on weight after a train loaded with five hundred wounded soldiers headed cautiously toward the White House. It returned after going only three or four miles—far enough for the engineer to see Confederates on the opposite side of the river. Other people began to worry about what the rebels could see. Captain John D. Frank's Battery G, 1st New York Light Artillery, trained its guns on a Southerner in a tree a mile away. The third shot hit the tree, and the scout was carried away in the blast.

Some Federals remained optimistic. Major Paul J. Revere of the 20th Massachusetts, grandson of the Revolutionary War hero, wrote home: "The army is in as good condition as it ever has been, full of confidence, and should it become necessary to move to the left to James River will still present a determined front to the enemy." Others shared the opinion of Theodore Dodge of the 101st New York, who wrote, "I suppose it is for the best." But many of the men were depressed when the truth came. A soldier in Sedgwick's division wrote in his diary, "*What sad news!! Commenced retreat!!!*" Another called it "*Blue Saturday*" and said, "This a day never to be forgotten." A third, watching the artillery leave, noted, "This circumstance with the reports we hear makes things look bad to us."[22]

That night McClellan ordered Sumner, Heintzelman, and Smith to fall back to an interior line of fortifications covering Savage Station. Thomas Osborn, commander of Battery D, 1st New York Light Artillery, which was covering the III Corps retreat, was told that if a wagon blocked the road and the Confederates should attack he was to do anything—including blowing up the wagon or a whole train, men, horses and all—to keep the road clear. Some of the artillery did not reach Savage Station until the next morning. Birney's train of forty-two wagons left its camp around 9 P.M. and crossed White Oak Swamp at daylight on the twenty-ninth, moving only about eight miles during that period. Smith received the order to move after waiting "in a terrible anxiety" all night. He wrote later: "To be on the march and to know there was an intelligence guiding us that our resistance might be made effective, and that it was not a disorderly retreat was so exhilarating that fatigue was forgotten"—which is impressive, since Smith had not slept since the night of the twenty-fourth. Others were not so impressed. One diarist wrote, "It now becomes apparent that it is a regular skaddadle," and added that confidence in McClellan was "a little shaky."

The men also worried because they could find no one on their left and knew nobody was on their right. They feared being cut off, and every tick of the clock increased those worries. Some of them did not get the order to retire until first light on the twenty-ninth. Several pickets in the 33rd New York had given up hope of escaping capture before the order finally came. All the pickets left, "hardly letting a canteen clink," while a detail from the 1st Minnesota stayed behind to destroy the remaining stockpiles of supplies. In the 19th Massachusetts, men "left the breastworks gloomy" and abandoned their knapsacks. Some of the men in Hooker's division took their knapsacks, but not until first filling them with food.

Slocum's division fell back to Savage Station to act as reserve. Some men left the front lines about 11 P.M. Others waited until 1 A.M. to draw rations and begin the retreat. Naglee's men stayed where they were at Bottom's Bridge, experiencing a mostly quiet night except for a solitary blast about midnight that some did not even notice.[23]

McClellan thus kept only two brigades—Meagher's and Naglee's—covering the approaches from the north and east to the Union rear, while three corps—Sumner's, Heintzelman's, and Franklin's—covered the approaches to the west. Lee had a great opportunity; all he needed to do to take advantage of it was move his forces to the north side of the Chickahominy farther east. However, this did not happen. By evening he felt sure that McClellan was headed for the James, and he expected to cross the Chickahominy on the morning of the twenty-ninth to pursue the Unionists. Yet he did not move any units from their positions to be in better position for the pursuit. Perhaps the uselessness of Confederate maps, seen since Gaines's Mill, helped Lee decide that night marches would not be expedient. Instead he moved to Longstreet's headquarters at Dr. Gaines's house so he could get the pursuit going first thing in the morning. Two of Longstreet's engineers, Maj. R. K. Meade and Lt. Samuel R. Johnston, went across the river to reconnoiter. Lee got to bed relatively early that night, and when Brig. Gen. Jubal A. Early attempted to report to Lee at about 11 P.M. to be assigned to command, he found the army commander already in bed.[24]

McClellan had remained at Savage Station all day, and with no major conflicts that was the proper place for him. He worked to get the army's trains and supplies out of harm's way. Evacuating casualties was also a priority. The last train to make it to the White House left at about 8 A.M. with four hundred wounded on it. As many sick and wounded as could be taken were put into wagons and headed for the James, and those who could walk were told that if they could keep up with the trains, they should, or else they would be captured. Circulars went out from headquarters ordering commanders to give their men three days' rations and keep full supplies of ammunition for both infantry and artillery. All wagons that could be spared were to be sent to Savage or Orchard Station (between Fair Oaks and Savage Stations) to be loaded with food and then sent to White Oak Swamp. It is no wonder that McCall's division, marching in the evening, was so delayed by traffic that it didn't even come close to reaching White Oak Swamp.

Entrenching tools were to be sent with the wagons. Any nonessential supplies were to be destroyed, including unnecessary officers' baggage. Lieutenant Colonel Barton Alexander, the engineer, asked McClellan to rescind this order, saying it would seriously affect the troops' morale—in fact, it would tell them they were really running for their lives. McClellan asked Alexander if that truly was his opinion, and Alexander said it was. McClellan apparently agreed—he later did not remember anything about the order—but it was too late for some units. The sick and wounded who could not walk and for whom there was no room on any of the transports were to be left with liberal quantities of medical stores. McClellan knew they would be captured, and he wanted to make sure they would receive proper attention. Several doctors were ordered to stay with the casualties.[25]

Before the capture of Dispatch Station cut McClellan's telegraph communication with Washington, Little Mac received the answer to his 12:20 telegram to Stanton. The answer came from Lincoln, and its tone no doubt surprised McClellan, who did not know of the deletion of the last two sentences. "Save your army at all events," Lincoln began. He promised reinforcements as fast as he could get them together, and he only mildly criticized McClellan for complaining that Lincoln was not getting troops to him fast enough. The president explained that McClellan's reverse was the price to be paid for keeping the Confederates out of Washington—a highly debatable point, given the facts. He also passed along the advice of Maj. Gen. John Pope—now in command of the forces around Washington—that McClellan should fall back toward the York River instead of the James. That advice was too late and was wrong anyway. Even if Porter could have held off the Confederate assault, the rebels were in position to move to his east, cutting him off from the Pamunkey and York Rivers. The rest of the Army of the Potomac would have to cross the Chickahominy, possibly in the face of the enemy.

McClellan's last telegram before 11 A.M., when communications were cut off, let Washington know that he had no idea where he would wind up. He said he was not sure he could save his army. Lincoln, meanwhile, followed up on his promise to McClellan by telegraphing Brig. Gen. Ambrose Burnside, on the coast of North Carolina: "I think you had better go with any re-enforcements you can spare to General McClellan." McClellan also wanted Burnside to come to him. He telegraphed Brig. Gen. John A. Dix, in command at Fort Monroe, to tell Burnside to have his force ready to move to the Peninsula. Stanton wired Maj. Gen. Henry W. Halleck, commander of Union forces in the western theater: "The enemy have concentrated in such force at Richmond as to render it absolutely necessary, in the opinion of the President, for you immediately to detach 25,000 of your force, and forward it . . . to Richmond." Meanwhile, Lincoln telegraphed Dix and the navy's Goldsborough that communication with McClellan had been cut and told them to reopen communication "any way you can."

McClellan probably worked well into the night, as many elements of the army were on the move that evening. He personally told Sumner, Heintzelman, and Franklin where he wanted their corps either late on the twenty-eighth or after midnight on the twenty-ninth.[26] Thus, while the Confederates were resting, Union soldiers were marching, trying to get away from a situation that had the potential to get worse before it got better.

CHAPTER 10

"But What Do You Think? Is the Enemy in Large Force?"

JOHN MAGRUDER DID NOT sleep the night of June 28–29. Still suffering from indigestion, and perhaps also suffering somewhat from the medication given by his doctor, he was troubled by his position—just his troops and those of Benjamin Huger, fewer than twenty-four thousand men, facing the entire Union army. Lee's notes on the night of the twenty-eighth repeating commands to remain vigilant, even to the point of making the men sleep on their arms, could only have increased his anxiety. He knew that the Yankee entrenchments were occupied as late as 3:30 A.M. It must have been with great relief, then, that Prince John got word around dawn on the twenty-ninth that those entrenchments were being abandoned. Major Meade and Lieutenant Johnston, James Longstreet's engineers, had reported back from their reconnaissance, and Lee himself knew that the Yankees had begun their retreat in earnest. Chilton had been sent to tell Magruder and bring him to Lee, who by then would have formed a plan for the pursuit.

Magruder's view abruptly changed at this news, brought almost simultaneously by one of his own staff officers. If the Federals were retreating, he must attack, or at least advance on the rear guard. Riding with Chilton toward New Bridge, Magruder gave the orders to advance. Richard Griffith, a forty-eight-year-old Pennsylvania-born teacher, banker, U.S. Marshal, and Mississippi state treasurer, led his brigade of men from his adopted state down the road toward Fair Oaks Station. David Jones's division, on Griffith's left, advanced over the fields they had fought for during the last two days.[1]

Meanwhile, Joseph Kershaw had received orders from his division commander, Lafayette McLaws, to find out whether Yankees were still in front of him. Kershaw had turned forty five months before. A lawyer who fought in Mexico, Kershaw had been a delegate to the secession convention in his native South Carolina and then joined the army, becoming a brigadier in early 1862. He sent Col. John D. Kennedy's 2nd South Carolina, supported by the 8th South Carolina, toward the Union lines through the fog lying on the fields. William L. Daniel of the 2nd South Carolina remembered that the day "dawned brightly upon us, and none knew that the beautiful day of rest was to become a day of blood and death." When Kennedy reported that the Unionists were gone, McLaws ordered Kershaw to take his other three Gamecock regiments to support the 2nd in an advance on Fair Oaks.

Magruder sent notice of his intent to Lee, no doubt reasoning that he would be delayed in meeting the commanding general by ensuring that his orders were carried out. The courier, a member of Magruder's staff, found Marse Robert with Longstreet at Dr. Gaines's house and in an unusually good mood. He now knew that McClellan was retreating—Longstreet called his engineers' report "the first information we had from a reliable source." As he had not heard from either Stuart or Ewell that the Yankees were moving toward the Chickahominy, he could act on his surmise that Little Mac was headed for some forward point on the James River. Lee had a relatively good road network and his forces well in hand, and he thought the opportunity to strike McClellan a hard and perhaps fatal blow was within his grasp. As Longstreet later wrote, Lee thought the enemy's move "not practicable; that General McClellan's army was in his power and must be our prize, never to reach the new base."

When Lee received Magruder's message, he was putting finishing touches on his pursuit plan. After hearing that Magruder was set to assault the empty entrenchments, Lee gave Prince John's staff officer the message, "My compliments to General Magruder, and ask him not to hurt my young friends, Major Meade and Lieutenant Johnston, who are occupying that fort."[2]

Lee did seem to have McClellan in a tight spot. Four roads left Richmond in an easterly or southeasterly direction. The northernmost one was the Williamsburg road, which basically paralleled the Richmond and York River Railroad from the capital to Bottom's Bridge, heading almost due east. The next road to the south was the Charles City road, which turned southeasterly from the Williamsburg road between Richmond and Seven Pines and intersected with the Long Bridge road at the Glendale intersection. The third road was the Darbytown road, actually named for a family named Enroughty that lived in the area. The Enroughtys, through some past dispute about an inheritance, pronounced their name Darby but retained the old spelling. This road left Richmond and paralleled the Charles City road at a distance of a mile or two, ending at the Long Bridge road about three miles west of Glendale. The final, most southerly road was the New Market road, which followed the southeasterly course of the

Charles City and Darbytown roads about two miles west of the latter. It split into two roads near its intersection with the Kingsland road at New Market. One branch became the Long Bridge road, which collected the Darbytown and Charles City traffic on its way to the Chickahominy. The other became the James River road, or simply the River road, which skirted the western and southern sides of Malvern Hill as it paralleled the river.

Three other roads were also important to the Union army and thus to Lee. The White Oak road ran south from Bottom's Bridge across White Oak Swamp to the Long Bridge road about a mile east of Glendale. Most Union forces left around Savage Station would cross White Oak Swamp on it. The other two roads led south from the Long Bridge road. The Carter's mill road left the Long Bridge road a little more than a mile west of Glendale. It intersected with the Willis Church road (called by some the Quaker road), which headed south from Glendale itself, just north of Malvern Hill. The combined road then crossed Malvern Hill and joined with the James River road.

All these roads thus led to the same place if the traveler decided to stay west of the Chickahominy, and they described a rough rectangle. The north side was the Williamsburg road, the west and south sides were the New Market and James River roads, and the White Oak and Willis Church roads formed the east side. The key areas were the east side and the southeast corner. McClellan first needed to get his army across White Oak Swamp. If any units were caught between rebels and that tortuous watercourse, which had several fords but at most two bridges useful for crossing artillery and wagons, they could be trapped by the numerically superior Confederates. The White Oak road thus had to be kept open.

The second key point was Malvern Hill, a potentially strong defensive position. If the Confederates could establish a strong position there, McClellan's whole army could be caught between two rebel forces and forced to fight its way to either the James or Richmond. As seen by Keyes, the area around the Glendale intersection was important to both of these key points for McClellan. Southern soldiers there would control the outlet of the White Oak road and the entrance to the roads leading to Malvern Hill.

Lee's plan thus needed to aim at two objectives. First, he needed to slow the Yankees down. Second, he needed to get some substantial force to the Glendale–Malvern Hill area. He needed to slow the Northern retreat because McClellan's most advanced units (Erasmus Keyes's IV Corps) were seven miles closer to the James than the nearest Southern unit (Huger's division). Also, since most of the Confederate forces were still north of the Chickahominy, Lee needed time to get them in position. He could count on McClellan moving slowly because the Federals would be encumbered by the army's trains. Even so, if he wanted to trap McClellan's entire army—his ultimate goal—he would need to slow it enough so that some Confederate units could reach the

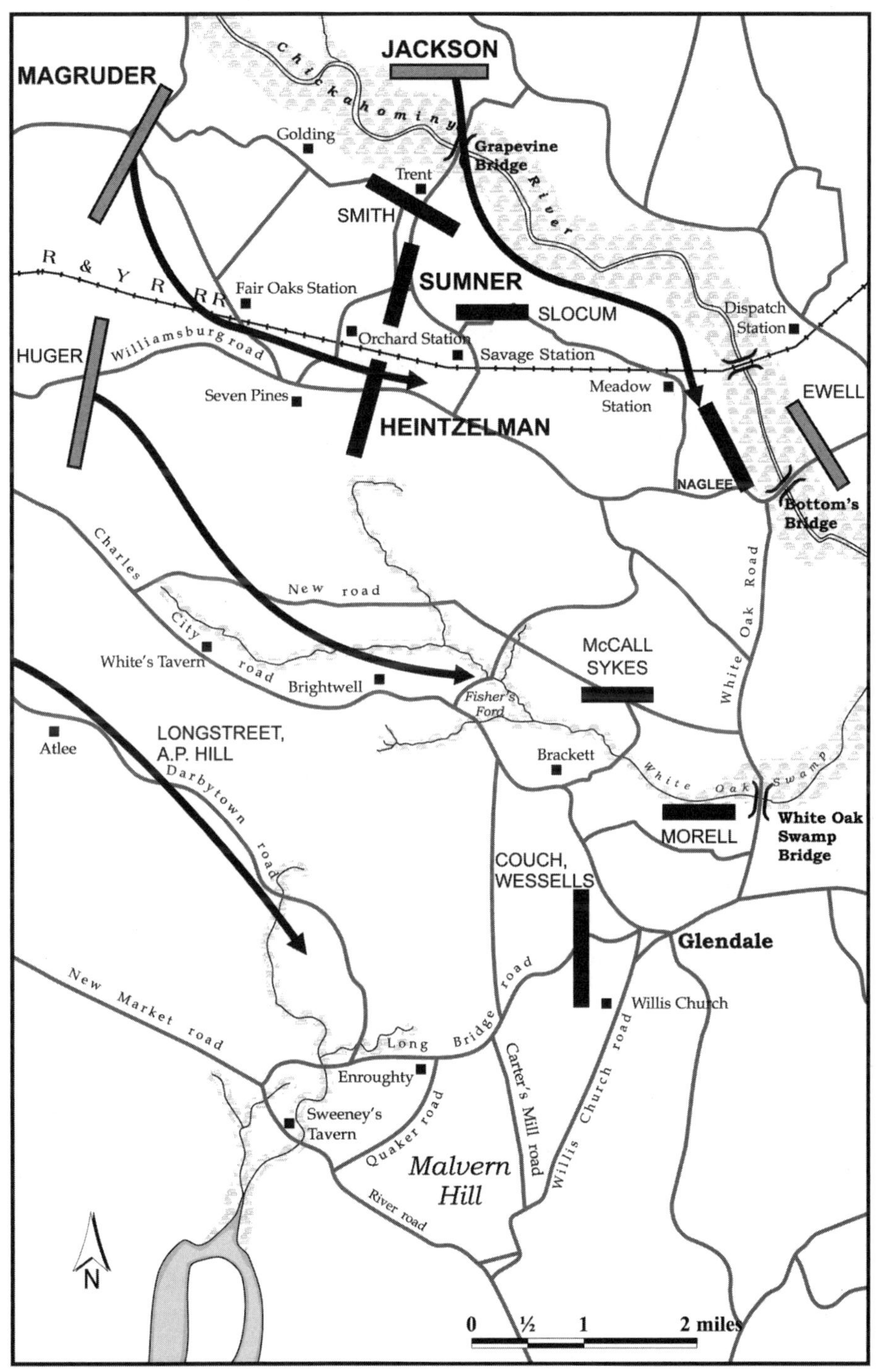

Lee's plan for June 29, 1862

area around Glendale and Malvern Hill before McClellan could occupy it in force and get his trains south of there.

Picking the Confederate units to point toward Glendale was difficult for Lee, given his two objectives. His nearest units, as little as eight miles from Glendale, were Huger's and Magruder's men. By using them, Lee could move a substantial force south of the Yankees on the twenty-ninth. However, that choice would uncover Richmond until other forces could take their place, expose all Confederate units to the possibility of flank attack as they moved south, and eliminate any quick strike at the Union rear guard (needed to slow the Northerners). The other units—Longstreet's, A. P. Hill's, D. H. Hill's, and Jackson's—were still north of the Chickahominy, some seventeen miles from Glendale via New Bridge and the Darbytown road. It would be a safe march, but those men who made it would be in no shape to attack on the twenty-ninth. The rebels north of the river would have a difficult time attacking the Union rear as well. Until Grapevine Bridge was repaired, they would have to march about eight miles to reach Savage Station, predicating a late afternoon attack on a rear guard that might have disappeared.

Lee resolved this dilemma by using Huger and Magruder to fix the Union rear guard in place. Perhaps they could slow the rest of the Army of the Potomac enough to allow his other forces to get into place for a decisive attack on the thirtieth. Huger, whose lines extended from the railroad to south of the Charles City road, was to move down the latter road, pursuing any Federals who had taken it and flanking any Northerners still on the Williamsburg road. Magruder, who had started the day between the railroad and the Chickahominy, was to move to the Williamsburg road, following any retreating Unionists and perhaps coming up in the rear of units that had turned south.[3]

It was still barely possible, of course, that McClellan would attempt to recross the Chickahominy and retreat down the Peninsula. Lee had Ewell in place at Bottom's Bridge to watch for any Union movement that way, and he thought that Stuart had the bridges south of that point covered. Ewell, with his division, could put up a determined resistance at Bottom's Bridge, but Stuart would not be able to do much with a few regiments of cavalry against McClellan's army in an attempt to cross at the lower bridges. Jackson and D. H. Hill were the closest to these areas. They could perform a dual function for Lee. First, assuming McClellan did what Lee thought, Jackson could repair Grapevine Bridge and others near there. Once across the Chickahominy he would be in perfect position to hit the right flank of any stubborn Northerners still in the Savage Station area. If all the Yankees had departed, Stonewall could follow the south bank of the river past Meadow Station, a little more than a mile east of Savage Station, from which a road would connect with the White Oak road. Jackson, with fourteen of the army's thirty-five brigades and nearly twenty-five thousand infantry, could get into position to flank any retreating Union troops if he moved fast enough. He was about eight miles from White Oak Swamp Bridge.

If McClellan did head down the Peninsula, Jackson could march to cut off the bridges on the lower Chickahominy. The two most important of these were Long Bridge, about nine miles away, and Jones's Bridge, about sixteen miles away. Jackson would have to move fast to block these bridges, but Ewell at Bottom's Bridge would have nearly a five-mile head start and would be closer to the bridges than most of the Union army. If Jackson could get enough men to the bridges to keep McClellan on the south bank of the Chickahominy, the rest of the Army of Northern Virginia could pursue from the northwest.

Lee did not tell Jackson of the second, less probable part of his mission. Instead, he told Stonewall that once Grapevine Bridge was repaired he should cross and march down the road to Savage Station, past McClellan's old headquarters at the Trent house, and then move east as best he could to keep the Chickahominy close. He was to guard against any northern thrust by Federal troops, and not to leave the road heading east (the Meadow road, paralleling the Williamsburg road north of the railroad) until he had gotten around the flank of any Yankees still in the area. Lee must have assumed that Magruder and Huger would fix in position at least part of the Union rear guard, for otherwise Jackson—even with a good march—would have a hard time turning the Army of the Potomac's right flank.

A. P. Hill's and Longstreet's divisions, which remained on the north bank of the Chickahominy, had the least dangerous but perhaps most taxing task of the hot day. They were to cross the river at New Bridge and march by the shortest route to the Darbytown road. From there they would head to the Long Bridge road, putting them in position to cut off any of McClellan's men still north of Glendale the next day. It would be a long march, at least sixteen miles, but the men had rested almost all day on the twenty-eighth. Longstreet would command both his and Hill's divisions on the march, and Old Pete's division would lead the way.

Lee's plan was a reasonable improvisation based on the information he had at the time. It was not as complex as the plan to open the fighting. No definite timetable was set. Most of his units would be within six miles of each other (the distance between Savage Station and the junction of the Darbytown and Long Bridge roads), so distance would not retard communication. Lee used all the available roads and had put his finger on the decisive area, as he sent Longstreet and A. P. Hill to the Glendale-Malvern Hill area. Marse Robert likely knew this area better than the area north of the Chickahominy through earlier travels in the region.

Porter Alexander argued that Lee's placing of the largest forces—by which he meant Jackson's fourteen brigades—on the shortest road would naturally mean that Stonewall would encounter the most difficult obstructions and defense. His alternative was to send the whole force then north of the Chickahominy on the flanking march, bring Maj. Gen. Theophilus Holmes's force from Drewry's Bluff south of the James, and place everyone near Malvern Hill to cut off McClellan's retreat. This way, Alexander said, Lee could keep all the important forces under his own eye and possibly pressure McClellan to attack to reach his new base.

Alexander had been extremely critical of Jackson's conduct during the Seven Days, and the idea of having Jackson where Lee could keep an eye on him must have appealed to the artillerist in hindsight. But there was no reason for Lee to be especially upset with Stonewall's actions on June 26 and 27, so there would be no reason for Lee to assume that Jackson needed special watching. Lee was probably more likely to spend time with Magruder and Huger if he felt the need to supervise anyone. Alexander's idea should be considered on its merits, however. Placing a larger force as far south as possible would enhance the chances of cutting the Army of the Potomac off from its new base. But adding Jackson to Longstreet's command would mean having more than forty thousand men, including artillery, trying to march down one road and cross the Chickahominy on one bridge. The head of the column might get as far in either case, but most of the men would be slowed by the immense amount of traffic. Since speed was important in getting somebody to Glendale, perhaps Alexander's suggestion is not particularly helpful.[4]

Lee also had to consider the possibility that McClellan would not help him by acting as Lee thought. In this case, some large force north and east of the Yankees could keep Little Mac from heading north around the Confederates and also help bottle him in between the Chickahominy and the rest of the Army of Northern Virginia. Jackson's command was best suited for this duty, and Lee was prudent in keeping Stonewall north and east of the Federal rear guard.

While Longstreet and A. P. Hill got their men moving, Lee rode to find Magruder. The two generals met on the Nine Mile road, and Lee explained his plan to Prince John as they made their way toward the front lines south of the Chickahominy. Magruder misunderstood one important detail: He thought Lee was sending Huger forward on the Williamsburg road instead of the Charles City road, Huger's actual route. In fact, Magruder must have misunderstood Lee twice, because once the generals and their staffs reached Fair Oaks Station, Lee repeated his instructions before leaving for Huger's headquarters.

Before Lee left Magruder, he noted the Confederate positions. Kershaw's brigade occupied the old Union entrenchments near Fair Oaks Station on the south side of the railroad. Four companies of the 2nd South Carolina led the way, and William Daniel recalled that the men "moved cautiously through the dense woods," but they encountered no Yankees in the entrenchments except a few stragglers. William Crumley, a fifteen-year-old courier serving with

Kershaw, bluffed three Federals into surrendering after he cut down the U.S. flag still flying above the works. The South Carolinians looked around the empty fortifications with great pleasure. They were "40 feet thick at the base, 20 feet on top, 15 feet high, with moats in front 15 feet deep and 20 feet wide," a rebel noted. Another wrote home, "I don't think we ever could have stormed them successfully." Other brigades came later. As Toombs's men moved toward the lines, bayonets fixed, they "looked for a dreadful time." When the Georgians found their opponents no longer there, "Some of us were not less gratified than surprised to find the enemy entirely gone." Others started singing, "Thou art gone from my gaze."[5]

More rebel units were headed toward the area in response to Magruder's earlier orders. After Lee left, Prince John began to place these units. Kershaw consolidated his brigade on the south side of the railroad. Brigadier General Paul J. Semmes's brigade of Georgians, Louisianans, and Virginians moved to Fair Oaks Station. Griffith's brigade was split in half, two regiments (possibly the 17th and 21st Mississippi) moving behind Kershaw to support him, and the other two moving alongside him on the north side of the railroad. Brigadier General Howell Cobb's Georgia brigade of Magruder's own division followed Griffith. It went in next to Griffith's regiments on the north side of the railroad.

While the rest of the Southerners were getting into position, Magruder ordered Kershaw and his own two brigades to send forward skirmishers and find out what was in their front. He must also have told Kershaw about Jackson's part in the day's activities to ensure that rebel did not fire on rebel as Jackson's men came marching from Grapevine Bridge on the road to Savage Station. That road was about two miles east of Fair Oaks Station, and uniform colors could easily be mistaken at such distances. The South Carolinian was certainly impressed with the "repeated cautions" about Stonewall. He advanced his command about a mile, with skirmishers in front, and began to receive infantry and artillery fire from his left front. Troops could also be seen about a mile away in that direction. Knowing that Jackson would be coming from there, he sent a color-bearer (who probably thought the order crazy and dangerous) to wave a regimental flag so Stonewall's men could see their fellow countrymen.[6]

The troops Kershaw saw were not Confederates, but part of the Federal rear guard. McClellan no doubt knew it would be necessary to fight Confederates around Savage Station, and he gave orders alerting his commanders to that possibility. Baldy Smith was to cover the departure of the last trains and hold the line against any movement from the Grapevine Bridge area. He moved from his position near Golding's farm to the Trent house. Elder's battery left Savage Station about 9 A.M.—the last unit of the artillery reserve to start the retreat (Carlisle's brigade had left the Courtney house about midnight). Once the trains had departed the Trent house area, Smith sent Winfield Scott Hancock's brigade to cover the approach to Savage Station from a Union-built bridge known as Sumner's Lower Bridge, not quite two miles downstream from Grapevine Bridge. One man remembered stopping every half-mile or so and forming line, "as if fearful of being attacked." John Davidson's brigade moved a little less distance to the east, going into line near the Dudley farm, again to cover a possible avenue of Confederate approach. With William Brooks's brigade remaining at the Trent house, Smith covered all the approaches to Savage Station from the north. Henry Naglee's brigade still covered the railroad bridge and Bottom's Bridge, and Thomas Meagher's brigade was in between near Meadow Station.

Samuel Heintzelman's troops were to move about a mile to their rear, and they did so slowly, in case the Confederates followed too closely behind them. Joseph Hooker's men covered the Williamsburg road and the railroad. Cuvier Grover's brigade moved into position with its right next to the railroad. Dan Sickles's brigade filed into place on Grover's left, with the Excelsiors' left near the Williamsburg road. Joseph Carr's brigade, having been relieved of picket duty by Sickles's men an hour before the retreat started, arrived at the new entrenchments first. After the rest of the division showed up, Carr moved farther east and formed the reserve. Phil Kearny moved his division back past Anderson's sawmill to positions south of the Williamsburg road, with Hiram Berry on the left, John Robinson in the center, and David Birney on the right next to the road. Some of the men still wondered about the movement. One wrote that morning, "I cannot imagine that we shall really have to retreat, and am of opinion that this movement is some ruse or other." They may also have been grumbling, because Kearny ordered them to carry 150 rounds of ammunition each, more than twice the usual allotment. Kearny's officers were wearing red patches on their caps, perhaps the first use of what later became the standard corps badge throughout the army.[7]

The Yankees thus had the approaches to Savage Station covered on the north and west-southwest sides. The men assigned to cover the gap between Heintzelman and Smith were from Edwin Sumner's II Corps. Brigadier General Israel B. Richardson had posted his division, minus Meagher's Irish Brigade, north of Fair Oaks Station. Richardson, a forty-six-year-old Vermonter, was known as "Fighting Dick" and had proved his valor in the Mexican War after graduation from West Point. He resigned in 1855 but reentered the military with the outbreak of war. That morning he pulled his men back about two miles past Orchard Station (where the 1st Minnesota detachment was waiting to destroy the forward depot) to the vicinity of the Allen farm on the north side of the railroad. William French's brigade formed the first line of battle, with Brig. Gen. John C. Caldwell's brigade of New Hampshire, New York, and Pennsylvania infantry behind it. This position covered the Meadow road.

Caldwell, twenty-nine, was a Vermont native like Richardson. However, unlike his division commander, he had no military experience before the war, having been a teacher before becoming colonel of the 11th Maine. Upon getting Richardson's order to put a regiment out on picket, Caldwell selected the 5th New Hampshire for the job. At about the same time, French noticed some buildings about three hundred yards in front of his lines, probably the Allen homestead and outbuildings. Figuring they could be useful for artillery spotters or sharpshooters, and wanting to prevent the Confederates from occupying them, French asked Richardson if he could use the buildings. The division commander checked with Sumner, who agreed, and the 53rd Pennsylvania moved into its temporary shelter. Richardson also stationed half of Capt. George W. Hazzard's eight guns from Batteries A and C, 4th U.S. Artillery, on a small hill behind the 53rd Pennsylvania's position. Apparently Richardson did not worry about really serious fighting, because he sent the batteries' other four guns and caissons to Savage Station with Capt. Rufus D. Pettit's Battery B, 1st New York Artillery.

Sumner's other division, John Sedgwick's, retreated to the area south of Richardson's men, hooking up with Grover's brigade of Hooker's division. Brigadier General William W. Burns's Pennsylvania soldiers moved to French's left. As they did so, a company commander ordered an officer to call in his pickets. The man, who had been a good officer, hesitated and said, "I am a coward and cannot do this work." He was arrested immediately. Napoleon Dana's brigade of Massachusetts, Michigan, and New York troops lined up on Burns's left. Alfred Sully took his Minnesota, Massachusetts, and New York men into a position as the division reserve.

Sedgwick, three months shy of his forty-ninth birthday, was from Connecticut. A West Pointer, he had fought the Indians and in Mexico and served as a major in the 1st U.S. Cavalry under Robert E. Lee. Like Richardson, Sedgwick put out one regiment for picket duty. Burns, an Ohioan who was twelve years younger than his superior and a West Point graduate who had served on the frontier during much of his prewar career, chose the 71st Pennsylvania. The division's two batteries, Capt. John A. Tompkins's Battery A, 1st Rhode Island Light Artillery, and Lt. Edmund Kirby's Battery I, 1st U.S. Artillery, also went into line. On his own, Dana—just turned forty, and a native of Maine who after West Point and the Mexican War became a banker in Minnesota—moved the 20th Massachusetts about six hundred yards in front of his position to hold a line of trees.[8]

The Union line thus ran from near Anderson's sawmill south of the Williamsburg road to the Allen farm north of the railroad. A gap that Heintzelman estimated to be three-quarters of a mile wide existed between Richardson's right flank and Brooks's position. A small creek ran through the unguarded area, but overall it would be relatively easy terrain for a large

Confederate force to march over—meaning that the Union rear guard had a serious weakness.

Kershaw, however, did not find it, as he was marching straight toward Hooker's division. The time was about 9 A.M., and the sunlight in the Confederates' eyes may have made it difficult for them to see the Yankees east of them. But those Yankees, particularly the two regiments sent out by the II Corps division commanders, had no such problem. Lieutenant Colonel Samuel G. Langley of the 5th New Hampshire took his regiment to a point near Fair Oaks Station. From there he saw the South Carolinians in the old Federal works—many more men in gray than he had in blue. He sent word back to Richardson, who told Langley to stay where he was. Langley did not literally obey that order. Instead, he moved his main force back into a tree line. Likewise, the 71st Pennsylvania of Burns's brigade moved forward to the brigade's old camps. The 71st was known as the "California Regiment," having been recruited in Philadelphia by California's U.S. senator, Edward D. Baker, who was subsequently killed at Ball's Bluff. It was a large regiment, consisting of fifteen companies instead of the usual ten. Lieutenant Colonel William G. Jones saw the same thing Langley had. As the Confederates advanced, Jones fell back to some trees near the Allen house. These men probably were the skirmishers whose firing Kershaw reported receiving, and the rebels responded for about half an hour after Kershaw's flag-waving signal did no good.

Tompkins's and Kirby's batteries opened fire on the rebels from their positions around Allen's farm. Tompkins used his four Parrott rifles to hit Capt. Delaware Kemper's Alexandria (Virginia) Artillery battery, which was advancing with Kershaw, while his two howitzers fired into the woods at the infantry. Kirby's six guns also aimed at the woods. A Union gunner said the Yankees' fire was "sharp and hot." However, Col. Charles H. Tompkins, the division's artillery chief, soon found that the fuses being used by the guns firing into the woods might burn short, putting Yankee troops in danger from their own artillery. He ordered those guns to cease firing. John Tompkins's four Parrotts kept up the fire, two of them moving on Sumner's order to a position on the railroad. Kemper's battery apparently did not return the fire, but Capt. Henry H. Carlton's Troup (Georgia) Artillery battery took up the fight. The Union fire was enough to convince Kershaw and McLaws that the Federals were there in some force. McLaws reported the information to Magruder. Kershaw, meanwhile, fell back a little.[9]

At about the same time that Kershaw engaged the Northerners, David Jones emerged from the area between his lines and Golding's farm (known as Labor-in-Vain Swamp). Magruder had ordered Jones to incline southward toward Fair Oaks Station to give Jackson a clear field of fire. If Jones had moved straight southeast, the day might have ended differently, for Jones would have

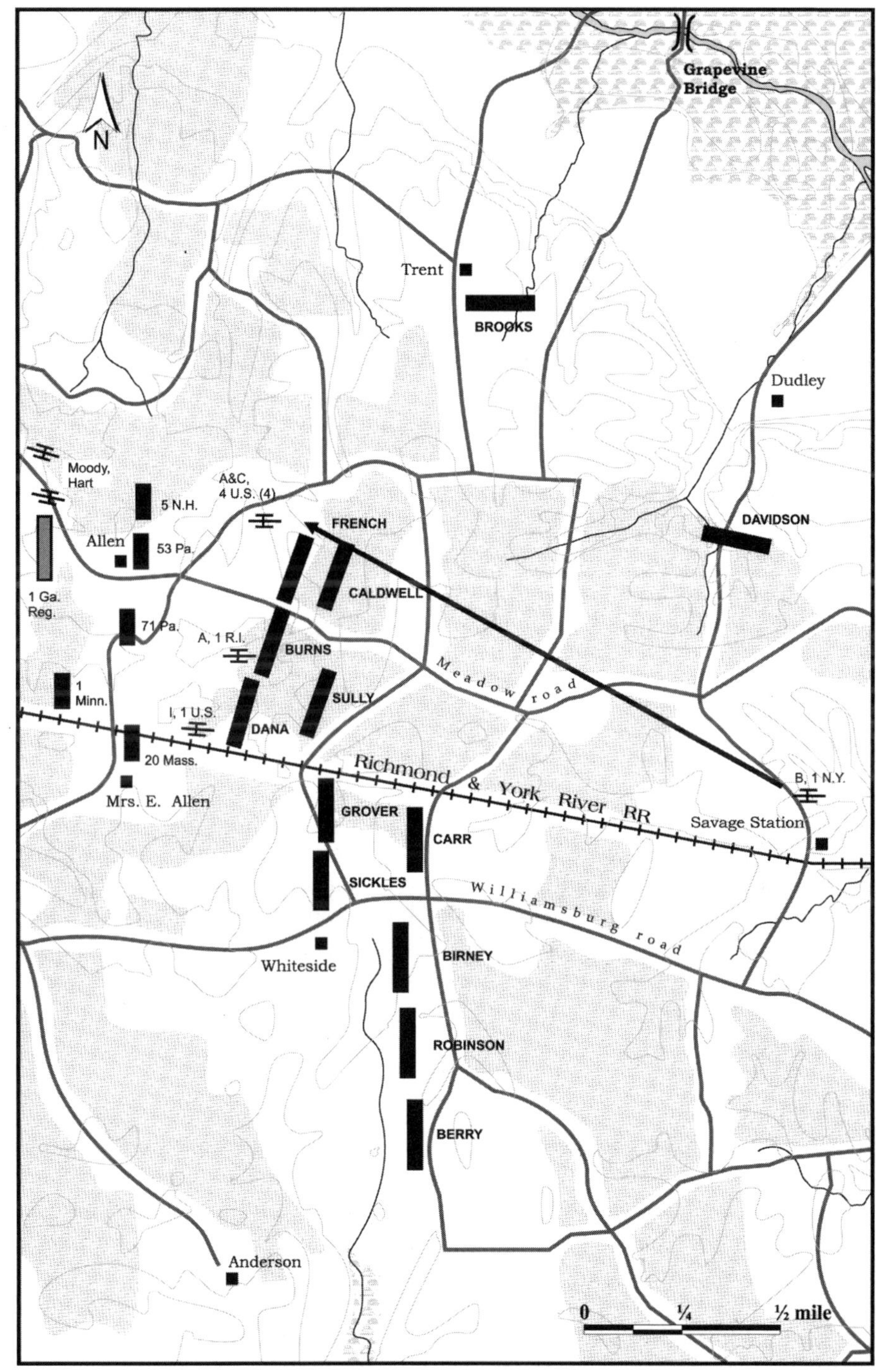

Allen's Farm, June 29, 1862

hit the gap in the Union line between Allen's farm and the Trent house. Even his small, two-brigade division could have caused great harm by hitting both Sumner's right flank and Smith's left flank. Instead, Jones made it to near Fair Oaks Station and turned east, George T. Anderson's brigade leading and Toombs on Anderson's left rear. On the way, the men picked up all sorts of abandoned food and quenched their thirst with leftover ice. Colonel W. J. Magill's 1st Georgia Regulars took the lead as skirmishers, with the 7th Georgia supporting them and the rest of the brigade in line of battle. After a short march, the Regulars met with fire from the Union skirmishers—probably the 53rd Pennsylvania, occupying the Allen buildings—and the firefight provoked a larger response from the Northern line. Hazzard's battery threw a hundred rounds into the rebel lines. Captain James F. Hart's South Carolina battery and Moody's battery added their guns to the din.

Magill's men pushed through a patch of woods into the clearing, where they saw at least three regiments from French's brigade: the 53rd Pennsylvania and two regiments Richardson had placed to support Hazzard. The Southerners moved back to the shelter of the trees, helped by a volley that one Pennsylvanian said "set them a thinking." The artillery fire kept up, however. Hazzard used up all the ammunition he had kept with him. He sent back for two caissons, and Richardson called for Pettit's battery to come to Hazzard's aid. Sumner, too, had been monitoring the situation, and he sent four of Captain Tompkins's guns to relieve Hazzard. Tompkins got there first and set up, despite being "thoroughly trotted out and shook up." Pettit's guns and Hazzard's caissons arrived shortly, and Pettit began firing while Hazzard retired to Savage Station. The Union guns "gave us a warm reception," one of the 1st Georgia Regulars remembered. Other Yankee regiments involved included the 1st Minnesota from Sully's brigade, the 63rd New York from Meagher's, the 20th Massachusetts from Dana's, and the 71st Pennsylvania and 5th New Hampshire, which must have fallen back to this position. Fire kept up for about two hours in this "brisk" fight, the Federals "letting them have the bullets just as fast as they wanted them" until 11 A.M., when "we drove them back and at once began our backward march"—each side moving away from the other.[10]

Thus ended the engagement known as Allen's Farm, sometimes called the Peach Orchard for the area of the farm in which the fighting between Anderson and French took place. It was mostly an artillery duel conducted in two different areas. There was little infantry combat except for the firing between Kershaw's men and the Union skirmishers as the latter retreated, and the fight between Magill's men and the Northerners around the Allen farm buildings. The Yankee losses were quite high in the 5th New Hampshire and 71st Pennsylvania, which suffered from Kershaw's fire and fought Magill, and the 53rd Pennsylvania, which was Magill's principal opposition. The 5th New Hampshire suffered 7 killed and 45 wounded, the 71st Pennsylvania (the California

Regiment) had a total of 96 killed or wounded, and the 53rd Pennsylvania lost 1 killed and 12 wounded. Anderson's rebel brigade lost 3 killed and 25 wounded, 22 of those casualties suffered by the 1st Georgia Regulars. Kershaw probably lost a few men, but no separate losses were reported. One man in Moody's battery was wounded, and a single man in Griffith's brigade was mortally wounded: Griffith himself. Edward Duffey of Kemper's battery dodged an incoming shell. When it exploded, a piece of it wounded Griffith in the thigh while he was sitting on his horse awaiting orders. Jefferson Davis saw Griffith being carried off. Griffith had been Davis's adjutant in the Mexican War, and the Confederate president said to Griffith, "My dear boy, I hope you are not seriously hurt." He was taken to Richmond, where he died. "All in the brigade loved him," one man wrote. Major Joseph Brent of Magruder's staff called Griffith's death "a singular dispensation," especially since about twelve thousand men were standing on and around the Williamsburg road.[11]

Meanwhile, Magruder was still hard at work. He was planning to use a new weapon: a thirty-two-pound rifled gun mounted on two rail cars and pushed by a locomotive. On the front of the car, rails protected the gun and its crew. They curved around to offer some protection on the sides as well. An opening in the front allowed the gun to fire. The rear was unprotected, but cotton bales had been piled on the cars to protect Confederate riflemen. Lee had suggested something like this shortly after taking command. He thought it could help stop McClellan's movement of heavy ordnance on the railroad. The "battery" had been constructed, but now it was being used as an offensive weapon under Lt. James E. Barry's command. The rebels called it "the Land Merrimac," and it had fired during the Allen's Farm artillery duel. Now it was to accompany the continued advance, but something was obstructing the railroad. Magruder had the obstruction removed.

Prince John also sent Maj. Henry Bryan of his staff to check on Jackson's progress, figuring that Stonewall had already crossed the Chickahominy. While he was waiting for word to come back, he received McLaws's message about the size of the Union force to his front. Another message to the same effect came from Jones at about the same time. Jones's information was gained from both his own skirmishers and a Union prisoner. The Yankees thus held the ground in front of Magruder and were obviously there in greater force than a simple rear guard. This meant two things. First, Magruder's pursuit with only his three understrength divisions would accomplish little except possibly to get those divisions chewed up. In fact, they might get chewed up anyway if the Northerners attacked—as Magruder somehow gained the impression they were doing. Second, a good bit of the Union army was north of White Oak Swamp, and a movement down the Charles City road to Glendale might trap those units. If that possibility were to be realized, then Huger's division—to whom the Charles City road had been assigned—must be moved quickly, and Magruder must again convince the Union commanders that he was ready to attack with large numbers to fix them in place.

Prince John sent Major Brent to tell Lee of the situation and request that Huger's division be ordered to reinforce him. Magruder was still under the delusion that Huger was supposed to march on the Williamsburg road, so it was natural that he ask for Huger's help as Magruder thought he should have been there anyway. Brent found Lee at Huger's headquarters near the Williamsburg road. When the commanding general arrived there, he had found Huger's men already advanced to the deserted Union lines. The 4th Georgia of Brig. Gen. Ambrose R. Wright's brigade had been on picket duty the night before with orders from Wright to report any Yankee movements. The pickets were not to talk above a whisper for fear the Unionists would hear them and attack. Later, getting reports of wagons moving, Huger ordered all pickets to push forward in the morning. Shortly after sunrise, not hearing from any of the pickets, Huger rode to the area and met Col. George P. Doles of the 4th Georgia. Doles believed that the Federals were gone, and Huger went with a company of the Georgians to the works. He found only some hospital attendants, who pointed him toward a surgeon staying with some sick soldiers. Huger told the surgeon that as long as he remained with the sick he would not be considered a prisoner of war.

Wright had not received any reports from the pickets, either, so he sent his assistant adjutant general, Capt. V. J. B. Girardy, to get them going. Girardy returned at about 8 A.M. with the news that the Northerners had retreated. At that information, Wright ordered his whole brigade after the Yankees. Instead he found Huger, who told him to take his men the one and one-half miles back to camp and let them eat breakfast. After that they were to go from the Williamsburg road to the Charles City road and move cautiously down it. Once the brigade was ready, however, Wright received orders to move down the Williamsburg road instead. He again rode to meet Huger, and after a short time was once again ordered to go to the Charles City road. If Wright's report is any indication, Magruder was not the only confused Confederate commander.

Lewis Armistead's and Robert Ransom's pickets had similar experiences. One man in the 57th Virginia said he advanced through the trees "fully expecting to have a little fun," only to discover that the enemy had departed. The pickets kept moving to the area around Seven Pines, and, after meeting a Yankee with a flag of truce, turned around and went back. Some pickets from Ransom's 26th North Carolina climbed a tree to reconnoiter. They saw nothing but a bunch of tents, and twenty minutes later were in the Federal works. After observing the devastation around Seven Pines they also went back to camp to get ready for the day's march.

When Huger got his men in motion, William Mahone led, with Armistead behind him and Wright and Ransom bringing up the rear. Lee and Huger talked briefly, then Huger went with his men. Lee stayed at Huger's headquarters, a good central point for dealing with the forces trying to come to grips with the Union rear guard and within easy communication range of Longstreet's column.

Finding Lee there, Brent gave him Magruder's message. Marse Robert was nonplussed. He thought McClellan was in full retreat and would hardly tell his rear guard to give battle anywhere near Fair Oaks Station. "Major," he asked Brent, "have you yourself seen and formed an opinion upon the number of the enemy?" Brent could only reply that he had not seen the Yankee lines. "But what do you think?" Lee pressed. "Is the enemy in large force?"

Brent, surprised at this question coming from Lee, answered, "Genl. Magruder has instructed me to say that he finds the enemy in strong force in his front." Lee seemed amused by this response, and Brent thought that Lee appreciated his loyalty to Prince John. After some consideration, Lee thought he saw a solution that would ease Magruder's mind while not hurting his plans. He told Brent he would order Huger to send two brigades to the Williamsburg road. If they were not engaged by 2 P.M. they would need to return to the Charles City road. Brent, in no hurry to deliver a message that Magruder probably considered vital, had "a very pleasant conversation" with Lee's staff.[12]

Actually, nearly two full army corps were in Magruder's path, while another division was nearby facing Jackson. If Lee had believed his subordinate, he could have ordered Magruder to go on the defensive and Huger to hurry down the Charles City road. He might have realized that a large part of the Army of the Potomac would be caught between the Chickahominy, Jackson, Magruder, and Huger. If Magruder were not attacked, he could move cautiously forward, slowing the enemy without actually attacking, ensuring that the Northerners did not escape. Another opportunity, the second that day to present itself to the Confederates, passed.

CHAPTER 11

"He Has Other Important Duty to Perform"

Almost as if playing a game of leapfrog, Yankees moving from Savage Station and the Trent house took up covering positions while other units kept marching toward the James River. In the morning there was a small disturbance south of White Oak Swamp. The IV Corps was still in position covering the Glendale crossroads. The troops were making coffee when they heard Confederate cavalry approaching. Colonel Lawrence S. Baker of the 1st North Carolina Cavalry was in charge of those horse troops not with Stuart. He and five of his companies had arrived on the twenty-eighth from North Carolina. That evening, Lee decided he might as well make use of them and told Baker to scout south of the Chickahominy. Baker moved with his five companies and the 3rd Virginia Cavalry down the Charles City road to the Long Bridge road, intending to get as far as the Willis Church road if he could. Rumor had it that the Yankees were camped near the church.

Baker ran into pickets from Col. William W. Averell's 3rd Pennsylvania Cavalry, which was providing a screen for Keyes's men. The Union pickets saw the size of the rebel force and moved back to the main position—where Innis Palmer's brigade from Couch's division was waiting with two sections of artillery. Lieutenant William Munk's two-gun section from Battery C, 1st Pennsylvania Light Artillery, was on the Long Bridge road, supported by the 2nd Rhode Island and 7th Massachusetts, as well as more cavalry. Lieutenant Edward Dougherty's section from Battery D, 1st Pennsylvania Light Artillery, was just off the road in a concealed position. One rebel wrote that it was "a question of who was more surprised, our regiment or the Yankees." But Averell's scouts had seen the approaching column. The Confederate horsemen followed the Union pickets almost into the line, when the infantry and artillery opened fire at a distance Munk said he had "carefully measured" and which Baker said was only a few yards. The cannon were loaded with case shot, then with canister, and after two rounds—"a noise by no means pleasant to listen to" according to one cavalryman—the Southerners had had enough and turned tail. Confusion followed as the rear troopers kept trying to get forward and the lead troopers tried to get to the rear. Dougherty's cannon fired a couple more rounds and then two companies from the 3rd Pennsylvania Cavalry pursued the retreating rebels for two miles, clearing the area. Baker had discovered where some Federals were, but that knowledge came at a high cost. Major Thomas N. Crumpler of the 1st North Carolina Cavalry was mortally wounded, another officer and 11 enlisted Tar Heels were wounded, and a man from the 3rd Virginia was wounded as well. Two officers and 46 enlisted men were missing and presumed captured, wounded, or killed (perhaps as many as 7 of them killed). The only reported Yankee loss was 1 killed and 5 wounded in the 3rd Pennsylvania Cavalry. Elisha Rhodes of the 2nd Rhode Island noted in his diary that the rebels "did not hit even one of our men." The whole thing was crazy enough that some people assumed Baker had charged not to get information but because he had drunk too much whiskey. This slight incident in some way became known as the skirmish on the James River road. It, or perhaps what might be lurking behind the Confederate cavalry, concerned Keyes enough that he ordered George Morell to march from his camp at the Britton farm, a mile and a half away, to support IV Corps if necessary. Some of George Sykes's men, coming from Brackett's Ford, got into line just in case.[1]

McClellan came up from his headquarters, now at the Britton farm, after the incident. Averell had ridden to headquarters and given the army commander some information. He concluded his report by saying that because the road to Richmond seemed fairly clear, the Army of the Potomac could advance upon the city. McClellan responded, "The roads will be full enough tomorrow. Averell, if any army can save this country, it will be the Army of the Potomac, and it must be saved for that purpose." Once at the front, and with the Prince de Joinville as a companion, Little Mac expressed his approval of both the fight and Keyes's dispositions. "The general seemed pleased with everything he saw," Keyes later recalled, "and the tone of confidence and approval in which he addressed me was in absolute contrast with his previous salutations to me during the campaign." He was happy enough that he told Capt. Thomas Ruffin of the 1st North Carolina Cavalry, who had been among those captured, that the charge had won his admiration.

After the skirmish, Keyes's men were ready to move to the river, but obviously other troops needed to replace them. Morell put his men in partial line of battle just west of Glendale, at a point specified by Porter, and kept them

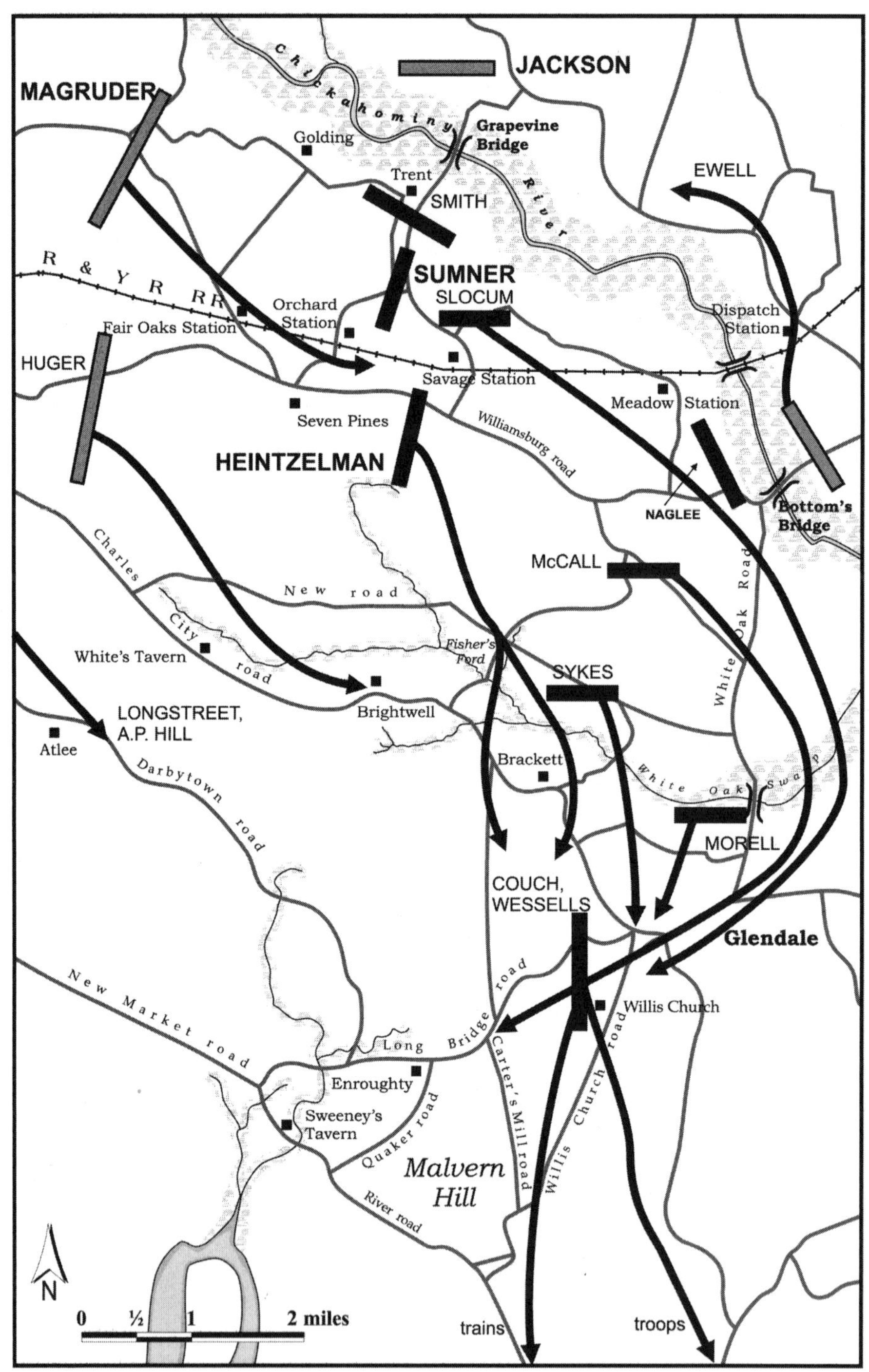

Troop movements, June 29, 1862

there all day. John Martindale reported that his men got nothing to eat but hard bread and coffee. Still, many were in good spirits. The end of their march had been back toward Richmond, and they thought McClellan was making a grand strategic move. They could hear the sounds of battle on their right, and if they had thought the movement a retreat, "panic would have resulted."

Sykes, having bivouacked at least some of his men at 2 A.M., began the march again at dawn, crossed the swamp at Brackett's Ford, and moved into position on the Charles City road on Couch's right. He also stayed in line of battle all day. John Ames of the 11th U.S. Infantry fell fast asleep under the trees, awakening to "peace and sunshine and great heat." Jonathan Hager of the 14th U.S. Infantry, after a "very refreshing" breakfast of hard crackers and swamp water, kept in the shade and rested—probably like many others.

George McCall's division, still retreating with only brief rests, did not reach White Oak Swamp until about noon. McClellan at that point ordered McCall to get his men in position to repel a Confederate attack, and McCall stayed near the swamp until 5 P.M. Some of the Pennsylvania Reserves marched almost all day to get past the swamp.

The artillery reserve made somewhat faster progress. Hays's batteries made it to the Glendale area in the morning, having moved all night. Captain Henry Benson's Battery M, 2nd U.S. Artillery, joined the 3rd Pennsylvania Cavalry and the 8th Pennsylvania Reserves of John Reynolds's brigade (commanded since Reynolds's capture by Col. Seneca G. Simmons of the 5th Pennsylvania Reserves) on picket duty along the Long Bridge road. George Getty's brigade probably also reached Glendale in the morning. Two batteries were detached from it that afternoon—Samuel Elder's battery (just arrived) for service with Keyes, and Lt. Alanson M. Randol's Battery E, 1st U.S. Artillery, for service with McCall. Ames's brigade crossed White Oak Swamp Bridge about 4 A.M. and parked around Glendale. Two of his batteries, Capt. Otto Diederichs's Battery A and Capt. John Knieriem's Battery C, 1st Battalion, New York Light Artillery, were given to McCall at about 5 P.M. Major Petherbridge's batteries made it to White Oak Swamp around noon and set up camp there. Captain Howard Carlisle's battery survived a "stampede of teamsters" about 3 A.M. to make it to White Oak Swamp around noon. At 3 P.M., Brig. Gen. Randolph Marcy ordered Carlisle's guns to guard the approaches to White Oak Swamp Bridge. By early afternoon the artillery reserve, except for those batteries detached for other service, was back together in the area between White Oak Swamp and Glendale. Carlisle's batteries unhitched their horses that night for the first time in three days.

Henry Slocum's division arrived at Savage Station at about 5 A.M., having moved only some three miles in six hours because of the mass of men, artillery, and wagons around the Trent house and roads south. Despite having little rest, the men were ordered to White Oak Swamp Bridge. The last five or six miles took several more hours because of the crowded roads, but Slocum finally arrived at 2 P.M. Around 5 P.M. he received orders to relieve Keyes's corps in its positions guarding the Long Bridge road approach to Glendale, and he reached that position about 7 P.M. after an exhausting two days. Half of Slocum's men immediately went on picket duty, a post that would not allow them much rest.[2]

When IV Corps was relieved that afternoon, McClellan ordered Keyes to march to the James River, establish communications with the navy gunboats operating there, and guard the bridge used by the River road to cross Turkey Island Creek south of Malvern Hill. The whole army would use this bridge to reach whatever place would be designated as the new base. McClellan gave Keyes the discretion to use whatever roads he wished—probably in response to information from Keyes that routes nearer the Chickahominy than the Willis Church road could be used.

Since Keyes understood the road network in the area as well as any Union officer, this was a wise move on McClellan's part. The Willis Church road was the most direct and by far the best route from Glendale to the James. It ran into the River road just north of Turkey Island Creek Bridge. Captain Peter Keenan of the 8th Pennsylvania Cavalry brought a second route to Keyes's attention. This road, which was little more than a grass-covered path, had not been used much in recent years. It was covered with vines and bushes, and fallen trees hindered movement in many places. But it roughly paralleled the Willis Church road, running north and south between one and two miles east of that road. Keyes, with the knowledge gained from the local farmer, knew that this road would lead around the eastern slopes of Malvern Hill to the area around Turkey Island Bridge. He could certainly move more quickly by two roads than one, and he did so. The trains went by the Willis Church road, guarded by the 8th Illinois Cavalry. The infantry, artillery, and 8th Pennsylvania Cavalry moved down the abandoned road, Couch leading and Wessells as rear guard. The cavalry and artillery were spread throughout the column. Pioneers cleared the road by the light of lanterns. By the time they were done the road was passable by any sort of vehicle, and the Comte de Paris later reported that four hundred carriages, five hundred ambulances, 350 field guns, fifty siege guns, and twenty-five hundred head of cattle used it.

This was the real significance of Keyes's move. It was not that troops could move on it. Once it was cleared, the trains could use it and be at least a mile farther east, that much farther away from Confederate attack. But why was the road not more generally known? Members of the 3rd Pennsylvania Cavalry made a reconnaissance before the Seven Days. Several officers explored the region between the Chickahominy and the James and, after comparing notes, made a map of the region. Averell, the regimental commander, said, "[O]ur commander knew the country to be traversed through the seven days far better than any Confederate commander." Given the Confederates' lack of knowledge, that is faint praise. The map drawn after the reconnaissance shows the start of a road at about the right place, almost exactly one mile east of Glendale, and puts houses in the area south of where the road is shown to stop. There thus seems to have been some knowledge in the army of the road network. McClellan might be faulted less for ignorance than for not foreseeing possibilities and having the abandoned road cleared earlier. Clearing the abandoned road would be a signal that it might need to be used for a retreat. Nonetheless, it is a precaution McClellan should have taken. If the road had been used from the beginning of the retreat, all the trains and artillery could have been out of the way a day earlier, freeing the roads for combat troops.[3]

Before the trains could use any road to the James they first had to cross White Oak Swamp. To do so they were to use both bridges built on the twenty-eighth, but there is a difference of opinion as to their readiness by daylight on the twenty-ninth. Bliss, supervising the movement of the trains, wrote that only one bridge was ready and that it was not approachable. John Barnard, McClellan's chief engineer, noted only that the corduroy at the bridge over Brackett's Ford was difficult to keep in good shape. The bridge and approaches were finished (by quartermaster LeDuc no less, along with Capt. R. N. Batchelder, another quartermaster) and a couple of hours after sunrise the trains could cross in both places. Nevertheless, travel was still slow. Short movements would be followed by long halts despite Bliss's work. Trains would try to pass each other, and quartermasters fought for the right of way and threatened to shoot the teamsters. Some fights even wound up with wagons overturned. One quartermaster called it "the grandest 'skedaddling' ever I saw." Bliss was so frustrated with the teamsters that he secured troopers from the 6th Pennsylvania Cavalry to enforce discipline at the points of their lances. Some of the trains did not cross White Oak Swamp until late afternoon, but they all eventually made it.

McClellan spent the day "examining the ground, directing the posting of troops, and securing the uninterrupted movement of the trains." He believed that the most important aspect of the day was to look to the safety of the trains by keeping troops positioned to protect them and picking their final destination. After establishing his headquarters at the Britton farm early that morning, McClellan was able to get only a couple of hours' sleep at the most as he and his staff had made the move around 2 A.M. Although he had slept very little during the previous five days, he could still be pleasant, even to his enemies. McClellan stopped during the day's exertions to rest on the veranda of a house. The lady of the house came out to complain to him. His men were eating her cherries, she exclaimed. McClellan smiled at the woman and ordered the "pillage" stopped. He also found time to write to John Dix at Fort

Monroe that he hoped to be at the James by that night. Venting his anger, he wrote, "May God forgive the men who have caused the loss this army has experienced. . . . I for one can never forget nor forgive the selfish men who have caused the lives of so many gallant men to be sacrificed. . . . If we get through this it will be better for you to keep this to yourself as confidential—if I lose my life make such use of it as you deem best."[4]

His work certainly was important, but he could have left it to subordinates. In fact, he had entrusted one important aspect to his engineer, Barton Alexander. On the afternoon of the twenty-eighth, Barnard, acting on McClellan's orders, told Alexander to take Lts. Cyrus B. Comstock and Francis U. Farquhar to the James River to find a suitable place for the army's new base. Alexander and Comstock left Savage Station about midnight and (after stopping to confer with Brig. Gen. Daniel P. Woodbury, the engineer brigade commander, near White Oak Swamp Bridge) moved to Keyes's headquarters. There they picked up a detachment of the 2nd U.S. Dragoons under Maj. Alfred Pleasonton as their escort. Alexander then heard the James River road skirmish and tried to get some roads cut through the woods so that troops could move more easily. He failed in that and then returned to McClellan for some reason. After sketching his view of the road structure for the army commander, he again left headquarters around noon, reaching Carter's Landing at the Shirley plantation on the James—the original home of Robert E. Lee's mother—around 5 P.M. He procured a boat and went to confer with navy officers near that point, returning around 7 P.M. to report in writing to McClellan. After that, Alexander got Commodore John Rodgers of the *Galena* to send supplies and transports for the wounded as far as Harrison's Landing, three miles east of Shirley. Rodgers thought it would be impossible to keep the supply boats safe that far up the river and said he preferred that the new base be at the mouth of the Chickahominy, more than fifteen miles downstream. Alexander did not like this idea very much, but it was too late to reconnoiter, so he stayed at Shirley that night. Perhaps McClellan selected positions and posted units himself because his engineers had not returned with detailed information.

Little Mac also left one other important duty to his subordinates: the management of the rear guard. McClellan had ordered Edwin Sumner, Samuel Heintzelman, and Baldy Smith (through William Franklin) to fall back to predetermined positions, hold those positions until dark, and then cross White Oak Swamp. However, he left no one specifically in charge of the overall force. This has been described as a deliberate move. Perhaps it was, for McClellan had little confidence in Sumner, who was the senior corps commander. At sixty-five, Sumner was the oldest corps commander on either side during the war and almost thirty years older than McClellan. Born in Boston, he joined the regular army at age twenty and never left the service, spending time in the dragoons and cavalry and distinguishing himself in Mexico. When war broke out, Sumner became one of three brigadier generals in the Regular Army. Called "Bull Head" after a musket ball supposedly bounced off his head, Sumner was known as a straight-ahead fighter with little fear and not much more judgment. Earlier in the month, McClellan had written his wife that he feared being forced to give up command of the army because "Sumner would ruin things in about two days." However, by neither staying at Savage Station nor placing someone in command there, McClellan set up the real possibility of confusion among several independent commanders who needed to work closely together to prevent a disaster.[5]

In fact, the seeds of disaster had already been sown with the gap in the Union lines. Fortunately for the Yankees, no Confederate force took advantage of it. Sumner, it seems, did not know of the gap because he was "occupied . . . with the desire to get at it again with Magruder, who had assailed his front; so reluctant was he to seem to give an inch to the enemy." Baldy Smith knew of the gap, but thought Sumner was supposed to fill it. Sumner, however, was nowhere to be seen, and neither was Slocum, who Smith thought was supposed to be on his right. McClellan had, in fact, ordered Slocum south of White Oak Swamp, but neither Smith nor Franklin, his corps commander, knew that. Franklin came by shortly and a cavalry reconnaissance revealed the problem, in addition to finding some stray parties of rebels already in the gap. The two generals rode back to Savage Station seeking word of Slocum and found only the 15th Massachusetts there and Thomas Meagher's II Corps brigade close by.

As Smith later put it, "Here was a muddle." Not only could any Confederate force on the south bank of the Chickahominy that found the gap exploit it, but Jackson's men (or any other large force) crossing at Grapevine Bridge could also flank Smith at their leisure. Franklin ordered Smith to move to Savage Station while he attempted to get Sumner to fall back. Franklin wrote a note telling Sumner that Smith's division was exposed and in great danger, and asked that Sumner fall back to support him. Sumner responded that he could not do so immediately, as he was engaged, but that he would as soon as he could. Smith remembered, "To any appeal for aid he [Sumner] was prompt to respond," and sure enough, II Corps soon could be seen marching toward the station. Israel Richardson moved on a road he had cut through the woods, halting on some hills east of Savage Station, and John Sedgwick relocated to some high ground south of it. His men moved at the double-quick and threw away everything they did not need so as to reduce their suffering on that hot day. Some on the march were overcome by the heat and fell by the roadside, where they were taken prisoner later in the day. Napoleon Dana sent the 42nd New York about a thousand yards to the front into the woods to observe any Confederate moves.

Franklin may have laid it on a bit thick in his appeal, for Sumner reported that he received information that a large body of Confederates was crossing the river and moving on him. Heintzelman also reported receiving this information, perhaps first from Lt. Col. Caspar Trepp of Berdan's Sharpshooters, who was supposed to be with Smith's division and was falling back because cavalry had told him that rebels were in possession of the Trent house. The III Corps commander did not know where Smith was at the time, but he later saw the division show up at Savage Station. He subsequently met with Franklin and Smith, who told him of their situation and of rebels crossing at Grapevine Bridge. Heintzelman rode to see Sumner and found the latter's men coming through III Corps's lines. Sumner told Heintzelman he was falling back to Savage Station and asked Heintzelman to help him decide on the exact place. Since Sumner's withdrawal uncovered Heintzelman's right flank, III Corps was also to move back. Phil Kearny, on the left of the line, was to move back as soon as II Corps cleared the area, followed by Joseph Hooker's division.[6]

Then came a moment of confusion that resulted from the fact that no one was in charge. Sumner must have thought he was, for he ordered Heintzelman to guard the Williamsburg road. In fact, Sumner later said that he and Heintzelman had "a distinct understanding" on the matter. Heintzelman, however, did not understand things that way. He found Sumner and, according to his own report, "learned that the course of action had been determined on." Heintzelman nevertheless determined his own course of action. First he ordered all the excess supplies, ammunition, and railroad cars remaining near him to be fired. Lt. Henry Norton of his staff and some cavalry carried out those instructions. Then, noting that the area around Savage Station was jammed with more men than he thought could be brought into action easily, Heintzelman decided not to add to the mess. Remembering a road that led to Brackett's Ford (by which some of Kearny's men and artillery had already traveled) pointed out earlier by one of McClellan's aides, Heintzelman sent his whole corps down it. Only two batteries, Thomas Osborn's Battery D, 1st New York Light Artillery, and Lt. Joseph E. Nairn's 4th New York Light Artillery battery, stayed behind to help Smith, who had sent his own artillery to White Oak Swamp. They stayed even though Heintzelman was not thrilled about the prospect of having his batteries hurt while fighting for other generals. Kearny, retiring first, left the 20th Indiana of Robinson's brigade and Capt. James Thompson's Battery G, 2nd U.S. Artillery, in the works west of the road to White Oak Swamp and south of the Williamsburg road to slow down any pursuit. When Robert Everett, the assistant surgeon of the 5th Michigan in Hiram Berry's brigade, went to saddle his horse, it kicked him in the leg, numbing it. A soldier helped him onto the horse so he would not be captured.

Heintzelman was wrong in part of his analysis. His position was far enough from Savage Station that congestion would not have been a problem. He was not needed for defense, but he might have been in position to launch a flank attack on Magruder if he had stayed. Even with two aggressive division commanders, however, Heintzelman may not have launched that attack. And Heintzelman was correct in saying that if he had been forced by a retreat after a battle to use the same roads as Sumner and Smith, losses would have been far greater than they were.[7]

By 2 P.M., Sumner had made it back to his new positions, leaving Savage Station itself uncovered. That hastened the process of destroying or abandoning all supplies that could not be taken on the retreat, which had started the day before. The 1st Minnesota detachment at Orchard Station piled up sugar, coffee, salt, and dried apples, poured vinegar and whiskey over the pile, and shoved everything onto the railroad before the Confederates forced the detachment's withdrawal. Major Brent of Magruder's staff saw Union camps near Fair Oaks Station with commissary stores piled in three or more tiers lining both sides of the railroad. Tents were filled with bedding materials and even furniture. Trunks and camp chests were abundant, but no ammunition or guns could be found.

Those were farther east at Savage Station, the main supply depot near the army and also the location of the main Union field hospital. The 15th Massachusetts, sent to Savage Station the night before, had begun the work of destruction there at about 9 A.M. The troops worked all day in the hot sun and threw all sorts of supplies into the fires. A VI Corps officer recalled that "fires and explosions were the order of the day." He saw a pile of burning hardtack that he thought was enough "to feed a province of starving Russians for days." Other people who saw this particular pile thought it was as big as a forty-foot barn, or as long as a city block and high as a two-story house, or, according to a Bostonian, comparable to Faneuil Hall. An estimated one million rounds of ammunition was burned. The army also reportedly destroyed millions of dollars worth of property. An artilleryman wrote that the explosions of the burning ammunition reminded him of an artillery duel. Boxes of rifles were smashed and shells and cartridges were thrown into wells and pools of water. Coffee and sugar were knee-deep in some places. Whiskey from broken barrels "run down the hill like a river," one man said. Another wrote that while some soldiers were smashing in whiskey barrels, others were drinking the contents from pools on the ground. Josiah Favill of the 57th New York thought the fire was magnificent, but it was "a sad sight" to witness the destruction of so much material. J. J. Marks called the sight "altogether unearthly and demoniac." Walter Eames of the 15th Massachusetts told his wife, "It was an awful waste but better that than to have it fall into the hands of the enemy."

Not all hospital stores and clothing were burned. A VI Corps surgeon arriving with Smith's division saw open boxes of clothing and shoes, with men taking what they wanted. Even with that, however, the surgeon noted that when the Army of the Potomac returned to the Peninsula two years later, it found residents who wore clothes and shoes they had saved from Savage Station. What the civilians did not keep for themselves they sold in Richmond or someplace else. An officer in Kearny's division saw a pile of knapsacks, perhaps those of a whole regiment, burning. Hunks of leather cut to pieces by axes were lying everywhere, as were all sorts of clothes. On the railroad, a twenty-five-car train sat blazing away. The explosion of that locomotive's boiler, or perhaps that of another train, was particularly noteworthy.[8]

Another train contained anywhere from four to seventeen carloads of ammunition that had been sent from White House Landing and unloaded. The material was put back on the cars and the train was sent on. Officers in Richard Ewell's division east of the Chickahominy near Bottom's Bridge had been watching columns of Unionists marching south all day while their men were tearing up the railroad. Then an officer reading from the Bible looked up to see a train, the locomotive with steam up and several cars attached, near Savage Station. Ewell, Isaac Trimble, and others got their field glasses out, but the Yankees cut down a tree so they could not see what was happening. In half an hour the tree was removed and the train came roaring down the tracks at top speed. The cars were on fire, and explosions rocked them. Exploding shells went everywhere. Most of the men in the group stampeded, either because they forgot that the bridge had been burned or because they feared that the train would jump the river at such a speed. Campbell Brown told the men around him to run for it.

The train had no chance of crossing the river, and it plunged off the end of the bridge into the river, hissing, roaring, screaming, and exploding. The explosions broke windows three-quarters of a mile away and shook the ground for miles around. A mushroom cloud billowed a thousand feet high, causing a rebel artilleryman with Magruder to think that a magazine had exploded. The Federal pickets on the west side of the bridge threw themselves onto the ground, and a solid shot buried itself about ten feet from one soldier. Another man wrote that it was as if the ground had opened up underneath him. Both men and horses used to battle panicked for a bit. Some horses still hitched to an ambulance ran off with it and the wounded men inside in tow. Ewell recovered his wits first and, stating the obvious, said: "That was an ordnance train. Have the troops formed immediately, for the enemy is retreating and we will be of no further use on this side of the Chickahominy." A Federal recorded in his diary that "the Rebs did not get much of value out of that train."

Different Confederates profited to different degrees from the abandonment of the depots. One man from the 15th Virginia in Brig. Gen. Paul Semmes's brigade said that at various places he and his buddies "got everything we wanted," including food, clothes, and oilcloths. On the other hand, a man in Col. J. Thompson Brown's 1st Virginia Artillery told his wife that the rebels were able to get relatively little from the Yankee camps. One Confederate thought the destruction was a signal of demoralization in the Army of the Potomac.[9]

More demoralizing than the destruction of stores was the abandonment of some three thousand sick and wounded soldiers at the hospital. Many of the men might have died during transport, but they had a chance to live if they remained behind. That did not make the decision any easier to take. A number of doctors and nurses decided to stay with the men, but still there were scenes of parting as the various units left the area. J. J. Marks also chose to stay put. Urged to leave by one colonel, Marks had found Heintzelman and told the corps commander of the situation at Savage Station. Marks was not sure whether to stay or join the retreat, and Heintzelman said he could not advise the chaplain, adding that no orders kept him there. Deciding his duty was with the wounded, Marks stayed. Others, like Isaac and P. H. Taylor of the 1st Minnesota, stayed to help the invalids as best they could. Even Southerners pitched in—for a price. A black woman and her children saved three barrels of flour from the burning supplies, made cakes, and sold them to the wounded for twenty-five cents each.

Going back to the hospital, Marks told all who could walk that they should leave, and if they could carry their guns to take them, since they might feel better in the morning. He found some supplies, then returned to see a long line of wounded and sick taking his advice—men supporting each other or leaning on staffs, one man carried on the shoulders of two others, some fainting and then rising again. Joseph Baker of the 57th Pennsylvania saw many men moving down the road who "would not have felt able to walk two rods if the secesh had not been after them." George Barr, a surgeon with the 64th New York, told his wife that the thought of being taken prisoner "struck horror and dismay" into the wounded and sick and motivated them "to exertions which no other circumstance would have compelled them to make."

Marks witnessed fathers leaving sons and friends taking leave of friends, neither group expecting to see the other again. Then the invalids realized they were being left. One man yelled, "O my God! Is this the reward I deserve for all the sacrifices I have made, the battles I have fought, and the agony I have endured from my wounds." Others cried and fainted, and still more drew on every ounce of strength they had to attempt their escape. One surgeon estimated that two thousand Yankees left the hospital of the five thousand who had been there the night before.[10]

Their escape window was closing, though, because Magruder would attack again. However, the road to that attack was long. Prince John was waiting for his officers to return with information about Benjamin Huger and Stonewall

Jackson. Besides asking Lee for help, Magruder sent directly to Huger for two brigades. The South Carolinian responded by ordering Ambrose Wright and Robert Ransom from the Charles City road back to the Williamsburg road. After going about two miles, Wright put his men in reverse yet again, stopping in the old Federal entrenchments near the French house on the Oak Grove battlefield. Ransom, who had just begun marching, moved up to Seven Pines.

Magruder met Huger as the latter was coming up with Ransom's brigade. Huger, probably frustrated with the day's events and skeptical of Magruder's reports, may have said something to that effect, and Prince John insisted that the enemy was about to attack him. Could Huger form into line of battle to help him? The left should be on the railroad and the right at Seven Pines. Huger agreed and began to get Ransom's brigade into position.

By this time, Magruder had heard from Jackson. Major Bryan of his staff returned about noon with Capt. J. K. Boswell, Stonewall's chief engineer, and the news that Jackson would have Grapevine Bridge finished in two hours. At the same time, Bryan told Magruder that only about three companies of Jackson's men at most had crossed the river so far. If any sort of coordinated attack were to occur, Magruder would have to wait for Jackson.[11]

Jackson was repairing not one bridge but two. The original Grapevine Bridge had been built by Sumner, along with another bridge farther down the Chickahominy. These bridges, for all intents and purposes, had been destroyed by rising water around the time of the battle of Seven Pines. Grapevine Bridge was repaired. Another, called Alexander's Bridge, was constructed by the engineers about three hundred or four hundred yards above Grapevine Bridge. The Yankees destroyed both, along with all the other bridges in that area of the Chickahominy, when Porter crossed after Gaines's Mill. While almost all the available evidence points to the reconstruction of Grapevine Bridge, Jackson's efforts most likely were directed toward both bridges. With twenty thousand infantry plus artillery and wagons, Jackson could not have expected one bridge to handle the traffic. With another one so close at hand, and a better one at that judging by the evidence, it only makes sense he would work to repair both. Alexander's Bridge was deemed fit by Union engineer Barnard for use by all arms, whereas Grapevine Bridge was to be used by all arms only in an emergency. If this was the case after weeks of intermittent Yankee effort, making Grapevine Bridge suitable for heavy traffic in a few hours would be impossible unless the Federals were worse at destroying things than they were building them.

Brigadier General Wade Hampton, who took command of Fulkerson's brigade in Jackson's division, remembered that a lieutenant and not more than twenty men repaired one bridge that morning. It may be assumed that this was Grapevine Bridge and the major effort was directed at Alexander's Bridge. For some reason never to be fathomed, Jackson assigned this task to Major Dabney, who "was not so good a builder as he was a preacher." One explanation is that no engineers were around, but Captain Boswell was close enough to be sent to Magruder later that day. No other explanation makes any sense. Dabney tried—and failed. He called the men he was using "shilly-shally."

Not so shilly-shally were the people Jackson called on next. Captain C. R. Mason, who ranked as an acting quartermaster but was actually a railroad contractor, was a pretty fair pioneer detachment leader for Stonewall. One report filed after the war stated that Mason and his men were at Ashland just starting breakfast when Jackson sent for them; it took three couriers before Mason would finally get his men started on what turned out to be a fifteen-mile trip. If true, this story would partially explain why Jackson was late crossing the river.

As soon as he reached Stonewall's location, Mason got to work. Jackson told Mason that engineers would give him plans for the bridge, and Mason stopped him. "Never mind pictures, General!" he said. "If you will send me men enough who will wade in the water and tote poles, I will have the bridge ready by the time the engineers can prepare pictures." Mason worked not at the Grapevine Bridge site itself, but between Grapevine Bridge and New Bridge. That site could have been either Alexander's or Woodbury's Bridge, but was most likely Alexander's. D. H. Hill's pioneer detachment, commanded by Capt. William P. Smith, worked on what he called Grapevine Bridge, but it could have been either one.

Jackson must have felt pretty good about his men's progress if he let Magruder know that he could begin crossing around 2 P.M. The slim evidence available indicates that he indeed thought he would be able to cross sometime that day. Charles Winder's brigade moved to the vicinity of the bridges so it could cross as soon as possible after they were finished. William Whiting's troops also had orders to be ready to march. Magruder took that confidence to heart. Knowing that Huger was in position and Jackson would soon arrive seemed to eliminate from Prince John's mind the possibility of a Union attack and open up the possibility of bagging at least part of the Union rear guard. He did not keep the second possibility in mind for long, though. Reports came that the Northerners were advancing. They were confirmed by a reconnaissance by Stephen D. Lee. After meeting with Huger, Magruder moved back to his own division and ordered Howell Cobb's brigade to advance about four hundred yards to the edge of a wood so it could command a field over which the Unionists would have to march. The left of Richard Griffith's brigade (now commanded by Col. William Barksdale of the 13th Mississippi) would move up in support. Then Magruder received a note from Huger stating that he was withdrawing his men for other service.[12]

Huger was acting on Lee's orders. While positioning his two brigades, Huger saw another battle line a little ahead of him. He asked who they might be and was told they were part of Lafayette McLaws's division. This force could have been either Semmes's brigade or Kershaw's brigade, as Magruder had ordered McLaws to put Kershaw in front and Semmes right behind. In either case, Huger probably figured that Magruder had lost his head by placing him directly behind another unit, and he also could see no evidence of a Federal attack—since none was occurring. Just then he received a note from Lee, which in essence reiterated Lee's earlier decision that if Huger was not needed he was to move down the Charles City road. Huger concluded he was not needed and sent the note to Magruder. Wright, waiting at the French house, was told to go to the Charles City road for the third and final time. Ransom already had his men in motion from Seven Pines down the Charles City road, having waited three hours.

Huger's movements were correct. He was following a direct order from Lee, and he was not needed on the Williamsburg road. The waste of time that resulted was not Huger's fault. Magruder, however, was still under the impression that Huger was supposed to be on the Williamsburg road, and the withdrawal of his troops must have been a severe blow, even after Major Brent returned with information regarding Lee's order to Huger. Another was soon to come. David Jones sent Magruder a message in which he informed Prince John of his position, left and in front of Cobb's brigade, and that there were plenty of Yankees in front on his right. It was no good to attack, Jones said, unless everybody did. Finally, he told Magruder that he had hoped for cooperation from Jackson, "but he sends me word that he cannot, as he has other important duty to perform."[13]

Much speculation has arisen over that "other duty." A soldier such as Jackson would naturally want to help his fellow commanders, but Stonewall's orders seem to preclude that possibility by forcing him to stay near the Chickahominy and flank the Yankees. This explanation is marred only by Lee's statement that Jackson had been ordered to support Magruder. That Lee and Jackson could be at such variance in reading the same orders seems far-fetched. Jackson would have been frustrated by not being able to get the bridges repaired and, being usually reticent, he might merely have remarked to Jones's courier that he had other important duty—to get the bridges finished. Absent evidence that Jackson indeed had other duty, this is a possibility.

Porter Alexander, with characteristic antipathy toward Jackson, says that the fact the twenty-ninth was the Sabbath was reason enough for Jackson. This canard can be dealt with by pointing out two facts. First, Jackson had fought on the Sabbath before, although he certainly did not like the idea. Second, he assigned Dabney, a minister who could be expected to perform services on Sunday if Jackson were as maniacal about it as Alexander suggests, the task of rebuilding a bridge. It might have been possible to use the ford at Grapevine Bridge, but one of Jackson's veterans recalled that the river at the time was "quite wide and too deep to wade." In any case, it is harder to get artillery through a ford than infantry, and Jackson, a gunner by training, would have wanted his guns with him in any action. Stonewall could have used New Bridge for at least part of his force, although he would have needed to ask Lee or disobey a direct order. Also, Longstreet and A. P. Hill were using New Bridge for at least part of the day.[14]

A. L. Long gave a tantalizing hint after the war by writing that Jackson, Ewell, and Stuart were to "remain in observation lest the Federals might change their line of retreat" by recrossing the Chickahominy, and Jackson was ordered in the afternoon to take over the pursuit from Magruder. However, the evidence leads to a conclusion exactly opposite of what Long says. Lee's original orders as remembered by Dabney include Jackson in the units crossing the river. But the best evidence comes in an order from Col. Robert H. Chilton to Jeb Stuart, telling the cavalry commander (in Lee's name) to watch the crossings as far as Jones's Bridge to see if the Yankees were headed that way. If so, he was to advise Jackson, who would then defend the crossings. If the Northerners were beyond any of the crossing points, Stuart was to leave a detachment to watch for any movements and cross the river himself to operate on the correct side of the Chickahominy. Jackson was to be advised of these orders.

Chilton wrote this message on the Charles City road, which indicates that it was not written first thing in the morning. It found Stuart at White House Landing. Jeb left the main body about two miles away from the burned house and took Rooney Lee, a few men, and a howitzer under Pelham's command to the landing early in the morning. A Union gunboat, the *Marblehead*, was still at the landing. While giving the cavalry commander a tour of his estate, Rooney convinced Stuart that a few sharpshooters could get the gunboat out of his hair. About seventy-five men from the 1st and 4th Virginia Cavalry and the Jeff Davis Legion advanced in pairs about forty paces apart. When some Yankees came ashore to fight the cavalrymen, Stuart decided such a waste of time and men would be pointless and ordered Pelham to fire. A couple of well-placed shots convinced those in the gunboat to leave, and the Yankees were recalled. Pelham gave chase for a while, more to worry the Federals than for any other reason.

Stuart found a gold mine at the landing, for despite Union efforts and claims, many provisions and sutler's stores had been left unharmed. Oranges and lemons, white and brown sugar, salt fish, eggs, bacon, arms, uniforms, and even hoopskirts, among other things, were found. The material left behind may even have included a pontoon train, some railroad cars, and a locomotive. John Esten Cooke, an accomplished writer, said he would not try to describe the chaos there.

Stuart's men were out of rations and, unaccustomed to such luxury, started getting carried away. Several men began to get drunk on various types of liquor the Northerners left behind, hiding the bottles in their clothing. Rooney Lee started a rumor that the Yankees had poisoned the liquor, leaving it as a trap, and that one man died in great agony after drinking it. Soon bottles of all sorts—including champagne, beer, and whiskey—flew into the air, exploding on impact. A number of men held their hands to their stomachs, bracing themselves for the inevitable.

Stuart did not move much the rest of the day. Getting rations for his men and completing the destruction the Northerners had started occupied him. He received a note from Lee sometime that morning. It might have been Chilton's message, but that is doubtful. Jeb described the note he received as coming directly from Lee. He specifically said that a later message came from Chilton, and one would expect him to be as precise as this in recording the sender of all messages. The note he mentions might also have been the one Lee sent the previous day. Stuart probably received Chilton's message later that morning or early in the afternoon. In response to it, he sent Fitzhugh Lee's 1st Virginia Cavalry to observe the river crossings and forwarded the note to Jackson. Stonewall received it around 3 P.M. He endorsed it with the comment, "Genl. Ewell will remain near Dispatch Station & myself near my present position." The note and the courier who brought it probably returned to Stuart.

This is clear and convincing evidence that Jackson saw his "other important duty" as staying north of the Chickahominy in case Stuart needed him. The question then becomes whether Lee truly meant those orders to be followed in the way Jackson followed them. Chilton's message might have been a contingency plan. Lee wanted Jackson to cross the river when he could and, if he heard from Stuart, resist the Yankees on the south (or west) bank. But that would have put Stonewall with his back to a river if the Federals came at him, not a pleasant predicament. Lee could have meant that Ewell would resist the crossing, but then why not simply say Ewell instead of Jackson? Moreover, as these orders must have been written after Jackson got his original orders of the day, why did Lee not write Jackson directly to tell him of this possible change in plan? Perhaps Lee, as an engineer, thought that it would take time to rebuild the bridges and so did not foresee a conflict. But if that were the case, his orders for the day would not have given Jackson the task they did.

No explanation here is entirely satisfactory. Lee could have received information to make him react in that way. That information and its source are unknown. However, since Lee reacted that night and later (by referring to Jackson's message to Jones as "originating in some mistake") as if he had not sent the message to Stuart, it is impossible to reconcile the orders, messages, and reports. Jackson never mentioned any orders for the twenty-ninth, merely saying that he spent the twenty-eighth and twenty-ninth burying the dead, caring for the wounded, and repairing the bridge. Blame for his actions on the twenty-ninth cannot be laid at his door. It must belong to either Lee or

Chilton—Lee for sending the order or Chilton for writing something different from what Marse Robert intended.[15]

In the end, it did not matter. Whoever worked on Alexander's Bridge did not complete it until nightfall. The original construction had taken five days on the bridge and three additional days on the approaches. Although repairing the bridge would not take as long as building it, doing so in one day was an impressive accomplishment. Jackson could have used Grapevine Bridge to put his infantry across, but it is doubtful that the reconstructed Grapevine Bridge could have handled artillery. Since the original orders contemplated Jackson resisting attacks and flanking the Northerners, artillery would be important.

The bridge could handle a few horses and riders, and Jackson crossed it with his staff sometime in the afternoon. He rode up to the Trent house, from where he could observe the lay of the land. He also inspected the recently abandoned telegraph office. According to one account he talked with Toombs; according to another he saw Magruder and Lee together. He then rode back to his troops and Winder's men went back to their camps. When Stonewall at last lay down for the night, he heard firing from the south bank. Telling his staff that everything should be ready for a dawn march, he went to sleep for what Dabney called "a short repose," probably "the best thing he could do."[16]

CHAPTER TWELVE

"Why, Those Men Are Rebels!"

By the time Stonewall Jackson crossed the Chickahominy, Magruder's units were attacking once more. Assuming that Jackson's message to Jones citing "other important duty" followed his receipt of Lee's orders from Stuart (Magruder's report carries no mention of time), Magruder could not have received Jones's message until nearly 4 P.M. Between the time of Huger's departure around 2 P.M. and the time he got Jones's message, Magruder was waiting for Jackson to appear. Brent reported that Magruder was making plans to advance. But the fortune swings of the day, and the strength of the Yankee force in front of him, probably made him decide he could not press the enemy rear guard as vigorously as Lee wanted unless he had help.

Once he got word that Jackson would not arrive, however, Magruder seemed to throw caution to the wind. Perhaps he remembered Lee's original order to press the Yankees vigorously, or perhaps he was so frustrated with the day's problems that he could not think of anything else to do. He ordered all his units to the front and told his commanders to attack any enemy who could be found, in works or in the open, no matter how many of them there were.

This order may seem suicidal, but the Yankees were cooperating. There could have been two corps and a division waiting for Magruder. But III Corps had left, II Corps was east and south of Savage Station, and Baldy Smith's division was on its way toward White Oak Swamp. After arriving at Savage Station, Smith had formed a line of battle north of Israel Richardson's division. After a couple of hours, however, someone—either William Franklin or Smith himself, most likely—decided Smith was no longer needed, since the rebels were showing no sign of attacking. Instead of remaining in position, the division followed Henry Slocum toward White Oak Swamp.

Thus, when Magruder decided to attack with 14,500 troops, he faced only Edwin Sumner's 16,000 instead of about 40,000. Joseph Kershaw once again had the honor of advancing first. He moved forward at about 3 P.M. in response to an earlier order. The South Carolinians moved past Orchard Station before their right-flank skirmishers became engaged. When they popped through the woods south of the railroad they saw the 20th Indiana and James Thompson's battery, left by Phil Kearny to slow down any Confederate pursuit of Samuel Heintzelman's corps, behind fortifications. Kershaw stopped his men under the brow of a hill and called up Capt. Del Kemper's battery. Meanwhile, he sent the 2nd and 3rd South Carolina to the south to flank the bothersome Federals.

Thompson fired on the advancing Southerners, but the Hoosiers did not. Thompson thought they did not have loaded muskets, but in reality they carried 150 cartridges each. Perhaps they held their fire because trees screened the rebels. Kemper's battery came up and opened fire on the Yankee position, finding the exact range but getting little in response. Meanwhile, the 2nd and 3rd South Carolina made a difficult approach to the fortifications, got ready to charge, and found the Northerners gone. Kearny had ordered his men to hold in position for forty-five minutes, and that is exactly what they did. The infantry followed the rest of the corps, but Thompson and his guns were almost to Savage Station before he realized he was going the wrong way. He corrected that mistake when the real fighting began.

Kershaw got moving again after Major Brent delivered Magruder's order to advance and engage any enemy troops he could find. Nevertheless, he worried about his right flank, which only went as far south as the Williamsburg road, and told Brent he would like some support. A few minutes later, Paul Semmes responded by moving two of his regiments, the 10th Georgia and 32nd Virginia, to Kershaw's right.[1]

The rebel advance was discovered in quite an unusual way. Franklin and John Sedgwick rode to the hospital at Savage Station to visit some friends around 4 P.M. with no idea what was happening. Franklin had even sent McClellan a message wondering about a withdrawal of all troops, saying, "The danger of an attack is over." Sedgwick and Franklin decided to pay a visit to Heintzelman's headquarters, which they supposed was to their left somewhere. Riding into a field, they saw some men coming out of a patch of woods north of the railroad. This must have been Cobb's brigade, but Franklin thought they were fellow Yankees, even though they were some distance from where Heintzelman should have been. Sedgwick took a closer look, pulled up, and said, "Why, those men are Rebels!" Franklin later remembered, "We then turned back in as dignified a manner as the circumstances would permit." But the rebels had seen them and trained a couple of cannon on them, marking the official opening of the battle of Savage Station.

As Franklin and Sedgwick made their somewhat dignified exit, Union signal officers reported the Confederate advance. Captain Kemper moved his men to the road and opened fire, and the rebels' railroad gun joined in. Other Yankees were surprised. One man in the 1st Minnesota said the Southerners opened up "before we were aware of their presence." Captain Thomas Osborn drew part of this fire. He and Lt. Joseph Nairn were ready to rejoin Joseph Hooker's division (as Smith, to whom they had reported earlier when Heintzelman moved to the south, had left the field), but Osborn found the way blocked by rebels. While reconnoitering, he was seen and fired upon. Sumner ordered the battery into firing position without knowing that infantry was with the rebel guns. When Osborn told him, Sumner yelled, "Where is Heintzelman? Where has he gone?" and other similar questions Osborn could not answer.

There was no time to find the answers. The nearest brigade was William Burns's, which had been facing Bottom's Bridge to repel an attack expected from that direction. Whoever posted Burns that way must not have known of Henry Naglee's brigade at the bridge and Thomas Meagher's brigade at Meadow Station. Sumner had Burns move two regiments, the 72nd and 106th Pennsylvania, back half a mile into the woods west of the station and between the railroad and the Williamsburg road. As Burns was getting his men into position, a scout told him there were many Confederates on the Williamsburg road—Semmes's men. Sitting in the woods filled with dense undergrowth, Burns's troops could hear rebel officers in front of them giving commands. As rebels could be seen north of the railroad as well, Burns saw he could be hit on three sides and sent back to Sumner for some help. Sumner told Sedgwick, back from his adventurous exit, to send the 1st Minnesota of Alfred Sully's brigade to Burns's left. It arrived, after having to dodge Southern cannon fire on its march through an open field, before the Confederate's launched an attack. One Minnesotan remembered not only the rebel fire but the Union fire as well. "They seemed hot enough to scorch us," he said of his own gunners' shells. Burns posted the 1st Minnesota in reserve about 150 yards to the rear with its left flank somewhat refused. He was still concerned about the right, however, and moved Col. DeWitt C. Baxter's 72nd Pennsylvania to cover the railroad with its right flank refused. This move, although necessary in Burns's view, created a gap in the line between the 72nd and 106th Pennsylvania.[2]

At the same time, word went back to Baldy Smith's division, now two miles from Savage Station, to return. Winfield Scott Hancock's brigade led the way, moving to the right of the road while William Brooks's men moved to the left. John Davidson had suffered from sunstroke and was forced to relinquish command to Col. Robert F. Taylor of the 33rd New York; his brigade formed the reserve. The 7th New York from John Caldwell's brigade supported the right flank, while the 81st Pennsylvania of the same brigade moved to the left flank. William French was at the rear of the line along the railroad.

Meagher's brigade was with the rest of Richardson's division by that point, having been ordered back to Savage Station around 4 P.M. It was not under Meagher's command, however. He had been placed under arrest earlier in the day for not obeying Richardson's order to rejoin the division (even though McClellan told Sumner he did not want the Irishmen moved). It may have been that the orders were confusing enough that Meagher decided the prudent course was to do nothing. Colonel Robert Nugent of the 69th New York, which had joined its brethren that morning, had taken command after Meagher's arrest, and he sent the 88th New York toward Burns's position. Richardson also wanted French to advance, but French could not be found. One

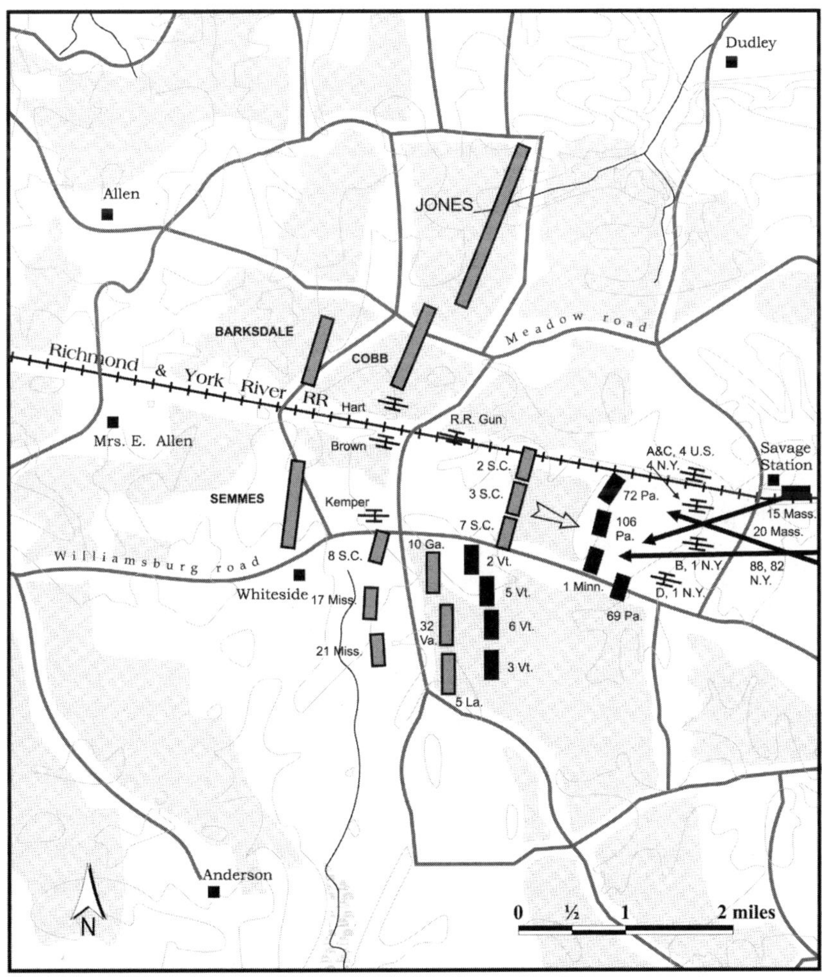

Savage Station, June 29, 1862

man wrote that French was "trying to save the surplus whiskey to keep it from falling into Rebel hands."

Batteries also went hurriedly to the front. Captain Rufus Pettit's battery was already set up near the Williamsburg road, as were Capt. George Hazzard's guns. Pettit moved to a position within three-quarters of a mile of the Confederates under their fire, and Hazzard took half his battery a little distance to the right. Captain John Tompkins's and Lt. Edmund Kirby's batteries of Sedgwick's division had marched with Baldy Smith, and they turned around when he did—"not in accordance with our wishes exactly," one gunner wrote. Tompkins put his rifled guns on Hancock's left, the "shells flying 'right smart'" around them, and his howitzers and Kirby's battery moved to Hancock's right. Nairn, Pettit, and Hazzard were on Osborn's left and right.[3]

The rebels tried to answer this massing of artillery. Kemper's battery switched targets, Kemper guiding fire from an advanced position, but the Union guns won that battle in about five minutes. Captains James Brown and James Hart came from David Jones's position to the railroad, and Hart opened up with his two Blakely rifles, but again the Yankees overpowered the Confederates. Captains John Lane and E. S. McCarthy both came under fire, but neither could answer from their disadvantageous position near the railroad. McCarthy's Richmond Howitzers tried two different positions, one just past a bridge over a railroad cut and another south of that position, but the first was given up after "a perfect hailstorm of shot and shell" met the Virginians, and the other suffered from "a murderous fire" from the right flank. Finally moved again to a position south of the Williamsburg road, McCarthy's battery fired no guns. The railroad gun opened on the Yankee reserves from the railroad cut where McCarthy had first set up, occasionally landing shells near the field hospital (and perhaps a battery set up there). This prompted a flag of truce and a note that any rebel fire into the hospital would likely hit some of their own men. Kemper's battery provided the Confederates' only effective artillery support after moving to a position on the Confederate right.[4]

The infantry action began when Kershaw moved the 8th South Carolina south of the road to provide protection for Kemper's battery and his right flank, and the whole brigade advanced. The 2nd and 3rd South Carolina, having returned to the brigade, led the charge, with the 2nd's left on the railroad. The 7th South Carolina, following immediately behind, extended the line south to the Williamsburg road. They went into the woods from a ravine, with Kershaw calling "Charge!" as soon as Union fire passed over his men's heads.

Kershaw then passed through about two hundred yards of heavy timber before getting into thick underbrush "in which it was impossible to discover either friend or foe over 20 yards," according to Col. James D. Nance of the 3rd South Carolina. Thomas Pitts described the woods as "the thickest undergrowth of bushes you ever saw. . . . [Y]ou could not see a man ten paces ahead of you and it was utterly impossible to keep anything like a line of battle." When the Gamecocks finally emerged into the open they were just thirty steps away from the Federals. That was too close for one Northerner, who threw his gun down and ran into the Southern line yelling, "I'm a prisoner, let me go to the rear." Sergeant Robert Shand of the 2nd South Carolina could not find his own company as he moved left and right through the heavy fire. He finally gave up and started firing back. Colonel D. Wyatt Aiken of the 7th South Carolina advised the men who could hear him, "Load advancing and fire at will." Private Ben Taylor of Aiken's regiment turned to the rear and yelled, "Give it to them, boys!" He was then shot in the head, and his brother Jim saw the scene in sorrow. The Taylors's captain, John Hard, put his hand on Jim's shoulder and said, "I have no consolation to offer you, except that Ben has fallen at his post; there he lies, yonder is the enemy, avenge him." Later, Captain Hard himself was hit in the hand and then in the breast. A pocket Bible saved his life by taking the bullet's blow.

Robert Shand thought it was the hottest fire he was ever in. "The bullets whistled past my ears without interruption and not singly, but in two's and three's at a time," he recalled. Pitts estimated the distance between the two forces at about twenty-five paces, while a fellow South Carolinian put it at fifteen paces and said, "You may be sure that they poured a fire into us." The grapeshot fired by Union artillery was "dreadful," according to one veteran. But the rebels pushed back the 106th Pennsylvania in the center of the Union line, wounded Burns in the face, killed Capt. Charles McGonigle of the 72nd Pennsylvania, broke the line, and reached the fence at the edge of the wood. A Confederate color-bearer waved the flag across the fence, and the Southerners prepared to continue the pursuit.[5]

A combination of things caused Kershaw to halt. One was Semmes's charge south of the Williamsburg road. Semmes was a Georgia banker and planter just turned forty-seven. He had been active in the state militia before the outbreak of war and was colonel of the 2nd Georgia before becoming a brigade commander in the spring. Semmes noticed the sound of firing moving to his right after he sent the 10th Georgia and 32nd Virginia that way. The sound would have naturally tended that way, since the Williamsburg road and the railroad both run somewhat southeasterly from Fair Oaks Station to Savage Station, but Semmes was concerned and moved forward with the 5th Louisiana to the right of the 32nd Virginia. South of the road, where Semmes was, the woods were as thick as they were north of the road. Someone spotted troops not more than forty yards ahead and could not tell who they were in the lowering sun and thick underbrush. Semmes sent Pvt. John Maddox of Company K, 5th Louisiana, to check. Probably muttering to himself, Maddox moved forward and yelled, "Who are you?" The answer came back,

"Friends." Semmes heard that and thought he had better find out just whose friends they were, so he shouted, "What regiment?" When the someone responded, "Third Vermont," Semmes yelled who he was and gave the order to fire.

The 3rd Vermont was from Brooks's brigade in Smith's division, which was supporting Burns's left flank. The 1st Minnesota had moved up when its commander on the field, Lt. Col. Stephen Miller, noticed that the Pennsylvanians' left was in danger. However, the rebels extended far enough to the south that the Minnesotans found themselves outflanked as well. They stood their ground as the Pennsylvanians to their right retreated. Miller called, "Minnesota, stand firm! Don't run, Minnesota!" But they needed help on both sides. It was, as one veteran recalled, "an extremely tense situation."

Brooks advanced his men into the woods, the 5th Vermont just south of the road and the 6th Vermont to its left. The 2nd Vermont supported the 5th, and the 3rd Vermont supported the 6th. As the 5th Vermont advanced, the 1st Minnesota's color guard heard the command "forward" and, thinking it was for them, advanced with the Vermonters. If Semmes's account is correct, he was on or near what became the Yankee left flank with the 5th Louisiana, but he was outnumbered.

The two sides struggled in the woods, with Brooks's two support regiments joining the fray. This was a brutal fight given the size of the forces. At least part of it was hand-to-hand. One Yankee tried to capture the 10th Georgia's colors but was knocked down and killed. The 1st Minnesota's color guard (minus its color sergeant, who was killed earlier) wound up in the midst of the Confederates but somehow managed to escape. The sides were within forty yards of each other most of the time, and the woods were so thick that when Col. T. G. Hunt of the 5th Louisiana wanted to charge, Semmes would not let him. A man from the 2nd Vermont reported that bullets fired by friends who were shooting through them in the dense woods hit many men in the front line. The Confederates were using old "buck and ball" muskets, useless at long range but horrific at short range, and they made the lead fly "thick and fast" around the Vermonters. Robert Hatrick of the 10th Georgia, who was wounded and later died of his wounds, called the Yankee ranks "terribly broken" from the fire. Isaac Burton of the 5th Vermont wrote that in his company only five of fifty-nine men were unhurt. Some men in the 5th Vermont used all sixty rounds of ammunition they carried with them. Several muskets overheated and became useless, to be exchanged for those of killed or wounded comrades. Brooks himself was wounded in the leg but stayed at the front. He later reported to his father that it was "just enough to call it a wound but not enough to amount to anything else." The men of Davidson's brigade, marching to Brooks's support, heard their comrades shout, "Let's give them the bayonet!"

When Semmes's advance was stopped, Magruder ordered Major Brent to take two of William Barksdale's regiments, the 17th and 21st Mississippi, to support him. Brent braved the storm of shells and bullets to get the men moving. Once the Mississippians were in position, Brent headed back through the same storm to Magruder's position north of the railroad. As he did so, he watched the railroad gun firing away. Magruder soon ordered it to advance, which brought it out of the railroad cut that had protected its sides. Burns's Yankees started firing at those sides, which were less protected than the front, and tried to tear up the track so the gun could not move. The train and gun beat a hasty retreat.

The fight between Semmes and Brooks occurred in Kershaw's rear. Colonel Aiken of the 7th South Carolina heard the firing and thought his right flank may have lagged behind, because, he said, "it was impossible in the thicket to see half the length of the regiment." He sent his sergeant major to check on his lieutenant colonel, who was in charge of the right flank. The sergeant major returned with the news that the lieutenant colonel had been wounded, two companies were cut off, and the Yankees were in his rear. Aiken immediately ordered a withdrawal, but only two companies heard the order. He took these to a crossroads and then gathered the others together. After finding the two companies that had been cut off, he brought them to the crossroads. Hearing no firing on his left, he moved the whole regiment backward about fifty yards. When no Yankees followed, he turned the command toward the rear and came out of the woods, where he saw the 2nd and 3rd South Carolina and formed on their right.

At about the same time, the 3rd South Carolina heard an order to halt and cease firing. Colonel Nance went to the right of the regiment, where he had heard the order spoken, and asked the officer there by what authority he had given it. The officer said it came from his right and that he understood they were firing on friends. Others in the regiment also heard that fellow Southerners were in their front. The 7th South Carolina was on the right and disjointed, so the message could have come from there. Nance repeated the order. The 2nd South Carolina also heard the order and fell back.

Meanwhile, the 8th South Carolina was having all sorts of troubles. It moved to the right to make room for Kemper's battery to fire, but when the artillery was forced to retire, Col. John W. Henagan moved the regiment more to the right to get it out of the way of the Union shells. The regiment started to advance but had to move back to the left because in the intervening time the 10th Georgia had passed through its lines on the way to a meeting with Brooks's brigade. Within a short time the 8th South Carolina was hit by Yankees from its front and a couple of rebel regiments from behind—probably from Semmes's brigade, as the 53rd Georgia, 10th Louisiana, and 15th Virginia had not advanced with the other three regiments and were directly behind the

Gamecocks. Major D. McLeod of the 8th and Capt. C. R. Holmes of Lafayette McLaws's staff got the people behind the 8th settled down, and the Gamecocks prepared to advance again. However, the 10th Georgia, which was in their way, stopped them again. Giving up, Henagan moved his men back to a point near Kemper's battery and stayed there until after the battle.[6]

By then Burns's men had rallied and counterattacked, and they had been reinforced. The first unit to arrive was the 88th New York of the Irish Brigade, running across the field and cheering. Sumner had sent it, along with Caldwell's 5th New Hampshire, in response to Burns's request, but the 5th New Hampshire never made it to the front line. Burns put the Irish along the road between the 106th and 69th Pennsylvania, which had been sent to the left of the line earlier. One man wrote that the Irishmen's charge was "a splendid sight," while another remembered them "yelling like Satans."

The 82nd New York of Sully's brigade moved into the breach in the center of the line. Sully, who was commanding the brigade because of the illness of Brig. Gen. Willis A. Gorman, had left one of his horses with a servant. A round of solid shot took off part of a man's head, and the horse bolted, throwing the servant and heading toward the Confederate lines. Volleys turned it around, and it reached the Northern lines, where soldiers corralled it. Despite the distraction, the two New York regiments drove Kershaw's lone remaining regiment, the 3rd South Carolina, back through the woods into the ravine.

The 106th Pennsylvania was "somewhat disordered" after the rebel charge, according to Col. John W. Kimball of the 15th Massachusetts. Kimball's regiment, after having destroyed stores at Savage Station all day, replaced the 106th in line. The Bay Staters got into "a smart fight" supporting the 82nd New York and 1st Minnesota. On the south side of the road, the 20th and 49th New York of Davidson's brigade went to Brooks's assistance, led by Baldy Smith himself. But nightfall ended the battle before these troops became engaged.

North of the road, the 20th Massachusetts from Napoleon Dana's brigade relieved the 72nd Pennsylvania, while Burns's 71st Pennsylvania and Dana's 7th Michigan also went to the front. The 7th Michigan moved forward at the double-quick at dusk, but it was not needed. The 71st Pennsylvania avoided dangerous fire as "the bullets were flying very thick but all over our heads," one diarist in the regiment noted. Hancock's men also were not engaged. One man said, "[W]e thought we were in for a good fight but they did not show," but the Yankees were close enough to see the artillery fire "mowing them down in winrows."

Barksdale's two Mississippi regiments were not as fortunate as the Union reserves. They got a couple of rounds off around sundown before they were asked to stop lest they fire into Semmes's men. Then an artillery officer begged them to start up again. They did, and got another message that they were hitting fellow rebels. The Mississippians received heavy fire while this confusion was being sorted out, perhaps from the Georgians, and almost every man hit was shot through the brain. Finally even that fire died down, and the battle of Savage Station ended.[7]

It had been a bloody affair. On the Confederate side, nine regiments were engaged—Kershaw's four, Semmes's three, and Barksdale's two. Semmes reported that his three regiments went into action with 755 men, and Kershaw reported 1496 officers and men in his brigade. Barksdale's two regiments probably totaled about 850 men, and they were engaged late in the fight. On the Union side, Burns's regiments probably totaled around 2400; the four regiments in Brooks's brigade also probably numbered about 2400; and the other regiments involved (1st Minnesota, 82nd and 88th New York, and 15th Massachusetts) would have had about 2,300 engaged. So, including artillery, 2,300 Confederates charged 5,000 Yankees initially, another 2,300 Northerners and 850 Southerners came in as reinforcements, and they all fought to a draw.

Kershaw's brigade lost 48 killed, 236 wounded, and 9 missing; the 3rd South Carolina, having advanced the farthest, suffered the most with 23 killed and 108 wounded. In Semmes's three regiments, 11 were killed and 53 wounded, with 10 of the dead and 47 of the wounded coming from the 10th Georgia. Barksdale's losses were not reported separately, but they could not have been large. Union losses were heavier. The 5th Vermont, having charged almost into the Confederate lines, had 45 men killed, another 27 mortally wounded, 116 wounded, and 26 missing. The rest of Brooks's brigade suffered 37 men killed outright, at least according to one source. The reported total casualties of the Seven Days for the four regiments involved were 455, almost all of which occurred at Savage Station. The 72nd Pennsylvania lost 14 killed, 10 more mortally wounded, and 75 wounded. Reasonable estimates place total rebel losses at approximately 375 and total Federal losses at approximately 600. These losses do not count the 3,000 or so sick and wounded given up at the Savage Station field hospital, about half of the total number of captured or missing reported for the Army of the Potomac for the entire Seven Days. A member of Kershaw's brigade, writing after the campaign, said of Savage Station, "I do hope never again to be a participant in such a terrible battle. It was heart-rending indeed." The artillerymen, however, got a little break because of the thick undergrowth and trees. One Rhode Island gunner even went to sleep during the battle.[8]

The cannoneers would have been busier if either side had put in anywhere close to all its forces. Of the twenty-eight Confederate regiments under Magruder, only nine participated in the battle, or thirty-one hundred of his thirteen thousand infantry. David Jones's division did not enter the battle at all. On Magruder's left, south of the Trent house, Jones was perfectly placed to hit the Yankee right flank. He seems to have recognized this, but his mood reflected Magruder's anxiety. Jones moved George T. Anderson's brigade to face south "so as to take the enemy in flank and rear, should he advance on General Cobb's position." This does not sound like a man who was getting ready to attack any enemy found anywhere, as Magruder had ordered. But Jones had barely gotten Anderson in line when he received an order from Magruder to move to a bridge over the railroad between Orchard Station and Savage Station and be ready to support the right flank. That order may have included a prohibition on forward movement. Magruder said he wanted Jones relatively early but could not find Jones's men until it was too late. Jones said he obeyed the order to reach the bridge but could not find Magruder. Either way, Jones's men were out of the fight, which would have been unfortunate if Jones had shown any sign of offensive activity.

Bob Toombs did not even mention the twenty-ninth in his report, and his two regimental commanders who did both noted merely the pursuit of the Northerners. Anderson wrote, perhaps complaining, of "marching in line of battle all day through woods, swamps, and open field" without getting into the fight. At least one of his regiments heard the sound of the fighting, but those men were well to the north of any action. Howell Cobb also did not see the battlefield at Savage Station. His men, though hit by enemy fire, "had no opportunity of participating actively in the fight." Magruder moved one of Cobb's regiments (he does not say which) to the same railroad bridge to which he ordered Jones, but that was all. Barksdale's other two regiments remained in support of Cobb, marching back and forth across the railroad. Kershaw and Semmes showed themselves to be fighters, but this cannot be said of the rest of Magruder's command.[9]

It is easy and partially correct to blame Magruder for these failures. His final attack order was in one sense crazy and in another sense correct, but Prince John did not ensure that it was carried out. He should have coordinated the attack better, he should have confirmed the reports of a Union attack personally before asking for reinforcements, and he should have been more decisive in his actions. However, he had reasons for his indecision. He thought Benjamin Huger was going to be on the Williamsburg road and made his dispositions accordingly. He also thought that Stonewall Jackson would be moving from the north to join him in the attack and did not find out to the contrary until relatively late in the day. These misconceptions could have been cleared up with better communication from Lee and Jackson. He was right in his assessment of the forces facing him, at least more nearly right than was Lee. Magruder's problems may have saved Lee from a severe handling, and in reality Magruder could have done little more than he did.

Lee, of course, did not see it that way. After the battle, Prince John sent Walter Taylor of Lee's staff (who had informed Magruder of Jackson's ordered cooperation) back to Lee while Rev. L. W. Allen of Magruder's staff took a message to Jackson. Taylor must have reported the day's result, and Marse Robert was not happy. That evening he wrote Magruder: "I regret much that you have made so little progress today in the pursuit of the enemy. In order to reap the fruits of our victory the pursuit should be most vigorous. I must urge you, then, again to press on his rear rapidly and steadily. We must lose no more time or he will escape us entirely." Taylor also must have told Lee of David Jones's note, for in a postscript Lee told Magruder that Jackson had indeed been ordered to support Prince John and push the pursuit as well. It is this message that has caused much confusion regarding Jackson's other duty. But overall, Lee was wrong. A vigorous pursuit by Magruder may have decimated his command.

Three opportunities were lost on June 29, and Lee lost one of them himself. The first lost opportunity, missing the original gap in the Union lines between Sumner and Smith, was no one's fault. But the second, the possibility of sending Huger down the Charles City road quickly, was ruined by Lee's order to reinforce Magruder with two brigades. Magruder may shoulder some of the blame, but Lee should have corrected him immediately or gone to see for himself. Huger deserves little if any blame. Lee caused his slowness. A third missed opportunity that is often mentioned was Jackson's failure to cross the Chickahominy, and it is at least questionable whether any opportunity really existed there. There was no missed Confederate opportunity at Savage Station; if anyone missed an opportunity there, it was the Yankees.[10]

In fact, the equally ineffective Union command helped save Lee. Even after Heintzelman's retirement, the Yankees had forty regiments in and around Savage Station. At most, fourteen regiments participated in the battle, but even that would be a stretch, as the 20th and 49th New York did not get to Brooks's support until after the fighting. Sumner acted more like a brigade or division commander than a corps commander, sending individual regiments in willy-nilly. His actions helped save Burns, but several entire brigades stayed in reserve instead of being fed to the front lines, where they could have dealt Magruder a severe blow. Burns, in Sedgwick's words, "showed himself a splendid soldier," and Brooks and his men deserve credit for taking a hard blow, but the rest of the Union command had nothing of which to be proud.[11]

The Yankees were lucky that no further damage was done. Without the fortunate discovery made by Franklin and Sedgwick, Kershaw and Semmes would have been able to get nearer to Savage Station and perhaps surprise the Federals before they could get in line. Even the seven rebel regiments may have inflicted serious harm in that circumstance. The Southerners were also lucky because Heintzelman moved. Had he stayed where he was, he could have taken Semmes in the flank and rolled up both Confederate commands.

But Heintzelman was not there. In fact, that evening some of his men met other Southerners elsewhere. Kearny, leading III Corps on its march, had decided to cross White Oak Swamp at Jordon's (or Jordan's) Ford, three miles from Kearny's camp and about three miles upstream from White Oak Swamp Bridge. He rightly figured that the area around White Oak Swamp Bridge and the bridge at Brackett's Ford would be jammed with men and vehicles. The road from Jordon's Ford led to the Charles City road, which he could take to Glendale. He had scouted the road that morning and found it clear of Confederates.

That afternoon, Kearny ordered Hiram Berry to check out the condition of the fords in the area. Berry was a thirty-seven-year-old Mainer who had been a carpenter, contractor, banker, politician, and militia captain before the war. He thought Jordon's Ford and Fisher's Ford, between Jordon's and Brackett's, needed work and put the 4th Maine, his old regiment, on the job. Berry returned to find that the corps was marching. The men found it hard going with the extra ammunition they carried, and many fell out in the heat. Charles D. Haydon of the 2nd Michigan wrote in his diary that batteries passed the infantry at a full gallop, regiments tried to pass each other, and part of his regiment got cut off from the rest. The three companies with him gave up, along with the 38th New York of David Birney's brigade, and waited for everyone else to pass. Theodore Dodge of the 101st New York was more understanding, believing the guns needed to be protected more, and his men got out of the batteries' way. But Dodge's company got lost and had to march through knee-deep water twice to regain the right road. Kearny rode along the line watching over the men. Coming up on Haydon's band, he told the men to go slow, as they were "the rear guard of all God's Creation."

Birney's brigade, in the lead, crossed the two forks of the swamp at Jordon's Ford. Once the men were south of the swamp, however, they encountered fire from William Mahone's brigade, which was leading Huger's column down the Charles City road. Mahone and Lew Armistead had never turned around, and they marched somewhat anxiously as they looked for Northerners who had crossed the swamp at either Jordon's or Fisher's Fords. At one point the 12th and 49th Virginia mistook each other for the enemy, but fortunately they each discovered the mistake before many shots were fired. At the intersection of the Charles City road and the road from Jordon's Ford, Mahone's skirmishers met a Union cavalry patrol. This really made Mahone suspicious, and he sent a scouting party to the ford. The scouts saw Birney's men crossing the swamp and reported back to Mahone, who got his brigade into line of battle and sent skirmishers to fire on the Unionists.

Skirmishers from the 3rd Maine returned fire, but it was obvious to the Yankees that there was a substantial body of Confederates supported by artillery to the south of them. Kearny took a look at the situation and, while Mahone advanced two of his regiments toward the ford (and fought off another cavalry scouting party), decided for once that discretion would be the better part of valor. Learning that the road to Brackett's Ford had little traffic, he backed Birney's men away from Mahone's oncoming rebels.

Kearny's men crossed at Brackett's Ford (except for Berry, who crossed at Fisher's), and by 10 P.M. the entire division was camped around the Charles City road, moving through Porter's men along the way. However, Huger thought that the Jordon's Ford encounter meant that Kearny was still in position, and going any farther down the Charles City road would put Kearny in his rear. The road that Kearny had used, called the New road, paralleled the Charles City road from south of Seven Pines about six miles to the White Oak road. Huger, not knowing of Kearny's withdrawal, was concerned that the Yankees might use the New road to get behind him. The 44th Alabama of Ambrose Wright's brigade and an artillery battery went to the intersection of the two roads, five miles from any Northerner. Wright, who had barely reached White's Tavern on the Charles City road (two miles from Mahone's position) after all his comings and goings, would march down the New road in the morning. Mahone's brigade slept in line of battle, as did Armistead's behind it. Robert Ransom's men brought up the rear on the Charles City road, having passed through much debris on the march.[12]

Huger's command was thus strung out over several miles on the Charles City road. Magruder had his forces in the area between Orchard Station and Savage Station. Jackson got Alexander's Bridge repaired sometime late on the twenty-ninth, and D. H. Hill crossed the Chickahominy that night. The other divisions made ready to cross. Richard Ewell left Bottom's Bridge around 6 P.M. to rejoin Jackson, having posted Bradley Johnson's command at the bridge. On the march, Campbell Brown passed a house and asked for a drink. The man there said that the Yankees had poisoned the spring, although he could not figure out how. Brown tried it and found it had medicine in it. The medicine had come from a nearby Union hospital, where the Northerners had dumped the stores they could not take with them into a creek. "It is hard to realize the value of all the stores destroyed by McClellan," Brown later wrote.

James Longstreet's and A. P. Hill's divisions marched all day in the heat and humidity. The men kicked up so much dust that everything, including the trees along the roads, was covered with it. Suffering from the intense heat but joined by Jefferson Davis for part of the march, those who stayed in the ranks reached at least as far as the Atlee house on the Darbytown road, six miles south of New Bridge and about seven miles' march from Glendale. The 3rd Virginia Cavalry, recovered from the morning's ambush, camped about a mile ahead of Longstreet's force.[13]

While most of the Confederates spent the stormy night trying to sleep, many Yankees were on the march. Hooker's men, following Kearny, crossed the swamp at Brackett's Ford and bivouacked near the Charles City road. The movement was not without adventure. The 2nd New Hampshire and 26th Pennsylvania took a different road from the rest of Cuvier Grover's brigade, a wrong turn that caused some anxious moments until the men found their brethren at the swamp. One diarist wrote that evening, "Everyone looks downcast and sad." On the way, Pvt. Charles C. Perkins of the 1st Massachusetts needed to get rid of some clothes to make it in the heat. He took off his dark blue shirt, cut it into strips, and threw it and a second pair of socks away—along with a jar of pepper he had been carrying. After wiping his body off with a towel, he put on a clean shirt, put his wet blouse in his knapsack, and started off again. Others probably followed Perkins's example, given that the march was through woods that cut off air circulation on a hot day. The air was so dusty that the men's uniforms and hair all became the same color. At one spring filled with struggling men, those who chose not to join the fight dipped "liquid mud" out of footprints and kept marching. Captain Edward Acton only made it to camp because a surgeon offered the sick Acton his horse. Perkins heard that Unionists had been passing along the road since eleven the previous evening.[14]

Keyes's men marched all night to reach Haxall's Landing on the James River below Turkey Island Bridge. Darius Couch called it "one of the most fatiguing marches imaginable," and George Hagar of the 10th Massachusetts said that no one said a word during the night. At any stop the men would fall to the ground, and many of them marched while asleep. Naglee's brigade and the artillery with it started leaving the Bottom's Bridge area about 5 P.M., shortly after the train blew up, and arrived at White Oak Swamp Bridge the next morning. The cavalry pickets on the east side of the river crossed after dark to rejoin McClellan's headquarters. Slocum's division, which had relieved Keyes's men, stayed in position all night—except for the 1st New Jersey, which headed back to White Oak Swamp Bridge to protect the crossing. Some of the men got their first rest for three nights. Slocum was in his tent that night dreaming of a banquet—he had not eaten in thirty-six hours—when Col. Calvin E. Pratt of the 31st New York in Newton's brigade awakened him. Pratt, who had been severely wounded at Gaines's Mill and left for dead there, walked for two days to find his unit. He had heard of Slocum's lack of food intake before he came to the tent and woke the general with some French soup. Slocum, who did not recognize Pratt because he was covered with his own blood, later said that the soup was worth waking up for.[15]

At 5 P.M. McCall moved from his position near White Oak Swamp to cover the Glendale crossroads. William Averell covered the movement with his 3rd Pennsylvania Cavalry, Henry Benson's battery, and the 8th Pennsylvania Reserves of Simmons's brigade. The roads were jammed with wagons, cattle, wounded, and stragglers. During the rainy night the division passed its position at the junction of the Darbytown and Long Bridge roads and continued down the latter road. McCall's men made contact with rebels, probably the 5th Virginia Cavalry, about midnight.

Before that, however, the commanders had realized their mistake. George Meade, moving with the front of the column, became convinced they were on the wrong road. The entire V Corps was off track, actually. George Morell and George Sykes had left at sundown for Turkey Island Bridge. All the units had been told to move by the Quaker road (meaning the Willis Church road). McCall would stop on the New Market (in reality Long Bridge) road near the Quaker road, while Morell and Sykes would continue on to the bridge. But they were really marching toward another Quaker road, which left the Long Bridge road about two miles west of Glendale. Meade stopped his brigade and went to explore this other Quaker road. It turned out to be overgrown, with ditches and fences across it that made it unusable. He reported this to McCall, who in turn told Porter.

A guide misled Fitz John into thinking the road Meade had found was the right Quaker road. One account had Porter marching Morell and Sykes to the Quaker road, where they tried to go down it but were forced to turn around. This may or may not be true, as it seems that Meade ran into Confederate pickets at about that spot. Perhaps the Confederates came forward after Porter left, which he did after telling McCall to stay where he was—even though he thought he no longer commanded McCall's men. Porter's confusion arose because McClellan had ordered McCall to guard the trains instead of telling Porter to give the order. Little Mac also had given McCall the order to guard Glendale.

Orders or no, McCall could do little but stay where he was. Alanson Randol's battery parked in a field just off the road. As some men went to get water from a stream a few hundred yards behind them, others wandered the field. One of them heard a musket being cocked and called out, "Look out, there! What do you mean?" The ensuing conversation convinced the Union artilleryman that the man was a rebel picket. The Yankee said he belonged to a battery that had just come in—not mentioning that the battery was Northern. The horses were kept hitched all night. A soldier from the 7th Pennsylvania Reserves found out the next day that he had been inside Southern lines all night. The Confederates had let the Yankees come into the lines, hoping to capture them, but enough other Northerners were around that they thought better of it.

The men in Seneca Simmons's brigade in particular suffered as they spent the night in line of battle. Three days after their first fight, they seemed to be adversely affected by it, as sleeping men plagued by nightmares would yell out, "Fall in! Fall in!" There were numerous other distractions: Horses from a battery broke free, firing caused by a false alarm was heard in the rear, and dogs at nearby houses barked all night. Sleep was not to be found.

Longstreet, who was relatively close to the Federals, could have launched a night attack in hopes of doing severe damage to the Army of the Potomac. However, the rainy night, the difficulty in mounting a night attack, the men's exhaustion after marching throughout the hot day, and the fact that they probably would have taken a long time to get in any sort of battle order suggests that this possibility was slim.[16]

Meanwhile, Morell and Sykes, having found the right Quaker road, made it to Malvern Hill by about 9 A.M. Some units did not even start until 6 A.M., having endured a night filled with shots from nervous pickets. John Bancroft of the 4th Michigan wrote in his diary: "March and wait and march and wait and then countermarch. May you never experience how tired we were." Once they reached the hill, the two divisions positioned themselves to cover the River and Willis Church roads.

The troops around Savage Station had been ordered to cross White Oak Swamp that night. But when Franklin told Sumner he was going to obey the order and get Smith's division across, Sumner was indignant. He forbade Franklin to execute a retreat. "No, General, you shall not go, nor will I go—I never leave a victorious field," Sumner exclaimed. "Why! if I had twenty thousand more men, I would crush this rebellion." Franklin found a candle and showed Sumner McClellan's order. "General McClellan did not know the circumstances when he wrote that note," Sumner said after reading it. "He did not know that we would fight a battle and gain a victory." Franklin left, knowing that if the Yankees stayed they were courting disaster.

Baldy Smith came to the rescue. His aide, Maj. Caspar M. Berry, delivered McClellan's order, which Smith had requested because he did not trust Sumner to fall back by himself. Berry went with Franklin back to Sumner and assured Sumner that yes, McClellan did know of Savage Station, and yes, he still wanted the men to cross White Oak Swamp that night. Colonel Delos Sacket, McClellan's inspector general, showed up with two orders, one written and another private. Colonel A.V. Colburn, Little Mac's assistant adjutant general, had told Sacket that if Sumner did not obey he was to be arrested. Bull Head, somewhat disappointed, turned to his staff and said, "Gentlemen you hear the orders; we have nothing to do but obey." Franklin then began his movement, with Sedgwick and Richardson following.[17]

It was a memorable experience for men who had marched and fought all day, then had to march all night with little food. "The rain the wind and the dark was exceeding anything of the kind I ever before witnessed," one soldier remembered of the thunderstorm. Thomas Hyde remembered that water was "scarce and poor" along the way, and that men chewed on twigs to ease their thirst. One Vermonter told his sister he would have paid twenty-five cents for one drink of decent water. Hyde himself fell asleep on his horse and awoke in another brigade when some runaway horses were thought to be rebel cavalry.

Many others slept while riding, and one man thought the horses understood this and took special care to keep their places in the line. Captain Osborn went to sleep on some ammunition chests. Two of his men kept him from rolling off. Some men in the 5th Wisconsin were separated from the rest by the trains and did not rejoin the regiment until the next day. Smith's division crossed the swamp around daybreak.[18]

Some in Sedgwick's division found the scene around Savage Station exhilarating, particularly after sunset, with the fires at the station and the guns lighting the sky. But the night was rather less so. Before they left, some of the 1st Minnesota's men heard the Southerners taking their wounded off the field as well as the cries of their own wounded, who had to be left on the field "to the tender care of the Rebels." Then, as late as 3 A.M., the march started. The roads were filled with infantry and artillery. The march was mostly through dense, swampy forests, and the thunderstorm did not help matters. The only light came from burning wagons and caissons, except for a few candles fastened to trees. The rain stopped at midnight, which helped, but the men hardly halted all night, and there were few sounds but the tramp of feet and the rumble of artillery fire. The men slipped and slid on the road. No drinking water could be found. Some worn-out men would fall out of line and be asleep in a moment. Cavalrymen kept waking the sleepers up and telling them that the Confederates were close. Another said that he had never suffered so much in his life. Confusion reigned, especially after the infantry got mixed in with the wagons. At one point, four or five regiments tried to march with each other on the narrow, muddy road.[19]

Matters also were confused at Savage Station. Some pickets, such as those of the 20th Massachusetts, did not get the word to retire and were almost captured. Richardson's division, serving as the army's rear guard, did not leave the area until 1 A.M., and Hazzard's battery did not leave until daybreak on the thirtieth. One man remembered that nothing above a whisper was heard. The scenes that imprinted that night's march on the minds of men from Smith's and Sedgwick's divisions made the same mark on Richardson's men. The rain and mud were everywhere. Some men slept as they marched. The cavalry awakened those sleeping by the side of the road to keep them from being taken prisoner. The exhausted men dropped fast asleep once White Oak Swamp was crossed.[20] But they had to continue. The Confederates were not about to give them time to rest.

CHAPTER THIRTEEN

"We've Got Him"

George Hazzard and his men spent the night of June 29 at Savage Station, resting from the day's exertions. Four of Hazzard's eight guns had fought at both Allen's Farm and Savage Station, and the men were so tired they slept through the night's rain. Awakening that morning, they heard drums and bugles, apparently unusual sounds to the Yankees. They looked around and found they were the only Northerners left on the field—the noises they heard were coming from Confederate camps.

Hazzard wasted no time, at least after he said, "They have sacrificed my battery to save themselves." He got the men moving and the teams in harness. First the caissons, then the guns started down the road. Telling Lt. Rufus King Jr. to keep the column closed up, he stayed at the rear of the column with a couple of twelve-pound smoothbores in case rebels followed him. First at a walk, then at a trot, the batteries headed toward White Oak Swamp. The road itself was in good shape. Many stragglers from other units lined it, however. The artillerymen told these Unionists that rebels were not far behind, "saving probably many an able-bodied soldier from spending the balance of the summer in a Southern prison," King later reported.

When the batteries finally reached White Oak Swamp Bridge it was ready to be fired, as William French's brigade had crossed and French thought no one was behind him except Confederates. King got that straightened out, and the batteries crossed by 10 A.M. Their crossing reminded the 50th New York Engineers that their camp equipment was on the north side of the swamp. They ran over, got what they could, and returned to the bridge. French had already set it ablaze, and the engineers crossed the burning structure. They caught their breath, and the artillerymen were congratulated on their escape.

After Hazzard's crossing, every unit in the Army of the Potomac was south of White Oak Swamp. Confederates also crossed to the south bank of a watercourse that morning. D. H. Hill's division, Stonewall Jackson's advance force, began crossing the Chickahominy at about 3 A.M., followed by William Whiting, Jackson's own division, and Richard Ewell. The Army of Northern Virginia was together south of the Chickahominy for the first time.

McCarthy's battery, with Magruder, was waiting along the Williamsburg road to begin the day's march. Suddenly the gunners heard the sound of horsemen coming down the road leading from Grapevine Bridge, past McClellan's old headquarters at the Trent house, to Savage Station. One was in advance of the others. It was Jackson, on his little sorrel, and it looked as if he were waiting for someone to come down the Williamsburg road. His appearance, according to one artilleryman, was "worn down to the lowest point of flesh consistent with effective service. His hair, skin, eyes, and clothes were all one neutral dust tint, and his badges of rank so dulled and tarnished as to be scarcely perceptible. The 'mangy little cadet cap' was pulled so low in front that the visor cut the glint of his eyeballs."

The dead of the 17th and 21st Mississippi were laid out near Jackson's position, but Stonewall was so intent upon the road that he gave the ghastly scene barely a glance. Soon Robert E. Lee and his staff rode up, the immaculately attired and strikingly handsome Lee a strong contrast to the beaten down Jackson. The commander recognized his famous subordinate, rode on with a courier, and both generals dismounted.

Greetings were warm but brief. One of the men, somewhat jerkily, began talking and tracing a diagram with the toe of his right boot. Two lines he drew with firmness. Then, starting at the end of the second line, he began to move his toe toward the first. The draftsman would look at the other, then down at the ground, talking all the while, as he completed the triangle. When his toe reached the first line he raised his foot, stamped it, said, "We've got him"—the only words Robert Stiles, about thirty feet away, heard—then signaled to his staff for his horse. Jackson and Lee shook hands, the little sorrel came back, and Jackson got on the horse a little awkwardly and rode off. As Marse Robert watched Stonewall depart, his courier brought his own horse, and Lee also rode away.[1]

What was being drawn, and who was drawing it? Lee's plan was, in most respects, the natural continuation of the plan for the twenty-ninth. James Longstreet and A. P. Hill were to march from Atlee's farm on the Darbytown road to the Long Bridge road, take that road to the east, and engage the Federals wherever they might be. Benjamin Huger was to keep going down the Charles City road and find the enemy, firing upon the Yankees as soon as he made contact. One slight deviation came as a result of his encounter with Phil Kearny the day before. Ambrose Wright's brigade headed down the New road to make sure no Yankees were on his left flank. Jackson was to maintain his position along the road closest to the Chickahominy. He would head down the Williamsburg road to the White Oak road to the Long Bridge road and thus to the area of the Glendale intersection, where he expected to find Longstreet. These three columns would attack nearly simultaneously, which was why Huger would fire guns on his approach.

Magruder's role was the one change from the plan of the twenty-ninth. Prince John seemed to Lee to need personal attention. Magruder had asked for reinforcements in case Jackson was headed elsewhere. He had no idea where Jackson was, and he was feeling lonely because he was sure (correctly so) that he had faced several Union divisions. He gave orders and instructions all night, at least until Stonewall showed up at about 3:30 on the morning of the thirtieth. After Jackson told Magruder his men would be in the area around daylight, Prince John finally relaxed enough to go to sleep. It was his first rest in forty-eight hours.

Lee visited Magruder, probably after both men had talked with Jackson, and laid out Prince John's part in the day's plan. Instead of joining Jackson along the Williamsburg road, Magruder would march to the Darbytown road and become Longstreet's and A. P. Hill's reserve. Sending Prince John to Brackett's Ford, where most of Kearny's division had crossed White Oak Swamp the night before, would have put pressure on what proved to be a weak point in the Federal defense. But it was not the key point to Lee. That point was south of Glendale, where Longstreet and Hill were headed. Lee had two choices. The first was to heavily weight the northern part of his force, trying to pin down the Unionists while Longstreet and Hill cut the line of retreat. The second was to weight the southern part, ensuring that Longstreet and Hill could break any defense opposing them. He concluded that the second strategy was better, and he relied on Huger and Jackson to provide enough pressure on the Yankees to keep reinforcements from heading south.

Sending Magruder south may have been an indication of Lee's lack of confidence in Prince John. However, this does not have to be so. If Lee were to emphasize the southern part of his plan, a large rebel force needed to be on the Long Bridge road. Lee could have sent Huger there to be the reserve and given Magruder the Charles City road assignment. Such a plan would have forced Huger's most distant brigade, Wright's, to march about five miles to the junction of the Darbytown and Long Bridge roads. But most of his units were closer than that. Magruder's men would need to move about seven miles to get to where Huger's advance was. If Magruder went to the Darbytown road, he would march at least nine miles, perhaps more like twelve, depending on which roads he took. Obviously, moving Huger to the Darbytown road would allow the reserve force to get to Longstreet more quickly. But Lee had less need for speed than power. If he really wanted the majority of his men on the Darbytown–Long Bridge road, Magruder's force was the right one to send, as

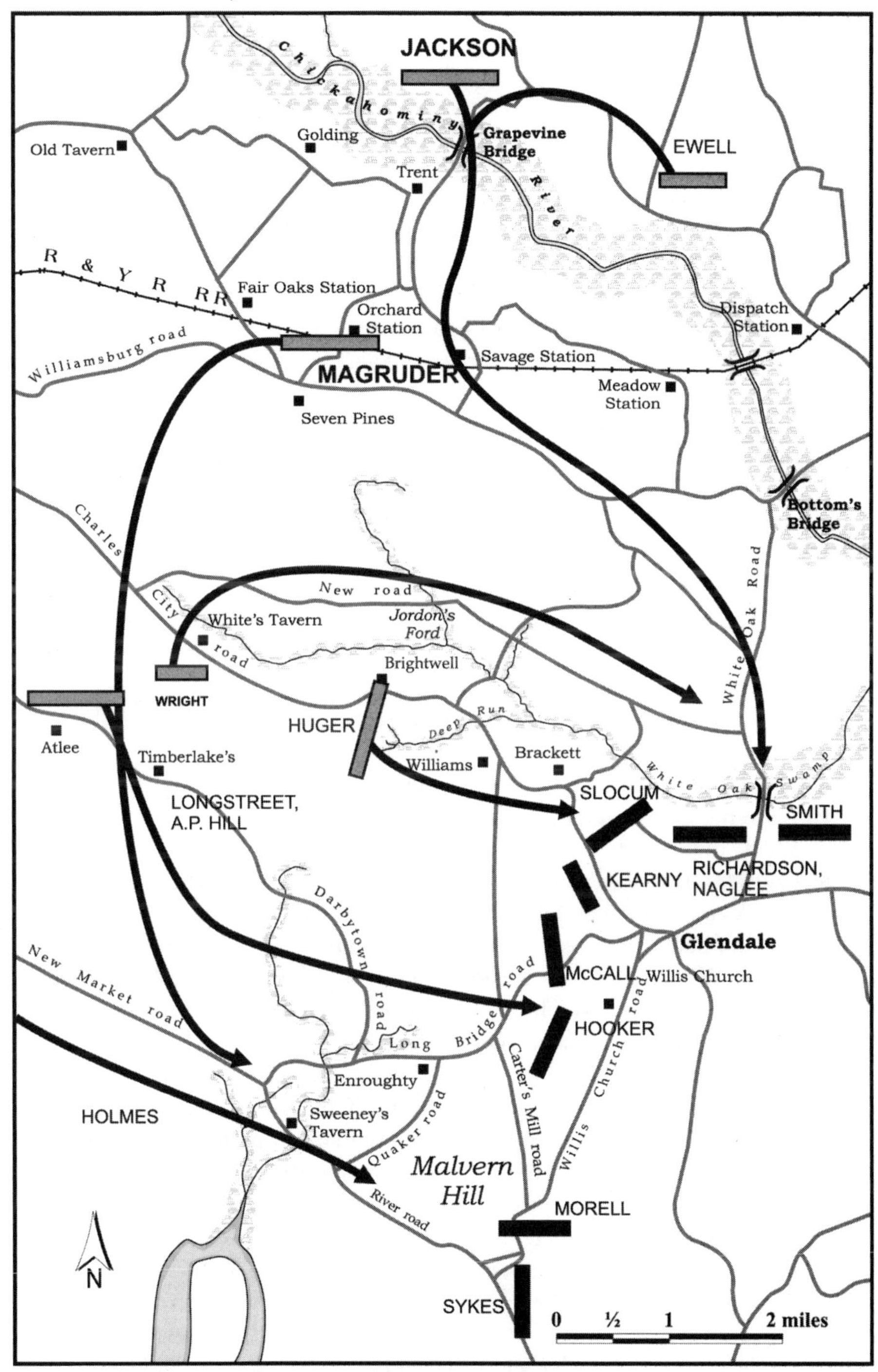

Lee's plan for June 30, 1862

it outnumbered Huger's force by a few thousand men, and it could be in position by early afternoon.[2]

These four columns, containing the whole of Lee's army (about seventy thousand men), would thus be headed to Glendale. Lee probably had heard reports from Savage Station of Magruder's taking prisoners from three different Federal divisions and realized that a substantial Union force had been north of White Oak Swamp until late the previous evening. That meant the Yankees probably would have to fight at Glendale. Pressure on that point from three sides could lead to great problems for McClellan, perhaps even the loss of a substantial part of his army if Longstreet and A. P. Hill could cut the Willis Church road.

Lee had one further piece on this chessboard. Theophilus Holmes, commanding the Confederate Department of North Carolina, had been ordered to move north of the river from Petersburg on the twenty-sixth. By the twenty-seventh he was at Drewry's Bluff on the south bank of the James. However, by the twenty-eighth he was back at Petersburg, asking Secretary of War Randolph if he and his men were wanted. Two of his brigades had already been detached. Robert Ransom and his men had been with Huger's division since Oak Grove, and John Walker had been with the army since the twenty-sixth. Holmes brought three regiments from his other brigade—the 43rd, 45th, and 50th North Carolina under Col. Junius Daniel—across the James with two batteries and three companies of cavalry on the afternoon of the twenty-ninth. That night Walker, back from his excursion north of the Chickahominy, rejoined Holmes's men along with two batteries. The next morning, the combined force moved to and down the New Market road to its junction with the Long Bridge road, reaching that spot around 10 A.M. There it was joined by Brig. Gen. Henry A. Wise with two regiments, the 26th and 46th Virginia, and two more batteries from Chaffin's Bluff opposite Drewry's on the north bank of the James. Holmes had asked Wise whether the brigadier could join his force, and Wise brought most of his men with him. This heterogeneous force included about sixty-three hundred infantry, 130 cavalry, and six batteries of artillery.

Holmes was on the New Market road, which became the River road and joined up with the southern end of the Willis Church road south of Malvern Hill. Thus Holmes, with a quick march, could be in position to threaten a flank attack on any Yankees moving toward the James. His orders did not call for that, though, and he took a defensive position around the junction of the New Market and Long Bridge roads. Jefferson Davis was there, and the president approved both Holmes's position and Wise's joining him without orders. Holmes was in position to be used if Lee could find something for him to do.

It is not clear what roads were represented by the triangle drawn in the dirt on the Williamsburg road. One side could have been the White Oak road–Willis Church road axis; another could have been either the Darbytown or

New Market–River road. In that case, however, the third side would mean nothing. Alternatively, the two sides drawn decisively could have been the White Oak–Willis Church axis and the Williamsburg or Charles City road, with the third side the Darbytown or River road being the road that would be taken by the force that would cut the Yankees off. That is not necessarily a triangle, and one account has the drawing as three sides of a square, which could fit. The witnesses were far enough away that the figure could have been either. The drawing might also have been of positions: Jackson's with the first line, Huger's with the second, and Longstreet and Hill cutting off the retreat with the third. This would explain why the third side was drawn tentatively, and it would also fit with Lee's plan. In any event, it seems that Jackson understood the plan and was ready to execute it.

It also does not matter much who the draftsman was. If the two men were talking, which is certain, Lee could have been explaining the plan and drawing at the same time, or Jackson could have been talking and drawing to show he understood what was to happen. No matter what was drawn or who was drawing it, the Confederate leaders had a large opportunity. Lee anticipated results "most disastrous to the enemy" from the day's activity.[3]

Certainly more than George McClellan's rear guard was at stake—or McClellan's rear guard was one of the largest in history in proportion to the size of the army it was protecting. Of Little Mac's eleven divisions, seven full divisions plus one brigade of another were in the area between White Oak Swamp Bridge and Willis Church itself, describing a rough triangle about one square mile in area covering the approaches to Glendale. Two divisions and one brigade were near White Oak Swamp Bridge. Baldy Smith's division was covering the trains' movement south. Smith himself saw a man, perhaps Mr. Britton, who owned a house near where the division stopped—probably the house McClellan had used until that morning as his headquarters. The Union general told the Confederate citizen it would be a good idea to leave, but the civilian stayed, perhaps because his wife—younger than the husband and pretty, according to Smith—was exhausted. She also was worried about her fruit trees, her fences, and other possible harms that could come with so many Yankee soldiers camped on her property.

Apparently the man started taking Smith seriously, because about 10 A.M. he went to see William Franklin. The man asked if there would be a fight that day. Franklin thought there certainly would, and he told the man it probably would start in about a half-hour. "Then I will have time to take my wife and child to my brother, who lives about half a mile down the swamp, and get back before it begins," the man replied. "Yes," said Franklin, "but why come back at all?" The man responded, "Why, if I don't your men will take all my chickens and ducks."

Smith, too, was exhausted, but he could not get to sleep. He eventually gave up and decided to take a cold bath. Others did get to sleep, and still more moved to picket positions. Food was brought up, and one man noted, "Everything seems to indicate a day of rest."

Joining Smith at the bridge site were Henry Naglee's brigade, which after retreating from Bottom's Bridge had been placed under Smith's orders, and Israel Richardson's division. Richardson, who had been the last (besides Hazzard's batteries) to leave the Savage Station area, found a mass of stragglers trying to cross White Oak Swamp Bridge. Knowing that rebels would not be far behind him, Richardson told them they were liable to be the cause of the destruction of the army. He and his aides got the stragglers, and his division, across in time. Charles Nightingale of the 29th Massachusetts was one of the stragglers, having fallen asleep on the march. He wrote that trying to find his regiment in the chaos was "like looking for a needle in a haystack"—everyone else was doing the same thing. Finally organized, the division got into position on Smith's left, and like their VI Corps brethren the men tried to get some sleep. Some were ordered to rest, but that may have been the most unnecessary order of the campaign. Smith's artillery covered the bridge, with Capt. Thaddeus Mott's battery joined by Capt. Romeyn B. Ayres's Battery F, 5th U.S. Artillery, in forward positions. Lieutenant Andrew Cowan's 1st New York Light Artillery battery was a little in back of those two batteries. Captain Charles C. Wheeler's Battery E, 1st New York Light Artillery, which had been reduced to two guns, was placed in reserve. Hazzard rested at the top of the hill south of White Oak Swamp.[4]

Two more divisions were near the Charles City road. Franklin, on orders from McClellan, moved Henry Slocum's division from his position on the Long Bridge road to a point on the Charles City road midway between Glendale and Brackett's Ford. Emory Upton's, Josiah Porter's, and William Hexamer's batteries set up in front of a road leading from the Charles City road to the White Oak road, with the infantry in supporting positions. One of Col. Joseph Bartlett's aides called the setup "a '*nice little arrangement*' for the Rebs."

Kearny's men also wound up on the Charles City road. Their march was a little longer than Slocum's. Kearny headed northwest on the Charles City road from his campsite near Brackett's Ford to a tributary of White Oak Swamp called Deep Run, a position he described as "very strong." But he was supposed to be on Slocum's left, spread from the Charles City road to the Long Bridge road. Kearny's actual position, according to Samuel Heintzelman, was "very favorable for an advance upon Richmond, but much too far forward for the object we had in view," and Heintzelman moved the division to its proper place with "much difficulty." Kearny, undoubtedly miffed, complained that his division had to cover a front of more than two miles. This probably was an exaggeration, for the actual distance between the two roads where he was posted is not much more than a mile. James Thompson's battery was on the left, supported by John Robinson's brigade, while Capt. George E. Randolph's Battery E, 1st Rhode Island Artillery, moved forward a little and to the right with David Birney in support. Hiram Berry's brigade formed Kearny's reserve. Heintzelman sent the 87th New York of Robinson's brigade and one of Hexamer's guns to Brackett's Ford, where the bridge had been destroyed, to keep watch. Some of the men found blackberries for breakfast while they rested.[5]

Joseph Hooker was supposed to be next to Kearny, covering the area between the Long Bridge road and the Willis Church road. McClellan had set the Yankee dispositions early in the morning while talking with Edwin Sumner, Franklin, and Heintzelman. His vision of the line seems to have been, from right to left: Smith, Naglee, Richardson, Slocum, Kearny, and Hooker, with John Sedgwick in reserve. But that left George McCall's division unaccounted for. Perhaps the confusion of the night before, with Porter ordering McCall to hold his position yet not thinking McCall was under his orders, contributed to this omission. McCall reported that someone ordered him to move back from his exposed position to Glendale, and he halted near the Willis Church road to hold the position until the army's trains had passed. But the Pennsylvania Reserves believed they were not on the front line. The regiments were drawn up for muster, since it was the last day of the month. Doctors began working on wounded soldiers who had arrived in ambulances. Truman Seymour noted that the men expected to follow the rest of V Corps south at any moment, but they were pleased to be able to rest even a little after two days of hard fighting and two more days of marching. "There was evidently no expectation of an attack or of the division being required to be engaged during the day," one officer remembered.

Whether they knew it or not, the Pennsylvania Reserves were between Kearny and Hooker. With McCall were five batteries. The two remaining batteries of his own division, Mark Kerns's battery (reduced to four guns and commanded by Lt. Frank P. Amsden since Kerns's wounding at Gaines's Mill) and James Cooper's battery, had been joined by Alanson Randol's, Otto Diederichs's, and John Knieriem's batteries the previous day. At least some of the Reserves' artillerymen woke up slightly refreshed, having had a night's rest for the first time since the twenty-fifth.

Hooker was to McCall's left, and Fighting Joe did not even know the Pennsylvanians were there (although his men knew McCall was in front of them). After reconnoitering the area with Kearny, Hooker picked out his defensive position parallel to and about a half-mile west of the Willis Church road. Cuvier Grover, on the right of the line, posted his right even with the church about three-quarters of a mile south of Glendale. Joseph Carr was in the middle, and Daniel Sickles moved in on the left. The division artillery kept going south toward Malvern Hill. Hooker, after finding a good spot for a

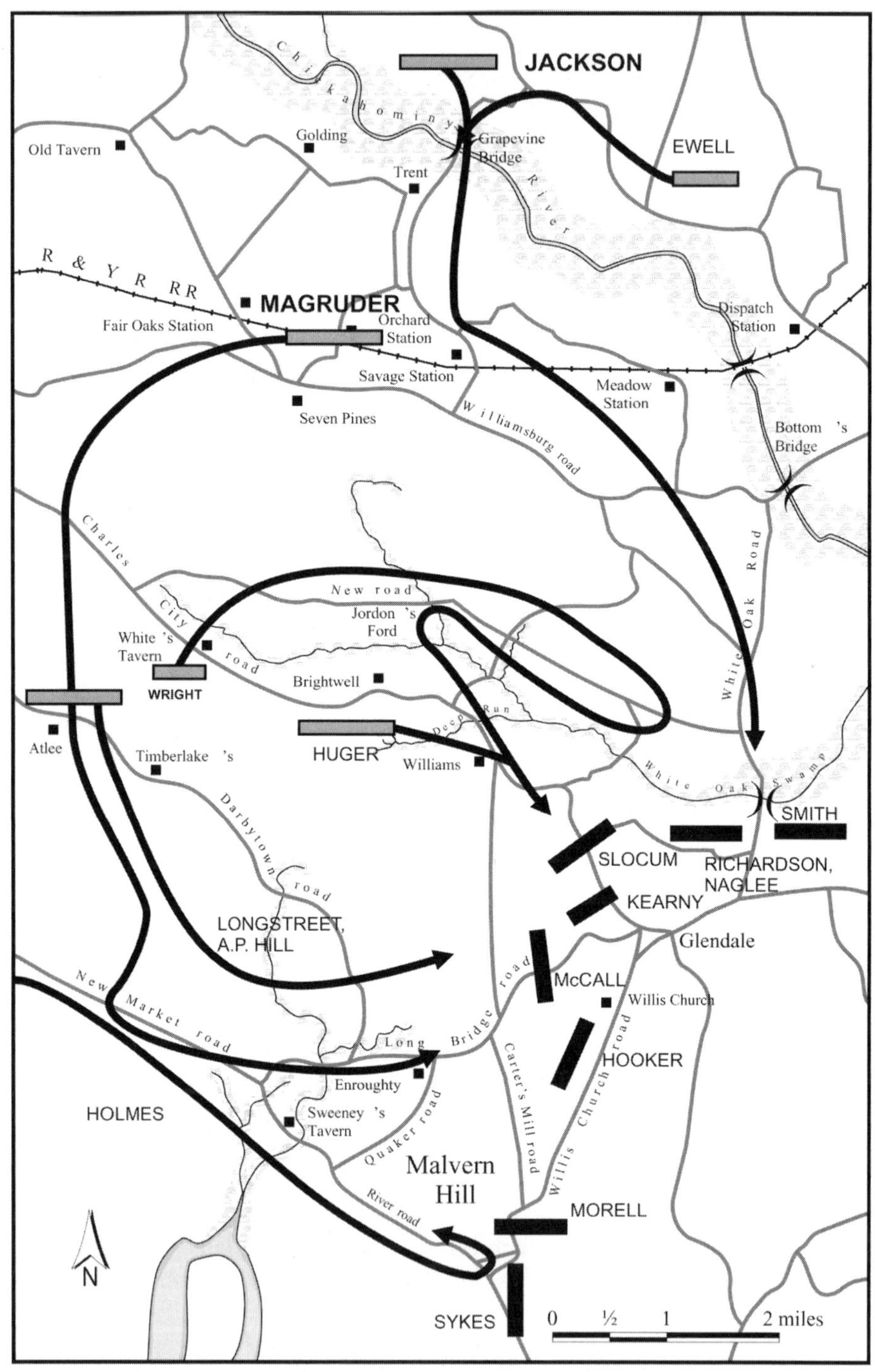

Troop movements, June 30, 1862

battery, said, "I guess we won't need it today." He established the line by 9 A.M., which meant he might not have seen McCall's men in the woods west of the Willis Church road as he moved down it. His first notice of McCall came around 11 A.M., when he saw some wagons belonging to the Pennsylvania Reserves. He investigated and found McCall's left between five hundred and six hundred yards north of his own right, angling off to the northwest. However, this discovery caused no change in Hooker's dispositions.

Between Hooker and McCall, the Yankees had the Long Bridge road approach to Glendale covered. In reserve, an important role given the length of the line and its proximity to the Willis Church road, was Sedgwick's division, which moved from White Oak Swamp to the area around the Nelson farm at Glendale in fits and starts, resting at every opportunity. The stops let some of the division's stragglers find their units. The day once again was hot, and probably humid after the night's rains. No breeze stirred the air.[6]

All the approaches to Glendale were being watched by substantial numbers of Federals, and there was a reserve in case of problems. In fact, 125,000 men were either headed toward or guarding Glendale—with 70,000 rebels moving toward the crossroads, and 55,000 Northerners guarding the approaches to it. In sheer numbers, the battle of the thirtieth promised to be the largest of the war thus far.

The rest of the Unionists were south of the Glendale area. Darius Couch's division and Henry Wessells's brigade from John Peck's division were near Haxall's Landing. Having marched all night, the men were worn out and "expected" (perhaps hoped) to stay where they were, according to George Hagar of the 10th Massachusetts. The 2nd Rhode Island and 7th Massachusetts of Innis Palmer's brigade were guarding the bridge where the River road crossed Turkey Island Creek, just south of Malvern Hill and the last key point in the Army of the Potomac's path to the James. Porter sent George Morell's division south of the bridge, where it made camp. George Sykes halted on Malvern Hill with the artillery reserve. Porter posted the guns facing west and north. Robert Buchanan went to the right of the line, Charles Lovell was next to him, and Gouverneur Warren moved down the hill's west side into a valley from which his brigade could engage any Confederates coming down the River road.

The commander of all these men, George McClellan, also was having a busy morning. After telling the commanders of the three corps around Glendale where he wanted the troops posted, he rode the length of the line. He undoubtedly understood the importance of this crossroads, recognizing what any knowledgeable military man would have by looking at any good map of this part of the Peninsula, but if he had not, Erasmus Keyes's note would have informed him.

The roads in the area were clogged with the army's trains. A member of John Tompkins's battery noted that thousands of wagons were still on the road to the

James, all trying to get there as soon as possible. One quartermaster at Glendale that morning said no officer was present to give any directions. As a result, the various brigades, divisions, and corps fought for the right to use the Willis Church road. Every narrow place in the road caused conflict. Every place where other trains came in caused fighting, sometimes physical, between the harassed teamsters, officers, and others. Some fights were so violent that wagons were damaged and animals killed. A soldier in Hooker's division watched wagons that became disabled pulled out of the line and burned without anyone's taking the time to unload them first. Observing this scene, McClellan knew he had to buy time for the wagons to reach safety. He ordered the roads leading to Glendale obstructed, and Heintzelman followed these orders by cutting trees along both the Charles City road and the road from Brackett's Ford to the Charles City road.

McClellan was more concerned about his trains than he needed to be. Keyes had already found and used the secondary road from the Glendale area to the area around Haxall's Landing, but the IV Corps commander had not yet told McClellan of his discovery. Little Mac said repairing the road delayed Keyes's relaying of information to McClellan, but Keyes could have told anyone in the Glendale area, sent an aide to the Britton farm, or left someone at Glendale to make sure other officers knew of the road. The engineers Alexander, Comstock, and Farquhar had not returned from their mission to find a suitable base for the army, but it is likely that they would have traveled by roads McClellan already knew.

At least for a while, then, most of the trains would go by the Willis Church road (some trains had found Keyes's road, or some other road). Alexander Bliss diverted the trains to Keyes's road during the battle of Glendale after some trains were formed into hollow squares for protection. Even with this diversion, the teamsters and others with the trains were in for what Joseph Elliott, quartermaster of the 71st Pennsylvania, termed the "most exciting day ever experienced." At one point, Elliott thought he certainly would be captured. But he made it past the danger point to his appointed resting place by 5 P.M., as did Frank Young and the 15th Massachusetts's trains. Sometime that evening, all the trains made it to their destination, either in the Malvern Hill–Haxall's Landing area or at the Berkeley plantation at Harrison's Landing, several miles down the James from Haxall's.

The Glendale area would need to be protected all day anyway, because if Glendale were taken the troops at White Oak Swamp Bridge and the trains would be in jeopardy. McClellan knew this. He also knew that he could not form a solid line to protect the area from White Oak Swamp Bridge to the James because he did not have the troops. By bringing Keyes's men up from Haxall's Landing and Morell's division from Turkey Island Bridge, McClellan could extend the Yankee line from Hooker's left flank to the River road. However, that move would require using the reserve force and a breakthrough could then be disastrous.

Seeing this, McClellan took a calculated risk in posting his troops. If a substantial Confederate force came down the Carter's mill road, which was left uncovered, it could attack Malvern Hill, held by many guns but few troops at that point. Alternatively, it could turn back up the Willis Church road and roll up Hooker's left flank, virtually assuring the destruction of a major part of McClellan's army. Little Mac had to be hoping this would not happen; if it did, Hooker might see such a move in the relatively open ground and counter it, or a force from Malvern Hill could attempt to intercept the rebel force.

McClellan's general plan was good, covering the important roads at Glendale in strength and seizing the important positions at Malvern Hill and Turkey Island Bridge. Gaps existed not only between Malvern Hill and Hooker's division, but also between Slocum's right and Richardson's left, as well as small holes caused by the misunderstanding regarding McCall's division. The opening between Slocum and Richardson was less consequential than it might have been because it contained no roads for Southerners to use. The other gaps could cause problems.[7]

Whether by design or default, McClellan had given key roles to two divisions that had already suffered horrendous losses in the campaign. McCall's division lost 1,949 men at Mechanicsville and Gaines's Mill, and Slocum's division lost 1,975 men at Gaines's Mill. Both had been marching for the better part of two days since Gaines's Mill, with little chance to lick their wounds. Yet Slocum was posted on the Charles City road, a key road for any Confederate advance. McCall—compared by one student of the campaign to a "proverbial stepchild" because he was always posted where the fighting was fierce—wound up on the Long Bridge road, another key rebel route. Of the seven divisions around Glendale, these two were the least ready for hard duty and should have been in reserve roles if possible.

There also was no clear command structure in place. McClellan must not have discussed the command structure at his meeting with Sumner, Heintzelman, and Franklin, because after that meeting Franklin received an order putting him in charge of Richardson, Smith, and Naglee (of the three only Smith being in Franklin's own corps). This move unified the command at White Oak Swamp Bridge. But how did it affect Slocum's division on the Charles City road? Franklin could not be in two places at once. Not only that, but Heintzelman's two divisions were separated in line by McCall's division, and no one was in charge of McCall. Sumner was left with only one division (Sedgwick's) to control, since Richardson had been placed under Franklin's control. Perhaps McClellan did not give Sumner any more to do because he distrusted the II Corps commander. The same motivation probably underlay McClellan's not naming any overall commander on the field. Any success arising out of these command conditions would require cooperation among several different generals and good staff work.[8]

The command problems could have been solved easily if McClellan had remained on the field. However, as he had the day before, Little Mac left his rear guard to fend for itself and headed south, according to one account as soon as he heard that Lee's men were approaching the Willis Church road from the west. His own explanation was that he wanted to examine the ground all the way to Haxall's Landing—during which he may have talked with Keyes and found out about the secondary road. He and his staff rejoiced at seeing the James River. He then returned to Malvern Hill to realign some troops and get the trains moving faster. After sending aides from Malvern Hill to the corps commanders near Glendale informing them of his actions and asking about their positions, McClellan moved back to Haxall's Landing and boarded the *Galena* to discuss with Commodore Rodgers the location of the new base.

Perhaps Alexander's written report had not reached McClellan, or perhaps Little Mac wanted to reason with Rodgers himself—he could not have liked Rodgers's notion to retreat all the way to the mouth of the Chickahominy, twenty air miles from Haxall's Landing. Alexander was no longer with Rodgers. The two had headed up the James to the bend north of the mouth of Turkey Island Creek, and then went down the river to Carter's Landing. After changing boats, Alexander headed to the mouth of the Chickahominy to look around. His boat ran aground on a sandbar, and he stayed there that night. Rodgers moved back to Haxall's.

The naval officer told McClellan that because the river's main channel came so close to City Point, on the south side of the James at the mouth of the Appomattox River and controlled by the Confederates, he could not guarantee the transports' safety in that area. The base would have to be downriver from that point, ruling out the use of Haxall's Landing (located upriver from City Point) as a base. Rodgers conceded that Harrison's Landing would be suitable, even though he had not liked the idea when Alexander suggested it.

McClellan then got off the boat, although not before eating dinner with Rodgers in the commodore's well-appointed mess. One of his first acts once on land was to send Randolph Marcy a message that the army's headquarters was to move to Haxall's as a temporary measure and advising him that Malvern Hill would not be held permanently. Little Mac wanted to know how many of the wagons had not begun moving and what roads led from the Glendale area to Long Bridge and Jones's Bridge across the Chickahominy. He was contemplating having to make another stand between Malvern Hill and his final position, and he probably wanted to know if he would have to cover the lower bridges. He finally moved back to Malvern Hill, where he stayed until the next day. On his way, he stopped at the new headquarters and sent Stanton and his wife messages. The one to Stanton demanded large reinforcements quickly and more gunboats to protect his army. "If none of us escape we shall at least have done honor to the country," he wrote. "I shall do my best to save the Army."

Lincoln had not heard from McClellan in two days. The messages the president did receive on the twenty-eighth and twenty-ninth, from Rufus Ingalls and an army paymaster, were encouraging but wrong. The paymaster reported that Porter had retired from the Gaines's Mill battlefield only under orders, and Ingalls said McClellan was going to concentrate near Richmond. Stanton, hearing all of this, estimated that Little Mac would be in Richmond in two days. On the thirtieth, Lincoln heard from John Dix that McClellan intended to abandon White House Landing for the James River, and later that day Lincoln grew increasingly worried over the lack of news from McClellan's headquarters.

Washington was alive with rumor, as three days passed before most of the city had reliable news. New York was worse. George Templeton Strong worried at everything from the War Department's silence to the term "*strategic movement*; polite language, I suppose, for a retreat." Secretary of State William Seward, in town to pass along a secret message from Lincoln asking Northern governors to volunteer more troops, was "very jolly," but Strong was not: "The indications taken all together—the 'totality of the symptoms'—are of disaster and ruin," he wrote.

McClellan was not that pessimistic. His message to his wife said, "I am well but worn out—no sleep for many days. . . . I still hope to save the army." He had chosen a peculiar way of accomplishing that, however. For the second day in a row, McClellan had decided that his efforts with the head of the army were more important than making sure the tail kept Lee at bay. In fact, for the second day in a row he was going over ground that the engineer Alexander was supposed to be working on. More than any other day, McClellan's judgment on the thirtieth is suspect. Whereas on the twenty-ninth it is at least possible that his army was not in danger, and on July 1 he was at least on the field, there seems to be no excuse for his actions on the thirtieth. He had to know that Lee would be after him and that Glendale would be the focus of Lee's assault. He had arranged for signal communication between Malvern Hill and the river, but that is a poor substitute. To leave units from five different corps at a vital point with no overall commander is to court disaster, and McClellan would have been subject to severe criticism if disaster had resulted.

There are a few possible explanations. Lack of physical courage is not one, though. At Oak Grove he was not averse to being on the field. One possibility is that McClellan was so exhausted that he could not function properly. Andrew Humphreys of McClellan's staff wrote to his wife: "[N]ever did I see a man more cut down than Genl. McClellan was. . . . He was unable to do anything or say anything." McClellan could have been "cut down" at this point by the lack of sleep.

Another possibility is that McClellan had lost his will to command. He could function as a staff officer, which was exactly what he was doing, but no longer as a leader of men in battle. Perhaps he thought that he could do his best for his army by scouting ahead, making sure the Malvern Hill position was set, and choosing the new base. William Franklin and McClellan's aide William Biddle both wrote long after the war that Little Mac thought the situation at Glendale was well in hand and that his proper place was with the head of the army, although Franklin expressed doubt that McClellan was correct. Heintzelman seemed to support this explanation in his testimony before the Joint Committee on the Conduct of the War when he said of McClellan: "[H]e was the most extraordinary man I ever saw. I do not see how any man could leave so much to others; and be so confident that everything would go just right." Perhaps he could see only the river and the protection of the gunboats; or perhaps his messianic complex and worry for his country combined to keep him from putting himself in danger. It is impossible to be sure.[9]

While McClellan was examining a new base for the Army of the Potomac, Confederate units were moving to intercept the Yankees. Jackson's men continued on the road to White Oak Swamp. Stonewall wanted and got an early start, but he was still concerned with speed. Before he met Lee, he was waiting at a crossroads for Col. Thomas Munford and his 2nd Virginia Cavalry, which was to be at the crossroads at daylight to lead the march. But the rainstorm that had caused Union soldiers misery that night had scattered the horse soldiers as well. By sunrise Munford could gather together only about fifty men and he was still half a mile from his appointed place. Jackson was not late. When Munford rode up, Stonewall said, "Colonel, my orders to you were to be here at sunrise." Munford tried to explain, including the fact that he had no food for his men. Jackson was not moved. "Yes, sir," he repeated. "But, Colonel, I ordered you to be here at sunrise. Move on with your regiment. If you meet the enemy drive in his pickets, and if you want artillery, Colonel [Stapleton] Crutchfield [Jackson's artillery chief] will furnish you."

Probably wondering how he would drive in pickets with fifty men, Munford rode off. The rest of his men kept riding by, trying to catch up, and Jackson noticed. Two couriers came to Munford with Jackson's message that the cavalrymen were "straggling badly." Munford rode back, again trying to explain his problems. "Yes, sir," Stonewall replied. "But I ordered you to be here at sunrise, and I have been waiting for you for a quarter of an hour." Munford finally gave up, told his adjutant to form up the stragglers where they were, and went on with his fifty men, making a bold charge and pushing the Yankee pickets across the swamp.

Unlike Munford, D. H. Hill had been ready at dawn. When Reverend Dabney, pleased that Stonewall's orders were being carried out in this division, said that Jackson could never have his men ready at dawn as Hill had and asked how he did it, Hill responded, "Well I suppose I do it by hard scolding only." Hill was not happy about the day's plan. "If it does not end in disaster," he told Dabney, "it will only be our luck or a kind Providence."

As he approached Savage Station at the head of the column, Hill thought he saw some Northerners in line of battle. It turned out to be the men from the hospital, all of whom were now prisoners. Jackson stopped as he passed through the area and talked with Cpl. Patrick Taylor of the 1st Minnesota. When he asked Taylor how many Yankees had been at Savage Station the day before, Taylor replied, "I don't know, sir." Jackson pondered Taylor's response for a moment and said, "I don't suppose you'd tell if you did know." Wade Hampton wrote Taylor a pass so he could get water for the wounded.

Hill and his men also marched past the area where Paul Semmes and William Brooks had fought, and saw the 5th Vermont's casualties looking like a whole Union regiment of death. The Yankee dead were "thicker than on any of the fields around Richmond," a North Carolinian remembered. Every house the men passed was filled with wounded soldiers. As he passed Savage Station, Hill began to pick up Federal stragglers, eventually gathering about a thousand of them. He detailed the 4th North Carolina of George B. Anderson's brigade and the 5th North Carolina of Samuel Garland's brigade to take care of them. Jackson, being congratulated on the taking of so many prisoners, was told that the rebels might have a hard time taking good care of them. "It is cheaper to feed them, than to fight them," he replied with a smile.

As they marched through the area that McClellan's army had occupied for weeks, the Valley veterans saw the supplies the Yankees left behind. The Army of the Potomac had taken all it could and destroyed as much as possible, but there was still a lot left. Abandoned mules came out of the trees. Ruined wagons and pontoon trains, mounds of food, tools, cooking utensils, medicines, and clothing were strewn on the ground. Mounds of coffee beans had been burned, and some were done just enough to be used. The road was "a map of clothing, crackers, and letters and things taken out of the knapsacks."[10]

Huger, moving down the Charles City road with William Mahone's, Lew Armistead's, and Robert Ransom's brigades, also captured many Union stragglers. He started his men from the Brightwell house at daylight. Mahone, in the lead, first covered the road to Fisher's Ford in case the Northerners had not left the area. He found a copy of orders on a dead Yankee telling Kearny to retire and keep a strong battery with him, but they did not specify to where Kearny should retire. As several fords crossed White Oak Swamp, Huger was still concerned for his left flank. The men halted several times to form into line of battle just in case. But Mahone, talking to a civilian in the area of Fisher's Ford, learned that no large enemy force was close, and the column again began advancing down the Charles City road. He immediately ran into two things: Yankee pickets, and obstructions on the road (particularly fallen trees) put there by men from Slocum's division. Mahone estimated that the obstructions lasted for more than a mile, which meant that they would have extended as far as the Brackett field, owned by the family that had given its name to the nearby ford. He may have learned that by riding down the Charles City road and being fired upon by Union skirmishers, temporarily losing his straw hat in the process. The corner of the Brackett field closest to the Confederates was about a mile from Slocum's position and about two miles from Glendale.

Mahone had a decision to make. He could go over the obstructions or around them, either of which would have meant leaving his artillery (plus all of Huger's) behind as the infantry passed through the trees. He could clear the obstructions, which would mean cutting up the fallen trees while under Federal fire—or perhaps lifting them out of the way, as one person who examined the road two years after the fact claimed could have been accomplished by one company of troops. He could also cut a road through the woods, which might have been the best choice with experienced woodsmen, since cutting a tree down is probably quicker than cutting it up once it has fallen. Mahone, the one-time railroad construction engineer, should have been able to make this decision wisely.

He chose to either cut a road through the woods or cut up the fallen trees (the record is unclear). But his men lacked proper equipment for either task, or perhaps the Virginians may have had little experience or skill in chopping trees. For whatever reason, as both sides cut down trees in this "battle of the axes," the Confederates lost. Moreover, not wanting to risk men when he did not know where the main Federal line was, Huger did not send anyone down the road to chase off the Northerners doing the cutting. With all these problems—concern for his left flank, dealing with the obstructions, and enduring Union skirmishers—Huger knew he would be delayed. Sometime that morning he sent a note to that effect to Lee. By late morning he had advanced little more than a mile and some of his units had not moved at all.

Huger's fourth brigade—Wright's—was marching north of the swamp. At dawn, Wright moved from the junction of the New and Charles City roads down the New road, leaving Capt. H. M. Ross's battery of Georgia's Sumter Artillery behind to come when called. Wright also learned that Kearny had left the immediate vicinity, and by 8 A.M. he was at the northern part of Jordon's Ford. He found Yankee pickets just west of the ford, the bridge broken down, and the approach to it obstructed by fallen trees.

Wright took this situation seriously. Skirmishers fell out to drive in the pickets. Lieutenant L. F. Luckie of the 3rd Georgia headed north to find a path and ford that Wright's guide had told him was half a mile away. Luckie then crossed the swamp to look at the enemy's position. Colonel Doles of the 4th Georgia sent men south about three-quarters of a mile to another crossing. But that proved unnecessary, as Wright found out when his skirmishers captured two Federals. They told him that their main force was headed for White Oak Swamp Bridge. Luckie came back with the same story, and Wright ordered the whole column forward. The rebels dispersed the pickets and a somewhat more substantial rear guard, crossed the swamp, and moved into the deserted Union camp, where they found much abandoned equipment. Wright kept marching well into the afternoon, continuing east along the New road, occupying camps, taking prisoners, and probably marveling at the amount of equipment left behind.[11]

Longstreet and A. P. Hill ran into no empty Yankee camps during their morning march from Atlee's farm. After talking with Magruder, Lee joined this column, which had the crucial task of cutting the Willis Church road. The men marched down the Darbytown road and turned left at its junction with the Long Bridge road. At about 11 A.M. they reached the area about a mile west of Glendale where they were to wait for the sound of Huger's and Jackson's guns before attacking. Hill took advantage of the wait to get his brigades, which were behind Longstreet's, closed up. Dorsey Pender's men, for example, marched between ten and twelve miles on a hot day with very little water. Ominously for the men, Little Powell also established field hospitals.

Magruder, meanwhile, was also on the road, although he personally was still not feeling well. Up until 3:30, he managed to sleep for only an hour before Lee's visit. Prince John was, as Major Brent put it, "under a nervous excitement," getting himself involved with every aspect of the movement and probably delaying its start. After his men finally got moving, Magruder and his staff stopped at a stream to water their horses. Brent, prompted by Henry Bryan, Magruder's chief of staff, went up to his commander. "General," he said, "I am sorry to see that you are not feeling well this morning." Magruder asked Brent why he thought that, and Brent replied that he had never seen Prince John act quite this way. Queried as to specifics, Brent began, "Well, General, I hope you will pardon me, but I have never seen your usual calmness so much lost by an extreme irritability, sometimes exhibited without any apparent cause, and hence I inferred that you must be feeling badly."

Magruder then confessed. "Well, Major," he said, "you are right. I am feeling horribly. For two days I have been disturbed about my digestion"—stress probably had something to do with that—"and the doctor has been giving me medicine, and I fear he has given me some morphine in his mixture, and the smallest quantity of it acts upon me as an irritant. And beside that, I have lost so much sleep that it affects me strangely; but I fully appreciate your kindness in speaking to me, and I will endeavor to regain my self control."

Why Magruder did not question his doctor, or indeed let him know that no morphine was allowed, is an unanswerable question. He might have been calmer the day before without the morphine (if indeed he took any, his behavior not merely being a result of stress and lack of sleep), perhaps showing better judgment. But the march itself, once started, seemed to go well. Lafayette McLaws complained about the lack of guides, but Magruder had a guide sent by Lee, and at least the front of the column knew where it was going, reaching the Darbytown road and following Longstreet and Hill.[12]

All of Lee's forces were headed toward Glendale except for Holmes, who was waiting on the River road. Lee's plans were coming together; the trap was being built. What remained to be seen was whether the builders could complete the trap before the quarry escaped.

CHAPTER FOURTEEN

"He . . . Rose and Walked Off in Silence"

The Union unit at Glendale most exposed to the enemy attack was not ready for it. The Pennsylvania Reserves's historian wrote, "Most of the men were fitter subjects for the hospital than for the battle-field." Even the healthy ones were waiting to march down the Willis Church road. There is some question about how George McCall first figured out that rebels were nearing him. He reported that he had heard cannon fire from the north at about 9 A.M. (probably a mistake as to the time). Because he did not think he was in any danger from the north, he reasoned that he had better protect against an attack from the west. He thus sent an infantry regiment to join the 4th Pennsylvania Cavalry on picket and formed the division in line. However, Truman Seymour wrote that he and George Meade rode to the front and found only the cavalry screen between them and the rebels. Their ride had apparently been inspired by reports of a Southern advance, and the reports were correct. The two brigade commanders reported to McCall, who sent the 1st and 3rd Pennsylvania Reserves out to picket and got the rest of the division in line.

Whichever account is right, the result was the same. McCall surveyed the area between the Long Bridge road and Willis Church, then deployed Meade to the north of the Long Bridge road. Seymour was on Meade's left, covering the area from the Long Bridge road to the Whitlock farmhouse, about a third of a mile northwest of Willis Church. Colonel Seneca Simmons's brigade formed the reserve. Alanson Randol's battery went with Meade, Mark Kerns's and James Cooper's batteries were in the middle near the Long Bridge road, and Otto Diederichs and John Knieriem moved to the left of Seymour's line. In Col. R. Biddle Roberts's opinion, the line was "a magnificent appearance."

McCall liked the ground he was to fight over. In general it was open, forming the Whitlock farm, with some trees parallel to the Long Bridge road. The open ground formed a rectangle eight hundred yards wide and a thousand yards deep, offering excellent fields of fire. The ground was gently sloping with a small stream flowing through it. It was, McCall thought, "a beautiful battle ground, but too large for my force to find cover or protection on both flanks." Joe Hooker and Phil Kearny could have provided that protection, but there was a gap between Hooker's right and McCall's left, and Kearny's left was to the rear of McCall's right. If the rebels came straight up the Long Bridge road, McCall would be in good shape, but if they got off the road any distance in either direction he could be in a desperate situation.

The 3rd Reserves made it into position south of the Long Bridge road without incident at about 11 A.M. The 1st Reserves, however, had more of an adventure. Colonel Roberts was given a black guide who was supposed to know the country. As the regiment kept advancing, Roberts dropped companies off to take their positions. But when the last company reached its position, Roberts realized that the guide had led him straight into the enemy's lines (probably a picket line). Moving back at the double-quick, Roberts gathered his regiment, got back to the road, and set up his picket line in a safer area. The guide was shot.[1]

The enemy Roberts found probably was the 3rd Virginia Cavalry, which was leading Longstreet's column up the Long Bridge road. Someone reported to Longstreet about noon that Yankee skirmishers were advancing. With Longstreet commanding the entire column, Richard Anderson was in field command of the division, and Micah Jenkins of the Palmetto Sharpshooters took command of Anderson's brigade. At the head of the column, Jenkins checked what was in front of him, found the 1st and 3rd Reserves in place, and some fighting ensued. Meade responded to the firing by heading to the 1st Reserves's area. Roberts had been trying to draw the rebels out of the woods, even galloping along his line with some cavalry to draw fire, and had figured out that a lot of Confederates were in the trees. The officers heard firing in the 3rd Reserves's direction, and Meade told Roberts to get back to the line. Roberts told McCall that the rebels were near. McCall did not believe him at first, then ordered Roberts to draw an attack by firing on the enemy.

Colonel Horatio G. Sickel of the 3rd Reserves had seen the Southerners when they tried to flank his regiment. Sickel counterattacked until the rebels retired. He then pulled his men back toward the main line, completing McCall's dispositions. The Confederates were completing theirs, as well. Longstreet was away from the field, having either stayed behind at his campsite when the men began their march or left the column for some reason. He or Lee (who was still with the troops) gave A. P. Hill an order to take overall command for the present. Little Powell went to Richard Anderson, and the two generals positioned the troops. Longstreet's division made ready for either attack or defense. Jenkins remained on the Long Bridge road, with one regiment to the south of the road. James Kemper's men filed to Jenkins's right. Cadmus Wilcox and Pryor went north of the road, supported by Winfield Featherston. George Pickett's brigade, commanded by Eppa Hunton after Pickett was wounded at Gaines's Mill, was near the center of the line. Lawrence Branch moved his men to support Kemper, while the rest of Hill's division stayed on the road. Lee sent a message to John Magruder asking how far he had marched. Without hearing from Magruder, however—perhaps after noticing the number of troops on the Long Bridge road or receiving Benjamin Huger's notice of the delay that officer was encountering—Marse Robert sent another message to Magruder telling him to halt and rest his men, keeping them ready to move at once. Longstreet, meanwhile, had rejoined his men and was near the front. Sometime between 2:30 and 3 P.M., he heard artillery fire to the north. Figuring it was Huger's signal, Longstreet ordered several batteries in the area to answer it.[2]

Old Pete was mistaken. The guns were Stonewall Jackson's, opening on William Franklin's position at White Oak Swamp Bridge. Colonel Stapleton Crutchfield, Jackson's artillery chief, had reached the bridge area just after the Yankees fired the bridge. He examined the area and observed Federal guns on the hill south of the swamp and sharpshooters hidden in some trees near the bridge site. Backing up, he found a good position about a thousand yards from the Union guns on a hill north of the swamp and west of the road, as well as a way to get cannon to that position without being seen. The first division on the road, and thus the first available artillery, belonged to D. H. Hill, so Crutchfield brought the batteries forward.

There is little agreement about the number of guns actually moved into line—Crutchfield reported 23, Jackson reported 28, and D. H. Hill reported 31—but there is no question that they came from Hill's and William Whiting's divisions. They certainly included Capt. Thomas H. Carter's King William (Virginia) Artillery battery, Capt. G. W. Nelson's Hanover (Virginia) Artillery battery, Hardaway's and Rhett's batteries, all of Hill's division, and Capt. William L. Balthis's Staunton (Virginia) Artillery battery and James Reilly's Rowan Artillery battery of Whiting's division. Other artillery from D. H. Hill's division that may have participated included Bondurant's battery, Clarke's battery, and the Orange (Virginia) Artillery battery, commanded by Lt. C. W. Fry due to Peyton's sickness. The fact that at most thirty-one guns were used would indicate that not all of these were employed. Captain Rhett, who went with Crutchfield on his reconnaissance, took some pioneers and cut a road through some trees to the position. The artillerymen followed, set up, and between 1:45 and 2 P.M. according to their watches, began firing on the unsuspecting Federals.[3]

Few of those Federals were ready. James Miller of the 2nd Delaware had seen a Southerner climb a tree. Miller pointed out the man just before the

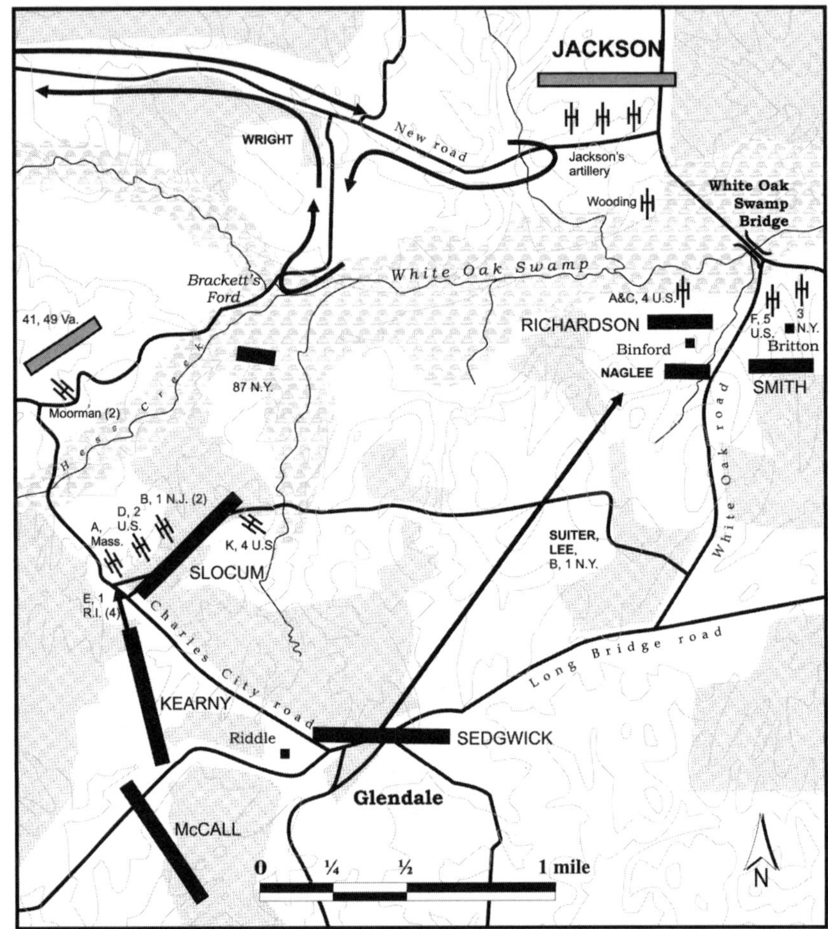

White Oak Swamp and Brackett's, June 30, 1862

shelling started, and perhaps those within earshot were the only ones who knew something was up. The firing caught Baldy Smith dressing after his bath. Overcoming the shock and opening the door of the outhouse he had used, Smith saw Jackson's guns almost literally filling the air with shot and shell. The general tried to get his groom to bring his best horse, but he soon found that the groom had taken the animal and skedaddled. Neither would be seen for two days. An Englishman who was Smith's servant at the time coolly saddled another horse, by which time Smith had hurriedly finished dressing—leaving his watch behind.

The men in the ranks were just as shocked. J. B. Pollard of the 2nd Vermont said, "Our men being taken by surprise and the most of us asleep scattered like a flock of sheep at the first fire." Many soldiers counted that unexpected wake-up call among their "most memorable experiences," and one man wrote home, "Twas the most terrific scene I ever witnessed, and I feel entirely unequal to the task of describing it."

Some of the artillerists and teamsters still near White Oak Swamp had watered their horses and mules in the swamp. The cannonade, as might be expected, startled the animals—between two hundred and three hundred in number, one man said—and they bolted into Thomas Meagher's brigade, hurting more men than did Confederate fire. Infantrymen laughed in the midst of the shelling at the teamsters' troubles. Many teams left as quickly as they could—"their departure seemed to be hurried," one diarist noted. Some cut the traces, leaving the wagons behind, to get out faster. The teamsters were threatened with death if they did not slow to a walk, and the trains soon were brought under control. The 5th Wisconsin's hospital corps was on the dead run when the surgeon, Alfred Castleman, yelled what he remembered as "a great mouthful of oaths." Apparently Castleman was not usually given to such language, and the men stopped and returned immediately—a little unconvinced that Castleman had uttered such words.

The men of the 7th Maine had gone to sleep immediately upon crossing White Oak Swamp earlier that morning. Someone eventually woke them up, and Major Hyde went with two hundred men to picket the right part of the Union line. They had just settled into their places when the rebel guns opened up. Romeyn Ayres's and Thaddeus Mott's batteries tried to respond to the Southern activity. At the same time, Ayres told Charles Wheeler and Andrew Cowan to take their guns to the edge of a wood to the rear—probably since the chances of setting up shop under such a fire were slim. Apparently the Yankees could not see their opponents clearly even after the firing started, but in any case the contest was bound to be unequal, with just two batteries pitted against as many as thirty-one guns. Ayres reported that Mott's battery was "thrown into confusion," "useless," and leaving the field "broken up and in disorder, the horses, many of them, scattered." An ammunition chest exploded, destroying William Moore's knapsack, which he had strapped to the caisson. Moore later recalled that he did not get a change of underwear until October. Mott left a gun on the field. Ayres's own men kept to their posts a little longer, but Smith, dressed and ready for action by now, ordered the battery away from danger.[4]

Meanwhile, Smith's infantry had retreated. The Confederates were about three-quarters of a mile from the Union lines, at about the same elevation as the Yankees—about 50 feet above the swamp and its flood plain—with no obstructions to hurt their aim. The Northern foot soldiers were sitting ducks. One shot went through the Britton house, wounding its owner—who had stayed despite Smith's and Franklin's warnings. Hit in the leg, he bled to death. "He had sacrificed himself for his poultry," wrote Franklin.

Smith ordered the infantry back nearly half a mile to the same woods that sheltered the artillery. Brooks remembered the move as being "in great haste," but Hyde remembered the retreat as relatively slow. A few men complained, "Why don't they double-quick?" Some of the men did, and one of Winfield Scott Hancock's men wrote home, "There was not a knapsack on one of the men in our company." One regiment, the 20th New York in John Davidson's brigade, had more than it could take. The Germans in this regiment wore black top hats, but as they broke for the rear the hats came off, dotting the plain wherever they lay. Hyde related the tradition in the 7th Maine that the New Yorkers were still running, and their colonel was rumored to be operating a beer garden in Cincinnati. Hyde blamed the officers for this poor performance. Smith remembered that the regiment "scattered like chaff." Davidson (a thirty-seven-year-old Virginian and second-generation West Pointer who allegedly declined a Confederate commission) was back in command of his brigade. He, Smith, and Capt. Edward Martindale of Davidson's staff rallied most of the New Yorkers. Smith, though, said that almost half the regiment did not show up until hunger forced the men in two days later.

Israel Richardson's men sought what shelter they could while still supporting their batteries. The rebel metal "came in amongst us like hail stone," according to one account. Some lay down in hollows to escape the fire. A woman whose husband was in the Irish Brigade would grab by the neck any retreating soldier and drag him back into the ranks with several choice comments—a large umbrella serving as her only physical weapon. Naglee's men hid behind some rails thrown up at the edge of a wood and watched the "terribly sublime" scene.[5]

Jackson could see this retreat. He could not, however, see to the west of the road, where Richardson's men were basically in their positions. Stonewall ordered Munford, whose regiment was reassembled by then, to cross the swamp and retrieve Mott's abandoned gun. D. H. Hill, Jackson, and some staff officers went with Munford to get a better view of things. As the rebels crossed the swamp and attempted to charge, Union troops poured a heavy fire into the cavalrymen. A Federal battery, thought to be the guns that had been seen retreating, also fired at the rebels. Hill and Jackson decided it might be better if they turned around, and they did so—"retiring rapidly," Hill remembered, adding, "Fast riding in the wrong direction is not military, but it is sometimes healthy."

One Yankee, an obviously drunken Irishman of the 7th Maine, was close enough to be "captured" by the Southerners. He refused to cross the swamp, however, and was ready to fight for his freedom with his fists. A Confederate asked Hill if he should shoot the Federal, and Hill said to let him be. The Irishman, guarded only by his coat hung on a stick, survived four shots fired from fifty yards by Rev. L. W. Allen. Getting back to his company the next day, he told his fellows "if he had had one more canteen of whisky he could have held the position all day."

Munford also decided he had better get back to the northern side of the swamp, but he did not want to have to cross the stream—which was running high with water from the previous night's rain—under fire. He moved his men downstream about a quarter of a mile to a cow path that led to a ford. Franklin later remembered that the rebels fell back "much faster than [they] advanced." On the way, Munford passed through a few of Smith's campsites, finding knapsacks, blankets, and other items—including recent Washington newspapers. After getting across the stream, which he recalled he did "with great difficulty," Munford let his men take the knapsacks and blankets, but he sent the newspapers to Jackson, letting him know where and how he had regained the north bank. Stonewall congratulated him on getting back safely. Skirmishers from D. H. Hill's division, crossing with Munford, stayed on the south bank the rest of the day and all night. At the same time Jackson sent Munford forward, he ordered Capt. George W. Wooding's Danville (Virginia) Artillery battery to fire on the Yankee sharpshooters from near the bridge site. Wooding was recalled to join the guns on the ridge when Munford left the area.

George Hazzard's guns, in the area west of the White Oak road that was screened from the rebels' view, had shelled Munford and Wooding. That, of course, had drawn the interest of the rebel artillery. The Southerners even sent iron rails toward Hazzard. Richardson ordered the guns to advance a little and four of them moved forward and to the west, into a little gorge that offered them shelter and let them command the bridge area. They stayed about fifteen minutes, when the entire battery received an order to retire. It began doing so, but got only four hundred yards when it received an order to take its original position and commence firing. The combatants could not see each other through the trees, but they could aim at the smoke, so the artillery duel continued. Hazzard was supported by Ayres, who after the retreat had set up again only to have Hazzard move in front of him. Ayres then moved to the east a little. There he saw the gun left by Mott's men—which surprised him, since he had ordered a corporal and two lieutenants to remove it from the field.[6]

The casualties caused by the opposing gunners have been described as "trifling," but artillery firing for hours will do some damage. In Meagher's brigade, still under Robert Nugent's command, a round shot ricocheted, killing a soldier. The two men on either side of the dead Yankee rose up, lifted his body, carried it to a tree, and put it down underneath the tree's protection. After they covered the man's face with a blanket, they left the spot, went back to the line, and lay down in the spots they had vacated. A Captain O'Donohoe in the same brigade was lying down when a solid shot buried itself six inches from him. The hole was big enough to bury a baby in. A comrade suggested that O'Donohoe move to where the shot had hit the ground, since another one would not hit there, but O'Donohoe decided to stay where he was. Soon another solid shot hit the exact same spot as the first, going even deeper into the ground. Summing up the Federals' feelings, one of Smith's men said the Confederates blazed away "to our entire satisfaction."

Hazzard's batteries suffered from a "very rapid and very precise" Confederate fire. The ground protected them because they had been placed just behind the brow of a hill, and the solid shot mostly hit the hill and ricocheted over the Yankees' heads. Hazzard himself sighted guns, delivered ammunition, and disentangled horses after they had been shot. This activity eventually cost him his life. He was supervising the unloading of ammunition when a shell burst nearby, and a fragment hit him in the leg, breaking the bone. Hazzard was taken off the field; he died from complications a few months later.

The artillery contest continued until dark. The Union guns, outnumbered all afternoon, got some help when Rufus Pettit's battery came up on Richardson's orders from the Glendale area. Lieutenant Rufus King Jr., who had taken over Hazzard's battery when Hazzard was wounded, continued to battle it out with the rebels. Once, he saw Confederate infantry near the swamp, perhaps pioneers who Jackson had sent out to try to rebuild the bridge, but who King thought might be trying to assault him. He loaded canister and fired, forcing them to seek cover in the woods on the other side.

Meagher, still under arrest and not commanding his brigade, was nonetheless on the scene and helped work a gun. When King began to run low on ammunition, Meagher volunteered to go find Richardson and get more sent up. Before it arrived, however, King had run out and was forced to retire into a hollow. When his caissons had been filled, King sent three guns back up to a position just left of his former spot.

Pettit arrived at that point and set up to King's right. King pointed out the target area, but his own gunners were so exhausted they did not fire again until almost dusk, when they heard trees being felled. Case shot was sent into the trees. Finally, King took one gun back to the rest of the battery, leaving Lt. Edward Field to fire "slowly and surely" with the other two guns. Meanwhile, Pettit fired to get the range, zeroing in at about a mile and, according to his report, blowing up an ammunition chest. Pettit used nearly sixteen hundred rounds of ammunition in what one artilleryman called a "warm" engagement.

Crutchfield experienced some of the same problems as the Federal gunners, particularly the inability to see the target. As did the Yankees, Crutchfield reported the enemy's fire as accurate, although not as effective as it could have been because of the nature of the ground. He said that no carriages or guns were lost and claimed to have blown up a caisson himself. Although Franklin remembered the firing slowing after the first half-hour, rising again at intervals but never with the original force, Crutchfield reported that the duel lasted until dark "without intermission."[7]

No accurate count can be made of the Union casualties at White Oak Swamp Bridge, but they cannot have been heavy. The infantry were almost all protected by either trees or the ground, and only a few regiments moved after the initial rush. Franklin wrote long after the war, "The fight at White Oak Bridge was entirely with artillery, there being little musketry firing." No reports of any substantial number of casualties were made. The highest reported loss was in the 5th New Hampshire of Caldwell's brigade, which had 5 men killed and 9 wounded. Total Union casualties may have amounted to as many as 100. On the Confederate side, the losses were even fewer: only three batteries, those of Clark, Peyton, and Rhett, reported losses, and those totaled 3 killed and 12 wounded. Wooding's battery reported 1 killed and 3 wounded for the campaign, and some of those may have occurred at White Oak Swamp Bridge.

Such low casualty figures are to be expected, given that (as Porter Alexander said) the guns were firing "at random," even if there were as many as 31 guns on one side and about 12 more powerful guns at any one time on the other. Alexander thought that Jackson, if he was going to use only artillery, should have assembled 75 cannon, but he had no more than 72 with him. In fact, the historian of the Confederate artillery said that Jackson brought up all his guns for the engagement, although Stonewall reported that only batteries from D. H. Hill's and Whiting's divisions (plus Wooding's battery) were used.[8]

After Jackson returned to the north bank of White Oak Swamp, he ordered Hill and Whiting to move their men to a pine forest for cover. He also ordered pioneers to repair the bridge, but "the men would not work" under the Union fire. Jackson, seeing the repair would cost him many men, ordered it discontinued. The ford that Munford used was available. Munford wrote long after the war, despite his difficulty in crossing the swamp on horseback: "I know that I thought, all the time, that he could have crossed his infantry where we recrossed. I had seen his infantry cross far worse places, and I expected that he would attempt it." One of Munford's officers remembered that they had encountered little difficulty crossing the swamp at the ford. Munford could not remember what he had written to Jackson in his note, but given Stonewall's congratulatory response on the crossing, it may be assumed that Munford had reported the passage was difficult. It could be that the note was pessimistic enough to keep Jackson from further investigating that ford. Stonewall certainly did not use it.

Wright, continuing to move down the New road during the afternoon, reached the White Oak road shortly after the artillery duel began. He went to Jackson for orders, as Huger's covered only the movement to the bridge. Stonewall told him to find a way to cross upstream if he could, since the Yankees were in place at the bridge itself. Wright began retracing his steps, and his guide showed him the road that led south to Brackett's Ford. After a company from the

3rd Georgia took its place as skirmishers on the west side of the road and a company of the 1st Louisiana did likewise on the east side, Wright moved forward. Reaching the swamp, he found the bridge destroyed and the road south of the swamp blocked. The rebel skirmishers moved through the water and fallen trees until they encountered pickets from the 87th New York of Robinson's brigade.

The New Yorkers fell back slowly before Wright's men, allowing the Confederates a good look at what they faced. The road led into a meadow surrounded by hills, and on the hills to the southeast sat artillery with infantry support—Slocum's division, facing the Charles City road but well able to see any movement Wright might make and respond to it. One regiment, the 1st New Jersey, was facing the swamp itself. Two Yankee pickets captured by the Southerners confirmed the observations. Wright had not ordered Ross's battery to join him from the Charles City road, so he had no guns to help him with an assault. He decided against attacking, moved his men back across the swamp, kept moving west, and crossed at Fisher's Ford (the next available crossing). The brigade stopped for the day near the Fisher house south of the swamp. Wright apparently never let Stonewall know of his findings, although he did tell Huger of Jackson's predicament.

Although Wright was convinced he could not make headway at Brackett's Ford, Franklin, the Union commander, thought that Jackson could have done severe damage by using it. Writing twenty years after the events, Franklin said simultaneous attacks at White Oak Swamp Bridge and Brackett's Ford "would have embarrassed us exceedingly." For that matter, any strong advance would have caused Slocum anxiety for his right flank.

Franklin also wrote that Stonewall should have known about Brackett's Ford. But Jackson's men were moving in from the north and probably would not have learned about it on the march. Wright arrived at about the time Stonewall might have become interested in other crossings, so it is possible that Jackson used him as a scout. Still, Stonewall should have ensured that Wright communicate any findings to him. The failure to press any advantage the rebels had at Brackett's Ford must be shared by Jackson and Wright—Jackson for not pushing harder to see the possibilities to the west, and Wright for not communicating the situation to him.[9]

While Wright was scouting, Franklin was bringing up more men. He became concerned about the gap between Slocum and Richardson as soon as he rode up, which was shortly after Jackson's guns opened fire. He was returning from his meeting with McClellan, and rushed to the sound of the guns. Finding the situation not to his liking, Franklin asked Edwin Sumner for help. The II Corps commander promptly sent two of John Sedgwick's brigades—two of the three reserve brigades near Glendale—to Franklin's aid. These two brigades were Napoleon Dana's and Alfred Sully's, with Dana in command of the force and Col. William R. Lee of the 20th Massachusetts taking charge of

Dana's brigade. Sully felt ill, so command of his brigade fell to Col. James A. Suiter of the 34th New York. The men, having rested for a couple of hours, moved quickly to Franklin's aid, and the VI Corps commander told Dana to put one brigade on Richardson's left and hold the other in reserve. Dana sent Suiter to the front. Franklin must have felt better about his left flank then.[10]

Meanwhile, Wade Hampton was examining Franklin's right flank. His brigade was in line east of the White Oak road, extending from the road to the swamp in a pine forest. Wanting to see his opponents, Hampton took a staff officer and his son Wade, who was serving with him at the time, across the swamp. At that point it was only ten or fifteen feet wide, shallow with a sandy bottom, and easily crossed. The three men saw a line of Union troops in a ravine facing toward the bridge site. Their position was strong against an attack coming from the bridge, but not so good against an attack from where Hampton was, as its flank was exposed.

Hampton recrossed the swamp and went first to Whiting, then to Jackson. Stonewall asked Hampton if he could build a bridge at the site. Hampton replied that he could make one for infantry without being noticed, but one for artillery would attract attention because he would have to cut down trees to get a road wide enough for wheeled vehicles. Build the bridge, Jackson said, presumably meaning one for infantry. Hampton detailed fifty soldiers to cut pines for poles and take them to the bridge site. The bridge was finished quickly, and Hampton went south of the swamp again to see if the Federals had been disturbed by anything. They had not, and Hampton found that he could get within 150 yards of them without their hearing him. The South Carolinian then headed back to Jackson.

Stonewall was sitting on a fallen pine tree next to the White Oak road. Hampton sat next to him and told him that the bridge was finished and the Northerners were still there and exposed to flank attack. Jackson listened with his eyes closed and his cap drawn over his eyes. When Hampton finished, Jackson "sat in silence for some time, then rose and walked off in silence."

Stonewall did little else the rest of the day. Major J. W. Fairfax of Longstreet's staff came over from the Glendale area to ask for reinforcements. Jackson presumably told Fairfax that he was stymied. At some point during the day he wrote his wife, implying that he was tired but pressing her to give at least 10 percent of their income to the church. Later in the afternoon he fell into a sleep so sound that nothing would arouse him. He awoke in time for supper, but fell asleep with food between his teeth. Finally, after supper, he looked at his staff and said, "Now, gentlemen, let us at once to bed, and rise with the dawn, and see if to-morrow we cannot *do something!*"[11]

"Our delay at White Oak was unfortunate," Whiting noted. Jackson said the marshy ground, the bridge's destruction, and the Union position's strength caused it. This has satisfied almost no one, with the possible exceptions of and Lee. Porter Alexander called the statement “farcical.” is wife of an illness in a letter obviously written shortly after likely written later in the same week: “During the past week I well, have suffered from fever and debility, but through the ever-kind Providence I am much better to-day.” Again, not many d sickness as a complete explanation, although most observers be-lie... n suffered from fatigue or the stress of campaigning. D. H. Hill, who rejected physical debility as an issue, believed Stonewall was taking it easy on his men, who had experienced a hard campaign and a tough march to the Richmond area. Hill also identified a supposed tendency of Jackson’s to not perform as well when under another general as he did when entrusted with independent command. Jackson’s brother-in-law only implicitly criticized Jackson. Alexander credited Hill’s first explanation and also said that Jackson’s “failure is not so much a military as a psychological phenomenon. He did not try and fail. He simply made no effort.”[12]

Like Alexander, most people believe that Jackson failed at White Oak Swamp.[13] There is also a consensus of opinion that Jackson failed at Mechanicsville, Gaines’s Mill, and Grapevine Bridge. However, these alleged failures do not stand up to close examination. Jackson’s supposed failure at White Oak Swamp thus deserves equal treatment. There are several possible points of failure in this case. He could have forced his way over the swamp. If he did not cross at White Oak Swamp Bridge, he could have used another crossing to accomplish the same objective. If he did not feel he could get across the swamp, he should have immediately sent a messenger to Lee with the news and a request for further orders. Finally, if he really was incapacitated, he should have recognized this fact and given up command for the day.

The evidence clearly shows that Jackson did not get across White Oak Swamp, and he also did not try hard. He seemed to understand his orders, which came directly from Lee. Those orders, even if they were merely to pursue the Yankees, would not have precluded an attack. The question is whether the casualties would have been worth it. They might not have been if a failed effort left Franklin able to send a good part of his force away from White Oak Swamp to help other Union forces in the Glendale area, or if a successful effort had left the Confederates too disorganized to add their force decisively to the mass at Glendale. It is unlikely that Jackson could have forced a crossing. There are contradictory reports of the difficulty posed by White Oak Swamp, so it is best to leave that out of the equation. Jackson could have had nearly 27,000 men at the swamp, if all of Richard Ewell’s division had been available. But Isaac Trimble’s brigade did not arrive until 4 P.M., and the Maryland Line probably was not there at all. Thus, early in the afternoon Jackson had about 24,000 men. Facing him on rising ground in a good defensive position oriented against an attack from the bridge site, was Franklin with nearly 19,000 men plus artillery support. By later in the afternoon, counting most of Ewell's men and Wright's (since Stonewall could have kept him), Jackson could have had 29,000 men. But Franklin, reinforced by two of Sedgwick's brigades, would have increased his total force to nearly 24,000. Even given Jackson's numerical advantage in artillery—an advantage somewhat lessened by the rebels' lesser-quality cannon—these numbers do not sound encouraging.[14]

It was not necessary to engage Franklin completely to affect the day's fortunes, however. Stonewall needed to keep Franklin occupied as long as possible. He needed to make him worry about the possibility of attack, perhaps get him to ask for reinforcements, but at all costs keep him from sending troops to other threatened sectors of the battlefield. Jackson made a good enough start that Franklin had indeed asked for reinforcements and had received two of the army's three reserve brigades. He needed to keep that effort up throughout the day.

He could have done that by demonstrating with infantry at either the bridge site or some other crossing. This gets to the second possible criticism: that he did not investigate other crossings or act on information he received. Brackett's Ford perhaps was problematic, but other crossings were available. Hampton's crossing site sounded promising, and Munford's less so. Either could have been investigated if a crossing were the goal, and Hampton's crossing sounds as if he might have been able to do some real damage. But Jackson not only did not investigate these crossings personally, he ignored information given to him by subordinates. In Hampton's case, he basically wasted his men's effort in building an infantry bridge that probably did not need to be built even if the crossing were to be used.

The only possible answer to this criticism is that Jackson's orders restricted him to the White Oak road until further orders came. Perhaps Jackson saw it that way, but if so, he was wrong. Lee would have wanted an advance down the White Oak road, or perhaps anywhere to the east of that road, but not west of it. Moving to the Charles City road would have brought Jackson too near Huger and away from a place where he could seal roads to prevent a Federal escape. This would have precluded a mass crossing at Brackett's Ford. But it should not have prevented a crossing at Hampton's bridge—an attempt to drive the Unionists away from the bridge site so Stonewall could get going down the road again.[15]

Moreover, it should not have prevented demonstrations at all possible crossings, including Brackett's Ford. Ostentatious feints by infantry toward the several crossings would have kept Franklin's attention, and his men, in the area. A strong move by Wright (which Jackson could have ordered) would have divided Slocum's attention between that force and the force heading down the Charles City road. These actions would have fixed the Yankees in place, keeping them from giving the other forces around Glendale their support.

If Jackson, confronted by the circumstances, had wanted to cross or even demonstrate somewhere besides White Oak Swamp Bridge but thought his orders prevented him from doing so, he should have communicated with Lee. Major Fairfax, Longstreet's aide, had made it to Jackson (and presumably back). Lee was with Longstreet much of the day. D. H. Hill sent his engineer officer, Capt. W. F. Lee, to Huger to see if that officer could attack Franklin, and the engineer brought back to Hill the message that Huger was slowed by obstructions in the road. So communication was possible. A forty-minute ride would take a courier from Lee to Jackson (and the reverse as well), most likely by Fisher's Ford. If Jackson had any questions regarding his role and his proper course of action, he was obligated to send an officer to Lee, but he did not do so—something even Dabney wondered about.[16]

The first two areas of criticism can be collapsed into one: Jackson did not keep Franklin occupied. This cannot be denied. Franklin was able not only to release Sedgwick's two brigades, but also to send two of Richardson's brigades to the Glendale area. This was almost half Franklin's peak strength, or about 10,000 men, who Jackson could have kept near White Oak Swamp Bridge with aggressive action. Slocum was able to detach a brigade from his line late in the day, and while the blame for this possibility cannot be laid completely at Jackson's door, he could have helped fix that brigade, keeping another 2,000 men away from the area immediately around Glendale. Stonewall thus had at least some responsibility for the 12,000 reinforcements the Yankees received at the most crucial point of the day, and primary responsibility for 10,000 of them.

The third area of criticism—that Jackson should have communicated with Lee if he was unable to cross at White Oak Swamp Bridge—also cannot be denied. Jackson was among the first to point out that blame in this case must be shared. Two weeks after the battles, just as Lee was about to shift the area of fighting from the Richmond area to the Washington area, Hunter McGuire (Jackson's physician), Crutchfield, and Sandy Pendleton were discussing whether Stonewall should have marched to Longstreet's aid. This action itself was clearly outside Jackson's orders, and it would have been a mistake if it involved going all the way around Huger to reach Old Pete's side. Jackson came near the three men, heard the conversation's nature, and said, "If General Lee had wanted me at Frayser's Farm he could have sent for me." Lee indeed could have sent for Jackson, although he would not have wanted to. He also could have checked on Jackson's situation, which he did not. Nonetheless, Jackson must take primary responsibility for the lack of communication. He was the commander on the scene, he was the one who could paint the picture for Lee to understand, and he was the one who needed advice. This two-way lack of communication is typical of the Confederates' problems in this area throughout the campaign.[17]

One historian has called Jackson's failure at White Oak Swamp "complete, disastrous and unredeemable." That is an accurate description. But suggestions that Jackson was saving his infantry or was uncooperative as a subordinate are ridiculous. They are not supported by anything in Stonewall's character. It is more likely that physical problems—a combination of lack of sleep, stress, and the resulting exhaustion (both physical and mental)—are to blame for Jackson's strange behavior on June 30. There is a difference of memory between Dabney and McGuire concerning the amount of rest Jackson got on the night of the twenty-ninth, but even with the few hours' sleep McGuire says he got, Stonewall would have run out of energy at some point. He seemed in good shape the morning of the thirtieth; perhaps the breaking point came that afternoon. A courier with Jackson wrote after the war, "General Jackson had been in a bad humor for several days; the truth of the matter is that he and his men had been completely worn out by what they had gone through." Lack of food may have entered into it as well, although again there is a difference of memory concerning how much Jackson ate that day.[18] Everything seems to have come together to affect him on this, perhaps the worst of all possible days.

If Jackson had realized his condition, he could have temporarily relinquished command. Ewell and D. H. Hill, both of whom Jackson trusted, were available. Hill in particular was with Jackson and was familiar with the situation and orders. Perhaps this course of action would have been the best one for Stonewall to follow.

CHAPTER FIFTEEN

"I Thought I Heard Firing"

Benjamin Huger was attempting to reach the Union line on the Charles City road. After working through nearly two miles of obstructions created by Yankee pickets, the men with the axes "cutting them out as best they could," William Mahone's brigade came to the Brackett field near the Williams house. The timing is uncertain, but it must have been after Ambrose Wright investigated Brackett's Ford and rejected it as a crossing point for his brigade.

Coming into the field, Mahone saw many Federals on the next ridge, about three-quarters of a mile away. Between the two was a creek lined with trees. Henry Slocum, whose VI Corps division was in position there, wrote his wife that he had tried to save lives by "carefully posting my troops and using my artillery." Mahone decided to shell the Yankees, but he brought up only two guns of Capt. M. N. Moorman's battery. These opened fire on the Union position.

Slocum's batteries quickly responded. Emory Upton and Josiah Porter put all their guns into action, and William Hexamer fired two guns. Some Northern pickets within a hundred yards of the rebel guns yelled, "Good! Good! Give it to them!" to the gunners. Hexamer's guns were not particularly well served, but the others were, and Mahone described their fire as having "great energy and effect." One of Mahone's men said the brigade changed position during the shelling, but that it did not help much. "It really seemed as if our precise position was known to their gunners," he wrote. An artillery officer remembered, "It was a hot day and a hot fight, too." It was even hot for the Federals' infantry supports; one man recalled that the fire "fairly burned my face."

Gustavus De Russy's battery added its fire for a while. Porter's guns became so hot they would fire as soon as the vent was uncovered without any spark added. As a result, four guns from Capt. George E. Randolph's Battery E, 1st Rhode Island Artillery, were brought forward to relieve him. Lieutenant Colonel A. S. Cutts, commanding the Sumter (Georgia) Battalion of the Confederate reserve artillery, moved his three batteries to the front line, but he never received an order to fire. Moorman's two guns made the Unionists lie down to escape the grape and canister, but they did little else.[1]

This unequal contest, called the Action at Brackett's, continued for several hours—in fact, Slocum said he nearly ran out of ammunition—and it accomplished nothing except to add men to the casualty rolls. Slocum reported that his killed and wounded numbered no more than 25, and the rebel losses totaled 78, all but 2 in Mahone's brigade. The 41st and 49th Virginia regiments, supporting Moorman's guns, suffered 36 and 30 casualties, respectively. Slocum's men chuckled at the results, figuring the shelling paid the Confederates back some for Gaines's Mill.

Mahone called this loss "serious, considering that [the engagement] was confined exclusively to the artillery." But, as with Jackson, more than artillery could have been applied. Both sides thought about it. Huger and Mahone investigated possibilities after the artillery fire started, and although Huger thought White Oak Swamp was too close to do anything on his left, to his right the ground looked open enough for a flanking maneuver. However, by the time he reached that conclusion it was nearly dark, so he contented himself with ordering Lew Armistead and Wright, who had joined up by now, to head south in the morning. Huger spent the night at the Fisher house. The men lay on the wet ground, some of them dreaming of battle, most of them sleeping soundly.

Slocum's inspiration came later, with news that his Federal brethren were hard pressed near Glendale. As the gun battle on his front had stopped, he ordered Joseph Bartlett's brigade to take the Brackett field position. Just after Bartlett started his men moving, a body of Southerners appeared in line a little distance behind Hass Creek, the stream that separated the two fields. Upton's battery came up and fired canister at the Confederates, who beat a hasty retreat. Slocum was ready to advance again when Samuel Heintzelman showed up with a request for a brigade to help Phil Kearny. George Taylor's brigade, such as it was after Gaines's Mill, was given that mission. With only two brigades present and an unknown number of rebels to his front, Slocum decided to stop Bartlett.

Huger's feeble attempt at an advance was not what Lee had in mind that morning. Lee treated Jackson's and Huger's failures differently in his report of the campaign. Jackson was, Lee said, "unable to force the passage of White Oak Swamp," implying that he had indeed tried. In the same sentence Lee wrote that Longstreet and A. P. Hill had no support at Glendale partially because of "Huger not coming up." Lee clearly thought Huger *could* have come up but did not, and many have agreed with him. The most sympathetic portrayal of his behavior has been that it was an attempt "to save lives."[2]

To blame Huger solely for Confederate failures on June 30 is overly harsh, however. Jackson's failure allowed 10,000 Union soldiers to fight at Glendale, whereas Huger's failure only allowed Taylor's brigade to join the struggle there. Until Wright's brigade joined him, Huger had about 6,500 men to Slocum's 6400. After Wright arrived, Huger's force would have risen to about 8,500. As with Jackson, Huger had little chance of any great success in an assault. Nevertheless, he should have moved more quickly and at least demonstrated with his infantry as soon as he got within sight of the Federals.

Huger did tell Lee he was facing obstructions. But that communication, while a better effort than other Southern generals (including Jackson) gave, left a lot to be desired. He apparently did not indicate the nature of the obstruction or the length of time he would be obstructed. There is no record of Lee's attempting to communicate with Huger to get matters clarified—something that could have been accomplished easily by Lee or a member of his staff. But that failure on Lee's part does not lessen the blame to be placed on Huger.

Unlike Jackson, Huger had few options as to where to place his men or demonstrate against the enemy. A road did lead from the Williams house south to the Long Bridge road, but taking it would merely have placed Huger's division alongside Longstreet and A. P. Hill and possibly exposed it to attack by Slocum on the march. Lee could have sent Huger down the Carter's mill road to Malvern Hill, but he would have arrived too late to get anything accomplished. Huger's task that day was, at the very least, to add to the pressure on the Yankees around Glendale. He failed miserably at this. Still, to award him the lion's share of the blame for the results of events on June 30 is wrong.

While Jackson and Huger struggled with demons both Yankee and personal, Lee continued to observe the field around Longstreet's position. Longstreet and A. P. Hill were also in the area, and Longstreet's order to the batteries to fire in reply to the supposed signal from Huger was being delivered when Jefferson Davis rode up. "Why, General," Davis said to Lee, "what are you doing here? You are in too dangerous a position for the commander of the army." Davis no doubt had his encounter with Lee at Mechanicsville in mind and wanted to get in the first word.

Lee was not deterred, however, from his concern for Davis. "I am trying to find out something about the movements and plans of those people," he told the president. "But you must excuse me, Mr. President, for asking what you are doing here, and for suggesting that this is no proper place for the commander-in-chief of all our armies." Davis, not to be outdone this time, returned the explanation: "Oh, I am here on the same mission that you are."

The two strong-willed men tacitly decided this confrontation was a stalemate and began talking about the plans for the day. Longstreet joined them and remembered the discussion as a "pleasant conversation, anticipating fruitful results from the fight." But Yankee batteries replied immediately to the rebel guns' signal firing, and Powell Hill decided to take matters into his own hands. "This is no place for either of you," he told his army commander and commander in chief, "and, as commander of this part of the field, I order you both to the rear." Davis responded, "We will obey your orders," and moved back in company with Lee a little ways. The distance was not far enough for Hill, however. He came up to them again and said, "Did I not tell you to go away from here? and did you not promise to obey my orders? Why, one shell from that battery over yonder may presently deprive the Confederacy of its President and the Army of Northern Virginia of its commander." After a few more well-chosen words, Davis and Lee moved far enough back for Hill's taste. It was none too soon, as the Federal guns began sweeping the road with their shells. In fact, one shell burst close enough to the generals that a courier was wounded and several horses were hit.

Longstreet decided to silence the guns, which were in Cooper's battery near the Long Bridge road. Richard Anderson's men, now commanded by Micah Jenkins, were close to the battery—Capt. William H. Chapman's Dixie (Virginia) Artillery battery, attached to the South Carolina brigade, had drawn some of the Yankee fire—and Old Pete ordered Jenkins to shut it up. Longstreet thought Jenkins would use the Palmetto Sharpshooters to shoot the gunners without bringing on a general engagement. As he put it, he was "under the impression that our wait was understood." But Jenkins decided that the orders were not to "silence" the guns but to "advance and silence" them, and he moved his whole brigade forward, less four companies of the 6th South Carolina that did not get back from the skirmish line in time to reform.

By this time, Lee was moving to the River road. Colonel Thomas L. Rosser and the 5th Virginia Cavalry had engaged enemy skirmishers in the morning on the Long Bridge road, withdrawing when Longstreet arrived. At the same time, Rosser's pickets on the River road reported Yankee movement in that area, and Longstreet told Rosser to go there and assess the situation. Rosser saw something no Confederate wanted to see: Union troops, either George Morell's or George Sykes's men, moving toward the James across Malvern Hill. If Lee were to catch the Federals, he needed to keep them from the James. Any who got past Malvern Hill were probably safe. Rosser sent word of this sighting to Longstreet and Theophilus Holmes at about 1 P.M. Apparently neither got that word, however, so Rosser went to confer with Lee.

Marse Robert decided to see for himself. He and Rosser rode to the River road, after Lee first informed Longstreet that Holmes had Yankees in front of him and sent Major Meade, the engineer at Longstreet's headquarters, to

Holmes with Rosser's information. When he reached the River road, Lee probably saw Northerners on top of Malvern Hill, and perhaps he could see the Union wagons crossing the hill on their way to the river.[3]

Not only were Sykes's men still posted on the hill and in the valley, but eight batteries of artillery—Howard Carlisle's, John Edwards's, Stephen Weed's, James Robertson's, and Joseph Nairn's, along with Capt. John E. Beam's Battery B, 1st New Jersey Artillery, Capt. John R. Smead's Battery K, 5th U.S. Artillery, and Capt. Adolph Voegelee's Battery B, 1st New York Light Artillery—were with them. Aside from Gouverneur Warren in the valley, the Federals were on a plateau seventy to eighty feet above the River road with a clear field of fire. Sykes later wrote, "Nothing could be more commanding than the line I held." Morell's men had been recalled from their camp just south of Turkey Island Bridge, and they were in line facing north to Sykes's right. Next to Morell were two regiments from Innis Palmer's brigade and Albion Howe's brigade, all of Darius Couch's division, which McClellan had recalled to Malvern Hill. John Abercrombie's brigade had moved to support the 7th Massachusetts and 2nd Rhode Island at Turkey Island Bridge, and Henry Wessells's men also moved away from Haxall's Landing a little to support the artillery reserve parked south of Malvern Hill.

Fitz John Porter reported that the last of the trains and artillery got through his command about 4 P.M. The sight of Unionists in position on Malvern Hill and trains crossing the hill would have told Lee he could not hope to keep McClellan's entire army from the James River. The most he could hope for would be to destroy the "rear guard" around Glendale. He could, however, at least harass the trains and perhaps cause some destruction by using Holmes.

That officer, a fifty-seven-year-old North Carolinian, served in the army from his graduation from West Point in 1829 until he resigned in 1861 to serve the Confederacy. He was a veteran of action in Florida and Mexico. After commanding a brigade at Manassas, Holmes had been assigned to head the Department of North Carolina. Major Meade had suggested to Holmes that a battery of rifled cannon, posted at the edge of a wood about a half-mile from the Yankee lines, would "greatly embarrass his retreat." Walter Stephens, Lee's chief engineer, agreed with Meade's assessment, so Holmes ordered Col. James Deshler, his artillery chief, to take six rifled guns—one section each from Capt. James R. Branch's Virginia battery, Capt. T. H. Brem's North Carolina battery, and Capt. Thomas B. French's Virginia battery—to the area. Meade and Stephens pointed out the position, but Deshler had to move his guns off the road through the trees and underbrush to work them into position. In the end, he was able to put only five guns where he wanted them. The 30th Virginia from John Walker's brigade advanced with the artillery, but Holmes wanted some personal knowledge of the situation, so he moved forward and ordered the rest of his force to advance at the same time.

When Holmes arrived he found Lee. The army commander heard what Holmes had done, agreed with it, and told Holmes to wait until his whole force was in position before opening fire. Then Lee left and Holmes was on his own. Unfortunately for him, however, he was not unobserved. The dusty Virginia roads betrayed the Southerners' movement, and a signal officer sent a message to the gunboats. A Union sailor climbed up a mast to check the Confederate positions. When Deshler commenced firing, sometime between 4 and 5 P.M., the Union guns responded immediately. In addition to the eight batteries with Sykes, Thomas Osborn's battery added its fire from Morell's position on the north side of Malvern Hill. Augustus Martin's Massachusetts artillerymen moved up to support Warren's men in the valley. The contest thus rapidly became unequal: at least forty-four guns against five.

Some Confederates thought the first shells were from navy gunboats, but the *Aroostook* (first into action) and *Galena* both responded to the sound of the rebel guns. The fire had a profound effect on the rebels. "Shells burst all over us, covering some of us with dirt, crashing the trees, and throwing limbs and splinters about us in every direction," Henry Graves of the 2nd Georgia Battalion wrote his mother, and a Yankee observer called the result "perfect pandemonium." Major Edgar Burroughs's cavalry was routed, the horses knocking a fence onto some infantry taking shelter behind it. Some artillery that had been left in reserve also quickly quit the field. This caused a minor controversy later. Holmes blamed Branch for the rout of his four reserve guns, although Branch had gone to the front with his other section and so was not present. Lieutenant R. G. Pegram, an otherwise highly praised officer, was in command of the four guns at the time. Also breaking was Capt. Edward Graham's Virginia battery. Its guns and caissons became caught in the underbrush, and some of the drivers cut the traces and took off on the horses, leaving two guns and three caissons behind. Deshler and Graham went back that night to recover the guns and caissons, but they could find only one caisson. The next morning Graham tried again but found Union pickets on the ground. By the time the pickets left, the guns were gone, having been captured by Warren's men—along with some hardtack that was probably even more welcome to the hungry Federals. Holmes brought charges against the artillery officers, leading to a protest from Capt. Joseph Graham, who took over Brem's battery upon Brem's retirement and who was being confused with Edward Graham.

Jefferson Davis rallied the broken troopers and gunners. However, just after he succeeded in doing so, another shell exploded in the top of a tree, sending metal and tree limbs all over the men and causing them to again fly. Davis remembered that their manner of departure "plainly showed no moral power could stop them within the range of those shells." An infantry soldier's comment was, "They ran back like a flock of sheep with a pack of dogs after them."[4]

Just after the cavalry and artillery broke, Holmes asked Junius Daniel for an infantry regiment. Daniel sent his own, the 45th North Carolina, under the command of Lt. Col. J. H. Morehead, telling him to have the men lie down in the road. As they moved off, they were hit by enemy artillery shells and friendly gunners headed directly for them on the road at the same time. The infantry broke and ran off the road. A picket from the 5th New York was within earshot and could hear one of the officers trying to get his men organized, but it was no good. "They ran like sheep," he said. One Tar Heel, Nathan Frazier, wrote, "We were all frightened a good deal and every man was trying to get to the best place and behind the biggest tree." Frazier hid behind a white oak but saw a pine tree as big as the oak cut in two by a shell. Benjamin Rawlings of the 30th Virginia and several others moved from one side of an oak tree to another, depending upon where the shells were coming from. Rawlings saw his lieutenant doing the same thing, and the look on the man's face made Rawlings burst out laughing—a fit that only increased when he saw his colonel take a drink from a flask. What made Rawlings laugh was the scared look on everyone's face, and the more he laughed the more scared he got. One brave Confederate, the 50th North Carolina's color-bearer, took his flag to an open field and held it there defiantly.

Daniel eventually got the men reformed and headed to Holmes's position. Holmes himself had been in a nearby house. The old officer was hard of hearing, but he had sensed something happening. He came out of the house, put his hand behind his right ear, and said, "I thought I heard firing."

Deshler kept up the contest for about an hour. By that time enough gunners had been hit that the guns could not be served, and enough horses had been hit that the caissons had to be left so the guns could be brought off. Either Yankees or rebels blew up some of the caissons. Most Union batteries ceased firing when Deshler withdrew, but the gunboats kept up the shelling for several hours. Their shells threw up dust and smoke as if a powder keg had exploded. Signal officers on land guided the naval gunners—a case of "beautiful cooperation of forces," according to Maj. Albert Myer, the army's chief signal officer. A Regular Army officer up on the hill called the scene "indescribably grand."

One land-based Union battery also kept firing—apparently with canister, which it had been using during the entire combat. Weed reported it to be the 4th New York Light Artillery battery temporarily commanded by Lieutenant Nairn. But that battery's regularly assigned commander, Capt. James Smith, who was sick during the battles, issued firm denials based on an investigation he conducted after his return. Whatever battery it was, its effect was probably worse on the Federal infantry than on the Confederates. Lieutenant Woods McGuire of the 3rd U.S. Infantry in Col. Robert Buchanan's brigade and two corporals from the same regiment were killed, apparently by the battery's fire. Few other Unionists became casualties in this action, known as the engagement at Malvern Cliff or Turkey Bridge. Of the battery commanders, only Weed reported any casualties: 2 men killed. On the Confederate side, 17 artillerists were wounded. Daniel's brigade lost 2 killed and 22 wounded by enemy fire, and several more hurt by stampeding horses. Walker's brigade lost 20 wounded, 1 of whom later died.[5]

Many believe that Holmes should have shown more aggressiveness and possibly could have taken Malvern Hill instead of asking for reinforcements while facing a small brigade of infantry in the lowland. However, these claims make no sense. Holmes could not have taken Malvern Hill at any time on the thirtieth. His force of sixty-three hundred infantry faced not only Warren's brigade but also all of Sykes's division, with Morell, Couch, and Wessells close by—a total of 23,500 men—along with most of the reserve artillery. Almost all of these units were around Malvern Hill before Holmes arrived at the junction of the Long Bridge and River roads. He would have been either attacking up a steep hill after crossing a creek or marching south of the hill and opening his flank to assault. Holmes called the idea of an attack "perfect madness," and a soldier in Daniel's brigade wrote home saying, "if our generals had persisted in charging the battery, our ranks would have been cut down like grain." Reinforcements did arrive, but the only discussions of the order to attack seem to indicate clearly that the idea came from either Lee or Longstreet, not Holmes.

It is hard to see what Holmes could have done to delay the Federals on June 30. The earliest he could have reached the area from which he opened fire would have been early afternoon. He could have brought up more guns, but he still would have been operating at a disadvantage and the Yankees would still have been in position. His fire might have delayed the trains, but that delay would have lasted only as long as the Confederate fire lasted. It is doubtful that such a delay would have caused McClellan any real problems. Porter was so unconcerned about his position that he slept through the entire engagement. That sums up the chances Holmes had of accomplishing anything.

By 9 P.M., Holmes had given up any ideas of offensive action and began withdrawing to a position between his furthest point of advance and the Long Bridge–River road junction, where he spent the night. Like Huger and Jackson, he got only his guns into action on June 30. Unlike them, he accomplished as much as he could.[6]

The reinforcements involving Holmes came from Magruder's command. Magruder had been at Timberlake's store, just under a mile southeast of Atlee's farm on the Darbytown road, when he received Lee's message asking where he was. Prince John had been held up by the rear of A. P. Hill's division—an indication he had moved quickly that hot day—and had not moved far when he received Lee's order to halt where he was. He spent at least two and a half hours there before receiving an order to march to Holmes's aid.

Magruder reported that the order came from Longstreet. Old Pete, in his memoirs, wrote that "the Confederate commander" ordered Magruder to go to Holmes—a choice of words that would indicate that Lee had issued the order. Lee might have written the order in response to Rosser's information, but why would he do that before he saw the situation? Lee also might have told Longstreet to order Magruder to move to ensure that Longstreet knew Magruder would not be available to him. Lee could have had only two reasons to want Magruder with Holmes. One would be that Holmes's force was disintegrating and needed support if it were attacked. This wound up being at least partially true, but Lee had not seen anything of the sort when he was in the New Market area. The second would be that Lee saw a chance for an attack if Magruder could bring his force of more than fourteen thousand men to join Holmes's total force (including infantry and cavalry) of seven thousand soldiers. But Lee's orders to Holmes did not imply an attack. Instead of merely telling Holmes to get all of his men into position, Lee would have explained his plan and pointed out the part Holmes was to play. Lee may have had this idea in mind. He wrote that Magruder, being farther away from Holmes than Lee had thought, "did not reach the position of the latter [Holmes] in time for an attack." If that were the case, however, why did Lee communicate with Longstreet, who the commander knew was busy on his own front, instead of just ordering Magruder to the proper point? On the other hand, why did Magruder say the order was from Longstreet?

Whatever the case, the order set off a series of events that brought no credit to anyone on the Confederate side. A rumor circulated that Holmes's force had been driven back and needed support. A second note from Longstreet arrived, indicating that Holmes did need assistance and telling Magruder to leave his artillery so as to move more quickly. Should he need artillery support, Prince John could request it from Old Pete. This postscript makes little sense, for Longstreet had to know, even if he was not engaged when he wrote the note, that he would be engaged shortly. Perhaps he thought the terrain would not allow for proper use of guns in any attack he would make.

Shortly after Magruder received the order to support Holmes, he heard from Robert Chilton that the army's chief of staff wanted to show Prince John his positions. This would imply that the order originated with Lee, although Magruder reported Chilton indicated the order came from Longstreet. It could be that Chilton had remained with Longstreet when Lee went to Holmes. After getting Chilton's message, Magruder sent Major Brent to report the situation to Holmes and get any advice the older general might have regarding positions. Since Chilton was going to show Magruder the positions, there was no reason for Prince John to get Holmes's advice, but at least he was communicating—something few rebel generals did well in this campaign. While Magruder went to meet Chilton, Magruder's men started in motion. A man who owned a farm near New Market had pointed out a road that would shorten the march, so all but Paul Semmes's brigade took that road. Semmes, guarding the artillery, took the Darbytown road, which was clear of A. P. Hill's men by that time.

Brent also took the shortcut. Finding Holmes, he delivered Magruder's message and asked for the advice Magruder wanted. Holmes answered "very brusquely" that he did not have any advice to give. Brent then asked if Holmes could show him where the Yankees were, and Holmes said no. Exasperated, Brent said he was returning to Prince John and offered to take a message to him. Holmes said he had no message. After talking with a few others at Holmes's headquarters Brent left, "almost paralyzed by amazement" that Holmes was in command of any Southern troops. Brent thought Holmes was upset at getting a message from Magruder, but that is unlikely. Perhaps Holmes was upset at his men's performance; Brent arrived after the cannon fire.

Magruder met Chilton at the intersection of the Darbytown and Long Bridge roads. The two men exchanged information—Magruder advising Chilton where his men were and what they were doing, and Chilton telling Prince John where they were supposed to wind up. They moved to the intersection of the Long Bridge and River roads, which was where Magruder's right flank was to be. He then was to march toward Malvern Hill from there to support Holmes.

Magruder was all energy. He had a staff officer summon Semmes's brigade. Another staff officer went to hurry along the rest of the troops. A third staff officer stayed at the intersection to post troops as they came up. Prince John himself rode to find Holmes—"galloped" was the term he used. Magruder spent an hour trying to find Holmes, until it was close to sunset. Giving up, he ordered another staff officer (perhaps Brent, although the stories do not mesh perfectly) to find Holmes while Magruder rode back to Semmes's position.

Meanwhile, the rest of his command arrived near the Long Bridge–River road intersection around 6 P.M. The troops had not been there long, however, when an order came from Lt. Col. John B. Cary, Magruder's inspector general, to move to the area Chilton had designated. As Lafayette McLaws traveled down the River road he met Henry Wise and told him the point they were moving toward. Wise was horrified; he said that point was fully exposed to gunboat fire. McLaws was saved by another messenger from Magruder, who said he was to march down the Long Bridge road.

One mile along that road, east of its intersection with the River road, McLaws saw Magruder. Prince John had found Semmes in position and ordered him to take his brigade into the woods. Semmes recognized the real possibility of losing whatever organization his men had by marching them through thick woods in the gathering darkness. Magruder insisted, however, noting that Chilton had given him the order—implying that it came from

Lee. Semmes said he would try. Magruder, after seeing the Southerners head into the trees, again "galloped" toward the River road. Along the way he got yet another order from Longstreet to bring half his men to the Glendale area. Still moving west, he encountered McLaws. Prince John ordered McLaws, whose men had been marching in the hot sun all day, to rest them while Jones's and Magruder's own divisions headed to Glendale. While the two generals were together, Semmes came up. He had been separated from part of his brigade and all but one member of his staff during the advance into the woods.

Magruder returned to the Long Bridge–River road intersection, where he received his seventh message of the day. This one, from Chilton, told him to bring his entire command to the Glendale area. By this time, both Magruder and his horse must have been exhausted, and they both got a little rest by remaining at the intersection until his men got there. More staff officers rode to his various commands. Finally, his short stationary period over, Magruder moved "rapidly" to meet Lee and Longstreet. When he arrived, Lee told him to relieve Longstreet's men as soon as he could, and Prince John directed his troops into position until 3 A.M., when he retired for some much-needed sleep.

Magruder's men also must have been in need of sleep. David Jones and George T. Anderson both said the march took more than eighteen hours, and Lt. Col. William Luffman of the 11th Georgia in Anderson's brigade reported its duration to be twenty hours. Colonel J. B. Cumming of the 20th Georgia in Robert Toombs's brigade recorded the distance traveled as twenty miles—not much of an exaggeration, as the distance was at least seventeen miles, depending on the route taken. June 30 was a hot tidewater Virginia day. Howell Cobb called the march "most fatiguing," while Colonel Aiken of the 7th South Carolina remembered it merely as "fatiguing."[7]

It was also unnecessary. More than 20 percent of the Army of Northern Virginia had spent the day marching when it might have been fighting. But where might it have fought? The Federals had 23,500 men and most of the artillery reserve in the Malvern Hill area, plenty of strength to deal with Holmes and Magruder combined. Truly such an attack, particularly one beginning in the middle of the afternoon, would have cost Magruder many of his men.

The more likely place for Magruder to fight, given his place in Lee's original plan, was Glendale. According to Magruder's own report, a march of twelve miles had placed him at Timberlake's store by 2 P.M. From Timberlake's, a march of about six miles would have placed his lead elements at the Glendale battlefield. He would not have been too late, as he could have followed A. P. Hill's division, which reached the battlefield in plenty of time to participate in the day's events. Some extra infantry at Glendale would have been helpful to Lee and Longstreet in following up the gains the Confederates undeniably made there. Magruder's absence "grievously weakened" Lee's chance of accomplishing anything on June 30 only to the extent that Southern failures elsewhere made it so. If Jackson and Huger had fulfilled their part of the bargain, Magruder would have been free to move to support Longstreet, help Holmes, or even march down the Carter's mill road. From there he could have attacked Malvern Hill from the north or completely cut off McClellan's forces around Glendale from their retreat route.

The concern expressed by Lee and/or Longstreet in moving Magruder to Holmes's support was completely inaccurate. Holmes was in no danger except from artillery shells, and Lee should have realized that from his reconnaissance. If, instead of marching to New Market, Magruder had kept going down the Darbytown road to its junction with the Long Bridge road, he would have been in position to aid the Southern cause. A guide did not mislead Magruder into taking a wrong road. The evidence is that he did just what he was ordered to do: get to the River road by the quickest route and move down it to support Holmes. He took the guide's shortcut to arrive more quickly. Going down the Darbytown road, as Semmes and the artillery did, would have placed Prince John in a better position, but Magruder's orders did not allow that. It is hard to justify these orders with any possible result. Thus, another failure must be added to the Confederate ledger for June 30. This one, at least, was not due to the mistakes of a subordinate—unless Longstreet in truth was the source of the orders.[8]

Robert E. Lee, after examining Holmes's position, returned to Longstreet's position southwest of Glendale. When he got there, he found the major battle of the day under way. Jenkins's brigade, under orders to silence Cooper's battery in front of it, had moved out at nearly 4 P.M. Moxley Sorrel of Longstreet's staff was with Lord Edward St. Maur, a member of the British house of Somerset and a neutral observer. When the firing began, the Britisher quite coolly said to Sorrel, "This is not my place, and with your permission I shall retire." Moving deliberately, St. Maur found a place where he could watch the action without unnecessarily exposing himself.

Jenkins was headed toward the right-center of McCall's line with the 4th and 5th South Carolina on the left and the Palmetto Sharpshooters and 2nd South Carolina to the right. The 9th Pennsylvania Reserves of Truman Seymour's brigade formed up behind Cooper's battery, Jenkins's target, to support it. The 10th Pennsylvania Reserves formed a line perpendicular to the 9th Reserves, with the 10th's right near the 9th's left. The 12th Reserves were posted to the left of the 10th. Seymour moved six of the 12th's companies to a hastily formed breastwork at the Whitlock farmhouse on the left of the line, two hundred yards in front of the first positions. Both regiments were supporting Otto Diederichs's and John Knieriem's batteries, and Seymour sent two guns to the rear of the 12th Reserves's initial position to a small hill. The remaining four companies of the 12th Reserves moved to the rear of these two guns.

On McCall's right, Alanson Randol got his battery in position. Four guns went into line in a field to the northwest of the Long Bridge road. Randol felt there was not enough room where he was for Lt. E. W. Olcott's two guns, so he initially kept them limbered. James Thompson's battery from Kearny's division was posted to Randol's right, and George Meade and Seymour asked Thompson to change his front to help beat off the rebel attack along Long Bridge road. Thompson told them that he was on the left flank of Kearny's division and needed to support his own men first. Then Kearny rode up and Thompson explained the situation. Kearny told Thompson to change position so he would be aimed to the west, nearly perpendicular to Randol's guns. After Kearny left, Thompson decided to place his guns in echelon, with his right guns farthest forward, to attempt to cover all the ground he could. When Randol saw Thompson's new position he moved one of Olcott's guns to the Long Bridge road on his own left. The 4th Pennsylvania Reserves moved to Randol's rear. The 7th Pennsylvania Reserves and the remaining hundred or so men of the 11th Pennsylvania Reserves lined up behind the 4th Reserves. The 2nd, 5th, 8th, and 13th Pennsylvania Reserves of Seneca Simmons's brigade were in reserve in the center, and the 4th Pennsylvania Cavalry was behind Seymour's line on the left.[9]

As Jenkins advanced, the 1st and 3rd Pennsylvania Reserves continued to fall back. The 1st Reserves made it through the lines to a position near Cooper's battery. That prompted Jenkins to tell the 5th South Carolina to shoot the battery's horses, and the Gamecocks' volley triggered a response from the Federals. The 9th Reserves was ordered to change its front to stop a possible rebel attack on its left flank. This took it away from any possibility of supporting Cooper's guns. Fortunately for the Yankees, the 1st Reserves took the 9th Reserves's place in line.

The men of the 3rd Reserves allowed the rebels to close within fifty paces of their line, then delivered a volley that Horatio Sickel claimed decimated the 9th Virginia (which would have been difficult, since the 9th Virginia was with Armistead's brigade somewhere on the Charles City road). Another volley hit the onrushing Southerners and stopped them momentarily. Artillery and more infantry opened fire as Jenkins's men resumed the charge, and the 3rd Reserves tried to get out of the way. The 3rd Reserves was hit by fire from other Yankees and broke, heading to the rear "in great confusion" according to Sickel. The regiment was basically done for the day as an organized fighting force, although the soldiers continued to fight individually.

Jenkins was advancing without support since Longstreet, who had ordered him only to silence a battery, was still waiting for the certain engagement of Huger and Jackson before launching a general advance. He attracted the attention of all Federal units within range. Lieutenant Olcott's gun from Randol's battery joined Cooper's guns and those belonging to Frank Amsden, who

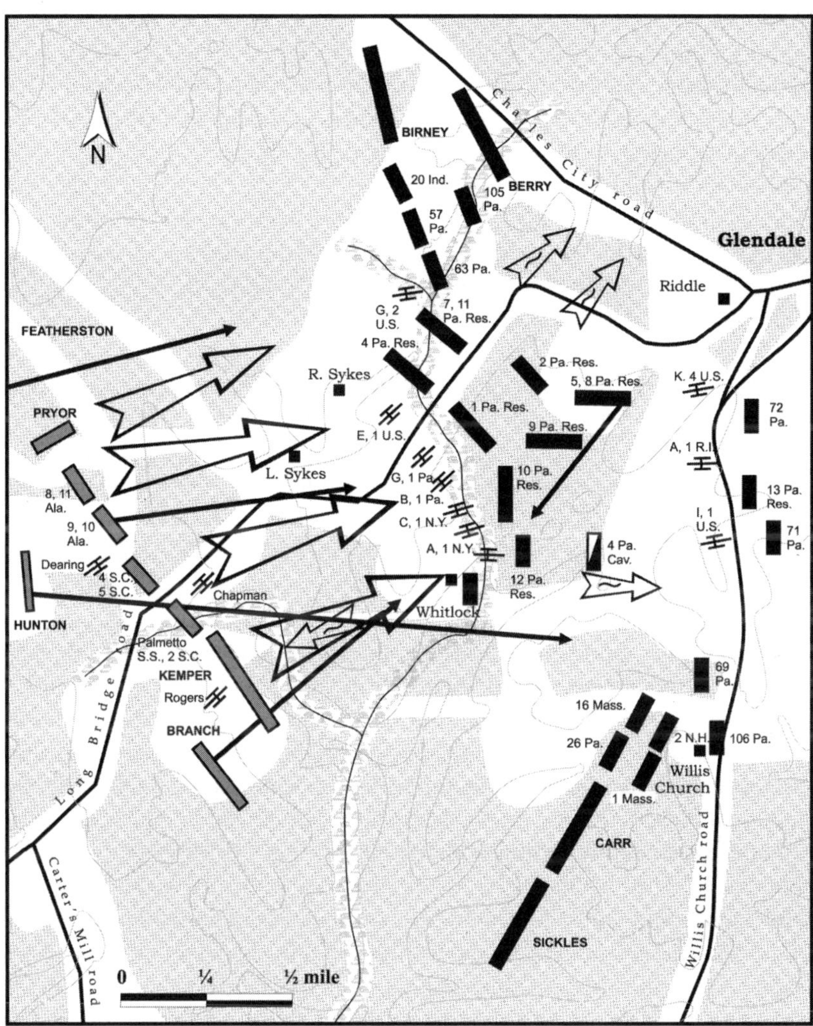

Longstreet's assaults, Glendale, June 30, 1862

had moved into position between Randol and Cooper on the battle line. Jenkins tried to respond by getting Chapman's battery to the front, but three guns had no chance against thirteen and Chapman soon was forced to retreat.[10]

Longstreet once called Jenkins "the best officer he ever saw," but Old Pete also said that Jenkins on this day was "only too anxious for a dash at a battery." This anxiety cost him and his men. It was difficult for infantry to charge artillery in an open field without taking horrendous losses. Jenkins, riding along the line, miraculously escaped serious injury. He wrote his wife that his sword was shot off and then broken, the sword knot cut, his bridle rein and saddle cloth both hit, and his overcoat cut in a dozen places by shell fragments. He sent the sword and overcoat home. He neglected to mention that he was hit in the shoulder and breast by spent fragments, or that he had two horses shot from under him. His brigade's losses affected him enough that he prayed for a bullet to strike him so he would die alongside his men.

Lieutenant Elihu W. Cannon of the 6th South Carolina had broken his right leg in the charge and lay between the lines. Before anyone could get him out of harm's way, he was hit in the right hip and the left foot. His wounds to the right leg necessitated its amputation. Private Charles M. Amos of the Palmetto Sharpshooters was more fortunate. Hit in the hand and arm, he made it safely to the rear. Stopping at a small stream, he saw a group of mounted officers and civilians nearby and asked if he could get his wounds treated. A surgeon came up, along with a civilian who asked about the battle. Amos responded that they would take the fort—even though there was no fort to be taken—but that they could not hold it without help because the Sharpshooters had been cut to pieces. The civilian responded, "He is a beardless youth and excited." Amos did not like that much and said, "If you were over there where I am from, you would be excited, too." An officer tapped him on the shoulder and told him to quiet down, since he was addressing the president of the Confederacy (apparently Davis had not gotten too far away from the battle). Amos refused offers to hold his arm while the surgeon removed the bullet, and the surgeon commented that the "beardless youth" was a better soldier than they had thought. Davis again asked about the battle, and Amos repeated his answer. The president decided to gather up some troops in the rear and lead them forward. He was persuaded to let a staff officer do it instead.

Porter Alexander, watching Jenkins's efforts, met up with one regiment's color-bearer. The man had been shot through both lungs. Alexander gave him some brandy and pointed him toward an ambulance. The soldier responded to the kindness by asking Alexander if he had any chance of recovery. Alexander told him that Major Wheat of the Louisiana Tigers had been shot in the same way at Manassas and recovered (although he subsequently died at Gaines's Mill). The young man was cheered at this news. "Of course, I'm willing to die for my country, if I must," he said, "but I'd a heap rather get well & see my mother & my folks again." By the time Alexander recorded the story he could no longer remember the man's name and never knew if he had indeed recovered.

Jenkins, although appalled at his men's losses, was determined to capture the battery. As he looked at his men they would look back with an expression that said, "We can't go any farther." Yet when Jenkins waved his hand, the Confederates would charge. Three times they assaulted the Federal positions, and three times the batteries and the six companies of the 1st Reserves in the line beat them back (one company had been detached earlier, and three had gone the wrong way and joined the 5th Reserves in another action). The Pennsylvania infantrymen fired their muskets so fast their hands blistered. Eventually they were ordered to use only the bayonet, perhaps to avoid shooting their own cannoneers, and the fighting between foot soldiers was hand-to-hand. The V Corps historian wrote of this struggle, "No pen will ever write the details of this strife, in which bayonet and butt were freely used." The Union gunners, veterans now, courageously stood by their guns and fired round after round of grape and canister at point-blank range into a half-mile-wide clearing of destruction. One artilleryman said of the Southerners, "Many of them kissed the ground not ten feet from the mouths of the cannon." The rebels were not silent, and one soldier of the 1st Reserves wrote his wife, "It appeared to me they [bullets] flew in every square inch of air around me except the little space I stood in."[11]

With two batteries working together, the Federals might have held the line until dark. But Seymour had ordered Amsden's caissons to the rear at the start of the artillery firing, and the three soldiers Amsden sent to bring them forward could not find them. Finally running out of ammunition, Amsden located McCall, who told him to move to the rear. Amsden did so with tears in his eyes. Seymour may have had good reason to withdraw the caissons—they might have been exposed enough to be hit by rebel artillery, for example—but he should have made sure Amsden knew where they were.

The South Carolinians took heart from Amsden's withdrawal because it meant they only had one battery to contend with now. They redoubled their efforts, particularly on the 1st Reserves's left flank. Cooper kept firing canister, but this time the Confederates pushed through the lead storm and forced the Unionists away from the guns—perhaps all the way to the Willis Church road.

The rebels had little time to celebrate the capture. The 1st Reserves found some trees to use as shelter and kept up a steady fire. The 9th Reserves was coming back to its original position after its ill-conceived move to the left when Col. C. Feger Jackson, the regiment's commander, came upon Cooper. Captain Robert Taggart thought the artillery captain looked "down-spirited"—as were his men, one writing home that he "never felt so horror stricken in my life." When Cooper told Jackson his guns had been taken, the men of the regiment heard it and wanted to take them back. They charged as the rebels were turning the guns, and again the fighting became hand-to-hand, with bayonets, clubbed muskets, knives, pistols, and probably any other weapon at hand being used on both sides. The 9th Reserves drove the Confederates back with the help of Randol's battery, which changed front to the left and blazed away at the Southerners. Cooper's gunners carried their dead and wounded to the rear.

The Yankees finally halted, although the officers had difficulty stopping them. Captain John Cuthbertson had to take hold of the 9th Reserves's color-bearer to get him to stop. No sooner had they reformed than the rebels were back.

The 9th and 10th Alabama of Cadmus Wilcox's brigade joined Jenkins's men. The fire from the cannon almost scorched the Alabamians, but they returned minié balls for canister at about ten yards and forced the gunners to leave their guns, which could not be moved because of the lack of horses. The 2nd Pennsylvania Reserves charged the Southerners but was broken and reformed in its original position. The 9th Reserves had to retire as well. Taggart tried to rally a bunch of Confederates who he thought were Yankees, but he was able to escape them. According to one account, Pvt. William F. Gallagher of Company F killed the 10th Alabama's color-bearer during the hand-to-hand fighting and captured the regiment's colors, presenting them to McCall after the charging had stopped.[12]

This phase of the struggle for Cooper's battery had been bloody. The 1st Reserves lost 14 killed, 83 wounded, and 10 missing, and the 9th Reserves suffered 17 killed, 84 wounded, and 36 missing. Both were among the five regiments with the most losses in the battle. Cooper's battery lost 4 killed and 10 wounded. But the Confederates suffered even more. The Palmetto Sharpshooters lost 39 killed and 215 wounded. The total of 254 of 375 men engaged was doubtless the single highest regimental loss in the battle. One company had just one man left unhurt, and two other companies had three unhurt men each. The 9th Alabama lost 31 killed, 95 wounded, and 4 missing. Jenkins's brigade of 1,200 men lost at least 500. Porter Alexander listed Jenkins's casualties as 562 killed or wounded and 27 missing, and Wilcox's losses, including the 10th Alabama, numbered 213.[13] But this fight did not even take first place among the many fights that made up the battle of Glendale. Moreover, the rebels failed to accomplish their objective: to break the Union line and cut off the Federals from their line of retreat.

CHAPTER SIXTEEN

"It Is Nothing When You Get Used to It"

When James Longstreet saw Micah Jenkins become heavily engaged, he ordered his other brigades to attack. James Kemper, on Jenkins's right, received that order at about 5 P.M. His regiments were in line, the 24th Virginia on the left with the 7th, 1st, 11th, and 17th Virginia extending the line to the right. Longstreet had previously warned Kemper against Union moves on his right flank, and Kemper changed the 17th's front to face toward the right. He also moved some skirmishers several hundred yards so they could see a field to his front and put Capt. Arthur L. Rogers's Loudoun (Virginia) Artillery battery on a small hill near the 17th's position.

A Virginian who had turned thirty-nine only two weeks previously and in brigade command only a week longer, Kemper fought in the volunteer service in Mexico. He returned home after that war to practice law and became involved in politics. Near the right of his line when he received Longstreet's order, Kemper immediately got the 17th faced forward and sent his staff to the rest of the line with the word to advance. The brigade was posted just west of a wood. The forests in the Glendale area were dense and filled with underbrush, and Kemper found it impossible to move any distance with any sort of order. The shells Otto Diederichs and John Knieriem sent the Virginians' way increased his difficulties. Soon the Federal pickets were driven in, and something seemed to take hold of the rebels. Kemper attributed it to the men's idea that they had reached their enemy's main line, which is possible since the troops were in their first large battle. The men began to move at the double-quick, cheering as they advanced, contrary to Kemper's orders never to move that fast without seeing the enemy first. As they could not have seen any substantial number of Yankees in the woods, they obviously were not obeying orders, but Kemper excused the error as being "upon the side of bravery."

The Virginians ran through two stretches of woods, a total of between one thousand and twelve hundred yards, and then popped out into the Whitlock field. Diederichs, Knieriem, and six companies of the 12th Pennsylvania Reserves awaited them amid the broom straw. By accident, Kemper had hit upon a key point in the Union line. Given the Yankees' imperfect coordination, Joseph Hooker's men just south of the Whitlock farm might not help George McCall's men in the field. If Kemper could roll up the forces in front of him he might be able to reach the Willis Church road. If he were reinforced there, the Confederates might actually be able to cut the Yankees' escape route.

The two German batteries kept up their firing, and James Cooper's battery (not yet heavily engaged with Jenkins's men) also shelled Kemper's brigade. Kemper described the artillery fire as "incessant." The Pennsylvania infantrymen fired three volleys, but the Virginians were undaunted. One of them later remembered: "It looked like sure death to cross that field, and I looked for a broom straw big enough to hide behind, but there was no stopping, and on we had to go, taking chances who should be shot down." McDowell Creek, a small watercourse between the lines, had stymied seven companies of the 17th Virginia. Others, particularly the 1st and 7th Virginia, had kept their order. Those men forced the Federals away from their positions after a short hand-to-hand combat. The Germans abandoned their guns—Knieriem (probably with only two guns, his other two being the ones farther back) when the Confederates got within sixty yards of him, and Diederichs shortly afterward when he ran out of canister and explosive shells. Sergeant T. P. Mays of the 7th Virginia planted his regiment's colors on the guns. The 12th Reserves abandoned the breastworks around the Whitlock house as Kemper's force threatened to surround them. The 4th Pennsylvania Cavalry, posted behind the 12th Reserves, was dismounted. Lying on the ground to dodge flying bullets, the men could not get to their horses before the infantry and artillery stampeded them. The cavalrymen retreated on foot.

The 12th Reserves, cavalry, and German artillerymen streamed to the rear, getting the attention of the Federals on both sides. One was Joe Hooker, whose men were in the woods south of the Whitlock farm near the Willis Church, as they had been since earlier in the morning. Another was Edwin Sumner, who had only one brigade of his corps left in the Glendale area. When Sumner heard the first sounds of the rebel attack, he put William Burns's brigade into line and, apparently having nothing better to do, posted the regiments himself. The 72nd Pennsylvania went to the right of the line, the 69th Pennsylvania occupied the middle, and the 106th Pennsylvania went to the left. The 71st Pennsylvania was behind Edmund Kirby's battery, which set up on a small rise near the R. H. Nelson house half a mile east of the Whitlock house across the Willis Church road. Soon, however, Sumner pulled the 69th out of the line and sent it to Hooker, also moving the 106th Pennsylvania to a position from which it could support Cuvier Grover's brigade. That brigade, which was on the right of Hooker's line, had been set to attack the flank of any Southerners moving toward the Willis Church road with the 26th Pennsylvania and 16th Massachusetts in front and the 1st Massachusetts and 2nd New Hampshire behind. The last-named regiment had marched half a mile to the right to support Gustavus De Russy's battery (by then commanded by Lt. Francis W. Seeley), which had moved from Henry Slocum's line to Hooker's, and then returned. Grover's fifth regiment, the 11th Massachusetts, was on the far left of Hooker's line guarding against an attempt to turn his flank.

George McCall saw the retreat of the 12th Reserves as he moved the 13th Reserves to the left of the line. McCall told Seneca Simmons to take two regiments to support the line, and Simmons picked the 5th and 8th Reserves. Three companies of the 1st Reserves joined them. Looking back at McCall for a moment, Simmons faced front again and called out, "Brigade! Forward! Charge!" The 10th Reserves also headed toward the rebels' left flank from the 12th Reserves's right rear.

Kemper's advance had been quick enough that no other Confederate unit kept up with him. Lawrence Branch's brigade, Kemper's right-flank support, was ordered to advance at the same time as Kemper. The order caught the North Carolinians fixing supper. Branch moved slowly without a guide and fell behind Kemper. Jenkins had been on Kemper's left, but he had advanced earlier and in a different direction. The Virginians were in an exposed position, and Kemper knew it. So did the men. One soldier later described the individual rebel infantryman as "his own general when he got into battle." Sergeant Allen M. Bane of the 7th Virginia climbed on the wheel of a Union cannon and yelled, "Retreat." Kemper officially ordered a withdrawal.

Simmons's charge and that of the 10th Reserves hit Kemper before that withdrawal could be completed. "The Rebel ranks were quickly broken," a Pennsylvanian recalled. As the Confederates tried to extricate themselves, some of the units offered resistance, and many of these men were captured, perhaps as many as 165. One man from the 1st Virginia was taken prisoner as he sat on a captured cannon smoking a pipe. Some accounts had the Yankees running after the rest of the rebels into the woods west of the Whitlock field. Another report was that the 5th Reserves somehow lost its flag (it was retrieved by the 10th Reserves). Kemper attempted to reform his men, sending out details to find soldiers and posting the regiments along the Long Bridge road so it would be easier for stragglers to find them. His brigade had numbered 1443 soldiers before the charge, and he lost 414 of them, including 100 in the 11th Virginia, 111 in the 7th Virginia, and 113 in the 17th Virginia—including 73 from the last-named regiment who were captured. These men had gone back in good order after their belated advance was stopped and, according to Porter Alexander, they walked directly into a Union brigade posted about a hundred yards south of and parallel to their line of march which otherwise did not enter the action. This brigade could have been Dan Sickles's on the left of Hooker's line, as Sickles's skirmishers took many prisoners. Some of the 17th's prisoners surrendered after diving into a ditch to escape being trampled by a Yankee charge.[1]

The problems were not over on McCall's left. As Kemper fell back, Branch's brigade arrived. Kemper pointed the North Carolinians to the spot he had just left, and Branch continued his advance. George Pickett's brigade, commanded by the still-ill Eppa Hunton, also entered the fight. Hunton's Virginians had started to Jenkins's left west of the Long Bridge road. Captain James Dearing's Latham (Virginia) Artillery battery had set up in front of them and started shelling the Yankees, whose artillery responded in kind, causing some casualties among Hunton's men. At 5 P.M. they started to advance, marching to the right instead of straight ahead. They crossed the Long Bridge road, straightened up, and headed forward. On the way, the men encountered McDowell Creek and Kemper's retreating men, both of which threw Hunton's soldiers off line.

By this time, the Pennsylvanians had reformed around the Whitlock house, some of the 10th Reserves taking cover behind the same breastworks the 12th Reserves had used. McCall was able to rally Diederichs's and Knieriem's men to their guns after his assistant adjutant general, Capt. Henry J. Biddle, was mortally wounded while attempting to get them orders. Biddle had looked at the advancing rebels and said they were Yankees. The 8th Reserves's Col. George B. Hays had his horse cut to pieces by a shell during the charge. Private Wilson Cooper pulled the severely bruised Hays out from under the animal and helped him off the field, but that regiment was without its leader as the next rebel onslaught came.

As Hunton's brigade advanced, Hunton himself fell behind due to exhaustion. Command of the brigade passed to Col. John B. Strange of the 19th Virginia. Strange came under fire from his right and moved the Virginians a little to the left into a wood to reform. Then they came on to Branch's right. With Strange was Capt. Charles Pickett, George's brother and assistant adjutant general. Charles Pickett and Capt. W. Stuart Symington, a volunteer aide to George Pickett, had been ordered to report to Richmond while General Pickett was recovering from his wound, but they volunteered to go with Hunton and stayed with Strange when Hunton fell behind. Pickett lost his horse, but he still carried the rebel flag as he walked beside Strange. The flag, as it always did, drew Union fire, and Captain Pickett was hit. Others began to take him off the field, but Pickett told them to keep charging if it was not convenient to get him to safety. He did ask, however, that they let him keep the flag so he could die underneath its folds (Pickett survived his wound).

Both sides were somewhat confused. Each thought the other group of men was friendly. Kemper's men had probably confused their fellow Virginians, and the portion of the 10th Reserves at the breastworks may have given the rest of the Yankees pause. As the men at the breastworks were killed or taken prisoner, the rest of the 10th Reserves plus the 5th and 8th Reserves rose from the ground to charge. Instead, they got a volley that scattered them and decimated their officers. "Every officer to whom the troops looked for orders fell almost at the same time," one man recalled. The Confederates pushed the 5th, 8th, and 10th Reserves back and eventually broke them after "terrific" fighting. Simmons was mortally wounded and Truman Seymour's horse was shot, throwing the brigade commander to the ground. That was the final straw for the Yankees. The German artillerymen did not wait this time, but left their guns early enough that Strange saw several of them deserted as he charged. The rebels not only forced Knieriem's forward two guns and Diederichs's battery to limber up and ride off, they chased the remaining four companies of the 12th Reserves from Knieriem's other two guns and captured those, along with some human prisoners.

The 13th Reserves had just made it to the Nelson house when their comrades broke. Major Stone put his troops in line and ordered them to lie down. As the broken infantry ran past him, Stone yelled at the officers to reform them behind the Bucktails. Once all the friendly forces were behind them, the 13th Reserves gave the Confederates a volley. Stone, however, soon realized he could not hold the line by himself, particularly since the six companies present had lost 206 men in the previous five days. The Bucktails thus turned tail. At this point, Branch and Strange were very close to breaking the Union line and seizing the Willis Church road.[2]

John Sedgwick had sent for Napoleon Dana's and Alfred Sully's brigades at the first sign of trouble. Those men, after marching part of the way from Glendale to White Oak Swamp at the double-quick a few hours before, moved at double time part of the way back. One regimental commander said his men could not move at that pace in the heat, but they moved as fast as they could. Charles Curtiss of the 7th Michigan said the dust was so thick a man could not see ten feet. Many men broke down on the march and were left behind. Sumner kept sending messages to hurry up. Sedgwick also sent at least one message to that effect, and he worried that even if his men arrived in time they would be demoralized by the sight of the Pennsylvania Reserves.

Sully, although ill, tried without success to rally some of the Pennsylvanians. They would only reform four hundred yards behind the line, where Stone set up the 13th Reserves. Seymour apparently had left the field. One witness had seen him sitting calmly on his horse before the battle, but evidently his fall and his men's collapse had unnerved him. He was seen walking along the road to White Oak Swamp Bridge, seemingly dazed, with a bullet hole in his hat, calling his brigade "entirely dispersed." Seymour was looking for help from Franklin, and when the two met Seymour needed brandy to calm down. He returned to the battlefield area after dark, but for the moment the Pennsylvania Reserves were attempting to reform with Simmons killed and Seymour gone.

Kirby's battery fired shot and shell at the rebels. They seemed to react to the fire by moving a little to their left as if to attack Kirby, and Burns led the 72nd Pennsylvania to the woods between Kirby and the Southerners. Captain Tompkins's battery, less than half a mile north of Kirby, added its fire to the Union efforts. The minié balls came on the gunners "like rain." Seeley's battery opened fire as well. As the Confederates advanced, one gunner in Tompkins's battery wrote, "Things for a few minutes looked desperate."

Then the 19th Massachusetts from Dana's brigade arrived, doubtless huffing and puffing, but yelling at the artillerymen, "Give it to 'em boys! We're coming! Give it to 'em." The Bay Staters put aside everything but what they needed for fighting, headed for the woods at the double-quick, lay down just short of them for five minutes, then rushed straight into the trees. The 20th Massachusetts was not far behind and soon passed the 19th, which had been slowed by a battery passing in front of it. Another of Dana's regiments, the 7th Michigan, moved to the south of the Bay Staters, and the 42nd New York extended the line even farther southward. These regiments had been placed under the command of Col. William R. Lee of the 20th Massachusetts during the march, and they moved into the space between the 69th Pennsylvania, next to Hooker, and the 72nd Pennsylvania.

The next regiment to arrive was the 1st Minnesota, Dana's old regiment and Sully's regiment as well. "I will place my old regiment, general," Dana told Sumner. Sumner then told the Minnesotans, "Boys, I may not see all of you again, but I know you will hold that line." Dana led them into the woods south of the 72nd Pennsylvania, and the rest of Sully's men went to the Minnesotans' right, with the 15th Massachusetts and 34th and 82nd New York arrayed from south to north. As the 15th passed Sumner, Bull Head shouted: "Go in, boys, for the honor of old Massachusetts! I have been hit twice this afternoon, but it is nothing when you get used to it." They responded with "cheering that drowned for a time the terrible musketry."[3]

To the south of the Reserves, Hooker saw the broken elements of the Pennsylvania Reserves streaming past and even through his men. He also worried that the beaten Pennsylvanians would cause his own line to waver. Soon the rebels appeared, and the 16th Massachusetts, on the right of Grover's front line and the only one of Grover's regiments to have a clear field of fire, opened up. Hooker told the men, "Give them hell, boys," and the 16th Massachusetts gave three cheers for their state. The 69th Pennsylvania of Burns's brigade on the Bay Staters' right, and one company of the 26th Pennsylvania on the 16th

Massachusetts' left—the only company that could fire on the Southerners because of the ground—also began shooting. This fire, concentrated on the flanks of Strange's small brigade (only 723 muskets), was destructive, and the Virginians broke, leaving their newly taken prisoners behind. Captain Symington, the only officer in the brigade still on his horse, rode to the 56th Virginia's color-bearer, seized the flag, and held it high while trying to rally the men. His horse was shot seven times and finally died. As the rebels fell back, Grover attacked with the 1st Massachusetts, pushing Strange back across the field and into the woods he had just charged from. Meanwhile, the 69th Pennsylvania had advanced with fixed bayonets up the rise previously occupied by the German artillery and joined in the pursuit. The 26th Pennsylvania also advanced, but just to clear its front of rebels.

While Strange's men struggled to rally, Branch was heavily engaged with Sedgwick's men. Branch's brigade, about two thousand strong, was able to withstand the Union onslaught without much breaking, and a hot firefight began. Some of the Yankee muskets overheated enough that the men had to put their ramrods against trees to force the charges down the barrels. One estimate was that only two-thirds of the muskets would fire. Even so, the Federals gave the Confederates a "murderous fire," which some of the rebels had to endure with no cover. But the Southerners' fire was just as strong—and came from different angles. The 7th Michigan broke when hit on the left flank. One diarist wrote, "The right wing would have held the ground but when the colors and colonel leave the men are not apt to dwell long." The 42nd New York also broke—perhaps partially because of the confusion resulting from the regiments' going in piecemeal as they arrived on the scene. Burns rushed the 71st Pennsylvania and 19th Massachusetts to hold the line. The 19th was told that the 7th Michigan was in front of it. It instead encountered two Southern regiments, lost an estimated one-third of its men, and fell back to a rail fence at the edge of the woods. Just before the storm hit, Col. Edward Hinks turned to George Mace, one of the rank and file, and said, "We are not going to be killed this time, are we, Mace?" The soldier replied, "No sir, the bullet is not made for us yet." Just then, the Confederates fired. Hinks was wounded and Mace was killed. The same burst of fire mortally wounded Maj. Henry How.

The 20th Massachusetts advanced farther than the rest of Dana's brigade—perhaps spurred on by the example of Lt. James Lowell, who was mortally wounded but swung his sword in the air urging his men on. The Bay Staters passed some abandoned guns, probably Cooper's, and Colonel Lee was knocked down by a wounded artillery horse and taken out of the fight. Left in an exposed position and fired on by Jenkins's and Wilcox's men, the 20th fell back in good order to avoid being surrounded, firing twice on its way back to the Willis Church road. Burns was all over the field, his face covered with blood, keeping his men to their work. Sedgwick, on the same mission, was hit in the arm and leg (neither wound was serious) and had two horses hit under him but stayed on the field.

The Confederate right, as had the center, had failed to break the Union line decisively. All four of McCall's regiments in this area had broken, having lost 31 killed, 184 wounded, and 88 presumably captured, but the timely arrival of Sedgwick's brigades and the steadiness of Grover's line had kept the line from collapsing completely.[4]

Meanwhile, another savage engagement took place on the Confederate left. Cadmus Wilcox's Alabamians had been in position for several hours, with artillery shells flying over their heads in both directions, when Hunton moved his brigade out from Wilcox's right. After several contradictory orders, Richard Anderson told Wilcox to attack.

The 9th and 10th Alabama moved to the east of the Long Bridge road and participated in the struggle for Cooper's battery. The 8th and 11th Alabama advanced west of the road, joined by four companies of the 6th South Carolina that had not advanced with Jenkins. Wilcox asked Maj. James L. Coker of the 6th South Carolina if the enemy could be seen from the hill Coker occupied, then came up and took a look. A solid shot hit the tree on the hill. Coker asked Wilcox if he had gotten a good view, and the general replied, "Too good for me." He then gave the order to attack. Randol's battery, including Olcott's guns, was the target. The latter had returned during the fight for Cooper's guns. Having changed front to fire at the rebels attacking Cooper, the battery now changed front again to defend itself against Wilcox. At least one artilleryman thought the movement was poorly executed. The 4th, 7th, and 11th Pennsylvania Reserves were between Randol's limbers and caissons, lying down ready to fire. Randol had cautioned the infantry that if in repulsing an enemy attack it got in front of the cannon and had to retire, it should do so by a flank so the artillery would have a clear field of fire. Thompson's guns were also ready to help against any Southern attack.

The 8th Alabama, on the left of Wilcox's line, was the first to make contact. Just before they jumped off, these men had received an order to move to the left. They then missed the order to charge, but Lt. Col. Y. L. Royston, in command of the regiment, saw the rest of the brigade advance and ordered an advance himself. During the charge Charley Tisdale, the youngest soldier in the regiment, had his knee knocked out of joint by a shell—the second battle in a row (Gaines's Mill was the first) in which he was wounded. An officer saw Tisdale crying and told him not to cry just because he was wounded. Tisdale told the officer, "I am not crying because I am hurt, but because these damned Yankees won't let me get a shot at them." The rest of the 8th got within perhaps fifty yards of Randol's battery when the combined power of twelve guns firing canister and more than two regiments of infantry forced it to stop and fall back, Royston being wounded in the process. The 8th tried again, but failed.

The 11th Alabama charged on the 8th's right. Again the artillery and infantry blasted away, and the 11th staggered—one man wrote, "the crossfire on this occasion was never equaled before on earth." A few men came on, including a drunken officer who shouted, "Dixie is gone up! Dixie is gone up!" These men were captured and the rest fell back. The Yankee infantrymen, who could see better lying down because they were under the smoke hanging in the air, saw the Confederates fall back and sprang up after them. But the Southerners were not finished. Despite Randol's call, "Keep in the rear of the guns," the Federals kept going until they received a volley. They staggered and broke for the rear—but not by the flanks, as Randol had instructed them.

The rebels followed them. Randol could not fire because he would have decimated his own supports, so he waited helplessly. Nor could he limber up and get out. Thirty-eight of his horses were dead and many others wounded. The horses of one caisson were maddened by a volley and rushed through the 7th Reserves, running over Colonel Harvey of that regiment and bruising him badly enough that he had to be carried from the field. The battery finally fired when the Alabamians were within thirty yards of the guns, but it was far too late at that point. The Confederates chased the gunners at bayonet point, killing some of them and mortally wounding and capturing Lt. Edward B. Hill, the head of one of Randol's sections. Charley McNeil, the 11th Alabama's color-bearer, climbed onto one of the guns waving the regimental colors, but he was wounded and fell, still waving the flag. His nephew, Billy McNeil, tried to get the flag but was killed. About seventy or eighty Unionists escaped capture by walking through a gap in a fence. George Meade, the brigade commander on this part of the line, was severely wounded during the battle and rode to the Union rear. A spent ball may have hit McCall, who was also in the vicinity.

Randol rallied a few companies of infantry, and charged Wilcox's men with Company B of the 4th Reserves and some others who had stayed on the line. As often happened at Glendale, the fighting became hand-to-hand. "Greek had met Greek," McCall observed. Another veteran of the combat wrote, "The scenes enacted in this horrible contest for the mastery beggar description." Captain Walter C. Y. Parker of the 11th Alabama got the best of two Yankee officers with his sword but suffered two bayonet wounds in his chest, another in his side, and a musket wound in his thigh. Lieutenant T. J. Michie, also of the 11th Alabama, fought hand-to-hand with a Union officer, gave his opponent a mortal wound, then fell, cut in the head by a saber. He then received three bayonet wounds in the face and two more in the chest. He survived for three days, encouraging his fellow wounded before succumbing to blood poisoning. Captain Thomas Taggart of the 4th Reserves killed two rebels in sword-to-sword combat.

Randol and his rag-tag group of infantry finally forced the 11th Alabama away from his guns, gathering up the stricken Lieutenant Hill in the process. Charley McNeil was bayoneted and killed, and the Yankees took the colors. The rebels retreated to the same woods on the east side of the road where the 9th and 10th Alabama had taken refuge after the fight over Cooper's guns. The 8th Alabama kept firing, however, and Randol saw Confederate reinforcements coming, so he withdrew his men. Both sides stared at each other, exhausted.[5]

The 11th Alabama lost 49 killed, 121 wounded, and 11 missing in this fight. The 8th Alabama lost 16 killed and 57 wounded, plus 1 missing. Company B of the 11th Alabama went into the fight with 28 officers and men. Eight were killed, 15 were officially listed as wounded, and the other 5 had slight wounds or bullet holes in their clothing. The 4th Reserves suffered 8 killed, 33 wounded, and 96 missing. The 7th Reserves wound up with 9 killed, 62 wounded, and 33 missing. The two companies of the 11th Reserves present lost 4 killed, 18 wounded, and 10 missing. The Pennsylvania Reserves were pretty well used up. Almost every regiment had broken at least once, and all three brigade commanders were gone (Simmons killed, Meade wounded, and Seymour wandering in search of help). On the right and in the center, where they still held the front line, rebel reinforcements would surely sweep them off the field.[6]

Fortunately for the Northerners, the next assault did not hit the Reserves. The Confederates Randol saw approaching probably were from Roger Pryor's brigade. But Pryor was not headed for Randol. Lined up just to the left of Wilcox, Pryor got the order to advance when Wilcox did. But he ran into tougher ground than did Wilcox, so his assault was somewhat delayed. By the time his men made it to the front, Wilcox had attacked and fallen back. Pryor headed forward, toward James Thompson's battery and John Robinson's brigade on Kearny's left.

Also in this area was Lt. Pardon S. Jastram's section of George Randolph's battery. Jastram had been left behind when Randolph went to Slocum's support. After Jastram spent about half an hour at Kearny's headquarters, one of Kearny's orderlies ordered him to head to the front and "save the day." Jastram and his men moved into a field south of the Charles City road, probably between Thompson and Randol. Jastram got no definite information regarding either Federal or rebel dispositions, and when he asked what he should do he was told, "Fire toward the sun." He could barely see anything because of the smoke and had to shoot one gun in the air when it was loaded with canister, not wanting to risk hitting his own men. Jastram undoubtedly was an unsettled lieutenant by the time combat started, as were his men, seeing what one remembered "we had never seen before": a battle from up close.

Union soldiers (probably from McCall's division) began to retreat through and to the left of Jastram's section. He had to place his few shots carefully, did not know if he was hitting anything, and feared capture. The two guns got off five shots before he decided to get out of there. At that same moment, an officer ordered him out so he would not be surrounded, but a horse in one of his teams had been hit and in falling had tangled the harness so badly it could not be used. Jastram ordered one gun spiked and got the other off the field.

After the battle, Kearny was contemptuous of Jastram's decision. He claimed that he never saw Jastram but that he and his officers were conspicuously mounted, and that his orderly was intelligent (meaning that he could not have made a mistake). Kearny suggested a court of inquiry, which met and issued a report after Kearny's death later in the summer. The court censured Jastram in several respects but praised his activity and noted extenuating circumstances. It decided that no further action should be taken.

The other Northern artillery, Thompson's battery, would see plenty of action. It was on Robinson's left, just west of the Long Bridge road. The 63rd Pennsylvania was posted near the guns, with the 57th Pennsylvania in the middle and the 20th Indiana on the right with two companies deployed as skirmishers. The 105th Pennsylvania formed Robinson's reserve. The Hoosier skirmishers moved back when the fighting started and joined their brethren, who had constructed a breastwork. At one point, an unknown officer ordered the 63rd Pennsylvania to charge. The regiment sprang forward but found it was a false alarm.

Forced by the terrain to march in column, Pryor sent his regiments in one by one. The 14th Alabama went forward first, Lt. Col. D. W. Baine telling Pryor that his men could take the battery. Thompson called out that his guns were in danger, and the 63rd Pennsylvania moved fifty feet in front of the battery, lay down, and "opened a perfect storm of rifles." The cannon blasted double canister over the Pennsylvanians' heads, and the first charge was stopped, as were two more. At one point the Yankee color-bearer was by the corner of a slave cabin between the lines while the rebel color-bearer was at the opposite corner. The regiment was shattered and fell back "reluctantly." Colonel Baine was killed, the Alabamians' major was wounded, and only two captains escaped unhurt. As the 14th Louisiana prepared to attack, Pryor rode along the line. Thompson fired at the target, and a shell blew a leg off Pryor's horse. Another one exploded in the top of a cherry tree, dropping George Zerr of Company C to the ground. In the charge, James McCann, the regiment's color-bearer, was killed, and in one company only nine of forty-two men were not hit. Pryor could make no headway. The rebels found what cover they could and kept up the fight.[7]

Winfield Featherston's small Mississippi brigade, Longstreet's last brigade, was held in reserve at first, but after Wilcox and Pryor had gone in, Featherston was called forward. At one point he thought that the Yankees were attacking, but he got to Pryor without incident. Pryor asked him for support, and Featherston quickly saw the necessity. He was on the Confederates' extreme left, however, and he could see Federals to his left. Sending Lt. William G. Sykes of his staff to ask Longstreet for reinforcements for that flank, Featherston advanced his men to a fence at the edge of a field. He was inclined to order a charge but decided that the force he faced was larger than his own and might try to flank his men. Instead he waited for support to come up, meanwhile continuing to fire at Robinson's men—probably the 57th Pennsylvania, part of the 20th Indiana, and the 105th Pennsylvania (brought up during

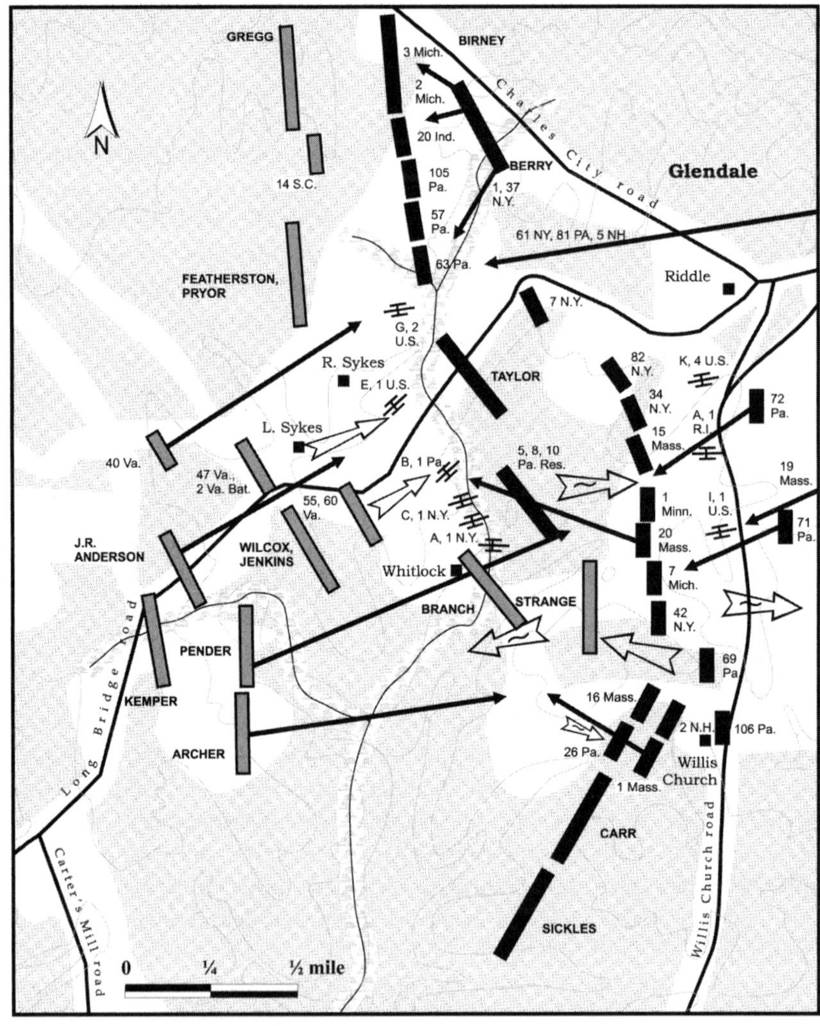

A. P. Hill's assaults, Glendale, June 30, 1862

the struggle). At some point Featherston was wounded in the shoulder and left the field.

Longstreet's men had all joined the battle. They had struck hard and had broken McCall's line in three places, but they had not been able to sustain any of the breakthroughs. Four of the six brigades were either exhausted or retreating. The other two, Pryor's and Featherston's, were holding their own, but, if Featherston could be believed, were in danger of being flanked. If the Federals pushed hard they might break the rebel line. Longstreet, in charge of the battle, had to decide whether to break contact completely or put the rest of A. P. Hill's men into the fight (Branch already being engaged). Hill's men were to apply the coup de grâce, but the plan for the day had failed. Huger and Jackson had not done their parts, and Longstreet's men were hard-pressed. Longstreet, probably in consultation with Lee, decided Hill had to go in not to crown success but to relieve pressure.[8]

One of Hill's brigades, Maxcy Gregg's South Carolinians, joined the fight quickly. Gregg had arrived on the field after marching all day, and he was told there was an attack on the Southern left. The 14th South Carolina was the lead regiment, and Col. Samuel McGowan sent Capt. A. P. West with some skirmishers to the left front to find out the situation. West found Featherston wounded and in the neighborhood of enemy skirmishers. Featherston told West the South Carolinians should advance at once. McGowan gave the order, and the 14th moved through trees to the edge of a field. Pryor gave Gregg a battle flag that belonged to a Louisiana battery, and asked that he take it into action. McGowan called for a color-bearer, and Pvt. T. W. Carwile volunteered (he survived, but the flag was hit five times). The 14th discovered the 20th Indiana behind its breastwork, and the two regiments settled down for an intense firefight. Some of the Confederates fired as many as seventy times, and the Hoosiers fired so much that they were forced to pour water on their muskets to cool them off.

The 13th South Carolina moved to the 14th's left. Perhaps because there were friendly units to its front, the 13th could not fire safely, so it waited for an hour until it was ordered to fix bayonets and charge. Before the regiment could start, however, the order was canceled because of darkness and the fear of charging on fellow Southerners. Gregg's other three regiments went either to the 13th's left or to support positions. None of them became heavily engaged.

The 14th, however, was still engaged with the 20th Indiana. Just after sunset a lull occurred. Perhaps, in the gloom and smoke, nobody knew whether friend or foe was to their front. During this lull an officer from the 20th Indiana, possibly Capt. Alfred Reed, approached the South Carolinians wondering who they were. McGowan replied by asking to whom the officer belonged. When he said 20th Indiana, he was told he was in the midst of the 14th South Carolina and taken prisoner. That caused the fighting to start up again.

Fighting also continued on Pryor's front. The men of the 57th Pennsylvania fired between eighty and 130 rounds each, and Robinson thought the situation there was serious enough to ask for reinforcements from Hiram Berry's brigade. The 1st and 37th New York went to support Thompson and the 63rd Pennsylvania, and the 2nd Michigan went to help the 20th Indiana. The 3rd Michigan went to support David Birney's brigade, which stretched from Robinson's right to Slocum's left. The 5th Michigan was held in reserve for the moment. Artillery and rifle fire flew around Birney's men "in torrents," but few men were harmed.

Thompson finally told Col. Alexander Hays of the 63rd Pennsylvania that he had run out of canister and case shot and would have to leave the field. Hays ordered a charge, and once again hand-to-hand fighting broke out—"muzzle to muzzle," Hays called it. The Southerners fell back, as did Hays, noticing as he did so that one of Thompson's pieces remained in position. When Thompson tried to bring it off the field a trace broke, and while his men were replacing it the horses that had been pulling it were shot. He then spiked the gun and left it. Kearny asked for a court of inquiry to review Thompson's actions as well, saying the artilleryman should have come to him for help and that a few men could have removed the gun, particularly since the infantry support never faltered.

Soon Robinson's men got help from John Caldwell's brigade, summoned from White Oak Swamp along with Thomas Meagher's brigade, which was still commanded by Colonel Nugent. These men also left their knapsacks. One Irishman put his carefully by a tree so he could retrieve it, but it was gone when he returned. Nugent's men stopped at Glendale, but Caldwell moved to the front, urged on by Kearny. Yankees were firing upon each other, and the 61st New York got separated from the rest of the brigade. The New Yorkers found Robinson, who used them to relieve the 63rd Pennsylvania. Colonel Francis C. Barlow put the 61st in line behind a fence, waited for other Union regiments to stop firing, and then hopped over the fence to charge. But the 61st met no enemy in the field, just a rebel flag on the ground, which the men picked up and forwarded to Sumner's headquarters. They finally ran into men who asked who the New Yorkers were. When told, the strangers responded, "Throw down your arms, or you are all dead men." The New Yorkers did not like those alternatives much and opened fire, which was returned immediately. The Federals aimed at the flashes of rebel muskets in the dusk. Barlow asked for reinforcements and got the 81st Pennsylvania from the same brigade, which "pitched into the Rebels with a will," according to Sgt. James Mitchell. "We was needed for they was gaining ground on our boys," he added. Noticing rebel movement on his left, Barlow pulled both regiments back to the fence, which he held for the rest of the battle with the 5th New Hampshire.

The regiment Barlow charged was probably the 40th Virginia of Charles Field's brigade. Field advanced to Gregg's right, with the 55th and 60th Virginia on the east side of the Long Bridge road and the 47th Virginia and 2nd Virginia Battalion on the west side of the road. The 40th Virginia was to have been on the brigade's left, but the ground separated it from the rest of the Virginians. Field got word to the 40th to keep going and attack the Yankee right, which Col. John M. Brockenbrough described as "a vastly superior force" and probably was Robinson's left. Soon cheering was heard on the far left of the Federal line, and those Federals in front of Brockenbrough charged. They got within twenty feet of the Virginians before they were forced back.[9]

The rest of Field's men kept going toward Randol's and Cooper's batteries. There were still Unionists there. After Randol's countercharge, McCall had searched for some Yankees to fill in the gap. He found two of Berry's regiments—one was probably the 5th Michigan—and asked them to move up. Their commanders said they could not without Kearny's orders, but just then Phil himself rode up. Things quickly were set, and Kearny told McCall, "If you can bring on another line in a few minutes I think we can stop them." McCall rode off.

At that point, the 47th Virginia and 2nd Virginia Battalion charged Randol's guns. Randol got off some canister—one wounded man pulling a cannon's lanyard as Field's men were on top of him (the shot went over the rebels' heads)—but the Virginians pushed the Northerners away from the guns and into the woods. Hit by flanking fire, Col. Robert M. Mayo of the 47th turned one of Randol's guns to his left, where the heaviest fire came from, and formed his regiment in the road to better protect the guns. Field then arrived and told Mayo to stop firing the cannon because the troops there might be rebels.

Shortly afterward, horses were heard to the east along the Long Bridge road. McCall had found Major Stone of the 13th Reserves with about five hundred men from six different regiments who had rallied behind the Union left. Stone was moving them toward the area of most danger when McCall came out of the trees, moved to the head of the column, and led it toward the batteries. Near the batteries, about where his original line had been, McCall halted the men and rode forward with Stone and two others. The party had not gone far when they met soldiers. "What command is this?" McCall asked. "General Field's, sir," replied Lieutenant W. Roy Mason of Field's staff. "General Field! I don't know him," McCall said. "Perhaps not, as you are evidently in the wrong place," Mason responded. McCall later told his wife he "was a prisoner before I knew where I was," but he had wits enough to try to ride off. Private S. Brooke Rollins grabbed McCall's horse's bridle and said, "Not so fast." Stone was quicker; two volleys followed, but he escaped only slightly wounded. McCall, seeing Colonel Mayo, said, "For God's sake,

Colonel, don't let your men do me any harm." Mayo asked McCall if the Yankee general thought the rebels were barbarians. The question may or may not have relieved McCall's mind.

Field's other two regiments took Cooper's battery. Colonel William E. Starke of the 60th Virginia ordered his men to fix bayonets and, after a brief combat, the Virginians drove the nearby Federals back about a mile. These rebels also became threatened with flanking fire, probably from George Taylor's brigade of Slocum's division. Samuel Heintzelman had ridden over to Sumner's position (in the process getting his left wrist bruised) after McCall was attacked. Satisfied with what he saw there, he returned to the Glendale crossroads, where he had been since the meeting with McClellan. Receiving a request for help from Kearny, Heintzelman turned to Slocum, since Slocum had offered to help after finding that Huger's cannon were causing few problems. Heintzelman rode up the Charles City road, saw that Slocum's men were not being pushed, and got Taylor headed toward Kearny.

Kearny's report reads as though he did not ask for help, but a history of Taylor's brigade reported that one of Kearny's staff officers told Taylor Phil "desired the assistance of his old brigade." Kearny had found a hole in his line. Riding to his left, where he figured McCall would be, he ran into some Southerners. Fortunately for Kearny, the dark concealed the color of his uniform—and probably the fact that he lacked an arm. When a rebel captain rode up and asked what he should do next, the quick-witted Kearny growled, "Do, damn you, why do what you have always been told to do." He then rode away.

Taylor told his staff officer, Lieutenant Grubb, "Keep ahead of them and keep them from going too far." Kearny told the men what the situation was, and they headed through the woods at the double-quick cheering. For a while they lay under heavy fire, the balls passing over their heads, but the rebels eventually pulled back so Taylor moved the brigade to the rear of the two abandoned batteries. Caldwell got his remaining regiments in position behind Taylor, and the fighting ended on the Union right, except for an incident that occurred about an hour after sundown. The 2nd Michigan, having relieved the 20th Indiana, sent up a tremendous shout after its foes from Gregg's brigade stopped shooting. The Confederates did not like the cheer much, and they fired again, which was returned by the Michiganders. Then both sides gave three cheers and quieted down for the night.[10]

Farther to the Confederate right, James Archer moved his brigade to the support of Strange and Branch. As the 56th Virginia of Strange's brigade fell back, it met Archer's men. "They got you boys," one of Archer's soldiers said, "but get out of the way and we will give them hell." Archer met the 1st Massachusetts of Grover's brigade. The Bay Staters thought the unit was Federal, perhaps from Sickles's brigade, until Archer's troops gave them a volley. "To remain there was certain death," one of the 1st Massachusetts men recalled, and the regiment fell back to behind the 15th Massachusetts of Sully's brigade, which had relieved the 69th Pennsylvania when that regiment's ammunition ran out. The 26th Pennsylvania finished clearing its front of rebels at about this time, and although Strange turned Knieriem's two abandoned guns on the Yankees and firing continued well after dark, meaningful activity had ceased on Hooker's front.

North of Hooker, Pender's brigade had advanced after spending the afternoon dodging shells. Passing a group of Confederate wounded and stragglers who told the North Carolinians the men up front needed support, Pender saw some Yankees apparently oblivious to his presence. The rebels fired from seventy-five yards, scattering the Federals. Pender skirmished with other Northern units for a while, then pushed his men into the woods and the 1st Minnesota and 72nd Pennsylvania on the right of Sedgwick's makeshift line. Leaving some men to protect his right flank from Hooker, Pender advanced, but he ran out of ammunition and the Yankee fire was strong. In the 22nd North Carolina, seven of the nine members of the regimental color guard were killed or wounded, and the flagstaff itself was broken twice in the fighting. Pender pulled back, not knowing that Field was somewhere ahead of him.[11]

Hill, concerned about Federal pressure, decided to put in his last brigade, Joseph Anderson's. As Anderson's men got ready, Jefferson Davis rode along the line and was greeted with cheers. The 3rd Louisiana Battalion and the 14th Georgia were on the west side of the Long Bridge road, and the 35th, 45th, and 49th Georgia to the east of it. The 3rd Louisiana Battalion advanced first, followed in a few minutes by the rest of the brigade. Anderson moved the men forward, cautioning them that other Confederates were ahead of them. As he crossed a fence, Anderson saw some troops marching toward them. He knew they were Yankees (perhaps some of Taylor's men, who would have been in the area), but the men were not sure after hearing the shout, "For God's sake, don't fire on us; we are friends." Anderson ordered a bayonet charge, but the men were demoralized by having to charge their supposed brethren. To raise their spirits, some yelled, "Three cheers for Jefferson Davis!" A command of "Fire!" rang out from seventy-five yards away and a "solid sheet of fire" flared to the rebels' front. The 45th Georgia took the brunt of it. "Never in my life did balls fly so thick around me," wrote one man. Anderson was hit in the forehead by a spent bullet and fell. Hill, worried, saw some of Wilcox's men who had rallied and went to them. Some began to shrink back, and Little Powell rode forward, grabbed the regiment's flag, and yelled, "Damn you, if you will not follow me, I'll die alone!" A soldier shouted back, "Lead on, Hill!" The general told the men to "cheer long and loudly" while moving to the front, and soon all firing stopped.

Behind the Confederate lines, a meeting of old friends took place. George McCall and James Longstreet had known each other in the U.S. Army. McCall had been a captain in the 4th U.S. Infantry, and Longstreet a lieutenant in the same company. As McCall's captors brought him to the rear, Longstreet heard McCall's name announced. McCall dismounted, and Longstreet removed his glove and offered to shake hands. McCall, as Longstreet later put it, "drew up with haughty mien, which forbade nearer approach." One account had McCall saying, "Excuse me, sir, I can stand defeat but not insult." Longstreet had a couple of staff officers escort the captured Federal into Richmond. The next day McCall talked with William Sydnor of Hanover County, and cried when discussing the deaths of every member of his staff.[12]

Called by many names, including Nelson's Farm, Charles City Crossroads, New Market Road, Frazier's (or Frayser's) Farm, Willis Church, even White Oak Swamp and Turkey Bend, Glendale was a relatively short engagement. It started no earlier than 4 P.M.—most troops were not engaged until 5 P.M. or later—and ended just after nightfall. Instead of involving as many as 125,000 men, as it might have, only about 19,500 Confederates and 23,500 Federals were engaged. Total casualties are hard to pin down, since both armies totaled losses from June 29 through July 1, but some distinctions were made for Confederate units and Federal losses can be estimated. McCall's division, down to 6,000 men before the battle, lost 1,118 killed, wounded, or missing. Grover's brigade suffered 195 casualties. Sedgwick's division lost nearly 700 men, Robinson's and Berry's brigades more than 300 each, and Caldwell's brigade probably suffered close to 200 casualties. So the total Union loss can be estimated at about 2,800 killed, wounded, or missing. The 1st New York of Berry's brigade may have suffered as many as 230 casualties. The Northerners also lost sixteen guns: Randol's and Cooper's batteries, two of Knieriem's cannon, and one each of Thompson's and Jastram's.

On the Southern side, in addition to Jenkins's estimated losses of 589, Kemper's 414, and Wilcox's 468, Strange's brigade lost 228, while Pryor and Featherston lost an estimated 800 or more men, making Longstreet's estimated loss about 2,500. A. P. Hill's losses are hard to estimate, but probably numbered between 900 and 1,200, so the total Confederate loss seems to have been around 3,500. One of Porter Alexander's estimates put Longstreet's and Hill's casualties at about 2,000 men each; another one credited Longstreet with 2,600 casualties and Hill 1,700. In five days McCall had lost more than 3,000 men out of about 9,000, Longstreet had lost 4,600 out of 9,000, and A. P. Hill had lost more than 4,000 out of 14,000. For all practical purposes, those three divisions were out of the campaign.

The fighting at Glendale was some of the most savage of the war. Many reports mention hand-to-hand combat or volleys at less than a hundred yards. Porter Alexander wrote, "[N]owhere else, to my knowledge, [occurred] so much actual personal fighting with bayonet and butt of gun." An officer in the 1st Minnesota said that in some cases the artillery could not fire with effect because of the hand-to-hand fighting. He described the musket fire as "incessant, one terrific roar, no cessation or pause anywhere."[13]

At the end of the day, the lines were about where they had been at the start of the battle. Lee had not broken through to the Willis Church road or cut off the Union line of retreat. In fact, given the size of the forces, Lee had not much chance of that in the first place.

No Confederate combat soldier or commander can be criticized for this battle. As at Gaines's Mill, almost everyone from private to division commander did what could be done. The rebel attacks seemed poorly coordinated, but this was partially the result of the beginning of the battle, which was not specifically ordered but brought on by Jenkins's charge. The ground and some confusion also contributed to the poor coordination. Longstreet criticized Branch for not supporting Kemper, but the ground the Tar Heels covered provides ample justification for their delay. Hunter McGuire, perhaps showing the rivalry between Jackson's and Longstreet's staffs after the war, said Longstreet was slow and waited until Hill had done most of the fighting before committing his division. Yet exactly the reverse took place, with all of Longstreet's men engaged before five of Hill's six brigades entered the battle. Longstreet could have applied more force at a specific point by attacking in column, but no one knew where the weakest point was. It makes more sense to attack everywhere with one division and follow up success with the other than to attack in column hoping to find the weak point.[14]

Rebel conduct at Glendale was not the problem on June 30. Cadmus Wilcox wrote after the war, "It could not have been expected that two divisions should have accomplished what was intended to be achieved by the whole army." The conduct away from Glendale caused what one writer called "the bitterest disappointment Lee had ever sustained." Lee's plan was not overly complex. No great feat of timing was required. Longstreet's force, which had the farthest to march of the major players, would be in place in plenty of time. Magruder's men, who might be needed as reinforcements, could get to their proper place by midafternoon. All Jackson and Huger had to do was put pressure on the Yankees in front of them; all Longstreet had to do was wait for that pressure to show.

Lee spent his time with Longstreet when, at least at the beginning, he might have been elsewhere. Huger's was the central position, and if Lee wanted Huger to open the battle he might have been there to make sure it got off to a proper start. But on this day more important problems were the lack of communication with Huger and Jackson and the wanderings of Magruder, prompted by perhaps too much communication. Both of these problems were at least partially caused by Lee. He had not yet honed his army into a coordinated fighting force. If Jackson had notified Lee of his delay, and if Lee had had a better picture of Huger's delay, he might have changed his plans. He could have moved Longstreet and Hill down the Carter's mill road, used Magruder to block any Union attack from Malvern Hill on his rear, and cut McClellan's lines of retreat that way. This idea, using Longstreet and Hill to free up Jackson and Huger instead of using Jackson and Huger to push the Federals into Longstreet and Hill, was riskier than Lee's original plan in that it placed much of his army in between the two parts of McClellan's force. But it might have produced a similar possibility of surrounding a substantial part of the Army of the Potomac. Yet without the knowledge that his original plans had been stymied, Lee would not have considered it. Moreover, he made no effort to acquire such knowledge, instead riding to Holmes's area—the least important sector of the field.[15]

But if Lee can be blamed, so can Jackson. As previously discussed, ten thousand men reinforced the Federals in the Glendale area entirely because Jackson was inactive. Without those men—in particular, without Sedgwick's two brigades—the battle of Glendale becomes much different. The force of the attack on the Confederate right increases in weight relative to the number of Union defenders. Two brigades of Hooker's division played little part in the fight and could have been used either as support (but perhaps arriving too late) or to attack the rebels' flank (with uncertain results). Only Burns's brigade would have been in the Southerners' direct path. Also, Caldwell's brigade would not have been able to help stiffen Kearny's resistance. One of Kearny's brigades was not engaged, and Taylor's men might have been available to Kearny, but overall, a slight numerical advantage goes to the rebels. Lee's plan then would have had a better chance of working. Thus, the majority of the blame for the Confederate failure on June 30 must fall on Stonewall Jackson's shoulders.

One Union officer wrote long after the war, "The results of this day were not flattering to the Confederacy, or especially so to us." While true regarding the Army of Northern Virginia's high command, this comment at first seems less so when examining the Army of the Potomac's work. At Glendale, most of the officers and men deserve commendation. Sumner, Heintzelman, and Franklin moved troops to threatened points. Franklin wasted no time in sending Sumner's men to Glendale when they were needed, and Sumner and Heintzelman were active behind the lines. The division commanders responded well to the various crises of the day.

Alfred Sully said some of the Pennsylvania Reserves "behaved shamefully." But the controversy over the Reserves at Glendale heated up with Hooker's report of the battle. In the published version, which he had revised, Hooker claimed that McCall's entire division was routed. In a prolonged exchange of letters with McCall, Hooker maintained that claim, although he did qualify the statement with the admission that some of his information came from others and not his personal observation. Both generals marshaled their forces in this battle of words. McCall appended excerpts from no fewer than ten supporting letters and reports to a supplemental report he filed. Hooker, for his part, referred to conversations with John Reynolds (who was not present at the battle), Kearny, Berry, Robinson, Sumner, and Sedgwick.

Both men made exaggerated statements. McCall got the sequence of events wrong and said that only the 12th Reserves and the 4th Reserves failed to maintain their positions. This is in one sense true, but every regiment in the Reserves retired or broke at some point. Hooker's characterization of the division as completely routed is no less false. Many regiments, having broken, rallied either entirely or in part—including, perhaps, some of the 12th Reserves. One of Hooker's statements—that he threw the rebels on to Kearny's front after McCall had given way—is best answered by McCall himself, as quoted by Longstreet: "[B]y a little stretch of the hyperbole he could have said that he threw Longstreet over the moon." None of the forces engaged on the Confederate right—where Hooker was—ever fought any of Kearny's forces. In fact, Hooker must accept some of the blame for the routing of the 12th Reserves. He took his position without knowing that McCall's men were near him, but he found out in plenty of time to adjust his line to protect the Pennsylvanians' flank. Yet he did nothing. This left the 12th Reserves's left flank effectively in the air.

A look at the casualty lists shows that if routs occurred, in most cases they happened only after some tough resistance. A unit does not suffer about 10 percent of its force killed or wounded without fighting. Longstreet was certainly impressed with his old commander's unit. He said that McCall was "more tenacious of his battle" than any other leader Longstreet knew of except D. H. Hill at Antietam. The next day, Old Pete asked N. F. Marsh, a surgeon with the 4th Pennsylvania Cavalry who had stayed with the wounded, which Yankees had fought at Glendale. Marsh said all he knew of belonged to McCall. Longstreet replied, "Well, McCall is safe in Richmond; but if his division had not offered the stubborn resistance it did on this road we would have captured your whole army." He added, almost as an aside, "Never mind; we will do it yet." McCall's men, of course, were not the only Yankees at Glendale. Having previously lost 20 percent of their strength and made a tough march, however, they were worn out. A member of the 7th Reserves wrote that "many of the men were scarcely able to walk," and Meade attributed their breaking to their lower morale after almost a week of constant battle or marching with little sleep or food. Their conduct at Glendale is understandable.

The other units criticized at Glendale are the German artillery units. One contemporary observer wrote that they "were among the most admired of the troops," but Alexander Webb of McClellan's staff had noted their "inefficiency" before the battles started. Seymour reported that as soon as they received some musket fire the artillerymen limbered up and rode off. But McCall rallied them at least once, and Kemper (who attacked this part of the line) wrote that they "poured an incessant fire of shell, grape, canister . . . upon my line, and did much execution." Criticism of these batteries is somewhat harsh.

There were few strategic options for the Yankees. Perhaps a holding action around Glendale combined with an assault up the River road on July 1 might have turned the tables on Lee. But McClellan would have needed a different character than the one he had to consider this option. An attack at Glendale on the night of June 30 would have been a disaster, given the darkness and the nature of the ground. Even in the battle that was fought there are many reports of men either mistaking the enemy for friends or firing on their friends. An attack in the area on July 1 would have found fresh troops—Magruder's—in place.[16]

In fact, there were still more rebels in the Glendale–White Oak Swamp area than there were Yankees. The inactivity that occurred on two fronts on June 30 might not have been repeated on July 1. Perhaps the man who worried the most was the one most exposed: William Franklin. He could only sit and hope he was not cut off by rebels seizing the Glendale area, and at the same time keep watch on Jackson's men across the swamp. His orders apparently were to hold the crossing until nightfall, and he had done that. He figured it was high time to get out of the possible trap.

Sometime during the day, Capt. Preston C. F. West of Baldy Smith's staff had found a road Franklin could use in his withdrawal. From the brief description Franklin gave, it is likely that this road was the same one that Keyes used—showing that communication was a widely shared problem in this campaign. The discovery was crucial; it is doubtful that all Union troops north of Malvern Hill could have used the Willis Church road and still gotten cleanly away. Sometime shortly after dark, Franklin sent word to Heintzelman that he was withdrawing, told Richardson to watch the crossing with French's brigade and Ayres's battery until everybody else was gone, and put Smith's division on the road, followed by Naglee's brigade at around 10 P.M.

After the order of march had been determined, Smith laid down to sleep, telling his staff to get him up in an hour. The staff fell asleep also, however, and by the time everybody got up the rest of the men had gone. "We did not loiter along the road till we had caught up," Smith later recalled. Two of Naglee's regiments were briefly left behind as well. One of the marchers remembered the night as another "of tramping, of dust, of thirst, of smothered objurgation, of weary struggle with sleep." Another wrote that he marched fifteen miles (an exaggeration) in five hours and said it was "one of the hardest marches I ever marched." At one point in the march the men of Davidson's brigade were leaning on their muskets, waiting to move or lying in the road, when something spooked them and every man—Franklin and Davidson included—was off the road and into the trees. Davidson never did see Franklin again that night. Before French and Ayres left, they could hear rebel workmen trying to repair the bridge, and they responded with musket balls and cannon shot. At last, however, French brought his men away from White Oak Swamp, and Jackson's route was open.[17]

So was Heintzelman's flank, and he was not happy about it. He had received no orders to withdraw, but he had sent word to McClellan that he thought it best to do so. His situation was even worse than Franklin's. Including Slocum's division, Heintzelman's troops were much farther from Malvern Hill than a bunch of Confederates. Without support on his right, he was in danger of being surrounded by the entire Army of Northern Virginia.

Franklin's move was the correct one. McClellan wanted to stay in the Glendale area and only decided otherwise after hearing of Franklin's retreat. But without fresh troops he would have been courting disaster for part of the army, for the situation would have been the same except that Magruder would have been on hand. Besides, the Malvern Hill defensive position was much stronger. Even so, at first Heintzelman could not believe Franklin had left. Seymour, back from Franklin's headquarters, told Heintzelman it was true. Heintzelman wanted Franklin to stay until he heard from McClellan, because without orders he felt he could do nothing. He thus sent Lt. Leavitt Hunt of his staff to find VI Corps. But Hunt saw only Naglee's brigade, and by the time he got back to Heintzelman it was close to midnight. Slocum had sent his own message to headquarters because he was nearly out of food and ammunition and then joined Heintzelman. They must not have received the word to withdraw that McClellan had sent in response to Heintzelman's message. On their own they decided they had better get away as soon as they could. Slocum, having the farthest to go, left immediately. Some members of the 32nd New York heard a cowbell and, having understood that a cowbell was a rebel ruse, tensed up. The bell actually was on a cow, however. Bartlett's men had to go back to get their knapsacks, and they left "just as quietly as possible and thank God we got out without harm," one man from the 16th New York reported. Porter's battery left under orders not to speak a word or strike a horse, to leave anything that got stuck, and to drive on the grass so as to muffle the sound. One officer actually ordered Confederate skirmishers off the road so the guns could get through. The infantry, also forbidden to talk, moved with doubts of the outcome, knowing they were nearly surrounded. "This was the darkest hour I have ever witnessed," Robert McAllister of the 1st New Jersey wrote. Kearny followed Slocum, some of his men having seen Southerners approach their flank before they left around 2 A.M. Jastram's bad day ended appropriately: nobody told him about the retreat.[18]

After arranging for the retreat, Heintzelman went to see Sumner. The II Corps commander probably was quite irritated about having to retreat from a successful battle for the second night in a row. He later wrote that he "certainly should not have [retired] without orders from the commanding general if these generals had not fallen back and entirely uncovered my right flank." But he had no choice, and Caldwell, Nugent, Sedgwick, and Seymour followed Kearny. "We did little more than drag ourselves along," one man wrote home. "Everything was as still as a funeral procession," another noted. Some artillery officers from the Pennsylvania Reserves wanted to get their guns, which were still on the field between the two sides, but apparently Heintzelman had orders from McClellan by then to do nothing to start fighting, so the guns stayed where they were.

That left only Hooker, with one of the best divisions in the army, to hold the road. He stayed in position until about daylight, when his brigade commanders quietly called in their pickets and headed south on the Willis Church road. Before they left, Hooker's men saw rebels with torches looking for their wounded and heard the cries of men seeking help. "The unbroken, mournful wail of human suffering was all that we heard from Glendale during that long, dismal night," Hooker remembered. "That was a horrible night," a soldier in the 2nd New Hampshire wrote his parents. A member of the 5th New Jersey told his wife of the sounds, "They are ringing in my ear now with awful distinctness, and will ring there for many a day to come." On other parts of the line the story was the same. Soldiers of the 1st Minnesota could hear comrades calling for each other before midnight. Burns's men heard the groans of men mixed with the hum of insects and the cries of the whippoorwill. The Confederates at times came within a few feet of Kearny's pickets, "but we did not trouble them," one man wrote. Neither did the 15th Massachusetts' pickets.[19]

The surgeons worked through the night. At the Willis Church, where Benjamin Roher of the 10th Pennsylvania Reserves had set up a hospital, amputated arms and legs were piled in a corner. At 2 A.M. the hospital was broken up and some surgeons were detailed to stay with those too badly wounded to move. Robert Everett of the 5th Michigan stayed until daylight, after first having gone to look for wounded and encountering rebels doing the same. Then, just as he and his fellow surgeons had decided to stay with their patients, an orderly came with word to head for the James with their ambulances. Only one surgeon stayed behind.

At midnight, Alexander Bliss was awakened and told to bring the ammunition trains from near Harrison's Landing to Haxall's. Earlier in the evening, Howe's and Palmer's brigades of Couch's division were ordered toward Glendale. They got into a supporting position and stayed until about midnight, when they moved back to Malvern Hill. Henry Wessells's brigade in John Peck's division also was to move to the front, but Erasmus Keyes had moved

Wessells to the far right of the line and Peck could not be found. At least one of the couriers McClellan had sent to Heintzelman and Franklin to find out information, Lt. Walter Newhall of the 3rd Pennsylvania Cavalry, spent all night going between Franklin and headquarters, riding past and through rebels on the way.[20]

While the Yankees were moving, the Southerners were reorganizing. Magruder's men, completing their daylong march, took over the front line. Hearing the wounded crying (which one man called "most lamentable"), they forgot their weariness and did what they could for both blue and gray casualties. One Southerner caring for Northern wounded found a Yankee with his brother's cap and learned that his brother had died during the battle. A sutler with William Barksdale's brigade said the dead and wounded "were so numerous that it was difficult to walk in the dark. The scene was horrifying." William Whiting's men repaired White Oak Swamp Bridge while Jackson slept. Huger stayed where he was. Bradley Johnson and the Maryland Line, still on the north bank of the Chickahominy, got orders to leave the Bottom's Bridge area. Holmes camped on the River road. Meanwhile, Robert E. Lee probably was attempting to figure how a day filled with such promise could go so wrong.[21]

George McClellan, however, must have thought the campaign was progressing well, given his perspective. His army was intact and occupying a strong defensive position, his new base was picked out, and his trains were secure. He probably also knew he would face at least one more day of fighting.

CHAPTER SEVENTEEN

"We Had Better Let Him Alone"

July 1 found the Army of the Potomac for the most part consolidated on Malvern Hill. Samuel Heintzelman reached Malvern Hill at about 1:30 in the morning. McClellan told him to consult with John Barnard and Fitz John Porter regarding his position, but there was no reason to try to point it out in the dark, so they waited until daylight. At that point, McClellan came onto the plateau. After riding the length of the line with Heintzelman, Little Mac left a couple of staff officers to post the men. Phil Kearny, the first to arrive, took his place along the eastern crest of the hill. Joe Hooker's division, the last of the Union units to reach the hill, settled in south of Kearny. One man wrote of the scene he encountered, "I could hardly conceive *any* power that could overwhelm us." Edwin Sumner's corps trudged past George Morell's line to rest near the southern end of Malvern Hill and the Malvern house. Some could see the James, "'our glittering goal,' 'our haven of rest'" in the distance. George McCall's shattered division, now commanded by Truman Seymour, stopped near the same house. Henry Naglee, with his "wearied mortals," joined Henry Wessells's men to reunite John Peck's division near Haxall's Landing. Henry Slocum's men found "the long-looked-for River" and halted on Peck's left, and Baldy Smith stopped on Slocum's left.

The Union line on the morning of July 1 formed an inverted U. George Sykes's division held the west side. Gouverneur Warren guarded the River road along with the 11th U.S. Infantry of Charles Lovell's brigade. The rest of Lovell's command was on the hill within easy supporting range, and Robert Buchanan's brigade was just north of Lovell. Morell's division formed part of the north side. Charles Griffin's brigade held the front line, just north of Dr. J. H. Mellert's house in a field facing north toward the Long Bridge road. John

Martindale and Dan Butterfield were behind Griffin in a patch of trees west of the Willis Church road. Butterfield's men were together again; the 83rd Pennsylvania had been supporting Griffin, but in the morning Griffin's own 4th Michigan took the Pennsylvanians' place supporting some artillery. Hiram Berdan's sharpshooters were acting as skirmishers a couple of hundred yards in front of the line.

Darius Couch's division was on the northeastern corner. Couch was less than a month from turning forty and was an 1846 West Point graduate, as were so many other officers prominent in this campaign. After serving with the artillery in Mexico and elsewhere, the New Yorker worked in his wife's family's copper business until war broke out. One of his brigades, Innis Palmer's, had only two of its four regiments on the field (the 2nd Rhode Island and 7th Massachusetts were covering Turkey Island Bridge on the River road behind Warren's men). The 10th Massachusetts and 36th New York were near a wooded ravine east of the Willis Church road and north of the West house. These regiments (and Albion Howe's brigade as well) originally faced west toward Griffin, but eventually they turned to the north and northeast. One company from the 10th Massachusetts went forward to observe the ravine, while four companies of the 36th New York went into the western edge of an oat field east of the ravine. Three of Howe's regiments were to Palmer's right rear, facing the oat field, with the 93rd Pennsylvania's right resting on another ravine. The 62nd New York was to Palmer's left rear supporting artillery, and the 102nd Pennsylvania was in reserve. John Abercrombie's brigade was behind Howe's line.

The II and III Corps were on the east side. These men looked out over the valleys of Western Run and Turkey Island Creek, watercourses that (like Beaver Dam Creek and Boatswain's Swamp) might not look imposing but would cause attacking Confederates problems. This line was extended by William Franklin's and Peck's men on the River road southeast of Turkey Island Bridge.

Perhaps the most important part of the Yankee defense was not the infantry, but the artillery. The entire Army of the Potomac was assembled for the first time in the campaign, which meant that fifty-three batteries and 268 guns were available for use, not including the siege artillery. Six of the eight batteries (with twenty-eight guns) that had bombarded Theophilus Holmes the day before were still on the west side of the line. James Robertson's battery had left the front after the engagement at Turkey Bridge, and John Beam's battery had moved to a position with III Corps. Augustus Martin's battery was posted with Warren in the lowland along the River road, with two guns near the James River and the other three on the road itself. On the north part of the line, under the command of Regular Army artilleryman Griffin, were thirty-one guns from seven batteries. Capt. La Rhett L. Livingston's Batteries F and K, 3rd U.S. Artillery, and Capt. Walter M. Bramhall's 6th New York Light Artillery were there, along with Adelbert Ames's, Henry Kingsbury's,

William Weeden's, John Hyde's, and Thomas Osborn's batteries. Some of Hyde's men who had lost their guns at Gaines's Mill volunteered to fill the ranks in other batteries.

The II and III Corps artillery (minus Joseph Nairn's, Osborn's, and Bramhall's batteries) were on the east part of the line. Rufus Pettit's and Rufus King's batteries rejoined Israel Richardson's division in the morning. Charles Tompkins and Edmund Kirby had parked their guns with John Sedgwick's division on their arrival at Malvern Hill, along with Capt. John D. Frank's Battery G, 1st New York Light Artillery. George Randolph's and James Thompson's batteries were with Kearny's division, while the rest of the III Corps artillery parked with Hooker's men. This meant that ten batteries and sixty guns were protecting the approaches from the northeast.

Hunt's remaining guns—John Tidball's, James Roberton's, and Henry Benson's batteries in William Hays's brigade; Otto Diederichs's and John Knieriem's batteries along with Battery D, 1st Battalion, New York Light Artillery, and all of Albert Arndt's brigade; and E. R. Petherbridge's brigade—were in park near the Malvern house. Two batteries (12 more guns) of the 1st Connecticut Heavy Artillery—5 thirty-pound Parrott rifles, 5 four-and-a-half-inch Rodman guns, and 2 ten-pound Whitworth cannon—also were near the Malvern house. Men struggling on ropes along with the mule teams had dragged them up the steep south slope of Malvern Hill the previous evening. These ten batteries and 52 guns completed the artillery setup on Malvern Hill itself. The Yankees had 171 guns on the hill, all within a mile and a half of one another. Besides the 5 guns with Warren near Turkey Bridge, another seventeen batteries with 86 guns were with Peck's division and VI Corps near Turkey Island Creek Bridge.[1]

This line resulted from the labors of several Northern officers. Porter had selected the original line for Sykes's and Morell's divisions and probably had posted Couch's men, since as a corps commander he would have outranked Couch. McClellan pointed out the general outline of the position. The engineer staff, including Barnard but principally Humphreys of the topographical engineers, put Sumner and Heintzelman in their positions. Henry Hunt, a forty-one-year-old Michigander who had attended West Point, fought in Mexico, and served in the artillery ever since (including helping to revise the army's light artillery tactics), posted his artillery reserve batteries as well as the army's other guns.

Those people had done their jobs well. On the left, Sykes had a commanding view of the River road—the effectiveness of which he had demonstrated in bombarding Holmes the previous day. On the right, Sumner and Heintzelman had a position similar to those held by Porter at Mechanicsville and Gaines's Mill: on a hill forty feet above a swampy stream (in this case Western Run, a tributary of Turkey Island Creek), the ground rising on the other side of the stream. Some strengthening of the position there was accomplished by cutting timber and blocking roads northeast of Western Run. In the middle, Couch and Morell had less elevation advantage than their brethren on the flanks, but they did have wide-open fields of fire to the north and northwest. A large field ran west of the Carter's mill road for about half a mile north of Morell's position. A smaller field ran along the Willis Church road north of Couch's men. The terrain was gently sloping, with only one or two depressions to shelter attackers. Artillery had a wide and clear field of fire; any battery could support any other battery. Finally, the divisions covering the likely Confederate attack routes were relatively well rested. Morell's and Sykes's divisions had not fought since Gaines's Mill, and Couch's men had not fought in a major engagement during the campaign.

Everyone on the field knew this position's strength. General Lee, who probably knew the area well from visits to the Shirley plantation just down the River road, noted that it possessed "great natural strength." Porter, whose men had fought at Mechanicsville and Gaines's Mill from excellent defensive positions, called it "better adapted for a defensive battle than any with which we had been favored." Unlike at Gaines's Mill, where inferior numbers held a strong defensive position, the Yankees on top of Malvern Hill would outnumber the rebels attacking up the slope. About 53,000 Federals were on top of Malvern Hill, and Warren had about 1,000 more in the lowland. Heintzelman wanted 20,000 more men to hold the line, but it is hard to figure out where they could have been placed except in reserve. Facing them, according to Lee's plan for the day, were about 48,000 Confederates, and Holmes was on the River road with roughly 7,000 men.[2]

Whether the Union command structure was as good as the position is open to dispute. McClellan had put Porter in charge of his area of the line, including Couch's division, so for the third day of seven Fitz John headed the defense at the likely point of rebel attack. Sumner and Heintzelman had charge of their corps, although Bull Head Sumner seemed put out by the whole situation (barely reporting any activity at Malvern Hill, and specifically pointing out that he was no longer in command—of what he did not say). Meanwhile, McClellan, after his ride around the hill, was nowhere to be seen.

As Jackson might have put it, Little Mac was on other important duty. Cheered by the men as he rode around the lines—one soldier wrote, "as yet to our feeble ken he had done all things well"—he returned to Haxall's Landing and sent several telegrams. In a message to his wife, he said the men "cheer me as of old as they march to certain death." He also reported being "completely exhausted—no sleep for days—my mind almost worn out—yet I *must* go through it." To Brig. Gen. Lorenzo Thomas, the adjutant general of the U.S. Army, he expressed his hope that Lee would not attack him and said he would move to Harrison's Landing that night if possible. His men, he said, were very tired, and he could not stay in position or advance on Richmond because he was "overpowered by superior numbers." He asked John Dix at Fortress Monroe to forward any reinforcements he could find to Harrison's Landing.

By midmorning, McClellan had finished his paperwork and boarded the *Galena* so he and Commodore Rodgers could pinpoint the army's final resting places. On the way, he and Franklin, who was also on board, slept. Two hours later McClellan got off the *Galena* at Harrison's Landing to personally inspect the ground and perhaps satisfy himself about the site's suitability before reboarding the gunboat. Later in the afternoon he was back on Malvern Hill. After staying with Porter for less than an hour, he rode along the line to what he considered his most worrisome point: his right flank. Porter moved him in that direction, saying, "General, everything is all right here and you are not needed; if you will look after our center and right that would help us here more than you can by remaining." By "center and right" Porter probably meant anything to the right of his lines: Sumner, Heintzelman, Peck, and Franklin. There McClellan went, and there he stayed until late—posting some batteries, perhaps watching the battle through a field glass as did surgeon Robert Everett of the 5th Michigan, who was near Little Mac, and also perhaps getting a message from Porter that read in part, "The enemy has renewed the contest vigorously, but I look for success again."

Moving back to Haxall's Landing, McClellan stopped at Erasmus Keyes's headquarters, described the battle, and told Keyes the rebels were not likely to reach his men. He then said he was going back to the *Galena* to direct fire. McClellan's brother Arthur, a member of the army's staff, told an inquirer that the army commander had found everything to his liking. However, Little Mac did not get back to the gunboat until after the battle was over, and he stayed on it through the night as it moved downriver.

This day's activities were great fodder during the 1864 presidential campaign pitting McClellan against Lincoln. McClellan was portrayed as timid as well as incompetent in editorial cartoons, supposedly living it up on the gunboat while men died on the hill. A few people have used these actions to question McClellan's courage; many have used them to question his competence. Yet on both counts McClellan's actions on July 1 are less questionable than his actions on June 30. He was away from the action the entire day on the thirtieth—a day that could have resulted in the destruction of up to half his army. On July 1, he returned to the field. His stated reason for not remaining at the point of attack, that he was not worried about the other parts of his line, probably was prompted by his confidence in his friend Porter and the strength of the position. Lee's ride to check out Holmes's situation on June 30 was less productive than McClellan's gunboat trip, and it also removed a commander from a vital point just before a major battle.

Whether born of timidity or not, McClellan's activities did not reflect good military judgment. Although Barton Alexander of the engineers was not around—he was checking out the navigability of the Chickahominy and did not see Little Mac again until July 2—plenty of other engineers could have been detailed to examine Harrison's Landing. McClellan said he could not entrust the job of selecting the army's resting place to anyone else. By this he must have meant that he needed to know firsthand that the army had a safe haven. But his need for assurance was too strong. He also said he went where he would be of most benefit to the army. Yet his presence still electrified most of his troops. Given his perceived situation—beset by superior numbers, in a good defensive position but in danger of being outflanked and cut off from a base he had not really established yet, and with some subordinates he could not trust—anything he could do to enhance his men's fighting capabilities would be helpful. Of course, he once again was leaving a muddled command situation, one that might not be damaging as long as Lee concentrated his attack from one direction. But it could explode on McClellan if Lee assaulted both Porter's line and the east side of Malvern Hill. Who would decide the issue if both sides needed reinforcements? McClellan returned before the battle was fully underway, but he could not have known that would be the case. Fatigue possibly clouded Little Mac's judgment. Again, however, he was risking much on the field to ensure that he was satisfied with his new base, assuming that the army would in fact survive to reach that base. And his subordinates once again would need to cooperate fully to ensure that outcome.[3]

Robert E. Lee also was tired. His exertions, his disappointment, and perhaps a lack of sleep prompted by that disappointment had worn him down. D. H. Hill and James Longstreet both noted Lee's disappointment and said the commander bore up well under the circumstances, but one can imagine the strain that effort caused him. Jubal Early, somewhat recovered from a wound he had received at the battle of Williamsburg in May (although he still could not get on a horse by himself), reported to Lee to be assigned to command. Early had found Lee the night before and presented him a letter from Secretary of War Randolph suggesting that Early take over Arnold Elzey's brigade. On the morning of July 1, Early came again to Lee for the official assignment. Noting that something had gone amiss the previous day, Early worried out loud that McClellan might escape after all the Southern efforts. Lee replied impatiently, "Yes, he will get away because I cannot have my orders carried out!" Now he had to improvise once more to try to salvage what he could from a campaign that had begun with high hopes, perhaps boosted those hopes even higher, and then saw them dashed in a single day.

As with its opponents, the Army of Northern Virginia would be concentrated on July 1 for the first time in this week of battles. William Whiting's men repaired

White Oak Swamp Bridge and crossed to the south side before daylight, followed by D. H. Hill, Charles Winder, and Richard Ewell. Whiting's van met John Magruder's skirmishers near Glendale. These skirmishers had awakened to sights they had been spared the night before. The guns standing silent and unmanned, the dead of the Pennsylvania Reserves around the fence, the Whitlock house with the slain piled in heaps and amputated limbs thrown into a pile, all greeted Magruder's soldiers—as well as Mrs. Whitlock, who had taken her young child to safety before the battle but had returned that morning to the ghastly sight. The roads were "full of grim terrors to one unaccustomed to bloodshed," one man wrote. Another said, "Hundreds of dead bodies were lying on the hill as we marched along. We stepped over their bodies and seemed to have no more feeling than if they had been so many logs."

Magruder had also come in contact with Hooker's rear guard and forced the Yankees' retirement. The 21st Mississippi captured some men who had slept so soundly their comrades' leaving did not disturb them, as well as some musical instruments. No one knew if more Unionists were near, so Magruder advanced in line. Lee and his staff joined Magruder, and Major Brent of Magruder's staff was sent to the front to observe and report. Brent recognized Whiting's approaching force as Confederate. Finding they were Jackson's troops, Brent asked for Jackson. Stonewall was at a house nearby and just mounting his horse when Brent approached and introduced himself. The first question Jackson asked concerned Lee's location. He and Brent soon met up with Lee, Magruder, and their staffs. Jackson's men had continued marching down the east side of the Willis Church road, and with Magruder's men on the other side of the road, Lee, Jackson, and Magruder were running a friendly gauntlet. Shout after shout rang out from both sides of the road. Embarrassed by the attention, Lee periodically touched his cap in acknowledgment. He, Stonewall, and Prince John discussed the coming day, Lee showing the other two their positions on a map. Jackson was to be on the left of the Quaker road (as Lee called it), with Magruder on the right. Jackson's relatively fresh troops would lead the advance, and Magruder would follow Stonewall down the road.[4]

Lee also wanted Benjamin Huger on the front line. Huger had started Lew Armistead and Ambrose Wright south at 3 A.M. This was probably a flanking move, because Huger had no idea that the Federals had vacated their lines. After Wright left, following Armistead into the woods south of the Charles City road, Huger heard from Longstreet that the Charles City road was clear of Northerners all the way to Glendale. Huger thought William Mahone, his frontline commander, should have discovered this, but Mahone told him Yankee pickets had been in his front and had surrendered when Mahone advanced, saying they had received no orders to fall back. Once Huger knew the road was clear, perhaps as late as 9 A.M., he pushed Mahone and Robert Ransom down it. These men also saw evidence of battle, which surprised some of

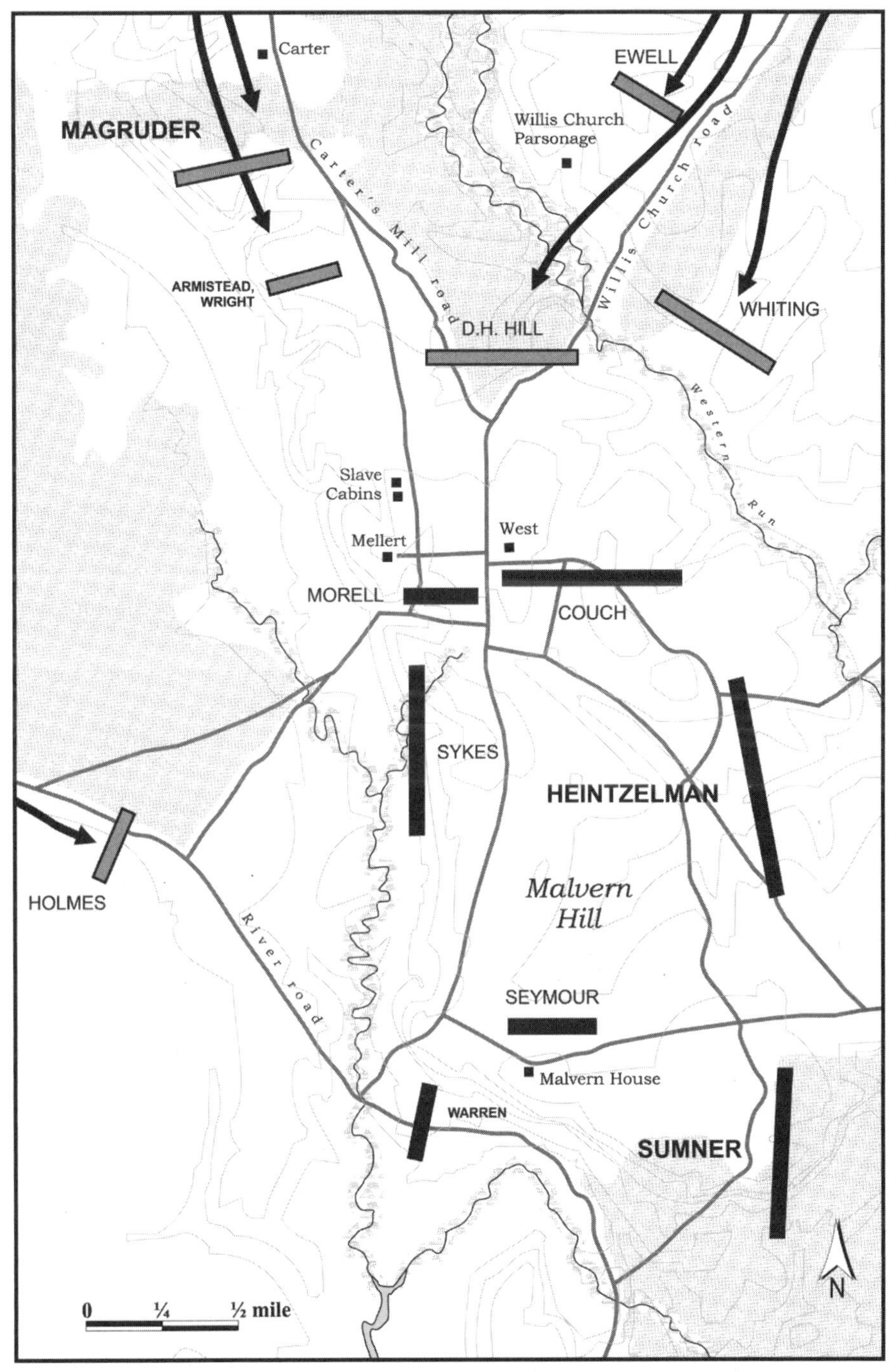

Troop movements, July 1, 1862

them (evidently they had not heard the roar of muskets at Glendale) and sickened others. "Here the carnage exceeded anything I had yet beheld," wrote Henry Burgwyn of Ransom's brigade. "In places the Yankees were lying almost in heaps." Some of the men were more interested in the Union knapsacks and what was inside them.

The roads around Glendale were "filled with columns of troops pushing ahead," one of Mahone's men said, slowing Huger's progress. He also was not sure where to go. Eventually Walter Taylor of Lee's staff found Huger and directed the South Carolinian toward the front. Armistead and Wright continued south along a country road—Armistead called it a "blind road"—to the Long Bridge road west of Glendale. Armistead found Lee there, who told him to head down the Carter's mill road. After about a mile of marching, Armistead met Maj. Thomas M. R. Talcott of Lee's staff. Talcott told Armistead the Federals were not far off, and Armistead deployed his skirmishers and put the rest of his men in a wooded ravine about three-quarters of a mile north of the Mellert farm. Wright stopped his men behind them. For the moment these brigades formed the Confederate right. Longstreet and A. P. Hill, the former engaged heavily twice, the latter three times in the previous five days, stayed pretty much where they were in reserve. Holmes advanced from the intersection of the Long Bridge and River roads with some of his force.[5]

Lee had chosen well, putting rested troops in the front. The sight of them should keep the Federals in place and give Lee a chance to form a plan. An important question was whether Malvern Hill should be attacked. D. H. Hill told Lee not to attack. Reverend L. W. Allen had described the position to Hill, who repeated the description to Lee and Longstreet with the comment, "If General McClellan is there in force, we had better let him alone." Longstreet laughed and told Hill, "Don't get so scared, now that we have got him whipped." This was a strange comment to make after Glendale's slaughter, but Old Pete probably thought the Yankees were demoralized, and the evidence of that in the form of abandoned knapsacks, muskets, and other supplies was strewn from Beaver Dam Creek to Malvern Hill.

Alternatives to a frontal assault could be explored without commitment. Lee decided to investigate. He had asked Longstreet, whose division was to be in reserve, to accompany him on the field—either because Lee was tired or because he wanted another competent officer with him as a sounding board. Telling Longstreet to examine the situation on the Confederate right, Lee went to the left, where Whiting's men were on the Willis Church road near the Willis Church parsonage.[6]

Longstreet found some fertile possibilities and a major mistake. The possibilities emerged as Old Pete came onto a plateau near Armistead's position, where Armistead, Wright, and Col. Edward C. Edmonds of the 38th Virginia were sizing up the situation. This area was at nearly the same elevation as the Union guns, and Longstreet could see as far as the field near Whiting's position east of the Willis Church road. Between forty and sixty pieces of artillery could be massed where Longstreet was, and their fire would hit the flank of the Yankees opposite Jackson. Longstreet also could see that Jackson could concentrate up to a hundred guns, if available, to fire as the infantry advanced, thus creating a cross fire that would not only hurt the Northerners but further demoralize them, setting up a Gaines's Mill–type charge by Jackson's divisions. As he put it, "the tremendous game at issue called for adventure." If Longstreet's plan worked, destruction of at least part of McClellan's army might result.

As Old Pete was pondering this, he saw Magruder observing the same scene while Magruder's column marched southwest along the Long Bridge road. Magruder agreed with Longstreet about the artillery, but Longstreet said that Magruder was marching away from the position he was to occupy. Prince John's three guides, all of whom had been born in the area, confirmed that the road they were ready to turn onto was the Quaker road. This road ran from near Nathan Enroughty's farmhouse to near Sweeny's Tavern on the River road. Several other roads led from the Long Bridge road to the River road, and this one had fallen out of general use. But it was the only road called the Quaker road anywhere near there.

Unfortunately for the Confederates, it was not what Lee meant by the Quaker road. Lee's map showed the Willis Church road as the Quaker road. The Willis Church road was the best route for Magruder to take to reach his assigned position, although the Carter's mill road could have been used as well. But the road Magruder was getting ready to enter would reach the River road a mile southeast of the junction of the Long Bridge and River roads, nearly two miles west of where Lee wanted him and closer to Holmes's force than to Malvern Hill. Either the map Lee had used in his discussion with Magruder was faulty or Prince John did not pay attention.

Magruder told Old Pete he would obey an order to retrace his steps, but Longstreet did not feel comfortable ordering Magruder to essentially disregard an order from Lee. So Magruder turned into the Quaker road. Longstreet communicated with Lee regarding the artillery concentration and Magruder's march. Lee agreed with the concentration and sent pioneers to clear the way through some trees along the Carter's mill road so batteries could get to the chosen spot without having to expose themselves to Yankee gunners. As Longstreet began to find batteries to fill the positions, he had second thoughts about not ordering Magruder to his proper place and rode back to Prince John, finding him about one and a half miles down the Quaker road. At about the same time, Robert Chilton, Lee's chief of staff, arrived. Lee agreed with Longstreet about Magruder, and Chilton told Prince John he needed to move to a different road. Magruder immediately turned his men around. The line of march had been David Jones's, Magruder's, and Lafayette McLaws's divisions.

McLaws had barely reached Carter's mill road when Longstreet directed him down that road, and some of McLaws's men did not even know of the mistake. The other two divisions reversed course.[7]

Magruder's adventure obviously cost Lee some time in getting his forces arranged. It also cost them a coherent deployment. Lee's vision was Jackson to the left, Magruder on the right, and Huger wherever he was most needed. But Magruder would not be on the right for quite a while as a result of the mistake, so part of the line had to be improvised. This might mean a tangled command, because Lee still had not seen Huger and so might be forced to either act like McClellan and let each unit control its own moves, or name an overall commander with authority that might not be recognized. If this problem could be overcome and Longstreet's plan was followed, then not much would be lost by the confusion.

Lee's approval of Longstreet's other suggestion, regarding artillery, was at most a contingency. Lee needed to understand the situation before he could formulate a definite plan. Neither he nor anyone else could have that understanding before they had a good look at Malvern Hill. D. H. Hill's famous quotation contains the phrase "If McClellan is there in force" because he did not know. Jackson apparently was present when Hill made that comment, and there are statements that Jackson wanted to turn the Union right and was overruled by Lee, but neither Jackson nor Lee knew where the Union right rested. Once Lee saw McClellan's army in position, he could see that Longstreet's idea would cost him little. If the guns had an effect, he could attack. If they had no effect, he could do something else—that something to be determined by further reconnaissance, particularly to the east where turning McClellan's flank could cut him off from his new base.[8]

On the left, Whiting came under artillery fire from the Yankees as his men neared the Willis Church parsonage, about three-quarters of a mile from the West house and the Yankee guns, just after 11 A.M. Jackson received Lee's order to start massing artillery and started rounding up guns. The first to show up was James Reilly's Rowan Artillery, followed by William Balthis's Staunton Artillery. Shortly afterward, William Poague's Rockbridge Artillery from the Stonewall Brigade came down the Willis Church road. As the Valley gunners arrived, the Rockbridge Artillery's Edward Moore was seized with the feeling he would be killed that day, so he got off his seat and ran along with the battery to shake it off. Whiting told Balthis to cut down some trees so more guns could be gathered before they all moved into position at the same time, saying he wanted fifty guns ready to go before one moved into the field. Jackson arrived and ordered the batteries already there into the field. "These few guns will not be able to live in the field five minutes," Whiting observed. "General," Stonewall snapped, "obey orders." To which Whiting replied, "I always obey orders promptly but do not obey these willingly."

Reilly's guns went first, but the Tar Heels found the field untenable in the face of a Yankee cross fire. Kingsbury fired his guns from the front of the Union line, as did Osborn and Bramhall, while Beam, Thompson, and Randolph opened fire from their positions with III Corps and Capt. John W. Wolcott's Battery A, Maryland Light Artillery, joined in from the II Corps position. The big siege guns at the Malvern house began firing as well. One infantryman watching the action said, "It was pretty lively work I can tell you."[9]

Two ministers were visiting rebel friends in the area, and when the shelling started they headed to the rear—first at a brisk walk, then at a run. They were physical opposites—one large, one small—and a soldier called out, "Run little preacher—the big preacher'll catch you." The rest of the men in the area picked up the line and sang it to the tune of a spiritual song until the ministers were out of earshot. Jubal Early, Colonel Walker of the 13th Virginia, and Willy Field, Walker's aide-de-camp, were lying down eating when a Yankee shell passed through the body of a soldier in front of them and hit the ground just under Field's side. The impact lifted Field off the ground and the concussion killed him without the shell's touching him. John Brown of Poague's battery, detailed to take care of the wounded, had put an oak tree between himself and the Yankees and sat down, no doubt thinking he was safe. But a round went right through the tree and took his head almost completely off, only a few ligaments keeping it lying on the man's right shoulder.

Early in the day Jackson, Ewell, and Whiting were riding into the Poindexter field when a round of solid shot just missed them, throwing up dust and drawing more Union fire. Several shells hit near the group, which included some staff officers. A couple of the shells landed close to Jackson's horse. After another horse was hit in the head by shell fragments, Jackson's sorrel took off, and Jackson—who must have been holding the reins—was pulled down to his hands and knees. His horse kept going, but Stonewall got to his feet, stopped it after twenty or thirty yards of travel, and moved to a less exposed place. The horse later regained its poise, and both horse and rider merely looked up when a shell burst about twenty feet in front of them. D. H. Hill, talking with John Gordon of the 6th Alabama, tossed aside worries about his safety. "I am not going to be killed until my time comes," he said as he sat facing the incoming missiles with his back to a tree. Just then a shell exploded near him and a fragment tore his coat. Hill moved to the far side of the tree. Some of Whiting's men, having moved into position supporting their artillery, dodged shells and grapeshot for two hours. One shell killed a man in the 2nd Mississippi and showered another with enough dirt pellets that he thought for a moment he had been torn to shreds.

Reilly was shelled out of his position. The other two batteries, Poague's at least posted by former artillery instructor Jackson in Whiting's absence, were somewhat better protected and kept a small barrage going. One or two other rebel batteries arrived (including Capt. Wilford E. Cutshaw's Jackson Artillery battery, arriving late from the Valley), scattering Whiting's infantry, who were still on the road. Someone ordered the batteries off the field. Poague (and apparently Balthis and Cutshaw) refused to obey the order, but at least one battery left. That unknown battery came in contact with Lt. John C. Carpenter and two guns from the Allegheny (Virginia) Artillery battery, headed south in response to Jackson's order. Carpenter looked for a position for his guns, but the guns turned around and left with the other battery. Finding them again, Carpenter heard what happened. Whiting then arrived on the scene and ordered Carpenter to the front. He set up to Poague's right, but soon Balthis—who had "found a beautiful position" after running through the fire—ran out of ammunition and left. One of Poague's guns, a six-pounder, was pulled out of the line because there were not enough artillerymen to work the piece. Two guns from George Wooding's Danville Artillery battery arrived. The others had no ammunition but may have entered the fight later.[10]

The Confederate artillery fire had some effect. Beam was killed by a shell that pierced his body late in this combat, Tompkins's and Kirby's batteries (although not engaged) changed position several times to avoid the fire, and Wolcott called the fire "galling" near the Malvern house. It might have been particularly galling for Pettit's battery, which was not allowed to return fire but suffered from the incoming shells. In Abercrombie's brigade, one soldier remembered, the shelling "cut us up terribly." Charles Haydon of Berry's brigade was almost buried by the sand and stubble thrown up by one shell's explosion, caught a ball from a shrapnel shell with his hands before it stopped rolling, and dodged two others that hit close to him. He noted that most of the rebel shells burst 150 feet in the air, scattering fragments everywhere. Although the fire killed a few people, it did not frighten the Federals much. In fact, Haydon went to sleep during the shelling. One of Kearny's men noted in his journal, "They don't aim as well as we do." Only Capt. Alonzo Snow's Battery B, Maryland Light Artillery, came from the artillery reserve to help. Snow had first been ordered to Griffin's side of the line, then moved to Howe's right and opened fire on the rebels in the field in what one gunner remembered as "a very hot place."

Sumner's men moved from a camp position into line of battle to support the guns when the firing started, Hooker also took position under the fire, and Birney's brigade on the front of Kearny's line entrenched as a result. Sumner, that noted straight-ahead fighter, moved away from the crest to get some protection from the shells, which were beginning to exact a toll, especially in Sedgwick's sector. A hospital was moved to get the wounded out of range, but none of the infantry left the line or became demoralized. The foot soldiers were hot and tired, and the commanders worked to help boost their spirits. Morell's bands played, while Kearny gave his men iced lemonade and water. Thomas Hyde of the 7th Maine actually wanted the Confederates to attack, deciding that even a fight would be better than what he had just been through.[11]

The Confederate artillery fire did not have the desired effect because the 80 to 100 guns Longstreet had envisioned could not be brought to bear. Instead, only 20 guns were lined up in the Poindexter field. Of those, 4 left quickly, and 4 more ran out of ammunition. Not more than 14 guns were in action at any one time, and they faced 32 Union guns on an equal elevation at relatively short range, as well as part of the heavy artillery from a longer range. No guns could be effective in such a situation.

On the rebel right, Wright and Armistead had four batteries attached to their brigades. But the gunners had not marched with the infantry, so when the generals decided artillery was necessary, they needed to send to the rear for it. Those four batteries would have helped the Confederates mass the 30 guns Magruder thought were necessary and the 40 to 60 that Longstreet wanted.

Other batteries were also available. Mahone, leading Ransom down the Charles City road, encountered someone—probably Longstreet or an aide—who said Armistead needed artillery. Captains M. N. Moorman and Carey F. Grimes both were there, and both went to the front. Willie Pegram's battery in A. P. Hill's division, despite the rough handling it had received at Mechanicsville and Gaines's Mill, also advanced. Moorman seems to have arrived first, but he was concerned about the situation. Armistead, a forty-five-year-old Tar Heel who, despite having been dismissed from West Point (supposedly for breaking a plate over Jubal Early's head), had spent his entire adult life in the Regular Army before joining the Confederate army, wanted less concern and more work—and drove Moorman off the field. Grimes, having come up in the meantime, was directed to report to Wright. Before he could deploy his guns, however, Armistead met with him and Wright. Armistead told Wright he needed an artillery commander who would fight. Wright responded that Grimes's battery was available. Armistead asked Grimes if he could get to a hill just south of the ravine where his men were located. Grimes said that if any battery could, his could. Armistead had pushed Yankee pickets back with the 14th Virginia to clear the way for the cannoneers, and Grimes, guided by Wright, moved to the north end of the Mellert field.

Union guns occupied the south end of that field, and they opened fire as soon as the rebels came into sight. Livingston indeed may have begun by bombarding the Southern skirmishers. He, along with Ames, Kingsbury (after that battery had shelled Reilly's men), Hyde, and perhaps Weeden and Nairn, blasted away with at least eighteen guns at close range to Grimes's two guns that could reach the Federals effectively. Some of the siege guns probably added their weighty shells to the Yankee side, as did Carlisle's six twenty-pounders and Voegelee's four twenty-pounders from along Sykes's line. Such an unequal contest could not last long—and it did not, according to Wright, although Grimes wrote that he was on the field for two hours. Pegram wheeled his pieces into line to the east of the road and continued firing for more than an hour until ordered to stop by Wright—even though by that time only one of the Purcell guns was firing. Two of Pegram's men were killed at their guns, and two lieutenants and fifteen privates were wounded, some several times. Perhaps Moorman's artillerists got into the act after Grimes retired, but if so, it was for just a few minutes. A Confederate watching the contest counted nineteen dead horses in the area.

Ames called the Southern fire "severe," as did some infantry officers from Morell's division. It was plenty severe enough for one teamster who had brought rations to the 14th U.S. Infantry in Buchanan's brigade. A shell took off part of his wagon bed before he even got to the infantrymen, and when the shells started falling again he begged the regulars to hurry. The hungry soldiers unloaded every ounce of food before they let him go. A soldier in the 13th New York had just received a rifle and was lying down when a shell ricocheted once, hit the ground again and burrowed its way under the man's body, went back into the air and exploded. The soldier came away with cuts and bruises, but his new weapon was ruined. The man asked his captain if he would have to pay for it.

However severe or heavy the Confederate fire might have been, however well the Confederate guns were served, the attempt was doomed. Armistead called repeatedly for more guns. He even saw Longstreet, who promised them to him. But it was not until Magruder's men arrived that any more artillery would be seen northwest of Malvern Hill.[12]

It is not as if there were no guns available. John McCreery, a gunner with Capt. Edward S. McCarthy's 1st Company, Richmond Howitzers, wrote later, "We had plenty of artillery to have filled the field with it." In the Army of Northern Virginia (not counting Holmes's or Stuart's batteries) there were 63 batteries, 46 of which were permanently assigned to brigades or divisions, and 17 of which were in Pendleton's reserve artillery. Of the latter, 11 were temporarily attached to infantry commands. Jackson and Longstreet were able to round up parts of 9 of these batteries for a total of 28 guns, 13 of which were forced out of action. Where did the failure arise?

On Jackson's side of the line, Stapleton Crutchfield, who had gotten the guns at White Oak Swamp Bridge into position without the Federals suspecting a thing, might have been able to accomplish the same thing at Malvern Hill. But he was ill and not on the field. Whiting had 2 batteries, Balthis's and Reilly's. Hill's division, next in line, had 5 batteries permanently assigned and 2 others temporarily attached, but all 7 had been sent back to Seven Pines, as they had exhausted their ammunition. Jackson's division had 5 batteries and Ewell's division 3, but all were attached to brigades and probably strung out along the line of march.

On Longstreet's front, Old Pete wrote in his memoirs that Magruder had said he would get thirty rifled guns from his own command, and Prince John commanded thirteen batteries in all (James Woolfolk's guns having been pulled out for refitting and recruiting). But Magruder himself seems not to have returned from his wanderings until at least an hour after Longstreet had left Armistead. If this were the point at which Prince John said he would get thirty guns, they would have been far too late to help Longstreet. If, on the other hand, Magruder had promised the guns at the earlier meeting, he and Stephen Lee would have suffered from a problem similar to Jackson's. Magruder's artillery was attached to infantry brigades and divisions, at intervals throughout the line of march, and not easily brought to the field. Stephen Lee reported that the guns could only move into position along a narrow lane in the open and subject to Federal fire, so the pioneers Robert Lee sent did not get their jobs done—perhaps another case of rebels having problems with axes. Only two of Magruder's batteries—a section of Hart's battery and McCarthy's battery—actually set up and engaged the Yankee guns. McCarthy ran a three-hundred-yard gauntlet of shot, shell, and case shot to get into position. Huger's artillery—aside from Grimes and Moorman, four batteries in all—must have been at the end of his line. Yet nothing was heard from them and, given the traffic, perhaps nothing was all that could be expected.

These problems leave two groups of gunners from which it might have been possible to send artillery to the field: the batteries in Longstreet's and A. P. Hill's divisions, in reserve near Glendale, and Pendleton's reserve artillery. Longstreet controlled seven batteries, and Little Powell had eleven. None of Old Pete's batteries were engaged, although they had not suffered much in previous battles. In fact, the Washington (Louisiana) Artillery, Longstreet's reserve gunners, had grumbled at the inactivity. Finally getting an order to move to the front, the men became excited, but when they got there about dark, Longstreet told them, "We have done all we can today." One of Armistead's men remembered hearing Longstreet promise to get his guns to the front. Longstreet sent a staff officer back to Glendale, and when the officer returned with the report that one battery commander would arrive as soon as the horses were watered, Longstreet exploded, "Water horses! Water horses! When I want his battery in action! Go back and tell him to take his battery to the rear and say to [another captain] to bring his battery here."

Pegram's guns and Capt. Greenlee Davidson's Virginia battery were noted by Hill as being engaged, but only Pegram reported any losses. One commander, Capt. William G. Crenshaw, reported that his battery was ordered to the rear to refit before Malvern Hill, and it is possible that others were under the same orders. If Crenshaw's is assumed to be the only battery not on the field, then sixteen batteries sat silent near Glendale, not more than a mile and a half from the area where Longstreet wanted the artillery concentrated. Since it is likely that Longstreet himself moved Pegram's guns to the front, one has to wonder what happened to the others—surely not all the battery commanders were watering their horses. Assigning responsibility for the failure is difficult, although Longstreet must share some blame for not using his own guns.[13]

Pendleton's reserve artillery included just six batteries under Pendleton's direct command. In the first six days of fighting, those six batteries did little work beyond some long-range shelling. Pendleton was an interesting story. The fifty-two-year-old Virginian was both an Episcopal minister and a West Pointer, graduating fifth in the class of 1830. His ministry kept him occupied until the war, when he shed the frock and picked up the saber as captain of the Rockbridge Artillery. He had been sick on the twenty-ninth, and on the thirtieth he mainly observed where the army was and changed his batteries' positions to try to make them useful. His largest rifled pieces traveled down the Darbytown road to its intersection with the Long Bridge road on the thirtieth. The remaining batteries of Col. J. Thompson Brown's command had moved to the same vicinity a day earlier, probably marching with Longstreet and Hill.

It was Pendleton's responsibility to get those guns into action on July 1, and he tried. Having been out of touch with the army, he first looked for Lee. He failed to find the commanding general, however—which is not really surprising since both men were on the move and few people could be expected to know where Marse Robert was at any point. Pendleton then tried to find a position from which his long guns could do some damage, but he could not find one that would not endanger fellow Southerners. At least one gun could not cross some of the streams in the area to get into any kind of position at all, so he moved back to his remaining men and waited for someone to tell him what to do.

Pendleton wasted his time. He should have been able to find someone, Jackson or Longstreet or even Armistead, who might have helped him find something to do, and he might have risked some Southern heads in the effort to hit some Northern ones. But two factors greatly reduce Pendleton's responsibility. First, he had only six batteries. Of all the commands on the field at Malvern Hill, his was the smallest in terms of artillery concentration. His contribution, even given that he had large rifled pieces, would have been negligible. Second, apparently no one tried to find him. It is almost as though the rest of the army forgot about Pendleton, including Lee, Longstreet, and Jackson, who all were trying to get guns concentrated.

The most important fact concerning the Confederate artillery at Malvern Hill is that it was underutilized. The major reason for this was inefficient organization and management. Porter Alexander, in making this charge, implicitly blamed Pendleton. The real culprit, however, seems to be the timing. Certainly the rebel artillery was not as well organized as the Union artillery, much of which was under Hunt's direct orders. Hunt was able to concentrate his guns at Malvern Hill, whereas the Confederates were not. Pendleton wanted to consolidate control, and Lee had approved his plan. But Pendleton's plan did not go far enough toward the Union model to enable him to control his guns the way Hunt did at Malvern Hill. Only if the batteries temporarily assigned to divisions or brigades had been kept in the reserve's control, to be retrieved after each engagement, could Pendleton have done materially more than he did on July 1.

Another problem with concentrating Southern guns was the simple difficulty of moving them into position. They were exposed to Union fire, coming down narrow roads clogged with infantry, with few good positions to choose from (and those positions no doubt had been spotted by the Yankees). Longstreet acknowledged after the war that a concentration such as he had imagined would have been impossible, for the above reasons and also because the ground the guns would have to roll over was too rough in many places. For all these reasons, the Northern guns were in a position to virtually annihilate the Southern guns before the latter could even get into position. It might have been nice had Longstreet found this out before he suggested the plan to Lee, but the idea itself was reasonable.[14] The execution was in part impossible and in part not accomplished. If Lee was dependent upon the Confederate artillery to make an attack, the day's work should have stopped early in the afternoon.

CHAPTER EIGHTEEN

"Press Forward Your Whole Line and Follow Up Armistead's Success"

THE REBEL INFANTRY continued to move forward. D. H. Hill's division, marching behind William Whiting, turned right off the Willis Church road toward a patch of woods at the foot of Malvern Hill, just north of the intersection of the Carter's mill and Willis Church roads. Hill's men had to cross an open field and Western Run to get to the trees, and as they did so, the same Union guns that had whipped the Confederate artillery found infantry as well. George B. Anderson's North Carolinians, on the left of Hill's line on the Willis Church road, came within range of Henry Kingsbury's canister along with the fire of Adelbert Ames's, La Rhett Livingston's, Walter Bramhall's, and Thomas Osborn's batteries. Innis Palmer's two regiments also opened fire. The 14th North Carolina got within a hundred yards of the guns, but the fire was too much, and the regiment's color-bearer fell. Palmer's men pursued, and some members of the 36th New York pounced on the prize. It was the only time during the war that the 14th lost its flag. Anderson was wounded, but his men rallied on the south side of Western Run.[1]

On the other side of the Confederate line, Lew Armistead saw a line of Union skirmishers (Hiram Berdan's sharpshooters, who formed George Morell's picket line, or perhaps the advance of John Martindale and Dan Butterfield with their men to better supporting positions) moving on his men. The Southern brigadier decided to meet force with force and ordered the 14th, 38th, and 53rd Virginia forward. Some of Ambrose Wright's men followed the

Virginians. Wright told them to stop, then found out Armistead had ordered the advance and put the whole brigade in motion.

Colonel Edmonds of the 53rd Virginia saw Armistead, "hat off and arm uplifted," ordering a continued charge, on what he did not know and could not imagine except the main Yankee line. So that is where he went. The commanders of the other regiments did not get any orders (because Armistead did not issue the order), but at least some of their men followed Edmonds toward the crest of the hill. Forcing the sharpshooters out of a depression about four hundred yards from the Federal lines, they took the Yankees' places and got some needed shelter from Union bullets and guns (those of Ames, Livingston, and perhaps Kingsbury and John Hyde). A shell wounded Fletcher Harwood, the 53rd Virginia's color-bearer. He waved the flag and called for someone to take over. Captain R. W. Martin grabbed it and yelled for the rest of the troops to follow. One of Wright's regiments had supported the 53rd Virginia, but Wright, seeing the disadvantage, had ordered his brigade back, and the Georgians left. Armistead tried to figure out how to withdraw his men from their advanced position or charge the Northerners with the rest of the brigade—finally deciding he could do neither until the artillery arrived.[2]

Armistead's advanced position helped Lee decide how to coordinate an assault if the supposed artillery concentration had its desired effect. If and when Armistead saw a Yankee retreat, he could signal the rest of the army to advance. Marse Robert told Robert Chilton to draft an order to that effect. Chilton's order read as follows: "Batteries have been established to rake the enemy's lines. If it is broken, as is probable, Armistead, who can witness the effect of the fire, has been ordered to charge with a yell. Do the same."

This order is ludicrous on its face, and it seems incredible that Lee told Chilton to write it that way or approved it after it was written—despite Longstreet's written testimony that Lee indeed had this plan in mind. The signal for the attack was ridiculous. A shout raised from one part of the line could be the result of any number of things—including a Yankee success prompting a yell from the Northerners. In the days before standard time it was hard to coordinate an advance, but Lee could have been with Armistead to observe the Yankees himself. If they began retreating he could order an advance with the troops near him, and Jackson's left (the farthest point from Armistead) was less than a mile and a half away. A courier with orders could reach it easily even by keeping to roads and going back to Glendale.

Lee's proper position was with Armistead if that was the best observation point. Armistead might have been a brigade commander for only four months, but he was a lifelong soldier and probably would not mistake the replacement of one battery by another for a retreat. Even so, Lee should have been there. It was the decisive point, and thus the place for the army commander. No one but Lee should have made the decision to attack or not to attack.

No time was written on the order, just the date. As with Magruder's wrong turn, this omission might not have severe consequences, but it might contribute to confusion in newly arrived units. A commander arriving late might not know whether the order was still in effect or had already been executed. To improvise a plan is dangerous, albeit usually necessary, but to improvise a plan and then communicate it through a strange order with no time written on it is to invite disaster.[3]

There is no easy explanation of this order. Lee seems to have been exhausted. At one point Jefferson Davis, on the field once again, prevented Lafayette McLaws from waking the sleeping commander, saying he needed the rest. Marse Robert had taken the precaution of keeping Longstreet with him just in case, but decided it was not necessary to relinquish command. Other evidence shows that Lee was thinking clearly despite his exhaustion.

Ironically, Armistead never mentioned receiving such an order or his important role in it. Perhaps the orders went to division commanders only. If so, Benjamin Huger would have been responsible for informing Armistead. The order did not affect Armistead's early actions. D. H. Hill had time to get all his brigades in place, examine the Yankee line and note it was as strong as he thought it would be, and remain in place for what he called "a long while" before he received the order. John Magruder did not get the order until after he had returned to the field following his misadventures. By that time the artillery concentration had failed, and Hill sent a message to Jackson that since the firing was "farcical," perhaps the order should be ignored. Stonewall wrote back that it was still in force.

Lee, awake enough to realize that Longstreet's idea was not working, was trying to find an alternative. Again riding with Longstreet, Lee investigated the possibility of turning the Malvern Hill position to the east. The two generals apparently found something to their liking—a road (perhaps Erasmus Keyes's road), relatively level terrain, some cover for marching troops, perhaps—and Lee ordered Longstreet to take his and A. P. Hill's divisions that way. Lawrence Branch, at the head of one of A. P. Hill's brigades, received orders to move down the Long Bridge road.

Malvern Hill's crest heads southeast from the junction of the Willis Church and Carter's mill roads for about a mile and a half, after which it slopes sharply down to a plain west of Turkey Island Creek. East of the creek the ground rises again and was wooded at the time of the battle. This elevated area extends onto the River road south of Malvern Hill and Turkey Island Bridge. A march of about six miles, using Keyes's road, would bring the Confederates to the River road south of Turkey Island Creek. It would not be a difficult march, and it would not come much closer than a mile and a half to the Yankee guns. Lee or Longstreet may have ridden far enough to see the Union VI Corps occupying the preferred area—Caspar Trepp of Berdan's sharpshooters, on duty with Baldy Smith's division, saw a lone horseman opposite his line. But even a position near the millpond northeast of Haxall's Landing would make life uncomfortable for the Unionists. John Bell Hood thought either this march or a movement down a vale that began north of the Poindexter field (which Robert Dabney thought was the best move) would have been possible earlier in the day. After a reconnaissance by some of his Texans, Hood, joined by Wade Hampton, suggested it to William Whiting, who turned him down.

A. P. Hill and Longstreet might have been able to get into position on July 1, although an attack would have been difficult to pull off before dark. It thus is not likely that Lee thought he could attain success that day. Perhaps some shifting of troops during the night could strengthen his left and he could attack the next day. He knew he could count on the Confederates at Malvern Hill to keep the enemy busy—possibly enough that he might once again have an opportunity to cut the Army of the Potomac in half.[4]

Meanwhile, Magruder came back to the field. This may have been the first or second time he showed up just north of Malvern Hill, but this time he had his men with him. Lee had told Prince John to move to Huger's right, and Longstreet had told him to support Armistead. William Barksdale's brigade, probably Magruder's first to arrive, was already at Armistead's right rear, so Magruder ordered up three regiments of Howell Cobb's brigade (the 24th Georgia, 2nd Louisiana, and 15th North Carolina, as Cobb's Legion was supporting the artillery and the 16th Georgia protected the rebel right). Cobb was one of the leading lights of the Confederacy. Nearly forty-seven years old, he had been the Speaker of the U.S. House of Representatives, governor of Georgia, and secretary of the treasury before secession. Afterward, he was presiding officer of the Montgomery Convention that organized the new country and a candidate for its presidency. He immediately advanced while Magruder went ahead to see the exact situation. At the same time, Prince John sent Major Brent to find Huger and see where the Southern commands connected.

Brent had previously climbed a tree to view the area. He saw the hill and its strength as a position, as well as the Union guns ringing the top of the plateau, and decided it was not likely that any movement to the right could accomplish much. He later wrote that it "was a beautiful and impressive scene." A rebel sentry, who said that he was half-surprised that Brent had been able to climb safely down, greeted Brent when he returned to the ground and pointed out that there were Yankee sharpshooters on the skirmish line. Finding Robert Ransom's brigade, Brent asked Ransom where Huger might be. Ransom did not know, but another officer pointed Brent in the right direction. Huger was a mile to the rear from that point. When Brent asked about troop positions, the South Carolinian said he had no idea where his lines ended, he had not been to the front, and since his brigades had been moved without his knowledge he could not tell where they were. His division was no longer his to command, and he was staying out of it.

Huger obviously was upset at having others give his units orders. Lee had ordered Armistead and Wright to their positions in the morning. That afternoon Marse Robert and Huger met as Huger brought his other two brigades onto the field. This must have been after Lee had seen Magruder, for Lee told Huger to send William Mahone to support Cobb (who was supporting Armistead and Wright). Lee, not making the mistake McClellan made, put his right wing under one commander: Magruder.[5]

Whatever Huger's reaction, his brigades were on the field. Brent then moved east along the supposed line and found D. H. Hill. The North Carolinian was in position between the Willis Church and Carter's mill roads, probably muttering about his brother-in-law Stonewall being such a stickler for following orders and hoping no one would raise a shout. He showed Brent his right flank, which was in the air, so the major had at least one useful piece of information when he reported back to Magruder.

Prince John was, as Brent put it, "much perplexed" by Huger's reaction. He may also have been perplexed by the Yankee position. The Northerners had not been idle while the Southerners were sorting themselves out. John Sedgwick's division had hooked up with Baldy Smith's VI Corps division guarding Turkey Island Bridge from a turning movement such as Lee was attempting. Napoleon Dana's brigade took the south end, with the 106th Pennsylvania of William Burns's brigade on Dana's right to fill a gap between Dana and Smith. Alfred Sully was on Dana's left. Charles Morgan's and Samuel Elder's batteries were moved to Smith's front. McClellan may have ordered these movements after he returned to the field. They strengthened his right while weakening the reserves for the left and center of the line.

Near the front line, John Abercrombie moved his brigade to form a line with the rest of Darius Couch's division. Almost as old as Edwin Sumner, Abercrombie had served in the army for forty years after graduating from West Point, and was a veteran of the war with Mexico. He ordered the 65th New York and 61st Pennsylvania to support Kingsbury's battery and the 62nd New York in Albion Howe's brigade. The 67th New York and 23rd and 31st Pennsylvania took position between Palmer and Howe's other regiments. Then, after Howe (a forty-four-year-old Maine native and West Pointer who taught there after serving in Mexico and had just achieved brigade command) advanced his men to a better position, the regiments were shuffled a little. The 65th New York and 31st Pennsylvania supported Palmer's two regiments near the ravine north of the West house while the 67th New York and 61st Pennsylvania filled the gap between Palmer and Howe. The 23rd Pennsylvania supported

Howe's right. Couch's line now curved from the Willis Church road to the northeast crest of Malvern Hill.

Artillery was also moving. Kingsbury, having fired more than 750 rounds already during the day, had only sixteen rounds per gun left. Three of his guns had enlarged vents as a result of the firing, and he moved out of the line. The three remaining guns in William Weeden's battery, commanded by Lt. Richard Waterman, and Hyde's two guns came from the far left of Charles Griffin's line near the Mellert house to replace Kingsbury. John Edwards's battery moved from the south end of George Sykes's line to replace Livingston, who had likewise run out of ammunition. Bramhall was ordered to Heintzelman's line, and Osborn moved first to Couch's line and then, without firing, to Joe Hooker's line.

These movements had to attract the Southerners' attention. But they misread the signs. In fact, Porter Alexander said the Yankee movements could not have worked better if they had been planned to deceive. Whiting had moved his men into the Poindexter field, working his way on the right to the edge of a wood that separated his field from the hill itself. Hampton supported Whiting, and Isaac Trimble extended the line to the southeast. Whiting interpreted the Union movements on top of the hill as evidence of the Northerners retreating and reported this to Lee.[6]

At about this time, David Jones's division was moving into position. Longstreet had put George T. Anderson's Georgians in the rear of Cobb's brigade, which was in the rear of Armistead. Robert Toombs was on Anderson's right and rear. When Magruder ordered Cobb to advance, he also ordered Anderson to advance. Toombs took over Anderson's old position, putting four brigades in column to the west of the Carter's mill road—a potentially powerful attacking force. Someone had ordered Anderson to move to the right of the Southern line, but Magruder got the Georgians back where he wanted them.

McLaws was in position at the Carter house on the Carter's mill road. The forty-one-year-old Georgian graduated from West Point with Longstreet and fought in Mexico, staying in the army after that until the beginning of hostilities. When Longstreet ordered McLaws to march down the Carter's mill road, McLaws went to reconnoiter the area. He found Armistead and Wright where Longstreet had ordered him to go. When he reported that fact, Old Pete told him to stay where he was. After Magruder returned from his trip to the Quaker road, McLaws joined the rear of the line with Paul Semmes to the west of the Carter's mill road and Joseph Kershaw to the east.

While his men were getting into place, Magruder studied the Union position. Perhaps he had stopped taking the medicine that had irritated him earlier in the campaign, but he had had very little sleep and very little food. Major Brent remembered that Magruder, despite being up nearly all night, had not eaten at all. Brent had a haversack full of food, which Prince John and the other members of his staff disposed of quickly. Magruder may not have eaten anything the rest of the day. Although his energy seemed undiminished, perhaps his judgment was not. He sent a message to Lee to the effect that he had arrived, his units were in place, and Armistead had driven a body of the enemy. Captain A. G. Dickinson, one of Magruder's aides, probably reached Lee with the message at about the same time the commanding general received Whiting's report of a Federal retreat.[7]

These pieces of information indicated to Lee that, contrary to other evidence, the Confederate artillery must have scared McClellan enough to make him retreat from his strong position. Perhaps some additional pressure might cause the Army of the Potomac to collapse, and the success Lee had sought since the beginning of the campaign could be achieved. McClellan was not retreating, however. He was reinforcing his front and replacing batteries, which had used up their ammunition, with fresh batteries. Armistead had not had any success; his assault merely succeeded in pinning down a few regiments of rebels. Nothing had changed since Lee decided that an assault was not possible. But Lee did not know that, so he dictated a message for Dickinson to give to Magruder. Dickinson wrote: "General Lee expects you to advance rapidly. He says it is reported that the enemy is getting off. Press forward your whole line and follow up Armistead's success." Dickinson also told Prince John in the note that he would move Mahone's brigade (supposedly already under Magruder's control) into Anderson's spot, and that Ransom was headed under orders to support Cobb. Lee, never having countermanded Chilton's orders, did not bother sending new orders to the other commanders—when they heard noise on the right, they would advance on the basis of the old orders.

While Dickinson headed from Magruder to Lee and back, Magruder received those orders. He was also grabbing all the troops he could find to put in against what he thought was the entire Federal army. When Brent ran into Ransom, the North Carolina brigade was near the Carter's mill road in some woods. Mahone was presumably a little to Ransom's right, perhaps across the Carter's mill road. After Brent returned from his errand, Magruder sent him back to Ransom to hurry that officer to the front. Ransom was a Tar Heel commanding Tar Heels. The thirty-four-year-old had learned about orders at West Point and in the Regular Army, and he had positive orders from Huger not to move until Huger issued the order. He thus told Brent that although he would like to move, he could not. Mahone, who Brent had observed on his way to Ransom, had the same orders at that time but was a little more hopeful, feeling the coming battle would change the situation.

Brent gave the replies to Magruder. Prince John told Brent to get back to Huger's brigadiers and not to leave until at least one came up. He was then to move that brigade to Wright's support. Brent went to Mahone first. By that time, Huger had received Lee's order giving command of that brigade to Magruder and had transmitted that order, so Mahone advanced—minus the 49th Virginia, which was detached to guard a battery. Ransom, however, had checked with his commander, and still had instructions to take orders only from Huger. Magruder himself had sent a message by another courier asking about a battery and again requesting him to move forward. Huger, meanwhile, had joined Ransom, and again told him to stay put.

Magruder received Lee's message during this period. There was no doubt about Lee's intent: he must attack and follow up whatever success Armistead had gained. Mahone and Ransom were his to command. He would attack at once, all along his line, with a force he estimated at fifteen thousand and which might have been twenty-three thousand men of all arms (counting Armistead and Wright, which Magruder may not have done). Included in that number were E. S. McCarthy's and Greenlee Davidson's batteries, the latter coming from A. P. Hill.[8]

Prince John examined the ground with Armistead and Wright, the two lead commanders. Wright by this time had most of his brigade together. During the abortive advance earlier in the day, the 4th Georgia and a few men from the 3rd and 22nd Georgia had found a hollow on the far right of the line. Wright joined them with the rest of the 3rd Georgia and the 1st Louisiana. The 22nd Louisiana was not to be found. Wright had seen its commander, Col. R. H. Jones, coming back toward the front after getting his face scratched by a shell fragment and falling out of line. The brigadier told Jones to collect his men and advance, but that did not happen.

After making arrangements for a simultaneous advance, Magruder met Mahone's men and made a few comments to the Virginians, who were busy watching for shot and shell sent by the Yankees. Sending Major Bryan of his staff to get Wright moving, Prince John went to Armistead to start that brigade forward. When Armistead informed him that the three regiments that had not yet advanced were untested, Magruder put Cobb's three regiments between Armistead's two detachments and ordered them to attack.

The Confederate guns renewed their work, joined by a couple of new batteries on Jackson's front: Capt. James M. Carrington's Charlottesville (Virginia) Artillery battery and Capt. Alfred R. Courtney's Virginia battery, both from Ewell's division. Jackson once again placed the guns, in this case Carrington's cannon, himself. These batteries were able to create a cross fire that affected Martindale's and Butterfield's men. But the Yankee guns "seemed to have the range before we got our first piece in position," according to one of the Charlottesville gunners. Even though Carrington was partially sheltered, Jackson ordered his three guns (the other three could not get into position because so many horses were wounded) to retire after about fifteen minutes.

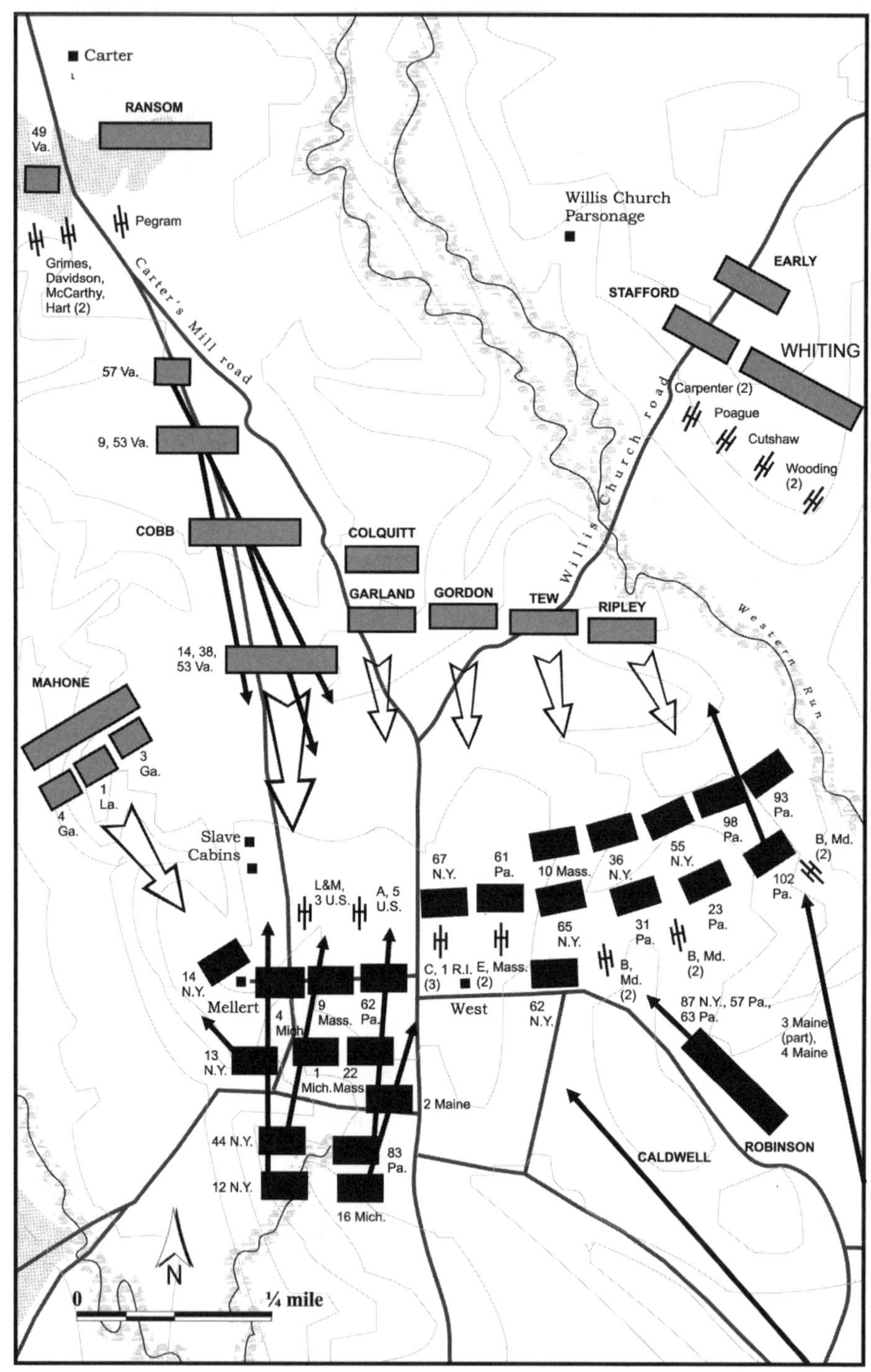

First assaults, Malvern Hill, July 1, 1862

One man getting some water from the ravine between the two armies returned to find the cannon gone. John Carpenter's guns, having been in position almost since the beginning of the artillery combat, kept firing for several hours and finally left after running out of ammunition.

On the Confederate right, rebel infantry attacks probably saved the guns there from a more severe shelling, although one man from McCarthy's battery remembered, "Never before had we experienced such fire," and another told his mother, "Shell and shot seemed to pour over in one incessant stream." McCarthy kept working until his ammunition was exhausted. Davidson could not believe the position he was supposed to occupy on the west side of the Carter's mill road, figuring he would be blown to bits in a few minutes, but he was able to put his guns in position while the opposing artillery was otherwise occupied. Even then, he could only keep up a fire by loading the guns on the far side of a small slope, then running them up to fire. One section of Hart's battery also entered the action, but the possibility of hitting their own men forced the rebel guns to cease firing. It thus would be Southern infantry against Northern artillery and infantry.[9]

Union gunners on the front line and in the Malvern house area were positioned where they could hit any Confederates marching down the Carter's mill road, since they were in the open for nearly a mile. However, there were ravines and steep slopes to the rebel right that could hide troops from much of the artillery except for three guns in Augustus Martin's battery on the River road. Wright, followed by Mahone, headed that way. The 4th Georgia was on the right of the line, the 1st Louisiana in the middle with those of the 22nd Georgia who were present, and the 3rd Georgia on the left. Wright estimated his force at less than a thousand men, and one company commander had about half his men, the others being either sick or "kept by absolute cowardice." The rebels jumped off yelling, "Remember Beast Butler and our women!"

Wright's men may have been few in number, but they were headed for a weak point just north of the Mellert house where the Federal line made a right angle and headed south along the bluff. The 14th New York in Griffin's brigade was stationed there, overlooking a ravine. In the wheat field to the north and west of Griffin's position were shocks of newly cut grain, and Berdan's green-clad marksmen had taken shelter behind them. The sharpshooters saw Wright and Mahone coming, and Berdan sent Lt. Col. William Y. W. Ripley to Morell with the information. Morell acted immediately, sending messages to Col. James McQuade of the 14th New York as well as Martindale, Butterfield, and Porter.

Morell had given Martindale and Butterfield discretion to support either each other or Griffin without further orders. Sheltered to only a small degree from rebel artillery, both brigades had suffered from such shelling as the Confederates could muster. While the Yankee guns returned fire with an intensity Martindale had never before experienced, he walked along the lines and told his men that they could not retreat from this position. On receiving the report of the Confederate advance, Martindale ordered the 13th New York to support its fellow Empire Staters, told the troops they would "prove the sincerity of our promise when we left Rochester," and led them in person.

Yet the rebel blows were about to fall on the 14th and part of the 4th Michigan (to the 14th's right). Wright saw the movement of the 13th New York and moved the 3rd Georgia to meet it. Meanwhile, the other two regiments charged to within three hundred yards of the Yankee lines, where they took shelter in a hollow. Mahone's troops caught up with them there after surviving an advance through sharpshooters' bullets coming from the wheat field to the west of the hill. They were protected from the Federals on the hill itself, but not from fire from Howard Carlisle, Adolph Voegelee, Weed, and Joseph Nairn to their south or the sharpshooters. The Southerners lay down in the hollow.[10]

Armistead's men in their forward positions saw Wright and Mahone advance and gave cheers of welcome. The Virginians charged as well, advancing to within seventy-five yards of the guns before they stopped to return the Union fire. After a brief exchange of fire they attempted the final leap to the guns. This assault was aimed right at Griffin's line. The Yankee artillerists, including Edwards's, Ames's, Weeden's, Hyde's, and perhaps two of Snow's guns, blasted the advancing rebels with canister. Griffin told his three regiments there—the 4th Michigan, 9th Massachusetts, and 62nd Pennsylvania, from left to right—to wait until they could see the rebels' eyes before firing. Most of the men did—although the 9th Massachusetts came close to picking off some of Edwards's gunners. The Southerners got close enough to Edwards's battery that Cpl. George Himmer shot one with his revolver. But the infantry sprang from their positions just behind the artillery and, joined by some of Berdan's sharpshooters (who had been withdrawn from skirmisher positions), drove the Virginians back.

This charge, although unsuccessful, gave confidence to Wright's and Mahone's troops, who had been wavering a bit without support in their hollow. Mahone seized a battle flag and ordered his brigade forward; Wright's men also advanced. The Federals wavered at first but stiffened and let the rebels climb part of the way up the hill before they let loose from between 150 and 200 yards. The shock drove the Southerners back down the hill. They rallied, charged again, and were broken again. This sequence continued through the afternoon. The Confederates suffered from "as terrible a fire of grape, canister and Minie balls as ever was rained and poured about mortal men," according to David Winn of the 4th Georgia. That fire put thirty-nine bullet holes in the 6th Virginia's flag. One Virginian with Mahone could barely hear his and his comrades' muskets because of the roar of the artillery just above them. Someone in Mahone's command yelled that they were firing on friends, and a colonel yelled back: "Firing upon our friends! They are damned Yankees. If you say we are firing on our friends, God damn you, I will cut you in two with my sword." He turned to the rest of the men and said, "Fire fast. Give it to 'em, boys. Give it to 'em. Fire fast. They are nothing but damned Yankees." Despite the colonel's entreaties, these commands made no more headway the rest of the day.[11]

Cobb's three regiments—the 2nd Louisiana, 24th Georgia, and 15th North Carolina—supported Armistead's leading three regiments. Armistead's trailing regiments, the 9th and 57th Virginia, followed Cobb. Eventually the 16th Georgia of Cobb's brigade joined the rush from its previous position protecting a flank. Armistead cried, "Ninth Virginia, charge!" and led his raw regiments forward. The attacks forced Griffin's men back into their lines. About twenty-five men from the 9th Massachusetts were captured when, having driven some of Armistead's men back, they did not hear the cry, "Back to your guns! Quick! Back to your guns!" The 4th Michigan's fire hit other Bay Staters as they retreated. At about this time David A. Woodbury, the 4th's colonel, was killed. A volley from the 57th Virginia hit the 62nd Pennsylvania's color-bearer—one of five times the regiment's colors fell. They were saved by an officer of the 44th New York in Butterfield's brigade, who returned them upon demand. Edwards had limbered up after his close call during the first charge, but the other Northern batteries were still firing canister, and the 57th's first battle turned sour when two captains were hit and the color-bearer, stunned by a shell, left the field. The men were confused, and when they were ordered back they "stampeded in all directions," one witness reported. Some rallied and participated in two more charges, but most were out of the fight.

Captain J. T. Kilby of the 9th Virginia grabbed some fallen colors of another regiment and tried to rally it; the flagstaff was shot from his hand. Lieutenant James F. Crocker, also in the 9th, admired the Yankees' poise but did his best to beat them anyway. He told a soldier who had taken refuge behind a stump that dodging metal was okay, but "do not fail to fire on the enemy." Just then Crocker was shot through the throat, shoulder, and arm. The 38th Virginia's color sergeant was killed, one corporal died, and three others were wounded bearing the flag. A private who picked it up was killed, and the regiment's lieutenant colonel and a captain were both wounded while carrying it. The flagstaff shattered while Colonel Edmonds was in the act of handing the flag to the last of the color guard. That man put it on his bayonet and made it through the battle.

Four men, including the major, in the 2nd Louisiana of Cobb's brigade were killed bearing its flag. Billy Malloy of that regiment went forward "into the jaws of death" expecting to be killed. He got about two-thirds of the way up the hill when he was shot. The 16th Georgia was fired on by some North Carolinians to its left rear and broke. This and the 57th Virginia's confused retreat were exceptions. But even though most of both brigades charged five or six times during the afternoon and evening, they never came as close to a breakthrough as they did in their initial effort.[12]

They pressed the Yankees enough, however, that Griffin's men and the sharpshooters started running out of ammunition and were replaced by Butterfield's brigade. Earlier in the day Couch and Butterfield decided the junction of Couch's and Morell's lines would be a weak point. Butterfield told Couch the IV Corps division would have his support and also ordered the 83rd Pennsylvania and 16th Michigan to the junction of Morell's and Couch's line. The Michiganders moved from that position to support some newly positioned guns just west of the Willis Church road. The 83rd Pennsylvania moved straight ahead, replacing the 9th Massachusetts and probably opposing one of Cobb's regiments. Butterfield was so ill that day that he took two doses of chloroform, but he stayed on the field, telling the Pennsylvanians, "When you advance let your war-cry be, 'Revenge for McLane,'" (the 83rd's colonel, who had fallen at Gaines's Mill). Moving to the left and through Martindale's right, they met the rebel advance and stopped it 150 yards from the line. The 44th New York, taking over for the 62nd Pennsylvania on the 83rd's left, launched a bayonet charge that forced other Southerners back. The Confederates dropped their colors, and Sgt. W. J. Wittich of the 83rd Pennsylvania won a race to grab them. Wittich handed them to Butterfield. Oliver Norton, having survived Gaines's Mill, picked up a tent on his way to the front and slung it over his shoulder. It later saved his life by stopping a bullet. The 16th Michigan stood its ground against the continual rebel assaults in what one diarist called "very desperate" fighting. It finally pulled back when the battery it supported was withdrawn.

Butterfield sent the 12th New York to the left of the line. Its commander, Lt. Col. R. M. Richardson, did not see any rebels there, so he marched to the front instead. Other troops were already supporting artillery in that area, and Richardson wanted "immediate work," so the regiment turned back to the left. Reaching the ravine in front of the Mellert house, it found the 4th Michigan out of ammunition and being attacked on the flank by Wright's and Mahone's men. The Michiganders had suffered from a "terribly effective" Confederate fire, creating gaps in its line. Frank Forncrook, a cook in Company E, dropped his food, grabbed a musket, and filled one of the gaps until he was killed. A. H. Boies was hit in the chest, the bullet passing through a diary and entering his body just below the heart. Boies did a backward somersault and lay on the ground senseless.

The New Yorkers charged through the 4th Michigan to push the rebels back. Their major, Henry A. Barnum, was hit in the charge and thought he was mortally wounded. Taken to the Malvern house, he said, "Tell my wife that in my last thoughts were blended herself, my boy, and my flag." He then asked about the battle. Told it was going well, he rose, said, "God bless the old fla—" and fell back apparently dead. He survived, however, and became a brevet major general before the war ended.[13]

Magruder's first attacks had little effect besides getting a few thousand men shot. It would have been better, at least for his command, if he had been allowed to continue along his Quaker road. From his force of less than 1,000 men, Wright lost 54 killed, 260 wounded, and 79 missing for a total of 393 casualties; he claimed he had fewer than 300 men with him by nightfall. Mahone, with 1,226 officers and men, lost 39 killed, 166 wounded, and 124 missing for 329 total casualties. The 3rd Georgia lost 157 men, including its major, a captain, and four lieutenants killed. The 12th Virginia and 4th Georgia both lost more than 100 men. One company of the 1st Louisiana lost all its officers, and Pvt. Thomas Rice was promoted to captain then and there. John W. Lash, in Company C of the 16th Virginia, was struck with a bullet, but the minié ball hit a picture of his baby boy and did not cause a serious wound. Lash wrote home asking his wife to rename the boy Malvern Hill.

Armistead's casualties, including the 5th Virginia Battalion (which suffered only from artillery fire), totaled 388 (49 killed, 272 wounded, and 67 missing) from perhaps 1,500 men who went into action. The 9th Virginia lost 66 of 150 men. The 57th Virginia lost 13 killed and 83 wounded. This included 27 casualties in Company H in about forty minutes. The 14th Virginia lost only 75 men, but 21 of them were in Company K—only 1 man escaped unhurt. The 14th's battle flag had forty-seven holes in it, and the 38th's flag was hit more than fifty times. Cobb also took into action about 1,500 men, and he lost even more: 413 killed or wounded. The 2nd Louisiana lost 182 killed or wounded, more casualties than in all but one other Confederate regiment at Malvern Hill. The 15th North Carolina lost 131.

Griffin's men also suffered, but not as much. The 14th New York, with the advantage of position, lost 21 killed and 100 wounded. The 13th New York, in reserve during the contest, had only 6 men wounded despite watching as "the bullets flew like hail over and around us," as Charles Brown put it. Griffin's other three regiments lost a total of 367 killed or wounded, 141 of them in the 9th Massachusetts—including Colonel Cass, who fell mortally wounded. The 4th Michigan lost its colonel, Dwight Woodbury, and 116 men. The 62nd Pennsylvania lost 110 men. But the regiments held against the shock of the first strong assault on the Union line at Malvern Hill. Fitz John Porter later said that the 4th Michigan (and perhaps by extension the rest of the brigade) saved the Army of the Potomac.[14]

At the time of Magruder's first attacks D. H. Hill and his brigade commanders were in conference north of Malvern Hill, discussing Chilton's order. Robert

Rodes was sick, and John B. Gordon of the 6th Alabama took his place. Col. C. C. Tew of the 2nd North Carolina replaced the wounded Anderson. The six men had watched the Confederate artillery's duel with the Yankee artillery. Since they saw no effect—Samuel Garland termed the firing "wild," as might be expected when the gunners were being shelled out of their shoes—they figured there would be no infantry fighting. The meeting was breaking up when, out of the woods to their right, one or two rebel brigades came yelling and charging toward the Federal lines. Hill turned to his subordinates and cried, "That must be the general advance! Bring up your brigades as soon as possible and join in it."

Hill's brigades had shuffled some during their earlier advance. Garland, originally behind Roswell Ripley's men, wound up on the right of the Southern line, his left on the Willis Church road. Ripley had maneuvered to Tew's left, forming the left of the line. Gordon, originally on the right, moved to his left and became almost the middle of the line. Alfred Colquitt's men were behind Garland on the right of the line. As soon as the commanders returned to their brigades, they sent the men forward. The advance was coordinated as well as possible—Chilton's order specified that they advance when they heard the signal, they had heard it at the same time, and none of them had far to go to reach their commands.

The Confederates headed up the hill against more than a full Union division and its accompanying artillery. After Butterfield and Couch met, Butterfield sent Porter word of the possible problem. In response, John Caldwell's brigade moved from near the Malvern house to behind Couch's line—some of the men being interrupted from supper by the order. When Gordon, Tew, and Ripley charged this part of the Federal line, the result was a Confederate disaster. Ripley's men, on the left, got to the brow of the hill and were blasted with a "leaden storm," according to Julien Cumming of the 48th Georgia. They held their ground for a while, but Howe's 102nd Pennsylvania hit the rebels, in particular the 1st North Carolina (one of the regiments decimated at Mechanicsville), in flank. About a hundred men of the 3rd North Carolina moved to the 1st's support, but their colonel, Gaston Meares, was killed in the "heavy fire of every kind of shot and shell," and Ripley retreated down the hill in some confusion. Four companies from the 3rd Maine and the entire 4th Maine of David Birney's brigade, plus the 23rd Pennsylvania of Abercrombie's brigade, reinforced Howe, while two guns from Snow's battery provided artillery support.[15]

On Ripley's right, Gordon fought through dense woods, marched through meadows, and traversed hills to get to his assault position. Joined by one of Tew's regiments, which had lost its way in the forest, Gordon moved the 5th and 26th Alabama to the left out of clear sight of the Union guns. Standing on a stump, he called, "Alabamians! There is a battery over on that hill, and Alabamians have got to take it. All that will follow me say I." When the brigade responded with a shouted "I," Gordon said, "Then follow me," and headed toward Abercrombie and Palmer with his four regiments (the 12th Alabama having gone to Richmond with Federal prisoners).

Tew's men charged just to Gordon's left. Before jumping off, one of the Tar Heels saw Hill looking "not satisfied." The Northern guns and muskets immediately began to chew up Gordon and Tew, stopping them two hundred yards from the batteries. "We murdered them by the hundreds but they again formed and came up to be slaughtered," one of Palmer's men wrote in his diary. "We willingly gave them what shells grape and canister they wanted but they did not seem to be satisfied with that so we thought we would introduce some musket balls," added Thomas Tanfield of the 61st Pennsylvania.

Seven men, the first six of whom died, had carried the 3rd Alabama's colors by the time they reached their furthest point of advance. One man wrote home that the best way to describe the Union fire was to compare it to a heavy rain. The 30th North Carolina had outstripped everyone else and for a moment was by itself. Then Abercrombie's 65th New York and 61st Pennsylvania and Palmer's regiments stepped out from behind the cannon to join the 67th New York and 31st Pennsylvania and press the Confederates down the hill. The Federal advance was not easy or without cost. One man from the 65th New York described the fighting as hand-to-hand. George Hagar of the 10th Massachusetts fired so fast he could no longer load his gun, so he picked up a dead comrade's weapon and kept going. Major Ozro Miller of the 10th Massachusetts fell during the charge. Nevertheless, Hill's men were forced to retreat under the pressure. "We offered them the last we had which was our bayonets and even offered to carry them over to them but they were so bashful that we could not get near them," Tanfield wrote. The seventh man to carry the 3rd Alabama's colors made it through the battle alive, but he had only a piece of the staff with him—the flag had been torn to shreds by the fire.

Gordon's pistol's handle was shot away, his canteen was hit and the water dumped on his pants, and part of the front of his coat was torn away during the charge. Later, a shell hit the ground, burrowed in, and exploded near him, covering him with sand and temporarily blinding him. Somehow he made it through the fight without permanent injury. He claimed his men got closer to the guns than any other Southerners, but if true, it was a hollow victory. Frank Parker of the 30th North Carolina wrote his wife, "I never before in all my life knew what it was to be thankful, truly thankful." Eugene Blackford of the 5th Alabama called it "the most shocking scene of butchery," adding, "We could not shoot a gun, but simply marched up to be mowed down by the storm of canister poured upon us."[16]

On Hill's right, Garland's men had been dodging shot and shell when the order came. Charley Powell of the 23rd North Carolina had grabbed one shell, the fuse still burning, and thrown it into a stream, extinguishing the fuse before the shell blew. He and his mates advanced up the west side of the Willis Church road, where there was less cover than on the east side (the ravine directly in front of the Yankee lines is not quite as deep there). They made even less progress than the other brigades—getting to within about four hundred yards of the Northerners when the men, contrary to orders but in accord with self-preservation, lay down and began firing. Before that happened, color-bearer Harry Williams of the 12th North Carolina was shot in the head and died. Two members of the color guard were killed and one wounded in the same volley. Seeing there was no chance of getting closer to the Union lines, Garland sent a message to Hill saying that he needed reinforcements just to hold his position. Hill sent the 6th Georgia from Colquitt's brigade and tried to find more troops.

But Hill's men had had enough. After their repulse, members of Ewell's staff herded them back to the front. Many complained of being shocked by the guns. Lieutenant Colonel John M. Jones of Ewell's staff got into an argument with one soldier and fired his gun at the poor fellow, who decided he would rather face an unseen enemy than a seen "friend" and turned back to the front. Campbell Brown yelled, "Great heavens Colonel, weren't you afraid of hitting him." Jones yelled back, "Oh no, I aimed a foot over his head—but it wouldn't have mattered much if I had killed him."

With due regard for Jones's opinion, the back of the line was the best place for D. H. Hill's division after its ordeal. Its assault was unnecessary and costly. By the time the brigades streamed back in disorder, to be reformed with difficulty in the dark, they had lost nearly 1,750 men, almost 20 percent of their strength. Gordon lost 425 of just over a thousand engaged, including 200 men in the 3rd Alabama, the highest loss of any Southern regiment in the battle and more than 56 percent of its strength. Another 264 casualties thinned Ripley's already depleted ranks. The 44th Georgia, having suffered so much at Mechanicsville, lost almost half of its remaining strength. Garland and Tew lost about 850 men between them. Colquitt, in reserve at the start of the charge, still suffered 200 casualties. Hill wrote his wife that his men were "most horribly cut up," and that the "blood of North Carolina poured out like water." His comment in *Battles and Leaders,* that "It was not war—it was murder," may not have applied completely to the battlefield, but it fits for his division.[17]

CHAPTER NINETEEN

"General Magruder, Why Did You Attack?"

By the end of D. H. Hill's assault, Darius Couch's line was even stronger than at the beginning. His men had suffered comparatively little—about six hundred casualties out of more than eight thousand engaged—and they had been reinforced. Three of John Robinson's regiments, the 57th and 63rd Pennsylvania (combined under the command of Alexander Hays of the 63rd) and 87th New York, supported artillery. John Caldwell's 5th New Hampshire also supported a couple of batteries near Howe's line. Three more batteries—John Frank's (from Sumner), Gustavus De Russy's under Francis Seeley (from Heintzelman), and Henry Benson's (from the artillery reserve)—hurried up to replace William Weeden and John Hyde. Frank and Seeley arrived first. Frank, finding no place where he could set up all eight of his guns together, moved four to Adelbert Ames's left and put the other four to Ames's right.

Confederate units also came onto the field. Robert Toombs's Georgians, advancing through thick woods filled with obstructions, relied on the sound of guns to guide their advance. This almost certainly would lead them toward the middle of the battle instead of the right-center supporting Howell Cobb and George T. Anderson. Toombs finally came out into the open and got the men as organized as he could under fire from the Federal artillery. Moving forward again, he came up to the advance units, stopped, and ordered the troops to lie down. Soon an order came—supposedly from David Jones, the division commander—calling for the regimental officers to move to the left. In fact, this "order" was a suggestion from Capt. Asbury Coward of Jones's staff to Toombs, who decided he did not like the idea. Before he could do anything about it, though, most of his brigade had crossed the Carter's mill road and entered the woods through which D. H. Hill had marched. The 20th Georgia, on the left flank, made this maneuver with few problems, but the 15th Georgia, which apparently heard the order first, cramped the 2nd Georgia. Toombs, seeing the brigade divided, ordered the 17th Georgia to follow the other regiments; the 17th was split in half during the change in front. Toombs tried to push stragglers back into line—perhaps because he found it hard to keep up with his men, as Coward saw him lagging behind them and able to "go no faster." But the brigade commander could not clear up the confusion. A soldier in the 17th Georgia reported, "I'm certain I was with a half a dozen different regiments at various times," adding, "It was a perfect scene of confusion at the time we were ordered in, and nobody seemed to know where they were going or what they were going to do."

It was in this position, near a fence and leaderless, that D. H. Hill found the Georgians. He reported ordering them to support Samuel Garland's men. They tried but could not stand the fire and fell back in disorder after they reached the brow of Malvern Hill. When Hill met Toombs on the field, he screamed at the Georgian, "Where were you when I was riding in front on my horse trying to rally your brigade?" Hill apparently meant no disrespect to the men themselves, and no regimental commander reported advancing as Hill said, but he definitely meant disrespect to Toombs, as he made clear in a July 6 letter: "My remarks were personal to yourself and not to your brigade. I did not in the slightest degree reflect on your men." Toombs understood clearly enough to challenge Hill to a duel, which Hill rejected. It may be that Toombs had been drinking. One man remembered seeing the brigadier reeling around a flagstaff calling for men to rally around him, and Thomas Cobb heard rumors of his drunkenness. Regardless of whether their commander was drunk or sober, Toombs's men gave Hill little support. They did suffer, however.

As George T. Anderson's Georgians moved forward on Toombs's right, west of the Carter's mill road, the left cleared the woods first and forged ahead of the rest of the brigade (which wound up near Ambrose Wright and William Mahone). Before Anderson could fix that problem, John Magruder (who was still galloping around the field) ordered the right-hand group—the 1st Georgia Regulars, and 7th and 8th Georgia—to attack. Anderson was with the 9th and 11th Georgia. Some of the 11th Georgia (Anderson's regiment) broke, and Anderson called out: "If I can't get the regiment to go with me I will take the Walton Infantry, my old company. I know they will go." He then told the men, "Boys, stick to your colors." None of his regiments got very far. The right-hand regiments reached the foot of Malvern Hill but no farther, and Anderson pulled them back. His assistant adjutant general, Lt. Charles C. Hardwick, risked his neck to deliver the order to the 8th Georgia. These Georgians' retreat, through the same fury of shot, shell, and canister they had just advanced

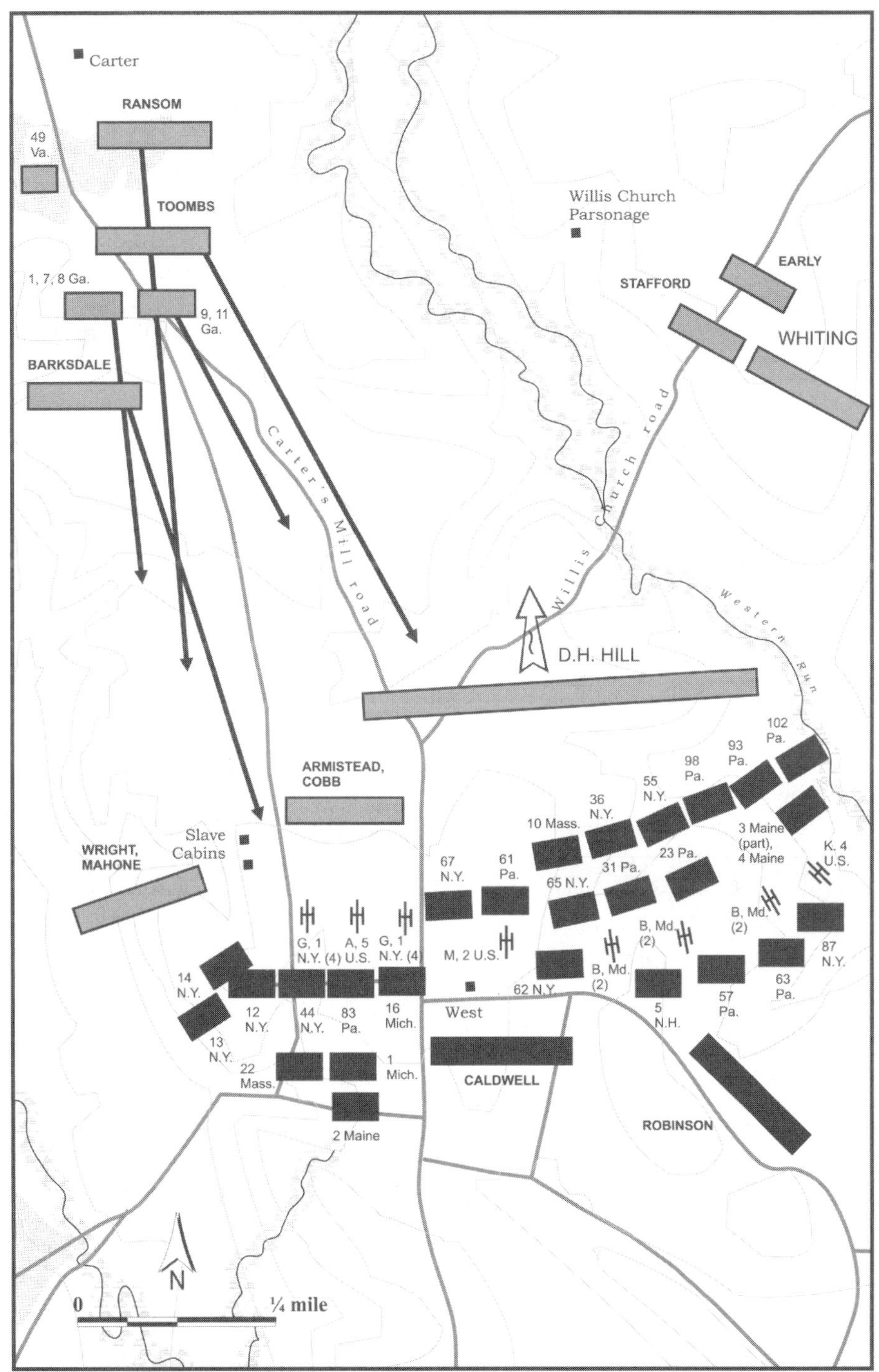

Second assaults, Malvern Hill, July 1, 1862

through, was made in some disorder. The 9th and 11th Georgia never charged the Yankees, instead finding shelter in a hollow for the duration of the battle.[1]

To Anderson's right, Magruder himself deployed William Barksdale's Mississippians. He sent them (and perhaps Anderson's three right-hand regiments at the same time) to support Wright and Mahone. The men had been suffering from the artillery fire—one man's clothes were set on fire—and Barksdale, mounting his horse, cried out, "Attention! This brigade must take that battery!" As they advanced, they took shelter in a ravine with clear fields of fire located between Lew Armistead and Cobb on their left and Wright and Mahone on their right. However, they lost some cohesion getting there.

As Barksdale's men advanced, they probably broke up a firefight between volunteers from Berdan's sharpshooters and some rebels who had participated in previous charges. The Yankees were trying to draw fire away from the guns, and the two groups fired at about fifty yards' distance. Brigham Buswell decided standing up was better than lying down. He figured that a marksman could hit the head of a prone man easily at that distance, but perhaps would hit a less deadly part of an upright man. He was wounded twice and headed toward the rear just before Barksdale's men came to the top of the hill.

They aimed at the 44th New York and 12th New York but got only to the brow of the hill, between one hundred and two hundred yards from the Federals. By that time, no batteries were directly in front of the Southerners, but those on George Morell's right and Couch's left—Ames's, Frank's, and Alonzo Snow's—turned their guns on Barksdale. The Northern gunners were impressed with the Southerners' determination, but that feeling only brought "the inspiration to do great deeds," one of them said, and the Mississippians' casualties showed it. One-third of Barksdale's men were hit, a total of at least four hundred casualties. Each regiment's field commander fell wounded. Lieutenant Colonel William Brandon of the 21st Mississippi went down with a wound to the ankle just moments after seeing his youngest son shot.

They pressed Dan Butterfield's men, however. The 83rd Pennsylvania and 44th New York were in continual firefights, and the Pennsylvanians fired almost every cartridge in the regiment (some men having fired more than a hundred times). The 12th New York, with less pressure, still was actively engaged for more than an hour. Meanwhile, John Martindale was getting his men into the fight. Like Butterfield, he had readied some troops to support Couch—in Martindale's case the 2nd Maine. As the pressure in front mounted, however, Martindale brought the 2nd Maine back to support the 22nd Massachusetts and 1st Michigan, which he moved to Charles Griffin's and Butterfield's support. The 1st Michigan helped the 83rd Pennsylvania and ran out of ammunition itself; the 22nd Massachusetts took its place and also ran out of cartridges. Fitz John Porter, watching with Martindale, noticed the wounded and stragglers streaming to the rear from the beleaguered line. He had what was left of the 25th New York set up as a straggler line to keep the stragglers to the front and take care of the wounded. Farther back, the 3rd Pennsylvania Cavalry performed the same function for the entire front.[2]

The pressure was strong enough that Porter asked for reinforcements. First, he told Henry Hunt to bring up John Tidball's and James Robertson's batteries and the thirty-two-pound howitzers of Battery D, 1st Battalion, New York Light Artillery. By then, however, Robert Tyler's siege guns had stopped firing, perhaps because of Porter's worries for his line, and were being tugged back down Malvern Hill's southern slope. They might also have retired because of the navy's fire. One of the most misunderstood aspects of the battle of Malvern Hill concerns the Union gunboats. Confederate survivors of the battle consistently wrote of the big shells and booms of the gunboats. John Rodgers of the *Galena* told his mother, "I feel quite sure we did good service." But the gunboats did not fire until late in the battle—according to Porter just before he asked for reinforcements—and when they opened up they hit Yankees as often as they hit rebels. The fledgling signal service attempted to direct the fire—one officer stood calmly amidst the artillery fire to send messages—but the smoke made signaling difficult, and Porter told the boats, "For God's sake, stop firing, you are killing and wounding our men." One shell exploded among the siege guns, killing one man and wounding three others, and another killed one and wounded four. A third landed in Weeden's battery, killing two and wounding three. Porter believed the fire the Confederates discussed actually came from the siege guns. Campbell Brown of Ewell's staff said the gunboats lost their prestige among the Confederates at Malvern Hill because they scared far more men than they killed. On the other hand, a Georgian who walked the field the next day saw many Northerners who had been killed by gunboat fire.

Porter told George Sykes he needed some infantry. In response, Robert Buchanan and Charles Lovell moved north toward Morell's left. After observing Couch's area and seeing that there was no end in sight to the struggle, Porter asked Edwin Sumner for two brigades. Sumner and Samuel Heintzelman were together on the Union right. Reading Porter's note aloud, and perhaps mindful of McClellan's concern for the Yankee right flank, Sumner mused on the propriety of sending two brigades. Heintzelman—who had been Porter's superior earlier in the campaign—said, "By Jove! If Porter asks for help, I know he needs it and I will send it." Thomas Meagher's Irish Brigade—Meagher had been released from arrest to command it—and Dan Sickles's Excelsior Brigade were selected.[3]

North of Malvern Hill, Robert Ransom's brigade joined the fight. Ransom had sent the 24th North Carolina to Magruder's aid in response to an urgent plea, and at the same time he sent a staff officer to Benjamin Huger for instructions. Huger responded that Ransom could go if he pleased but was not to put himself under Magruder's orders. This was the last act by the South Carolinian that would affect the day's results. In reality, Huger was as inactive at Malvern Hill as he had been the previous five days, but in this case he seemed purposefully inactive, his dander up in response to his men being taken from him. He was slow getting to the field, took no initiative, and hindered others from entering the battle. He did not notify Lee of his early moves, when he still thought Yankees were in front of him on the Charles City road, and he did not actively seek out information. None of these behaviors reflect those of successful generals. If Huger had been more prompt in moving, more active in gathering information and acting on it, and less indignant at having some of his men taken from him, the Southern line might have formed earlier and had more order to it. But for anything to have changed at Malvern Hill, the order that began the battle would have needed to be different or its execution better. Huger had nothing to do with either.[4]

Major Brent was with Ransom, having been sent again by Magruder, and once Ransom moved out, Brent went to find his chief once more. Instead he found Col. William B. Norris, the chief of Prince John's signal service. Norris, who was a little hard of hearing, decided the firing had stopped and shouted, "Hurrah, we have taken the batteries!" Brent himself said the noise at that time was the most tremendous fire he heard during the war.

As Ransom's men advanced, they began moving as individual regiments. The 24th North Carolina was already separated; then the 25th and 35th North Carolina charged on Magruder's direction. These last two regiments suffered severely, although it is difficult to tell exactly where. By the time Ransom got to them the 25th's colonel, Henry M. Rutledge, had been stunned by an exploding shell, and its major was seriously wounded. The 35th's colonel, Matt W. Ransom (Robert's brother), was hit twice and taken from the field, and its lieutenant colonel, O. C. Petway, was mortally wounded. All three regiments fell back, and Robert Ransom took them to the right of the line to reform under cover of the terrain. The other two regiments had already gone that way, although the 26th North Carolina lost its way and Lt. Col. Henry Burgwyn threatened a straggler with the sword to get him to lead the regiment into battle. Burgwyn said the man thought "it would be better to risk death from the enemy than to get it from his friends."

Magruder by this time was worried that he might be thrown back from his advanced positions and asked Lee for reinforcements. Marse Robert, who was with Lafayette McLaws's division, Magruder's sole uncommitted force, ordered it in. He also sent to A. P. Hill for two brigades, and those of Lawrence Branch and Col. Edward Thomas (commanding Joseph Anderson's men) moved to the front. They did not see action, however, although Branch got his men into position before nightfall. Longstreet in turn moved his division to Magruder's right and rear to secure that flank.

Lee sent Magruder a note telling Prince John he needed to press more toward his right (probably because of the favorable terrain), instead of shifting to the left as he had been. Magruder took this as an order to renew the assault and sent yet another aide to hurry McLaws's men and find a couple of batteries. The aide, Major Hyllested, did not find McLaws but did find Paul Semmes and Joseph Kershaw and told them Magruder's desires.[5]

On the east side of the Willis Church road, D. H. Hill also needed reinforcements. It would have been difficult for him to hold his positions on Malvern Hill against a Yankee attack. Stonewall Jackson responded to Hill's request by ordering his own and Richard Ewell's divisions to the front.

Ewell's division was behind William Whiting's, with Isaac Trimble on Whiting's extreme left, Col. Leroy Stafford on Whiting's right in a ravine (after having moved around some during the day), and Jubal Early (in command of Arnold Elzey's men) behind Stafford near the Willis Church road. Bradley Johnson's Maryland Line arrived from Bottom's Bridge and was on Early's right behind D. H. Hill's jumping-off positions. Early and Trimble moved immediately on receipt of the order.

Charles Winder, with Jackson's division, had halted near Willis Church but moved north to escape the Federal fire. After the battle started, the division had formed into line of battle. Alexander Lawton was on the east side of the road with the Stonewall Brigade next to him on the west side, and the brigade previously commanded by R. H. Cunningham (with Brig. Gen. John R. Jones back in command) behind the Stonewall Brigade. Jackson told Winder to move his and Lawton's brigades to the right of the road and find D. H. Hill. Jones followed Winder, stopping on the road to let the traffic clear.

His response to Hill was Jackson's last real contribution on July 1. Like Huger, Stonewall was relatively inactive. Perhaps the Jackson of the Valley campaign would have moved to his left to turn the Union right and so make a battle at Malvern Hill unnecessary. But Jackson was not in the Valley, he was not an independent officer, and he had his orders. He might have suggested the move to Lee earlier than Lee thought of it. More fundamentally, it is difficult to understand how Jackson could have forced McClellan to abandon Malvern Hill. If Stonewall moved his entire force, he opened his flank and rear and the rest of the Confederates north of Malvern Hill to assault. If the Yankees did not attack, he would have nearly twenty-seven thousand men with which to face the Union right—which extended all the way to the River road. By afternoon that force included John Peck's division, the entire VI Corps, John Sedgwick's division, and William French's brigade—nearly thirty thousand men with seventeen batteries in a good defensive position. Jackson thus would have been in danger of being cut up. If, on the other hand, he just moved part of his force, he would have protected the rest of Lee's army but exposed his detachment to even greater danger. Any turning movement would have to come from someone besides Jackson.[6]

Stonewall did not order all his troops forward during the battle. He presumably received Robert Chilton's order, and told D. H. Hill to obey it. However, he did not advance Whiting's men when Hill moved forward. Perhaps he thought it best to hold Whiting in place to protect the guns. He was prompt in sending reinforcements to Hill, and an attack by Whiting would not have accomplished at Malvern Hill what it accomplished at Gaines's Mill. That is because although the stage was set as it was on June 27, important circumstances were different. As at Gaines's Mill, some of Lee's men were holding advanced positions, having failed to dislodge the Yankees. Others were ready for one last effort, although it was not as well coordinated as at Gaines's Mill. Facing them in a strong defensive position were V Corps, some additional units (including the Irish Brigade coming as reinforcements), and lots of artillery. But there were nearly as many Unionists as at Gaines's Mill, more Yankee cannon, many fewer Confederates, and a smaller area for the Federals to cover—meaning fewer potentially weak points in the line and quicker reinforcement of any threatened sector.

Theophilus Holmes moved his entire force down the River road late in the afternoon, and it reached about the same area it had occupied the previous day. Wise's command moved to the left of the road and advanced to the junction of the Willis Church road with the River road. From there, less than a mile from the Yankee lines, the men could hear cheering from Malvern Hill. One soldier wrote his father, "Never did I hear anything equal" to the noise. The troops were ready for action, perhaps wanting to atone for the day before. But they did not join the battle, and Holmes moved some of them back to find a suitable campground that night. D. H. Hill and Magruder mentioned in their reports that Holmes did not get into the battle, both in contexts that implicitly blame Holmes for not doing anything. But that is ludicrous. There were plenty of guns to deal with Holmes if he attacked. As on June 30, he was in no position to alter the outcome.[7]

On Magruder's far right, Ransom formed his line under the western brow of Malvern Hill and sent it forward. As they began to move, the top of a pine tree cut off by a round of solid shot went through a Confederate's clothes and pinned him to the ground. No Federal seemed to notice Ransom; in fact, troops were moving away from him. Closing in on the batteries from the flank, guided by the flashes of the guns in the gathering darkness—"they were fast enough to leave very little doubt," one officer remembered—he approached to within a hundred yards of the artillery. Riding ahead with a white handkerchief tied around his cap, Ransom yelled, "Come on boys, come on heroes, your General is in front." The men, perhaps sensing a triumph in the making, shouted up and down the line.

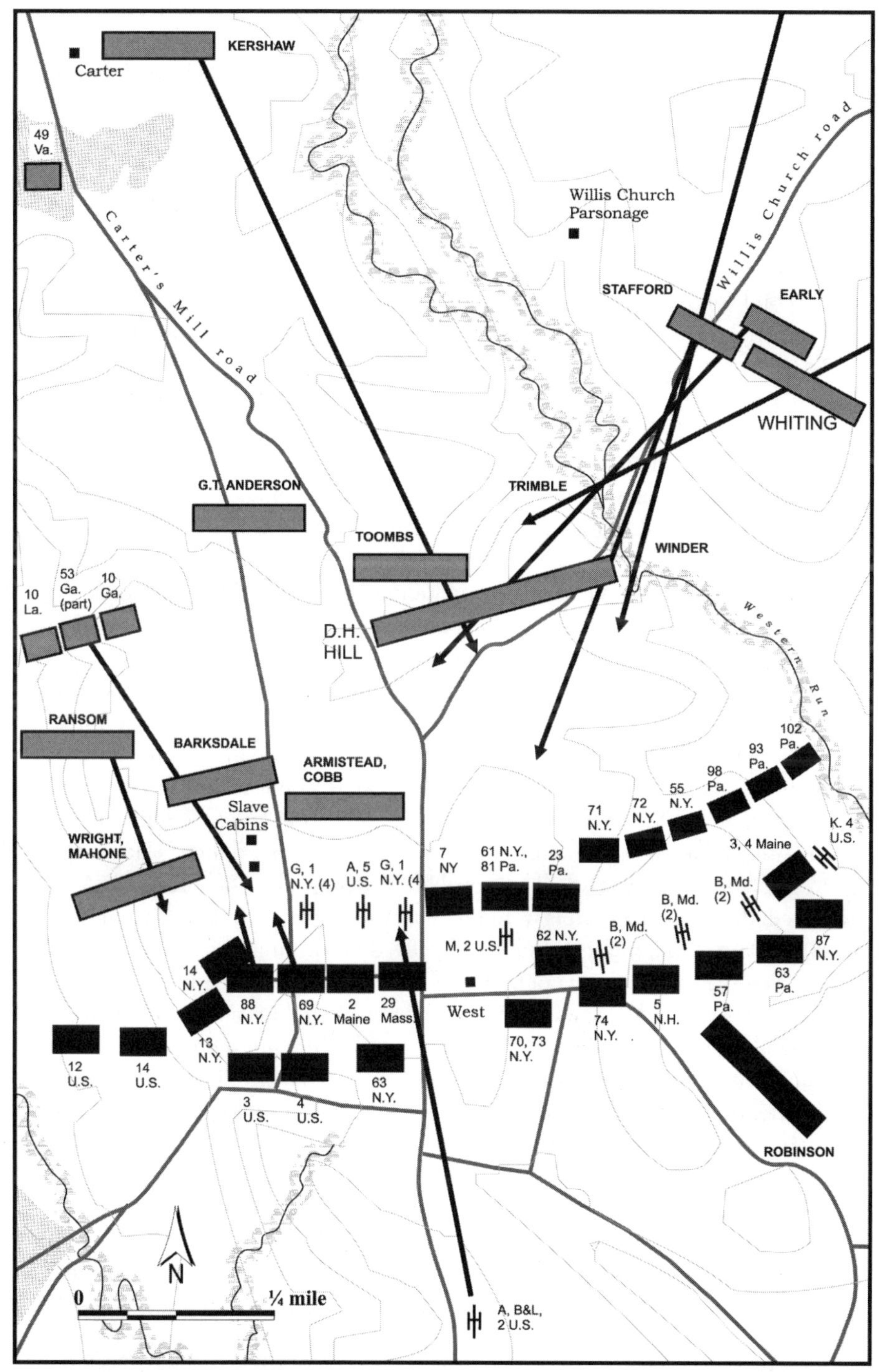

Final assaults, Malvern Hill, July 1, 1862

But Sykes's men were waiting. The 12th and 14th U.S. of Buchanan's brigade had moved down the slope to get a clear field of fire into the ravine Ransom's men were ascending. The wheat was high enough to block the regulars' vision. Sykes told Capt. John D. O'Connell of the 14th U.S. Infantry not to fire until he could hit the rebels full in the flank—which happened to be right after those rebels shouted. The Tar Heels got within twenty yards of the guns. The Unionists' faces could be seen in the gloom by the light the sheets of fire produced. But a second volley from the regulars and one from the 14th New York—repelling a third major attack on its line—was "beyond description" to Ransom. The Southerners finally broke, leaving the payroll of Company G, 26th North Carolina, behind. It had fallen out of the captain's pocket when a ball cut it open. Ransom rallied his men and marched most of them back to their original position on the Carter's mill road. They had marched perhaps the farthest under enemy fire of any Confederates and had come about as close as any to the Union line. But they paid dearly for the near success in what Col. Zebulon Vance of the 26th North Carolina said was the "most terrific and bloody charge of the war." They suffered 499 casualties, including 69 killed and 354 wounded—the highest brigade casualty total in the battle. The 25th and 35th North Carolina, engaged in two separate assaults, each had more than 100 men hit.[8]

To Ransom's left, Semmes's brigade made its delayed appearance. Semmes had six regiments, but he was able to bring together only 557 men. The Yankee artillery had thinned the ranks some, and was able to concentrate its fire on Semmes and Kershaw (moving to Semmes's left). One soldier from the 15th Virginia called the shelling "unsurpassed for severity in any conflict during the war." Colonel T. P. August of the 15th Virginia was wounded. He stopped to give some last words to his men before being taken off the field. As he talked, the stretcher-bearers were hit, and August unceremoniously fell into a ditch. A shell fragment stunned Col. Alfred Cumming of the 10th Georgia, and Semmes had his coat cut by another shell fragment. One man in the 53rd Georgia was killed by some grapeshot, which blasted his gun into bits.

Semmes also lost men due to the heavy straggling prevalent in Magruder's force that day. Kershaw was missing about 250 men from his brigade. George T. Anderson noted that many of his men had fallen by the wayside on the march to the field. Cobb's brigade, 2,700 strong on the morning of the twenty-ninth, had fewer than 1,500 in its charge. The straggling is understandable. Some of Magruder's men had fought on the twenty-ninth. All had marched all day and well into the night of the thirtieth, and then had spent time on the first marching and countermarching. Efforts were made to get the stragglers, as well as those falling back from the lines, to their posts. Magruder gave special mention to Lt. Benjamin H. Harrison, who eventually died leading some men back into the fight. But it proved impossible to gather up those scattered all over the roads.

Semmes finally moved the right of his line—the 15th and 32nd Virginia and the 5th Louisiana—to some cover to their left. They wound up behind the 10th and 53rd Georgia, and Semmes put himself in front of these two regiments and ordered their advance. Only Company K of the 53rd Georgia joined in, but the brigade's sixth regiment, the 10th Louisiana, followed the Georgians on their right. At the same time, one company of the 1st Georgia Regulars of Anderson's brigade, some North Carolinians (perhaps from Ransom), and some Mississippians (probably from Barksdale) joined the crowd. They filed between the 10th Louisiana and the Georgians. Other Confederates did not join in—they had beaten the odds once and probably did not want to try again. Even Semmes's second line did not advance, but it may have been placed to draw fire away from the charging regiments. The 15th Virginia's temporary commander, Maj. John S. Walker, took this ruse too far: he was shot when he stood up, drew his sword, and ordered, "Forward, charge!" About seven hundred men went forward with Semmes.

Fewer men had broken a strong line just four days before behind Boatswain's Swamp. But that line had no reserves, and this one did. The rest of Buchanan's brigade, the 3rd and 4th U.S. Infantry, was waiting behind the left of the north-facing line. The V Corps no longer held the front, however. The Irish Brigade had moved forward, some of the men without supper. A sheep was roasting for about twenty-five men when the order came, and Capt. Joseph O'Donoghue of the 88th New York said, "Ah, I think some of the 25 who engaged supper will not be on hand when it is ready." Meagher sent them in with the 69th New York leading, followed by the 88th New York, the 63rd New York, and the 29th Massachusetts. As they moved to the front they passed the Irish 9th Massachusetts. One group of Irish cheered the other.

Meagher's men got plenty of attention from corps commanders during their march. Sumner saw them off, and as they moved forward Porter met them. On the way, though, Fitz John's horse fell, throwing him in front of it. Remounting to the cheers of the men, Porter led them into the lines—but not before tearing up his diary and dispatch book, just in case the Irish did not get to the front in time. Butterfield grabbed the 69th's green flag and put the regiment into line, the 88th moving to its left.

Semmes and Meagher arrived at the front at the same time, the Confederates heading toward the guns at an angle that opened their right flank to the 69th and 88th New York. The 69th made contact first, firing as it advanced. Its volleys, combined with fire from rebels behind them, slowed Semmes's men. The 88th then hit the Southerners almost in their rear, and they broke backward, taking shelter behind some buildings (probably the Mellert house's slave quarters) about sixty yards from the Northern line.

One of Semmes's regiments, the 10th Louisiana, had reached that line. Its commander, Lt. Col. Eugene Waggaman, had asked the priest with the regiment if he could make confession the previous evening. Waggaman ordered his men forward at the double-quick but even then moved far ahead of them. The last fifty yards to the line took five minutes, according to one account, and then hand-to-hand combat between Irishmen ensued, with shouts of "Kill him" and "Bayonet him" all around. One historian of the 69th New York wrote that this up-close combat was "never surpassed in any battle of the war." In the end, Waggaman and thirty-seven others were captured; the rest fell back.

In the 88th New York, James Turner was encouraging his fellow Irishmen, telling them to "Never mind the bullets," when one of those bullets went through his straw hat. He thought the bullet hole made the hat "almost worth keeping." Robertson's and Tidball's batteries arrived, and the 29th Massachusetts supported them. The 63rd New York followed (after Meagher put Lt. Col. Henry Fowler under arrest because Fowler insisted he was under Sumner's special orders and so did not have to listen to his own brigade commander). Tidball could only get two pieces into action because of the infantry in front of him. By the time he and Robertson opened fire it was dark, and the musketry soon stopped. Semmes's two regiments and one company lost 135 men, including 63 captured. The 69th New York, the principal defender against this rush, lost 127 killed or wounded.

With Semmes's repulse, the action west of the Willis Church road ended. Parts of Confederate commands remained in their advanced positions, including those of Armistead, Wright, and Mahone, the first men to charge up Malvern Hill. With Wright was the 49th North Carolina from Ransom's brigade. Toombs, Anderson, Barksdale, and Cobb pulled their men back; Semmes was so exhausted that two men had to help him back to camp.[9]

Kershaw's brigade, the last of Magruder's command to get into the fight, started out east of the Carter's mill road and kept moving down its east side through the woods. This motion naturally pointed them toward Couch's line. Moving through three lines of their fellow rebels under "a perfect storm of shell, grape and canister shot" according to Thomas Pitts of the 3rd South Carolina, the Gamecocks advanced to within two hundred or three hundred yards of Couch's line. At least two of the regiments had other rebels between them and the Yankees, either Toombs's or D. H. Hill's men. The 2nd South Carolina, Kershaw's left-hand regiment, was in the open and began firing. The rest of the brigade was, as one man put it, "exposed to an awful fire without an opportunity of firing a gun."

The Yankee fire came from fresh troops. Caldwell moved the 61st New York and 81st Pennsylvania (which he had consolidated under Francis Barlow's command) and the 7th New York to Albion Howe's aid. But Howe, seeing that the pressure point was on his left, sent Barlow's force and the 23rd Pennsylvania of John Abercrombie's brigade that way. They wound up relieving the 67th

New York and 61st Pennsylvania of Abercrombie's brigade and the 36th New York of Innis Palmer's brigade, all of which had run out of ammunition. The 7th New York went to Barlow's left. Some of Caldwell's men began to kneel and fire, as the others along the line were doing, but Barlow got out in front and yelled, "Stand up boys, you can have a better shot at them." His troops stood up, as did those in other regiments, but the artillery fire from behind forced at least some of the Yankees to lie down to avoid the canister.[10]

Sickles's New Yorkers arrived from the III Corps lines. As the men headed for the front, Sickles told them, "Men, all I ask of you is to do as you always have done." Trying to report to Porter on the left of the line, Sickles found Phil Kearny, who first told him he was not needed on the left, and then—after word came that the right (Couch's line) needed help—told Sickles he would have to decide for himself. Sickles kept moving forward and found Porter, who told him to support batteries on Couch's side of the line. He barely had his men set up for this purpose, however, when one of Porter's staff officers told him to support Couch in any way necessary. Soon staff officers from Couch's units began asking for help, as their commands also were running out of ammunition. Sickles sent the 72nd New York, which relieved Abercrombie's 31st Pennsylvania, and the 71st New York, which took the 65th New York's place. The 74th New York supported the 72nd, while the 70th and 73rd New York stayed in reserve.

Kershaw's men, joined by the 2nd Georgia and part of the 20th Georgia of Toombs's brigade, could not advance into the hailstorm of fire thrown out by these Federals. Some of the rebels received fire from their backs as well. Kershaw and Colonel Nance of the 3rd South Carolina tried to get the fire stopped, and Cpl. T. Whitner Blakely of the 3rd dodged bullets from both sides to accomplish the task. One of the bullets got Charles Coker, the 8th South Carolina's ordnance sergeant, who could not resist joining the front line; his brother William saw him die.

Kershaw realized he could not go forward and accomplish anything. But by staying where he was he was risking true demoralization, so he ordered the brigade back. John Bowden of the 2nd Georgia did not hear the order. "Personally I had nothing in my mind but to take the battery," he remembered. Heading past the remnants of Hill's division, he looked around and noticed no one was with him. "It occurred to me that I could not take the cannon, so I retreated," he said. Others heard the order and took advantage of it. Four of the regiments kept going all the way back to their starting point, some in disorder. Only the 2nd South Carolina retreated to Kershaw's desired rendezvous point. The 2nd and 20th Georgia stayed in a little depression until sunset, when their commanders decided support was not coming and ordered a withdrawal. The retreat quickly became a rout under the Yankee fire. One officer wrote, "Another lieutenant and I walked off, determined not to set the example of flight, but it was very agreeable to us to walk fast."[11]

The rebel fire hitting Kershaw was from the 26th Georgia of Lawton's brigade, part of the last Confederate movement of July 1—that of Ewell and Winder in response to D. H. Hill's request for reinforcements. Ewell arrived at the front line first, since he was closer to the action than Winder. Ewell's troops may have been happy to advance after enduring the cannon fire, "laying on our faces as close to the earth as we could get" as one Virginian in Early's brigade put it. On the other hand, the bullets were flying fast enough that another Virginian pulled his cap down tight to keep it from flying off. Early's brigade moved to the wooded area between the Willis Church and Carter's mill roads from which Hill had started and attempted to make its way through the brush. Two things slowed the march: Ewell took Early across an old dam instead of going through the ravine, and the generals lost contact with their troops by doing so. Also, the wooded area was the nearest shelter for many men who had charged the hill, and the confusion was so great Early could not find out whether his men had reached that point. He often mistook groups of men coming back from the lines for his brigade. Four of his regiments, having been ordered by Ewell to move to the left at the double quick, went too far left; the other three, not getting that order, wandered into the open.

Early, Ewell, and some of their staff tried to rally other Confederates with varying degrees of success. Ewell asked Kershaw to support Early with the 2nd South Carolina. Kershaw was not very happy about it, but he acquiesced. Early himself could not persuade more than a few of Toombs's men to stay with him. Just then the 12th Georgia came within Early's sight, soon followed by the 25th and 31st Virginia. Captain G. W. B. Hale of Early's staff rallied some men whose officers had been shot during charges. Early advanced with this polyglot group, but he was told merely to hold his position on the west side of the Willis Church road and to by no means try to charge the Yankees. It was dark by then, but the Federal artillery was still working, and holding the position was all that could be hoped for.

Winder could not find D. H. Hill. McHenry Howard, sent to locate him, called the errand "the most disagreeable duty I was ever called on as a staff officer to perform." The masses were still in the woods, and Winder heard heavy firing to his left, so he took his Virginians that way, repeating his decision at Gaines's Mill. This was not Gaines's Mill, however, and Winder could not keep his men together through the "terrific storm of shell and musketry." The brigade commander and about a hundred men from the 4th and 33rd Virginia made it through a ravine on the left of the Confederate line to where a handful of the 1st and 3rd North Carolina of Roswell Ripley's brigade were still on the upslope. One participant wrote, "Perhaps it was fortunate for us that we could not see how many they [the Yankees] were." They could feel their enemy's efforts, though. Howe's men and Seeley's guns kept up a steady fire, hitting thirty-three of the fewer than one hundred men from the 33rd Virginia involved in the action. Colonel John Neff took two spent balls "but was not much hurt." The rebels were rattled enough to fire in the air and randomly, perhaps even hitting their own men. There was a rumor that one Southerner shot another's head off.

The 2nd and 5th Virginia moved into the open killing field west of the Willis Church road. A steady stream of men falling back told the newcomers the whole army was in retreat. Lieutenant Colonel Lawson Botts of the 2nd Virginia did not like what he saw, so he and Col. William S. H. Baylor of the 5th Virginia moved their men back to the Willis Church road.

Winder went to find the rest of his men and ran into Lawton instead. Following the Virginians down the Willis Church road, the Georgians had run into the same problem as everyone else. Lawton, marching with the 13th Georgia on the right of his line, had lost contact with the rest of his men, could not figure the best route to his destination, and relied on the Union artillery fire to guide him. In doing so, he followed Winder's path. Thus, when the Virginian came back, Lawton was there. Winder persuaded Lawton to join the little band of the Stonewall Brigade. Lawton allowed Col. Marcellus Douglas and part of the 13th Georgia (with only between seventy-five and a hundred men) to move straight ahead, while the rest of the regiment followed Winder. Even Douglas got separated from his group, but the Georgians were determined to attack.

This small group of Douglas's men met up with men from Stafford's brigade. Stafford had come under Whiting's orders, and an officer (exactly who is uncertain, because no general officer reported ordering Stafford to advance) criticized him for not attacking with other troops. The unknown officer then ordered the Louisianans to move forward. Three of the regiments—the 6th, 7th, and 8th Louisiana—followed the order, but the 9th Louisiana stayed behind, through either not getting the order or not understanding it, and the Louisiana Tigers were not ordered in at all after the carnage at Gaines's Mill. This charge on Couch's left failed just as the rest had. The Louisianans "fought like wildcats" according to one Federal, however, and they came as close as anyone on the east side of Malvern Hill to reaching the line before Sickles's and Barlow's men stopped them twenty paces away. The men of the 7th New York shot all eighty of their cartridges as well as those in the boxes of the dead and wounded. Then they were told, "All right, but you have got your bayonets." The 81st Pennsylvania also shot all its rounds and stayed on the field without ammunition until the battle was over. Barlow's muskets became too hot to hold and then too dirty to load, but they "jumped up to give them the bayonets." Only the 72nd New York actually had ammunition, and Col. Nelson Taylor had to run to the rear through shot, shell, and minié balls to get more, but the fire and bayonets proved to be enough to halt the rebel advance.

The Louisianans and Georgians tried to retire gracefully, but order was impossible to maintain. Some of them retreated to Winder's line. The 27th Virginia and the rest of the 4th and 33rd Virginia came forward at this time. As these men advanced Col. A. J. Grigsby of the 27th was hit in the shoulder and left the field. After the battle, he found a spring and asked to have some water poured on the wound. "Colonel, does it hurt?" a man asked. "Yes, damn it," Grigsby responded, "it was put in there to hurt." Grigsby's men did not get far, either.

Not comfortable with his few men, Winder went back and found the rest of Lawton's men, John R. Jones's brigade (commanded again by Cunningham after Jones was hit in the knee by a piece of shell), and Bradley Johnson's Maryland Line. Johnson had wanted to put J. B. Brockenbrough's battery into action against the Unionists, but Jackson forbade it. Winder put these men into line to his right, with Johnson on the extreme right, Cunningham next, then Lawton. Close enough to hear the Federal officers give commands, they were the only Confederate troops actually on Malvern Hill east of the Willis Church road after nightfall.[12]

Whiting also had ordered movement in response to D. H. Hill's problems. Trimble went around John Bell Hood and Evander Law to reach the crowded woods on Whiting's right. Not having been in a battle since Gaines's Mill, Trimble must have gotten his blood going again, and some of his men also were ready to fight. One of them told his family that instead of suffering under the artillery fire, "I had rather to walk in front [of the] enemy with my musket [and] shoot it out." After Trimble put the brigade into position, he and D. H. Hill rode within a hundred yards of the Yankees, and Trimble thought he saw a chance to take one of Couch's batteries in flank. Hill did not like the idea of a night attack when the guns were still firing. Trimble, however, would not take no for an answer, at least not from Hill, and Jackson found him readying an attack. Stonewall gave his brigadier some information and advice. "I guess you had better not try it," Jackson said. "General Hill just tried it with his whole Division and has been repulsed. I guess you better not try it, sir." So Trimble's men stayed in what one of them called "a trying position, for three batteries were playing on us."

Even after the infantry fight ceased, the Federals did not let up. Hunt, on the scene with two thirty-two-pound howitzers by nightfall, fired away with them. Lieutenants Alanson Randol and E. W. Olcott, not having anything better to do after the capture of their guns at Glendale, helped out and perhaps got some revenge in the process. The other guns continued to fire until well after dark.[13] Finally, even they stopped. The battle of Malvern Hill was over.

One staff officer in III Corps called Malvern Hill "a magnificent pageant. . . . The coming down of a great mass of the enemy on the open plain to their utter destruction by the awful artillery fire. It was indeed a cruel and bloody sight." Confederates were perhaps even more inspired. Captain Matthew Nunnally of the 11th Georgia believed the night action was "one of the grandest scenes ever witnessed. The 30 pieces of artillery belching forth missiles of death and destruction—and the burning fire and bursting bombs lighting up the heavens with it mingling the many thousand small arms—and you might see the terrible but grand scene." J. Wood Davidson of Gregg's brigade wrote that the night bombardment was "one of the most magnificent spectacles I ever saw. . . . Every flash of every gun flared up against the sky in secondal succession—nay, ten per second might often be counted! And the shells could be traced by a faint streak overhead; and when they burst, the pyrotechnic splendor was grander than any view of 'the lightning's red glare painting hell in the sky.' . . . Majestic murder."

No one can question the last part of that statement. Malvern Hill was a slaughterhouse. About 30,000 Confederates were actually engaged at Malvern Hill, although several thousand more endured the Yankee shelling. The rebel losses amounted to around 5,150 killed or wounded, with another 500 or so missing and probably captured. Even discounting the losses from those troops not engaged in infantry assaults—a bit more than 200 from Jackson's command—the ratio of men shot to men engaged was as high for the Confederates at Malvern Hill as it was at Gaines's Mill. Besides the losses already noted, Winder's brigade (with just over 1,000 men in the ranks) suffered 104 casualties in its brief work. The 13th Georgia of Lawton's brigade lost 9 killed and 46 wounded out of at most 100 men engaged. Stafford's Louisianans lost 116 in the battle's last charge. Toombs's and George T. Anderson's brigades lost 400 between them, and Kershaw and Semmes (even with their reduced numbers in action) suffered more than 200 men hit and another 92 missing. Even Whiting's division, in line early but participating in no attacks, lost 175 men from its two brigades.

D. H. Hill pointed out an unusual aspect of Malvern Hill's casualties: more than half the Southerners killed or wounded suffered from artillery fire. Any rebels attempting to form up or move to assault positions through the open fields came under the fire of several guns posted atop the hill. Then the guns on the front lines would fire canister and grapeshot into the advancing Confederate infantry. In fact, much of the time the artillery was the first line of defense.

Union casualties were much lower, especially given the number of men involved. A little more than 27,000 Yankees were engaged at Malvern Hill. In addition to Griffin's and Couch's losses, Butterfield and Martindale suffered about 500 casualties (146 in the 83rd Pennsylvania alone, the highest Union loss in the battle), Caldwell and Meagher about 350, the III Corps units a little more than 100, and the artillery fewer than 100. Just over 2,100 Unionists were hit—less than half the number of Confederates hit, and a very low percentage of the number engaged. Only a few Federals from other units became casualties as a result of artillery fire.[14]

The casualty figures make the battle look lopsided. Some participants did not see it that way, though. Henry Hunt testified: "The battle was desperately contested, and frequently trembled in the balance." A couple of times, particularly on Morell's front, rebels got dangerously close to the lines. But there was never a threat of a decisive breakthrough at Malvern Hill. Only a few brigades from Jackson's command were available for following up a breakthrough early in the day. A Gaines's Mill–type outcome—with the Confederates breaking the Federal line in a final all-or-nothing charge—was less likely because the artillery had better fields of fire, the area of likely attack was narrower, and the Union defense had more depth. At Gaines's Mill, no Yankee was left in reserve at the end of the day. At Malvern Hill, nearly the entire III Corps (more than ten thousand troops) was still on the hill and unused. One division and one brigade of the II Corps—another 10,000 or more men—were just south of the plateau within easy supporting distance. Even this does not count the Pennsylvania Reserves, although their usefulness as a fighting force on July 1 is questionable. A breakthrough might have caused panic in the Union lines, but following up on it would have been difficult at best. Even after Gaines's Mill, Porter's men crossed the Chickahominy without problems. A combined attack earlier in the day would have stood as little chance as one later, because the Army of the Potomac was in position well before the Confederates arrived.[15]

That night, Robert E. Lee rode through the camps. Seeing Magruder, he asked Prince John, "General Magruder, why did you attack?" Magruder did not hesitate: "In obedience to your orders, twice repeated." This was literal truth. Lee had ordered Magruder to go in three different times, once in response to Armistead's "success," a second time after Magruder had reported that "success," and a third time in telling Prince John to press the enemy on the Confederate right. Of course, the first order was conditional, Magruder himself triggered the second, and the third probably was an attempt by Lee to position Magruder's force better. And so is raised the question of responsibility for the day's successes and failures.

The successes were mostly on one side, and the failures mostly on the other. The Union defensive line was well set up, the men fought hard, and the field commanders cooperated. Credit for the setup must be shared by many people, including McClellan, Porter, and several engineers, most principally A. A. Humphreys. It is hard to imagine better use being made of the ground. All sides of the line were well manned, with the possible exception of the River road area, with only three regiments on the lowland. But reinforcements were close at hand. All the lines were within easy supporting distance of one another. The defense was in depth with plenty of reserve troops.

The stars of the battle were the artillerists. Hunt deserves much credit for this battle. He performed yeoman's work in getting fresh batteries to the front line. One possible problem for the Federals was being caught without enough guns at the front, and Hunt made sure that did not happen. There were no complaints about the gunners themselves. An engineer observing the men at work noted that they fired without sponging, "it being considered better to run the risk of bursting the guns than to lose a second's time." It took courage to fire in this way, for a bursting gun would do terrible damage to its crew. Some batteries stand out. Ames and his men, for example, launched nearly fourteen hundred rounds of ammunition and stayed at the front in a key position the entire day. The battery also suffered twenty-three casualties, but it kept firing until after dark. Snow's battery, on the right, was divided into three sections and posted at different parts of the line. It lost twenty men hit despite being at the front only part of the day. Lieutenant Samuel N. Benjamin of Carlisle's battery, who was hurt badly enough that he could only stand on crutches and had to ride on a gun carriage, kept at his post throughout the battle (and had done so earlier in the campaign as well).

The artillery drew the comments of many Confederates, of course. For example, Bradley Johnson (writing years after the war) called it "the most infernal fire that has ever been concentrated in America." Captain Wingfield of Jackson's command wrote in his diary: "So close were the reports that it seemed one constant roar." Jubal Early did not even know the infantrymen were fighting until he entered the contest, because the artillery drowned out the muskets' relatively pitiful reports. Samuel Hankins of the 2nd Mississippi was able to go to sleep during the battle, not awakening until the next morning. Despite that oddity, the battle has been cited as evidence of the power of concentrated artillery, along with such contests as Austerlitz, Friedland, Wagram, and Sedan.

Even more artillery could have been concentrated. Only 75 guns were stationed along the north side of the Union line. The highest number on the north side of the line at one time was 38, late in the day. During a good part of the day fewer than 30 guns were on the front line. They were supported by 25 guns on the left (five leaving to enter the front line) and 37 on the right (6 coming from the front line, and 6 others coming in late). The number on the left includes the 5 guns in Martin's battery on the River road, only 3 of which fired on infantry (the other 2 bothering rebel cavalry pickets). The 12 siege guns by the Malvern house were gone more than two hours before the firing stopped. Moreover, as many as 38 guns on top of Malvern Hill on July 1 seemingly did not fire a shot: most of these were in II Corps batteries waiting for an attack on the right that never came. This is not meant as criticism. The guns at the front were set up so their direction could be changed quickly without worry of hitting other Federal gunners. In fact, some of the late arrivals had a hard time finding room for all their guns. If more had been needed, they were available.

Credit also must go to the infantrymen. Unlike at Glendale, they stayed behind the guns most of the time and did not advance too far during countercharges. This behavior allowed the gunners a clear field of fire. Regiments such as the 14th New York on the far left and Howe's units on the far right stayed in position all day, despite facing multiple attacks. Couch's men, suffering in reputation after Seven Pines, redeemed themselves by not taking a step backward unless under orders.

As at Gaines's Mill, many infantry commanders reported running out of ammunition, but unlike at Gaines's Mill reinforcements always were at hand. Credit for that must go to the commanders. First among them is Fitz John Porter. In command of the north and west sides of the Union line, he had posted his men as early as June 30, called for reinforcements and put them in the right places, and did not get in Couch's way but supported him in any way possible. Couch funneled reinforcements to the proper areas, and if he wanted to claim too much in his report, saying that for a time he was in command of the entire line, not too much dishonor can be brought for that overstatement. Porter, in fact, gave Couch full credit for his management of the right side of the line, and a veteran later wrote, "No troops were ever better handled; never was better military skill displayed than by him." Couch also cooperated well with Morell and his brigade commanders, who were ready to aid Couch and supported each other in basically independent command. Griffin in particular deserves note. In command of the line in front of the Mellert house and also of the artillery posted there, he blunted the first determined rebel charges. Sumner and Heintzelman promptly responded to Porter's request for help.

The only real question is McClellan's role. His decisions—leaving the field to scout the army's resting place, staying on the right of the line when he came back to Malvern Hill instead of heading to the firing—can be questioned. However, as at Savage Station and Glendale, his real mistake was in not naming an overall commander on top of the hill. Porter was in command of his corps and Couch, and Sumner and Heintzelman were in command of their corps, but who would win an argument? This actually arose when Sumner ordered Porter off the hill early in the battle. Porter refused, pointing out that McClellan had approved his lines. The Confederates settled the matter by attacking. But what if they had not? Sumner might have pulled rank as the senior corps commander. Porter then would have been in a dilemma, and McClellan was far enough away that Fitz John did not feel it was possible to obtain an answer in a reasonable amount of time. Again McClellan, by not naming an overall commander in his absence, had flirted with disaster, and again cooperation among his chief subordinates and the efforts of his army had forestalled it.[16]

McClellan also had cooperation from the Confederates, for whom Malvern Hill could only be viewed as a debacle. As one rebel put it, "Some one again made a grievous mistake here." The men in the ranks fought hard. There was a lot of straggling, particularly from Magruder's command, but this is understandable: They had been marching for a day and a half in a Virginia summer, and many probably had difficulty keeping up. The brigade commanders in general did their parts. Ransom's unwillingness to commit his troops immediately and Toombs's problems were exceptions. The Confederates had thousands of men in a relatively small area between the Carter's mill and Willis Church roads just north of their junction because the woods there gave the best shelter to either organize for an attack or regroup after a repulse. The resulting confusion that struck Jackson's late efforts cannot be blamed on the brigadiers.

There are seven candidates for the blame for Malvern Hill: Lee, Magruder, Huger, Jackson, Longstreet, Holmes, and Pendleton. Pendleton, Jackson, Holmes, and Huger bear little responsibility except (in Jackson's and Huger's cases) in concert with others.

Longstreet was in one sense the instigator of the Confederate failure. His optimism regarding success and his suggestion about the artillery concentrations may have affected Lee's thinking, as evidenced by what actually happened. He did not order Magruder to turn around, although he was sure Prince John was headed the wrong way. He was not successful in setting up a grand battery on the rebel right, and what is more, he failed to use all the resources at his command. However, Lee also believed the Yankees were demoralized and probably shared Longstreet's optimism. Old Pete's suggestion to Lee was just that. It did not guarantee the success of a full-scale assault on the Malvern Hill position. If Longstreet did not order Magruder to reverse course, he at least told Lee about the problem—which is better communication than earlier during the Seven Days. Given the terrain north of Malvern Hill, any attempt to set up a battery where Longstreet wanted it was doomed to failure. His vision may have been clouded by his optimism, and perhaps he saw the failure and gave up the project as a bad job. But he also might still have been at it when Lee called him away to check on the possibilities to the left. Any mistakes by Longstreet were but slight contributions to the Confederate defeat.[17]

That leaves two men: John B. Magruder and Robert E. Lee. Magruder began badly by going down what proved to be the wrong road and ended with nearly three thousand of his men killed or wounded. Magruder's mistakes were many. He took a road different from what Lee wanted, and he continued down the road after Longstreet discussed the mistake with him. He failed to bring thirty rifled guns to the front lines. He misread Armistead's advance as a success on the basis of little firsthand information and reported it to Lee. His management of his forces meant that the most vulnerable spot on the Federal line—the northwest corner—was not heavily attacked. Finally, he did not coordinate his assaults well, particularly after the initial attack by Armistead, Cobb, Mahone, and Wright.

D. H. Hill, without mentioning names, scathingly criticized Magruder and others for not fighting, and he only modified that criticism in his writing twenty years later. Hill obviously was wrong. As for Magruder's going down the wrong road, if Lee's map was wrong, this mistake was made by the staff and not Prince John. He went down the Quaker road. He should not have gone as far as he did, since Lee had laid out the plan in person that morning and Longstreet questioned his route. Two, possibly three, major effects came from the resulting delay. First, Lee's ideas for the formation of the line were impossible to carry out. Second, Magruder's arrived on the field much later than anticipated, which was an important factor in his getting Chilton's order late in the day. Third, his artillery would have been more available, although there was not much chance of his getting thirty guns of any sort lined up in the field north of the Mellert house no matter when he started.

Magruder constantly was riding around, posting troops, looking things over, and encouraging men—to the point that his staff at times found it hard to find him. There were rumors in the army that he was drunk at Malvern Hill, which two of his staff were at pains to refute. He may still have been irritated by the medicine for his indigestion. Given his movements, he could not have investigated anything very long, and he might not have taken the time to really view the prospects.

When he sent his message to Lee regarding Armistead's advance, he did not know of Lee's earlier order and the importance it placed on Armistead. The message could have been simply that Armistead had advanced from his previous position. But Magruder, in reporting even that, should have noted the Yankees still on top of the hill. That information might have affected Lee's response, and Magruder could not assume Lee knew the situation. This mistake, therefore, was costly to the Confederate cause in that it gave Lee too much hope and an unrealistic picture of the field.

Magruder cannot be blamed for launching the attack. His orders were clear: he must follow up on Armistead's move. But Prince John might have been suffering from the effects of June 29. Lee had taken him to task that evening for not doing what he wanted, so if Lee wanted an attack, Magruder might have decided to oblige him. It would have been wiser to see if the situation matched Lee's desires. Again, however, Magruder cannot be blamed—any more than Stonewall Jackson can—when he was following orders. Although his attacks were uncoordinated, he did attempt a simultaneous initial assault. After that he continued feeding troops into the battle as they came in, and the confusion on the field resulted in their going every which way. Many units wound up too far to the left when the right would have made a better point of attack. But getting to the right cost Ransom many of his casualties, and such a movement by a larger force would have been seen and countered easily by Porter.[18]

Magruder must take some share of the blame for Malvern Hill. The attack began in part because he initiated it, and it was doomed from the start. But his responsibility and Lee's must be intertwined. Lee probably was exhausted on July 1, and he probably also was upset about the events of the previous day. But these two probabilities do not mean that Lee recklessly ordered a charge at Malvern Hill to get at the Yankees, or that he was so tired he could not think straight. In fact, Lee's thinking at Malvern Hill is not as bad as it might appear at first blush. He put relatively rested troops, or at least those who had not fought the previous day, in the front lines. His acceptance of Longstreet's idea was sound in principle and did not commit him to making an assault.

His fatigue might have affected his movements early in the day, when he relied on Longstreet. The two seem to have worked together well, and Old Pete kept in touch with his chief. But if Lee had examined the ground on the west side of the Carter's mill road, he might have reacted differently when Magruder's message reached him. This is where Lee's responsibility for the fiasco at Malvern Hill starts. Lee should have been observing the effects of the artillery on the right side of the line, no matter what his other thoughts. If he had been at his proper spot, the battle of Malvern Hill would never have taken place. Moreover, there had to be a better way to coordinate the advance than the idea of advancing at a yell. His division commanders were little more than a mile apart, and even with the difficulties of getting messages through a hail of fire and some rough terrain, it would have been better to send couriers than to depend on a yell above the roar of the guns.

Even this poor an order, however, did not commit Lee to a hopeless assault. In fact, he had given up on an assault and investigated the possibility of a turning movement. This action brings up two points. First, should Lee have investigated such a movement sooner? Looking back on the battle, it is easy to answer this question in the affirmative. However, as Lee brought his men together, he would have wanted to know the situation before investigating possibilities. Jackson or someone else on the left might have brought the idea to Lee's attention, but it is uncertain when anyone there (such as Hood) had the idea. And again, although the battle of Malvern Hill would not have occurred, a turning movement would have worked only if McClellan stayed in place on the night of July 1.

The second point concerns whether Lee should have countermanded the order. It is equally easy to affirmatively answer this question with the benefit of hindsight. If Lee had concluded that the artillery concentration had failed, he might have assumed his subordinates would reach the same conclusion. But it is always dangerous to assume things, especially when people's lives are at stake, and it would have been prudent of Lee to countermand the order, particularly since he was new to command of the army and its officers. If a countermand had reached Magruder in time, perhaps matters would have turned out differently.

When Magruder's message regarding Armistead and Whiting's message concerning a Yankee withdrawal reached Lee he again should have looked before leaping. Had Lee been on the far left of the line, he might have decided that the chance would be lost without an immediate response. In the time it took Dickinson to get to Magruder, though, Lee could have ridden about the same distance and made the decision on firsthand information instead of second- or even third-hand information. He could have stopped the attacks when he reached McLaws's headquarters in the early evening, once he realized that they were getting nowhere. Perhaps he could not have seen how the battle was progressing from the Carter's mill road, but a short ride would have enlightened him. As it was, he sent McLaws's men in, which was a mistake.

Magruder and Lee must share much of the blame for Malvern Hill, and neither man's actions alone would have produced the results they got. Lee's order issued by Chilton was bad, but Magruder got it far too late because he had not been on the field when it was dispatched. Bad maps obtained from Lee's staff apparently caused the delay. Magruder should not have told Lee about Armistead's "success," but Lee could have looked at the situation himself and indeed could have been on the right the entire time. Lee could have countermanded the order (and Chilton could have written the time on it), but Magruder should have checked to see if the order was current when he received it.[19] The whole affair would have been a comedy of errors had it not been so tragic.

CHAPTER TWENTY

"It Was a Very Tedious, Tiresome March"

As the sun was setting on Malvern Hill, Jeb Stuart and his cavalry arrived at the Rock house, three miles northeast of Turkey Island Bridge and four miles southeast of the Glendale crossroads. After receiving Lee's note on the twenty-ninth and responding to it, Stuart had completed his provisioning and destruction at White House Landing. On the morning of the thirtieth he left a Cobb's Legion cavalry squadron at the former Union depot and followed Fitz Lee toward the bridges across the Chickahominy. Lee took the 1st Virginia Cavalry to Long Bridge, where he saw some Yankee pickets, perhaps the 96th New York of Henry Wessells's IV Corps brigade and two sections of the 8th Battery, New York Light Artillery, across the river. He tried to shell them with a twelve-pound Napoleon gun, but its trail broke on the first shot.

Stuart took the rest of his force to Jones's Bridge, where Jeb had crossed the river on his ride around the Army of the Potomac. Things were a little lively there. William Averell had sent Capt. J. C. White with a squadron of the 3rd Pennsylvania Cavalry, two hundred infantry, and two guns from Battery M, 5th U.S. Artillery, under Lt. Valentine H. Stone to Jones's Bridge on the twenty-ninth. When Stuart arrived early in the afternoon on the thirtieth, John Pelham put his remaining two howitzers into position and opened fire (Stone reported facing eight rebel guns). The Northerners disappeared, and Will T. Martin crossed with part of his force to discover their movements. Pelham moved to the bridge to support Martin's men, but Stone opened up on Pelham from as little as four hundred yards away. The two gunners fired at each other for a while, with little result except a few men and horses hit, and then Stone and the rest of the Federals rejoined the army.

Stuart and his men spent the night where they were. At 3:30 in the morning on July 1, a courier awakened Jeb. Lee wanted him to rejoin the army, perhaps crossing the Chickahominy at Grapevine Bridge. Stuart asked when the message had been written and was told 9 P.M., after the fighting at Glendale was over. Jeb had heard sounds of combat and figured Bottom's Bridge would be clear if the Yankees were already at the Glendale crossroads. He started his men toward that bridge and, moving ahead of the column, crossed the river to learn the situation around White Oak Swamp. He saw columns of infantry moving south, with no signs or sounds of battle, and knew there was no reason for cavalry to come that way. Sending a note to Jackson telling Stonewall (with whom he had marched until Gaines's Mill) he would cross at Jones's Bridge, Stuart retraced his steps and found his men approaching Bottom's Bridge. He turned them around, and after fording the river at Jones's Bridge they headed west. Arriving at Rock's house after dark, Jeb scattered some Union pickets but found he could go no farther, as he could see campfires burning (probably Peck's division and the VI Corps between him and Haxall's Landing). He stayed at Rock's, his command having ridden forty-two miles, and sent Eugene Blackford of his staff to Jackson with the information. "That's good! That's good!" Stonewall replied gleefully. "Changing his base, is he? Ha, ha."

Stuart claimed his arrival at Rock's had precipitated the abandonment of the Malvern Hill position. The reality is somewhat different. The real issue is whether his movements helped or hurt the Confederate cause. Lee had some cavalry—the 5th Virginia Cavalry on the River road, the 1st North Carolina and 3rd Virginia Cavalry in Longstreet's rear, and the 2nd Virginia Cavalry with Jackson. The 5th Virginia Cavalry had found the Yankees at Malvern Hill (Thomas Rosser reported that to Benjamin Huger, who apparently did nothing with the information). It then rode to John Magruder's area and continued moving east throughout the day. The 3rd Virginia Cavalry and 1st North Carolina Cavalry, starting farther to the east, mirrored the 5th Virginia Cavalry's moves, gathering prisoners and trying to get to Jackson's left (which they could not do). The 2nd Virginia Cavalry apparently also moved to the east, as part of that regiment ran into Stuart at Jones's Bridge. Lee thus had troops available for reconnaissance, but his best cavalry commander was absent. What Stuart could have accomplished if he had been more easily available to Lee is an open question. He might have investigated the ground to the east of Jackson more fully while still leaving Lee enough cavalry to use as flank guards and advance scouts. He also might have been able to disrupt McClellan's rear enough to cause panic in the Union high command.[1]

While Stuart's men were approaching Malvern Hill, the Army of the Potomac was preparing to leave it. Not all the Yankees were happy about it. Fitz John Porter sent McClellan messages saying that if the men could get some food and ammunition, the army should stay where it was or even begin to make up the ground it had lost—to "reap the full fruits of their labors," as Fitz John put it. But Porter's messengers probably passed one headed to Malvern Hill with McClellan's order to move to Harrison's Landing. George Morell was to withdraw first, followed by Darius Couch, George Sykes, Phil Kearny, Joe Hooker, Edwin Sumner, William Franklin, and Erasmus Keyes.

Porter spent much of the night trying to change McClellan's mind. He was sure the Yankees could get to Richmond. Kearny was furious and said the withdrawal could be motivated only "by cowardice or treason." Some Confederates were of the same mind. Old friends turned enemies told John Reynolds, a prisoner in Richmond, that the way would have been clear. Joe Johnston thought the Federals would get to the rebel capital shortly.

McClellan, either headed for the *Galena* or already aboard the gunboat, was looking at a different picture. He was seeing hordes of Confederates coming around his right and cutting him off from Harrison's Landing. He was hearing Commodore Rodgers tell him the navy could not guarantee the safety of transports above that place. He was thinking that, as he told Averell earlier in the retreat, "[I]f any army can save this country, it will be the Army of the Potomac, and it must be saved for that purpose." The only way he could save the army was to get it to a position where the gunboats could help it, where he could be sure of supplies, and where the army itself could regroup, rest, and get ready for its next move. That place was Harrison's Landing. He had already chosen it, and that is where he would go—victory or no victory on top of Malvern Hill.[2]

There were elements in favor of staying in position, even advancing. For one, the Confederates were in disarray. Campbell Brown observed that the "moral effect of the day was decidedly that of a defeat." Magruder wrote Lee late in the evening: "The men in the fight are so entirely disorganized, arising principally from the darkness, that not an organized body exists." The Yankees themselves were tired but willing to stay where they were. Charles Haydon wrote in his diary, "If our army had been fresh I should have liked all to have been risked on a battle on this field," and Thomas Hyde remembered that his men would have been enthusiastic despite their ordeal if ordered to march on Richmond. In fact, many more Federals than Confederates were fresh. Almost all of III Corps, more than half of II Corps, all of VI Corps, and one IV Corps division had been out of the fight. A fair number of those men had not fought on the thirtieth, either. Every Confederate not straggling had at least been under fire on the thirtieth or the first. In Little Mac's mind, though, the Southerners must have fresh troops; after all, they had at least 180,000 of them.

McClellan was not on the battlefield by the end of the battle. Yet being there would not have changed the basic "facts" in his mind: He was far outnumbered, and he could not protect Harrison's Landing from where he was.

He could cover Haxall's with an extended line, but he would have no reserve force and the navy could not protect transports going to Haxall's. Although the gunboats had been ineffective at Malvern Hill, they would be more effective at Harrison's Landing where they would have better fields of fire, and McClellan wanted even more of them.

All these factors meant that Little Mac believed he had no choice. He did not have to be fixated on retreat, cowardly, or traitorous; he just had to be following the train of thought that had haunted him for months. He had insisted that the Confederates outnumbered him, and he had decided that he should not risk his army. His move was the right one from his point of view. It might have been right from a more realistic point of view as well. The rebels were disorganized that night, but a night attack would be dangerous to everyone. By the next morning, Lee probably would have his men in shape to defend themselves. A Federal advance might succeed, but it would not be a sure thing. Taking time to plan for an attack would give Marse Robert time to prepare for one. On the other hand, holding in position, even against Lee's actual numbers, risked allowing the Southerners to attempt once more to cut the Army of the Potomac from its supplies—this time with no easy fallback position. Besides, no matter the condition of the Confederates, McClellan's men had fought and marched for at least three days (four for some) with little food or sleep and so were not at peak efficiency—again, perhaps good enough for defense, but not for attack. The army also had no supplies (including both food and ammunition) other than what it carried in its wagons and on its backs.[3]

It was McClellan's decision to make, and he made it. For the third straight night, the Army of the Potomac would retreat from a field where it had at worst battled to a draw with its foe. The headquarters camp at Haxall's Landing was broken up, McClellan urging Alexander Bliss to make haste before he boarded the *Galena*. Henry Hunt's gunners were withdrawn shortly after they stopped firing except for a section from Henry Benson's battery, which stayed to cover the infantry's retreat. The engineers moved at about the same time. The Pennsylvania Reserves marched before midnight, the men having just started to sleep when they were ordered out. Morell's division, scattered along Malvern Hill, began pulling out about 11 P.M. John Martindale, told he would lead the division, arrived at a narrow, tree-lined passage filled with artillery. Morell told him to follow the guns, but other troops had the same idea. Martindale tried to stop them, but with no success. Then Dan Butterfield and Porter rode by and Martindale started his men forward, only to find that many of them had followed the tide instead of resisting it and were already ahead of him. The 14th New York, having fought in the first major action of the day, stayed well beyond everyone else in its division, not leaving the front until 2 A.M. Thomas Meagher (on Morell's front) went looking for relief near the end of the fighting. Instead he found Sumner, who ordered him to withdraw. All of his units did except the 29th Massachusetts, separated from the rest of the Irish and apparently forgotten. The Bay Staters did not leave until the next morning.

Couch's men also hit the road before midnight. At least a part of the 36th New York in Innis Palmer's brigade took the wrong road, getting within a quarter-mile of the Confederates before figuring out their mistake. John Caldwell and Dan Sickles, also on the front line, followed Couch. Sickles got no orders but fell back anyway. Someone forgot about the 5th New Hampshire in Caldwell's brigade, which stayed near the front lines waiting for a battery that never came. Finally, at about 5 A.M., Capt. Edward E. Sturtevant, in command of the regiment, decided there were better places to be since just about everyone else had left. The 63rd Pennsylvania in John Robinson's brigade also was left behind unintentionally, while Sickles's 71st New York was ordered to stay on the hill as part of the rear guard.

Sykes put Charles Lovell's brigade in motion sometime after midnight. With the Yankees went a Confederate officer and twenty-three men captured in a house (perhaps a Mellert slave cabin) by Lt. William H. Penrose and his men from the 3rd U.S. Infantry, and a Confederate officer who had wandered into the Union lines by mistake. Robert Buchanan's brigade stayed behind to function as a delaying force under Averell's command, along with the 3rd Pennsylvania Cavalry, the 71st New York, and perhaps the section of Benson's battery that had been left. Gouverneur Warren's three regiments and Augustus Martin's battery began marching down the River road about 1 A.M.

Samuel Heintzelman received his orders just before 11 P.M. He reported that the road off the hill—the extension of the Willis Church road—was so jammed that Kearny did not start until 3:40 A.M., and Cuvier Grover and Joseph Carr reported moving about that time. But Kearny reported moving about midnight, and several of his men also reported starting well before 3:40, so maybe part of III Corps clogged the road for the rest of it. The rest of Edwin Sumner's corps began moving after midnight, but the 1st Minnesota of John Sedgwick's division did not start until daybreak. William French did not even receive an order and also left about daybreak. William Burns's brigade at first moved north, and the men thought they were headed to Richmond. But after a half-hour's halt, an order came, and the men turned to go south again. Some men could barely stop crying after hearing the order to change direction.

Henry Slocum's division left its position around eleven, and Baldy Smith's men stayed behind to guard the bridges across Turkey Island Creek. The task of guarding the road east of Turkey Island Bridge fell to John Peck. Henry Wessells, a fifty-three-year-old Connecticut native, had served in Florida, Mexico, and the West after graduation from West Point and came from the western theater to command his IV Corps brigade. He formed his line on the heights east of Haxall's Landing shortly after midnight, and Henry Naglee's brigade took up a strong position about a mile to Wessells's rear.[4] By dawn on July 2 most of the Army of the Potomac was on the road to Harrison's Landing.

Most of the Army of Northern Virginia stayed in place the night of July 1, whether that place was on Malvern Hill or in a camp. Ambrose Wright and William Mahone stayed on the hill, along with the 49th North Carolina from Robert Ransom's brigade. Wright wrote Magruder, "for God's sake relieve us soon and let us collect our brigades." No relief was forthcoming, however, and the men listened as the Yankees withdrew under cover of darkness. Rebels found water and attempted to aid the wounded. The Federals were doing the same thing, their lanterns clearly visible. Lew Armistead's brigade, the other command involved in the earliest assault, also remained on the ground that night.

To Armistead's left, Jubal Early's men could hear the sounds of a retreating army and the cries of the wounded, and see Northerners with lanterns crossing the field. Charles Winder, having put his line together, told Jackson and D. H. Hill where he was, which was close to the Federal line. In the saddle all night, he knew nothing of the Union retreat. But Jackson's men could hear them. One of them noted that the "wagons and artillery made a great deal of noise."

Some of the division commanders in the rear, not hearing the wagons and guns, worried about an enemy attack in the morning. Richard Ewell fretted so much that he had Campbell Brown move between thirty and forty captured ammunition wagons to the north side of White Oak Swamp so they would be safe if the army needed to retreat quickly. Some officers discussing the situation decided to wake Jackson. Stonewall proved hard to wake, but he finally was able to hear the apprehension. When he did so, he dismissed it. "Please let me sleep," he said. "There will be no enemy there in the morning."

George T. Anderson, Robert Toombs, Paul Semmes, Joseph Kershaw, Howell Cobb, William Barksdale, and Ransom spent the night camped around the Carter house on the Carter's mill road. William Whiting's men, including Wade Hampton's brigade, stayed in their positions. About midnight Isaac Trimble, deciding nothing more would happen, pulled his regiments back into the woods. Leroy Stafford withdrew those of his men who had not joined with Winder to a gate by the Willis Church road. From there they went to Willis Church to get water and then came back to the gate. D. H. Hill's brigade commanders continued their efforts to organize their men throughout the night, most of them setting up camp near Willis Church. A. P. Hill's division moved back to the Long Bridge road, while James Longstreet's division stayed on the army's right rear.[5]

The cries of the wounded tore through the night air. Porter Alexander remembered they "could not fail to move with pity the heart of friend or foe." A soldier from the 4th Georgia said he heard "groans from some, prayers from others, curses from this one and the uncomplaining silence of the hero." Informal truces were agreed to along most of the lines, although in one place Yankees fired on Confederates trying to help their wounded. Other Yankees were fired on as they tried to find one man "alternately praying and cursing" in a high-pitched voice. The 1st Maryland tried to help George B. Anderson's North Carolinians, giving them water and moving them if possible. Everyone on the slopes could hear the cries, but some of the exhausted troops near the top of the hill could sleep despite them.

F. P. Ellis of the 13th Mississippi, wounded himself, saw a man moving among the bodies. Ellis finally figured out that the man and four or five others were robbing the dead, but he could not determine to which army they belonged. He also could see the litter-bearers with their lanterns, but as the sun rose he guessed he would lie on the field for several more hours before they reached him.

Brigham Buswell of Berdan's Sharpshooters, having reached the Malvern house late in the battle, lay in a room on the first floor. Just after midnight, Lt. Col. William Ripley of the sharpshooters entered and ordered anyone in the regiment who could move to fall in. He advised them that the army was retreating and anyone who stayed would be taken prisoner. Everyone who thought he could make it rose, including Buswell. A. H. Boies of the 4th Michigan, who also had spent the night at the Malvern house, left before getting his wound dressed.[6]

At about this time it started to rain. It often rained after Civil War battles, but in many cases both armies would stay near the battlefield and the men could get some shelter. On the night of July 1, however, the Army of the Potomac had more than seven miles to march to its new home, and most of the men would march most of those miles through a hard, driving rain. Even before the rain, one of Charles Griffin's men said, "It was a very tedious, tiresome march." Ira Spaulding of the engineers called it "such a march as I do not wish to make very often," given the darkness of the night and the condition of the roads, but the roads in particular would only get worse as time passed. Another man remembered, "Of all the nasty marches we ever made, I believe that beat them all."

Infantry, mounted men, batteries, and wagons were using the roads at the same time. John Peck had tried to order the march with infantry and artillery on one side of the road and wagons on the other, but that did not last. The vehicles would push the foot soldiers to the shoulders, and when the infantrymen tried to get back on the roads, cavalry teams would run them off so the vehicles could stay on course. Eventually the roads were no better than the shoulders. Hyde said he saw a mule drop into the mud until only its ears stuck out (the animal was pulled out). A regular officer twice fell into hip-deep mud. It took one unit six hours to go a mile and a half. Many of the marchers dropped out from exhaustion and lack of food. Fires built by the engineers lit the roads, but it was hard to lift the men's spirits; Capt. W. S. Sampson of the 22nd Massachusetts wrote the retreat was "a sad time for the remnant of the Twenty-second."[7]

Keyes sent trains on every road he could find from Haxall's, where many wagons had been parked, to Harrison's Landing. After dawn he even opened a road leading from Haxall's to the River road four miles southeast of Turkey Island Bridge that Naglee's men had obstructed. He later estimated that a thousand wagons had used that road to get to safety. Peck moved the wagons into fields whenever he could so that they could move more quickly. Even so, not even the most optimistic expected every gun, caisson, and wagon would make it. Heintzelman and Slocum claimed that all of their wagons made it from Savage Station to Harrison's Landing, but they were exceptions. An axle broke on one gun from Stephen Weed's battery. At one of the myriad bridges a caisson from Charles Morgan's battery, having fallen behind, tried to cross at the same time as a gun carriage from Samuel Elder's battery. The horses were forced into the stream—three of them drowned—and the gun was disabled. The limber was irretrievable, and the road was blocked. Elder worked the gun off the bridge, emptied a caisson, and attached the gun to the empty caisson to save it. Another artillery officer, revolver in hand, ordered infantrymen to throw their rifles into the road to form a sort of corduroy for his mired gun. A drummer boy fell off a wagon and was crushed by the wheels.

The march was conducted "in a perfect rush" according to Matthew Marvin of the 1st Minnesota. A soldier from the Irish Brigade called the army "a disorganized mob." The 6th New Jersey of Carr's brigade was cut in two by some of Sickles's men marching right through it. Warren, as far off as a Yankee could get from Harrison's Landing, could not move because of the mob on the River road and had to wait until everyone else had gone except the rear guard. John Ames, with Warren's force, wrote home: "I never endured such an intense strain of nervous expectation; the *tension* was fearful." Sykes, seeing his men's problems, held Lovell up until the three lonely regiments on the left could get through. Baldy Smith waited all night by the River road. Porter finally passed by about daylight, and Smith moved onto the River road. Some of Berdan's sharpshooters who had been left behind had to cross a bridge on the last timber still spanning the water. Smith soon came upon Wessells's brigade, which with Theodore Miller's battery was on the high ground east of Turkey Island Creek. Peck was there, and the two generals compared orders. Smith, although not under any directive to assist, told Peck he would come back if Peck needed help. That was at about ten in the morning on July 2, and all Peck awaited was Averell's command.[8]

Averell had waited for the dawn. It came foggy enough that a man fifty yards away was invisible. He then moved his horse soldiers toward the front. They came upon Buchanan, who told Averell the Confederates were moving forward

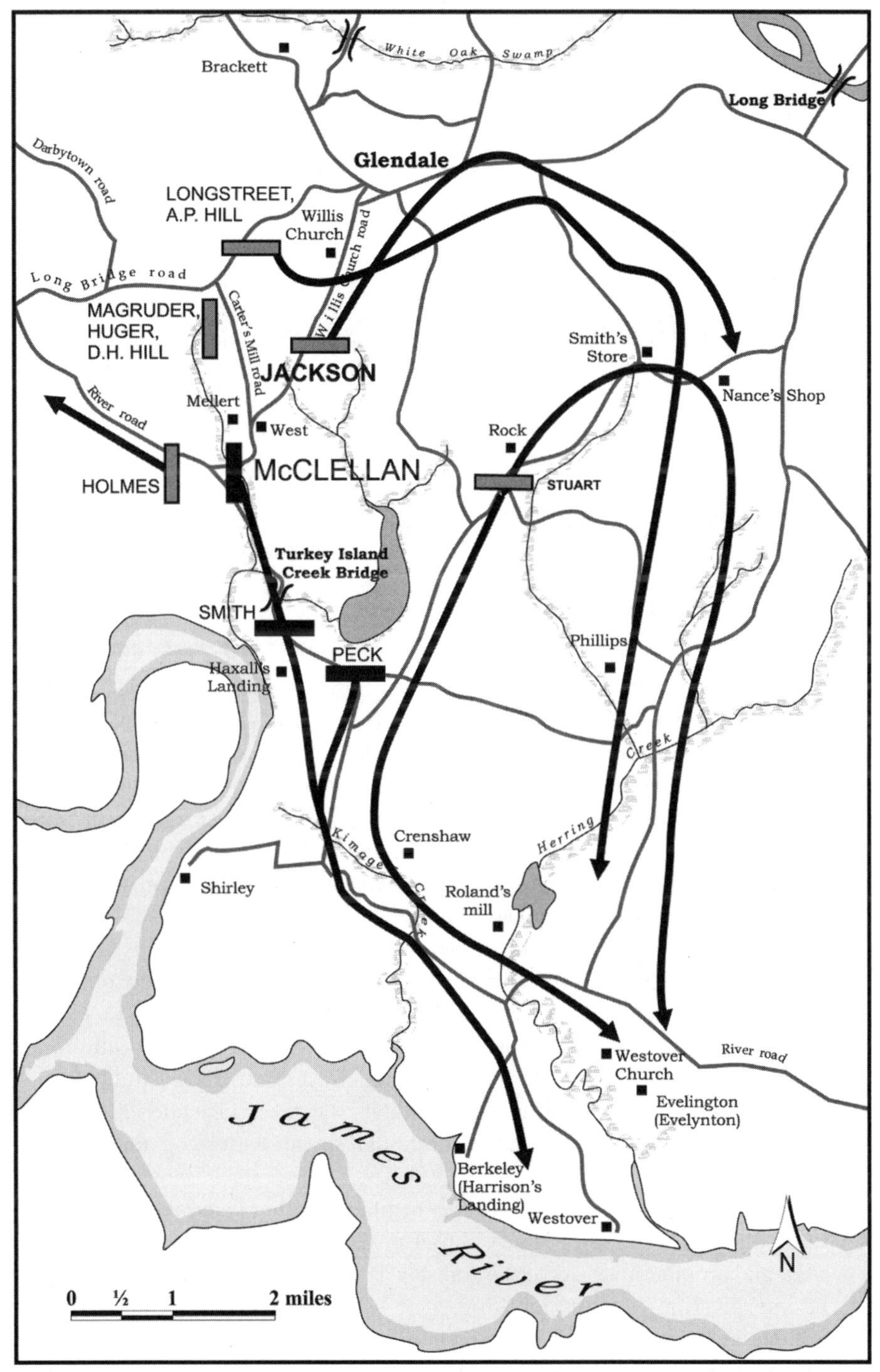

Troop movements, July 2 and 3, 1862

and working to flank the line. Averell put three of the regular regiments in line along with the 71st New York, and the 3rd Pennsylvania Cavalry covered the wings. He also sent for a battery (the two guns Benson left had apparently moved away with the main force). Then he went to the spot where the Yankee lines had been the previous day. His description, written twenty years later, is worth quoting at length:

> By this time the level rays of the morning sun from our right were just penetrating the fog, and slowly lifting the clinging shreds and yellow masses. Our ears had been filled with agonizing cries from thousands before the fog was lifted, but now our eyes saw an appalling spectacle upon the slopes down to the woodlands half a mile away. Over five thousand dead and wounded men were on the ground, in every attitude of distress. A third of them were dead or dying, but enough were alive and moving to give to the field a singular crawling effect. The different stages of the ebbing tide are often marked by the lines of flotsam and jetsam left along the sea-shore. So here could be seen three distinct lines of dead and wounded marking the last front of three Confederate charges of the night before. Groups of men, some mounted, were groping about the field.

Not yet having any artillery, Averell formed some troopers into squads and told them to impersonate gunners. Skirmishers from the 14th U.S. Infantry spread out to make their force seem larger. John Frank soon arrived with four guns, but by that time any forward movement the Confederates had been making was stopped, and the Southerners moved out to tend to their wounded and collect their dead. At 10 A.M. Averell learned that the rear of the army was two miles down the road. He moved his guns and reserve infantry regiment back, then his main line, then his skirmishers, and finally his cavalry. The infantry started as soon as they had retrieved their knapsacks.

As the Pennsylvanians withdrew they destroyed twelve wagons, lacking mules to pull them, and the entire Army of the Potomac was finally off Malvern Hill. After Averell crossed Turkey Island Bridge, Lt. Martin Reichenbacher of Battery C, 1st Pennsylvania Light Artillery, Lieutenant Gibson (a McClellan staff officer), Lt. Oswald Jackson (a Keyes staff officer) and twenty-five men of the 8th Pennsylvania Cavalry cut away the bridge and felled trees over it. The army once again had a substantial stream between it and its foe.[9]

The rebels on the hill were not ready to attack another Federal line. For one thing, there was the rain. Henry Burgwyn wore a Yankee overcoat, his own coat, and an oilcloth coat, yet he was so wet and the July air was so cool that he was shivering. For another thing, there were few rebels there. Jubal Early, waking on the morning of July 2, saw a small force that looked like friends. Moving to his right he stumbled across a dozen or fewer rebels, one of whom was Lew Armistead. Early asked Armistead where his brigade was, and Armistead replied, "Here are all that I know anything about except those lying out there in front." Armistead had also been eyeing the group of soldiers to the right, who proved to be the remnants of Mahone's and Wright's commands. They were ready to defend the details out caring for the wounded, but they were not going to attack even a rear guard, and as soon as they were able, everyone marched down the hill to recover.

The Maryland Line aimed a few shots at a Union cavalry officer, and there was some skirmishing. That was reported critically to Jackson, who responded, "He's right, that's his business there, attack them wherever he sees them! That's the way!" Stonewall, seemingly recovered from his stupor of June 30 and unperturbed by the fact that his prediction of the night before had not come exactly true, ordered the dead moved away from in front of his line. Asked why, he said, "I am going to attack here presently, as soon as the fog rises, and it will not do to march the troops over their own dead, you know; that's what I'm doing it for." Others were worried about defending, not advancing. Charles Winder, for instance, watched "anxiously" for a Federal attack and was "relieved" when none came.

When Jackson met Thomas Munford of the cavalry he said, "I wonder if I can get some buttermilk?" Munford took Stonewall to the house where he had procured some food and asked the lady there: "Can I get some breakfast for General Jackson, madam? He has had none today." The woman said, "For whom?" He repeated Jackson's name. "General Jackson! That is not General Jackson!" the woman cried, pointing at Stonewall. "Yes it is, madam," Munford replied. The woman burst out crying and gave Jackson everything she had—including some buttermilk.

Many people probably lost their appetites as they looked at Malvern Hill. Richard Ewell was beside himself. Moxley Sorrel of Longstreet's staff found him doubled up on the floor of a shack. Ewell rose when Sorrel entered and said, "Mather Thorrel, can you tell me why we had five hundred men killed dead on this field yesterday?" Major Brent saw Robert Toombs come out of the woods with a small group of men. Toombs was gloomy, believing the door to Richmond wide open. He talked of large losses, and when Brent asked him where his brigade was, all the Georgian could do was wave his hands toward his little band and shake his head. Brent himself was horrified by what he had seen. Many men lay just out of the woods, probably having been slain by artillery fire. From the Mellert slave cabins Brent could see a line of dead extending completely across the Mellert fields until the trees and ravines on the Southern right sheltered them from his eyesight. This line came forward to where he was, the sides angling in to form a right triangle with its apex at about where he stood on the west side of the Willis Church road. Surveying the point of furthest penetration, he saw the body of one Confederate about ten yards in front of the rest. He tried to find out at least what regiment the man had belonged to, but no one knew.

John Hinsdale, marching toward Malvern Hill with Longstreet's and Hill's divisions, noticed the trees damaged by grapeshot and shells, but he also saw the position of Willie Pegram's battery covered with dead horses. George Washington Hall of the 14th Georgia, also moving onto the field, noted in his diary that he could not find the words to describe the scene. Washington Hands of the Maryland Line found that shell fragments caused most of the "dreadful" wounds. "[M]ost of the killed were horribly mangled," and many suffered the increased indignity of having tree limbs weakened by artillery fire fall on top of them. Howard Walthall of the 1st Virginia wrote in 1913, "Thoughts of the ghastly sight sicken me to this day."[10]

While some Southerners pondered the past, others planned the future. Robert E. Lee was at the Poindexter house, where word reached him from local residents that the Yankees were demoralized. He also heard this from Stuart, who had taken the cavalry previously left with the army to find out where the Federals were. Jeb's troopers captured them by the score and found all sorts of equipment lying along the roads. With Jackson present, Lee was dictating messages when Longstreet came in from the rain. Old Pete wrote later that the day opened "heavy and oppressive," and his mood seemed to reflect it. He asked Marse Robert if any messengers were headed to Richmond. Told there would be, he asked Lee to send word to Mrs. Longstreet that her husband had survived. "Oh, General Longstreet, will you not write yourself?" Lee replied. "Is it not due to your good lady after these tremendous events?" Longstreet sat down and wrote a few lines. When he finished, Lee asked if he had ridden across the field. Longstreet said he had seen just about all of it. Lee inquired about his impressions, and Longstreet said, "I think you hurt them about as much as they hurt you." This was as charitable a way of putting the result as could be found, and Lee's response was only, "then I am glad we punished them well, at any rate."

Perhaps at this point orders for movements were given, for Longstreet and A. P. Hill began moving. Lee and Jackson continued to discuss pursuit possibilities, and after a while Jefferson Davis arrived, having tried in vain to find enough whiskey to give all the men some to ease the chill of the rain. Lee apparently was not expecting him, and forgetting the proper salutation said, "President, I am delighted to see you." Davis saw Jackson. The two had never met, but Jackson was unhappy with Davis because of a perceived slight, so when Lee introduced the two with the comment, "Why, President, don't you know General Jackson? This is our Stonewall Jackson," all Jackson did was salute, and Davis contented himself with a bow.

President and commander discussed possibilities while Jackson remained mostly silent. Eventually it was decided that, given the rain and confusion, large-scale pursuit was not a good idea. Jackson was the only person who disagreed, saying, "They have not all got away if we go immediately after them." A swift march could have overtaken some of the Federals if performed by the units closest to the enemy. Lee had ordered a similar maneuver the day after Gaines's Mill in sending Ewell to cut the railroad. Ewell's men had been in the thick of the Gaines's Mill fight, so it was possible to march the day after a major battle. But there were two crucial differences. First, Ewell on the twenty-eighth was not pursuing an entire army. Following McClellan on July 2 with only one division would have invited trouble; a substantial portion of the army would be needed to accomplish anything. Second, it did not rain the day after Gaines's Mill and the roads were in good shape. The day after Malvern Hill, even the roads not used by the retreating Yankees would have been terrible to start with and worse as the day went on. A fresh division, albeit a small one (Peck's), was waiting along the River road. Going east from Glendale and then turning south would be possible with some of Lee's force but not all of it. Moving everyone east would leave Richmond wide open in case the Unionists were in better shape than was supposed. It would also take longer, as the march from Glendale via the Long Bridge road and Nance's Shop to a position north of Harrison's Landing called Evelington Heights was about thirteen miles. The more direct route to Evelington Heights that split off the River road just east of Turkey Island Bridge was less than ten miles. Neither route would allow Lee to threaten the trains on the River road; instead they would place Lee in a position to threaten the Army of the Potomac in its new camp.

Then there is the undeniable fact that much of the Army of Northern Virginia was in no condition to march on the second. Jackson (minus D. H. Hill), Longstreet, and A. P. Hill (about 33,000 men) would be ready to move. The latter two (16,000 men) marched about two miles, camping near the Poindexter house. A march of the same distance by Stonewall's 17,000 men would have left them short of Turkey Island Bridge. This hardly would have been an effective pursuit, for even if they moved faster they would have had to fight Peck's men and probably Smith's division to reach the trains. Little could have been accomplished except to position the rebels a bit closer to the Yankees, and Lee decided to organize things first. It is hard to fault him for that.[11]

Jackson's men bivouacked near Willis Church. D. H. Hill spent the day—in fact the next week—removing the wounded, burying the dead, and generally cleaning up. Magruder's and Huger's men were engaged in the same activities on their parts of the field. Theophilus Holmes turned around at Lee's order and moved back to Drewry's Bluff, leaving Henry Wise's force at Chaffin's Bluff on the north side of the James. By the afternoon, Lee heard reports that McClellan might try to move the Army of the Potomac to the south side of the river, in which case Drewry's Bluff could be taken and the water route to Richmond opened for the Federal gunboats. He kept Magruder, Huger (including Ransom's brigade, only temporarily a part of the division), and D. H. Hill in the Malvern Hill area partially to guard against this possibility.[12]

While the Confederates were resting, burying the dead, and caring for the wounded of both sides, the Federals moved into their new campground. The headquarters camp and troops made it to the landing between 2 and 3 A.M. on July 2, missing the rain but enduring suffocating dust. The reserve artillery arrived beginning about 6 A.M. Morell, and probably Couch, pulled off the road beginning at sunrise as well. William Weeden's battery arrived at 4 A.M., but some regiments were on the road as late as 9 A.M. Slocum's division began arriving early in the morning after its relatively short march. One man was stuck in the mud on the way, and Slocum grabbed him by the coat collar, pulled him out of his too-large boots, and swung the soldier onto his horse. Once William Westervelt of the 27th New York arrived at the landing, he offered a quartermaster's department officer a silver dollar for four small biscuits, but the officer replied, "I don't keep a bake shop." Just then the officer's attention was diverted, and Westervelt grabbed six biscuits and left. Westervelt then encountered a black man carrying a boiled hog's nose and threatened to shoot him. The man gave Westervelt the meat, which tasted better than anything he could remember.

Some of Sumner's men made it to Harrison's Landing as early as 8 A.M. The 5th New Hampshire, left behind and not leaving the hill until 5 A.M., reached the river at about eleven. Sedgwick's men, though having started late, "went at a Hell of a rate" once they got going, according to one soldier. The head of the column arrived at 10 A.M., while some of the rear units took until 2 P.M. Heintzelman made it to the new base "early in the day." Some of his regiments were there by 8 A.M., although others did not arrive until the afternoon. Baldy Smith pushed his men to their assigned spot shortly after noon. Warren's men, at the rear of the main body, did not make it to camp until 5 P.M. Averell's force, having cleared Peck's positions, also made it to Harrison's Landing late in the day, the 3rd Pennsylvania Cavalry arriving after dark. On the way, some of Buchanan's regulars came upon several abandoned boxes of hardtack and dug in, hoping to find some dry pieces in the bottom of the box.[13]

As the men arrived they came upon what Alexander Bliss called a "deplorable" scene. The wheat field at the landing was, according to one account, "one of the most beautiful fields of grain the eye of man ever beheld." However, the rain and traffic had turned it and other fields into bogs. Soldiers huddled under any shelter they could find. Some sat in the rain for five or six hours. One camp was in a wood where the mud was three feet deep. Those who could gathered up straw for their beds and used the wheat for food. The new arrivals also met officers calling out the names of units and directing the soldiers to their proper locations. "It was like the hack-drivers at a railroad station in the city," recalled a member of the Irish Brigade. Even then, some men—like regular Jonathan Hager—could not find their units, walking back and forth across the fields with the mud oozing through their shoes.

Vermonter J. B. Pollard wrote in his diary, "What a sense of relief comes over us as we see the black hulls of the boats and their huge guns." William Burns of the 71st Pennsylvania wrote in his diary that he and his mates were "very thankful for being spared." Some were even willing to laugh at themselves, covered with smoke, powder, and probably mud. Porter wrote that "freed from care and oblivious of danger, all slept a long sleep." Baldy Smith slept from three in the afternoon until eight the next morning. Engineer Ira Spaulding went to bed in wet clothes without having eaten all day and slept for sixteen hours with only five minutes' wakefulness. Edward Acton of the 5th New Jersey lay on a rubber blanket with no pillow. "No feather bed or luxurious couch upon which I had ever rested gave so much comfort," he said later. Yet with the rainstorm, the knee-deep mud in what had been fields around the Berkeley and Westover plantations, the loss of comrades, and the retreat, the men could not help but be miserable and demoralized. A cavalryman wrote home, "this was the bluest Wednesday morning of my life." A chaplain called the men "a jaded, muddy, wet, and dirty looking crowd," and a surgeon said they were "drenched and tired, hungry, and dissatisfied."[14]

George McClellan stayed on the *Galena* the night after Malvern Hill and arrived at Harrison's Landing the next day. He probably found a message from Lincoln saying, "If you think you are not strong enough to take Richmond just now, I do not ask you to try just now." Lincoln promised to strengthen McClellan as fast as he could but told Little Mac that his request for fifty thousand troops was "absurd." McClellan, still exhausted, sent a reply to Lincoln announcing the army's arrival and explaining that he had yielded ground because he had been cut off from his supply base. He also wrote his wife, beginning to tell her about the battles, but cut it short, explaining that he was "very tired, & may require all my energies tomorrow." The 18th Massachusetts of Martindale's brigade had arrived on July 1 with the first boatloads of supplies from the White House. It and the 17th New York of Butterfield's brigade (which stopped at West Point on the York River to destroy the property there) rejoined their brigades on the second. Most important, Brig. Gen. Orris S. Ferry arrived with five thousand men of Brig. Gen. James Shields's division from the Shenandoah Valley. McClellan was grateful, telling Lincoln, "Every thousand men you send at once will help me much." Ferry's arrival as the vanguard of Shields's division not only lifted some spirits, it allowed some of the retreating Unionists to eat. The 5th Wisconsin procured twenty-three hardtack crackers a man from Shields's supplies.

The only Northerners not yet at Harrison's Landing by the evening of the second were Peck's two brigades and part of the army's trains. Peck ordered Wessells's troops to a position behind Naglee after Averell had passed. The 85th New York acted as the rear guard for the trains and destroyed some wagons that could not be removed. Once Wessells was in position again, Naglee's brigade crossed Kimage's Creek about three miles southeast of Haxall's, four miles from Turkey Island Bridge, and three miles from the Berkeley and Westover plantations. As Naglee's men marched, they saw deserted wagons, teams stuck in the mud, and dead mules all along the route.

By that point in the day, all the roads had been ruined. Kimage's Creek could be crossed only one wagon at a time in any event, so nearly a thousand wagons quickly accumulated west of the creek. By 5 P.M., Peck recognized there was no chance all the wagons could cross that evening, so he put Wessells's men in position just west of Kimage's Creek and supported them with some of the 8th Pennsylvania Cavalry and Miller's battery.

These Yankees had to put up with Stuart's men. Jeb kept busy picking up stragglers and equipment along the River road, but he sent Will T. Martin with the Jeff Davis Legion and the 4th Virginia Cavalry, accompanied by one of Pelham's howitzers, to bother the Federal rear guard. Martin had taken one detachment down to Haxall's Landing and captured some Yankees and mules right underneath the nose of the *Monitor*, if the reports can be believed. Martin then scattered some bluecoats near Shirley and followed them toward Harrison's Landing. He ran into Wessells's brigade, interrupting some Unionists who were boiling coffee. Some skirmishing occurred before the rebels moved back.[15]

In the morning, Stuart had scouted toward Charles City Court House with an eye toward harassing McClellan's flank if the Yankees were moving past Harrison's Landing down the Peninsula. No Union soldier had passed that way in the morning, and Stuart thought he could cause a disturbance if any came down the River road. He sent Pelham with the other howitzer and a squadron of the 1st Virginia Cavalry to the River road between Shirley and Charles City Court House to examine matters.

Pelham found the Yankees in their camps at Harrison's Landing and Evelington Heights. Stuart received the gunner's report early in the morning on July 3. He sent the information to Jackson, from where it would be forwarded to Lee, and he also put his men in their saddles. The 9th Virginia Cavalry headed to the heights by a northern route past Nance's Shop to watch for any Yankees coming from down the Peninsula. The rest of his men headed down the River road.

Lee had already started Longstreet and Jackson with their commands down the same road as the sun came out for the first time in twenty-four hours.

Longstreet took the lead. But when Lee heard Stuart's report, which included information about obstructions on the River road, he decided to backtrack and go by the Long Bridge road (presumably on a similar track to the 9th Virginia Cavalry through Nance's Shop and then southward to Evelington Heights). For some reason, instead of merely turning the column around so Jackson could lead, Lee halted Stonewall so Longstreet could get in front again.[16]

Meanwhile Stuart had reached Evelington Heights. This was the area of the plantation of Edmund Ruffin, the fire-breathing secessionist and innovative farmer. The heights were a great position from which to shell the Federals. Rising some sixty feet from Herring Creek, a tributary that separated Harrison's Landing from the mainland on its north and east sides, they extended for about two miles downstream on the east bank of the creek from Roland's millpond. Herring Creek was impassable from the millpond to the river as much of the land was swampy. The only road out of Harrison's Landing was the one by which the Army of the Potomac had moved, and the heights commanded that road and the Federals' camps. If Lee could occupy the heights in force, he would be in a position to pin McClellan to the banks of the James. Little Mac's safety would depend on the gunboats' subduing the rebel guns. As a defensive position, Evelington Heights would be even stronger than Malvern Hill, because the Unionists would have to cross not a small creek but a tidal stream to attack up the heights. If Lee could block the River road with sufficient force he would have McClellan trapped, the Federals' only possible salvation being the navy.

At 9 A.M., Stuart sent Martin down Herring Creek to its mouth, and he told Pelham to open fire despite a staff officer's suggestion that it would be better to wait. One howitzer was not going to do much damage, but the Yankees did not know what they faced, and they panicked. Only supermen could have moved so quickly through the muck. Some Unionists were still trying to find their regiments, and others had just had breakfast, when the shells began falling. The whole army fell into line, but for a while nothing happened, and some troops' spirits sank again, figuring they were leaving their defense to the gunboats. Reports came to McClellan of an advance by a large Southern force as Little Mac was saying good-bye to Randolph Marcy, who was headed to Stanton with an explanation of the week's events. David Birney wrote home that McClellan was surprised at the news of the attack. Perhaps he was, but not for the reason Birney supposed. Apparently Little Mac had given orders to occupy the heights. Certainly he would have noticed the need to do so on July 1, and even if he had not, John Barnard had seen that need and had let McClellan know of it on July 2. In a note the engineer said, "we must immediately push our forces further forward or we are bagged." Little Mac was upset that his orders had not been followed, but he calmed the troops by riding in

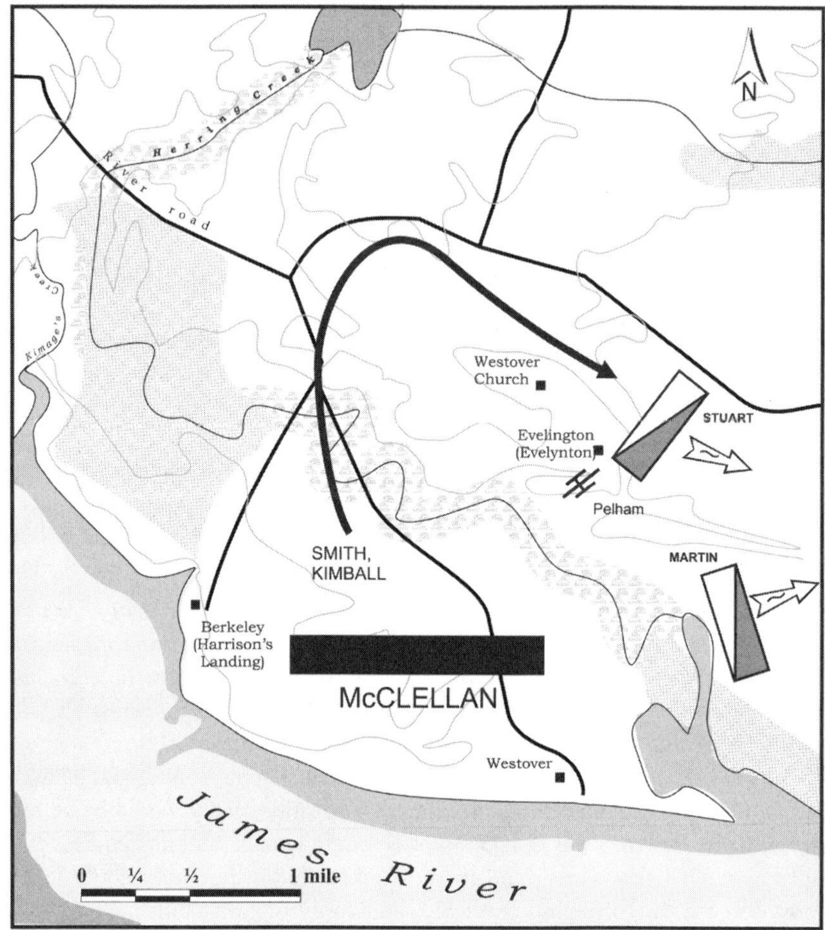

Evelington Heights, July 3, 1862

front of them, causing them to cheer as always. He also ordered Baldy Smith to take his men and a battery to the heights and take care of the rebels.

The commander of those rebels, Stuart, was hearing more from prisoners and residents about the Unionists' position and demoralization. Hearing also from Lee that help was on the way, he determined to hold his ground as long as he could. Pelham kept up his fire, but it would not stop much, and soon Smith arrived. Interestingly, Brig. Gen. Nathan Kimball's brigade from the Shenandoah was on the scene first, having been attached to Smith's division but taking orders from Erasmus Keyes to advance. Stuart's sharpshooters, posted in some brush along the road, fired into the newcomers, but Tidball's battery arrived and Jeb knew the game was up unless he got some infantry in position quick. At that point he learned that Longstreet was at Nance's Shop, still at least six miles away. Pelham fired his last two rounds at 2 P.M. and Stuart pulled back, as one veteran later wrote, "chuckling over the confusion he had produced in the camps of the enemy."[17]

It was no laughing matter. By firing with what he had to know was an impotent force, Stuart alerted the Federals to a major problem. Because of that, Lee lost the last opportunity of the campaign to inflict major damage on the Army of the Potomac. Yet there are several possible defenses for Stuart's actions. One is that Stuart believed infantry was close. But this is not much of a defense. He could have found out whether the infantry was close before firing. Even if reinforcements were close, what advantage would have been gained by waking up the Yankees before the foot soldiers were in position? A second defense is that McClellan certainly would occupy the heights on July 3. McClellan planned to do just that. But it had not been done, and whether it would be done would depend on McClellan's ability to inspire tired commanders to order the movement and tired troops to follow those orders in their disorganized state.[18]

It is possible that no infantry and artillery on the heights would be safe from gunboats or able to withstand their fire. The gunboats' reputation may have suffered after Malvern Hill, but with their large shells they still were capable of causing frightful damage, especially when the gunners could see their targets. Of course, no infantry were there to be tested. Stuart reported that guides had misled Longstreet, but the most likely route to take north, then east, then south from Malvern Hill to Evelington Heights does indeed pass Nance's Shop. Longstreet had moved perhaps eight miles after retracing his steps down the River road by 2 P.M. or a little before, not a bad march considering the road conditions. It is hard to believe he could have reached the heights much before nightfall unless he took a different road, and Lee had decided on the basis of information received that the River road (the only other possibility), although shorter, would be more difficult to use. Jackson covered less ground, and his command stretched out between Nance's Shop and Willis Church.[19]

None of this absolves Stuart from responsibility. It made little sense to open fire with only one gun. However, the great "opportunity" of the third was not really of the third but of the fourth, or the night of the third, and whether it truly existed depended entirely on the Federals. McClellan made sure there was no opportunity. He pushed Slocum to support Smith, put Heintzelman into position to the left of the VI Corps, and had Keyes on Heintzelman's left—three corps, more than half the army, on the heights or in supporting position—by late afternoon. Also by that point, the last of the trains were preparing to cross Kimage's Creek. Wessells, reinforced by the 56th New York and 104th Pennsylvania of Naglee's brigade, cut new roads, the engineers constructed new bridges, and new teams were hitched to the wagons. Still it took until 7 P.M. before Peck could report that all the wagons had crossed the creek. He then pulled Wessells's men back in stages, in absolute quiet—orders were whispered—and the 85th New York finally crossed the creek at 11 P.M. One man remembered a place where mattresses from a hospital wagon made an impromptu corduroy road across a particularly deep mud hole. The entire Army of the Potomac was finally in its new home.

Keyes and his subordinates deserved much of the credit for the trains, or most of them, getting to Harrison's Landing in decent shape. McClellan recognized this, telling Keyes so in person and praising him highly in his report of the campaign. It is interesting to note that despite hardly being used during most of the Seven Days, Keyes had a key role in two major parts of the retreat: finding a second road leading from the Glendale area to the James River and making every effort to speed the trains' passage from Haxall's to Harrison's Landing.

Robert E. Lee was still at Poindexter's. His fears for Drewry's Bluff had lessened with Stuart's reports, and he was keeping the rest of the army near Malvern Hill because he was not sure it would be needed. The next morning, the eighty-sixth anniversary of the signing of the Declaration of Independence, Marse Robert ordered David Jones's division to join Longstreet and Jackson and then headed down the River road himself.

Jackson, upset at the slow pace of the third, marched no later than dawn. Longstreet's advance had neared the heights the evening of the third, and Old Pete rode to the front the morning of the fourth to see where the Federals were. As units came in, Longstreet (apparently in direct charge of things as the senior division commander present) put them into line. Jackson moved directly in front of the heights, and A. P. Hill went to Stonewall's right to the Crenshaw farm between Herring and Kimage's Creeks. Jones's men, when they came on the scene, moved in on Jackson's left, extending the line along the heights.

Ewell's division, in front of Jackson's line, began engaging the Yankees with skirmish fire. These rebels came in contact with their old Valley enemies from Kimball's brigade. Longstreet was ready to attack but Jackson was not—or at least his men were not—so Old Pete asked Lee, who had arrived just after Jones's division, to decide the matter. Marse Robert saw a solid line of Federals on top of the heights, with artillery on the line and gunboats in the river. Instead of an easy push it would be a difficult attack. Lee was not sure his men could stand another hard battle at a time when a serious reverse could mean disaster. He walked the ground to confirm matters then made the only rational decision he could: to observe and not attack. He kept his headquarters a few miles north of the heights at the Phillips house in case further reconnaissance located a weak spot, but no such spot was found. On July 7 he ordered Ransom to rejoin Holmes's command and also sent Huger's division to the south side of the James River. On the eighth he ordered Jackson, Longstreet (including David Jones's division), and Hill back to the Richmond area, leaving Stuart to watch the Northerners. On the ninth he set up his headquarters back at the Dabbs house, already thinking of the next campaign, since this one was over.

For most of the men in the Army of the Potomac, July 4 was a day of reflection on what might have been and thankfulness that they were safe. One man wrote in his diary, "I expected by this date to be at home again if I lived." He described the celebration as "quiet," although McClellan ordered national salutes to be fired at noon and had the bands play. Little Mac wrote and delivered a congratulatory address to the men—one that a Wisconsin soldier called "entirely out of place." In a letter to his wife, McClellan said that if the rebels would let him alone for three days he could begin moving forward again. He told Marcy he was discouraged by a telegram from Lincoln. He asked the president for reinforcements.[20] Perhaps, having slept, he was the old George McClellan again, for better or worse. For him, too, the pages had turned and a new chapter opened.

CHAPTER TWENTY-ONE

"Under Ordinary Circumstances the Federal Army Should Have Been Destroyed"

THERE REMAINS THE SUMMING UP: the grim casualty numbers, the credit and blame, the importance of the battles in the war and for U.S. history. The angel of death had been busy on the Virginia Peninsula. The official totals for the Army of the Potomac were 1,734 killed, 8,062 wounded, and 6,053 missing for a total of 15,849 casualties. In addition, some of the missing, captured or not, were killed or wounded as well. Of the missing, 2,836 were from Gaines's Mill, including two regiments captured almost whole. Perhaps an equivalent number were captured when Savage Station was abandoned. Most of the rest would have been captured along the roads from that point to Harrison's Landing as the weak and wounded dropped out on difficult marches. Enough Yankee wounded fell into rebel hands that Lee reported taking more than ten thousand prisoners.

The Confederates, as the aggressors, suffered even more. Their numbers read 3478 killed, 16,261 wounded, and 875 missing, for a total of 20,614 casualties. Not only were they the aggressors and so would expect to experience higher losses, but they also occupied all the battlefields and so could account for their casualties more completely.

The casualty totals were extraordinarily high for that point in the war. Considered as one battle spread over seven days, it was not until Gettysburg that any campaign surpassed the total blood shed by Southerners. Only Antietam and Chancellorsville saw as many as ten thousand rebels hit. After Gettysburg, only Chickamauga as an individual battle came close to the Seven Days casualty total. The Army of Northern Virginia was never bigger than it was on June 26 after Jackson joined it, as the losses it sustained were never replaced.

The Army of the Potomac eventually recovered its losses, but that took time and the addition of units from other areas. Its official number of killed and wounded was surpassed, albeit slightly, by totals from several battles. But since some killed and wounded were almost certainly counted among the missing instead of their proper categories, it is likely that only Gettysburg, the Wilderness, and perhaps Spotsylvania Court House and Cold Harbor generated more Yankee killed and wounded than did the Seven Days. Truly a trail of blood ran from Beaver Dam Creek to Harrison's Landing, a distance of more than twenty-five miles.

Individual units suffered horrendous losses. The Palmetto Sharpshooters lost more than two-thirds of its strength at Glendale alone. The 1st South Carolina Rifles lost more than half its strength at Gaines's Mill, as did the 3rd Alabama at Malvern Hill and the 11th Alabama at Glendale. Four of Longstreet's six brigades lost at least 49 percent of their men during the campaign. Robert Rodes's brigade in D. H. Hill's division lost 41 percent at Malvern Hill alone. Longstreet's division as a whole lost more than 40 percent of its strength, D. H. Hill's division more than one-third, and A. P. Hill's division more than one-fourth. On the Union side, George McCall's division lost about one-third of its strength. George Morell lost more than one-fourth and George Sykes and Henry Slocum more than one-fifth of their men. The V Corps sustained more than half the total killed, and nearly half the wounded and missing, of the entire Army of the Potomac. The Pennsylvania Reserves in that corps suffered almost 20 percent of the entire army's casualties.[1]

When those numbers included a member of one's family they became far too personal. Newspapers were filled with lists of the killed and wounded. Both capitals turned into hospitals. Steamers came from the Peninsula to Washington bearing the wounded. They were taken off the ships and transported to hospitals with relief workers hovering over them. Families searched for the wounded and tried to reclaim the bodies of the dead. George Kenney, a lieutenant in the 71st Pennsylvania, was mortally wounded at Glendale. He died while under Confederate care on July 2 and was buried beneath an apple tree. His family tried for three years to bring his body home, but not until after the war could they retrieve it and bury it in Pennsylvania. Kenney's family was lucky: his grave marker was legible. Many others never saw their loved ones' resting place.

Richmond, nearer the battlefields, was even worse than Washington. "We lived in one immense hospital, and breathed the vapors of the charnel house," a woman remembered. People came from all parts of the Confederacy to nurse and comfort the wounded, but death still claimed its share, and graves could not be dug quickly enough to accommodate the dead. The hospitals and doctors were overwhelmed, and many wounded suffered from neglect. George Bagby wrote his son that people should be drafted to work in the hospitals and ease the suffering. Others' suffering could not be eased. At the same time the mother of Ellis Munford, a lieutenant in Greenlee Davidson's battery, was writing her daughters saying she would rather have her son a prisoner than in battle, Munford was killed at Malvern Hill. His body was delivered on a caisson to his home, where his unsuspecting family was on the steps trying to cool off in the evening sun.[2]

What did this suffering gain for the armies? The Army of the Potomac was safe after fighting a series of battles that each threatened at least a part of it, its supplies were secure, and it was in a strong position from which it had several strategic options. On the other hand, it was a lot farther from Richmond when the battles were over than it had been at their beginning, when the advance at Oak Grove had been seen as a preliminary to the final movement to seize the rebel capital.

McClellan thought it a success. He wrote in his report: "To the calm judgment of history and the future I leave the pronouncing upon this movement, confident that its verdict will be that no such difficult movement was ever more successfully executed; that no army ever fought more repeatedly, heroically, and successfully against such great odds; that no men of any race ever displayed greater discipline, endurance, patience, and cheerfulness under such hardships." In a letter to his wife he said, "You need not be ashamed of your husband or his army—we have accomplished one of the grandest operations of Military History." But he was writing from his own peculiar perspective, a world where nearly two hundred thousand rebels were consistently attacking with fresh troops, where his supplies were in imminent danger of being cut off, where his superiors did not support him, and where God had chosen him and his army to save his country, so it could not be risked for any possible gain. Many, and perhaps most, soldiers shared his perspective and so shared his view. One told his wife, "Under the circumstances I think he has accomplished a great feat," and another wrote that Little Mac had earned "a name not second to Napoleon." A Vermonter wrote his sister, "We have full confidence in McClellan yet; but wish that war department rest in Purgatory for not reinforcing him." The results even increased some men's trust. A Pennsylvanian wrote, "The troops have still greater confidence in General George B. McClellan than they have ever had."

Not all soldiers agreed with this judgment or held as high a view of McClellan as they had before the battles, however. A member of the Excelsior Brigade said, "McClellan was whipped," and later wrote, "I do not think McClellan has come up to the mark." And there was this comment from a Pennsylvanian: "He pretends that it was his intention to do just as he did but I believe he utters a falsehood when he says so, the boys do not have as much confidence as they used to."

The civilian reaction to McClellan split along partisan lines. Two groups emerged, one in favor of Stanton's hard-war approach and the other in favor of McClellan's opposing views. Democrats criticized Stanton and called for the politicians to stay out of military affairs. Yet many people had lost their confidence in the general. The press, despite restrictions, reported the results of the battles accurately, and most civilians could see when looking at a map that the army was much farther from Richmond after the week of battles than it had been. News of McClellan's July 1 trip on the *Galena* damaged his reputation. Even some conservatives abandoned McClellan. He was called either a traitor or an imbecile, and radicals criticized the administration for supporting him.

Abraham Lincoln continued to work with McClellan despite the criticism. To McClellan's July 2 telegram notifying Lincoln of the army's safety the president replied, "I am satisfied that yourself, officers and men have done the best you could. . . . Ten thousand thanks for it." But as McClellan continued to ask for reinforcements, particularly after Little Mac gave Lincoln a letter advocating limited war, Lincoln decided McClellan could never fight a decisive battle for Richmond and could not defeat the rebels with his form of warfare. McClellan's days in command of the army would end when Lincoln could find someone to replace him.[3]

More recent judgments have differed from Little Mac's not so much on the conduct of the campaign as it occurred as on the outlook that brought it about in the first place. The army was intact and had inflicted frightful losses on its opponent. It was in an undisputedly better strategic position. But he had given up the strategic basis of his campaign and had to start over. Because he was much farther from his objective, he essentially would have to pay for the same ground twice.

Most observers agree that the retreat or change of base (the word choice says something about whether one is for or against McClellan) was well executed. The army made it through safely. But it is difficult to give that credit to McClellan. He was bailed out when Erasmus Keyes found a second road to use. Had Keyes not done so, the trains would have been a larger impediment than they already were, and the Yankees would have had to hold on to their advanced positions far longer. McClellan also was helped by the fact that his corps commanders cooperated with each other in his absence. The mess at Savage Station, the potential disaster at Glendale, and possible problems at Malvern Hill all were directly traceable to McClellan's leaving the area and not designating a chain of command. The most critical day in this regard was June 30, and the three corps commanders involved in the action—Edwin Sumner, Samuel Heintzelman, and William Franklin—possibly saved the army by their willingness to work together. George McClellan had nothing to do with that. He did get the army moving, and he did guide its retreat in the general direction, but he had little choice in either of those areas.

The credit for the successful retreat must go to almost everyone but McClellan. Fitz John Porter was the principal Union field commander in three battles. In two of those battles he scored complete victories, and in the third he was overwhelmed after holding off superior numbers all day. He was not perfect during the campaign—his gaffe regarding McCall on the night of June 29 probably cost some lives—but his performance overall stood out brightly. Heintzelman led his corps well and pitched in elsewhere when needed, as he did at Glendale and Malvern Hill. He too was not without blemish, given his withdrawal from the Savage Station area on the twenty-ninth, but his record was close to Porter's, given the different opportunities. Sumner's tendency to be a field commander rather than a corps commander showed up at Savage Station, but at Glendale he also helped hold the Union line together. Franklin showed he might be a little timid, as at White Oak Swamp when he asked for reinforcements, but he returned those reinforcements and more to help at Glendale. Keyes, though not asked to fight, was the real reason the trains arrived at Harrison's Landing in as good a shape as they did. Henry Hunt, in command of the reserve artillery, was nearly flawless in the performance of his duties.

The division and brigade commanders almost without exception performed well. The breakthrough at Gaines's Mill and McCall's problems at Glendale were likely due more to the men's exhaustion than anything else, and very little else can be commented upon negatively. Most of all, any success achieved in the campaign has to be traced to the men, their fighting qualities, and their love for McClellan. The newcomers to the army, particularly McCall's division, performed admirably throughout the campaign. Few reports of regiments breaking without cause mar the record of either the infantry or artillery. Truly the Army of the Potomac showed its mettle during the week of battles.[4]

Whatever problems the Federals had were problems of perspective. McClellan could not see opportunities, and he could not bring himself to take advantage of opportunities he did see. Not only was he reluctant to shed blood needlessly, he tended to weigh the need to shed blood in an advance against the need to keep the army intact—and in that weighing, the need to save the army always came first.

His strategic vision seems sound until his version of reality is dropped and one closer to fact is adopted. He could have seized the strategic initiative on June 27 or even July 1 and possibly won the war, particularly on the twenty-seventh when the door to Richmond was at least ajar. At that point, Lee would have had to do some fast thinking and moving, the results of which are uncertain. That McClellan could not bring himself to do it, even when trusted advisers such as Porter urged him to, is his own fault—not Lincoln's, not Stanton's, and not Lee's. If his position was false, if his placement of troops was faulty through necessity, he had the chance to overcome those problems and did not.

In a July 10 letter to his wife, Little Mac wrote what may be his most truthful summary of the campaign: "My conscience is clear at least to *this* extent—viz: that I have honestly done the best *I* could; I shall leave it to others to decide whether that was the best that *could* have been done—& if they find any who can do better am perfectly willing to step aside & give way." Indeed, McClellan had done the best he could, but it was certainly not the best that could have been done, and in that sense the campaign and McClellan must be judged a failure.

The Northern public sensed that failure and reacted to it with a sense of despondency. Coming on the heels of the Valley campaign, McClellan's retreat gave even the festive Independence Day holiday a gloomy aspect. As the full story of the campaign became public, George Templeton Strong caught the country's mood by writing: "We are in the depths just now, permeated by disgust, saturated with gloomy thinking. I find it hard to maintain my lively faith in the triumph of the nation and the law." Democrats saw a chance to gain strength after the Republican-led failure, and radicals called for harder war even as Republicans throughout the country became discouraged.[5]

Perhaps as great as McClellan's sense of success was Lee's sense of failure. He was "deeply, bitterly disappointed" in the result. To his wife he wrote, "Our success has not been as great or complete as we should have desired." In his report he stated, "Under ordinary circumstances the Federal Army should have been destroyed." Since it was not, Lee must have considered the circumstances extraordinary. Yet by most measures, the campaign *was* successful. It forced an enemy army to fall back from the capital and regroup; resulted in the capture of many men, guns, and other supplies; and raised the morale of the people and the army. It is true that only one battle, Gaines's Mill, could reasonably be called a success. Three others could be called draws. One (Oak Grove) was a defensive battle, and the other two (Savage Station and Glendale) were parts of plans that failed with the inability to win the battles outright. Two others, Mechanicsville and Malvern Hill, were outright defeats. But despite the tactical failures, the Army of Northern Virginia had won the strategic campaign. Some of the soldiers recognized this. One wrote home, "We have whipped them badly but it has cost us thousands."

Civilian opinion mirrored military opinion. One man remembered the sentiment after the battles as joy chastened by sorrow and tempered by past events. There were regrets that the Yankees escaped, but thankfulness that the immediate danger was past. For some the disappointment was greater than for others. John B. Jones noted, "The people are too jubilant, I fear, over our recent successes near the city." Edmund Ruffin called the lack of complete victory "a great & mortifying disappointment." But even Ruffin celebrated the Union defeat. Politically, the victory lessened dissension within Confederate ranks. Jefferson Davis gained confidence and became more optimistic regarding possible European intervention, as did others. Overall, hope of final victory soared.

But Lee was not going for just those results. Trained in Napoleonic warfare, having seen Winfield Scott win against the odds in Mexico, Lee sought a knockout. Since he did not get it, especially after viewing the opportunities he had—opportunities that together have been called "the last and only opportunity for the Confederacy to win peace and independence"—he must have viewed the campaign as a failure—or at the very least, as one of his men put it, "We have gained a very complete victory but what good it is to do us is still to be seen."[6] Why was this the case? What were the extraordinary circumstances that prevented the destruction of the Army of the Potomac?

One was a circumstance not extraordinary at all: the changing nature of warfare. It had become almost impossible to destroy an opposing army. After the two major battles with discernible results—the Confederate victory at Gaines's Mill and the Union victory at Malvern Hill—the victors were in all likelihood too exhausted to follow up their success. It was no longer possible to wheel artillery to within two hundred yards of a defensive line, blast away, and then follow up with a bayonet charge. The gunners would be shot down and the attacking infantry would be decimated. Yet when faced with relentless attacks, the defenders became just as tired as the attackers, perhaps ran out of ammunition, and were often in need of reinforcement. Perhaps Lee had not seen enough of the consequences of the rifled musket to understand this yet.

Another less-than-extraordinary circumstance was the terrain. Full of good defensive positions behind little streams that created big problems and covered with woods and underbrush, the Peninsula was made for defensive fighting. The Northerners took full advantage of that. Even with complete information on enemy dispositions, Lee might have found it difficult to get troops down the few roads to the right places easily.

Another circumstance seems to have been problems with rebel subordinates. This is not to say that all of Lee's lieutenants were harshly criticized after the battles. Longstreet came out with an enhanced reputation, and deservedly so. Such criticism of Old Pete as existed for this campaign was probably due to his politics after the war, not his actions during it. The two Hills led their divisions in combat with great ferocity. Little Powell has been taken to task for his march across the Chickahominy, but in truth there is some evidence to acquit him of this charge and more evidence that Lee was not upset with him.

D. H. Hill's performance, like Longstreet's, left little to be desired. Jeb Stuart's escapades have been the subject of negative comment, but they likely had little effect on the results of the campaign. Theophilus Holmes's inactivity on the thirtieth and first likewise has been unduly examined. William Pendleton, the artillery commander, was a nonentity during the campaign, but because his force was split up, it would have been difficult for him to affect it much. The other brigade and division commanders did well except for some communication problems, such as Lawrence Branch and Richard Ewell on the twenty-sixth, the confusion in the area of Golding's farm on the twenty-seventh and twenty-eighth, and some missteps on the first.[7]

Benjamin Huger was almost a nonentity himself during the week of battles. His troops fought without him at Oak Grove, and on the twenty-ninth he seemed on a yo-yo not of his own making. On the evening of the twenty-ninth and thirtieth he was too tentative. At Malvern Hill he was again slow and eventually out of the fight, after holding up two brigades for some time. But only his inaction on the thirtieth had real consequences for the campaign. His share of the blame is small.

John Magruder's week could have been better. For example, the comedy of errors on the twenty-eighth, while not entirely his fault, occurred on his watch. But the blame he receives for his performance on the twenty-ninth—which certainly was not good—is overblown, as without Jackson nothing was going to be accomplished that day anyway. He did, through a misunderstanding, slow down Huger, but based on the latter's performance one is left to wonder what Huger might have achieved. It also is possible that by attacking even as late as he did Magruder did some of what he needed to do: hold up the retreating Unionists. He marched all over the Peninsula on the thirtieth, but he was ordered everywhere he went, so if he could have been used elsewhere, the fault is not his. On the first he took the wrong road, but given all the comments about the Confederate maps and the fact that his guides took him to the Quaker road, it is somewhat understandable. His actions that afternoon could have been improved upon, no question, and without them Malvern Hill might not have been fought, but the truth regarding that battle is more complex than simply saying, "Magruder messed up."

This was not how the soldiers themselves saw things. Both Huger and Magruder came in for criticism. When Robert Gray of the 22nd North Carolina wrote his father, "A part of our army was badly managed," he explicitly named Magruder and Huger. Another foot soldier said of Magruder, "Davis and Lee will never trust him again." And another North Carolinian remembered that Huger was the target of much criticism for slow movements. A Georgia mother who lost her son under Magruder's command wrote in a letter to Davis, Vice President Alexander Stephens, and the War Department, "The name of Butler is more agreeable in this bereaved neighborhood than

Magruder." Neither Magruder nor Huger would ever again command men in the Army of Northern Virginia, perhaps in part showing what Lee thought of their performances.[8]

One of these soldiers remembered that no one criticized Stonewall Jackson or Lee. In fact, Lee was seen as the savior of Richmond, and Jackson's star continued to ascend in the public's eye. More recently, however, Stonewall has received the lion's share of the blame for the failures of the Seven Days. Slow to get to Hundley's Corner, slow at Gaines's Mill, slow to cross the Chickahominy, stymied for no reason at White Oak Swamp, even inactive at Malvern Hill, Jackson is criticized for his actions (or lack thereof) on five of the seven days. But he did not set the timing at Mechanicsville, he was following orders and his understanding of the terrain at Gaines's Mill, he did as well as he could to repair the bridges and cross the Chickahominy, and his actions at Malvern Hill did not bring on the battle. Jackson's major failure was at White Oak Swamp, and there it was a complete failure with major costs for the Confederate cause. It was the only major failure of Stonewall's military career, and excuses regarding his health or mental state do not eliminate that black mark. Moreover, given his overall record, it was an extraordinary circumstance. Yet even this was not the sole cause of the failure of Lee's campaign.[9]

Lee himself looks good strategically. His plan at the beginning was a little complex in terms of timing, relying on a command many miles away to be at the right place at the right time. But it also was the right plan, the one plan that would get McClellan out of his lines and on the defensive. It took advantage of Little Mac's weakest point, concentrated force at that point, and used surprise in Jackson's arrival. His improvised plan of the twenty-ninth and thirtieth (the two days must really be considered the result of one plan) was masterful, bringing forces together at the decisive spot with a realistic chance of bagging part of the Union army. Again he was able to gather more men than his opponents had at that important spot. This was less complicated, with fewer timing problems, and if the Yankees beat him down the Willis Church road, more power to them. He did what he could with what he had. Even on the first, his strategic flexibility was not bad, although he could have investigated the eastern slopes of Malvern Hill and below earlier than he did. For Lee during the Seven Days, the devil was in the details, especially the tactical details of battle.[10]

It is not really correct to say that Lee failed tactically. He left those details to his subordinates, with a few exceptions, so the army's tactical failures must thus be laid at his subordinates' doors. Lee could, however, have paid more attention to this area, particularly given the organization of his army. This organization is one of the often-cited details. Others include the use of artillery and cavalry, Lee's staff, and the lack of information—particularly geographic information. The army was not as well organized as it could have been, with five or six independent commands depending on the period examined. Some of those were one division, others multiple divisions. The artillery, scattered among the brigades, was not as centralized as the more effective Union artillery. Lee inherited these problems. Inefficiency often exists in a transition period such as the Army of Northern Virginia experienced, and this inefficiency was one of the primary effects of the Seven Days being Lee's first battle. While the organizational problems did have an effect on the campaign, they were not crucial except in communication (which Lee could have overcome himself) and at Malvern Hill (where more centralized artillery might have been able to set up). Coordination between the infantry and artillery was a problem (although one caused by subordinates rather than Lee), but the ground and the fact that the Confederates were usually attacking prepared positions without much knowledge makes the lack of coordination understandable.

It is more difficult to see that the cavalry was misused. Certainly Stuart's movements could have been different, but Lee tried to get Jeb to reconnoiter the situation down the Chickahominy on the twenty-eighth, only to miss him. After that, however, the only possible misuse of cavalry was not to use it for reconnaissance on the first.

The only extraordinary circumstance Lee thought worthwhile to note in his report concerned information. The problems with maps cost Lee at Gaines's Mill, where adequate maps would have shown Boatswain's Swamp, and at Malvern Hill, where they would have shown roads to the east of the hill (not to mention clarifying the Quaker road issue). But it is unclear what might have changed. Lee's thinking at Gaines's Mill was that Porter would retreat down the north bank of the Chickahominy, something he would not have done. Jackson in an attacking position instead of a supposedly flanking position would have put more pressure on Porter's line earlier. This would have either caused a breakthrough earlier than actually happened, thereby creating the possibility of capturing much of Porter's force, or forced McClellan to send more reinforcements across the river in time to shore up Fitz John's line and prevent a breakthrough altogether. At Malvern Hill, Magruder would have arrived earlier, perhaps allowing a coordinated assault (which may or may not have succeeded), or perhaps merely making the uncoordinated assaults happen earlier and allow for even more killing in the fields. Otherwise, Lee's maps seem to have been adequate—they allowed him to point out the critical Glendale crossroads and get his men there. Perhaps better knowledge of the terrain might have helped at Malvern Hill, but the attacks did not happen until everybody could see the situation.

The problems with staff work show in three places: the lack of good guides, the lack of cooperation among units, and the lack of well-written orders. But at least two of these relate not only to Lee's staff, but also to Lee himself. The lack of good guides, at least early in the campaign, could have been solved by using Stuart's men. Jackson apparently had a good guide (Dabney's brother) on the road to Beaver Dam Creek, and his reticence prevented the guide at Gaines's Mill (a cavalryman) from picking the right route. Magruder's guides knew the area, they just did not know Lee's map. Other guides seem to have gotten the forces to the right places.

Lee picked the staff and had control of the officers. If there were coordination problems, they involved Lee. These problems resulted from bad communication between units and between Lee and his subordinates. It is hard to see what his staff could have done to change this without making things worse. If Lee had sent orders by his staff and those orders had been delivered in error or not delivered at all, then the staff could have taken the blame. The staff can take some of the blame for the lack of good information. But Lee should have made sure the information was gathered one way or another, and not assumed the staff he had picked would be as good as the staff Scott had in Mexico. After all, Lee was no longer on the staff; he was the commander. He did not communicate well throughout the campaign—principally with Jackson on the march to Mechanicsville, at Gaines's Mill, on the twenty-ninth, and at White Oak Swamp, but perhaps also with A. P. Hill at Mechanicsville and Huger on the thirtieth and the first. His communications with Magruder on the twenty-ninth, thirtieth, and first were manifestly problematic. This was not a staff problem, it was Lee's problem and that of other general officers, and it played a major role in much of the Seven Days.

The other major problem concerns orders. Beginning with General Orders no. 75, they were at least vague in spots, if not downright confusing. Jackson's role at the beginning of the campaign could have been spelled out more clearly. The order to Stuart on the twenty-ninth was seemingly at odds with Lee's thinking. The order for the possible assault at Malvern Hill was ludicrous on its face. Robert Chilton wrote all three orders, and this has caused much of the criticism of Lee's staff. But Chilton is only to blame if he wrote those orders and sent them himself, in which case he would have been worse than inefficient and Lee should have cashiered him quickly. Since he did not, one must assume Lee knew what Chilton was doing, which places the blame for the orders on Lee. Certainly that is the case with General Orders no. 75. The order on the twenty-ninth cannot be explained as easily, unless there was a misunderstanding between Lee and Chilton. Although that is possible, as the two had been working together for less than a month, there is no evidence of it. No one wants the order on the first to have come from Lee's mouth, but any other conclusion leads to incredulity. In the most realistic scenarios regarding these last two orders, Chilton and Lee must share responsibility.

In sum, Lee must bear a good bit of the blame for the disappointments of the Seven Days. Better communication and clearer orders would have helped his subordinates and men (who fought as hard and as well as their Northern counterparts) reap more from their efforts. Lee knew they deserved more: he noted in a letter that McClellan had escaped "notwithstanding our utmost efforts." Perhaps one of the extraordinary circumstances Lee meant was that he did not perform as well as he could have and would in the future.[11]

Most Southern newspapers did not see it that way. They, of course, did not have the perspective that Lee himself, writing eight months later, did. Their praise was high, except for a few anti-administration organs. Thus, one of the important military results of the campaign was its effect on morale. The campaign began a string of Confederate successes that would culminate in three separate invasions of Northern-controlled territory in the late summer and early fall (ending at Antietam, Perryville, and Iuka and Corinth). At least in the eastern theater of the war, the trend toward higher Southern morale and lower Northern morale would not turn around until Gettysburg. The Democratic gains in the 1862 elections in part stemmed from the Seven Days, although there is some question concerning that election's significance.

Another effect was the outcry in Europe over the very high casualty totals. This was particularly true in Great Britain and France, where the public clamor for intervention to stop the conflict (seen by many Southerners as necessary for victory) increased after the battles. In part this was a result of the casualties, but it was also due to pro-Southern sentiment. The British were joyous when the news arrived, and the press began cautiously to call for mediation between the two sides. The battles reinforced the British belief that the North could not defeat the South in a military sense. Some even believed the victory proved the South had made itself into a nation and should be recognized as such.

The French were, if anything, even more inclined to mediation. Their press issued repeated calls for this step. French emperor Napoleon III wanted to ask the British if the time for recognition was now, but he was persuaded to keep quiet. The pro-Union Russian government rejected a proposal for joint mediation by France, Great Britain, and Russia. Even so, the times were perilous for the Union. Lincoln may not have realized how close the British and French were to intervening in the conflict, but his representatives in Great Britain knew. Thomas H. Dudley, the consul in Liverpool, wrote that the danger of intervention had reached a peak. The U.S. ambassador in London, Charles Francis Adams, thought the North needed to link slavery explicitly to the war effort to prevent mediation by the antislavery British.

The British government was not prepared to intervene, however. Viscount Palmerston, the prime minister, and Lord John Russell, the foreign minister, believed that although the battles had brought mediation closer to reality, the time still was not right. To intervene, Palmerston believed, would mean supporting the South, and he was not ready to do that. In a speech during a long debate in August, Palmerston turned the pro-Southern Parliament to his view. Napoleon would not act without Britain, so mediation was again put on hold.[12]

These results are fairly important, yet the Seven Days has been ranked as one of the fifty-one most decisive battles in the history of the Western world, so there must be more to it than that. What makes the campaign so important in the history of the war, and in American and world history in general?

One decisive aspect is that it brought Robert E. Lee together with the Army of Northern Virginia. The combination would prove to be one of the most celebrated armies in world history. If the Seven Days had turned into a stalemate or a minor reverse for Lee, the combination may not have clicked as it did, or President Davis might have sought a different commander for the army. As it was, with a qualified success under their belts, Lee, his staff, his commanders, and the private soldiers got to know one another and gain confidence that would grow better over time. Lee also decided, with this campaign as his primary evidence, who he wanted in his army and how he wanted it organized. The results justified Lee's decisions. Without them, the war would not have lasted as long as it did.

The war also would have been shorter if the campaign had not undermined Lincoln's confidence in McClellan. After the Seven Days, Little Mac commanded the army in only one more active campaign—the Maryland campaign—and that was only because Lincoln felt he was the best man to pick up the pieces after John Pope's handling of the debacle at Second Manassas. This prolonged the war. McClellan actually was in a better position after the Seven Days (having a more secure base, for one thing) than he had been in before. If allowed to remain where he was, he might have chosen the strategy that ultimately led Ulysses Grant to victory over Lee: a move to the south side of the James River. But Lincoln had turned to others, and their attempts to take Richmond from the north would fail four times in the next seventeen months.

The most profound consequence of the Seven Days, however, was that its results forced the nature of the war to change, and with it the nature of the United States. McClellan's hopes for the Peninsula Campaign were simple: defeat the Confederate army, take Richmond, and force the radicals on both sides to retreat from their extreme positions so a peace could be negotiated. To think of what might have happened after a Northern victory, think of the following possibilities. Abraham Lincoln might have been a one-term president, perhaps in the league of James K. Polk. McClellan might have been elected president in 1864, as the peace he had won would have pleased moderates from both regions. Lee might at most have been a footnote in history, one of Scott's great staff officers, or perhaps the general who lost the Confederacy. Slavery might have continued past the Civil War, although it is likely that terms establishing a timetable for ending it would have been negotiated. The 14th Amendment to the Constitution, the basis of so much federal power, might not have passed. Reconstruction might not have occurred, and there thus might have been no basis for the Lost Cause myth.

Instead, the war went on. Lincoln issued a call for three hundred thousand troops while the battles were underway. The radical attacks on McClellan were aimed at Lincoln as well, and the Northern president heard the call for hard war. Democratic attacks on Stanton had little effect on Lincoln's thinking, and this response galvanized the administration's opposition. The "copperhead" movement of Southern sympathizers was a response to the tougher war policies, and they were a response to McClellan's failure to win the war without them. As the Confederate tide rose and foreign powers looked more closely at intervention, a window of opportunity opened for the South. The discussions regarding intervention reached their climax and the window began to close at Antietam Creek in September. One reason the window closed was that Lincoln explicitly linked the war to the end of slavery with the Emancipation Proclamation, which he drafted just three weeks after the Seven Days. That linkage had a profound effect on Britain and France. The Confederate reaction to Lincoln's move was the understanding that they were engaged in a fight to the finish. That chain of events started with the Seven Days.[13]

In the years that followed, Lincoln would become the nation's greatest president, Lee would become beloved by both sides, and McClellan would become both a failed general and a failed presidential candidate. Most importantly, the very idea of the United States changed. From a collection of states, or at most regions, each with a different basic loyalty, the country became a single nation during and following the Civil War, with sectional ties subordinated to the national government. It turned into a unified country with the most divisive question of its history settled. This change has taken a long time, and even now is not absolute. While complex, it can be stated simply: Before the Civil War, people said, "The United States are"; afterward they said, "The United States is." The beginnings of that transformation occurred on the Virginia Peninsula in late June and early July 1862.

APPENDIX A

Union and Confederate Troop Strengths

The question of troop strength during the Seven Days has been an issue since before the battles even took place. Allen Pinkerton's estimates were questioned even as they were given. Given Confederate claims of accomplishing great things with small numbers, and pro-McClellan claims that the Yankees were substantially outnumbered, the subject deserves exploration.

Union numbers are fairly straightforward, although they do require some adjustment. A return was reported on June 20 for McClellan's entire command, including the troops at White House and those at Fort Monroe. In that return, McClellan listed "aggregate present and absent," "aggregate present," and "present for duty, equipped" by division and other units. The most important number is "present for duty, equipped," and those numbers add up to 114,691.[1]

To find McClellan's effective strength on June 25 this number must be adjusted to remove troops not actually with the Army of the Potomac as well as noncombatants (engineers, provost and headquarters guards, and McClellan's general staff). Changes in numbers from June 20 to June 25 must be estimated, and attrition of several types taken into account to compare Union effective strength with Confederate effective strength. Thomas Livermore, in *Numbers and Losses in the Civil War*, has done most of this in what remains the most comprehensive analysis of Civil War numbers.[2] Livermore gives the army's effective strength as 91,169, with the note that estimating the cavalry at 85 percent instead of 93 percent would reduce this number by about 250.

The difference between Livermore's estimate and mine of 88,870 arises from minor disagreements, particularly with the number of troops at White House Landing (which are not broken out separately). Individually these disagreements amount to a couple of hundred men at most, with the exception that he does not reduce the June 20 number for sickness or casualties in the intervening five days. Since some skirmishing did occur and there was widespread reporting of sickness in the army, however, some adjustment must be made. The number is arbitrary, one-half of 1 percent loss per day, but much lower than Phil Kearny's note that the army was losing 1,500 men a day. It is safe to say that the Army of the Potomac had no more than 90,000 effectives on June 25. For any individual division the effective strength would be the June 20 number, minus about 3 percent for pre–Seven Days losses, minus the losses in any battles that had already occurred during the Seven Days.

Table 1: Estimate of Effective Strength, Army of the Potomac, June 25, 1862

Total present for duty, equipped, June 20	114,691
Staff, engineers, and guards	-2,585
At Fort Monroe	-9,246
At White House	-4,505
Present for duty, equipped, in combat units June 20	98,355
Loss in killed, wounded, and sick, June 20–25 (estimated)	-2460
Present for duty, equipped, in combat units June 25	95,895
Effectives (infantry at 93%, cavalry at 85% of previous number)	88,870

Confederate strength is at once easier and harder to pin down. No adjustments need to be made for troops in other areas, but there is no record of a return such as that provided by the Army of the Potomac until July 20, well after the battles were fought. Livermore's estimate for the Army of Northern Virginia was 95481, the highest estimate of anyone who does not have a pro-McClellan bias. But the problems with this estimate are greater than the problems with the Union estimate. He estimates that two brigades of Stonewall Jackson's division contain about seven hundred men per regiment. This number is too high considering the units' experiences during the Valley campaign and subsequent march to Richmond. Also, most Confederate commanders who reported strength reported "muskets," or "rank and file," or simply "men." What do these categories mean? Do they include officers? Do they include the artillery assigned to individual brigades or divisions? Livermore, with a few exceptions, believes that they mean neither. Since he is willing to add 7 percent to the effective strength for officers and up to a hundred men per battery, that decision is not insignificant on its face.

Other estimates that should be examined are those from Confederate officers themselves. Jubal Early estimated Lee's strength in some detail in a response to a letter from Joseph E. Johnston. Other detailed estimates from Porter Alexander and J. W. White exist.[3] These consistently show the Army of Northern Virginia as having eighty-five thousand or fewer men, and they consistently understate the numbers by not including officers and artillery. Early says that artillery is included in the published numbers and implicitly includes it in his estimates. One of Alexander's estimates says that it includes cavalry and reserve artillery. The other estimates are lists of numbers.

Alexander Lawton, D. H. Hill, John Magruder, four of James Longstreet's brigadiers, all of Benjamin Huger's brigadiers, A. P. Hill, and Theophilus Holmes all give strength figures in their reports, and most estimates use those numbers as their basis. Lawton does not include either artillery or officers. D. H. Hill does not seem to include either, although it is unclear. Magruder is unclear. Of Longstreet's brigadiers, James Kemper does not include either officers or artillery. Colonel J. B. Strange (reporting George Pickett's strength) includes officers but not artillery. Cadmus Wilcox does not seem to include either (he reports casualties among officers and men separately, but explicitly states only men with his strength figure). Roger Pryor also seems to include neither artillery nor officers. Of Huger's brigadiers, Robert Ransom seems not to include either (he refers to effective force). William Mahone includes officers but not artillery. Ambrose Wright seems to include only men in the ranks. Lew Armistead includes officers except for those of one regiment. A. P. Hill almost certainly includes artillery in his figure. Holmes is the most explicit, and he does not include artillery or officers in his report. All the estimates, including the ones used in this book, are given in the following table.

Table 2: Estmates of Effective Strength, Army of Northern Virginia, June 25, 1862

Unit	Early	Alexander (1)	Alexander (2)	White	Livermore	Burton
Whiting	4,000	4,000	5,300	4,000	4,182	4,186
Jackson	11,500	8,000	7,500	6,000	9,149	7472
Ewell	–	4,500	5,000	8,000	6,825	6,579
D. H. Hill	10,000	10,000	10,000	9,500	10,000	10,651
Longstreet	9,051	9,000	9,000	10,000	8,661	9,051
Magruder	13,000	13,000	13,000	9,500	13,000	14,179
Huger	8,930	9,000	10,500	8,000	8,138	8,564
A. P. Hill	13,000	14,000	14,000	10,000	14,000	14,000
Holmes	6,573	6,500	6,000	8,000	6,052	6,610
Pendleton	1,500	5,000	2,000	4,000	6,708	744
Stuart	2,500	–	3,000	3,000	–	2,500
Officers	–	–	–	–	5,859	5,236
Total	80,054	83,000	85,300	80,000	92,574	89,772

I have added artillery and officers (officers estimated at 7 percent) where my analysis above indicates either that they were not added or that it is unclear. Most of Livermore's artillery count shows up with Pendleton, whereas I count artillerymen with each division as appropriate. Early combines Jackson and Ewell, whereas Alexander (1) and Livermore combine Pendleton and Stuart. The principal differences between Livermore's number and mine are his estimate of Jackson's division and in the count of officers. Artillery and officers count for the principal differences between my estimate and those of the Confederates. I believe Livermore to be more correct in his method than are the Confederates, but surely he has overestimated the strength of Jackson's division.

In summary, the only certainty is that the two armies were very close in effective strength. My own view is that, including Holmes's command, Lee outnumbered McClellan by less than a thousand men. The difference was not as large in either direction as some partisans have wanted to believe.

APPENDIX B

Lee's General Orders no. 75

The following is the text of Lee's General Orders no. 75, dated June 24, giving the plan of battle that began the Confederate offensive of the Seven Days (*O.R.*, pt. 2, pp. 498–99).

I. General Jackson's command will proceed to-morrow from Ashland toward the Slash Church and encamp at some convenient point west of the Central Railroad. Branch's brigade, of A. P. Hill's division, will also to-morrow evening take position on the Chickahominy near Half-Sink. At 3 o'clock Thursday morning, 26th instant, General Jackson will advance on the road leading to Pole Green Church, communicating his march to General Branch, who will immediately cross the Chickahominy and take the road leading to Mechanicsville. As soon as the movements of these columns are discovered, General A. P. Hill, with the rest of his division, will cross the Chickahominy near Meadow Bridge and move direct upon Mechanicsville. To aid his advance, the heavy batteries on the Chickahominy will at the proper time open upon the batteries at Mechanicsville. The enemy being driven from Mechanicsville and the passage across the bridge opened, General Longstreet, with his division and that of General D. H. Hill, will cross the Chickahominy at or near that point, General D. H. Hill moving to the support of General Jackson and General Longstreet supporting General A. P. Hill. The four divisions, keeping in communication with each other and moving *en échelon* on separate roads, if practicable, the left division in advance, with skirmishers and sharpshooters extending their front, will sweep down the Chickahominy and endeavor to drive the enemy from his position above New Bridge, General Jackson bearing well to his left, turning Beaver Dam Creek and taking the direction toward Cold Harbor. They will then press forward toward the York River Railroad, Closing upon the enemy's rear and forcing him down the Chickahominy. Any advance of the enemy toward Richmond will be prevented by vigorously following his rear and crippling and arresting his progress.

II. The divisions under Generals Huger and Magruder will hold their positions in front of the enemy against attack, and make such demonstrations Thursday as to discover his operations. Should opportunity offer, the feint will be converted into a real attack, and should an abandonment of his intrenchments by the enemy be discovered, he will be closely pursued.

III. The Third Virginia Cavalry will observe the Charles City road. The Fifth Virginia, the First North Carolina, and the Hampton Legion (cavalry) will observe the

Darbytown, Varina, and Osborne roads. Should a movement of the enemy down the Chickahominy be discovered, they will close upon his flank and endeavor to arrest his march.

IV. General Stuart, with the First, Fourth, and Ninth Virginia Cavalry, the cavalry of Cobb's Legion and the Jeff Davis Legion, will cross the Chickahominy to-morrow and take position to the left of General Jackson's line of march. The main body will be held in reserve, with scouts well extended to the front and left. General Stuart will keep General Jackson informed of the movements of the enemy on his left and will co-operate with him in his advance. The Tenth Virginia Cavalry, Colonel Davis, will remain on the Nine-mile road.

V. General Ransom's brigade, of General Holmes' command, will be placed in reserve on the Williamsburg road by General Huger, to whom he will report for orders.

VI. Commanders of divisions will cause their commands to be provided with three days' cooked rations. The necessary ambulances and ordnance trains will be ready to accompany the divisions and receive orders from the respective commanders. Officers in charge of all trains will invariably remain with them. Batteries and wagons will keep on the right of the road. The chief engineer, Major Stevens, will assign engineer officers to each division, whose duty it will be to make provision for overcoming all difficulties to the progress of the troops. The staff departments will give the necessary instructions to facilitate the movements herein directed.

By command of General Lee:

R. H. CHILTON
Assistant Adjutant-General.

APPENDIX C
Jackson's Dabbs House Conference Memorandum

The following is the text of a memorandum kept by Stonewall Jackson of the June 23 conference at the Dabbs House, during which the plan for the Seven Days was finalized. Historians are unsure whether the memorandum is in Jackson's own hand, but Freeman's analysis, not contradicted by later writers, was that it was written either during the conference or very shortly afterward. The memorandum was first printed in Freeman, *Lee's Lieutenants*, vol. 1, pp. 499–500.

Maj Gen Jackson to be in position on Wednesday night on the Hanover Ct. Ho. Road, or near that road, about half way between Half Sink Bridge, and Hanover Ct. Ho. He will communicate to Maj Gen A. P. Hill, through Brig Gen Branch at Half Sink Bridge his position.

Gen Jackson will commence his movement, precisely at 3 o'clock Thursday morning, and the moment he moves, send messengers to Gen Branch in duplicate, to inform Gen Branch, who will immediately move himself.

Gen Jackson to move from his position down the second road from the Chickahominy, parallel to the first road, and near to it. Major Gen A. P. Hill, as soon as the movement of Jackson or Branch is shown on the other side of the Chickahominy, will push his columns across the Chickahominy at Meadow Bridge, turn to the right and move on Mechanicsville. Maj Gen Jackson will endeavor to come into the Mechanicsville Turnpike in rear of Mechanicsville.

Maj Gen Jacksons [*sic*] and Hill will unite here, and taking different roads bear down towards Coal Harbor, and on to York R. R. Maj Gen Longstreet to support Maj Gen A. P. Hill, and Maj Gen D. H. Hill to support Maj Gen Jackson. If practicable, it will be best for the supporting columns to take different roads from, but near to the main columns.

APPENDIX D
McClellan's June 28 Telegram to Stanton

The following is the complete text of the telegram sent by McClellan to Stanton at 12:20 a.m., June 28 (*O.R.*, pt. 1, p. 61).

HEADQUARTERS ARMY OF THE POTOMAC,
Savage Station, June 28, 1862—12.20 a.m.

I now know the full history of the day. On this side of the river (the right bank) we repulsed several strong attacks. On the left bank our men did all that men could do, all that soldiers could accomplish, but they were overwhelmed by vastly superior numbers, even after I brought my last reserves into action. The loss on both sides is terrible. I believe it will prove to be the most desperate battle of the war.

The sad remnants of my men behave as men. Those battalions who fought most bravely and suffered most are still in the best order. My regulars were superb, and I count upon what are left to turn another battle, in company with their gallant comrades of the volunteers. Had I 20,000 or even 10,000 fresh troops to use to-morrow I could take Richmond, but I have not a man in reserve, and shall be glad to cover my retreat and save the material and *personnel* of the army.

If we have lost the day we have yet preserved our honor, and no one need blush for the Army of the Potomac. I have lost this battle because my force was too small.

I again repeat that I am not responsible for this, and I say it with the earnestness of a general who feels in his heart the loss of every brave man who had been needlessly sacrificed to-day. I still hope to retrieve our fortunes, but to do this the Government must view the matter in the same earnest light that I do. You must send me very large re-enforcements, and send them at once. I shall draw back to this side of Chickahominy, and think I can withdraw all our material. Please understand that in this battle we have lost nothing but men, and those the best we have.

In addition to what I have already said, I only wish to say to the President that I think he is wrong in regarding me as ungenerous when I said that my force was too weak. I merely intimated a truth which to-day has been too plainly proved. If, at this instant, I could dispose of 10,000 fresh men, I could gain a victory to-morrow. I know that a few thousand more men would have changed this battle from a defeat to a victory. As it is, the Government must not and cannot hold me responsible for the result.

I feel too earnestly to-night. I have seen too many dead and wounded comrades to feel otherwise than that the Government has not sustained this army. If you do not do so now the game is lost.

If I save this army now, I tell you plainly that I owe no thanks to you or to any other persons in Washington.

You have done your best to sacrifice this army.

GEO. B. MCCLELLAN

Hon. E.M. STANTON

APPENDIX E
Chilton's June 29 Message to Stuart

The following is the complete text of the message sent by Robert H. Chilton, Lee's chief of staff, to Jeb Stuart and endorsed by Stonewall Jackson on June 29 (published in Chambers, *Stonewall Jackson,* vol. 2, pp. 59–60).

Gen'l Stuart

The Gen'l Comd'g requests that you will watch the Chickahominy as far as Forge Bridge, ascertain if any attempts will be made in that direction by the enemy, advising Gen'l Jackson, who will resist their passage untill reinforced. If you find that they have passed down below where they cannot cross, leave a force to watch movements which may be made, & recross yourself to this side for further operations. I am Sir Resply

yr obdt sert
R H Chilton
AAG

Hdqrs Charles City Road
June 29

3 h. 5 m. p.m. Genl. Ewell will remain near Dispatch Station & myself near my present position. T.J.J. [marginal note]

APPENDIX F
Orders of Battle

Army of the Potomac
Maj. Gen. George B. McClellan

II Corps
Maj. Gen. Edwin V. Sumner

1st Division
Brig. Gen. Israel B. Richardson

1st Brigade
Brig. Gen. John C. Caldwell

5th New Hampshire
7th New York
61st New York
81st Pennsylvania

2nd Brigade
Brig. Gen. Thomas F. Meagher
Col. Robert Nugent
Brig. Gen. Thomas F. Meagher

29th Massachusetts
63rd New York
69th New York
88th New York

3rd Brigade
Brig. Gen. William H. French

52nd New York
57th New York
64th New York
66th New York
53rd Pennsylvania
2nd Delaware

Division Artillery
Capt. George W. Hazzard

1st New York Light, Battery B
(Capt. Rufus D. Pettit)
4th U.S., Batteries A and C
(Capt. George W. Hazzard)

2nd Division
Brig. Gen. John Sedgwick

1st Brigade
Col. Alfred Sully

15th Massachusetts
1st Minnesota
34th New York
82nd New York
Massachusetts Sharpshooters (1st Company)
Russell's Sharpshooters

2nd Brigade
Brig. Gen. William W. Burns

69th Pennsylvania
71st Pennsylvania
72nd Pennsylvania
106th Pennsylvania

3rd Brigade
Brig. Gen. Napoleon J. T. Dana

19th Massachusetts
20th Massachusetts
7th Michigan
42nd New York

Division Artillery
Col. Charles H. Tompkins

1st Rhode Island Light, Battery A (Capt. John A. Tompkins)
1st U.S., Battery I (Lt. Edmund Kirby)

Corps Artillery Reserve
1st New York Light, Battery G (Capt. John D. Frank)
1st Rhode Island Light, Battery B (Capt. Walter O. Bartlett)
1st Rhode Island Light, Battery G (Capt. Charles D. Owen)

Corps Cavalry
6th New York, Companies D, F, H, and K

III Corps
Brig. Gen. Samuel P. Heintzelman

2nd Division
Brig. Gen. Joseph Hooker

1st Brigade
Brig. Gen. Cuvier Grover

1st Massachusetts
11th Massachusetts
16th Massachusetts
2nd New Hampshire
26th Pennsylvania

2nd Brigade
Brig. Gen. Daniel E. Sickles

70th New York
71st New York
72nd New York
73rd New York
74th New York

3rd Brigade
Col. Joseph P. Carr

5th New Jersey
6th New Jersey
7th New Jersey
8th New Jersey
2nd New York

Division Artillery
1st New York Light, Battery D (Capt. Thomas W. Osborn)
4th New York Light (Lt. Joseph Nairn)
1st U.S., Battery H (Capt. Charles H. Webber)

3rd Division
Brig. Gen. Philip Kearny

1st Brigade
Brig. Gen. John C. Robinson

20th Indiana
87th New York
57th Pennsylvania
63rd Pennsylvania
105th Pennsylvania

2nd Brigade
Brig. Gen. David B. Birney

3rd Maine
4th Maine
38th New York
40th New York
101st New York

3rd Brigade
Brig. Gen. Hiram G. Berry

2nd Michigan
3rd Michigan
5th Michigan
1st New York
37th New York

Division Artillery
1st Rhode Island Light, Battery E
(Capt. George E. Randolph)
2nd U.S., Battery G
(Capt. James Thompson)

Corps Artillery Reserve
Capt. Gustavus A. DeRussy

6th New York Light
(Capt. Walter M. Bramhall)
2nd New Jersey Light
(Capt. John E. Beam)
4th U.S., Battery K
(DeRussy, Lt. Francis W. Seeley)

Corps Cavalry
3rd Pennsylvania

IV Corps
Maj. Gen. Erasmus D. Keyes

1st Division
Brig. Gen. Darius N. Couch

1st Brigade
Brig. Gen. Albion P. Howe

55th New York
62nd New York
93rd Pennsylvania
98th Pennsylvania
102nd Pennsylvania

2nd Brigade
Brig. Gen. John J. Abercrombie

65th New York
67th New York
23rd Pennsylvania
31st Pennsylvania
61st Pennsylvania

3RD BRIGADE
Brig. Gen. Innis N. Palmer

7th Massachusetts
10th Massachusetts
36th New York
2nd Rhode Island

DIVISION ARTILLERY
1st Pennsylvania Light, Battery C
(Capt. Jeremiah McCarthy)
1st Pennsylvania Light, Battery D
(Capt. Edward H. Flood)

2ND DIVISION
Brig. Gen. John J. Peck

1ST BRIGADE
Brig. Gen. Henry M. Naglee

11th Maine
56th New York
100th New York
52nd Pennsylvania
104th Pennsylvania

2ND BRIGADE
Brig. Gen. Henry W. Wessells

81st New York
85th New York
92nd New York
96th New York
98th New York
85th Pennsylvania
101st Pennsylvania
103rd Pennsylvania

DIVISION ARTILLERY
1st New York Light, Battery H
(Lt. Charles E. Mink)
7th New York Light
(Capt. Peter C. Regan)

CORPS ARTILLERY RESERVE
Maj. Robert M. West

8th New York Light
(Capt. Butler Fitch)
1st Pennsylvania Light, Battery E
(Capt. Theodore Miller)
1st Pennsylvania Light, Battery H
(Capt. James Brady)
5th U.S., Battery M
(Capt. James McKnight)

CORPS CAVALRY
Col. D. McM. Gregg

8th Pennsylvania

V CORPS
Brig. Gen. Fitz-John Porter

1ST DIVISION
Brig. Gen. George W. Morell

1ST BRIGADE
Brig. Gen. John H. Martindale

2nd Maine
18th Massachusetts (detached with Stoneman)
22nd Massachusetts
1st Michigan
13th New York
25th New York
Massachusetts Sharpshooters (2nd Company)

2ND BRIGADE
Brig. Gen. Charles Griffin

9th Massachusetts
4th Michigan
14th New York
62nd Pennsylvania

3RD BRIGADE
Brig. Gen. Daniel Butterfield

12th New York
17th New York (detached with Stoneman)
44th New York
16th Michigan
83rd Pennsylvania
Michigan Sharpshooters (Brady's Company)

DIVISION ARTILLERY
Capt. William B. Weeden

Massachusetts Light, 3rd Battery (C)
(Capt. Augustus P. Martin)
Massachusetts Light, 5th Battery (E)
(Lt. John B. Hyde)
1st Rhode Island Light, Battery C (Weeden)
5th U.S., Battery D
(Lt. Henry W. Kingsbury)

DIVISION SHARPSHOOTERS
Col. Hiram Berdan

1st U.S. Sharpshooters

2ND DIVISION
Brig. Gen. George Sykes

1ST BRIGADE
Col. Robert C. Buchanan

3rd U.S.
4th U.S.

12th U.S.
14th U.S.

2ND BRIGADE
Maj. Charles S. Lovell

2nd U.S.
6th U.S.
10th U.S.
11th U.S.
17th U.S.

3RD BRIGADE
Col. Gouverneur K. Warren

5th New York
10th New York

DIVISION ARTILLERY
Capt. Stephen H. Weed

3rd U.S., Batteries L and M (Capt. John Edwards)
5th U.S., Battery I (Weed)

3RD DIVISION
Brig. Gen. George A. McCall
Brig. Gen. Truman Seymour

1ST BRIGADE
Brig. Gen. John F. Reynolds
Col. Seneca G. Simmons
Col. R. Biddle Roberts

1st Pennsylvania Reserves
2nd Pennsylvania Reserves
5th Pennsylvania Reserves
8th Pennsylvania Reserves
13th Pennsylvania Reserves (1st Rifles), Companies A, B, D, E, F, K

2ND BRIGADE
Brig. Gen. George G. Meade
Col. Albert L. Magilton

3rd Pennsylvania Reserves
4th Pennsylvania Reserves
7th Pennsylvania Reserves
11th Pennsylvania Reserves

3RD BRIGADE
Brig. Gen. Truman Seymour
Col. C. Feger Jackson

6th Pennsylvania Reserves (detached with Casey)
9th Pennsylvania Reserves
10th Pennsylvania Reserves
12th Pennsylvania Reserves

DIVISION ARTILLERY
1st Pennsylvania Light, Battery A (Capt. Hezekiah Easton)
1st Pennsylvania Light, Battery B (Capt. James H. Cooper)
1st Pennsylvania Light, Battery G (Capt. Mark Kerns)
5th U.S., Battery C (Capt. Henry V. De Hart)

DIVISION CAVALRY
4th Pennsylvania

CORPS CAVALRY
8th Illinois

ARTILLERY RESERVE
Col. Henry J. Hunt

1ST BRIGADE
Lt. Col. William Hays

2nd U.S., Battery A (Capt. John C. Tidball)
2nd U.S., Batteries B & L (Capt. James M. Robertson)
2nd U.S., Battery M (Capt. Henry Benson)
3rd U.S., Batteries C & G (Capt. Horatio Gibson, detached with Casey)

2ND BRIGADE
Lt. Col. George W. Getty

1st U.S., Battery E (Lt. Alanson M. Randol)
1st U.S., Battery G
1st U.S., Battery K (Lt. Samuel S. Elder)
4th U.S., Battery G (Lt. Charles H. Morgan)
5th U.S., Battery A (Lt. Adelbert Ames)
5th U.S., Battery K (Capt. John R. Smead)

3RD BRIGADE
Maj. Albert Arndt

1st Battalion New York Light, Battery A (Capt. Otto Diederichs)
1st Battalion New York Light, Battery B (Capt. Adolph Voegelee)
1st Battalion New York Light, Battery C (Capt. John Knieriem)
1st Battalion New York Light, Battery D (Capt. Grimm)

4TH BRIGADE
Maj. E. R. Petherbridge

Maryland Light, Battery A (Capt. John W. Wolcott)
Maryland Light, Battery B (Capt. Alonzo Snow)

5TH BRIGADE
Capt. J. Howard Carlisle

2nd U.S., Battery E (Carlisle)
3rd U.S., Batteries F and K (Capt. La Rhett L. Livingston)

SIEGE TRAIN
1st Connecticut Heavy (Col. Robert O. Tyler)

VI Corps
Brig. Gen. William B. Franklin

1st Division
Brig. Gen. Henry W. Slocum

1st Brigade
Brig. Gen. George W. Taylor
1st New Jersey
2nd New Jersey
3rd New Jersey
4th New Jersey

2nd Brigade
Col. Joseph J. Bartlett
5th Maine
16th New York
27th New York
96th Pennsylvania

3rd Brigade
Brig. Gen. John Newton
18th New York
31st New York
32nd New York
95th Pennsylvania

Division Artillery
Massachusetts Light, 1st Battery (A) (Capt. Josiah Porter)
1st New Jersey Light (Capt. William Hexamer)
2nd U.S., Battery D (Lt. Emory Upton)

2nd Division
Brig. Gen. William F. Smith

1st Brigade
Brig. Gen. Winfield S. Hancock
6th Maine
43rd New York
49th Pennsylvania
5th Wisconsin

2nd Brigade
Brig. Gen. William T. H. Brooks
2nd Vermont
3rd Vermont
4th Vermont
5th Vermont
6th Vermont

3rd Brigade
Brig. Gen. John W. Davidson
7th Maine
20th New York
33rd New York
49th New York
77th New York

Division Artillery
1st New York Light, Battery E (Capt. Charles C. Wheeler)
1st New York Light (Lt. Andrew Cowan)
3rd New York Light (Capt. Thaddeus P. Mott)
5th U.S., Battery F (Capt. Romeyn B. Ayres)

Division Cavalry
5th Pennsylvania, Companies I and K

Unattached Cavalry
1st New York

Army Cavalry Reserve
Brig. Gen. Philip St. George Cooke
6th Pennsylvania
1st U.S., Companies A, C, F, H
5th U.S., Companies A, D, F, H, I
6th U.S.

Volunteer Engineer Brigade
Brig. Gen. Daniel P. Woodbury
15th New York Engineers
50th New York Engineers

Battalion U.S. Engineers

Troops at White House, Virginia
Brig. Gen. Silas Casey
11th Pennsylvania Cavalry, Companies B, D, F, I, K
1st New York Light, Battery F (Capt. William R. Wilson)
93rd New York, Companies B, C, D, E, G, I

Troops at Gen. Headquarters
McClellan's Dragoons
Sturges's Rifles
Oneida, New York, Cavalry
93rd New York Infantry, Companies A, F, H, K
2nd U.S. Cavalry
4th U.S. Cavalry, Companies A and E
8th U.S. Infantry, Companies F and G

Army of Northern Virginia
Gen. Robert E. Lee

Jackson's Command
Maj. Gen. Thomas J. Jackson

Whiting's Division
Brig. Gen. William H. C. Whiting

Hood's (Texas) Brigade
Brig. Gen. John B. Hood

18th Georgia
1st Texas
4th Texas
5th Texas
Hampton (South Carolina) Legion

Law's Brigade
Col. Evander M. Law

4th Alabama
2nd Mississippi
11th Mississippi
6th North Carolina

Division Artillery
Staunton (Virginia) Artillery Battery (Capt. William L. Balthis)
Rowan (North Carolina) Artillery Battery (Capt. James Reilly)

Jackson's Division

Winder's Brigade
Brig. Gen. Charles S. Winder

2nd Virginia
4th Virginia
5th Virginia
27th Virginia
33rd Virginia
Allegheny (Virginia) Artillery Battery (Lt. John C. Carpenter)
Rockbridge (Virginia) Artillery Battery (Capt. William T. Poague)

Jones's Brigade
Lt. Col. R. H. Cunningham Jr.
Brig. Gen. John R. Jones

21st Virginia
42nd Virginia
48th Virginia
1st Virginia Battalion (Irish)
Richmond Hampden (Virginia) Artillery Battery (Capt. William H. Caskie)

Fulkerson's Brigade
Col. E. V. Fulkerson
Col. E. T. H. Warren
Brig. Gen. Wade Hampton

10th Virginia
23rd Virginia
37th Virginia
Danville (Virginia) Artillery Battery (Capt. George W. Wooding)

Lawton's Brigade
Brig. Gen. Alexander R. Lawton

13th Georgia
26th Georgia
31st Georgia
38th Georgia
60th Georgia (4th Battalion)
61st Georgia

Unattached Artillery
Jackson (Virginia) Artillery Battery (Capt. W. E. Cutshaw)

Ewell's Division
Maj. Gen. Richard Ewell

Elzey's Brigade
Brig. Gen. Arnold Elzey
Col. James A. Walker
Brig. Gen. Jubal A. Early

12th Georgia
13th Virginia
25th Virginia
31st Virginia
44th Virginia
52nd Virginia
58th Virginia

Trimble's Brigade
Brig. Gen. Isaac R. Trimble

15th Alabama
21st Georgia
16th Mississippi
21st North Carolina
1st North Carolina Battalion
Henrico (Virginia) Artillery Battery (Capt. A. R. Courtney)

Taylor's Brigade
Brig. Gen. Richard Taylor
Col. I. G. Seymour
Col. Leroy A. Stafford

6th Louisiana

7th Louisiana
8th Louisiana
9th Louisiana
1st Louisiana Special Battalion
Charlottesville (Virginia) Artillery Battery
(Capt. J. Carrington)

MARYLAND LINE
Col. Bradley T. Johnson

1st Maryland
Baltimore (Maryland) Artillery Battery
(Capt. J. B. Brockenbrough)

HILL'S DIVISION
Maj. Gen. D. H. Hill

RODES'S BRIGADE
Brig. Gen. Robert E. Rodes

3rd Alabama
5th Alabama
6th Alabama
12th Alabama
26th Alabama

G. B. ANDERSON'S BRIGADE
Brig. Gen. George B. Anderson

2nd North Carolina
4th North Carolina
14th North Carolina
30th North Carolina

GARLAND'S BRIGADE
Brig. Gen. Samuel Garland Jr.

5th North Carolina
12th North Carolina
13th North Carolina
20th North Carolina
23rd North Carolina

COLQUITT'S BRIGADE
Col. Alfred H. Colquitt

13th Alabama
6th Georgia
23rd Georgia
27th Georgia
28th Georgia

RIPLEY'S BRIGADE
Brig. Gen. Roswell S. Ripley

44th Georgia
48th Georgia
1st North Carolina
3rd North Carolina

DIVISION ARTILLERY
Jeff Davis (Alabama) Artillery Battery
(Capt. J. W. Bondurant)
King William (Virginia) Artillery Battery
(Capt. Thomas H. Carter)
Long Island (Virginia) Artillery Battery
(Capt. P. H. Clark, temporarily attached)
Capt. R. A. Hardaway's Alabama Battery
Hanover (Virginia) Artillery Battery
(Capt. George W. Nelson)
Richmond Orange (Virginia) Artillery Battery
(Lt. C. W. Fry, temporarily attached)
Capt. A. Burnet Rhett's (South Carolina)
Battery (temporarily attached)

MAGRUDER'S COMMAND
Maj. Gen. John B. Magruder

JONES'S DIVISION
Brig. Gen. David R. Jones

TOOMBS'S BRIGADE
Brig. Gen. Robert Toombs

2nd Georgia
15th Georgia
17th Georgia
20th Georgia

G. T. ANDERSON'S BRIGADE
Col. George T. Anderson

1st Georgia Regulars
7th Georgia
8th Georgia
9th Georgia
11th Georgia

DIVISION ARTILLERY
Wise (Virginia) Artillery Battery
(Capt. James S. Brown)
Washington (South Carolina) Artillery Battery
(Capt. James F. Hart)
Sumter (Georgia) Artillery, Company E
(Capt. John Lane, temporarily attached)
Madison (Louisiana) Artillery Battery
(Capt. George F. Moody)
Ashland (Virginia) Artillery Battery
(Lt. James Woolfolk, temporarily attached)
Capt. W. J. Dabney's (Virginia) Battery

MCLAWS'S DIVISION
Maj. Gen. Lafayette McLaws

SEMMES'S BRIGADE
Brig. Gen. Paul J. Semmes

10th Georgia
53rd Georgia
5th Louisiana
10th Louisiana
15th Virginia
32nd Virginia
Capt. Basil C. Manly's (North Carolina) Battery

Kershaw's Brigade
Brig. Gen. Joseph B. Kershaw

2nd South Carolina
3rd South Carolina
7th South Carolina
8th South Carolina
Alexandria (Virginia) Artillery Battery (Capt. Del Kemper)

Magruder's Division

Cobb's Brigade
Brig. Gen. Howell Cobb

16th Georgia
24th Georgia
Cobb's Legion (Georgia)
2nd Louisiana
15th North Carolina
Troup (Georgia) Artillery Battery (Capt. Henry H. Carlton)

Griffith's Brigade
Brig. Gen. Richard Griffith
Col. William Barksdale

13th Mississippi
17th Mississippi
18th Mississippi
21st Mississippi
1st Company, Richmond (Virginia) Howitzers (Capt. E. S. McCarthy)

Division Artillery
Col. Stephen D. Lee

Amherst (Virginia) Artillery Battery (Capt. Thomas J. Kirkpatrick, temporarily attached)
Magruder (Virginia) Artillery Battery (Capt. T. Jeff Page Jr.)
Pulaski (Georgia) Artillery Battery (Capt. J. P. W. Read)
James City (Virginia) Artillery Battery (Capt. L. W. Richardson)

Longstreet's Division
Maj. Gen. James Longstreet

Kemper's Brigade
Brig. Gen. James L. Kemper

1st Virginia
7th Virginia
11th Virginia
17th Virginia
24th Virginia
Loudoun (Virginia) Artillery Battery (Capt. Arthur L. Rogers)

R. H. Anderson's Brigade
Brig. Gen. Robert H. Anderson
Col. Micah Jenkins

2nd South Carolina Rifles
4th South Carolina
5th South Carolina
6th South Carolina
Palmetto Sharpshooters (South Carolina)

Pickett's Brigade
Brig. Gen. George E. Pickett
Col. Eppa Hunton
Col. John B. Strange

8th Virginia
18th Virginia
19th Virginia
28th Virginia
56th Virginia

Wilcox's Brigade
Brig. Gen. Cadmus M. Wilcox

8th Alabama
9th Alabama
10th Alabama
11th Alabama
Thomas (Virginia) Artillery Battery (Capt. Edwin J. Anderson)

Pryor's Brigade
Brig. Gen. Roger A. Pryor

14th Alabama
2nd Florida
14th Louisiana
1st Louisiana Battalion
3rd Virginia
Donaldsonville (Louisiana) Artillery Battery (Capt. Victor Maurin)

Featherston's Brigade
Brig. Gen. Winfield S. Featherston

12th Mississippi
19th Mississippi
2nd Mississippi Battalion
3rd Company, Richmond (Virginia) Howitzers (Capt. Benjamin H. Smith Jr.)

Division Artillery
1st Company, Washington (Louisiana) Artillery (Capt. Charles W. Squires)
2nd Company, Washington (Louisiana) Artillery (Capt. John B. Richardson)
3rd Company, Washington (Louisiana) Artillery (Capt. M. B. Miller)
4th Company, Washington (Louisiana) Artillery (Capt. Joseph Norcom)
Lynchburg (Virginia) Artillery Battery (Capt. James Dearing)
Dixie (Virginia) Artillery Battery (Capt. William H. Chapman)

Huger's Division
Maj. Gen. Benjamin Huger

Mahone's Brigade
Brig. Gen. William Mahone

6th Virginia
12th Virginia
16th Virginia
41st Virginia
49th Virginia
Portsmouth (Virginia) Artillery Battery (Capt. Carey F. Grimes)
Lynchburg Beauregard (Virginia) Artillery Battery (Capt. M. N. Moorman)

Wright's Brigade
Brig. Gen. Ambrose R. Wright

44th Alabama
3rd Georgia
4th Georgia
22nd Georgia
1st Louisiana
Company D, Virginia Light Artillery (Capt. Frank Huger)
Company A, Sumter (Georgia) Artillery (Capt. H. M. Ross, temporarily attached)

Armistead's Brigade
Brig. Gen. Lewis A. Armistead

9th Virginia
14th Virginia
38th Virginia
53rd Virginia
57th Virginia
5th Virginia Battalion
Fauquier (Virginia) Artillery Battery (Capt. Robert M. Stribling)
Goochland (Virginia) Artillery Battery (Capt. William H. Turner)

Hill's (Light) Division
Maj. Gen. Ambrose P. Hill

Field's Brigade
Brig. Gen. Charles W. Field

40th Virginia
47th Virginia
55th Virginia
60th Virginia

Gregg's Brigade
Brig. Gen. Maxcy Gregg

1st South Carolina
1st South Carolina Rifles
12th South Carolina
13th South Carolina
14th South Carolina

J. R. Anderson's Brigade
Brig. Gen. Joseph R. Anderson
Col. Edward L. Thomas

14th Georgia
35th Georgia
45th Georgia
49th Georgia
3rd Louisiana Battalion

Branch's Brigade
Brig. Gen. Lawrence O'B. Branch

7th North Carolina
18th North Carolina
28th North Carolina
33rd North Carolina
37th North Carolina

Archer's Brigade
Brig. Gen. James J. Archer

5th Alabama Battalion
19th Georgia
1st Tennessee
7th Tennessee
14th Tennessee

Pender's Brigade
Brig. Gen. William D. Pender

2nd Arkansas Battalion
16th North Carolina
22nd North Carolina
34th North Carolina
38th North Carolina
22nd Virginia Battalion

Division Artillery
Lt. Col. Lewis M. Coleman

1st Maryland Battery (Capt. R. Snowden Andrews)
Charleston (South Carolina) German Battery (Capt. William K. Bachman)
Fredricksburg (Virginia) Artillery Battery (Capt. Carter M. Braxton)
Capt. William G. Crenshaw's (Virginia) Battery
Letcher (Virginia) Artillery Battery (Capt. Greenlee Davidson)
Capt. Marmaduke Johnson's (Virginia) Battery
Capt. L. Masters's (Virginia) Battery
Pee Dee (South Carolina) Artillery (Capt. David G. McIntosh)
Purcell (Virginia) Artillery Battery (Capt. William J. Pegram)

Department of North Carolina
Maj. Gen. Theophilus H. Holmes

Ransom's Brigade
Brig. Gen. Robert Ransom Jr.

24th North Carolina
25th North Carolina

26th North Carolina
35th North Carolina
48th North Carolina
49th North Carolina

DANIEL'S BRIGADE
Brig. Gen. Junius Daniel

43rd North Carolina
45th North Carolina
50th North Carolina
Burroughs's Battalion (cavalry)

WALKER'S BRIGADE
Brig. Gen. John G. Walker
Col. Van H. Manning

3rd Arkansas
2nd Georgia Battalion
27th North Carolina
46th North Carolina
30th Virginia
57th Virginia (also in Armistead's brigade)
Goodwyn (cavalry)

DIVISION ARTILLERY
Capt. James R. Branch's Virginia Battery
Capt. T. H. Brem's North Carolina Battery
Capt. Thomas B. French's Virginia Battery
Capt. Edward Graham's Virginia Battery
Capt. Charles R. Grandy's Virginia Battery
Capt. W. P. Lloyd's North Carolina Battery

WISE'S COMMAND
Brig. Gen. Henry A. Wise

26th Virginia
46th Virginia
10th Virginia Cavalry (serving with Stuart)
4th Virginia Heavy Artillery
Capt. W. C. Andrews's (Alabama) Battery
Capt. A. D. Armistead's (Virginia) Battery
Capt. D. A. French's (Virginia) Battery
Nelson (Virginia) Artillery Battery (Capt. J. H. Rives)

RESERVE ARTILLERY
Brig. Gen. William N. Pendleton

1ST VIRGINIA
Col. J. Thompson Brown

Williamsburg (Virginia) Artillery Battery (Capt. John A. Coke)
Richmond Fayette (Virginia) Artillery Battery (Lt. William I. Clopton)
2nd Company, Richmond (Virginia) Howitzers (Capt. David Watson)

JONES'S BATTALION
Maj. H. P. Jones

Long Island (Virginia) Artillery (Capt. P. H. Clark)
Orange Richmond (Virginia) Artillery Battery (Lt. C. W. Fry)
Capt. A. Burnet Rhett's (South Carolina) Battery

NELSON'S BATTALION
Maj. William Nelson

Fluvanna (Virginia) Artillery Battery (Capt. Charles T. Huckstep)
Amherst (Virginia) Artillery Battery (Capt. Thomas J. Kirkpatrick)
Morris (Virginia) Artillery Battery (Capt. R. C. M. Page)

RICHARDSON'S BATTALION
Maj. Charles Richardson

Fluvanna (Virginia) Artillery (Capt. John J. Ancell)
Capt. John Milledge's (Georgia) Battery
Ashland (Virginia) Artillery (Lt. James Woolfolk)

SUMTER (GEORGIA) BATTALION
Lt. Col. A. S. Cutts

Company D (Capt. James Ap Blackshear)
Company E (Capt. John Lane)
Company B (Capt. John V. Price)
Company A (Capt. H. M. Ross)
Capt. S. P. Hamilton's Battery

CAVALRY
Brig. Gen. J. E. B. Stuart

1st North Carolina
1st Virginia
3rd Virginia
4th Virginia
5th Virginia
9th Virginia
10th Virginia
Critcher's Battalion (Virginia)
Cobb's Legion (Georgia)
Hampton Legion (South Carolina)
Jeff Davis Legion
Stuart Horse Artillery (Capt. John Pelham)
Capt. R. Preston Chew's (Virginia) Battery

NOTES

Abbreviations

AAS	American Antiquarian Society
ADAH	Alabama Department of Archives and History
Beinecke Library	Beinecke Rare Book and Manuscript Library, Yale University
BHC	Bentley Historical Collections, University of Michigan
BU	Department of Special Collections, Boston University
CMH	*Confederate Military History*, Clement A. Evans, ed.
CMU	Clarke Historical Library, Central Michigan University
CWMC	Civil War Miscellaneous Collection, U.S. Army Military History Institute
CWTI	*Civil War Times Illustrated* Collection, U.S. Army Military History Institute
Duke	Rare Book, Manuscript, and Special Collections Library, Duke University
ECU	East Carolina Manuscript Collection, J. Y. Joyner Library, East Carolina University
EU	Special Collections, Robert W. Woodruff Library, Emory University
FMC	Shadek-Fackenthal Library, Franklin and Marshall College
FSNMP	Fredericksburg and Spotsylvania National Military Park
GDAH	Manuscripts Collection, Georgia Department of Archives and History
Harrisburg CWRT	Harrisburg Civil War Round Table Collection, U.S. Army Military History Institute
Harvard	Houghton Library, Harvard University
HSP	Historical Society of Pennsylvania
HSWP	Library and Archives, Historical Society of Western Pennsylvania
LOC	Manuscript Division, Library of Congress
LV	Archives Division, Library of Virginia
MassHS	Library, Massachusetts Historical Society
MDAH	Manuscript Collection, Mississippi Department of Archives and History

MdHS	Manuscripts Division, Maryland Historical Society
MinnHS	Manuscript Collections, Minnesota Historical Society
MoHS	Manuscript Collections, Missouri Historical Society
NCCWRT	Northwest Corner Civil War Round Table Collection, U.S. Army Military History Institute
NCDAH	Archives and Records Section, North Carolina Division of Archives and History
NYHS	Manuscripts Division, New York Historical Society
NYPL	Manuscripts and Archives Division, New York Public Library
NYSL	Manuscripts and Special Collections, New York State Library
OCHS	Oswego County (New York) Historical Society
OR	*The War of the Rebellion: A Compilation of the Official Records of the Union and Confederate Armies*
ORN	*Official Records of the Union and Confederate Navies in the War of the Rebellion*
PC	*The Peninsular Campaign of General McClellan in 1862*, Papers of the Military Historical Society of Massachusetts
PSA	Pennsylvania State Archives, Pennsylvania Historical and Museum Commission
PSU	Historical Collections and Labor Archives, Pattee Library, Pennsylvania State University
RIHS	Manuscript Collections, Rhode Island Historical Society
Rutgers	Special Collections and University Archives, Archibald S. Alexander Library, Rutgers University
SCHS	South Carolina Historical Society
SHC	Southern Historical Collection, University of North Carolina, Chapel Hill
SHSW	Archives, State Historical Society of Wisconsin
Stanford	Department of Special Collections, Stanford University Libraries
UGa	Special Collections Division, Hargrett Library, University of Georgia
UM	James F. Schoff Civil War Collection, William L. Clements Library, University of Michigan
UNC-W	Manuscript Collection, William Madison Randall Library, University of North Carolina, Wilmington
UOkla	Western History Collections, University of Oklahoma, Norman
URL	Department of Rare Books and Special Collections, University of Rochester Library
USAMHI	U.S. Army Military History Institute
USC	South Caroliniana Library, University of South Carolina
UVa	Manuscripts Department, University of Virginia Library
UW-GB	Area Research Center, University of Wisconsin-Green Bay
VaHS	Virginia Historical Society
VtHS	Vermont Historical Society
WHMC	Western Historical Manuscript Collection, University of Missouri, Columbia
WRHS	Western Reserve Historical Society
Yale	Manuscripts and Archives, Sterling Memorial Library, Yale University

1. *"The Nation Has Been Making Progress"*

1. The general history in this book is taken from Long, *Civil War Day by Day;* McPherson, *Battle Cry of Freedom;* Weigley, *Great Civil War,* and other general studies of the war and period.

2. The most recent biography of McClellan is Sears, *George B. McClellan.* Brief biographical sketches of all Union generals are in Warner, *Generals in Blue* (pp. 290–92 for McClellan).

3. Ayres to father, June 26, 1862, Ayres Papers, Rutgers; Kenney to brother, June 25, 1862, Kenney Papers, Duke; Lincoln, *Collected Works,* vol. 5, pp. 155, 175, 179 (all citations will be from vol. 5 unless otherwise noted); McClellan, *Civil War Papers,* pp. 206–207; *OR,* ser. 1, vol. 5, pp. 41–45; *OR,* vol. 11, part 3, pp. 59–60, 62, 455–56 (all subsequent references will be to ser. 1, vol. 11, unless otherwise noted). All weather information not otherwise referenced can be found in Miller, "The Grand Campaign." See, for example, Williams, *Lincoln Finds a General,* vol. 1, pp. 103–51, for the argument that anyone could have done what McClellan did. Ropes ("General McClellan's Plans," p. 28) argues that McDowell's detention did not interfere with any of McClellan's plans of which Lincoln had approved. McCormick (*War Without Grant,* p. 84) wrote that it was not a hard blow to McClellan, who would have found a different reason to postpone an attack.

4. DeLeon, *Four Years,* pp. 168–69, 172, 191, 193; Putnam, *Richmond During the War,* pp. 121, 124–25, 129–30; Harrison, *Recollections Grave and Gay,* p. 80; Wickham to Rives and William H. to Rives, both May 15, 1862, John A. Lancaster and Son to Rives, May 14, 1862, all in the Rives Papers, LOC; Lange Memoir, Lange Papers, VaHS; Jones, *Rebel War Clerk's Diary,* vol. 1, pp. 123, 126 (all references will be to vol. 1); Mallory Diary, Mallory Papers, LOC; Fergurson, *Ashes of Glory,* p. 131; Davis, *Jefferson Davis,* pp. 417, 438, 446; Nevins, *War for the Union,* pp. 88–89; McPherson, *Battle Cry of Freedom,* pp. 428–30, 433; Ruffin, *Diary,* vol. 2, p. 308 (all references will be to vol. 2); Rable, *Confederate Republic,* p. 146. Sears (*To the Gates of Richmond,* pp. 87–88) notes the month of bad news.

5. Fergurson, *Ashes of Glory,* p. 134; Thomas, *Confederate Nation,* p. 159; Ruffin, *Diary,* pp. 290–91, 294–305; Lange Memoir, Lange Papers, VaHS; John B. Harvie to R. H. Meade, May 16, 1862, Meade Family Papers, VaHS; Putnam, *Richmond During the War,* pp. 130–31; Jones, *Rebel War Clerk's Diary,* p. 125; DeLeon, *Four Years,* p. 196; Seddon to Rives, May 10, 1862, Rives Papers, LOC.

6. *OR,* pt. 1, p. 276; *OR,* ser. 2, vol. 2, pp. 221–23; *OR,* ser. 3, vol. 2, pp. 2–3; Leech, *Reveille in Washington,* p. 189; Nevins, *War for the Union,* p. 88; McPherson, *Battle Cry of Freedom,* p. 422; Strong, *Diary,* vol. 3, pp. 223, 225 (all references will be to vol. 3); Lincoln, *Collected Works,* pp. 203, 210, 222–23; Donald, *Lincoln,* pp. 350–52, 355; Paludan, *People's Contest,* p. 96; Silbey, *Respectable Minority,* pp. 49–50.

7. Vanauken, *Glittering Illusion,* pp. 88, 90, 96; Owsley, *King Cotton Diplomacy,* pp. 295–305; Jones, *Union in Peril,* pp. 119, 121, 127; Strong, *Diary,* p. 226; Jones, *Rebel War Clerk's Diary,* p. 127; Crook, *North,* p. 206; Jenkins, *Britain,* vol. 2, pp. 81–82; Case and Spencer, *United States and France,* p. 285; Thomas, *Confederate Nation,* p. 177.

8. *OR,* pt. 1, pp. 749, 933–35; *OR,* pt. 3, pp. 190, 569; *OR,* vol. 12, pt. 1, pp. 281–83; Edmondston, *"Journal of a Secesh Lady,"* p. 183; Strong, *Diary,* p. 227, 229; Jones, *Rebel War Clerk's Diary,* pp. 128, 132; Ruffin, *Diary,* p. 312; Lincoln, *Collected Works,* p. 255; Sears, *To the Gates of Richmond,* p. 150; Putnam, *Richmond During the War,* p. 132; DeLeon, *Four Years,* pp. 198–99; Harrison, *Recollections Grave and Gay,* p. 84; Livermore, *Numbers and Losses,* p. 81. Woodworth (*Davis and Lee,* p. 148) infers Davis's opinion of Lee.

9. Harrison, *Recollections Grave and Gay*, p. 72; Davis, *Jefferson Davis*, p. 423. By far the most comprehensive biography of Lee is Douglas Southall Freeman's four-volume *R. E. Lee* (unless otherwise indicated, all references are to vol. 2). For a quick biographical sketch of Lee and all other Southern generals, see Warner, *Generals in Gray*.

10. Jones, *Life and Letters*, p. 184; Edmonston, *"Journal of a Secesh Lady,"* pp. 188–89 (emphasis in original); Jones, *Rebel War Clerk's Diary*, p. 133; Mallory Diary, Mallory Papers, LOC; Woodworth, *Davis and Lee*, p. 152; Cook, *Siege of Richmond*, p. 247; Freeman, *R. E. Lee*, pp. 86–88; *OR*, pt. 3, pp. 612–13.

11. Lee, *Lee's Dispatches*, p. 8; Pitts to Lizzie, June 9, 1862, Pitts Papers, SCHS; Hatton Memoir, Hatton Papers, LOC; unknown author to father, June 5, 1862, Haskell Family Papers, SCHS; Whitehorne to sister, June 11, 1862, Whitehorne Papers, LV.

12. McClellan, *Civil War Papers*, pp. 244–45; Williams, *Lincoln and the Radicals*, pp. 133–39; Lincoln, *Collected Works*, pp. 208–209, 236; Tap, *Over Lincoln's Shoulder*, pp. 105, 109; Paludan, *People's Contest*, p. 77; Strong, *Diary*, pp. 229, 231; Sears, *George B. McClellan*, p. 181; Leech, *Reveille in Washington*, p. 192; Donald, *Lincoln*, pp. 350–52, 355.

13. McClellan, *Civil War Papers*, pp. 299, 303, 305; Branch to A. P. Hill, June 4, 1862, Branch Papers, UVa; Bills to Calvin, June 6, 1862, Bills Papers, Leigh Collection, USAMHI; Thompson Journal, Thompson Papers, LOC; Babcock to his aunt, June 6, 1862, Babcock Papers, LOC; Lee, *Lee's Dispatches*, p. 8; Lee, *William Nelson Pendleton*, p. 188; McClellan, *McClellan's Own Story*, p. 387; Averell to father, June 8, 1862, Averell Papers, NYSL; Barnard, *Peninsular Campaign*, p. 33; Lewis to Maria, June 21, 1862, Lewis Papers, Harrisburg CWRT. Dowdey (*Seven Days*, p. 135) claims McClellan was playing politics.

14. Michie, *General McClellan*, p. 347; Pinkerton, *Spy of the Rebellion*, pp. 587–607; *OR*, pt. 2, pp. 484–89 (Fishel, in *Secret War*, p. 164, gives slightly different numbers); *Army of the Potomac*, p. 292; Livermore, *Numbers and Losses*, p. 86. Markle (*Spies and Spymasters*, p. 5) argues that the first possibility is correct, whereas Newton (*Seven Pines*, pp. 15–16) argues that the second possibility is correct.

15. *OR*, pt. 3, pp. 238–39; Graham to Ellen Lee, June 16, 1862, CWMC; Kearny to Courtland Parker, June 22, 1862, Kearny Papers, LOC; Wiley to family, June 18, 1862, Wiley Papers, PSU. For details on this estimate of Union strength, see Appendix A.

16. Winn to wife, June 14, 1862, Winn Papers, EU; Hill to wife, June 24, 1862, Miscellaneous Papers, UM. Sears (*George B. McClellan*, p. 179) argues the first point of view; Newton (*Seven Pines*, p. 16) argues the second. Campbell (*McClellan*, pp. 237–39) argues that Lee, with Jackson, would have had at least 153,000 men.

17. Hyde, *Following the Greek Cross*, p. 47; Taylor, *General Lee*, p. 70. Fishel (*Secret War*, pp. 102–64) treats the subject in minute detail. Palfrey ("Period Which Elapsed," pp. 153–54) expresses incredulity. Adams (*Our Masters the Rebels*, pp. 94–95) says McClellan had an inferiority complex (seemingly unlikely). Eckenrode and Conrad (*George B. McClellan*, pp. 74–75) say that since the Confederates could have concentrated 180,000 men at Richmond (a demonstrably false claim), McClellan merely assumed that they had.

18. Woodworth, *Davis and Lee*, p. 157; Hill to wife, June 16, 1862, Hill Papers, USAMHI; Alexander, *Military Memoirs*, pp. 110–11; Dowdey, *Seven Days*, p. 132; Lee, *Lee's Dispatches*, pp. 6–7; Marshall, *Aide-de-Camp*, p. 77.

19. Davis, *Rise and Fall*, vol. 2, pp. 130–31; Lee to Jackson, June 6, 1862, Lee Headquarters Papers, VaHS; *OR*, pt. 3, pp. 589–90; *OR*, vol. 12, pt. 3, p. 908; Simpson, *Hood's Texas Brigade*, p. 110. For details of this estimate of Confederate strength, see Appendix A.

20. *OR*, pt. 1, pp. 1036–40; *OR*, pt. 3, p. 590; Ruffin, *Diary*, p. 337; Borcke, *Memoirs*,

vol. 1, p. 37; Frayser, "Stuart's Raid," p. 505; Cooke, *Wearing of the Gray*, pp. 167–68; Mosby, "Ride Around General McClellan," p. 249.

21. *OR*, pt. 1, pp. 1008, 1020–23, 1036–37; Frayser, "Stuart's Raid," p. 506; McClellan, *I Rode with Jeb Stuart*, p. 56; Smith to Lenny, June 17, 1862, Smith Papers, HSP.

22. Cooke, *Wearing of the Gray*, pp. 169–70, 172–73; *OR*, pt. 1, pp. 1032, 1034, 1038–39, 1044; Frayser, "Stuart's Raid," pp. 507–509; Mosby, "Ride Around General McClellan," p. 252; Robins, "Stuart's Ride Around McClellan," pp. 272–73; Cook, *Siege of Richmond*, p. 284; Robertson, *Diary of the War*, pp. 32–33. Mosby ("Ride Around General McClellan," pp. 250, 253, 254), Frayser ("Stuart's Raid," p. 514), Reed (*Combined Operations*, p. 176), and Casdorph (*Lee and Jackson*, p. 259) criticize Stuart. McClellan (untitled address, pp. 442–43) and Thomas (*Bold Dragoon*, pp. 117–18) defend him.

23. Cooke, *Wearing of the Gray*, pp. 171, 174, 177; *OR*, pt. 1, pp. 1008, 1010, 1017, 1028; Frayser, "Stuart's Raid," p. 509, 511; Mosby, "Ride Around General McClellan," p. 253; Cooke, War Diary, Cooke Papers, Duke.

24. Frayser, "Stuart's Raid," p. 512; Cooke, *Wearing of the Gray*, p. 180; Jones, *Life and Letters*, p. 184; Longstreet, *From Manassas to Appomattox*, p. 119; Putnam, *Richmond During the War*, p. 141; Haden, *Reminiscences*, p. 13; Sears, *To the Gates of Richmond*, p. 173; Strong, *Diary*, p. 231; Lee, *Wartime Papers*, p.194. Casdorph (*Lee and Jackson*, p. 259) and Bearss ("Jeb Stuart's Ride," p. 140) agree with this view of the importance of the information. Starr (*Union Cavalry*, vol. 1, p. 273), Mosby ("Ride Around General McClellan," p. 254), McClellan (untitled address, p. 443), and Carmichael ("Stuart's Ride Around McClellan," p. 53) all emphasize the moral aspect of the raid. Cullen (*Peninsula Campaign*, pp. 66–67) at least mentions the value of the information. Cook (*Siege of Richmond*, p. 286) makes this point more strongly.

25. Stillman to parents, June 17, 1862, Stillman Papers, SHSW; "On to Prison," p. 29; Freeman, *R. E. Lee*, pp. 252–54; Robert Haile Diary, Freeman Papers, LOC; Potts to mother, June 14, 1862, Potts Papers, Harrisburg CWRT; Cobb to wife, July 14, 1862, Cobb Papers, UGa.

26. McClellan, *Civil War Papers*, pp. 301, 303, 307; *OR*, pt. 1, p. 47; pt. 3, p. 251; Catton, *Mr. Lincoln's Army*, p. 129; Cook, *Siege of Richmond*, pp. 275, 278–79, 301–302; Beals, letter to brother in law, June 19, 1862, Beals Papers, CWMC; Martin to mother and sister, June 25, 1862, Martin Papers, UM.

27. Webb, *Peninsula*, pp. 120, 128; Wead to father, June 16, 1862, Wead Papers, NYSL. Hassler (*General George B. McClellan*, p. 134), Dowdey (*Seven Days*, p. 136), and Wise (*Long Arm of Lee*, p. 206) all support this judgment. Sears (*To the Gates of Richmond*, p. 173) disagrees.

28. Dowdey, *Seven Days*, pp. 134, 164; McClellan, *Civil War Papers*, p. 261; *OR*, pt. 1, pp. 27–28, 30; *OR*, pt 3, p. 190. Myers (*General George B. McClellan*, pp. 295–96) uses the excerpt. Campbell (*McClellan*, p. 232) and Reed (*Combined Operations*, pp. 161–70) believe the order caused the delay.

29. *OR*, pt. 1, p. 27; pt. 3, p. 225; *OR*, vol. 51, pt. 1, pp. 680–81; McClellan, *Civil War Papers*, pp. 297–98; Lee, *Lee's Dispatches*, p. 8; McAllister to wife, June 6, 1862, McAllister Papers, Rutgers; Martin to mother and sister, June 19, 1862, Martin Papers, UM; Kearny to Courtland Parker, early June, 1862, Kearny Papers, LOC; untitled manuscript, Porter Papers, LOC. Macartney (*Little Mac*, p. 178) argues that McClellan's hand was forced. Of the three options open to McClellan, Reed (*Combined Operations*, pp. 169, 173) advocates keeping the line as it was. Reed (*Combined Operations*, p. 176) also believes McClellan was trying to lure Lee north by his dispositions. Cullen (*Peninsula Campaign*, p. 78) thinks the dispositions were caused by McClellan's decision to change his base if attacked.

2. *"How Are We to Get at Those People?"*

1. *OR*, pt. 1, p. 1000; Cook, *Siege of Richmond*, p. 254; "Memoranda of the Irish Brigade," Meagher Papers, Palmer Collection, WRHS; Tilley to wife, June 22, 1862, Tilley Papers, GDAH; Strong to Ben, July 21, 1862, Strong Papers, SHSW; Brooks to father, June 22, 1862, Brooks Papers, USAMHI; Tinsley Memoir, Tinsley Papers, VaHS; Dickert, *Kershaw's Brigade*, pp. 122–23; Everett to mother, June 22, 1862, Everett Papers, EU.

2. *OR*, pt. 1, p. 52, 1052–60; unpublished manuscript, Porter Papers, LOC.

3. Long, *Robert E. Lee*, p. 168; Stuart to Lee, June 4, 1862, Freeman Papers, LOC; Cooke, *Wearing of the Gray*, p. 166.

4. Longstreet, *From Manassas to Appomattox*, pp. 86, 114, 120. Walter Taylor (*General Lee*, p. 59) says anyone's notion of giving credit to anyone but Lee for the plan of the first part of the Seven Days is "foolish talk." However, if Longstreet did indeed make the suggestion he says he made, then it would be natural for Lee to discuss it with Longstreet. Taylor's comment probably is a case of the animus against Longstreet after the war breaking through to the surface. Sanger (*James Longstreet*, p. 64) points out that Lee and Longstreet both would reason this way.

5. Marshall, *Aide-de-Camp*, pp. 89–90, 97–98.

6. Davis, *Rise and Fall*, vol. 2, p. 132; memorandum of Dec. 17, 1868 conversation, Allan Papers, SHC.

7. Smith, *Autobiography*, p. 41; Kearny to Courtland Parker, June 22, 1862, Kearny Papers, LOC; *OR*, pt. 3, p. 247; Cook, *Siege of Richmond*, p. 303.

8. Maurice (*Lee the Soldier*, p. 116) makes the first point; Farwell (*Stonewall*, p. 340) makes the second.

9. Cooke, *Life of Stonewall Jackson*, pp. 202–204; Jones, "Reminiscences No. 6," p. 367; Whiting to wife, June 18, 1862, Whiting Papers, NCDAH; Pryor to Penelope, June 19, 1862, Pryor Papers, UGa; Polley, *Soldier's Letters*, p. 48; Erskine to wife, June 20 and 22, 1862, Erskine Papers, Center for American History, University of Texas, Austin; Stephens to Mary, June 20, 1862, Stephens Papers, EU; Johnson, "Memoir," p. 149.

10. Stephens to Mary, June 20, 1862, Stephens Papers, EU; Johnson, "Memoir," p. 149; Imboden, "Jackson in the Shenandoah," p. 297; Whiting to wife, June 18, 1862, Whiting Papers, NCDAH.

11. Dabney, *Life and Campaigns*, p. 434; Melhorn Diary, Melhorn Papers, Stanford; Vairin Diary, MDAH; Winder Diary, Winder Papers, MdHS; Polley, *Soldier's Letters*, p. 47.

12. Dabney, *Life and Campaigns*, p. 434; Douglas, *I Rode With Stonewall*, p. 103; Hill, "Lee's Attacks," pp. 348–49; Barger to parents, June 23, 1862, Barger Papers, *CWTI*; Brown, "Down the Peninsula," pp. 43–44.

13. Dabney, *Life and Campaigns*, p. 435; Douglas, *I Rode With Stonewall*, p. 104; Winder Diary, Winder Papers, MdHS; Vairin Diary, MDAH; Melhorn Diary, Melhorn Papers, Stanford; Wayland, *Stonewall Jackson's Way*, p. 159; Dabney memorandum, Mar. 31, 1896, Hotchkiss Papers, LOC. Among others, Farwell (*Stonewall*, p. 346) criticizes the rest; Greene (*Whatever You Resolve to Be*, p. 40) supports Jackson.

14. Jones, "Reminiscences No. 6," p. 150; Jones, "Career of General Jackson," p. 86. Alexander (*Fighting for the Confederacy*, p. 98) says Jackson should have left on the twenty-second so the meeting with Lee could take place earlier. However, it could not have taken place much more than a couple of hours earlier unless Stonewall had left twenty-four hours earlier than he did. That would have been possible, but Alexander's criticism only becomes valid after the meeting and the setting of the time for the attack.

15. *OR*, pt. 2, pp. 221–22; *OR*, pt. 3, p. 238.

16. Brent, *Memoirs*, p. 158; Marshall, *Aide-de-Camp*, p. 89. General Orders no. 75 (*OR*, pt. 2, pp. 498–99) is reprinted in Appendix B. Dowdey (*Seven Days*, p. 157) makes the point about confusion. Schenck (*Up Came Hill*, pp. 49, 62) believes that the order calls for Jackson to join in a "major assault" on the Yankees.

17. Longstreet, *From Manassas to Appomattox*, p. 121–22; Notes of Dec. 17, 1868 conversation, Allan Papers, SHC. D. H. Hill ("Lee's Attacks," p. 347) says that Jackson first specified the twenty-sixth and Longstreet questioned him on *that* date. Longstreet had the advantage of seeing Hill's article; perhaps that made his memory better.

18. Jones, *Life and Letters*, p. 185; Stovall, *Robert Toombs*, p. 246; Beaver to wife and sister, June 17, 1862, Beaver Collection, GDAH.

19. Jones, *Rebel War Clerk's Diary*, p. 135; Putnam, *Richmond During the War*, pp. 139, 145; Mallory Diary, Mallory Papers, LOC; Edmonston, *Journal of a Secesh Lady*, p. 192; Nevins, *War for the Union*, p. 131; Sears, *To the Gates of Richmond*, pp. 160–61; Strong, *Diary*, pp. 231–32; Lincoln, *Collected Works*, pp. 257, 259, 273, 284; Barker to sister, June 20, 1862, Barker Papers, RIHS; Dodge Journal, Dodge Papers, LOC; Burrill to parents, June 22, 1862, Burrill Papers, SHSW.

3. *"The Responsibility Cannot Be Thrown on My Shoulders"*

1. Smith, *Autobiography*, pp. 40–41; McClellan, *McClellan's Own Story*, p. 405; *OR*, vol. 11, pt. 1, p. 50; *OR*, vol. 51, pt. 1, pp. 677, 678, 684, 686.

2. *OR*, pt. 1, p. 50; *OR*, pt. 2, p. 108; *OR*, pt. 3, p. 250; McClellan, *McClellan's Own Story*, pp. 405, 408.

3. *OR*, pt. 2, pp. 96, 108, 120–21, 134–35; Wiley to family, June 28, 1862, Wiley Papers, PSU.

4. *OR*, pt. 2, pp. 121, 623, 787, 792, 798–99, 804–805; interview with Maj. William A. Towers, 4th Georgia Regiment, Towers Papers, GDAH.

5. *OR*, pt. 2, pp. 135–36, 155–56, 791, 804–805; Reese, "Private Soldier Life," p. 162; Evans to parents, June 28, 1862, Evans Papers, New Jersey Historical Society Library. Wright (*OR*, pt. 2, p. 804) says the troops were ordered up by Ransom, Ransom (*OR*, pt. 2, p. 791) says that he only ordered his men to report to Huger, and Huger (*OR*, pt. 2, p. 787) says merely that they were put into line and that Wright ordered them to support him.

6. *OR*, pt. 2, p. 96, 109, 121, 147, 179, 794, 796, 806, 818; *OR*, pt. 3, p. 238; Heintzelman to McClellan and Heintzelman to wife, June 25, 1862, McClellan Papers, LOC; Swanberg, *Sickles the Incredible*, p. 152; Marcy to Heintzelman, June 25, 1862, Heintzelman Papers, LOC; Hassler, *General George B. McClellan*, pp. 139, 141. Cook, *Siege of Richmond*, p. 297, characterized the order as conditional in nature.

7. *OR*, pt. 2, pp. 96, 137, 147, 201, 805; Wiley to family, June 28, 1862, Wiley Papers, PSU; Osborn, *No Middle Ground*, p. 55; Brewster, *Cruel War Is Over*, pp. 158–59.

8. *OR*, pt. 2, pp. 173–74, 184, 799, 802; Werstein, *Kearny the Magnificent*, p. 222; Doubleday, "Oak Grove," p. 7; Hays to sir, June 26, 1862, Hays Papers, HSWP; Hays, *Under the Red Patch*, p. 114. Robinson reported that he ordered Clark to withdraw; Grimes reported that he drove the Union artillerymen off, leaving the gun and its horses behind.

9. *OR*, pt. 2, pp. 174, 179–80, 184, 792, 799, 803, 806; Hays to sir, June 26, 1862, Hays Papers, HSWP; Doubleday, "Oak Grove," p. 7; unknown author (probably J. T. Gay) to Pupie, June 26, 1862, Nix Papers, UGa; Brown, *Reminiscences*, p. 11.

10. *OR*, pt. 2, pp. 121–22, 180, 792–93, 806; C. S. Powell, "War Tales," Rose Papers, Duke; Downes to mother, June 26, 1862, Downes Papers, CWMC; Burgwyn to mother, July 14, 1862, Burgwyn Family Papers, SHC.

11. Heintzelman Diary, Heintzelman Papers, LOC; Luckinbill Diary, NCCWRT; Burgwyn to mother, July 14, 1862, Burgwyn Family Papers, SHC; Dodge Journal, Dodge Papers, LOC; Hagar Diary, Lang Collection, USAMHI; Doubleday, "Oak Grove," p. 7.

12. *OR*, pt. 1, p. 50; *OR*, pt. 2, pp. 37–38, 97, 174, 807 981–83; Miller, "Battle of Oak Grove," p. 56. Williams (*Lincoln Finds a General*, vol. 1, p. 224) buys the Union view, whereas Freeman (*R. E. Lee*, p. 119) goes along with the Confederate side. Palfrey (*PC*, vol. 1, p. 149) finds Yankee claims more credible.

13. *OR*, pt. 2, pp. 490, 970; *OR*, pt. 3, pp. 251–52; Lee, *Lee's Dispatches*, pp. 13–14; Burgwyn to mother, July 14, 1862, Burgwyn Family Papers, SHC.

14. *OR*, pt. 2, pp. 623, 834, 756; Hatton Memoir, Hatton Papers, LOC; Hassler, ed., *General to His Lady*, p. 158.

15. Davis, *Chaplain Davis*, p. 71; Vairin Diary, MDAH; Melhorn Diary, Melhorn Papers, Stanford; Dabney memorandum, Mar. 31, 1896, Hotchkiss Papers, LOC; Moore, *Story of a Cannoneer*, p. 83; Dabney, *Life and Campaigns*, p. 439; Greene, *Whatever You Resolve to Be*, p. 41; Douglas, *I Rode With Stonewall*, p. 106.

16. Douglas, *I Rode With Stonewall*, p. 104; Dabney memorandum, Mar. 31, 1896, Hotchkiss Papers, LOC; Vairin Diary, MDAH; Winder Diary, Winder Papers, MdHS; Kearns Diary, Kearns Papers, VaHS; Davis, *They Called Him Stonewall*, p. 214.

17. Douglas, *I Rode With Stonewall*, p. 105. See *OR*, pt. 2, p. 498 for General Orders no. 75, which is reprinted in Appendix B of this book. Freeman (*Lee's Lieutenants*, vol. 1, p. 499) quotes the memorandum—kept by Jackson and found in his papers. The text is printed in Appendix C of this book. Freeman (*Lee's Lieutenants*, vol. 1, p. 500 n 35) concludes on the basis of knowledge of Lee's habits that the orders were written on the morning of the twenty-fourth. With a good courier, Freeman wrote, the orders could have gotten to Jackson by about 1 A.M. on the twenty-fifth.

18. Dabney memorandum, Mar. 31, 1896, Hotchkiss Papers, LOC; Pryor to Penelope, June 24–25, 1862, Pryor Papers, UGa; *OR*, pt. 2, p. 528; Vairin Diary, MDAH; Winder Diary, Winder Papers, MdHS; Kearns Diary, Kearns Papers, VaHS; Melhorn Diary, Melhorn Papers, Stanford.

19. Dabney memorandum, Mar. 31, 1896, Hotchkiss Papers, LOC; Winder Diary, Winder Papers, MdHS; Lee, *Lee's Dispatches*, pp. 14–15; Lee to Jackson, June 25, 1862, Dabney-Jackson Collection, LV; *OR*, pt. 2, p. 514; Dabney, *Life and Campaigns*, p. 440. Dabney records that Jackson spent most of that night praying and pacing.

20. *Annals of the War*, pp. 646–47. Bowers (*Stonewall Jackson*, p. 247) says Jackson was "on automatic pilot"; Farwell (*Stonewall*, pp. 342–43) says Jackson was physically incapable of getting his men moving as usual due to lack of sleep; and Chambers (*Stonewall Jackson*, p. 29) believes a more-rested Jackson would have pushed his force farther on the night of the twenty-fifth.

21. Untitled manuscript, Porter Papers, LOC; Powell, *Fifth Army Corps*, pp. 74–75; "Abstract of Statement made by Charles Rean," McClellan Papers, LOC; *OR*, vol. 51, pt. 1, pp. 693–95; *OR*, pt. 1, p. 49; *OR*, vol. 51, pt. 1, p. 696. Sears (*To the Gates of Richmond*, p. 182) agrees with Stanton and Pinkerton. French (*Army of the Potomac*, p. 95) criticizes McClellan for believing deserters' reports more than those of his own scouts.

22. Porter to Marcy, June 25, 1862, McClellan Papers, LOC; *Army of the Potomac*, p. 433; *OR*, pt. 1, p. 51; pt. 3, p. 259; Meade to Margaret, June 26, 1862, Meade Papers, HSP. Macartney (*Little Mac*, p. 182) believes McClellan's analysis correct, but admits that McClellan was too cautious because of his feeling that he and his army were the Union's only hope. Campbell (*McClellan*, pp. 207–208) argues that between eighty thousand and ninety thousand men could have gone to McClellan. Williams (*Lincoln Finds a General*, vol. 1, p. 225) makes the point about the division at Fort Monroe.

23. Alexander, *Military Memoirs*, pp. 111–12; Jones, *Life and Letters*, p. 171; Smith, *Autobiography*, p. 41; McClellan, *Civil War Papers*, pp. 310, 312; Newell, *"Ours,"* p. 121; Cook, *Siege of Richmond*, p. 320; Powell, *Fifth Army Corps*, pp. 75–76; untitled manuscript, Porter Papers, LOC; Hager Memoir, Hager Papers, UVa; Kautz Diary, Kautz Papers, LOC; *OR*, pt. 3, pp. 254, 257; Hassler, *General George B. McClellan*, p. 142.

4. *"Charging Batteries Is Highly Dangerous"*

1. Alexander, *Military Memoirs*, p. 111; *OR*, pt. 2, pp. 746, 970; pt. 3, p. 257; Fogel to sister, June 26, 1862, Fogel Papers, EU.

2. *OR*, pt. 2, pp. 756, 882; *OR*, pt. 3, pp. 619–20; Lee, *Lee's Dispatches*, pp. 15–17; Alexander, *Fighting for the Confederacy*, p. 99; Brent, *Memoirs*, p. 162.

3. Dabney, *Life and Campaigns*, p. 440; *OR*, pt. 2, pp. 552–53, 562; Winder Diary, Winder Papers, MdHS; Dabney memorandum, Mar. 31, 1896, Hotchkiss Papers, LOC; Melhorn Diary, Melhorn Papers, Stanford; Hunter McGuire to Hotchkiss, Apr. 14, 1896, Hotchkiss Papers, UVa; Douglas, *I Rode With Stonewall*, p. 105; Simpson, *Hood's Texas Brigade*, p. 113; Hood, *Advance and Retreat*, p. 25. In his memorandum, Dabney wrote that Jackson must have meant to signal with his artillery, but Stonewall never revealed his reasons for firing the guns.

4. Johnson, "Memoir," pp. 149–50; Graham, "Battle of Gaines' Mill," p. 1; "How the Seven Days Began," pp. 91–92; *OR*, pt. 2, pp. 881–82, 886.

5. *OR*, pt. 1, pp. 51–52; *OR*, pt. 3, p. 258; McClellan, *Civil War Papers*, pp. 313–15; Marcy to corps commanders, Marcy to Porter, Van Vliet to Rufus Ingalls, all June 26, 1862, McClellan Papers, LOC; "No. 1 Narrative," Bancroft-Bliss Family Papers, LOC.

6. Brent, *Memoirs*, p. 167; Smith, *Autobiography*, p. 41; McClellan, *Civil War Papers*, pp. 314–15; *OR*, pt. 1, pp. 57–58, 72. Barnard (*Peninsular Campaign*, p. 42) argues that nothing should have been expected.

7. Macartney (*Little Mac*, pp. 184–85) makes the argument about the cutoff of communications. Powell (*Fifth Army Corps*, p. 125) says the circumstances (including the lack of reinforcements) prevented McClellan from ordering an assault; Dowdey (*Seven Days*, p. 210) terms McClellan's actions defensive but sound and clearheaded.

8. *OR*, pt. 1, p. 59; *OR*, pt. 2, p. 499; Keith to friends, July 6, 1862, Keith Papers, VtHS; Dodge Journal, Dodge Papers, LOC.

9. *OR*, pt. 2, p. 835. Among the verdicts are: "precipitate but not insubordinate" (Robertson, *General A. P. Hill*, p. 76); only slightly early (Dowdey, *Seven Days*, p. 190); impetuous and injudicious (Hassler, *A. P. Hill*, p. 51); and rash (Eckenrode and Conrad, *James Longstreet*, p. 65; Cullen, *Peninsula Campaign*, p. 90). Schenck (*Up Came Hill*, p. 59) believes Lee would have approved. Cullen (*Peninsula Campaign*, p. 96) speculates on the possibility of a misunderstanding. Dowdey (*Seven Days*, p. 177) has given the final explanation.

10. Brent, *Memoirs*, pp. 160–1; Goree, *Longstreet's Aide*, p. 92; *OR*, pt. 2, p. 538. Richardson apparently sent his messages to D. H. Hill, who was with Lee.

11. *OR*, pt. 2, pp. 221–22, 289, 315–16, 384; Hager Memoir, UVa; Berry Diary, *CWTI*; *OR*, pt. 2, p. 491; Hotchkiss, *CMH*, vol. 4, p. 286.

12. Jones, *Rebel War Clerk's Diary*, p. 137; *OR*, pt. 2, pp. 414, 623; *OR*, vol. 51, pt. 1, p. 109; Sydnor, "Virginia Boy," p. 105; McAllister to Hennie, June 6, 1862, McAllister Papers, Rutgers; Cook, *Siege of Richmond*, pp. 230–31; Johnson, *CMH*, vol. 2, p. 259; *OR*, pt. 2, p. 623.

13. Sypher, *Pennsylvania Reserve Corps*, p. 208; *OR*, pt. 2, pp. 278, 312, 348, 384, 407, 411, 414; Powell, *Fifth Army Corps*, p. 78.

14. *OR*, pt. 2, pp. 841, 899; Dawson, *Reminiscences*, p. 48; "Annual Reunion," p. 12; "Purcell Battery," pp. 362–63; Hatton Memoir, Hatton Papers, LOC; Jones Diary, UM.

15. Sydnor to Hotchkiss, Dec. 27, 1897, Hotchkiss Papers, LOC. See, for example, Hassler, *A. P. Hill*, pp. 50–51, for the noted use of this letter.

16. *OR*, pt. 2, pp. 289, 385, 411, 419, 835, 841, 877–78; *OR*, vol. 51, pt. 1, pp. 110–11, 117, unidentified manuscript, McIntosh Papers, VaHS; Taylor, *Destruction and Reconstruction*, p. 99; Sypher, *Pennsylvania Reserve Corps*, p. 212. Other Confederates pointing out the deficiencies in maps include D. H. Hill, "Lee's Attacks," p. 352; Long, *Robert E. Lee*, p. 179; Johnson, *CMH*, vol. 4, p. 287, Taylor, *General Lee*, pp. 65–66; and Brent, *Memoirs*, p. 153.

17. Beall, *In Barrack and Field*, p. 364; *OR*, pt. 2, pp. 261, 399, 409, 411, 841, 897, Ledbetter, "With Archer's Brigade," pp. 350–51; Fulton, *War Reminiscences*, p. 34; "Army Correspondence," Bellefonte (Pa.) *Central Press*, p. 1; Fullerton to family, July 4, 1862, Fullerton Papers, CWMC; Roher to wife, July 6, 1862, Roher Papers, Leigh Collection, USAMHI.

18. *OR*, pt. 2, pp. 647, 835 (emphasis in original); Harrison, "Richmond Scenes in '62," pp. 447–48; memorandum of conversation, Dec. 17, 1868, Allan Papers, SHC; Marshall, *Aide-de-Camp*, p. 94.

19. *OR*, pt. 2, pp. 261, 399, 409, 899; Hinsdale Diary, Hinsdale Family Papers, Duke; Hill, *CMH*, vol. 5, p. 77, Flowers, "Thirty-Eighth North Carolina," pp. 249–50; John Faller to Cecelia, July 12, 1862, Faller Correspondence, Harrisburg CWRT; Hoke, "Organization and Movements of the Thirty-Eighth Regiment North Carolina Troops January 17, 1862–June 25, 1864," Hoke Papers, SHC.

20. *OR*, pt. 2, p. 623, 648, 835, 836. Woodworth (*Davis and Lee*, p. 165) makes the point that Davis bypassed a man in whom he supposedly had great confidence—Lee—in giving Hill this order.

21. *OR*, pt. 2, p. 623; Hill, *CMH*, vol. 5, p. 78 n; Avery, "Memorial Address," pp. 125–26. Dowdey (*Seven Days*, p. 187) makes the last point.

22. H. D. Dickens, "Some of My Recollections of the Civil War," D. H. Hill Jr. Papers, NCDAH; Alexander, *Military Memoirs*, p. 121; Robert Smith to Captain Neary or Captain Jordan, June 27, 1862, Jordan Papers, UGa; *OR*, pt. 2, pp. 623, 648, 654; Jackson et al., *Three Rebels Write Home*, pp. 23–24; Hill, *CMH*, vol. 5, p. 78; Faller to Cecelia, July 12, 1862, Faller Correspondence, Harrisburg CWRT, Alexander, *Fighting for the Confederacy*, p. 100; Edward Armstrong to father, June 29, 1862, Armstrong Family Papers, UNC-W.

23. *OR*, pt. 2, pp. 38–39, 399, 756; Porter to Mrs. Porter, June 26, 1862, McClellan Papers, LOC; Norris to mother, June 29, 1862, Norris Papers, USC; Livermore, *Numbers and Losses*, p. 82; Hill, "Lee's Attacks," p. 352. One regiment had been detached from McCall's division. Livermore gives the Confederate loss as 1484, but Fox (*Regimental Losses*, p. 550) gives it as 1,365. Both are estimates. Dowdey (*Seven Days*, p. 192) points out the need to cross the river, but it remains no excuse. Diket (*Pender*, p. 43) describes the suggestion as bad judgment.

24. Marshall, *Aide-de-Camp*, pp. 93–94; *OR*, pt. 2, p. 756.

25. Roher to wife, July 6, 1862, Roher Papers, Leigh Collection, USAMHI; Julius to father, July 14, 1862, Lilly Collection, NCDAH; "Army Correspondence," New Castle (Pa.) *Lawrence Journal*, p. 1; Allen to cousin, July 29, 1862, Allen Papers, LOC; Becker to home, July 6, 1862, Becker Papers, Pennsylvania "Save the Flags" Civil War Collection, USAMHI; "Family Record of John McAnerney," McAnerney Papers, VaHS; Blackford Journal, Blackford Papers, CWMC; Gilmer Diary, UVa.

26. *OR*, pt. 2, pp. 499, 614; Poague, *Gunner with Stonewall*, p. 28; Jones, "Reminiscences No. 7," p. 428; Melhorn Diary, Melhorn Papers, Stanford; Kearns Diary, Kearns Papers, VaHS; Vairin Diary, MDAH; Hotchkiss to G. F. R. Henderson, Apr. 6, 1896, quoting Dabney, Hotchkiss Papers, LOC; Henderson, *Stonewall Jackson*, vol. 2, p. 21 n 1; Blackford, *War Years*, p. 71. Thomas (*Bold Dragoon*, pp. 132–33) believes that this is how Stuart would have behaved.

27. *OR*, pt. 2, pp. 553, 614; Johnson, "Memoir," p. 150; untitled manuscript, Brazell Collection, UOkla; Handerson, *Yankee in Gray*, p. 44; Bradwell, "Soldier Life," p. 22. Later that night the Northerners came back and recaptured two guns they had left earlier, forcing Johnson to reinforce his own picket.

28. Freeman, *Lee's Lieutenants*, vol. 1, p. 500. Farwell (*Stonewall*, p. 347) criticizes his lack of support for Hill, whereas Dowdey (*Seven Days*, p. 196) defends Jackson. Cullen (*Peninsula Campaign*, p 95) and Robertson (*Stonewall Jackson*, p. 472) argue that Jackson did misunderstand his orders. Sears (*To the Gates of Richmond*, p. 199) notes the discrepancy. The criticism regarding tardiness has come from, among others, Long (*Robert E. Lee*, p. 171), Alexander (*Military Memoirs*, p. 116), and Michie (*General McClellan*, pp. 333–34). Cooke (*Life of Stonewall Jackson*, pp. 216–17) argues in Jackson's favor. Maurice (in Marshall, *Aide-de-Camp*, pp. 85–86, 86 n 6) argues that Jackson had plenty of time and simply did not perform as he should have.

29. Criticisms of staff and staff work come from Brent (*Memoirs*, p. 204), Dowdey (*Seven Days*, pp. 189–91), Freeman (*R. E. Lee*, pp. 233–34), and Hattaway and Jones (*How the North Won*, p. 195). The statements of Dabney (memorandum, Mar. 31, 1896, LOC) and McGuire (Mar. 30, 1896, UVa) are from the Hotchkiss Papers.

30. *OR*, pt. 2, p. 400; *OR*, pt. 3, p. 260; McClellan, *Civil War Papers*, p. 317; Thompson Journal, Thompson Papers, LOC; Wright, "Old Peninsular Days," p. 3; Marcy to Heintzelman, June 26, 1862, Heintzelman Papers, LOC; Perkins, "Civil War Diary," p. 163; Young Diary, CWMC; Thomas Carpenter to Mary, June 27, 1862, Bulkley Family Papers, MoHS; J. B. Oliver to father, June 27, 1862, Oliver Family papers, OCHS; Taylor Diary, WHMC; Lankton to Mrs. M. D. J. Gilman, 1864, Miscellaneous Papers, UM; Scandlin Diary, Scandlin Papers, AAS; Henry to wife, July 4, 1862, Henry Papers, MinnHS; Anderson Journal, Anderson Papers, UW-GB. Nichols (*Toward Gettysburg*, p. 92) makes the points about Reynolds and Seymour.

31. DeLeon, *Four Years*, p. 204; Jones, *Rebel War Clerk's Diary*, pp. 136–38; Putnam, *Richmond During the War*, p. 146; Lange Memoir, Lange Papers, VaHS; Strong, *Diary*, p. 233; *OR*, pt. 1, p. 53; *OR*, pt. 3, p. 260.

32. *OR*, pt. 2, p. 222; untitled manuscript, Porter Papers, LOC; Smith, *Autobiography*, p. 41; *Army of the Potomac*, p. 435. Smith's timing seems a bit off, or else he confused McClellan's coming from Porter with his going to Porter; he reported the conversation as occurring about midnight. Baquet (*History of the First Brigade*, p. 29), Grubb (*Notes of a Staff Officer*, p. 16), and Swinton (*Campaigns*, pp. 146–47) all believe that this was the best choice. Palfrey ("Seven Days' Battles," pp. 168–69) wrote, "This slight affair of the outposts, for it was hardly more than that, appears to have satisfied Gen. McClellan that his Peninsula campaign was a failure."

33. *Army of the Potomac*, p. 610; Powell, *Fifth Army Corps*, p. 82. Swinton (*Campaigns*, p. 140) criticizes Keyes's idea. The following agree with this assessment of McClellan's choices: Dowdey (*Seven Days*, p. 207), Eckenrode and Conrad (*George B. McClellan*, p. 87), and Hassler (*General George B. McClellan*, p. 145).

34. *OR*, pt. 2, p. 223 (emphasis in original); Powell, *Fifth Army Corps*, p. 83; Porter to Ropes, Feb. 11, 1895, Ropes Collection, BU; Frank B. Williams, "Reminiscence of the

Fiftieth New York Volunteer Engineers," Leigh Collection, USAMHI; untitiled manuscript, Porter Papers, LOC; Barnard, *Peninsular Campaign*, p. 40. Dowdey (*Seven Days*, p. 254) notes the correct term. Michie (*General McClellan*, pp. 347–48) has made the point about the trains.

35. Robertson, *Diary of the War*, p. 35; Ellis, *Leaves*, pp. 98–99; Marcy to Casey, June 26, 1862, McClellan Papers, LOC; Ashenfelter to Father Churchman, July 7, 1862, Ashenfelter Papers, Harrisburg CWRT; Sypher, *Pennsylvania Reserve Corps*, p. 222; Powell, *Fifth Army Corps*, p. 85; McCall to wife, June 28, 1862, McCall Papers, HSP; Brown to Caroline, July 7, 1862, Brown papers, URL.

5. *"Little Powell Will Do His Full Duty To-day"*

1. *OR*, pt. 2, p. 491; *OR*, pt. 3, pp. 620–21; memorandum of Dec. 17, 1868 conversation, Allan Papers, SHC; Lee, *Wartime Papers*, pp. 201–202; *ORN*, vol. 7, pp. 523–25.

2. *OR*, pt. 2, pp. 223, 386, 415; Report of Reynolds, Reynolds Family Papers, FMC; Powell, *Fifth Army Corps*, p. 86.

3. *OR*, pt. 2, pp. 426–27, 624, 756, 836, 853, 899–900; Wright to Dorothy, July 4, 1862, Wright Papers, VaHS; Hurst, *Fourteenth Alabama*, p. 11; Hinsdale Journal, Hinsdale Family Papers, Duke; anonymous memoir, Miscellaneous Papers, UM; Report of Reynolds, Reynolds Family Papers, FMC.

4. *OR*, pt. 2, pp. 569–70, 586; Melhorn Diary, Melhorn Papers, Stanford; Kearns Diary, Kearns Papers, VaHS. The criticism comes from, for example, Alexander, *Military Memoirs*, p. 122; Chambers, *Stonewall Jackson*, p. 43; Dowdey, *Seven Days*, p. 202.

5. *OR*, pt. 2, pp. 491–92, 624; Longstreet, *From Manassas to Appomattox*, p. 125; Alexander, *Fighting for the Confederacy*, pp. 100–101; Caldwell, *History of a Brigade*, p. 40; Jones, "Reminiscences No. 8," p. 557, Freeman, *R. E. Lee*, p. 138. The order is Freeman's; Jones only mentions that the three generals were together.

6. Dabney to Hotchkiss, Mar. 10, 1896, Hotchkiss Papers, LOC; Lee, *Lee's Dispatches*, p. 18. This note from Lee to Huger is the one record of Lee's ideas for the twenty-seventh. In their official reports, both Jackson and Lee note Jackson's role on this day as continuing in the spirit of the original orders—another indication that Jackson was to turn the Union flank, not fight a battle. This is also Dabney's surmise.

7. Longstreet, *From Manassas to Appomattox*, p. 125; *OR*, pt. 2, pp. 853–54; Caldwell, *History of a Brigade*, p. 39; Wise Journal, Wise Papers, Duke; Jones Diary, UM; Hinsdale Diary, Hinsdale Family Papers, Duke; Simpson Diary, Simpson Papers, SHSW.

8. *OR*, pt. 2, pp. 313, 535, 836, 854; Caldwell, *History of a Brigade*, pp. 40–41; Benson Memoir, Benson Papers, SHC; Freeman, *R. E. Lee*, p. 144.

9. *OR*, pt. 1, p. 118; *OR*, pt. 2, pp. 224, 272–73, 348, 371; Sypher, *Pennsylvania Reserve Corps*, p. 223; Vedder to family, July 20, 1862, Vedder Papers, CWMC; Slater, "Fray at Gaines' Mill," p. 1; Powell, *Fifth Army Corps*, p. 90; Sutton to brother, July 19, 1862, Sutton Papers, BHC; Swinton, *Campaigns*, p. 150; Jones, *Life and Letters*, p. 172. Cullen (*Peninsula Campaign*, p. 102) wrote that the lines "should have been impregnable."

10. Stevens, *Three Years*, pp. 84–85; George Batchelder to mother, July 5, 1862, Zadock Pratt Papers, BU; Ames to parents, July 5, 1862, Ames Papers, USAMHI.

11. *OR*, pt. 1, pp. 58, 118; *OR*, pt. 2, pp. 224, 348, 429; *OR*, pt. 3, pp. 264–65; untitled manuscript, Porter Papers, LOC; Powell, *Fifth Army Corps*, p. 92; *Army of the Potomac*, p. 622; Galloway, "Battle of Gaines' Mill," p. 1; Heintzelman to Marcy, June 27, 1862, McClellan Papers, LOC; McClellan, *Civil War Papers*, p. 367. Michie (*General McClellan*, p. 339) thinks the Barnard episode a "sad commentary" on the staff's compe-

tence. Powell (*Fifth Army Corps*, p. 122) says that Porter could have held his position if he had received the axes.

12. *OR*, pt. 2, pp. 660–61; Long, "John Bankhead Magruder," p. 110; Lee, *Lee's Dispatches*, p. 18; Dickert, *Kershaw's Brigade*, pp. 121–22; Bentley to wife, June 23, 1862, Bentley Papers, Leigh Collection, USAMHI; Berry Diary, *CWTI;* Townsend, *Campaigns*, pp. 119–22; brother to Lou, June 13, 1862, Wigfall Family Papers, LOC; Webb to father, June 9, 1862, Webb Papers, Yale; Lowe, "My Balloons in Peace and War," American Institute of Aeronautics and Astronautics Collection, LOC; Goss, *Recollections*, p. 59; George Batchelder to mother, July 8, 1862, Zadock Pratt Papers, BU. Bache (*George Gordon Meade*, p. 116) makes the argument that the deception should not have worked.

13. Sears (*George B. McClellan*, p. 211) and Williams (*Lincoln Finds a General*, vol. 1, p. 226) note that McClellan should have been with Porter. Sears (*To the Gates of Richmond*, p. 224) comments on McClellan's view of the situation.

14. Porter to Manton Marble, July 22, 1862, Marble Papers, LOC; Heintzelman Diary, Heintzelman Papers, LOC; *OR*, pt. 1, pp. 58–59; Porter to Ropes, Feb. 11, 1895, Ropes Collection, BU; Porter to McClellan, June 27, 1862, McClellan Papers, LOC (filed as June 26–28); McClellan, *Civil War Papers*, p. 321. Eckenrode and Conrad (*George B. McClellan*, pp. 95–96) say reinforcing Porter was the right thing to do no matter the real situation on the south side. Hassler (*Commanders*, p. 49) also says more troops could have been moved north.

15. Humphreys, *Andrew Atkinson Humphreys*, p. 164; *Army of the Potomac*, p. 623; Brent, *Memoirs*, pp. 170–71; Jones, "Reminiscences No. 8," p. 561; Putnam, *Richmond During the War*, p. 146; DeMotte, "Cause of a Silent Battle," p. 365.

16. *OR*, pt. 2, p. 836; Jones, "Reminiscences No. 8," p. 558.

17. *OR*, pt. 2, pp. 39, 356, 378, 836, 854–55. 862; "How the Seven Days' Battle Began," p. 95; Wilson Memoir, Harrisburg CWRT; Southwick, *A Duryee Zouave*, p. 75; Benson Memoir, Benson Papers, SHC; Caldwell, *History of a Brigade*, p. 43; McCrady, "Boy Heroes," pp. 237–38.

18. Southwick, A *Duryee* Zouave, p. 76; O.R., pt. 2, pp. 356, 367, 873–74; Mattison, "Orr's South Carolina Rifles," pp. 161–64; Capers, *CMH*, vol. 6, pp. 60–61; Davenport, *Camp and Field Life*, pp. 209–12; Mason, "What Regiment?" p. 3; Warren to Emily, July 8, 1862, Warren Papers, NYSL; Urban, *My Experiences*, pp. 119–20. Col. J. Foster Marshall, commander of the 1st South Carolina Rifles, noted that he fought seven Union regiments—only a slight exaggeration.

19. *OR*, pt. 2, p. 856; Caldwell, *History of a Brigade*, p. 46; Haskell, report, Haskell Papers, SHC; Benson Memoir, Benson Papers, SHC. Smith was mortally wounded, dying on Sunday the twenty-ninth.

20. *OR*, pt. 2, pp. 361, 367, 369, 372, 378, 856, 858–60, 885–86, 903; Capers, *CMH*, vol. 6, p. 61; "How the Seven Days' Battle Began," p. 96; Jones Diary, UM; unidentified manuscript, McIntosh Papers, VaHS.

21. *OR*, pt. 2, pp. 278, 313, 373, 883, 888, 891, 893, 896; Vedder to family, July 20, 1862, Vedder Papers, CWMC; Pindell, "Most Dangerous Set of Men," p. 42; Buswell, "Sharpshooter's Seven Days," p. 25; Kent, "Sharpshooting with Berdan," p. 9; Harrer, *With Drum and Gun*, p. 49.

22. *OR*, pt. 2, pp. 883, 900; Hinsdale Journal, Hinsdale Family Papers, Duke; R.W. York to Mrs. Benjamin Lacy, Lacy Papers, NCDAH; Gray to father, July 10, 1862, Gray Papers, NCDAH.

23. *OR*, pt. 2, pp. 296, 847, 849, 878–79; O'Connell Memoir, CWMC; Boies, "Brave

Old Woodbury," p. 3; "General Joseph R. Anderson," pp. 416–17; Anderson, "Anderson's Brigade," p. 450.

24. Ledbetter, "With Archer's Brigade," pp. 351–52; Fulton, "Archer's Brigade," p. 301; *OR*, pt. 2, pp. 296, 897; Ledbetter, "Mechanicsville and Gaines Mill," p. 245.

25. *OR*, pt. 2, pp. 282, 290–91, 897–98; Slater, "Fray at Gaines' Mill," p. 1. Powell (*Fifth Army Corps*, p. 115) agrees with Martindale.

26. *OR*, pt. 2, pp. 842, 845; "Purcell Battery," pp. 363–64; Hinsdale Journal, Hinsdale Family Papers, Duke; Wright to Dorothy, July 4, 1862, Wright Papers, VaHS; O'Connell Memoir, CWMC.

27. Porter, endorsement on Butterfield to Porter, June 27, 1862, McClellan Papers, LOC; Caldwell, *History of a Brigade*, p. 45; *OR*, pt. 2, pp. 874, 897, 982–83; Fox, *Regimental Losses*, p. 562. Schenck (*Up Came Hill*, p. 73) claims that Hill and his men had accomplished their primary mission of catching the enemy, engaging it, pushing it back, and holding it at bay. But this is at best an overstatement.

6. *"We're Holding Them, but It's Getting Hotter and Hotter"*

1. *OR*, pt. 2, pp. 316–17, 549–50, 679, 756–57, 767, 771–72, 868; Longstreet, *From Manassas to Appomattox*, p. 127; Wheeler, *CMH*, vol. 8, pp. 467–68; Pickett, *Soldier of the South*, pp. 16–17; Gilmer Diary, UVa; Withers, *Autobiography of an Octogenarian*, p. 186; Hotchkiss, *CMH*, vol. 4, p. 289; Frothingham to Maggie, July 4, 1862, Frothingham Papers, NYPL; Grannis, statement of service, Grannis Papers, SHSW.

2. Thurston, "Memoir of Richard H. Anderson," p. 148; *OR*, pt. 2, pp. 553, 624, 757; Longstreet, *From Manassas to Appomattox*, p. 127; Dabney, *Life and Campaigns*, p. 443; Robertson, *Stonewall Jackson*, p. 477; Dabney memorandum, Mar. 10, 1896, Hotchkiss Papers, LOC; Jones, "Reminiscences No. 8," p. 557; Hands Civil War Memoirs, UVa; Brown, "Down the Peninsula," p. 48; Blackford Journal, Blackford Papers, CWMC. Nowhere is the order of march specifically mentioned, but Jackson says Ewell was in the lead, and this was the order of divisions later in the day. The guide's words are not quoted, as Freeman (*Lee's Lieutenants*, vol. 1, p. 524 n 21) suggests that perhaps Dabney was not quite accurate concerning the guide's language. Dowdey (*Seven Days*, pp. 212–13) doubts Dabney's story, saying that the firing would have been coming from Boatswain's Swamp, not Gaines's mill, and that any guide who knew the area would have known that. But apparently no guides bothered to tell anyone of Boatswain's Swamp, since no one seemed to know of it, and there was indeed some firing at Gaines's mill at midday, so Dabney's story is not necessarily false. At least one other participant in the march, Campbell Brown of Ewell's staff ("Down the Peninsula," p. 47), noted that a wrong road was taken and that it cost Jackson two or three miles. Given that Dabney's story fits so well with what we know of Jackson's secrecy, it must be credited absent any specific information.

3. Dowdey (*Seven Days*, p. 215), Farwell (*Stonewall*, p. 348 n 1), and Sears (*To the Gates of Richmond*, p. 228) argue that Jackson should have kept going.

4. Jones, "Reminiscences No. 8," p. 559; Dabney memorandum, Mar. 10, 1896, Hotchkiss Papers, LOC; *OR*, pt. 2, pp. 243, 353, 515, 553, 624, 652; Polley, *Hood's Texas Brigade*, p. 64; Ardrey Diary, Ardrey Papers, Duke; Cooke, *Life of Stonewall Jackson*, p. 120; Dabney, *Life and Campaigns*, p. 444; Boswell to Hotchkiss, July 11, 1862, Hotchkiss Papers, LOC. Marshall (*Aide-de-Camp*, p. 99) wrote that Lee thought Jackson's movements would cause McClellan (actually Porter) to move his right flank to oppose Stonewall, whereupon A. P. Hill and Longstreet would hit the Union left.

5. *OR*, pt. 2, p. 553. Jones ("Reminiscences No. 8," p. 559) and McGuire ("General

Jackson," pp. 97–98) provide supporting evidence. Dowdey (*Seven Days*, p. 217) notes the lack of imagination. Alexander (*Military Memoirs*, p. 125) felt it unnecessary to comment on Jackson's report except to say that the inaction of Jackson's men was unlike anything Stonewall had ordered before or after the Seven Days.

6. *OR*, pt. 2, pp. 605, 610–11; Boswell to Hotchkiss, July 11, 1862, Hotchkiss Papers, LOC; Dabney memorandum, Mar. 10, 1896, Hotchkiss Papers, LOC; Brown, "Down the Peninsula," pp. 49–51; Jones, *Life and Letters*, p. 181; Jones, "Reminiscences No. 8," p. 562; Taylor, *Destruction and Reconstruction*, p. 96; "Family Record of John McAnerney," McAnerney Papers, VaHS; typescript, Buck Papers, Duke. Dabney does not give the exact orders from Jackson to Ewell, but the inference is obvious based on Dabney's discussion.

7. *OR*, pt. 2, pp. 371, 614–15, 856–57; Brown, "Down the Peninsula," pp. 50–51; Nisbet, *Four Years*, p. 110; Oates, *War*, pp. 115, 118–19. The Virginia regiment could have been any one of several, or it could have been the 7th North Carolina of Branch's brigade, which was ordered to support in the general area (*OR*, pt. 2, p. 888).

8. Taylor, *Destruction and Reconstruction*, p. 96; Douglas, *I Rode with Stonewall*, pp. 107–108; Wheat, "Memoir," pp. 57–58. Moore (*Louisiana Tigers*, p. 74) says that it is likely that Douglas did not catch the teasing nature of both men's remarks. Douglas knew Jackson at least pretty well, and Stonewall was unlikely to engage in banter on the day of a battle.

9. Sypher, *Pennsylvania Reserve Corps*, pp. 225–26; *OR*, pt. 2, pp. 401–402, 413; Bright and Bright, "*Respects to All*," p. 25; Veil Memoir, Veil Papers, CWMC; "Death of Col. Black," p. 3; Urban, *My Experiences*, p. 119; Slocum, *Life and Services*, p. 31; Pinto, *32nd Regiment*, p. 75; Powell, *Fifth Army Corps*, p. 100; Hawley to brother, July 14, 1862, Hawley Papers, CWMC.

10. Biddle to Ropes, Mar. 27, 1895, Ropes Collection, BU; *OR*, pt. 2, p. 313, 456–58, 605, 620; Galloway, "Battle of Gaines' Mill," p. 1; Pinto, *32nd Regiment*, p. 69; Douglas, *I Rode with Stonewall*, p. 108; Jones, *Lee's Tigers*, p. 104; Handerson, *Yankee in Gray*, p. 96; Hawley to brother, July 14, 1862, Hawley Papers, CWMC.

11. *OR*, pt. 2, pp. 457, 560, 606, 614; Galloway, "Battle of Gaines' Mill," p. 1; Brown, "Notes on Ewell's Division," p. 259; Brown, "Down the Peninsula," pp. 51–52; Davis Memoir, Davis Papers, UVa; James L. Dinwiddie to Bettie, June 29, 1862, Dinwiddie Family Papers, UVa.

12. Dabney memorandum, Mar. 10, 1896, and letter to Hotchkiss, Dec. 28, 1896, Hotchkiss Papers, LOC; *OR*, pt. 2, p. 563; Polley, *Hood's Texas Brigade*, p. 41.

13. Porter to McClellan and McClellan to Porter, June 27, 1862, McClellan Papers, LOC; *OR*, pt. 2, pp. 21, 401, 413, 421, 424; *OR*, pt. 3, p. 265; McClellan, *Civil War Papers*, p. 321; Sypher, *Pennsylvania Reserve Corps*, pp. 227–29; John Faller to Cecilia, July 12, 1862, Faller Correspondence, Harrisburg CWRT.

14. *OR*, pt. 2, pp. 420, 433, 438, 444, 445; Grubb, *Notes of a Staff Officer*, pp. 6–10; McAllister to Ellen, June 27, 1862, McAllister Papers, Rutgers; McCreight to sister, July 14, 1862, McCreight Papers, CWMC; Woodward, *Third Pennsylvania Reserve*, p. 89. The report of the 4th New Jersey's commander, Col. James H. Simpson, indicates that the aide was the Duc de Chartres, whereas Grubb named him as the Comte de Paris. Both were nephews of the Prince de Joinville, and all three had volunteered to serve with McClellan.

15. Westervelt Diary, CWMC; Potts to mother, July 3, 1862, Potts Papers, Harrisburg CWRT; *OR*, pt. 2, pp. 286, 447.

16. Park, "Sketch of the Twelfth Alabama," p. 230; Park, "Diary of Robert E. Park," p. 383; Blackford Journal, Blackford Papers, CWMC; *OR*, pt. 2, pp. 358, 365, 515, 624,

627, 652; Hager Memoir, Hager Papers, UVa; Reed, "Timely Sprint," p. 2; Brown, "Gaines's Mill," p. 3.

17. *OR*, pt. 2, p. 555, 570, 595, 624–25, 637, 640–41, 837; Dabney, *Life and Campaigns*, p. 449; Winder Diary, Winder Papers, MdHS; Garnett, "Personal Reminiscences," p. 148; Lawton to D. H. Hill, Jan. 13, 1885, Hill Papers, NCDAH; Bradwell Memoir, Bradwell Papers, MdHS; Melhorn Diary, Melhorn Papers, Stanford.

18. *OR*, pt. 2, pp. 451, 837; Cooke, *Life of Stonewall Jackson*, pp. 200, 226; Jones, "Reminiscences No. 8," p. 560.

7. *"I Have a Regiment That Can Take It"*

1. *OR*, pt. 2, pp. 348–49, 626, 630, 632, 635, 641–42, 644; *OR Supp.*, vol. 2, p. 437; Armstrong to father, June 29, 1862, Armstrong Family Papers, UNC-W; Ardrey Diary, Ardrey Papers, Duke; Blackford to mother, June 28, 1862, Blackford Papers, Leigh Collection, USAMHI; report of the 5th Alabama, Hobson Family Papers, VaHS. It is difficult to tell to which guns this refers. It could be the same guns that the 20th North Carolina took, but the reports do not completely reconcile.

2. *OR*, pt. 2, pp. 287, 621, 624, 649; Hands Civil War Memoirs, UVa; Johnson, "Memoir," pp. 151–53 (emphasis in original); Johnson, *CMH*, vol. 2, p. 86.

3. Cooke, *Life of Stonewall Jackson*, pp. 223–24; Howard, *Recollections*, p. 140; Worsham, *Foot Cavalry*, p. 99; Kearns Diary, Kearns Papers, VaHS; Grubb, *Notes of a Staff Officer*, p. 11; *OR*, pt. 2, p. 570, 575, 580, 584; Wallace, *5th Virginia Infantry*, p. 33; Booth, *Personal Reminiscences*, p. 47. It is not certain that the 5th Virginia took Hayden's guns. In an exchange of letters in the *National Tribune*, Alfred Davenport ("One of the Seven Days," p. 2) stated that the 5th Virginia took Hayden's guns, and Baylor (*OR*, pt. 2, p. 581) reported that he found wounded North Carolinians on the hill, but this is not certain evidence, for Garland (*OR*, pt. 2, p. 642) reported meeting Lawton and Winder's troops. Booth's story of the order is suggestive, as he notes, of the famous "Lost Order" of the Maryland campaign, also addressed to D. H. Hill, but there are many possible explanations for the order's being at the McGehee house after the battle.

4. *OR*, pt. 2, pp. 362, 365, 367–70; Hager Memoir, Hager Papers, UVa; Evans, "There is No Use," p. 44; Avery, "Memorial Address," p. 122. An exchange of letters in the *National Tribune* (Allen, "14th U.S.," p. 3; Facer, "Did Not Run Away," p. 3; Reed, "Too Busy to Run," p. 3; Allen, "Battle of Gaines's Mill," p. 3) addressed the question of whether the 14th U.S.'s withdrawal was really a rout, but the official reports seem to support the fighting withdrawal.

5. *OR*, pt. 2, pp. 39, 448, 451–52, 625; *OR Supp.*, vol. 2, p. 438; Curtis, *Bull Run to Chancellorsville*, pp. 120, 124, 126; Luckinbill Diary, NCCWRT; Martin to family, July 5, 1862, Martin Papers, UM; Dunning, "Gaines's Mill," p. 4; Porter, "Hanover Court House," p. 339 n; Walling to sisters, June 13, 1862, Walling Papers, CWMC; Westervelt Diary, CWMC; Hall, "Peninula and Antietam Campaigns," p. 173; Bicknell, *Fifth Regiment Maine Volunteers*, p. 103; Cyrus Stone to family, June 30, July 4, and undated, 1862, Stone Papers, MinnHS; Richards to Col. F. B. Kaercher, July 5, 1862, Richards Papers, CWMC. Westervelt wrote that the 16th New York lost a battery and then retook two guns. However, no official report mentions the regiment's losing any guns, and Bartlett's report (*OR*, pt. 2, p. 449) commends Howland for retaking two guns that had been lost by other troops. In an exchange of letters in the *National Tribune*, W. F. Wieland ("Did Not Lose Them," p. 3) stated that the guns were saved after a charge of the Irish Brigade. But there was no such charge, and the weight of evidence indicates that the guns were lost.

6. *OR*, pt. 2, pp. 284, 371–72, 375, 379, 401, 424, 447–48, 595–96, 600, 602; Murray, *South Georgia Rebels*, p. 61; Bradwell Memoir, Bradwell Papers, MdHS; Ames to parents, July 5, 1862, Ames Papers, USAMHI.

7. *OR*, pt. 2, pp. 313, 437–38, 443, 457, 460, 614–15; McCreight to sister, July 14, 1862, McCreight Papers, CWMC; Higgins Diary, FSNMP; Pinto, *32nd Regiment*, pp. 71–72; McAllister to family, July 1, 1862, McAllister Papers, Rutgers; "Flag of the 16th Mississippi Regiment," pp. 75–76; Dobbins, *Grandfather's Journal*, p. 87; Hawley to brother, July 14, 1862, Hawley Papers, CWMC; Baquet, *History of the First Brigade*, p. 287 (emphasis in original); Davenport, *Camp and Field Life*, p. 218.

8. *OR*, pt. 2, pp. 388, 401–402, 408, 410–12, 438, 615–16; *OR*, vol. 51, pt. 1, p. 115; Sypher, *Pennsylvania Reserve Corps*, p. 228; Nisbet, *Four Years*, p. 111; Fullerton to family, July 4, 1862, Fullerton Papers, CWMC; "Army Correspondence," New Castle (Pa.) *Lawrence Journal*, p. 1; Grubb, *Notes of a Staff Officer*, pp. 9–11; Hill, *CMH*, vol. 5, p. 81; Nabours, "Active Service," p. 69; Polley, *Hood's Texas Brigade*, pp. 66–70; Powell, *Fifth Army Corps*, p. 107; Sears, *To the Gates of Richmond*, pp. 55, 253.

9. *OR*, pt. 2, p. 563, 757; Hood, *Advance and Retreat*, pp. 25–26; Hamby, "Fourth Texas," pp. 183–84; Polley, *Hood's Texas Brigade*, pp. 45–46; Hunter, "At Yorktown in 1862," p. 113; Henderson, "General Hood's Brigade," pp. 302–304; Crozier, "Private with General Hood," p. 557; Polley, *Hood's Texas Brigade*, pp. 45–46, 51; Davis, *Chaplain Davis*, p. 88; Simpson, *Hood's Texas Brigade*, pp. 117–18; McMurray, *John Bell Hood*, pp. 46–49. Polley (*Hood's Texas Brigade*, p. 51) says that on the testimony of then-lieutenant, later colonel, William C. Oates, the regiment Warwick tried to lead was the 15th Alabama. But this is difficult to believe, for it was with Trimble's brigade and not in the field where the charge was made. This statement cannot easily be explained. Hood's men passed the 15th Alabama on their way to the battle site, but Oates in his history of the 15th says that the regiment was out of ammunition and charged when the Texans did.

10. *OR*, pt. 2, p. 563; Chambers, "Mississippians at Gaines Mill," p. 511; anonymous letter, July 3, 1862, 4th Alabama File, ADAH; R. L. Dabney to Hotchkiss, Feb. 15, 1897, Hotchkiss Papers, LOC; Vairin Diary, MDAH; Hanks, *Captain B. F. Benton's Company*, p. 9; Robert Coles, manuscript history, 4th Alabama File, ADAH; Haskell, "Reminiscences of the Confederate War, 1861–1865," Haskell Papers SHC.

11. *OR*, pt. 2, pp. 40, 322, 324, 757, 767; Withers, *Autobiography*, pp. 186–87; Wood, "Black Eagle Company," p. 56; Robert Scott to Fanny, Aug. 23, 1862, Keith Family papers, VaHS; Buchanan, untitled letter, p. 216; Apted diary notes, Apted Papers, CWMC; Hoyt, *Palmetto Riflemen*, p. 29; Pickett, *Pickett and His Men*, p. 94; Haskell, "Reminiscences of the Confederate War, 1861–1865," Haskell Papers SHC; Hotchkiss, *CMH*, vol. 4, p. 605. Col. John B. Strange of the 19th Virginia noted that he found out after the battle that Hunton did not leave the field even though he was sick, but he mentions nothing of Hunton's assumption of command on that day.

12. *OR*, pt. 2, pp. 282, 297, 302, 307, 309, 311; Christiancy Diary, Christiancy Papers, John Sutton to brother, July 19, 1862, Sutton Papers, and Newton Bibbins to family, June 28, 1862, Bibbins Family Papers, all in BHC; Parker, *Henry Wilson's Regiment*, pp. 120, 122; Fagan, "Imagination's Work," p. 3; Slater, "At Gaines's Mill," p. 3; Faller to Cecilia, July 12, 1862, Faller Correspondence, Harrisburg CWRT (emphasis in original); Jacob Heffelfinger Diary, *CWTI*. Martindale (*OR*, pt. 2, p. 291) attempts to shift the blame—if there is any—to other units. However, an analysis of the *Official Records* makes it clear that Hood's blow fell on him.

13. Burress, "Brave Mississippians," p. 111; anonymous memoir, Miscellaneous Papers, UM; Miller, "Letters of Lieutenant Robert H. Miller," p. 88; Williams, "Wilcox's

Brigade," p. 443; Patterson, *Yankee Rebel*, p. 32; O.R., pt. 2, pp. 773–74; Hilary A. Herbert, untitled manuscript, 8th Alabama File, ADAH.

14. *OR*, pt. 2, pp. 285, 317, 339–40, 344–45, 421; Grannis, statement of service, Grannis Papers, SHSW; Bevier to parents, July 5, 1862, Bevier Papers, Leigh Collection, USAMHI; *OR Supp.*, vol. 2, pp. 440–41; Hoyt, "Anderson's Brigade," p. 226; Norton, *Army Letters*, p. 93; Terrell, "Gaines's Mills," p. 3; Peacock to Sarah, July 5, 1862, Peacock Papers, CWMC; Waugh Memoir, FSNMP.

15. *OR*, pt. 2, pp. 563–64, 592; Polley, *Hood's Texas Brigade*, pp. 50–51; Davis, *Chaplain Davis*, p. 89; Haskell, "Reminiscences of the Confederate War, 1861–1865," Haskell Papers SHC; Frothingham to Maggie, June 28, 1862, Frothingham Papers, NYPL.

16. *OR*, pt. 2, pp. 41–42, 224, 226, 250, 272, 282, 408; *OR*, vol. 51, pt. 1, p. 115; Polley, *Hood's Texas Brigade*, pp. 50, 60; Davis, *Chaplain Davis*, p. 89; Law, "On the Confederate Right," p. 364; Cooke, "Charge of Cooke's Cavalry," pp. 344–45; Comte de Paris to Cooke, Feb. 2, 1877, Cooke Family Papers, VaHS; Hood, *Advance and Retreat*, p. 29. Swinton agrees with Porter (*Campaigns*, p. 152). Cullen (*Peninsula Campaign*, pp. 118–19), Dowdey (*Seven Days*, pp. 241–42), and Krick ("Battle of Gaines Mill," p. 63) criticize Porter's view. Sears (*To the Gates of Richmond*, p. 246) and Stine (*Army of the Potomac*, p. 83) believe that the charge saved some artillery, at least as much as it lost. Starr calls the charge "murderous and senseless" but says Porter's claim was "absurd" (*Union Cavalry*, vol. 1, pp. 277–78). Powell says the charge merely completed the disaster (*Fifth Army Corps*, pp. 103–104).

17. *OR*, pt. 2, pp. 39–40, 70–71, 76, 226, 250, 282; McCaleb, "Mississippi Brigade," p. 331; Butterfield to Porter, June 27, 1862, McClellan Papers, LOC; "Memoranda of the Irish Brigade," Meagher Papers, Palmer Collection, WRHS; Veil Memoir, Veil Papers, CWMC; Hard, *History of the Eighth Cavalry*, p. 146; Powell, *Fifth Army Corps*, p. 107, Roher to wife, July 6, 1862, Roher Papers, Leigh Collection, USAMHI; Conyngham, *Irish Brigade*, p. 186; Grubb, *Notes of a Staff Officer*, pp. 12–15; anonymous memoir, Faunce Papers, Duke; Noonan, manuscript history of 69th New York, Noonan Papers, Powers Collection, USAMHI. For the inflated claims see, for example, Conyngham, *Irish Brigade*, pp. 184–85; Lyons, *Meagher*, p. 156.

18. *OR*, pt. 2, p. 626; Hill, "Lee's Attacks," p. 357, Polley, *Hood's Texas Brigade*, p. 51; Stone to family, undated, Stone Papers, MinnHS.

19. Livermore, *Numbers and Losses*, p. 140; Wayland, *Stonewall Jackson's Way*, p. 162; Brooks to mother, July 4, 1862, Brooks Papers, GDAH; Worsham, *Foot Cavalry*, p. 99; Pickett, *Pickett and His Men*, p. 95; *OR*, pt. 2, p. 758; Longstreet, *From Manassas to Appomattox*, p. 129; "On to Prison," p. 30; Long, *Robert E. Lee*, p. 174.

20. *OR*, pt. 2, pp. 39–41, 558–59, 642, 780–86, 973–91; Livermore, *Numbers and Losses*, p. 83, 140-1; Fox, *Regimental Losses*, pp. 543–51, 562–63; Simpson, *Hood's Texas Brigade*, p. 119. Garland's report says "about 500 killed and _____ wounded," but in the casualty report, the total killed in the brigade for the entire series of battles is reported as 192, so it is reasonable to assume that the 500 figure refers to total casualties. In other battles, such as Gettysburg, Chickamauga, and Cold Harbor, the losses on one day of a multiday battle exceeded those at Gaines' Mill, and because of incomplete Confederate reporting not all battles are listed by Fox.

8. *"You Have Done Your Best to Sacrifice This Army"*

1. Hill, "Lee's Attacks," pp. 358–59; *OR*, pt. 2, p. 515; *OR*, ser. 3, vol. 3, pp. 252–319; Blackford, *War Years*, pp. 73–74; Polley, *Letters to Charming Nellie*, p. 55, and *Hood's*

Texas Brigade, pp. 61–62; Alexander, *Military Memoirs*, p. 172, and *Fighting for the Confederacy*, pp. 115–17.

2. Wise (*Long Arm of Lee*, pp. 211–13) criticizes the use of artillery, but this was a tough field for the Confederates regarding the guns, as shown by the difficulty that Jackson, a former artillery instructor, had in massing cannon. McCormick (*War Without Grant*, p. 86) takes Lee to task for having no organized force ready for pursuit, but Lee used everyone he had just to win the battle and probably (as in General Orders no. 75) expected all his units to pursue, which was impossible after most Civil War battles.

3. Alexander (*Military Memoirs*, p. 122, 132), Dowdey (*Seven Days*, p. 204), and Sears (*To the Gates of Richmond*, pp. 217–18) have made the argument that Jackson was late. Greene (*Whatever You Resolve to Be*, p. 56) argues that the delay was "irrelevant". Alexander believes Gaines's Mill would have been an easy victory if Jackson had attacked early.

4. Hassler, *A. P. Hill*, p. 57; Dickert, *Kershaw's Brigade*, p. 138; Longstreet to Lee, Mar. 20, 1866, Lee Headquarters Papers, VaHS; Longstreet, *From Manassas to Appomattox*, pp. 126–29. Farwell believes no Confederate general distinguished himself, citing in part the argument about unit cohesion, but that assessment is otherwise harsh (*Stonewall*, p. 354).

5. *Confederate Veteran* 6 (1898): pp. 472–73, 565–70, 580; *Confederate Veteran* 7 (1899): pp. 54–55, 170, 223–24, 227–28, 357–58; *Confederate Veteran* 8 (1900): p. 66; *Confederate Veteran* 15 (1907): p. 507; *Confederate Veteran* 23 (1915): pp. 161–62; Hill, "Lee's Attacks," pp. 355–57; Hotchkiss, *CMH*, vol. 4, p. 291; *OR*, pt. 2, p. 898; Longstreet, *From Manassas to Appomattox*, p. 129; Taylor, *General Lee*, p. 69; Henderson, "General Hood's Brigade," p. 304; Freeman, *Lee's Lieutenants*, vol. 1, pp. 532–35; Dowdey, *Seven Days*, p. 239; Simpson, *Hood's Texas Brigade*, p. 126. Avery ("Memorial Address," pp. 126–27) agrees with Hill. Avery's quotes from Jackson and Lee, in particular, do not make any claim that Hill's men were the first to break the Union line, they say only that they did in fact break it. Bridges (*Lee's Maverick General*, pp. 72–73) quotes a letter from Wilcox in which that officer said Hood told him Wilcox reached the guns before Hood did, but could not hold them.

6. Hill, "Lee's Attacks," p. 359; Kearny to Courtland Parker, July 20, July 31, 1862, Kearny Papers, LOC; Slocum to Stanton, July 19, 1862, Porter Papers, LOC. Sears (*To the Gates of Richmond*, p. 236, 246, 249) criticizes Porter, whereas Cullen (*Peninsula Campaign*, p. 120) defends him. Interestingly, Slocum, *Life and Services*, p. 26, says that committing forces piecemeal kept the line together longer than would otherwise have been possible.

7. "Brig. Gen. James T. [*sic*] Archer," p. 66; Porter, endorsement on Slocum to Stanton, July 19, 1862, and "A Cursory (but truthful) Narrative of my Recollections and Connections with the Rebellion," Porter Papers, LOC.

8. Porter, in a letter to Hiram Ketchum (quoted in Barnard, *Peninsular Campaign*, p. 81), wrote that with fifteen thousand more men he could have driven the Confederates back. Alexander (*Military Memoirs*, p. 130) and Eckenrode and Conrad (*James Longstreet*, p. 70) say that only one division was needed. Palfrey ("Seven Days' Battles," p. 152) claims that attacking Longstreet's south flank from south of the river would have been the best move.

9. *OR*, pt. 2, pp. 462–63, 688–89, 706, 831; Banes, *Philadelphia Brigade*, p. 73; Henry K. Burgwyn to mother, July 14, 1862, Burgwyn Family Papers, SHC; Westbrook, *49th Pennsylvania*, pp. 113–14; Barker to Annie, June 28, 1862, Barker Papers, RIHS; Battle and Adams, *Civil War Letters*, p. 8; Thompson Journal, Thompson Papers, LOC. Barker does not specify this action, but it is likely that the fifty rounds of shot and shell he said the battery fired were used here.

10. *OR*, pt. 2, pp. 237, 689; Smith, *Autobiography*, p. 41; Jones, *Rebel War Clerk's Diary*, p. 139; Hyde, *Following the Greek Cross*, p. 67; Charles P. Ives to Lee, July 9, 1862, Colonial Dames Collection, UOkla; Wright, "Old Peninsular Days," p. 3; Henry Burgwyn to mother, July 14, 1862, Burgwyn Family Papers, SHC.

11. *OR*, pt. 2, pp. 463, 661, 689, 695, 715, 748, 750; *OR*, pt. 3, pp. 621–22; Wyckoff, "Kershaw's South Carolina Brigade," p. 114; Henley Memoir, FSNMP; Hyde, *Following the Greek Cross*, p. 68; Trepp Journal, Trepp Papers, NYHS; Tyler to uncle, July 4, 1862, Tyler Papers, VaHS; Selkirk to parents, July 6, 1862, Selkirk Papers, USAMHI; Stovall, *Robert Toombs*, pp. 250–1.

12. *OR*, pt. 2, pp. 88, 467, 476, 695, 699–700; Clark, "Campaigning with the Sixth Maine," p. 408; Curtiss Diary, Curtiss Papers, CMU; Abbott, July 12, 1862 letter, Abbott Papers, Civil War Miscellany, Personal Papers, GDAH; Trepp Journal, Trepp Papers, NYHS; Thomas to friends, July 5, 1862, Thomas Papers, SHSW; newspaper article, DeClark Papers, CWMC.

13. *OR*, pt. 2, pp. 467, 696, 698, 700, 971, 977; *OR*, pt. 3, p. 238; *Army of the Potomac*, p. 623. It is not explicitly stated that the 7th Georgia was supporting the Wise battery. However, since only one regiment went to support that battery and three to support the howitzers of Lee's command to the north of Toombs's position (Toombs probably would have called all three regiments for help if he had found three), and the 7th Georgia went in on the right flank, it makes sense to conclude it. Stine (*Army of the Potomac*, pp. 86–87) makes the comment regarding the engagement's importance.

14. *OR*, pt. 3, p. 622; Putnam, *Richmond During the War*, p. 146; Edmonston, "*Journal of a Secesh Lady*," pp. 202–203; Banes, *Philadelphia Brigade*, p. 74; William Biddle to Ropes, Mar. 27, 1895, Ropes Collection, BU; Humphreys, *Andrew Atkinson Humphreys*, pp. 164–65; Porter, "Hanover Court House," p. 342. Porter also sent Col. Thomas L. Gantt with the same message to McClellan, and Gantt stayed for the same reason.

15. *OR*, pt. 1, pp. 59–60; *OR*, pt. 3, p. 266; Campbell, *McClellan*, p. 227; McClellan to Heintzelman, June 27, 1862, McClellan Papers, LOC (it is assumed that the other corps commanders got the same message); "Council of War evening of June 27, 1862," from "The Soldier of Indiana," Porter Papers, LOC; Eisenschiml, *Celebrated Case*, p. 38; Werstein, *Kearny the Magnificent*, pp. 224–25; Kearny, *General Philip Kearny*, p. 294; Heintzelman, notes on McClellan's report, Heintzelman Papers, LOC. This story was repeated by Heintzelman in testimony before the Joint Committee on the Conduct of the War (*Army of the Potomac*, p. 355).

16. *OR*, pt. 1, p. 60; *OR*, pt. 2, pp. 71, 76, 226, 274, 350, 389, 433; Marcy (?) to Keyes, June 27 or 28, 1862, McClellan Papers, LOC; Seth Williams to Heintzelman, June 27, 1862, McClellan Papers, LOC; Spaulding to Dunkle, July 14, 1862, Spaulding Papers, Duke; anonymous memoir, Faunce Papers, Duke; McMichael to Elizabeth Rooke, July 5, 1862, McMichael Papers, LOC; "On to Prison," p. 31; Apted diary notes, Apted Papers, CWMC; Bancroft Diary, Bancroft Papers, BHC; Judson, *History of the Eighty-Third Regiment*, p. 46; Fullerton to family, July 4, 1862, Fullerton Papers, CWMC; Thompson Journal, Thompson Papers, LOC; Osborne, *History of the Twenty-Ninth Regiment*, p. 150.

17. George Whatley to wife, June 28, 1862, 10th Alabama File, ADAH; Thomas Penn to mother, June 27, 1862, Penn Papers, Duke; Hinsdale Journal, Hinsdale Family Papers, Duke; Benson Memoir, Benson Papers, SHC; Westervelt Diary, CWMC.

18. Ellis, *Leaves*, pp. 97–99; Robertson, *Diary of the War*, p. 36; Braman to Kill, June 27, 1862, Braman Papers, NYSL; Ashenfelter to Father Churchman, July 7, 1862, Ashenfelter Papers, Harrisburg CWRT; Cook, *Siege of Richmond*, p. 322; Fuller, *Chaplain Fuller*, p. 269.

19. Alexander Bliss, "No. 1 Narrative," Bancroft-Bliss Family Papers, LOC; McClellan, *Civil War Papers*, pp. 321, 327; *OR*, pt. 1, p. 61; *OR*, pt. 3, p. 269; Bates, *Lincoln in the Telegraph Office*, pp. 109–10. The telegram is reprinted in full in Appendix D. Among those generally agreeing with McClellan are Campbell (*McClellan*, p. 223), Hassler (*General George B. McClellan*, p. 153), and Myers (*General George B. McClellan*, p. 301). Among those generally disagreeing, or at least finding fault with the sending of the message, are Cullen (*Peninsula Campaign*, p. 125), Dowdey (*Seven Days*, p. 256), French (*Army of the Potomac*, p. 101), Hassler (*Commanders*, p. 49), Sears (*George B. McClellan*, p. 214), and Williams (*Lincoln Finds a General*, p. 231).

9. *"His Only Course Seemed to Me Was to Make for James River"*

1. Lee, *Lee's Dispatches*, p. 202; Benson Memoir, Benson Papers, SHC; Jones, "Reminiscences No. 8," p. 562; Sypher, *Pennsylvania Reserve Corps*, pp. 235–36; Lange Memoir, Lange Papers, VaHS; DeLeon, *Four Years*, p. 205; Lucy Munford to Jennie, June 29, 1862, Munford-Ellis Family Papers, Duke; Putnam, *Richmond During the War*, pp. 147, 150; Jones, *Rebel War Clerk's Diary*, pp. 138–39; Mallory Diary, LOC.

2. Anonymous memoir, Miscellaneous Papers, UM; "Horrors of the Battlefield," p. 305; Branscomb to sister, July 15, 1862, Branscomb Family Papers, ADAH; Ardrey Diary, Ardrey Papers, Duke; W. A. Kenyon to brother, June 28, 1862, Kenyon Papers, Duke.

3. Reynolds to sisters, July 3, 1862, Reynolds Family Papers, FMC; Avery, "Memorial Address," p. 122; Hill, "Lee's Attacks," pp. 360–61; Hunter, "At Yorktown," p. 113; Westervelt Diary, CWMC. The story and Col. T. B. W. Stockton's brief report of his capture (*OR*, pt. 2, p. 323) sound similar, but Hunter said the colonel commanded the regiment defending against the 4th Texas, and that regiment was the 1st Michigan, not the 16th (which Stockton commanded). However, the commander of the 1st Michigan, Horace Roberts, was not captured.

4. Hood, *Advance and Retreat*, p. 28; Powell, *Fifth Army Corps*, p. 105 n 1; *OR*, pt. 2, p. 573; Lee, *Recollections and Letters*, pp. 73–74.

5. Alexander to father, July 24, 1862, Alexander Papers, SHC; Brent, *Memoirs*, pp. 175–76; Thomas Carpenter to Phil, July 7, 1862, Bulkley Family Papers, MoHS; *OR*, pt. 2, pp. 493, 515.

6. *OR*, pt. 2, pp. 493, 617, 758; Hill, "Lee's Attacks," p. 362 (emphasis in original). Trimble distinctly dates this incident as occurring on Sunday the twenty-ninth, not Saturday the twenty-eighth. However, no other report mentions anything about Trimble's brigade being left behind when Ewell moved on Dispatch Station. Freeman (*R. E. Lee*, pp. 163–64) and Martin (*Road to Glory*, pp. 111–12) tell the story as occurring on the twenty-eighth without comment. Hill's story refers to an answer given by a Professor Kendrick to Longstreet when the latter proposed to make carbonic acid by burning diamonds.

7. *OR*, pt. 2, pp. 200, 233, 493, 516, 524; Deloney to Rose, June 29, 1862, Deloney Papers, UGa; Brent, *Memoirs*, p. 176. Lee's report mentions the destruction of the bridge in such a way as to imply that Lee knew of that destruction earlier rather than later. Brent mentions only that Stuart sent a note telling of no enemy along the railroad.

8. *OR*, pt. 2, p. 493; Lee, *Lee's Dispatches*, pp. 20–21; Hill, "McClellan's Change of Base," pp. 385–86. Marshall (*Aide-de-Camp*, p. 89) mentions the two options Lee expected McClellan to choose from. Cullen (*Peninsula Campaign*, p. 128) and Dowdey (*Seven Days*, p. 252) think Lee was slow in believing in the change of base. For the opinion that McClellan had Lee's number this once, see (among others) Bache, *George Gordon Meade*, p. 117; Hassler, *Commanders*, p. 49; Macartney, *Little Mac*, p. 185; McCormick, *War Without Grant*, p. 86; Swinton, *Campaigns*, p. 154. Brent (*Memoirs*,

p. 174) says that he heard nothing at headquarters that indicated anyone thought McClellan was headed to the James.

9. *OR*, pt. 2, pp. 493, 621; Brown, "Down the Peninsula," pp. 55–56; Hands Civil War Memoirs, UVa; Johnson, "Memoir," p. 215. Naglee's report (*OR Supp.*, vol. 2, p. 413) says the cavalry on the east bank was the Oneida Cavalry, but Thomas Carpenter (letter to Phil, July 7, 1862, Bulkley Family Papers, MoHS) says that his men of the McClellan Dragoons were those on the east bank.

10. *OR*, pt. 2, pp. 198–200, 215, 351, 516–17; Johnson, "Memoir," p. 215; Thomas Carpenter to Phil, July 7, 1862, Bulkley Family Papers, MoHS; Seth Williams to Porter, June 28, 1862, McClellan Papers (telegram books), LOC; Blackford Journal, Blackford Papers, CWMC; Brent, *Memoirs*, p. 176.

11. McClellan, *Civil War Papers*, p. 302; *OR*, pt. 2, pp. 333, 482–83, 513, 516, 645; *OR*, pt. 3, p. 248; Robertson, *Diary of the War*, p. 37; Ellis, *Leaves*, p. 100; Kautz Diary, LOC; Blackford, *War Years*, pp. 74–75.

12. *OR*, pt. 2, pp. 333, 483; Ellis, *Leaves*, pp. 100–102; Robertson, *Diary of the War*, pp. 37–38; Braman to uncle, June 30, 1862, Braman Papers, NYSL; Ashenfelter to Father Churchman, July 7, 1862, Ashenfelter Papers, Harrisburg CWRT; Fuller, *Chaplain Fuller*, p. 271; Wilson, report, Wilson Papers, Leigh Collection, USAMHI.

13. Cullen (*Peninsula Campaign*, p. 134) suggests that Stuart should have crossed the Chickahominy below Bottom's Bridge.

14. *OR*, pt. 2, p. 360, 556, 565, 589, 642, 758, 874, 888, 891, 898.

15. Jones, *Life and Letters*, p. 174; *Army of the Potomac*, pp. 435, 610; Keyes, *Fifty Years' Observations*, p. 446, 480; *OR*, pt. 1, pp. 64, 118–19, 193, 216; *OR*, pt. 2, pp. 192–93, 202, 216–17; Spaulding to Dunkle, July 14, 1862, Spaulding Papers, Duke; Stewart, *Camp, March and Battlefield*, p. 186; Hatton Diary, CWMC (emphasis in original); Keyes to Marcy, June 27, 1862, McClellan Papers, LOC. McClellan's report mentions his knowledge of only one road. It must have been the Willis Church road, which is the only one shown on Plate 19-1, *OR*, Atlas, based on information gathered by Humphreys.

16. Powell, *Fifth Army Corps*, p. 131; Christiancy Diary, Christiancy Papers, BHC; *OR*, pt. 2, pp.242, 252, 265–66, 269, 274, 292, 309, 313, 319, 324, 340–41, 350, 365, 389, 971; Judson, *History of the Eighty-Third Regiment*, p. 46; Bancroft Diary, Bancroft Papers, BHC; Bliss, "Narrative," Bancroft-Bliss Family Papers, LOC; LeDuc, *Recollections*, p. 82; Ames to parents, July 5, 1862, Ames Papers, USAMHI; Evans, "There is No Use," p. 45; Young Diary, CWMC; Elliott Diary, CWMC; Donn, "With the Army of the Potomac," pp. 396–400; Hager Memoir, Hager Papers, UVa; Sypher, *Pennsylvania Reserve Corps*, pp. 248–50; McMichael to Rooke, July 5, 1862, McMichael Papers, LOC; Woodward, *Third Pennsylvania Reserve*, pp. 95–96; Gray, "Artillerist's Yarn," p. 7; Fullerton to family, July 4, 1862, Fullerton Papers, CWMC; "Battles before Richmond," p. 1.

17. Sears, *George B. McClellan*, p. 216; Lee, *Wartime Papers*, pp. 204–205; *OR*, pt. 2, pp. 535, 542, 548, 690; Brent, *Memoirs*, p. 175; Tyler to uncle, July 4, 1862, Tyler Papers, VaHS; Smith, *Autobiography*, p. 42; Hyde, *Following the Greek Cross*, p. 69.

18. *OR*, pt. 2, pp. 463, 465, 690, 694; newspaper article, DeClark Papers, CWMC; Thomas to friends, July 5, 1862, Thomas Papers, SHSW; Luckinbill Diary, NCCWRT; Keith to friends, July 6, 1862, Keith Papers, VtHS; Quimby to Emeline, July 12, 1862, Quimby Papers, FSNMP.

19. *OR*, pt. 2, pp. 468, 473–74, 477–75, 481, 661–62, 690, 706, 710–11; Lee, *Wartime Papers*, pp. 204–205; Brent, *Memoirs*, p. 192; Stevens, *Three Years*, pp. 92–93; "Gatling Gun," p. 1; Ingraham, "Correction," p. 4; Westbrook, *49th Pennsylvania Volunteers*, p. 115; Works to friends, July 11, 1862, Works Papers, URL; Selkirk to parents, July 6, 1862, Selkirk Papers, USAMHI; Franklin, "Rear-Guard Fighting," p. 369.

20. *OR*, pt. 2, pp. 535–36, 661–62, 788, 915; Charles Friend to wife, June 29, 1862, Blanton Family Papers, VaHS; Toombs, *Correspondence*, p. 600; Jordan, *Hancock*, p. 46; Pendleton to wife, June 28, 1862, Pendleton Papers, SHC.

21. *OR*, pt. 2, pp. 54, 71, 89, 151; anonymous memoir, Faunce Papers, Duke; Haydon, *For Country, Cause and Leader*, p. 258; Davis to Belle, July 5, 1862, Davis Papers, Yale; Ford, *Fifteenth Massachusetts*, p. 173; Marks, *Peninsular Campaign*, pp. 228–29; Banes, *Philadelphia Brigade*, p. 74; Batchelder to mother, July 8, 1862, Zadock Pratt Papers, BU; Dodge Journal, Dodge Papers, LOC.

22. Taylor Diary, WHMC; Elliott Diary, CWMC; Young Diary, CWMC; Perkins, "Civil War Diary," p. 165; Sypher, *Pennsylvania Reserve Corps*, p. 251; Banes, *Philadelphia Brigade*, p. 74; Revere to Lee, June 28, 1862, Revere Papers, MassHS; Dodge Journal, Dodge Papers, LOC; Stowe Diary, Stowe Papers, *CWTI* (emphasis in original); Scandlin Diary, Scandlin Papers, AAS (emphasis in original); Haines Journal, Haines Papers, Rutgers.

23. *OR*, pt. 2, pp. 22, 434; *OR*, vol. 51, pt. 1, p. 104; Osborn, *No Middle Ground*, p. 69; James Remington Diary, Remington Papers, RIHS; Smith, *Autobiography*, p. 42; Stillwell Diary, Stillwell Papers, SHSW; Taylor Diary, WHMC; Judd, *Thirty-third N.Y.S. Vols.*, p. 136; Hyde, *Following the Greek Cross*, pp. 69–70; Davis to Belle, July 5, 1862, Davis Papers, Yale; Patch to mother, July 5, 1862, Patch Papers, Leigh Collection, USAMHI; Haines Journal, Haines Papers, Rutgers; Luckinbill Diary, NCCWRT; Newcomb Diary, Newcomb Papers, Stanford; Thomas Carpenter to Phil, July 7, 1862, Bulkley Family Papers, MoHS.

24. Taylor, *Destruction and Reconstruction*, p. 102; *OR*, pt. 2, p. 494; Longstreet, *From Manassas to Appomattox*, p. 130; Early, *War Memoirs*, p. 76.

25. *OR*, pt. 1, p. 60; *OR*, pt. 3, p. 272; Cook, *Siege of Richmond*, p. 318; Westervelt Diary, CWMC; *Army of the Potomac*, pp. 436, 592; Frothingham to Maggie, July 4, 1862, Frothingham Papers, NYPL; Hager Memoir, Hager Papers, UVa. Sears (*To the Gates of Richmond*, p. 256) criticizes McClellan for putting his attention on the trains and thus being too cautious about getting the infantry out of the lines. This criticism is only warranted if the true size of the Confederate army is considered. Given McClellan's thoughts regarding Lee's forces, it makes sense that he should withdraw his units slowly and quietly.

26. *OR*, pt. 3, p. 269–71; McClellan, *Civil War Papers*, p. 324; Lincoln, *Collected Works*, p. 289. Franklin gave two somewhat conflicting versions in *OR*, pt. 2, p. 430, and *Army of the Potomac*, p. 623; Sumner did not move until the morning of the twenty-ninth but made no mention of when orders were given, and Heintzelman reported (*OR*, pt. 2, p. 98) that the orders were given on the evening of the twenty-eighth.

10. *"But What Do You Think? Is the Enemy in Large Force?"*

1. Brent, *Memoirs*, pp. 178, 191–92; *OR*, pt. 2, pp. 662, 707. Nowhere is the fact that Chilton received the information from Meade and Johnston specifically stated. However, as Magruder says that Chilton gave him the information, Chilton must have received it from somewhere. Longstreet (*From Manassas to Appomattox*, p. 130) says that Meade and Johnston gave Lee his first notice of the Union retreat. Chilton was most likely with Lee and would have been a natural courier to send to Magruder.

2. *OR*, pt. 2, pp. 90, 726, 744; Wyckoff, "Kershaw's South Carolina Brigade," pp. 115–16; Longstreet, *From Manassas to Appomattox*, pp. 130, 148–49; Lee, *Lee's Dispatches*, p. 20.

3. Sears, *To the Gates of Richmond*, p. 293; *OR*, pt. 2, pp. 494, 787. Hotchkiss, *CMH*, vol. 4, p. 295, points out the key nature of the Glendale crossroads. Lee's mentions of his orders for the twenty-ninth (the original has not been found) are somewhat

contradictory. In his official report (*OR*, pt. 2, p. 494) he says that Huger was to flank the Federals and Magruder was to take them in the rear. In his message to Davis on the morning of the twenty-ninth, however (Lee, *Lee's Dispatches*, p. 21), he mentions only pursuit of the enemy as the task assigned Huger and Magruder. The same move, of course, could accomplish both, depending upon the tactical situation.

4. Dabney to Jedediah Hotchkiss, Apr. 22, 1896, Hotchkiss Papers, LOC; *OR*, pt. 2, p. 837; Alexander, *Military Memoirs*, pp. 134–35. Longstreet ("'Seven Days'," p. 399) put the distance he would need to march at sixteen miles. Freeman (*R. E. Lee*, p. 172) figured it at about twenty miles. Cullen (*Peninsula Campaign*, p. 135) and Dowdey (*Seven Days*, p. 253) like Lee's plan. Farwell (*Stonewall*, p. 357), Sears (*To the Gates of Richmond*, p. 262), and Wycoff ("Kershaw's South Carolina Brigade," p. 127) do not. Sears (*To the Gates of Richmond*, p. 262) considers Alexander's idea without reference to his works and discards it. Dowdey (*Seven Days*, p. 253) relates that Lee had the plan thought up when he went to bed on the twenty-eighth, but he gives no source for this. Lee no doubt had considered his alternatives in case the Yankees disappeared from Magruder's front, but if the plan was set on the night of the twenty-eighth, Lee would have sent the orders out then, so the men could be ready to move at first light.

5. *OR*, pt. 2, pp. 662, 716, 726; Wyckoff, "Kershaw's South Carolina Brigade," p. 116; Shand Memoir, Shand Papers, FSNMP; Thomas Pitts to Lizzie, July 7, 1862, Pitts Papers, SCHS; letter of July 8, 1862, Duggan Papers, Civil War Miscellany, Personal Papers, GDAH; letter of July 12, 1862, Abbott Papers, Civil War Miscellany, Personal Papers, GDAH.

6. *OR*, pt. 2, pp. 662–63, 716, 726. Magruder's report does not say which of Griffith's regiments moved south, none of the regimental commanders reported on the action of the twenty-ninth, and Griffith, having been killed on the twenty-ninth, obviously did not submit a report. William Barksdale, who took command of the brigade after Griffith's death, did submit a report (*OR*, pt. 2, p. 750) and told of the 17th and 21st Mississippi's movement to the south side of the railroad, but the timing seems wrong. Reports from the various commanders under Magruder on the twenty-ninth are quite confusing as none of them completely coincide with the others. This description of the orders is from Magruder's report.

7. Bache, *George Gordon Meade*, p. 117; *OR*, pt. 2, pp. 71, 122, 137, 151, 257, 269, 463, 468, 481; *OR Supp.*, vol. 2, p. 415; Anderson Journal, Anderson Papers, UW-GB; Dodge Journal, Dodge Papers, LOC; Martin, et al., *Fifty-Seventh Regiment*, pp. 34–35. Kearny and his brigade commanders are vague about the exact places they wound up on the morning of the twenty-ninth. Berry reported that he occupied the left of the old earthworks and connected his pickets with those of Robinson, which ensured the defense of all approaches from the area of the sawmill to the Williamsburg road (*OR*, pt. 2, p. 185). That would seem to place Birney in reserve, but he reported only that he held the entrenchments, which does not sound as if he was in reserve (*OR*, pt. 2, p. 181). Kearny gave no indication of the order of his units.

8. *OR*, pt. 2, pp. 54, 57, 60, 77, 82, 87, 90, 93–94; Davis to Belle, July 5, 1862, Davis Papers, Yale; Banes, *Philadelphia Brigade*, pp. 76–77. It is not certain that the 1st Minnesota detachment worked at Orchard Station, but it is the logical inference given that the detachment had to march about half a mile to get behind the Union lines in the morning. Fair Oaks Station was farther away from the Allen farm than that. French reported that the 53rd Pennsylvania's movement took place after the Confederates started shelling his position, while Richardson reported the occupation as taking place before any Confederate firing. George Whitman of the 53rd Pennsylvania, in a letter to his wife (July 5, 1862, Whitman Papers, CWMC) does not mention the buildings but does

say he got into position before the Confederate firing began. No report specifies Sedgwick's formation, but Sully's report reads as if he was in reserve, and Dana's report makes it seem as if he were posted farther south than Burns.

9. *OR*, pt. 2, pp. 63, 82–84, 90–91, 98, 663–64, 726; Fox, *Regimental Losses*, p. 278; Thomas Pitts to Lizzie, July 7, 1862, Pitts Papers, SCHS; Barker to mother, July 6, 1862, Barker Papers, RIHS.

10. *OR*, pt. 2, pp. 54, 57, 83, 662, 691, 707, 709; *OR*, vol. 51, pt. 1, p. 108; McDaniel, *With Unabated Trust*, p. 85; Whitman to wife, July 5, 1862, Whitman Papers, CWMC; Stephen to Olive, July 6, 1862, Olney Papers, RIHS; Andrews, *Footprints of a Regiment*, p. 46; Burns Diary, Pennsylvania "Save the Flags" Civil War Collection, USAMHI; letter of July 6, 1862, Hospes Papers, SHSW.

11. *OR*, pt. 2, pp. 24–25, 694, 977; Banes, *Philadelphia Brigade*, p. 79; Duffey Diary, VaHS; Davis, *Jefferson Davis*, vol. 2, pp. 316–17; John Wise to cousin, July 4, 1862, Wise Papers, UVa; Brent, *Memoirs*, p. 180. The loss of the 71st Pennsylvania reported in Banes's history does not coincide with the official reported loss of 9 killed, 54 wounded, and 28 missing (91 total).

12. Brent, *Memoirs*, p. 181–83; *OR*, pt. 2, pp. 574, 663–64, 680, 788–89, 808–809; Sneden, "Pen and Sword," p. 49; Walker, *Second Army Corps*, p. 68; B. Wylie Scott to Ella, July 9, 1862, Merryman Papers, VaHS; Henry Burgwyn to mother, July 14, 1862, Burgwyn Family Papers, SHC.

11. "He Has Other Important Duty to Perform"

1. Sleight Memoir, Sleight Papers, BHC; *OR*, pt. 2, pp. 205, 207, 235, 274, 525–27; Harvey Davis diary extract, Harrisburg CWRT; Averell, "With the Cavalry," p. 431; Rhodes, *All For the Union*, p. 72; J. W. Biddle to father, July 15, 1862, Simpson-Biddle Papers, NCDAH; Powell, *Fifth Army Corps*, p. 132; Ames to parents, July 5, 1862, Ames Papers, USAMHI; Hager Memoir, Hager Papers, UVa. The reports submitted after this engagement are somewhat confusing as no one seems to have been entirely sure what road they were on. The roads used in the text are most likely the correct ones, but they are not always those referred to in the reports themselves.

2. Averell, "With the Cavalry," p. 431; Keyes, *Fifty Years' Observations*, p. 481; Hill, *CMH*, vol. 5, p. 83; *OR*, pt. 2, pp. 235, 243, 251–52, 265–66, 269, 274, 292, 350, 389, 417, 434; Frothingham to Maggie, July 4, 1862, Frothingham Papers, NYPL; Ames to parents, July 5, 1862, Ames Papers, USAMHI; Hager Memoir, Hager Papers, UVa; Roher to wife, July 6, 1862, Roher Papers, Leigh Collection, USAMHI; John Wittel to cousin, July 19, 1862, Wittel Papers, CWMC.

3. Keyes, *Fifty Years' Observations*, p. 481; Keyes to Marcy, June 28, 1862, McClellan Papers, LOC; *OR*, pt. 2, p. 193; Averell, "With the Cavalry," p. 431; Williams, *Lincoln Finds a General*, vol. 1, p. 232–33, 236. The map is Plate 19-1, *OR*, Atlas. Many historians have pointed out the fortunate nature of the discovery of the road; see, for example, Webb, *Peninsula*, p. 141; Hassler, *General George B. McClellan*, p. 155. Williams takes McClellan severely to task for the omission of the road on the map, but he falsely claims that no reconnaissances were made.

4. Alexander Bliss, "No. 1 Narrative," Bancroft-Bliss Family Papers, LOC; *OR*, pt. 1, pp. 62, 118–19; LeDuc, *Recollections*, p. 83; Adams, *Story of a Trooper*, p. 583; Elliott Diary, CWMC; Young Diary, CWMC; Joinville, *Army of the Potomac*, p. 93; McClellan, *Civil War Papers*, pp. 324–25.

5. *OR*, pt. 1, pp. 140–41; *OR*, pt. 2, p. 22; *OR*, pt. 3, p. 277; McClellan, *Civil War Papers*, p. 296. Hassler (*General George B. McClellan*, pp. 153–54) suggests that the

engineers' absence explains McClellan's behavior. Sears (*To the Gates of Richmond*, p. 265) describes McClellan's not assigning an overall commander as deliberate.

6. Walker, *Second Army Corps*, p. 66; Smith, *Autobiography*, pp. 42–43; Franklin, "Rear-Guard Fighting," p. 371; *OR*, pt. 2, pp. 50, 54, 80, 94, 98–99, 430; Banes, *Philadelphia Brigade*, p. 79; Trepp Journal, Trepp Papers, NYHS. Franklin's and Smith's accounts are subtly different, and this is a conjectured combination.

7. *OR*, pt. 2, pp. 50, 99, 161, 162, 170, 465; *Army of the Potomac*, pp. 356, 363; Osborn, *No Middle Ground*, p. 73; Everett to parents, July 6, 1862, Everett Papers, Leigh Collection, USAMHI. Walker (*Second Army Corps*, p. 68) and Palfrey ("Seven Days' Battles," p. 177) are among the critics. Bache (*George Gordon Meade*, p. 118), Cullen (*Peninsula Campaign*, p. 136), Sears (*To the Gates of Richmond*, p. 267), and Stanley (*E. V. Sumner*, p. 258) are less critical.

8. Davis to Belle, July 5, 1862, Davis Papers, Yale; Brent, *Memoirs*, pp. 180–81; *OR*, pt. 2, p. 89; Hyde, *Following the Greek Cross*, p. 71; Adams, *Story of a Trooper*, p. 580; Favill, *Diary of a Young Officer*, p. 136; Marks, *Peninsular Campaign*, p. 245; Eames to wife, July 5, 1862, Eames Papers, Smith Collection, USAMHI; Stillwell Diary, Stillwell Papers, SHSW; Miller, "Serving under McClellan," p. 28; Adams, *Reminiscences*, p. 33; Scandlin Diary, Scandlin Papers, AAS; Barker to sister, July 5, 1862, Barker Papers, RIHS; Stephen to Olive, July 6, 1862, Olney Papers, RIHS; Anderson Journal, Anderson Papers, UW-GB; Bowen, *Ball's Bluff to Gettysburg*, p. 106; Stevens, *Three Years*, p. 97; Dodge Journal, Dodge Papers, LOC.

9. Cook, *Siege of Richmond*, p. 325; Sneden, "Pen and Sword," p. 44; Sanborn, "Savage Station," p. 3; Hands Civil War Memoirs, UVa; Brown, "Down the Peninsula," pp. 56–57; Pryor to Penelope, June 27–30, 1862, Pryor Papers, UGa; Johnson, "Memoir," pp. 215–16; Francis Coker to wife, June 29, 1862, Heidler Papers, UGa; Newcomb Diary, Newcomb Papers, Stanford; O'Connell Memoir, CWMC; Jones Diary, Jones Papers, VaHS; Fogleman Diary, FSNMP; Haw Diary, Haw Papers, VaHS; Charles Friend to wife, June 29, 1862, Blanton Family Papers, VaHS; Allan, "Peninsula," p. 203.

10. *OR*, ser. 2, vol. 4, p. 798; Baquet, *History of the First Brigade*, p. 30; Sypher, *Pennsylvania Reserve Corps*, pp. 252–53; Taylor Diary, WHMC; Sanborn, "Savage Station," p. 3; Marks, *Peninsular Campaign*, pp. 237–48; Baker to Jimmie, July 9, 1862, Baker Papers, CWMC; Barr to Vinnie, July 4, 1862, Barr Papers, UM; Edward Stone to dear ones at home, July 8, 1862, Stone Papers, VtHS; Ford, *Fifteenth Massachusetts*, p. 174.

11. *OR*, pt. 2, pp. 663, 789, 809; Henry Burgwyn to mother, July 14, 1862, Burgwyn Family Papers, SHC. Both Magruder and Huger reported receiving messages but not sending any. Magruder nowhere says anything about asking for two brigades from Huger, but he also does not say anything about asking Lee for help or receiving his response from Major Brent.

12. *OR*, pt. 1, pp. 111, 114–15; pt. 2, pp. 571, 578, 627, 664, 748, 750; Alexander, *Fighting for the Confederacy*, pp. 105–106; Freeman, *Lee's Lieutenants*, vol. 1, p. 561; Dabney to Hotchkiss, Apr. 22, 1896, Hotchkiss Papers, LOC; Henderson, *Stonewall Jackson*, vol. 2, p. 47 n 1; M. A. Miller to Hotchkiss, May 20, 1862, Hotchkiss Papers, LOC; Jones, "Reminiscences No. 8," p. 564; Vairin Diary, MDAH. Sears (*To the Gates of Richmond*, p. 269) discusses two bridges being repaired.

13. *OR*, pt. 2, pp. 675, 716, 789; Henry Burgwyn to mother, July 14, 1862, Burgwyn Family Papers, SHC; Brent, *Memoirs*, p. 182. Brent makes it sound as though he had returned before Huger left, but the passage is not perfectly clear on that point.

14. Lee, *Wartime Papers*, p. 205; Alexander, *Fighting for the Confederacy*, p. 105, and *Military Memoirs*, p. 145; Cooke, "With Jackson Around Richmond," p. 248. Freeman (*Lee's Lieutenants*, vol. 1, p. 562) regretfully concluded that Jackson misread his orders

—before the evidence of the order to Stuart (to be detailed) came to light. Davis (*They Called Him Stonewall,* p. 232) suggests Jackson's duty was to get the bridge finished. Greene (*Whatever You Resolve to Be,* p. 60) takes Alexander to the figurative woodshed for the Sabbath theory. Alexander (*Military Memoirs,* p. 136) and Longstreet (*From Manassas to Appomattox,* p. 131) thought moving by New Bridge would have been best. More recently, Schenck (*Up Came Hill,* p. 82) suggested it.

15. Long, *Robert E. Lee,* p. 175; *OR,* pt. 2, pp. 516–17, 556, 680; McClellan, *I Rode with Stuart,* p. 78; von Borcke, *Memoirs,* vol. 1, p. 67; Beale, *Ninth Virginia Cavalry,* p. 26; Cooke Diary, Cooke Papers, Duke; Blackford, *War Years,* pp. 75–76. The complete text of these orders as printed in Chambers's *Stonewall Jackson,* including Jackson's marginal note, is reprinted in Appendix E. Sears (*To the Gates of Richmond,* p. 268) suggests that it was a contingency plan. Robertson (*Stonewall Jackson,* p. 490) puts the blame on Lee and his staff. Obviously not all the Confederate claims of plunder, particularly the more extreme, can be reconciled with Union claims.

16. *OR,* pt. 1, p. 114; *OR,* pt. 2, p. 571; *OR,* vol. 51, pt. 1, p. 688; Dabney, *Life and Campaigns,* pp. 459, 461; letter of July 8, 1862, Duggan Papers, GDAH; Farwell, *Stonewall,* p. 359. Eckenrode and Conrad (*Lee's War Horse,* p. 73) say Jackson should be praised for getting the repairs done so quickly. Dabney relates the story of Jackson's meeting with Magruder and Lee, as does Hunter McQuire (letter to Hotchkiss, Apr. 23, 1896, Hotchkiss Papers, UVa). However, the circumstances of at least McGuire's story seem implausible, as he has Lee dressing down Magruder, even though Lee wrote a note to Magruder with the same criticism that evening, and Major Meade of the engineers waving a white handkerchief on top of the Union works—something that might have occurred in the morning but not at night. A second implausible story is that the Stonewall Brigade, commanded by Winder, crossed with Jackson. Winder's report (*OR,* pt. 2, p. 571) and diary (Winder Papers, MHS) make no mention of this. Neither do any of his regimental commanders' reports, nor the diary of Watkins Kearns of the Stonewall Brigade (Kearns Papers, VHS). Dabney also tells the story of Jackson watching the ammunition train go into the river, which is more plausible.

12. *"Why, Those Men Are Rebels!"*

1. Brent, *Memoirs,* p. 182; *OR,* pt. 2, pp. 37–38, 170, 464, 664, 691, 716, 720, 726, 732, 735; *OR,* pt. 3, p. 238; Doubleday, "The Seven Days' Battles," p. 7.

2. Franklin, "Rear-Guard Fighting," p. 373; Franklin to McClellan, June 29, 1862, McClellan Papers, LOC; *OR,* pt. 2, pp. 50, 91, 727; *OR,* vol. 51, pt. 1, p. 108; letter of July 6, 1862, Hospes Papers, SHSW; Osborn, *No Middle Ground,* pp. 74–75; Banes, *Philadelphia Brigade,* pp. 79–80; Presnell, "Incidents in the Civil War," Pressnell Papers, MinnHS; Wright, "Old Peninsular Days," p. 3. Franklin's testimony before the Joint Committee on the Conduct of the War is somewhat different, in that his purpose in riding toward the front was that signal officers had told him of a large force of infantry headed toward them (*Army of the Potomac,* p. 623).

3. *OR,* pt. 2, pp. 56–57, 65, 69, 71, 77, 84, 86, 118–19, 464; Heintzelman to McClellan, McClellan to Sumner, June 29, 1862, McClellan Papers, LOC; Osborne, *History of the Twenty-Ninth Regiment,* p. 154; Conyngham, *Irish Brigade,* pp. 194, 197; Sigman Memoir, FSNMP; Decker to father, July 7, 1862, Decker Papers, CWMC; Stephen to Olive, July 6, 1862, Olney Papers, RIHS; Osborn, *No Middle Ground,* p. 75.

4. *OR,* pt. 2, pp. 694, 727, 732, 747; Andrus, *Brooke, Fauquier, Loudoun and Alexandria Artillery,* p. 11; McCreery Journal, McCreery Papers, VaHS; Brent, *Memoirs,* p. 188; Sneden, "Pen and Sword," pp. 49–50; Potter, *Reminiscences,* p. 5.

5. Dickert, *Kershaw's Brigade*, pp. 128–29; *OR*, pt. 2, pp. 91–92, 726, 735, 741; Pitts to Lizzie, July 7, 1862, Pitts Papers, SCHS; McDaniel, *Diary*, p. 7; Shand Memoir, Shand Papers, FSNMP; Wyckoff, "Kershaw's South Carolina Brigade," pp. 121–24; Suddath, "From Sumter to the Wilderness," p. 93; Franklin, "Rear-Guard Fighting," p. 374.

6. *OR*, pt. 2, pp. 464, 477, 479, 717, 721, 733, 737, 741, 744; *OR*, vol. 51, pt. 1, p. 108; Wright, "Old Peninsular Days," p. 3; Wright, "Rear-Guard Fighting," p. 375; Bloomer, "How the 1st Minn. Lost Its Colors," p. 3; Frye, "Savage Station," p. 5; Emery Diary, CWMC; Williams to parents, July 6, 1862, Williams Papers, VtHS; Burton, "Vermont Veterans," p. 7; Hatrick to mother, undated, Hatrick Family Papers, SHC; Brooks to father, July 5, 1862, Brooks Papers, USAMHI; Hyde, *Following the Greek Cross*, p. 72; Brent, *Memoirs*, pp. 184–88; Sneden, "Pen and Sword," p. 49; Pitts to Lizzie, July 7, 1862, Pitts Papers, SCHS. The accounts of the first contact between Semmes and Brooks are subtly different; this account is a combination.

7. Franklin, "Rear-Guard Fighting," pp. 374–75; Burns Diary, Pennsylvania "Save the Flags" Civil War Collection, USAMHI; Batchelder to mother, July 8, 1862, Zadock Pratt Papers, BU; *OR*, pt. 2, pp. 89, 91–92, 464, 737–38, 750; letter of July 14, 1862, Sully Papers, Beinecke Library; Eames to wife, July 5, 1862, Eames Papers, Smith Collection, USAMHI; Smith, *Autobiography*, p. 44; Curtiss Diary, Curtiss Papers, CMU; J. B. Oliver to father, July 4, 1862, Oliver Family Papers, OCHS; Stillwell Diary, Stillwell Papers, SHSW; Benjamin Humphries to R. Archer, July 9, 1862, Southall Papers, VaHS; Wiley, "Soldier's Life," p. 70; Stiles, *Four Years Under Marse Robert*, p. 98.

8. *OR*, pt. 2, p. 25, 35, 37, 721, 731, 751, 978–79; Fox, *Regimental Losses*, pp. 147–48, 150–51, 279, 430; Thomas Pitts to Lizzie, July 7, 1862, Pitts Papers, SCHS; Stephen to Olive, July 6, 1862, Olney Papers, RIHS. Barksdale's strength is estimated from his report that his brigade lost about one-third of its strength at Malvern Hill, and the reported casualties there were 525, making the brigade's strength about 1,600. As the two regiments at Savage Station were half of the regiments in the brigade, an estimate of 800 (plus officers) seems in the ballpark. The casualty figures for the 72nd Pennsylvania are for the entire Seven Days, but it was not engaged in other battles from Burns's report. Reports of the missing from these regiments include those left at Savage Station, so only a fraction of that total was included in the overall casualty figures.

9. *OR*, pt. 2, pp. 665, 691, 702, 705, 707, 713, 748, 750; Coward, *South Carolinians*, p. 41; Capers, *CMH*, vol. 6, p. 67; Henley memoir, FSNMP.

10. *OR*, pt. 2, pp. 665, 687. Alexander (*Military Memoirs*, p. 138) thinks Magruder should have pitched in, as does Long ("John Bankhead Magruder," p. 110), who believes Magruder lost the audacity he had possessed earlier in the campaign. Dowdey (*Seven Days*, pp. 268–69) makes the argument that Magruder saved Lee, whereas Cullen (*Peninsula Campaign*, p. 138) claims Prince John could accomplish little. Sears (*To the Gates of Richmond*, p. 274) says Lee's rebuke contained "considerable injustice." Casdorph (*Prince John Magruder*, p. 178) agrees with Lee's rebuke. Cullen (*Peninsula Campaign*, p. 139) and Freeman (*Lee's Lieutenants*, vol. 1, p. 563) disagree with my analysis of Lee's actions.

11. Winslow, *General John Sedgwick*, p. 25. Sears (*To the Gates of Richmond*, p. 271) calls Sumner's management of the battle "erratic," which may be kind.

12. *OR*, pt. 2, pp. 162, 181, 185, 789, 797, 809; Werstein, *Kearny the Magnificent*, p. 226; Dodge Journal, Dodge Papers, LOC; Haydon, *For Country, Cause and Leader*, p. 258; Bernard Diary, Bernard Papers, Duke; Heintzelman Diary, Heintzelman Papers, LOC; B. Wylie Scott to Ella, July 9, 1862, Merryman Papers, VaHS; Henry Burgwyn to mother, July 14, 1862, Burgwyn Family Papers, SHC; Day, *True History*, p. 18.

13. *OR*, pt. 2, pp. 556, 565, 571, 607, 622, 627, 775, 879; Brown, "Down the Peninsula,"

p. 57; Benson Memoir, Benson Papers, SHC; Wise Journal, Wise Papers, Duke; Hall Diary, Hall Papers, LOC; Leach, "Frazier's Farm," p. 162; Carter Diary, Carter Papers, Hampden-Sydney College. The reports of Wilcox and Joseph Anderson would seem to indicate that both divisions made it to near the Atlee house.

14. *OR*, pt. 2, p. 110; Haynes, *History of the Second Regiment*, p. 76; Haines Journal, Haines Papers, Rutgers; Perkins, "Civil War Diary," p. 167; Acton to Mary, July 5, 1862, Acton Papers, HSP; Smith, "Asa Smith Leaves the War," p. 56; Garnett, "Retreat to Malvern," p. 1.

15. *OR*, pt. 2, p. 199, 202, 431, 434; Hagar Diary, Lang Collection, USAMHI; Roe, *Tenth Massachusetts*, p. 116; Newcomb Diary, Newcomb Papers, Stanford; Thomas Carpenter to Phil, July 7, 1862, Bulkley Family Papers, MoHS; McAllister to family, July 1, 1862, McAllister Papers, Rutgers; Peter Filbert diary, Harrisburg CWRT; Slocum, *Life and Services*, p. 30.

16. Powell, *Fifth Army Corps*, pp. 133–34; Woodward, *Third Pennsylvania Reserve*, p. 98; Pennypacker, *General Meade*, pp. 38–39; *OR*, pt. 2, pp. 227–28, 389; Sypher, *Pennsylvania Reserve Corps*, pp. 254–55, 260–61; Faller to Cecilia, July 12, 1862, Faller Correspondence, Harrisburg CWRT. No one actually spelled out the orders for McCall's division or the route of the other two divisions, but the confusion regarding the Quaker road leaves this the best explanation. Eckenrode and Conrad (*James Longstreet*, p. 77) and Sanger (*James Longstreet*, p. 70) suggest Longstreet could have done more that night.

17. *OR*, pt. 2, p. 55, 228, 431; Hager Journal, Hager Papers, UVa; Evans, "At Malvern Hill," pp. 38–39; Bancroft Diary, Bancroft Papers, BHC; Franklin, "Rear-Guard Fighting," p. 375; Smith, *Autobiography*, pp. 44–45; Colburn to Sacket, June 29, 1862, McClellan Papers, LOC.

18. Henry to Dr. A. R. Avery, July 7, 1862, Henry Papers, MinnHS; Hyde, *Following the Greek Cross*, pp. 72–73; Quimby to Emeline, July 12, 1862, Quimby Papers, FSNMP; Favill, *Diary*, p. 140; Osborn, *No Middle Ground*, p. 77; Anderson Journal, Anderson Papers, UW-GB.

19. Batchelder to mother, July 8, 1862, Zadock Pratt Papers, BU; Smith to mother, July 6, 1862, Smith Papers, MinnHS; Burns Diary, Pennsylvania "Save the Flags" Civil War Collection, USAMHI; Waitt, *History*, p. 93; Banes, *Philadelphia Brigade*, pp. 82–3; Edward Davis to brother, July 5, 1862, Davis Papers, Yale; letter of July 6, 1862, Hospes Papers, SHSW; Marvin Diary, Marvin Papers, MinnHS; Ford, *Fifteenth Massachusetts*, p. 175.

20. *OR*, pt. 2, pp. 55, 58; Bruce, *Twentieth Massachusetts*, pp. 118–19; Sigman Memoir, FSNMP; anonymous memoir, Faunce Papers, Duke; Nightingale to mother, July 5, 1862, Nightingale Papers, Harvard.

13. "We've Got Him"

1. *OR*, pt. 2, pp. 57–58, 77, 627; Landugan, "At Savage Station," p. 7; Brainerd, *Bridge Building in Wartime*, pp. 76–77. Stiles (*Four Years with Marse Robert*, pp. 97–99) says Jackson was the draftsman. John McCreery in his journal (VaHS) says Lee was the draftsman. The discrepancy, given that both accounts are postwar reminiscences, accounts for the fact that no names are assigned in this version. Jackson's order of march in the text is not meant to be exact but is the most likely. It is certain that Hill was first and Ewell was last.

2. *OR*, pt. 2, pp. 495, 556, 665–66, 759; Allan, *Army of Northern Virginia in 1862*, p. 108; Brent, *Memoirs*, p. 190. No one has recorded the sequence of meetings, but this

one, presented by Freeman (*R. E. Lee*, pp. 179–80) seems the most likely. Cullen (*Peninsula Campaign*, p. 140) says Lee could have sent Magruder to Brackett's Ford and that Marse Robert lacked confidence in Prince John.

3. *OR*, pt. 2, pp. 495, 665, 788, 791, 906–907, 916; *OR*, pt. 3, pp. 619, 621, 623. Greene (*Whatever You Resolve to Be*, p. 62) arrives at the conclusion regarding Jackson. Alexander (*Military Memoirs*, p. 138, and *Fighting for the Confederacy*, p. 110), Allan ("Peninsula," p. 204), Dowdey (*Seven Days*, p. 304), and Hassler (*Commanders*, p. 50) all agree with Lee.

4. *OR*, pt. 2, pp. 55, 58, 431, 464–65; Smith, *Autobiography*, pp. 45–46; Adams, *Story of a Trooper*, p. 590; Franklin, "Rear-Guard Fighting," p. 379; Pollard Diary, Pollard Papers, VtHS; Anderson Journal, Anderson Papers, UW-GB; Tyler to uncle, July 4, 1862, Tyler Papers, VaHS; *OR Supp.*, vol. 2, p. 415; Nightingale to mother, July 5, 1862, Nightingale Papers, Harvard; anonymous memoir, Faunce Papers, Duke; Whitman to wife, July 5, 1862, Whitman Papers, CWMC. Eckenrode and Conrad (*James Longstreet*, p. 77) say McClellan only had a rear guard at Glendale.

5. *OR*, pt. 2, pp. 99, 162–63, 166, 431, 435; Richards to Kaercher, July 5, 1862, Richards Papers, CWMC; Dodge Journal, Dodge Papers, LOC. Kearny refers to the southernmost road as the New Market road. If he looked at a map for his mileage, that may account for the discrepancy.

6. *OR*, pt. 2, pp. 51, 81, 99, 111, 389–90, 402, 431; Powell, *Fifth Army Corps*, p. 137; Meade, *Life and Letters*, p. 284; Faller to Cecilia, July 12, 1862, Faller Correspondence, Harrisburg CWRT; Roher to wife, July 6, 1862, Roher Papers, Leigh Collection, USAMHI; Roberts, "Battle of Charles City," p. 1; Fullerton to family, July 4, 1862, Fullerton Papers, CWMC; Smith, "Asa Smith Leaves the War," p. 57; Batchelder to mother, July 8, 1862, Zadock Pratt Papers, BU; Burns Diary, Pennsylvania "Save the Flags" Civil War Collection, USAMHI; Marvin Diary, Marvin Papers, MinnHS. McClellan's report (*OR*, pt. 1, p. 65) indicates that McCall's division was posted with the rest, but Heintzelman's report and a note from him to Marcy (McClellan Papers, LOC) make it clear that Hooker's position had been determined without knowledge of McCall's location. McCall uses the terms "New Market road" and "Turkey Bridge road," but from the description they can only have been the Long Bridge road and the Willis Church road.

7. Hagar Diary, Lang Collection, USAMHI; *OR*, pt. 1, p. 64; pt. 2, pp. 99, 193, 213, 274, 350; *OR*, vol. 51, pt. 1, p. 104; Stephen to Olive, July 6, 1862, Olney Papers, RIHS; Smith, "Asa Smith Leaves the War," p. 57; Bliss, "No. 1 Narrative," Bancroft-Bliss Family Papers, LOC; Elliott and Young Diaries, CWMC; Heintzelman to Marcy, June 29, 1862, McClellan Papers, LOC. Sears (*To the Gates of Richmond*, p. 282) comments on the gaps.

8. *OR*, pt. 2, pp. 38–40; *OR*, pt. 3, p. 238; Dowdey, *Seven Days*, p. 285; Franklin, "Rear-Guard Fighting," p. 377. The critics have included Barnard (*Peninsular Campaign*, pp. 44–45), Cullen (*Peninsula Campaign*, pp. 143–45), Dowdey (*Seven Days*, p. 282), Michie (*General McClellan*, pp. 354–55), Sears (*To the Gates of Richmond*, pp. 281–82), Sypher (*Pennsylvania Reserve Corps*, p. 262), and Williams (*Lincoln Finds a General*, vol. 1, p. 237). Cullen (*Peninsula Campaign*, p. 145) called the lack of an overall commander "an open invitation to disaster."

9. Biddle to Ropes, Mar. 27, 1895, Ropes Collection, BU; *OR*, pt. 1, pp. 65, 141; Sears, *To the Gates of Richmond*, p. 280; McClellan, *Civil War Papers*, pp. 325–26; Lincoln, *Collected Works*, pp. 292–95; Leech, *Reveille in Washington*, p. 193; Strong, *Diary*, pp. 234–35 (emphasis in original); Humphreys to wife, July 11, 1862, Humphreys Papers, HSP; McClellan, *Civil War Papers*, p. 326; Franklin to Ropes, Mar. 23, 1895, Ropes Collection, BU; *Army of the Potomac*, p. 359. Critics have included Michie (*General McClellan*, pp. 354–55) and Sears (*George B. McClellan*, p. 218, and *To the Gates of*

Richmond, p. 281). Sears (*To the Gates of Richmond*, p. 281) notes that McClellan was acting as a staff officer. Dowdey (*Seven Days*, p. 286) suggests that his vision was limited. Sears (*George B. McClellan*, p. 218) mentions the messianic complex and its possible results.

10. Henderson, *Stonewall Jackson*, vol. 2, pp. 49–50; Dabney to Hotchkiss, Apr. 22, 1896, Hotchkiss Papers, LOC; Taylor, "Savage's Station," p.7; Potter, *Reminiscences*, p. 6; Hill, "McClellan's Change of Base," pp. 386–87; Ardrey Diary, Ardrey Papers, Duke; Watkins Memoir, FSNMP; Dabney, *Life and Campaigns*, pp. 460–62; Casler, *Four Years*, p. 94; Blackford Memoir, Blackford Papers, CWMC.

11. *OR*, pt. 2, pp. 495, 789, 797, 809–10; Bernard Journal, Bernard Papers, Duke; Hale and Phillips, *Forty-Ninth Virginia Infantry*, p. 35; Freeman, *R. E. Lee*, p. 194 n 57, quoting a letter from Col. W. H. Palmer to Walter Taylor of Lee's staff written July 24, 1905; Dowdey, *Seven Days*, p. 292; Henry Burgwyn to mother, July 14, 1862, Burgwyn Family Papers, SHC. Freeman (*R. E. Lee*, p. 193) favors leaving the artillery. Dowdey (*Seven Days*, p. 292) and Sears (*To the Gates of Richmond*, p. 285) like getting rid of the obstructions. Sears also speculates on the Virginians' capability with the ax. Huger says that Mahone cut a new road, but Mahone's report and Bernard's journal imply that the men marched down the Charles City road. Lee's report, which mentions Huger's note, gives no indication of the time it was sent or received, except that it must have been before 4 P.M.

12. Longstreet, "'Seven Days,'" p. 400; *OR*, pt. 2, pp. 495, 666, 718, 838; Hinsdale Journal, Duke; Brent, *Memoirs*, p. 192.

14. *"He . . . Rose and Walked Off in Silence"*

1. Sypher, *Pennsylvania Reserve Corps*, p. 261, 263–64; *OR*, pt. 2, pp. 389–90, 402–403, 420; Meade, *Life and Letters*, p. 285; Roberts, "Battle of Charles City Cross Roads," p. 1; Urban, *My Experiences*, pp. 148–50. McCall said only that he threw out the pickets toward Richmond, but as he was on the Long Bridge road, this is an easy assumption.

2. *OR*, pt. 2, pp. 527, 666, 675, 749, 759, 763, 768, 775, 785, 838; Roberts, "Battle of Charles City Cross Roads," p. 1; Longstreet, *From Manassas to Appomattox*, p. 134; Sypher, *Pennsylvania Reserve Corps*, pp. 264–65; Longstreet, "'The Seven Days,'" p. 400. No exact order of positioning was given by Longstreet, Hill, or any other commander. This is a likely positioning, given the reports of Wilcox and Featherston, here cited. Wert (*General James Longstreet*, p. 142) believes Longstreet stayed behind. Freeman (*R. E. Lee*, p. 181) attributes Lee's second note to Magruder to his receipt of Huger's message. In Longstreet's official report (*OR*, pt. 2, p. 759), Old Pete put the time of the firing at 3 P.M., while in "'The Seven Days'" (p. 400), written twenty years after the fighting, he said it was 2:30.

3. *OR*, pt. 2, pp. 557, 561, 627, 652, 655. Jackson reported that the firing began at 2 P.M., whereas Crutchfield said it started about 1:45. Neither completely agrees with Longstreet's reports or some Union accounts—a discrepancy to be expected during this period of inexact timekeeping.

4. Miller, "Serving under McClellan," p. 29; Smith, *Autobiography*, pp. 45–46; Stevens, *Three Years*, p. 105; Pollard Journal, Pollard Papers, VtHS; Walker, *Second Army Corps*, p. 72; Tyler to uncle, July 4, 1862, Tyler Papers, VaHS; Cullen, *Peninsula Campaign*, p. 145; anonymous memoir, Faunce Papers, Duke; Newcomb Diary, Newcomb Papers, Stanford; Barr to Vinnie, July 4, 1862, Barr Papers, UM; Davis, *104th Pennsylvania Regiment*, p. 122; Castleman, *Army of the Potomac*, p. 171; Hyde, *Following the Greek Cross*, p. 73; Moore Memoir, CWMC; *OR*, pt. 2, pp. 464–65.

5. Franklin, "Rear-Guard Fighting," p. 379; *OR*, pt. 2, pp. 477, 481; Thomas to friends, July 5, 1862, Thomas Papers, SHSW; Hyde, *Following the Greek Cross*, p. 73; Smith, *Autobiography*, p. 46; anonymous memoir, Faunce Papers, Duke; Whitman to wife, July 5, 1862, Whitman Papers, CWMC; *OR Supp.*, vol. 2, p. 416; Davis, *104th Pennsylvania Regiment*, p. 123; Newcomb Diary, Newcomb Papers, Stanford.

6. Dabney, *Life and Campaigns*, p. 464; Alexander, *Military Memoirs*, p. 149; Hill, "McClellan's Change of Base," pp. 388, 390; Watts to T. T. Munford, May 4, 1898, Watts Letter, FSNMP; Franklin, "Rear-Guard Fighting," p. 378; Henderson, *Stonewall Jackson*, vol. 2, p. 51; McClellan, *I Rode with Stuart*, pp. 80–82, 82 n 1; *OR*, pt. 2, pp. 58, 466, 557, 594, 627.

7. Alexander, *Military Memoirs*, p. 148; Conyngham, *Irish Brigade*, pp. 205–206; J. B. Oliver to father, July 4, 1862, Oliver Family Papers, OCHS; *OR*, pt. 2, pp. 55–60, 561, 566; Naisawald, *Grape and Canister*, p. 107; Decker to father, July 7, 1862, Decker Papers, CWMC; Franklin, "Rear-Guard Fighting," p. 378.

8. *OR*, pt. 2, pp. 63, 78–80, 557, 974, 984; Franklin, "Rear-Guard Fighting," p. 378; E. P. Alexander, "Confederate Artillery Service," p. 101; Wise, *Long Arm of Lee*, p. 219.

9. Dabney, *Life and Campaigns*, pp. 465–66; *OR*, pt. 2, pp. 566, 790, 810–11; Marshall, *Aide-de-Camp*, p. 111; Alexander, *Military Memoirs*, p. 149; Watts to T. T. Munford, May 4, 1898, Watts Letter, FSNMP; McAllister, report of movements, July 19, 1862, McAllister Papers, Rutgers; Franklin, "Rear-Guard Fighting," p. 381.

10. Franklin, "Rear-Guard Fighting," pp. 377–78; *OR*, pt. 2, pp. 51, 87, 89, 94; Batchelder to mother, July 8, 1862, Zadock Pratt Papers, BU. It can be inferred from these reports that Suiter's brigade was the one placed in the front line, but it is not stated directly.

11. Marshall, *Aide-de-Camp*, p. 111; Jackson, *Memoirs of Stonewall Jackson*, p. 297; Lamb, "Malvern Hill," p. 211; Dabney, *Life and Campaigns*, p. 467. Hampton's story is pieced together from two accounts he gave—one in a letter to Charles Marshall and published in Marshall, *Aide-de-Camp*, pp. 110–12, and the other in the letter quoted in Alexander, *Military Memoirs*, pp. 150–51 (emphasis in original). The two accounts are subtly different but only contradict each other in the name of the staff officer who accompanied Hampton.

12. *OR*, pt. 2, pp. 557, 566; Alexander, *Military Memoirs*, pp. 144, 147; Jackson, *Memoirs of Stonewall Jackson*, p. 302; Hill, "McClellan's Change of Base," p. 389. In *Fighting for the Confederacy*, p. 109, Porter Alexander wrote that Jackson's behavior was "enough to make one cry" given the opportunities of the day. Henderson (*Stonewall Jackson*, vol. 2, pp. 53–58) uses the illness as the complete explanation; Chambers (*Stonewall Jackson*, vol. 2, pp. 74–75), Davis (*They Called Him Stonewall*, pp. 243–44), and Robertson (*Stonewall Jackson*, p. 498) list it as a partial explanation. Those blaming fatigue and stress are Bowers (*Stonewall Jackson*, p. 256), Dabney (*Life and Campaigns*, p. 466), Davis (*They Called Him Stonewall*, pp. 243–44), Dowdey (*Seven Days*, p. 307), Farwell (*Stonewall*, pp. 362–63), Greene (*Whatever You Resolve to Be*, p. 73), Long (*Robert E. Lee*, pp. 175–76), Robertson (*Stonewall Jackson*, p. 498), Sears (*To the Gates of Richmond*, p. 289), and Vandiver (*Mighty Stonewall*, p. 317). Freeman (*R. E. Lee*, p. 199) thinks it a possibility. Cullen (*Peninsula Campaign*, p. 151) offers several reasons. Barnwell ("Stonewall Jackson at Richmond," p. 97) believes Jackson was confused by differences between his original orders and his orders for the thirtieth, but this is unlikely given the amount of communication between Lee and Jackson during this phase of the campaign.

13. Besides those already cited, see Allan, "Peninsula," p. 204; Garnett, "Personal Reminiscences," p. 149; Jones, "Reminiscences No. 8," p. 564; Taylor, *Destruction and Reconstruction*, p. 105.

14. *OR*, pt. 2, pp. 618, 622. Robertson (*Stonewall Jackson*, p. 497) says Jackson had no orders to attack, merely orders to pursue, and that Jackson obeyed those orders literally. Allan ("Peninsula," p. 204) complains of the lack of effort. Taylor (*Destruction and Reconstruction*, p. 105) says it would have been worth the cost; Henderson (*Stonewall Jackson*, vol. 2, p. 56) argues against this for the first reason, whereas Eckenrode and Conrad (*James Longstreet*, pp. 75, 78) argue against it for the second reason. McGuire (to Hotchkiss, Apr. 23, 1896, Hotchkiss Papers, UVa) believes that Jackson was careful with the lives of his men. Cooke ("With Jackson," p. 248) and McGuire ("General Jackson," p. 98) say the crossing would have been difficult. As previously noted, Hampton and Munford thought it could be done.

15. Greene (*Whatever You Resolve to Be*, p. 65), Henderson (*Stonewall Jackson*, vol. 2, p. 58), Jones (*Life and Letters*, p. 175 [quoting Jefferson Davis]), McGuire ("General Jackson," p. 98), and Dabney (Apr. 22, 1896, to Hotchkiss, Hotchkiss Papers, LOC) all think the orders answer the criticism at least partially. McGuire (Apr. 23, 1896, to Hotchkiss, Hotchkiss Papers, UVa) notes Jackson's views on orders. Longstreet (*From Manassas to Appomattox*, p. 150) suggests the move to the Charles City road, and Dabney (Apr. 22, 1896, to Hotchkiss, Hotchkiss Papers, LOC) says Jackson would have thought of it but was constrained by his orders. Greene, one of Jackson's most ardent modern defenders, concedes that Stonewall could have crossed at Hampton's bridge within his orders (*Whatever You Resolve to Be*, p. 73). Robertson (*Stonewall Jackson*, p. 497) says Jackson was covering contingencies through these moves but says nothing about the need to keep Franklin occupied.

16. Hill, "McClellan's Change of Base," p. 388; McGuire to Hotchkiss, Apr. 23, 1896, Hotchkiss Papers, UVa; Dabney to Hotchkiss, Apr. 22, 1896, Hotchkiss Papers, LOC.

17. *OR*, pt. 2, pp. 55, 61; McGuire to Hotchkiss, June 15, 1896, Hotchkiss Papers, UVa. McGuire (to Hotchkiss, Apr 23, 1896, Hotchkiss Papers, UVa) places the blame on Lee, not Jackson. Robertson (*Stonewall Jackson*, p. 498) says every commander must share the blame.

18. Dowdey, *Seven Days*, p. 308; Gill, *Courier for Lee and Jackson*, p. 28. Greene (*Whatever You Resolve to Be*, p. 66) notes the ridiculous nature of some of the explanations. For the Dabney-McGuire difference, see Dabney to Hotchkiss, Apr. 22, 1896, Hotchkiss Papers, LOC; McGuire to Hotchkiss, Apr. 23, 1896, Hotchkiss Papers, UVa.

15. *"I Thought I Heard Firing"*

1. *OR*, pt. 2, pp. 166, 435, 547, 789, 797–98; Day, *True History*, p. 19; Slocum, *Life and Services*, p. 31; Charles Ives to Lee, July 9, 1862, Colonial Dames Collection, UOkla; Kenney Memoir, CWMC; Bernard Journal, Bernard Papers, Duke; Shoemaker, *Shoemaker's Battery*, p. 17, Pinto, *32nd Regiment*, p. 86; John Briggs to Albert, July 25, 1862, Poriss Collection, USAMHI. Huger reported that it was evening before Mahone reached the clearing. However, Slocum (*OR*, pt. 2, p. 435) said the rebel artillery opened about 11 A.M. Wright (*OR*, pt. 2, p. 811) did not mention any artillery fire, so his reconnaissance must have been before Huger got in position. Huger reported that the Union guns fired first, as did George Bernard in his journal (Bernard Papers, Duke), but Mahone and Slocum both said that the Confederate guns were first to fire. Huger's report also reads as though more than two guns began the engagement and that he withdrew some of them; the account in the text follows Mahone's report.

2. *OR*, pt. 2, pp. 435, 495, 790, 798, 981; Richards to Kaercher, July 5, 1862, Richards Papers, CWMC; Bernard Journal, Bernard Papers, Duke; Hale and Phillips, *Forty-Ninth Virginia Infantry*, p. 36; John Briggs to Albert, July 25, 1862, Poriss Collection,

USAMHI; Rhoades, *Scapegoat General*, p. 95. It is hard to say which rebels Bartlett encountered, but perhaps Armistead was getting into position. See Allan, "Peninsula," p. 204; Alexander, *Military Memoirs*, p. 143; Dowdey, *Seven Days*, p. 306; and Freeman, *R. E. Lee*, p. 193, for the criticism.

3. Jones, "A Visit to Beauvoir," pp. 451–52; Longstreet, "'The Seven Days'," p. 400; *OR*, pt. 2, pp. 350, 410, 532, 759, 838, 907; *OR Supp.*, vol. 2, p. 442; Longstreet, *From Manassas to Appomattox*, pp. 134–35; *OR Supp.*, vol. 2, p. 442; Coker, *History of Company G*, p. 81. Cooper's report (*OR*, pt. 2, p. 410) reads in such a way as to imply that this battery shelled the generals. Rosser reported (*OR*, pt. 2, p. 532) that "no attention was paid" by Longstreet or Holmes to his message, but it is more likely that neither got the message, as neither mentioned receiving it but both discussed receiving information later.

4. *OR*, pt. 2, pp. 119, 202, 217, 228, 238, 250, 274, 284, 350, 380, 796, 907–11, 913; Hanifen, *History of Battery B*, p. 25; *OR Supp.*, vol. 2, p. 272; Nathan Frazier to wife, July 5, 1862, Frazier Papers, ECU; *ORN*, pp. 699, 709; Graves, *Confederate Marine*, p. 65; Ames to parents, July 5, 1862, Ames Papers, USAMHI; Carpenter, *War Diary*, p. 7; Davis, *Rise and Fall*, vol. 2, p. 123; W. D. Carr to mother, July 4, 1862, Herman W. Taylor Collection, NCDAH.

5. Fowler to friend, July 8, 1862, Fowler Papers, CWMC; Frazier to wife, July 5, 1862, Frazier Papers, ECU; Tribble, *Benjamin Case Rawlings*, p. 44; Carpenter, *War Diary*, p. 7; *OR*, pt. 2, pp. 354–55, 362, 910, 914–15; Hill, "McClellan's Change of Base," p. 390; *ORN*, vol. 7, pp. 699, 709; Thomas Carpenter to Phil, July 7, 1862, Bulkley Family Papers, MoHS; Myer to wife, July 17, 1862, Myer Papers, LOC; Hager Memoir, Hager Papers, UVa; Smith, *Famous Battery*, pp. 78–79.

6. *OR*, pt. 2, pp. 495, 667, 908; G. W. Watson to Fannie, July 10, 1862, Lyndall Papers, Duke; Longstreet, *From Manassas to Appomattox*, p. 139; Porter, "Battle of Malvern Hill," p. 411. Alexander (*Fighting for the Confederacy*, p. 106) and Hill ("McClellan's Change of Base," p. 391) criticize Holmes; Davis (*Rise and Fall*, vol. 2, pp. 122–23) defends him. Dowdey (*Seven Days*, pp. 297, 304) argues that delaying the Northerners was possible.

7. *OR*, pt. 2, pp. 495, 666–67, 675, 691, 705, 707, 715, 718, 742, 748; Longstreet, *From Manassas to Appomattox*, p. 139; Brent, *Memoirs*, pp. 193–94.

8. *OR*, pt. 2, pp. 666, 675; Sears, *To the Gates of Richmond*, p. 291. Brent (*Memoirs*, p. 193) calls the march "inexplicable," and Dickert (*History of Kershaw's Brigade*, p. 130) terms it "a wild goose chase." Dowdey (*Seven Days*, p. 304) also is critical. Sears (*To the Gates of Richmond*, p. 291) suggests an attack on Malvern Hill as a possibility without advocating it. Dickert (*History of Kershaw's Brigade*, p. 130) says Magruder was misled. Freeman (*R. E. Lee*, p. 193) thinks the orders were "justified."

9. *OR*, pt. 2, pp. 171, 255, 403, 421, 423, 425, 428, 759; *OR*, vol. 51, pt. 1, p. 114; Sorrel, *Recollections*, p. 77. Col. Albert L. Magilton, the 4th Reserves's commander, reported (*OR*, pt. 2, p. 421) that he was in front of Randol and to his left. It could be that Magilton was confused by another battery. Randol's report is supported by the report of Capt. Daniel S. Porter of the 11th Pennsylvania Reserves.

10. *OR*, pt. 2, pp. 255, 410, 412, 420, 423; *OR Supp.*, vol. 2, p. 442; Sypher, *Pennsylvania Reserve Corps*, p. 264; Alexander, "Records of Longstreet's Corps," p. 68. Most writers have assumed, in the absence of any evidence, that Lee ordered the assault that opened the battle of Glendale. See, for example, Dowdey, *Seven Days*, p. 298; Freeman, *R. E. Lee*, p. 184; Sears, *To the Gates of Richmond*, p. 293. However, Longstreet in his report (*OR*, pt. 2, p. 759) and in his memoirs (*From Manassas to Appomattox*, p. 135) stated that Jenkins's attack brought on the battle.

11. Jenkins to wife, July 4, 1862, Jenkins Papers, USC; Goree, *Longstreet's Aide*, p. 95; Longstreet, *From Manassas to Appomattox*, p. 135; Thomas, *General Micah Jenkins*, p. 17; Capers, *CMH*, vol. 6, pp. 431, 499; Alexander, *Fighting for the Confederacy*, p. 118; *OR*, vol. 51, pt. 1, p. 111; Urban, *My Experiences*, p. 157; Powell, *Fifth Army Corps*, p. 140; Fullerton to family, July 4, 1862, Fullerton Papers, CWMC; Murray and Hassler, "Gettysburg Farmer," p. 185.

12. *OR*, pt. 2, pp. 255, 396, 403, 410, 412; *OR*, vol. 51, pt. 1, p. 112; *OR Supp.*, vol. 2, pp. 442–43; Sypher, *Pennsylvania Reserve Corps*, pp. 269–70; Urban, *My Experiences*, pp. 157–58 (he identifies the commander as Kerns, but Kerns had been wounded at Gaines's Mill); Taggert Diary, Taggert Papers, PSA; "Army Correspondence," New Castle (Pa.) *Lawrence Journal*, p. 1; Patterson, *Yankee Rebel*, p. 48.

13. *OR*, pt. 2, pp. 32, 38, 40, 980–82; Alexander, "Records of Longstreet's Corps," p. 68 n; Fox, *Regimental Losses*, p. 563.

16. "It Is Nothing When You Get Used to It"

1. *OR*, pt. 2, pp. 86, 92, 106–107, 111, 123, 131, 138, 265, 390, 407, 425, 428, 759, 763–66, 883, 895; *OR*, vol. 51, pt. 1, pp. 111, 113; Caldwell, *History of a Brigade*, p. 48; Walthall Reminiscences, CWMC; Johnston, "Charge of Kemper's Brigade," p. 393; Sypher, *Pennsylvania Reserve Corps*, p. 266; Harris, *Historical Sketches*, p. 15; Warner Memoir, Pennsylvania "Save the Flags" Collection, USAMHI; Loehr, *War History*, p. 25; Sauers, "Pennsylvania Reserves," p. 39; Sherwood Diary, Sherwood Papers, VaHS; Alexander, "Records of Longstreet's Corps," p. 67 n; Hunter, *Johnny Reb and Billy Yank*, p. 191.

2. *OR*, pt. 2, pp. 390, 403, 417, 425, 428, 765, 769–70, 883; *OR*, vol. 51, pt. 1, p. 113; Sypher, *Pennsylvania Reserve Corps*, p. 279; Warner Memoir, Pennsylvania "Save the Flags" Collection, USAMHI; Pickett, *Pickett and His Men*, p. 101; "Army Correspondence," Bellefonte (Pa.) *Central Press*, p. 1.

3. *OR*, pt. 2, pp. 81, 87, 89–90, 92, 94–95, 417, 770; Curtiss Diary, Curtiss Papers, CMU; T. M. Key to Heintzelman, May 26, 1864, Heinztelman Papers, LOC; Sauers, "Pennsylvania Reserves," p. 42; Barker to sister, July 5, 1862, Barker Papers, RIHS; Stephen to Olive, July 6, 1862, Olney Papers, RIHS; *History of the First Minnesota*, p. 159; Waitt, *Nineteenth Massachusetts*, p. 85; Bruce, *Twentieth Massachusetts*, p. 127; Ford, *Fifteenth Massachusetts*, p. 176; Stowe to friends at home, July 6, 1862, Stowe Papers, *CWTI*.

4. Smith, "Asa Smith Leaves the War," p. 58; *OR*, pt. 2, pp. 32, 38, 40, 81, 92, 94–95, 111, 125, 133–34, 893, 895; Warner Memoir, Pennsylvania "Save the Flags" Collection, USAMHI; Pickett, *Pickett and His Men*, p. 101; Jeffreys, "'Red Badge' Explained," pp. 248–49; Banes, *History of the Philadelphia Brigade*, pp. 85–86; Palfrey, "Seven Days' Battles," p. 186; Holmes, *Touched with Fire*, p. 59; Curtiss Diary, Curtiss Papers, CMU; George Batchelder to Mary, July 10, 1862, Zadock Pratt Papers, BU; Waitt, *Nineteenth Massachusetts*, p. 96; Paul J. Revere to Lee, July 6, 1862, Revere Papers, MassHS; Milano, "Letters from the Harvard Regiments," p. 25; Sedgwick, *Correspondence*, p. 70.

5. *OR*, pt. 2, p. 172, 255–56, 391, 404, 421, 776–78; Coker, *History of Company G*, pp. 82–83; Powell, *Fifth Army Corps*, pp. 141–43; Hilary Herbert, untitled manuscript, 8th Alabama File, ADAH; Williford to friend, Sept. 11, 1862, Williford Papers, Harrisburg CWRT; Sypher, *Pennsylvania Reserve Corps*, p. 279; Hogan, "Battle of Frazier's Farm," p. 334; Hogan, "Thrilling War Experiences," p. 268; Woodward, *Third Pennsylvania Reserve*, p. 108. Major Stone of the 13th Reserves wrote that McCall was wounded when the two met (*OR*, pt. 2, p. 416), but McCall told his wife (July 1, 1862, McCall Papers, HSP) that a spent ball hit his breastbone, causing only a few moments' discomfort.

6. *OR*, pt. 2, pp. 32, 38, 40, 980; Mundy, "Thrilling Battle of Frazier's Farm," p. 87.

7. *OR*, pt. 2, pp. 166, 168–71, 175–76, 781; Lewis, *History of Battery E*, pp. 62–63; Hurst, *Fourteenth Alabama*, pp. 12–13; Alexander Hays to John B. McFadden, July 7, 1862, Hays Papers, HSWP; Hays, *Under the Red Patch*, p. 127; Leach, "Frazier's Farm," pp. 163–64; Jones, *Lee's Tigers*, pp. 106–107.

8. *OR*, pt. 2, p. 175–77, 179, 786; Longstreet, *From Manassas to Appomattox*, p. 137.

9. *OR*, pt. 2, p. 61, 65–66, 163–64, 171–73, 177–78, 186, 188, 786, 842, 844, 862, 865, 867, 870–71, 874; Caldwell, *History of a Brigade*, p. 47; Doubleday, "Seven Days' Battles," p. 7; Dodge Journal, Dodge Papers, LOC; Hays to John B. McFadden, July 7, 1862, Hays Papers, HSWP; Nightingale to mother, July 5, 1862, Nightingale Papers, Harvard; Conyngham, *Irish Brigade*, p. 208; Spencer, "How I Felt in Battle," p. 138; Mitchell to parents, July 9, 1862, Mitchell Papers, USAMHI; Barlow to mother, July 4, 1862, Barlow Papers, MassHS. The 20th Indiana's report listed Reed among the dead, but McGowan's report mentioned Reed by name in such a way as to imply that he was alive, and Reed was mentioned (albeit by the wrong spelling and in a nonexistent regiment, the 2nd Indiana) in a list of exchanged officers (*OR*, ser. 2, vol. 4, p. 440).

10. *OR*, pt. 2, pp. 100, 163–64, 391, 418, 842, 845, 847, 850; Dunaway, *Reminiscences of a Rebel*, pp. 31–32; Longstreet, "'The Seven Days'," p. 402 n; McCall to wife, July 1, 1862, McCall Papers, HSP; Baquet, *History of the First Brigade*, pp. 30–32; Kearny to wife, July 9, 1862, Kearny Papers, LOC; Grubb, *Notes of a Staff Officer*, pp. 20–21; McAllister to Henrietta, July 8, 1862, McAllister Papers, Rutgers; Haydon, *For Country, Cause and Leader*, p. 260.

11. Jeffreys, "'Red Badge' Explained," p. 249; Cudworth, *History of the First Regiment*, p. 221; Perkins, "Civil War Diary," p. 169; *OR*, pt. 2, pp. 90, 124, 133–34, 769, 901; *OR*, vol. 51, pt. 1, p. 109; Hinsdale Journal, Hinsdale Family Papers, Duke; report of Edward Bishop, July 14, 1862, Hinks Papers, BU; Gray to father, July 10, 1862, Gray Papers, NCDAH. Jeffreys says a North Carolinian from Huger's division said they would give the Yankees hell. The man may have been from Pender's brigade of North Carolinians, but it is more likely he was from Archer's brigade given the positions of the two units.

12. *OR*, pt. 2, pp. 838–39, 879–80; Jasper Gillespie to wife, July 5, 1862, Gillespie Family Papers, GDAH; Fitzpatrick, *Letters to Amanda*, p. 17; Longstreet, *From Manassas to Appomattox*, p. 139; Dickert, *Kershaw's Brigade*, p. 130; Sydnor to brother, July 2, 1862, Sydnor Papers, VaHS. Schenck (*Up Came Hill*, p. 88) tells the story of Wilcox's men without attribution. Robertson (*General A. P. Hill*, pp. 91–92) says the 7th North Carolina of Branch's brigade was involved, basing this claim on a 1934 newspaper article. Hill himself tells of rallying Wilcox's men and sending them in without mentioning the theatrics. It is likely that the incident would have happened at this point.

13. *OR*, pt. 2, pp. 24–27, 32–34, 37–40, 979–80, 982–83; Alexander, "Longstreet's Corps," p. 71, and *Military Memoirs*, pp. 154–55; Davis to brother, July 5, 1862, Davis Papers, Civil War Manuscripts Collection, Yale. Some accounts of the battle recount the taking of both German batteries, but it seems clear that Diederichs got all his guns off and Knieriem got two of his off. Henry Hunt of the artillery reserve states only that two of Knieriem's guns were captured, and Albert Arndt, commanding the artillery brigade the two batteries were part of, discusses both batteries in action at Malvern Hill (*OR*, pt. 2, pp. 237, 265). Naisawald (*Grape and Canister*, p. 119) agrees with this assessment.

14. *OR*, pt. 2, p. 759; McGuire to Hotchkiss, Apr. 23, 1896, Hotchkiss Papers, UVa; Sanger, *James Longstreet*, p. 73. Alexander ("Longstreet's Corps," p. 66) discusses the factors leading to the poor coordination. Robertson (*General A. P. Hill*, p. 93) calls

the coordination "unusually good" given the circumstances. Alexander (*Military Memoirs*, p. 154) suggests Lee could have been driven from the field if there had been more daylight.

15. Wilcox, manuscript review of "The Campaigns of Robert E. Lee," Wilcox Papers, LOC; Freeman, *R. E. Lee*, p. 199. Cullen (*Peninsula Campaign*, p. 149) argues that the plan was too complex, but Dowdey (*Seven Days*, p. 304) calls it "nothing complicated." Alexander (*Fighting for the Confederacy*, pp. 110–11) discusses Lee's positioning. Alexander (*Military Memoirs*, p. 143) also wrote that the army at that time "compared with an organized and disciplined army about as a confederacy would compare with a nation."

16. Hyde, *Following the Greek Cross*, p. 75; Sully to wife, July 5, 1862, Sully Papers, Beinecke Library; *OR*, pt. 2, pp. 111–13, 390, 394, 397, 403, 425, 764; Longstreet, *From Manassas to Appomattox*, pp. 138–39; Colwell to wife, July 30, 1862, Colwell Papers, CWMC; Meade to Randol, July 12, 1862, Hunt Papers, LOC; Cook, *Siege of Richmond*, p. 260; Webb to James, June 23, 1862, Webb Papers, Yale. Cullen (*Peninsula Campaign*, p. 151) makes the points regarding the corps commanders. Seymour says the 12th Reserves should not have been driven from its position, but Seymour had posted the regiment there and so may not be a credible witness—especially since he also says the regiment had support, which is not completely accurate. For examples of the criticism of the German artillery see Sears, *To the Gates of Richmond*, pp. 294–95; Cullen, *Peninsula Campaign*, p. 148. Hyde (*Following the Greek Cross*, p. 75) says the Federals should have counterattacked.

17. Smith, *Autobiography*, pp. 46–47, Franklin, "Rear-Guard Fighting," pp. 379–81; *OR*, pt. 2, pp. 77, 101, 431, 466; Newcomb Diary, Newcomb Papers, Stanford; *OR Supp.*, vol. 2, p. 416; Hyde, *Following the Greek Cross*, p. 76; Horton Keith to friends, July 6, 1862, Keith Papers, VtHS; Stevens, *Three Years*, pp. 105–106. Williams (*Lincoln Finds a General*, vol. 1, p. 238) makes the point regarding the Willis Church road.

18. *OR*, pt. 1, p. 67, *OR*, pt. 2, pp. 101, 436; *OR*, pt. 3, p. 281; Pinto, *32nd Regiment*, p. 87; Stone to parents, July 4, 1862, Stone Papers, MinnHS; Kenney Memoir, CWMC; McAllister to family, July 1, 1862, McAllister Papers, Rutgers; Dodge Journal, Dodge Papers, LOC; Butts, "Organization and First Campaign of Battery E," p. 293. Barnard (*Peninsular Campaign*, p. 45) says that McClellan's force probably would have been destroyed the next day if he had stayed. Dowdey (*Seven Days*, p. 321) says McClellan should have reinforced Franklin and fought at Glendale.

19. *OR*, pt. 2, pp. 51–52, 61, 101, 112, 124, 139, 151, 404; George Batchelder to Mary, July 10, 1862, Zadock Pratt Papers, BU; Sypher, *Pennsylvania Reserve Corps*, p. 277, "Army Correspondence," New Castle (Pa.) *Lawrence Journal*, p. 1; Burrill to parents, July 11, 1862, Burrill Papers, SHSW; Acton to Mollie, July 7, 1862, Acton Papers, HSP; letter of July 6, 1862, Hospes Papers, SHSW; Banes, *History of the Philadelphia Brigade*, p. 87, Haydon, *For Country, Cause and Leader*, p. 260; Stowe to friends, July 6, 1862, Stowe Papers, *CWTI*. It is difficult to figure the exact order of Kearny's march. This order assumes that the brigades left from west to east.

20. Roher to wife, Roher Papers, and Everett to parents, Everett Papers, both July 6, 1862, Leigh Collection, USAMHI; Bliss, "No. 1 Narrative;" Bancroft-Bliss Family Papers, LOC; *OR*, pt. 2, p. 202; *OR*, pt. 3, p. 284; Hagar Diary, Lang Collection, USAMHI; Newhall to father, July 4, 1862, Newhall Papers, HSP.

21. *OR*, pt. 2, pp. 557, 622, 667, 790, 908; Black, "After the Battle," p. 20; Pitts to Lizzie, July 7, 1862, Pitts Papers, SCHS; Warfield, *Confederate Soldier's Memoirs*, p. 93; Hubbert Diary, Confederate States of America Records, Center for American History, University of Texas, Austin.

17. *"We Had Better Let Him Alone"*

1. *OR*, pt. 2, pp. 52, 60, 83, 102, 116, 119, 166, 202–203, 208–209, 211, 213, 217, 238, 250, 265–67, 274–75, 279, 284, 293, 319, 350, 404, 431, 969, 971, 972; Acton to Mollie, July 7, 1862, Acton Papers, HSP; Batchelder to Mary, July 10, 1862, Zadock Pratt Papers, BU; Newcomb Diary, Newcomb Papers, Stanford; McAllister to family, July 1, 1862, McAllister Papers, Rutgers; Hanifen, *History of Battery B*, p. 25; Waugh Memoir, FSNMP. Three batteries are listed in the Union order of battle but not accounted for during the Seven Days: Batteries B and G, 1st Rhode Island Light Artillery, and Battery G, 1st U.S. Artillery.

2. *OR*, pt. 1, pp. 120–21; *OR*, pt. 2, pp. 22, 102, 228, 496; Porter, "Battle of Malvern Hill," p. 409–10; Brainerd, *Bridge Building*, p. 78. Freeman (*R. E. Lee*, p. 204) notes that the Yankees "could not have found ground more ideally set for the slaughter of an attacking army" if they had looked everywhere below Richmond. Sears (*To the Gates of Richmond*, p. 312) says the north part of the Malvern Hill line was necessarily too narrow; the plateau was not wide enough to hold the number of troops the Yankees would have needed to feel absolutely safe.

3. Porter, "Malvern Hill," p. 414; *OR*, pt. 2, p. 52; Hyde, *Following the Greek Cross*, p. 77; McClellan, *McClellan's Own Story*, p. 424, 434; McClellan, *Civil War Papers*, pp. 328–29 (emphasis in original); John Rodgers to Anne, July 1, 1862, and July 2, 1862, Rodgers Family Papers, Naval Historical Foundation Collection, LOC; Biddle to Ropes, Mar. 27, 1895, Ropes Collection, BU; Averell, "With the Cavalry," p. 431; Everett to parents, July 6, 1862, Everett Papers, Leigh Collection, USAMHI; Porter to McClellan, July 1, 1862, McClellan Papers, LOC; Keyes, *Fifty Years' Observation*, pp. 482–83; Mehaffey to mother, July 16, 1862, Mehaffey Papers, UM; *Army of the Potomac*, p. 437; McClellan to Johnson, Mar. 9, 1864, Johnson Papers, LOC. Sears (*George B. McClellan*, pp. 221–22) analyzes this decision. French (*Army of the Potomac*, p. 106) says that McClellan was trying to avoid capture. Macartney (*Little Mac*, p. 195) and Michie (*General McClellan*, p. 361) note McClellan's effect on the men.

4. Hill, "McClellan's Change of Base," p. 391; Longstreet, *From Manassas to Appomattox*, p. 142; Early, *War Memoirs*, p. 76; Goode, *Recollections*, p. 58; *OR*, pt. 2, pp. 566, 667; Winder Diary, Winder Papers, MdHS; Black, "After the Battle," p. 20; "Horrors of the Battlefield," p. 306; Scarborough Barnsley Diary, Barnsley Family Papers, SHC; William Brandon, "Military Reminiscences," Claiborne Papers, SHC; Ruth to wife, July 13, 1862, Ruth Papers, FSNMP; Brent, *Memoirs*, pp. 197–203. Black does not specify the Whitlock house in his narrative, but since it is the only one mentioned by combatants, it is the most likely structure.

5. *OR*, pt. 2, pp. 760, 790, 811, 818, 917; Bernard Journal, Bernard Papers, Duke; Burgwyn to mother, July 14, 1862, Burgwyn Family Papers, SHC; Hinsdale Journal, Hinsdale Family Papers, Duke; George Wills to father, July 3, 1862, Wills Papers, SHC. Freeman (*Lee's Lieutenants*, vol. 1, p. 612) puts Huger's meeting with Taylor later in the day, but it seems that it must have taken place earlier, and that Huger did not stop and wait long if at all. For a long wait to have happened, it would be necessary for Lee to have forgotten Huger, an unlikely occurrence. The Mellert farm is usually referred to as the Crew farm, for a former owner.

6. Hill, "McClellan's Change of Base," p. 391; Longstreet, *From Manassas to Appomattox*, p. 142; *OR*, pt. 2, p. 557. Longstreet implied that Lee wanted him there because of the commander's weariness, but the conclusion is not certain.

7. *OR*, pt. 2, pp. 668, 676–77, 691, 719, 823; Longstreet, *From Manassas to Appomattox*, pp. 142–43; G. W. Finley to Hotchkiss, Mar. 17, 1897, Hotchkiss Papers, LOC; Pitts

to Lizzie, July 7, 1862, Pitts Papers, SCHS. No report mentions the order of march, but none mentions getting the order changed, either. Because Magruder's division was the first to the front, this reconstruction seems likely. Brent (*Memoirs*, p. 206) says that Lee's map labeled the Long Bridge road as the Quaker road, but as Brent himself did not know the area, he might have misread it. The exact map Lee used is not known, but it was not the one drawn by Albert H. Campbell and printed in the atlas accompanying the *OR*, because that one (correctly labeling the Willis Church road and not showing Magruder's Quaker road) was not completed until 1863.

8. Dowdey (*Seven Days*, p. 329) says that nothing was hurt by the mere fact of the missing road. Brent (*Memoirs*, p. 207) says the delay was beneficial. For Jackson's presence during Hill's comment, see *OR*, pt. 2, p. 628. For his supposed views, see, for example, Henderson, *Jackson*, vol. 2, p. 61; Robertson, *Stonewall Jackson*, p. 499. Alexander (*Military Memoirs*, p. 161) makes the point about scouting to the east.

9. *OR*, pt. 2, pp. 105, 116, 120, 165, 166, 266, 287, 557, 566, 573, 653, 972; Moore, *Story of a Cannoneer*, p. 87, Balthis, "Recollections," Hotchkiss Papers, LOC; Perkins to Elizabeth, July 7, 1862, Perkins Papers, *CWTI*. It is conjecture that these were the Yankee batteries opposing Reilly, but their reports fit Whiting's description. The Union artillery reports discuss many actions during the day without always distinguishing the direction of fire or the number of Confederate guns opposing them. Major Elisha Kellogg of the 1st Connecticut Heavy Artillery reported opening fire early in the day without specifying direction; his guns probably shelled in all directions throughout the day.

10. Jones, "Reminiscences No. 8," p. 567, Brown, "Down the Peninsula," pp. 61–62, 64–65; Moore, *Story of a Cannoneer*, pp. 89–90; Hill, "McClellan's Change of Base," p. 392; Herndon, "Infantry and Cavalry Service," p. 174; L. W. Cox to Hotchkiss, Aug. 3, 1897, Hotchkiss Papers, LOC; Gordon, *Reminiscences*, pp. 67–68; Vairin Diary, MDAH; *OR*, pt. 2, pp. 566, 573–74, 594; Bohannon, *Giles, Allegheny and Jackson Artillery*, p. 73. The artillery commanders' reports mention two batteries leaving, but one may have been Reilly's.

11. *OR*, pt. 2, pp. 64, 81, 83–84, 88, 95, 116, 151, 165, 182, 228, 266–67, Rhodes, *History of the United States*, p. 101; Sleight Memoir, Sleight Papers, BHC; Haydon, *For Country, Cause and Leader*, p. 261; Dodge Journal, Dodge Papers, LOC; Gray, "Artillerist's Yarn," p. 7, Batchelder to Mary, July 10, 1862, Zadock Pratt Papers, BU; Neill to wife, July 4, 1862, Neill Papers, MinnHS; Powell, *Fifth Army Corps*, pp. 158–59; Hyde, *Following the Greek Cross*, p. 77. It is possible that Wolcott was referring to other fire, but he moved to get away from it fairly early in the day. Sumner wanted Porter to withdraw during the shelling, but Fitz John refused.

12. *OR*, pt. 2, pp. 260, 269–71, 283, 285, 287, 351, 802, 812–14, 818–19, 823, 972; Longstreet, *From Manassas to Appomattox*, p. 143; "Purcell Battery," p. 364; Shoemaker, *Shoemaker's Battery*, p. 17, McCreery Journal, McCreery Papers, VaHS (emphasis in original); Johnson, "Barksdale-Humphreys Mississippi Brigade," p. 206; Hager Memoir, Hager Papers, UVa; Slater, "Scenes at Malvern Hill," p. 1. The accounts of the artillery going into action do not completely reconcile, and Grimes's is followed for the most part. Weeden reported firing into some woods in the bottom on his left, which does not really sound like Grimes's position, but it is unclear what else he would have been bombarding. No report mentions Nairn's battery, but if it were still in position it would have fired as well.

13. McCreery Journal, McCreery Papers VaHS; *OR*, pt. 2, pp. 542, 562, 629, 669, 747, 819, 839, 904, 979–83; Owen, *In Camp and Battle*, pp. 90–93; G. W. Finley to Hotchkiss, Mar. 17, 1897, Hotchkiss Papers, LOC; Longstreet, *From Manassas to Appomattox*, p. 143. The reports are unclear as to when Magruder made his promise.

14. *OR*, pt. 2, pp. 483–89, 533–36, 539, 549; Francis Coker to wife, July 3, 1862, Heidler Papers, UGa; *OR*, pt. 2, pp. 537, 547, 550; *OR*, pt. 3, pp. 612–13; *OR*, vol. 51, pt. 2, pp. 577–78; Dowdey, *Seven Days*, p. 335; Freeman, *Lee's Lieutenants*, p. 616; Alexander, *Military Memoirs*, p. 160. Dowdey (*Seven Days*, pp. 334–35), Freeman (*Lee's Lieutenants*, p. 617), and Sears (*To the Gates of Richmond*, p. 318) are critical, but even the most noted defender of Pendleton, Wise (*Long Arm of Lee*, p. 227), makes the mistake of giving Pendleton command of all his batteries. If he did retain nominal command, the batteries were scattered to the winds in the various columns of infantry, so effective command was lost. In addition to the previously cited works, Cullen (*Peninsula Campaign*, p. 156) notes the forgetfulness of Lee, Longstreet, and Jackson. Alexander's charge drew a stinging retort from Wise (*Long Arm of Lee*, p. 227). The points regarding difficulties are made by Brown ("Down the Peninsula," p. 63), Alexander ("Longstreet's Corps," p. 73), and Longstreet ("'The Seven Days'," p. 403). Cullen (*Peninsula Campaign*, p. 156) says it would have been better if Longstreet had been enlightened earlier regarding the possibilities of his idea succeeding.

18. *"Press Forward Your Whole Line and Follow Up Armistead's Success"*

1. *OR*, pt. 2, p. 105, 119, 213, 260, 271, 287, 627; anonymous memoir, Schaub Papers, Troup County (Georgia) Archives; Hill, "McClellan's Change of Base," p. 392. The memoir indicates that the 14th's flag was taken later in the day, but the Union reports clearly indicate it was lost during the first action on the right. Kingsbury left before D. H. Hill's main assault, yet he reported the taking of the flag.

2. *OR*, pt. 2, pp. 260, 271, 275, 285, 288, 812–13, 819, 821, 823, 824, 828, 829; Ripley, *Vermont Riflemen*, pp. 53–54; Finley to Hotchkiss, Mar. 17, 1897, Hotchkiss Papers, LOC. Again, the Union batteries in action at this time are difficult to establish with precision, as most commanders' reports indicate that they fired at anything that moved.

3. *OR*, pt. 2, p. 677; Longstreet, *From Manassas to Appomattox*, pp. 143–44. Hill ("McClellan's Change of Base," p. 392) gives the order with only slightly different wording. Observers who have expressed incredulity that Lee approved it include Brent (*Memoirs*, p. 221) and Sears (*To the Gates of Richmond*, p. 317). The critics of the signaling mechanism include Cullen (*Peninsula Campaign*, p. 156), Greene (*Whatever You Resolve to Be*, p. 69), and Sears (*To the Gates of Richmond*, p. 317). Dowdey (*Seven Days*, p. 331) and Sears (*To the Gates of Richmond*, p. 317) comment on Armistead's inexperience. Sears (*To the Gates of Richmond*, p. 317) also criticizes the omission of time on the order.

4. McLaws to Longstreet, Nov. 30, 1885, Longstreet Papers, SHC; Hill, "McClellan's Change of Base," p. 392; *OR*, pt. 2, pp. 628, 669, 883–84; Longstreet, *From Manassas to Appomattox*, p. 144; Hood, *Advance and Retreat*, pp. 30–31; Trepp Journal, Trepp Papers, NYHS; Dabney to Hotchkiss, Mar. 10, 1897, Hotchkiss Papers, LOC. Longstreet mentions the order in both his official report (*OR*, pt. 2, p. 760) and in "'The Seven Days'" (p. 403) without discussing his ride with Lee, but Goree (*Longstreet's Aide*, p. 96) corroborates Longstreet's memoirs. For the VI Corps's position, see *OR*, pt. 2, pp. 431, 464. Freeman (*R. E. Lee*, p. 210) believes that Lee could have occupied such a point. Cullen (*Peninsula Campaign*, p. 158) considers an attack at that point difficult as both Franklin and Sumner were in the area. Branch's report (*OR*, pt. 2, pp. 883–84) merely says "down the road on which we had previously been moving," but when he was ordered to return and turned around he heard firing on his left, which would have been south, and the Long Bridge road was the one he had moved on the previous day, so this seems a logical inference. Dowdey (*Seven Days*, pp. 335–36) calls Longstreet's

account into question on the basis that no evidence but Longstreet's own postwar writings exists for an order to move his and Hill's divisions, but Branch's account seems clear. Sears (*To the Gates of Richmond*, p. 322) says it was too late to accomplish anything on the first when Lee thought of the movement. Alexander (*Fighting for the Confederacy*, p. 111) and Greene (*Whatever You Resolve to Be*, p. 71) both argue that such a movement earlier on July 1 would have led to success that day.

5. *OR*, pt. 2, pp. 496, 668, 749, 790; Brent, *Memoirs*, pp. 211–12. Most observers have put Magruder on the field for the first time at about 4 P.M. (see, for example, Freeman, *Lee's Lieutenants*, vol. 1, p. 598; Sears, *To the Gates of Richmond*, p. 322), yet Colonel Edmonds's report (*OR*, pt. 2, p. 823) indicates that Magruder had been on the field and had discussed the need for artillery before Armistead made his initial assault. This contradicts the general sense of Magruder's own report (*OR*, pt. 2, pp. 668–69) but not the literal words, as Magruder does not specify times or (clearly) a sequence of events. Cobb's report says he moved to Armistead's support at first in response to a message from that officer. Huger wrote that he could make no report as others commanded his force, and he complained that the same thing had happened at Seven Pines. The exact timing of this series of orders by Lee is questionable, as is whether they came before or after Lee's trip to the left flank and his decision to attempt a turning movement. It need not be assumed that the orders came before the decision, because even if Lee had decided on the turning movement, he would need to hold the Yankees in place. Thus, he needed to maintain the line north of Malvern Hill. One might wonder that both Lee and Longstreet were giving orders on the right, yet Magruder was put in overall command. This indicates that the timing was just before Lee's trip to the east—perhaps his journeys had confirmed that nothing was working—and that Lee and Longstreet were communicating well. But Old Pete's proper place was with the reserve, especially if a turning movement were in the offing.

6. Brent, *Memoirs*, p. 215; *OR*, pt. 2, pp. 88, 95, 105, 119, 120, 209, 211–12, 257–59, 267, 271, 275, 283, 285, 288, 293, 314, 319, 357, 566; Alexander, *Military Memoirs*, p. 162. It is uncertain whether McClellan ordered Sedgwick's redeployment, but he did move the artillery himself (*OR*, pt. 2, p. 197), so the inference can be made. It could be that Abercrombie misidentified the regiments. Otherwise, there would have been lots of marching and countermarching. Howe reported that he took a new position after he repulsed a Confederate advance, but no early Confederate assault really fits; he could have meant after George Anderson's advance, but that does not mesh with the report of Col. Thomas A. Rowley of the 102nd Pennsylvania.

7. *OR*, pt. 2, p. 691–92, 707, 719; Brent, *Memoirs*, p. 196. No such message is known to exist, but Dickinson went to Lee, and no one else is known to have reported any "success" by Armistead. Lee must have heard of it because he referred to it in his reply to Magruder, which is quoted below.

8. Brent, *Memoirs*, pp. 215–17, *OR*, pt. 2, pp. 669, 677–78, 747, 751, 794, 800, 839; Hale and Phillips, *Forty-Ninth Virginia Infantry*, p. 38. Brent's and Magruder's accounts do not completely mesh, but the differences are not great except for Mahone's role (in which I have followed the *OR*). The timing differences between Brent's account and Magruder's report, mentioned by Freeman (*Lee's Lieutenants*, vol. 1, p. 600 n 60) do not seem as great as Freeman makes them. Magruder did not give a time of receipt of Lee's order, but given the timing of the battle it must have been after he had arrived on the field for good, which was late in the afternoon.

9. *OR*, pt. 2, p. 275, 567, 609, 618, 669–70, 694, 749, 813–14, 819; Brent, *Memoirs*, p. 217, Bernard Diary, Bernard Papers, Duke; Cox to Hotchkiss, Aug. 3, 1897, Hotchkiss Papers, LOC; Herndon, "Infantry and Cavalry Service," pp. 173–74; Beeler Diary,

CWMC; Davis Memoir, Davis Papers, UVa; Randolph Fairfax to mother, July 3, 1862, Fairfax Family Papers, LV; James L. Dinwiddie to Bettie, July 3, 1862, Dinwiddie Family Papers, UVa; McCreery Journal, McCreery Papers, VaHS; *OR Supp.*, vol. 2, pp. 464–65. Cobb's report mentions a Union advance that was repulsed, perhaps the 13th New York's change of front or the repulse of Armistead's first charge. However, neither the timing nor the positioning seems right. Major John Garnett says Hart's battery only fired a few rounds.

10. *OR*, pt. 2, pp. 270, 275–76, 294, 314, 350–51, 355, 814; David Winn to Fanny, July 4, 1862, Winn Papers, EU; Baxter, "Battle Flag of the Third Georgia," p. 211; Bernard, "Malvern Hill," p. 60; Brown to Caroline, July 7, 1862, Brown Papers, URL. The artillery fire is speculative, especially that of Voegelee and Nairn, but Carlisle reported firing in that direction and Weed reported being able to fire a few rounds at "effective range." Given that Voegelee seems to have fired when Carlisle did, and that Nairn seems to have been near Weed, it is at least possible that they added their guns to the din.

11. *OR*, pt. 2, pp. 203, 267, 314, 357, 814, 824, 826; Ripley, *Vermont Riflemen*, pp. 57–58; Tuffs, "Malvern Hill," p. 4; Winn to Fanny, July 4, 1862, Winn Papers, EU; John Shipp diary, Shipp Family Papers, VaHS; Brown, *Reminiscences*, p. 14; Bernard, "Malvern Hill," pp. 61–62, 67; Porter, "Battle of Malvern Hill," p. 417 n. Couch's report refers to three batteries, probably meaning those of Edwards, Ames, and Kingsbury (or his replacements). Snow had one section on the left, one on the center, and one on the right of Couch's line, and the first two sections could have added their fire as well. Wright and Mahone (*OR*, pt. 2, p. 800) both reported driving the Unionists back in disorder, and it is possible that they either mistook the 14th New York's wavering for disorder or that one of their attacks hit the 4th Michigan as it was retiring after its counterattack. Whatever the case, the 14th New York did not break on July 1 (*OR*, pt. 2, p. 315).

12. *OR*, pt. 2, pp. 260, 314, 357, 749, 820, 824, 833; Macnamara, *History of the Ninth Regiment*, p. 156; Gilmore, "With the 4th Mich.," p. 7; Crocker, "Personal Experiences," p. 117; "On to Prison," p. 58; B. Wylie Scott to Ella, July 9, 1862, Merryman Papers, VaHS; Lichtenstein Memoir and Hutchins Memoir, *CWTI*.

13. *OR*, pt. 2, pp. 294, 320–21, 325, 328–29, 342, 345–46; Ripley, *Vermont Riflemen*, p. 58; Frothingham to Maggie, July 7 and 9, 1862, Frothingham Papers, NYPL; Norton, *Army Letters*, p. 94; Berry Diary, *CWTI;* Luce, "Brave Cook," p. 7; Boies, "Malvern Hill," p. 1; Porter, "Battle of Malvern Hill," pp. 425–26. The 16th Michigan's report lists the battery it supported as Capt. John Wolcott's Battery A, Maryland Light Artillery, but it most likely was part of Snow's battery. Butterfield reported the colors as belonging to a South Carolina regiment, but that is unlikely, as Kershaw's brigade was engaged later and to the east, while Richard Anderson's brigade was not engaged.

14. Robert, "Justice to General Magruder," p. 250; *OR*, pt. 2, pp. 30, 38–40, 276, 310, 801, 812, 815, 821, 834, 979, 981–82, 985; Dimitry, *CMH*, vol. 13, p. 222 n; Hotchkiss, *CMH*, vol. 4, pp. 993, 1128; Stewart, "Colonel John Bowie Magruder," p. 207; Crocker, "Colonel James Gregory Hodges," p. 190; Fox, *Regimental Losses*, p. 563; Brown to Caroline, July 7, 1862, Brown Papers, URL; Taylor to mother, July 4, 1862, Taylor Papers, BHC.

15. *OR*, pt. 2, p. 208–209, 634, 643, 650, 659; Barlow to mother, July 4, 1862, Barlow Papers, MassHS; Edward Armstrong to father, July 6, 1862, Armstrong Family Papers, UNC-W; Cumming to mother, July 3, 1862, Cumming Family Papers, Augusta State University. Howe reported that all of Snow's battery was with him, but Snow's report is clear that his battery's sections were split up and posted all along Couch's line. Sears (*To the Gates of Richmond*, p. 326) discusses the lack of coordination in Hill's assault.

16. Wall, *Pee Dee Guards*, p. 35; Henry Muldoon to father, July 3, 1862, 3rd Alabama File, ADAH; James Branscomb to sister, July 15, 1862, Branscomb Family Papers, ADAH; Ardrey Diary, Ardrey Papers, Duke; Hagar Diary, Lang Collection, and Thomas Tanfield to sister, July 7, 1862, Tanfield Family Papers, USAMHI; Sleight Memoir, Sleight Papers, BHC; Parker to wife, July 3, 1862, Parker Papers, NCDAH; *OR*, pt. 2, pp. 212–14, 634, 635, 637, Gordon, *Reminiscences*, p. 74; Blackford Journal, Blackford Papers, CWMC.

17. *OR*, pt. 2, pp. 628, 634, 643, 650, 976, 977, letter from father, July 7, 1862, Williams Papers, CWMC, USAMHI; Brown, "Down the Peninsula," p. 66; Fox, *Regimental Losses*, pp. 557, 563; Hill to wife, July 3, 1862, Hill Papers, NCDAH; Hill, "McClellan's Change of Base," p. 394.

19. *"General Magruder, Why Did You Attack?"*

1. *OR*, pt. 2, pp. 28–29, 52, 64, 107, 176, 251, 283, 628, 697, 700, 703, 705, 707–709, 712, 713, 715; Hays, report of July 4, 1862, Hays Papers, HSWP; Coward, *South Carolinians*, p. 43; Butler to wife, July 5, 1862, Butler Papers, EU; Stovall, *Robert Toombs*, pp. 254–58; Cobb to wife, July 23, 1862, Cobb Papers, UGa; Bowden Reminiscences, *CWTI*; Austin, *Georgia Boys*, p. 40; McDaniel, *With Unabated Trust*, p. 87. Frank's report does not specify which battery he sandwiched, but Ames's seems the most likely.

2. *OR*, pt. 2, pp. 52–53, 260, 267, 293–94, 297, 305–308, 311–12, 324, 342, 347, 660, 751–55; Johnson, "Barksdale-Humphreys Mississippi Brigade," p. 206; Brandon, "Military Reminiscences," Claiborne Papers, SHC; Buswell, "'Blood and Feathered'," pp. 27, 30; Ames, *History of Battery G*, p. 35; Judson, *History of the Eighty-Third Regiment*, p. 48; Averell, "With the Cavalry," p. 431. It is not certain that this action is when Buswell was wounded, but he made it to a hospital by sundown, so it would not have been later. He also mentions three charges, Barksdale's being the third on his area of the line.

3. *OR*, pt. 2, pp. 72, 204, 230, 238, 283, 351, 972; Rodgers to mother, July 22, 1862, Rodgers Family Papers, Naval Historical Foundation Collection, LOC; Porter, "Battle of Malvern Hill," pp. 416 n, 422; Myer to wife, July 29, 1862, Myer Papers, LOC; Porter to commander of gunboats, July 1, 1862, McClellan Papers, LOC; Brown, "Down the Peninsula," p. 61; Bradwell, "From Cold Harbor to Cedar Mountain," p. 223.

4. *OR*, pt. 2, p. 794. Dowdey (*Seven Days*, pp. 318, 342), Freeman (*Lee's Lieutenants*, vol. 1, p. 612), and Sears (*To the Gates of Richmond*, p. 335) grade Huger's performance low. Sears (*To the Gates of Richmond*, p. 335) believes Huger could have made a difference.

5. Brent, *Memoirs*, pp. 218–19; *OR*, pt. 2, pp. 671, 678, 680, 760, 794, 839, 884; Burgwyn to mother, July 14, 1862, Burgwyn Family Papers, SHC; Harris, *Historical Sketches*, p. 15. The order is misprinted in the *OR* as telling Magruder to press the Yankee right.

6. *OR*, pt. 2, pp. 558, 571, 585, 587, 597, 607, 611, 618, 620, 622. The first criticism is made explicitly by Sears (*To the Gates of Richmond*, p. 318), and implicitly by Longstreet (*From Manassas to Appomattox*, p. 144). Alexander (*Military Memoirs*, p. 167) and Hassler (*General George B. McClellan*, p. 167) make the second point. Robertson (*Stonewall Jackson*, p. 503) seems puzzled by the criticisms—and rightly so.

7. *OR*, pt. 2, pp. 629, 672, 908, 914, 915, 917, George Wills to father, July 3, 1862, Wills Papers, SHC. Hill repeated the criticism more explicitly in "McClellan's Change of Base," p. 391. Freeman (*Lee's Lieutenants*, vol. 1, p. 614) disagrees with Hill.

8. *OR*, pt. 2, p. 351, 360, 794–95, 984; Evans, "At Malvern Hill," p. 40; C. S. Powell, "War Tales," Rose Papers, Duke; Day, *True History*, p. 20; Henry Burgwyn to mother, July 14, 1862, Burgwyn Family Papers, SHC; Hager Memoir, Hager Papers, UVa;

Underwood, *Twenty-sixth North Carolina*, p. 31; Vance to Scott, July 25, 1862, Scott Papers, Duke. Ransom's brigade, at about three thousand men, was one of the largest involved in the battle.

9. *OR*, pt. 2, pp. 73–74, 245–46, 250, 670–71, 698, 708, 717, 719, 723–24, 749–51, 800, 815, 819, 978; Moore, "Malvern Hill," pp. 122–23; Wiley, "Soldier's Life," p. 70; Haw Diary, Haw Papers, VaHS; Conyngham, *Irish Brigade*, pp. 212–13; Porter, "Battle of Malvern Hill," p. 421; Noonan, manuscript history of 69th New York, Noonan Papers, Powers Collection, USAMHI; Gache, *Frenchman*, p. 121; "Colonel Eugene Waggaman," pp. 449–50; Turner to family, July 16, 1862, Turner Papers, NYSL; Fox, *Regimental Losses*, p. 204. The 69th reported 203 casualties for the entire Seven Days after Gaines's Mill, and the Irish Brigade as a whole 479. Of these, 232 were missing and probably captured at Savage Station and elsewhere.

10. *OR*, pt, 2, pp. 68, 209, 212, 214, 728, 734, 737, 742; Pitts to Lizzie, July 7, 1862, Pitts Papers, SCHS; Suddath, "From Sumter to the Wilderness," p. 94; Mitchell to parents, July 9, 1862, Mitchell Papers, USAMHI; Wray, "Malvern Hill," p. 4. Neither Abercrombie nor Palmer explicitly states that Barlow's men relieved his, but as the 23rd Pennsylvania moved into Abercrombie's line, it is probable that Barlow took position nearby.

11. *OR*, pt. 2, pp. 140–41, 698, 700, 705, 728, 734, 737, 738, 742; Garnett, "Retreat to Malvern," p. 1; Wray, "Malvern Hill," p. 4; Coker, "A Story of the Confederate War," Coker Papers, VaHS; Bowden Reminiscences, *CWTI;* letter of July 12, 1862, Abbott Papers, Civil War Miscellany, Personal Papers, GDAH.

12. *OR*, pt. 2, pp. 107, 209, 571–72, 576, 582, 587, 598, 601, 612, 620, 622, 729, 973; Jones Journal, Jones Papers, VaHS; Boggs, *Hammers and Allied Families*, p. 76; Early, *War Memoirs*, pp. 80–81; Hale, "Recollections of Malvern Hill," p. 333; Howard, *Recollections*, p. 151; Kearns Diary, Kearns Papers, VaHS; Neff to parents, Aug. 4, 1862, Neff Papers, *CWTI;* Garnett, "Personal Reminiscences," pp. 150–51; Gerrish Memoir, *CWTI;* Brown, "Down the Peninsula," p. 65; Stevenson, *History of Excelsior*, p. 32; Mitchell to parents, July 9, 1862, Mitchell Papers, USAMHI; Fuller, *Personal Recollections*, p. 43; Barlow to mother, July 4, 1862, Barlow Papers, MassHS; Casler, *Four Years*, p. 94; Johnson, "Memoir," p. 216.

13. *OR*, pt. 2, pp. 238, 240, 567, 598, 618–19, 815; Richardson to family, July 12, 1862, Richardson Papers, Alexander H. Stephens Museum Collection, GDAH; Dobbins, *Grandfather's Journal*, p. 89; letter of Maj. Samuel E. Baker, quoted in "Flag of the 16th Mississippi Regiment," p. 76.

14. Grubb, *Notes of a Staff Officer*, p. 24; Nunnally to sister and brother in law, Nunally Papers, Civil War Miscellany, Personal Papers, GDAH; "Horrors of the Battlefield," p. 306; *OR*, pt. 2, pp. 24–41, 973–84; Fox, *Regimental Losses*, pp. 460, 563; Hill, "McClellan's Change of Base," p. 394. Fox (*Regimental Losses*, p. 550 n) estimates Confederate losses at Malvern Hill to be 5,355, including the missing. Alexander ("Longstreet's Corps," p. 25) estimates the loss at 5,062. Union missing have not been added because of the difficulty in separating those captured at the hospital at Savage Station from those captured in battle. Fox (*Regimental Losses*, p. 543) estimates Union losses at 2489.

15. *Army of the Potomac*, p. 574. Dowdey (*Seven Days*, p. 344) and Freeman (*R. E. Lee*, p. 217) write as if success were possible. Cullen (*Peninsula Campaign*, p. 158) calls the attack "hopeless and useless." Sears (*To the Gates of Richmond*, p. 335) says a loss would have had grave consequences for McClellan's army, but only a loss that demoralized all the men on the hill could have had such consequences. Alexander recommended an early attack (*Military Memoirs*, p. 163).

16. Freeman, *R. E. Lee*, p. 218; Spaulding to John Dunkle, Aug. 16, 1862, Spaulding

Papers, Duke; *OR*, pt. 2, pp. 52, 204, 229, 245, 270, 380; Powell, *Fifth Army Corps*, p. 171; Johnson, "Memoir," p. 216; Wayland, *Stonewall Jackson's Way*, p. 163; Early, *War Memoirs*, p. 87; Hankins, "Simple Story of a Soldier—V, VI," p. 21; Wise, *Long Arm of Lee*, p. 221; untitled manuscript, Porter Papers, LOC; Slater, "Malvern," p. 3. Powell (*Fifth Army Corps*, pp. 173–77) takes Couch severely to task for his claim. Couch, as a division commander, would of course have been subordinate to Porter, and he would have known it. It is possible that Couch merely meant that he was commanding troops besides his own on the right of the Willis Church road. Swinton (*Campaigns*, p. 163) praises Couch's conduct. Palfrey ("Battle of Malvern Hill," p. 215) says the battle was fought without a commander.

17. Bradwell, "Soldier Life," p. 24. Hill, "McClellan's Change of Base," p. 391, says Lee believed with Longstreet that his opponents were demoralized. Sanger, *James Longstreet*, p. 74, thinks Longstreet did not communicate with Lee, but the fact that Chilton of Lee's staff showed up to tell Magruder the correct route seems to indicate that Old Pete did send a messenger. Freeman, *Lee's Lieutenants*, vol. 1, p. 592, thinks this probable. Dowdey, *Seven Days*, p. 333, criticizes Longstreet for supposedly giving up.

18. *OR*, pt. 2, p. 629; Hill, "McClellan's Change of Base," pp. 393–94; Brent, *Memoirs*, p. 216. Various of these criticisms have been made by Cullen (*Peninsula Campaign*, p. 157), Dowdey (*Seven Days*, pp. 329, 338, 345), Freeman (*Lee's Lieutenants*, vol. 1, pp. 591, 600, 601, 602), and Sears (*To the Gates of Richmond*, pp. 314, 332, 335). For the rumors of drunkenness see, for example, Benjamin Humphries to friend, July 29, 1862, Southall Papers, LV. For the rebuttals, see *OR*, pt. 2, p. 683; Lamb, "Malvern Hill," p. 217. Dowdey (*Seven Days*, p. 329) and Sears (*To the Gates of Richmond*, p. 315) absolve Magruder of most of the blame for hitting the wrong road. Dowdey (*Seven Days*, p. 337) mentions the effect of the twenty-ninth. Brent (*Memoirs*, p. 225) defends his chief by saying he followed orders "loyally and energetically." Hill ("McClellan's Change of Base," p. 394) and Taylor (*Four Years with General Lee*, p. 49) blame Magruder for the lack of coordination. Dowdey (*Seven Days*, p. 339) interprets Magruder's purpose as getting to his right, but if this is the case he did a poor job of it.

19. Dowdey (*Seven Days*, p. 330) and Sears (*To the Gates of Richmond*, pp. 314, 317) blame Lee's performance on exhaustion. Freeman (*R.E. Lee*, p. 210) implies that his investigation of a turning movement was a result of his frustration. Swinton (*Campaigns*, p. 163) says Lee never ordered "a battle so ill-judged in conception, or so faulty in its details of execution." Cullen (*Peninsula Campaign*, p. 155) disagrees with Swinton at least in part. Dowdey (*Seven Days*, p. 331) says that Lee stayed where he was to watch over Jackson; but since he moved around later this seems a bit much. Alexander (*Fighting for the Confederacy*, p. 112) points out the difficulties in communicating. For just one example of the judgment that the battle was hopeless, see Maurice, *Lee the Soldier*, p. 118.

20. *"It Was a Very Tedious, Tiresome March"*

1. *OR*, pt. 2, pp. 201, 216, 234, 517–18, 525, 527, 529, 533; Blackford, *War Years*, p. 79. Peck's report mentions this particular force at Long Bridge on the twenty-eighth; part or all of it may have still been there on the thirtieth. Averell ("With the Cavalry," p. 433) speculates on the possibilities of Stuart's being south of the Chickahominy during the Union retreat across White Oak Swamp. Stuart might have "annoyed" the Yankees, but it is hard to see how he could have "embarrassed" them given the infantry's movements on the twenty-eighth and twenty-ninth.

2. Porter to McClellan, July 1, 1862, McClellan Papers, LOC; Heintzelman Diary, Heintzelman Papers, LOC; Smith, *Autobiography*, pp. 47–48; Woodward, *Third*

Pennsylvania Reserve, pp. 124–25; Averell, "With the Cavalry," p. 431; *OR*, pt. 2, p. 23. Heintzelman says Porter for Morell, and Smith for Franklin, but he likely just wrote some wrong names.

3. Down the Peninsula," p. 64; *OR*, pt. 3, p. 282; Haydon, *For Country, Cause and Leader*, p. 262; Hyde, *Following the Greek Cross*, p. 80; LeDuc, "McClellan and Richmond," p. 7. Dowdey (*Seven Days*, p. 348) says McClellan did not have a fresh corps, and this is literally but not really true unless by "fresh" he means not having marched or fought for a few days. French (*Army of the Potomac*, p. 106) says McClellan was oblivious to the Confederates' suffering, but the more likely explanation is also mentioned by French: that McClellan thought they continued to use fresh forces. Eckenrode and Conrad (*Man who Saved the Union*, p. 116) say it is possible McClellan would have stayed if he had been on the scene. Sears (*To the Gates of Richmond*, p. 338) says McClellan could think only of retreat. Williams (*Lincoln Finds a General*, vol. 1, p. 239) says that there is no reason to speculate on what might have been done after Malvern Hill, since another commander would not have been at Malvern Hill in the first place. Cullen (*Peninsula Campaign*, p. 161) claims that since no plans for an advance were in place, they would have to be made. Plans could be improvised, as Lee had shown, but perhaps not by McClellan. Cullen also makes the point about the Federal exertions.

4. Bliss, "No. 1 Narrative," Bancroft-Bliss Family Papers, LOC; *OR*, pt. 2, pp. 64, 80–81, 90, 103, 107, 124, 141, 144, 151, 165, 182, 186, 189, 204, 217, 234, 246, 250, 251, 267, 276, 294–95, 315, 351, 364, 381, 436, 464; Taggert Diary, Taggert Papers, PSA; Spaulding to Dunkle, Aug. 16, 1862, Spaulding Papers, Duke; Sypher, *Pennsylvania Reserve Corps*, p. 306; Osborne, *History of the Twenty-ninth Regiment*, pp. 168–69; Miles to a friend, July 6, 1862, Miles Papers, Brown University; Heintzelman Diary, Heintzelman Papers, LOC; Dodge Journal, Dodge Papers, LOC; Davis to Belle, July 5, 1862, Davis Papers, Civil War Manuscripts Collection, Yale; Favill, *Diary*, p. 149; Banes, *History of the Philadelphia Brigade*, pp. 88–89; Dunn to sister, July 10, 1862, Dunn Papers, *CWTI*. As might be expected, the times of withdrawal vary greatly. For example, Couch says that Sickles left about midnight, while Sickles himself says he moved around 2 A.M.; Dana's report (*OR*, pt. 2, p. 95) indicates he received the order to withdraw at around 11 P.M. The times used are the consensus. Bernard ("Malvern Hill," p. 67) confirmed that in Mahone's area several men became lost and wandered into enemy lines. Averell's report names the New York regiment as the 65th, but his "With the Cavalry" (p. 432) names it as the 71st, which tallies with Sickles's report and that of Col. George Hall of the 71st. Averell's report also names the battery as Tidball's, which does not fit Tidball's own report, so it can be concluded with some assurance that the "battery" was the section from Benson's battery.

5. *OR*, pt. 2, pp. 567, 612–13, 619–20, 643–44, 650, 686, 692, 724, 729, 751, 760, 795, 800, 814, 819, 867, 884; Bernard Journal, Bernard Papers, Duke; Hands Civil War Memoirs, UVa; Winder Diary, Winder Papers, MdHS; Vairin Diary, MDAH; Brown, "Down the Peninsula," p. 67, "General Thomas J. Jackson," p. 311. Dabney, in a memorandum for G. F. R. Henderson, tells a similar story about Jackson with slightly different wording. It is likely that the gate mentioned is the same gate as the one Jackson and Lee were near during the day, on the lane leading into the Poindexter field, but this is not certain.

6. Alexander, "Longstreet's Corps," p. 75; Winn to Fannie, July 14, 1862, Winn Papers, EU; Ormsby to family, July 5, 1862, Ormsby Papers, Brigham Young University; Evans, "At Malvern Hill," p. 40; Johnson, "Memoir," p. 218; Bernard, "Malvern Hill," p. 69; Ellis, "Wounded Boy's Night," p. 456; Buswell, "'Blood and Feathered'," pp. 32, 76; Boies, "Malvern Hill," p. 2.

7. *OR*, pt. 2, pp. 124, 193, 217, 307; Bancroft Diary, Bancroft Papers, BHC; Spaulding to Dunkle, Aug. 16, 1862, Spaulding Papers, Duke; Erie L. Ditty Memoir, Stearns Family Papers, Virginia Polytechnic Institute; Hyde, *Following the Greek Cross*, pp. 81–82; Marvin Diary, Marvin Papers, MinnHS; Batchelder to Mary, July 10, 1862, Zadock Pratt Papers, BU; Evans, "At Malvern Hill," p. 42; Rhodes Journal, Rhodes Papers, Civil War Manuscripts Collection, Yale; Acton to wife, July 11, 1862, Acton Papers, HSP; Frank Williams, "Reminiscence of the Fiftieth New York Volunteer Engineers," Leigh Collection, USAMHI.

8. *OR*, pt. 1, p. 70; pt. 2, pp. 60, 103, 155, 194, 217–18, 220, 246, 258, 351, 355, 381, 436, 464, 481; Newcomb Diary, Newcomb Papers, Stanford; Marvin Diary, Marvin Papers, MinnHS; anonymous memoir, Faunce Papers, Duke; Ames to parents, July 5, 1862, Ames Papers, USAMHI (emphasis in original); Smith, *Autobiography*, p. 48; Trepp Journal, Trepp Papers, NYHS.

9. *OR*, pt. 2, pp. 206, 235–36, 360; Averell, "With the Cavalry," pp. 431–32; Hager Memoir, Hager Papers, UVa. Averell ("With the Cavalry," p. 432) discusses a formal truce, but no Confederate makes note of such a truce and his report describes the rebels as "gaining confidence" to come out onto the field, which does not sound much like a truce was declared.

10. Burgwyn to mother, July 14, 1862, Burgwyn Family Papers, SHC; Early, *War Memoirs*, p. 83; *OR*, pt. 2, pp. 801, 815, 816, 819; Johnson, "Memoir," p. 218; Blackford, *War Years*, p. 82; Winder Diary, Winder Papers, MdHS; Cooke, *Life of Stonewall Jackson*, pp. 248–49; Sorrel, *Recollections*, p. 47; Brent, *Memoirs*, pp. 229–30, 232–35; Hinsdale Journal, Hinsdale Family Papers, Duke; Hall Diary, Hall Papers, LOC; Hands Civil War Memoirs, UVa; Walthall Reminiscences, CWMC. The man Brent saw probably was from the 10th Louisiana.

11. *OR*, pt. 2, pp. 519, 760; Dabney, *Life of Stonewall Jackson*, pp. 474–75; Dabney, undated memorandum for G.F.R. Henderson, and McGuire to Hotchkiss, May 28, 1896, both in Hotchkiss Papers, LOC; Davis, *Rise and Fall*, p. 128. Longstreet (*From Manassas to Appomattox*, p. 146) says his command advanced toward Nance's Shop, which would have required him to move on the Long Bridge road east of Glendale and then turn south, but his report says he camped near the Poindexter house, which does not mesh. Also, the accounts of his and Hill's men indicate they moved to Malvern Hill on the second. Most likely he was confusing the march on the second with that of the third when he wrote his memoir. Cullen (*Peninsula Campaign*, p. 163), Dowdey (*Seven Days*, p. 348), Freeman (*R. E. Lee*, p. 225), and Sears (*To the Gates of Richmond*, p. 340) all agree with Lee.

12. *OR*, pt. 2, pp. 568, 572, 587, 619, 629, 713, 790, 908; Lee, *Lee's Dispatches*, pp. 23–25. Jackson's own report, pp. 558–59, says that his men started the pursuit on July 2, but this must have been a misstatement, as no one else mentions any forward movement.

13. Mehaffey to mother, July 16, 1862, Mehaffey Papers, UM; Alexander Bliss, "No. 1 Narrative," Bancroft-Bliss Family Papers, LOC; *OR*, pt. 2, pp. 64, 80–81, 88, 103, 147, 160, 246, 259, 262, 276, 283, 310, 383, 436, 464; Hall, "Peninula and Antietam Campaigns," p. 176; Westervelt Diary, CWMC; Bowen, *Ball's Bluff to Gettysburg*, p. 108; Edward Davis to brother, July 5, 1862, Davis Papers, Civil War Manuscripts Collection, Yale; Averell, "With the Cavalry," p. 432; Hager Memoir, Hager Papers, UVa.

14. Bliss, "No. 1 Narrative," Bancroft-Bliss Family Papers, LOC; Hyndman, *History of a Cavalry Company*, p. 55; Stephen to Olive, July 6, 1862, Olney Papers, RIHS; Dodge Journal, Dodge Papers, LOC; Sleight Memoir, Sleight Papers, BHC; anonymous memoir, Faunce Papers, Duke; Hager Memoir, Hager Papers, UVa; Pollard Diary, Pollard Papers, VtHS; Burns Diary, Pennsylvania "Save the Flags" Civil War Collection,

USAMHI; Gerrish Memoir, *CWTI*; Porter, "Battle of Malvern Hill," p. 423; Smith, *Autobiography*, p. 49; Spaulding to Dunkle, Aug. 16, 1862, Spaulding Papers, Duke; Acton to wife, July 11, 1862, Acton Papers, HSP; Mehaffey to mother, July 16, 1862, Mehaffey Papers, UM; Neill to wife, July 4, 1862, Neill Papers, MinnHS; Barr to wife, early July, 1862, Barr Papers, UM.

15. McClellan, *Civil War Papers*, pp. 329–30; *OR*, pt. 2, pp. 218, 220, 299, 334, 530, 531; Lincoln, *Collected Works*, p. 301; Stillwell, "Incidents of McClellan's Retreat," p. 7; Newcomb Diary, Newcomb Papers, Stanford; Wead to parents, July 7, 1862, Wead Papers, NYSL; Dunn to sister, July 10, 1862, Dunn Papers, *CWTI*.

16. *OR*, pt. 2, pp. 519–20; Dabney, *Life of Stonewall Jackson*, pp. 475–76. Freeman (*R. E. Lee*, p. 225) says Lee put Longstreet in front because his men had marched better than Jackson's, but without evidence to support that conclusion. The name of the plantation on the heights is Evelynton, but it is universally called Evelington Heights in the *OR*, so that name will be used.

17. *OR*, pt. 2, p. 246, 464, 482, 520, 922; Lee, *General Lee*, p. 165; Smith, *Autobiography*, p. 49; Hager Memoir, Hager Papers, UVa; McAllister to family, July 1–3, 1862, McAllister Papers, Rutgers; Charles Ives to Lee, July 9, 1862, Colonial Dames Collection, UOkla; McClellan, *Civil War Papers*, pp. 334–35; Birney to George Gross, July 20, 1862, Birney Papers, USAMHI; Barnard to McClellan, July 2, 1862, McClellan Papers, LOC; Jones, "Reminiscences No. 8," p. 569.

18. The accusers include Alexander, *Military Memoirs*, p. 169; Cullen, *Peninsula Campaign*, p. 165; Eckenrode and Conrad, *George B. McClellan*, p. 119; Jones, *Life and Letters*, p. 176; Lee, *General Lee*, pp. 165–66; Taylor, *Four Years with Lee*, pp. 41–42; and Taylor, *General Lee*, p. 83. Jones ("Reminiscences No. 8," p. 569) and Thomas (*Bold Dragoon*, p. 138) refer to the proximity of the infantry. McClellan (*I Rode with Jeb Stuart*, pp. 84–85) and Thomas (*Bold Dragoon*, p. 138) say McClellan would have occupied the heights. Sears (*To the Gates of Richmond*, pp. 340–41) uses the fact that McClellan did order their occupation to excuse Stuart. "Jackson and Ewell," p. 31, cites a comment from John Barnard that McClellan would have had to surrender if the Confederates could have occupied the heights that morning because the army was in such a disorganized state.

19. *OR*, pt. 2, pp. 520, 760. Freeman (*Lee's Lieutenants*, vol. 1, p. 643) and McClellan (*I Rode with Jeb Stuart*, p. 85) cite the power of the gunboats. Dabney (*Life of Stonewall Jackson*, p. 476) echoes the charge regarding Longstreet's wrong route, and Alexander (*Military Memoirs*, p. 169) also mentions it. Hotchkiss (*CMH*, vol. 4, p. 301) criticizes Longstreet's march on both the second and third, but he was not in the area at the time and so cannot give a firsthand report of the difficulties. Alexander, who was on the ground and who does not hesitate to criticize Jackson, had no negative comments about the march in either of his books. Dabney (*Life of Stonewall Jackson*, p. 476) puts Jackson's march at three miles, which would have put Stonewall at about the junction of the White Oak and Long Bridge roads. This seems to have been a median position. Trimble (*OR*, pt. 2, p. 619) says he camped eight miles from the James River opposite Westover. If "opposite" means north of, then the campsite would have been just west of Nance's Shop. Ewell was in the advance on July 4 (*OR*, pt. 2, p. 607). Captain B. W. Leigh (*OR*, pt. 2, p. 591) of the 1st Virginia Battalion in Jones's (Cunningham's) brigade puts the march at only a mile or two and his camp on the Long Bridge road, as does Cunningham (*OR*, pt. 2, p. 587). Whiting (*OR*, pt. 2, p. 568) says that Jackson missed the road and that he camped near Willis Church. Diaries from Jackson's command echo these reports. Lee (*General Lee*, p. 166) criticizes the decision to not use the River road.

20. McClellan, *Civil War Papers*, pp. 334–39; *OR*, pt. 1, p. 70; *OR*, pt. 2, pp. 218–21, 568, 588, 607, 619, 622, 713, 761, 922; *OR*, pt. 3, pp. 636–37, Dickey, *History of the 103rd Regiment*, p. 28; Davis, *History of the 104th Pennsylvania*, p. 133; Keyes, *Fifty Years*, p. 484; *Lee's Dispatches*, pp. 24–32; Dabney, *Life of Jackson*, p. 476; Haines Diary, Rutgers; Anderson Journal, Anderson Papers, UW-GB. Alexander (*Military Memoirs*, pp. 170–71) is a rare critic of Lee's decision not to attack, but he wrote under the impression that only one Federal division was on the heights.

21. *"Under Ordinary Circumstances the Federal Army Should Have Been Destroyed"*

1. *OR*, pt. 2, pp. 24–37, 40–41, 497, 498, 629, 835, 973–84; *OR*, pt. 3, p. 238; Livermore, *Numbers and Losses*, pp. 140–41; Fox, *Regimental Losses*, pp. 556–58.

2. Nevins, *War for the Union*, p. 140; Leech, *Reveille in Washington*, p. 231; Kenney Papers, Duke; Putnam, *Richmond During the War*, pp. 151–54; Bagby to son, July 8, 1862, Bagby Family Papers, VaHS; Elizabeth Munford to girls, July 1, 1862, Munford-Ellis Family Papers, Duke; Harrison, *Recollections Grave and Gay*, p. 161.

3. *OR*, pt. 2, p. 23; McClellan, *Civil War Papers*, p. 341; Tuttle to wife, July 5, 1862, Tuttle Papers, LOC; Moore to sister, July 15, 1862, Moore Papers, Suffolk (N.Y.) County Historical Society; Quimby to Emeline, July 12, 1862, Quimby Papers, FSNMP; Kiester to father, July 5, 1862, Kiester Papers, ECU; Wiley to family members, July 6 and July 25, 1862, Wiley Papers, PSU; Granger to wife, July 6, 1862, Granger Papers, CWMC; Leech, *Reveille in Washington*, pp. 193, 195; Nevins, *War for the Union*, pp. 142–43; Tap, *Over Lincoln's Shoulder*, pp. 123–25; Sears, *George B. McClellan*, p. 221; Williams, *Lincoln and the Radicals*, p. 143; Lincoln, *Collected Works*, p. 303; Donald, *Lincoln*, pp. 358–59; Williams, *Lincoln and his Generals*, p. 144.

4. Beringer et al. (*Why the South Lost*, p. 152) and Jones (*Civil War Command and Strategy*, pp. 69–70) emphasize that the army was intact, but the former notes that it had to start over. Swinton (*Campaigns*, p. 165) notes the strategic situation. Those who praise the change of base include Bache, *George Gordon Meade*, p. 108; Eckenrode and Conrad, *George B. McClellan*, pp. 120–21; Hassler, *General George B. McClellan*, p. 171; Myers, *General George B. McClellan*, p. 300; Powell, *Fifth Army Corps*, p. 180; Swinton, *Campaigns*, p. 164; and Taylor, *Destruction and Reconstruction*, p. 109. Eckenrode and Conrad (*George B. McClellan*, p. 100) call McClellan the best American general ever at logistics. Cullen (*Peninsula Campaign*, p. 179) thinks McClellan was good at logistics. Hagerman (*American Civil War*, pp. 50–51) and Williams (*Lincoln Finds a General*, vol. 1, p. 232) are more critical. Bache (*George Gordon Meade*, pp. 108, 143), Sears (*George B. McClellan*, p. 225), and Weigley (*Great Civil War*, p. 133) say credit cannot go to McClellan. Eisenschiml (*Celebrated Case*, p. 40) discusses Porter's part. Michie (*General McClellan*, p. 365) and Webb (*Peninsula*, p. 189) echo the praise of the men in the ranks.

5. McClellan, *Civil War Papers*, pp. 348–49 (emphasis in original); Leech, *Reveille in Washington*, p. 193; Williams, *Lincoln and the Radicals*, p. 140; Strong, *Diary*, p. 241; Silbey, *Respectable Minority*, p. 66; Tap, *Over Lincoln's Shoulder*, p. 121. Those who agree with my assessment of McClellan's basic problems include Adams (*Our Masters the Rebels*, p. 88), de Trobriand (*Four Years*, p. 272), McMurray (*Two Great Rebel Armies*, p. 38), Michie (*General McClellan*, pp. 320–21), Sears (*George B. McClellan*, pp. 225–26), Walker (*Second Army Corps*, p. 59), and Webb (*Peninsula*, p. 121). Among those who disagree are Hassler (*General George B. McClellan*, p. 171), Powell (*Fifth Army Corps*, p. 180) and Swinton (*Campaigns*, pp. 141–42). Cullen (*Peninsula*

Campaign, p. 179), Jones (*Civil War Command and Strategy*, pp. 69–70) and Rhodes (*History of the United States*, p. 453) agree with the overall assessment. Hassler (*Commanders*, p. 52) disagrees.

6. Alexander, *Fighting for the Confederacy*, p. 96; Jones, *Life and Letters*, p. 185; *OR*, pt. 2, p. 497; R.W. Mills to brother, July 3, 1862, Hugh Harrison Mills Collection, ECU; DeLeon, *Four Years*, p. 207; Putnam, *Richmond During the War*, p. 149; Jones, *Rebel War Clerk's Diary*, p. 144; Ruffin, *Diary*, p. 370; Rable, *Confederate Republic*, pp. 154–55; Woodworth, *Davis and Lee*, pp. 173–74; Taylor to brother, July 9, 1862, Taylor Papers, FSNMP; Thomas, *Confederate Nation*, pp. 163–64; Wellman, *Giant in Gray*, p. 80; Grady to wife, July 6, 1862, Grady Papers, EU.

7. Hattaway and Jones (*How the North Won*, pp. 199–200), Jones (*Civil War Command and Strategy*, pp. 69–70), and Weigley (*Great Civil War*, p. 134) discuss changes in war. Terrain problems are noted by Early, *War Memoirs*, p. 90; Taylor, *General Lee*, p. 74; and Wert, *Longstreet*, pp. 150–51. Chamberlayne ("Address on Character of General R. E. Lee," p. 34), Freeman (*R. E. Lee*, p. 239), and McMurray (*Two Great Rebel Armies*, p. 133) are among many to mention subordinates as contributing factors. Eckenrode and Conrad (*James Longstreet*, p. 86) call Longstreet's "failure" to take Malvern Hill before the morning of the thirtieth the great missed opportunity of the campaign, but their assessment is in the minority. I agree with Freeman's assessment of Longstreet and D. H. Hill; he is harsher in his view of A. P. Hill and Holmes (*R. E. Lee*, p. 245–46). More detailed but similar critiques of the Confederate officers can be found in Freeman, *Lee's Lieutenants*, vol. 1, pp. 606–59. Sears (*To the Gates of Richmond*, p. 343) also is more critical of Holmes.

8. Gray to father, July 10, 1862, Gray Papers, NCDAH; Benjamin Humphries to R. Archer, July 9, 1862, Southall Papers, LV; Foard Memoir, Foard Papers, NCDAH; Jones, *Heroines of Dixie*, p. 177. Sears (*To the Gates of Richmond*, p. 343) basically agrees with my view of Huger. Freeman (*R. E. Lee*, p. 246) gives Huger even less credit. Gallagher ("Fall of Magruder," p. 15) seconds my assessment of Magruder. Sears (*To the Gates of Richmond*, pp. 343–44) takes a balanced view, and Freeman (*R. E. Lee*, p. 246) is not unkind.

9. Foard Memoir, Foard Papers, NCDAH; Harrison, *Recollections Grave and Gay*, p. 89. Greene (*Whatever You Resolve to Be*, p. 74) and Robertson (*Stonewall Jackson*, p. 504) make a similar general judgment. More critical comments are made by, among many, Freeman (*R. E. Lee*, p. 247, although both there and in *Lee's Lieutenants* Freeman was writing without the benefit of the order found in Stuart's papers), Jones (*Civil War Command and Strategy*, pp. 69–70), Maurice (*Lee the Soldier*, p. 116), and Sears (*To the Gates of Richmond*, p. 344).

10. Freeman (*R. E. Lee*, p. 242) and Jones (*Civil War Command and Strategy*, pp. 69–70) agree with the general assessment of Lee's strategy; Cullen (*Peninsula Campaign*, pp. 166–67) agrees in part (he does not like the strategy of the twenty-ninth and thirtieth); and Hagerman (*American Civil War*, p. 110), Maurice (*Lee the Soldier*, p. 116), and Sears (*To the Gates of Richmond*, p. 344) disagree. Regarding details, Cullen (*Peninsula Campaign*, p. 168), Freeman (*R. E. Lee*, p. 241), Maurice (*Lee the Soldier*, pp. 119–20), Sears (*To the Gates of Richmond*, p. 344), and Taylor (*Destruction and Reconstruction*, pp. 111–12) all take this position.

11. Lee to Rives, July 4, 1862, Rives Papers, LOC. Among others, these problems are noted by Alexander (*Fighting for the Confederacy*, p. 104), Cullen (*Peninsula Campaign*, p. 166), Dowdey (*Lee*, p. 272, and *Seven Days*, pp. 349–50), Freeman (*R. E. Lee*, pp. 232–41), Hagerman (*American Civil War*, pp. 108–10), Hattaway and Jones (*How the North Won*, p. 195), J. W. Jones ("Visit to Beauvoir," p. 452), Archer Jones (*Civil War

Command and Strategy, pp. 69–70), Maurice (*Lee the Soldier*, pp. 116–17), R. Taylor (*Destruction and Reconstruction*, pp. 99–100, 107), W. H. Taylor (*General Lee*, p. 74), Weigley (*Great Civil War*, p. 133), Wert (*Longstreet*, pp. 150–51), and Wise (*Long Arm of Lee*, pp. 239–40). Lee's mention of information problems is in *OR*, pt. 2, p. 497. Swinton (*Campaigns*, p. 164) agrees with my general assessment of Lee. The praise of the rank and file comes from Freeman (*R. E. Lee*, p. 242), among many.

12. Andrews, *South Reports the Civil War*, p. 194; Freeman, *R. E. Lee*, pp. 243–44; Beringer et al., *Why the South Lost*, p. 153; McPherson, *Battle Cry of Freedom*, pp. 490–1, 560–2; Crook, *North*, p. 206; Vanauken, *Glittering Illusion*, pp. 101, 110; Owsley, *King Cotton Diplomacy*, pp. 295–96, 310–26; Jones, *Union in Peril*, pp. 127–28, 132; Case and Spencer, *United States and France*, pp. 307–309; Donald, *Lincoln*, p. 414; Jenkins, *Britain*, vol. 2, pp. 93–96, 100. Andrews (*North Reports the Civil War*, p. 215) notes that army reporters did not criticize McClellan himself. Adams (*Our Masters the Rebels*, p. 98) argues that McClellan's failure produced a lasting feeling of inferiority among Yankee soldiers and civilians, but this is difficult to sustain given the soldiers' letters after the campaign. For the Southern reliance on foreign intervention see, among many examples, Chamberlayne, *Ham Chamberlayne—Virginian*, p. 85.

13. J. F. C. Fuller includes the Seven Days in his list of the most decisive battles in world history. Various aspects of the decisive nature of the campaign are pointed out by Crook (*North, the South, and the Powers*, p. 206), Dowdey (*Seven Days*, pp. 355–57), Fuller (*Military History of the Western World*, vol. 3, p. 47), McPherson (*Battle Cry of Freedom*, pp. 471, 490–91, 504–505, 556), Nevins (*War for the Union*, pp. 143–47), Paludan (*People's Contest*, p. 90), and Sears (*To the Gates of Richmond*, p. 355). Dowdey (*Seven Days*, p. 358) notes the "training ground" aspects of the campaign for Lee and his men. McCormick (*War without Grant*, p. 88) says Lincoln learned McClellan's limitations in the campaign. Halleck (*OR*, pt. 3, p. 337) reports on a conversation with McClellan in which the latter suggested the movement across the James. Whether he would have done so in reality is, of course, another question.

Appendixes

1. *OR*, pt. 3, p. 238.
2. Livermore, *Numbers and Losses*, pp. 82–86 contains his entire analysis.
3. "Strength of General Lee's Army," pp. 407–24; Alexander, estimate of Confederate troops in battles around Richmond 1862 (version 1 and 2); White to Lee, Aug. 16, 1865; Venable to Lee, Mar. 1, 1866, all in Lee Headquarters Papers, VaHS.

BIBLIOGRAPHY

Manuscript Collections

Alabama Department of Archives and History, Montgomery
3rd Alabama File
4th Alabama File
8th Alabama File
10th Alabama File
Branscomb Family Papers
R. T. Coles Papers

American Antiquarian Society, Worcester, Mass.
William G. Scandlin Papers

Atlanta Historical Society
Zachariah A. Rice Papers

Augusta State University, Augusta, Ga.
Cumming Family Papers

Department of Special Collections, Boston University
Edward Winslow Hinks Papers
Zadock Pratt Papers
John C. Ropes Collection

Special Collections, Harold B. Lee Library, Brigham Young University, Provo, Utah
R. J. Ormsby Papers

Manuscripts Division, John Hay Library, Brown University, Providence, R.I.
William R. Miles Papers

Clarke Historical Library, Central Michigan University, Mount Pleasant
Charles H. Curtiss Papers

Rare Book, Manuscript, and Special Collections Library, Duke University, Durham, N.C.

William E. Ardrey Papers
George S. Bernard Papers
Samuel D. Buck Papers
John Esten Cooke Papers
S. E. Faunce Papers
Hinsdale Family Papers
George W. Kenney Papers
Moses W. Kenyon Papers
Mary A. Lyndall Papers
Munford-Ellis Family Papers
Green W. Penn Papers
H. V. Rose Papers
William Lafayette Scott Papers
Ira Spaulding Papers
George Newton Wise Papers

East Carolina Manuscript Collection, J. Y. Joyner Library, East Carolina University, Greenville, N.C.

Nathan R. Frazier Papers
Jacob S. Kiester Papers
Hugh Harrison Mills Collection

Special Collections, Robert W. Woodruff Library, Emory University, Atlanta

Troup Butler Papers
John A. Everett Papers
Theodore T. Fogel Papers
Henry W. Grady Papers
William Anderson Stephens Papers
David Read Evan Winn Papers

Shadek-Fackenthal Library, Franklin and Marshall College, Lancaster, Pa.

Reynolds Family Papers

Fredericksburg and Spotsylvania National Military Park, Fredericksburg, Va.

Isaiah Fogleman Diary
Albert W. Henley Memoir
James M. Higgins Diary
George W. Quimby Papers
William W. Ruth Papers
Robert W. Shand Papers
Martin Sigman Memoir
Thomas S. Taylor Papers
Thomas J. Watkins Memoir
J. W. Watts Letter
William A. Waugh Memoir

Manuscripts Collection, Georgia Department of Archives and History, Atlanta

John T. Beaver Collection
Noble John Brooks Papers

Civil War Miscellany, Personal Papers
Benjamin Franklin Abbott Papers
Ivy W. Duggan Papers
Matthew Talbot Nunally Papers
Jasper A. Gillespie Family Papers
Alexander H. Stephens Museum Collection
Sidney J. Richardson Papers
John M. Tilley Papers
William A. Towers Papers

Eggleston Library, Hampden-Sydney College, Hampden-Sydney, Va.
William R. Carter Papers

Library and Archives, Historical Society of Western Pennsylvania, Pittsburgh
Gilbert A. Hays Papers

Houghton Library, Harvard University, Cambridge, Mass.
Charles Nightingale Papers

Historical Society of Pennsylvania, Philadelphia
Edward Acton Papers
Andrew A. Humphreys Papers
George A. McCall Papers
George G. Meade Papers
Walter S. Newhall Papers
Thomas W. Smith Papers

Manuscripts Division, Library of Congress, Washington, D.C.
Samuel E. Allen Papers
American Institute of Aeronautics and Astronautics Collection
John C. Babcock Papers
Bancroft-Bliss Family Papers
Theodore A. Dodge Papers
Douglas Southall Freeman Papers
George Washington Hall Papers
John William Ford Hatton Papers
Samuel P. Heinztelman Papers
Jedediah Hotchkiss Papers
Henry J. Hunt Papers
Reverdy Johnson Papers
August V. Kautz Papers
Philip Kearny Papers
Stephen Russell Mallory Papers
Manton M. Marble Papers
George C. McClellan Papers
J. C. McMichael Papers
Albert J. Myer Papers
Naval Historical Foundation Collection
Rodgers Family Papers
Fitz John Porter Papers
William Cabell Rives Papers

Rodgers Family Papers
Gilbert Thompson Papers
Dennis Tuttle Papers
Wigfall Family Papers
Cadmus M. Wilcox Papers

Archives Division, Library of Virginia, Richmond

Dabney-Jackson Collection
Fairfax Family Papers
Valentine Wood Southall Papers
J. E. Whitehorne Papers

Manuscripts Division, Maryland Historical Society, Baltimore

I. G. Bradwell Papers
William Winder Papers

Library, Massachusetts Historical Society, Boston

Francis Barlow Papers
Paul Joseph Revere Papers

Manuscript Collections, Minnesota Historical Society, Minneapolis

John N. Henry Papers
Matthew Marvin Papers
Edward Duffield Neill Papers
Thomas H. Pressnell Papers
Orrin Fruit Smith Papers
Cyrus R. Stone Papers

Manuscript Collection, Mississippi Department of Archives and History, Jackson

A. L. P. Vairin Diary

Manuscript Collections, Missouri Historical Society, St. Louis

Bulkley Family Papers

New Jersey Historical Society Library, Newark

William James Evans Papers

Manuscripts Division, New York Historical Society, New York

Caspar Trepp Papers

Manuscripts and Archives Division, New York Public Library

William Frothingham Papers

Manuscripts and Special Collections, New York State Library, Albany

William W. Averell Papers
Waters W. Braman Papers
James B. Turner Papers
Gouverneur K. Warren Papers
Frederick F. Wead Papers

Archives and Records Section, North Carolina Division of Archives and History, Raleigh

Fred C. Foard Papers
R. H. Gray Papers

Daniel Harvey Hill Papers
Daniel Harvey Hill Jr. Papers
Mrs. Benjamin R. Lacy Papers
Lilly Collection
Frank M. Parker Papers
Simpson-Biddle Papers
Herman W. Taylor Collection
William H. C. Whiting Papers

Oswego County Historical Society, Oswego, N.Y.
Oliver Family Papers

Pennsylvania State Archives, Pennsylvania Historical and Museum Commission, Harrisburg
Robert Taggert Papers

Historical Collections and Labor Archives, Pattee Library, Pennsylvania State University, State College
William Campbell Wiley Papers

Manuscript Collections, Rhode Island Historical Society, Providence
William C. Barker Papers
Jeremiah M. C. Olney Papers
James H. Remington Papers

Special Collections and University Archives, Archibald S. Alexander Library, Rutgers University, New Brunswick, N.J.
Alfred N. Ayres Papers
William K. Haines Papers
Robert McAllister Papers

South Carolina Historical Society, Charleston
Haskell Family Papers
Thomas Henry Pitts Papers

Department of Special Collections, Stanford University Libraries, Stanford, Calif.
John Wesley Melhorn Papers
Lemuel E. Newcomb Papers

Archives, State Historical Society of Wisconsin, Madison
John H. Burrill Papers
Charles D. Grannis Papers
Horace W. Hecox Papers
Adolphus Conrad Hospes Papers
John Hemphill Simpson Papers
Ellicott Rogers Stillman Papers
Almeron W. Stillwell Papers
Benjamin Franklin Strong Papers
George B. Thomas Papers

Library, Suffolk County Historical Society, Suffolk, N.Y.
Cornelius L. Moore Papers

Troup County Archives, LaGrange, Ga.
Schaub Papers

Archives, United States Military History Institute, Carlisle Barracks, Pa.

John W. Ames Papers
David Bell Birney Papers
William T. H. Brooks Papers
Civil War Miscellaneous Collection
  Alfred M. Apted Papers
  Joseph D. Baker Papers
  Solomon F. Beals Papers
  James Beeler Diary
  Eugene Blackford Papers
  James S. Colwell Papers
  James Edson Decker Papers
  James DeClark Papers
  Jeremiah Downes Papers
  Joseph P. Elliott Diary
  Edson Emery Diary
  Frederick Fowler Papers
  John M. Fullerton Papers
  James Lee Graham Papers
  Luther A. Granger Papers
  Thomas Hatton Diary
  Edmund Hawley Papers
  James W. Kenney Memoir
  Robert McCreight Papers
  William A. Moore Memoir
  John O'Connell Memoir
  William H. Peacock Papers
  M. Edgar Richards Papers
  Timothy Vedder Papers
  Charles H. Veil Papers
  William Henry Walling Papers
  Howard Malcolm Walthall Reminiscences
  William B. Westervelt Diary
  George Whitman Papers
  Solomon Williams Papers
  John H. Wittel Papers
  Frank R. Young Diary
Civil War Times Illustrated Collection of Civil War Papers
  Jacob Barger Papers
  John Berry Diary
  John Malachi Bowden Reminiscences
  William E. Dunn Papers
  Henry Gerrish Memoir
  Jacob Heffelfinger Diary
  Clarence L. Hutchins Memoir
  Wolf Lichtenstein Memoir
  John F. Neff Papers
  Charles E. Perkins Papers
  Jonathan P. Stowe Papers
Harrisburg Civil War Round Table Collection

Benjamin F. Ashenfelter Papers
Harvey A. Davis Papers
John and Leo Faller Correspondence
Peter A. Filbert Diary
Andrew Lewis Papers
Clement D. Potts Papers
Joseph G. Williford Papers
Philip L. Wilson Memoir
Daniel Harvey Hill Papers
Wendell W. Lang Jr. Collection
George E. Hagar Diary
Lewis Leigh Jr. Collection
Henry Bentley Papers
Isaac Bevier Papers
George Bills Papers
Eugene Blackford Papers
Robert A. Everett Papers
James H. McIlwain Papers
George H. Patch Papers
Benjamin Roher Papers
George S. Wilson Papers
James H. Mitchell Papers
Northwest Corner Civil War Round Table Collection
Lewis Luckinbill Diary
Pennsylvania "Save the Flags" Civil War Collection
Charles Becker Papers
William J. Burns Diary
Adoniram J. Warner Memoir
Ralph G. Poriss Collection
John Briggs Papers
Kenneth H. Powers Collection
J. Noonan Papers
George H. Selkirk Papers
Murray J. Smith Collection
Walter J. Eames Papers
Tanfield Family Papers

Department of Special Collections, University of Chicago Library

Lincoln Collection Manuscripts
Herbert Mason Diary

Special Collections Division, Hargrett Library, University of Georgia, Athens

T. R. R. Cobb Papers
William Deloney Papers
Florence Heidler Papers
Fleming Jordan Papers
Mary B. Nix Papers
Shepherd G. Pryor Papers

Bentley Historical Collections, University of Michigan, Ann Arbor

John Bancroft Papers

Bibbins Family Papers
Henry Clay Christiancy Papers
Jerome John Robbins Papers
William E. Sleight Papers
John A. Sutton Papers
Edward Taylor Papers

William L. Clements Library, University of Michigan, Ann Arbor

James F. Schoff Civil War Collection
  Anonymous memoir
  George W. Barr Papers
  William Ellis Jones Diary
  Lewis J. Martin Papers
  Calvin Mehaffey Papers
  Miscellaneous Papers

Western Historical Manuscript Collection, University of Missouri, Columbia

Isaac L. Taylor Diary

Southern Historical Collection, Wilson Library, University of North Carolina, Chapel Hill

Edward Porter Alexander Papers
William Allan Papers
Barnsley Family Papers
Berry G. Benson Papers
Burgwyn Family Papers
J. F. H. Claiborne Papers
George C. Gordon Papers
Alexander Cheeves Haskell Papers
John Cheeves Haskell Papers
Hatrick Family Papers
William J. Hoke Papers
James Longstreet Papers
William Nelson Pendleton Papers
William H. Wills Papers

Manuscript Collection, William Madison Randall Library, University of North Carolina, Wilmington

Armstrong Family Papers

Western History Collections, University of Oklahoma, Norman

James Brazell Collection
Colonial Dames of the XVIII Century Collection

Department of Rare Books and Special Collections, University of Rochester Library, Rochester, N.Y.

Charles Curtis Brown Papers
Adam Clark Works Papers

South Caroliniana Library, University of South Carolina, Columbia

Micah Jenkins Papers
William Norris Papers

Center for American History, University of Texas, Austin
Confederate States of America Records
    Mike M. Hubbert Diary
Andrew N. Erskine Papers

Manuscripts Department, University of Virginia Library, Charlottesville
Lawrence O'Bryan Branch Papers
Wilbur Fisk Davis Papers
Dinwiddie Family Papers
Z. Lee Gilmer Diary
Jonathan B. Hager Papers
Washington Hands Civil War Memoirs
Jedediah Hotchkiss Papers
John B. Wise Papers

Area Research Center, University of Wisconsin-Green Bay
James Sibree Anderson Papers

Vermont Historical Society, Montpelier
Horton Keith Papers
J. B. Pollard Papers
Edward P. Stone Papers
Lyman S. Williams Papers

Virginia Historical Society, Richmond
Bagby Family Papers
Blanton Family Papers
Hannah (Lide) Coker Papers
Cooke Family Papers
Edward S. Duffey Diary
Richardson Wallace Haw Papers
Hobson Family Papers
Benjamin Anderson Jones Papers
Watkins Kearns Papers
Keith Family Papers
John Gottfried Lange Papers
Robert E. Lee Headquarters Papers
John McAnerney Papers
John Van Lew McCreery Papers (Recollections)
David Gregg McIntosh Papers (Reminiscences)
Meade Family Papers
Ella Merryman Papers
William W. Sherwood Papers
Shipp Family Papers
William Barrett Sydnor Papers
Fanny W. Gaines Tinsley Papers
John Steele Tyler Papers
Gilbert Jefferson Wright Papers

Special Collections, University Libraries, Virginia Polytechnic Institute and State University, Blacksburg
Stearns Family Papers

Western Reserve Historical Society, Cleveland
William P. Palmer Collection
Thomas Francis Meagher Papers

Beinecke Rare Book and Manuscript Library, Yale University, New Haven, Conn.
Alfred Sully Papers

Manuscripts and Archives, Sterling Memorial Library, Yale University, New Haven, Conn.
Civil War Manuscripts Collection
Edward E. Davis Papers
William B. Rhodes Papers
Alexander S. Webb Papers

Articles

Abbreviations

BL Johnson, Robert Underwood, and Clarence Clough Buel, eds. *Battles and Leaders of the Civil War.* 4 vols. New York: Century, 1887–88. Reprint, Secaucus, N.J.: Castle (1989–90).
CV *Confederate Veteran*
CWTI *Civil War Times Illustrated*
NT *National Tribune*
PC *The Peninsular Campaign of General McClellan in 1862.* Papers of the Military Historical Society of Massachusetts. Boston: James R. Osgood, 1881.
SHSP *Southern Historical Society Papers.* 52 vols. Richmond, Va.: Southern Historical Society, 1876–1959.

Alexander, E. P. "Confederate Artillery Service." *SHSP* 11 (Feb.-Mar. 1883): pp. 98–113.
———. "Records of Longstreet's Corps, A.N.V." *SHSP* 1 (Feb. 1876): pp. 61–76.
Allan, William. "The Peninsula—McClellan's Campaign of 1862, by Alexander S. Webb." *SHSP* 10 (May 1882): pp. 193–206.
Allen, James. "The 14th U.S. at Gaines's Mills." *NT,* Jan. 3, 1901, p. 3.
———. "The Battle of Gaines's Mill." *NT,* May 2, 1901, p. 3.
Anderson, Joseph R. Jr. "Anderson's Brigade in Battles Around Richmond." *CV* 31 (Dec. 1923): pp. 448–51.
"Annual Reunion of Pegram Battalion Association in the Hall of House of Delegates, Richmond, Virginia, May 21st, 1886." *SHSP* 14 (Jan.-Dec. 1886): pp. 1–34.
"Army Correspondence." Bellefonte (Pa.) *Central Press,* July 25, 1862, p. 1.
"Army Correspondence." New Castle (Pa.) *Lawrence Journal,* July 26, 1862, p. 1.
Averell, William W. "With the Cavalry on the Peninsula." *BL,* vol. 2, pp. 429–33.
Avery, A. C. "Memorial Address on the Life and Character of Lieutenant-General D. H. Hill." *SHSP* 21 (Jan.-Dec. 1893): pp. 110–50.
Barnwell, Robert W. "Stonewall Jackson at Richmond." *CV* 39 (Feb. 1931): pp. 94–97.
"The Battles before Richmond." *Hartford (Conn.) Daily Courant,* July 31, 1862, p. 1.

Baxter, Alice. "Battle Flag of the Third Georgia." *SHSP* 38 (Jan.-Dec. 1910): pp. 210–216.
Bernard, George S. "Malvern Hill." *SHSP* 18 (Jan.-Dec. 1890): pp. 56–71.
Black, A. L. "After the Battle of Frazier's Farm." *CV* 2 (Jan. 1894): p. 20.
Boies, A. H. "Brave Old Woodbury." *NT,* Mar. 19, 1896, p. 3.
———. "Malvern Hill." *NT,* Feb. 13, 1896, pp. 1–2.
Bradwell, I. G. "From Cold Harbor to Cedar Mountain." *CV* 29 (June 1921): pp. 222–25.
———. "Soldier Life in the Confederate Army." *CV* 24 (Jan. 1916): pp. 20–25.
"Brig. Gen. James T. [*sic*] Archer." *CV* 8 (Feb. 1900): pp. 65–67.
Brown, Campbell. "Notes on Ewell's Division in the Campaign of 1862." *SHSP* 10 (June 1882): no. 5, pp. 255–61.
Brown, Theo. V. "Gaines's Mill." *NT,* July 12, 1900, p. 3.
Buchanan, G. G. Untitled letter. *CV* 7 (May 1899): p. 216.
Burress, L. R. "Brave Mississippians in Virginia." *CV* 21 (Mar. 1913): p. 111.
Burton, Isaac M. "Vermont Veterans." *NT,* June 28, 1883, p. 7.
Buswell, Brigham. "'Blood and Feathered' at Malvern Hill." *CWTI,* Apr. 1996, pp. 24, 26–27, 30, 32, 76–77.
———. "A Sharpshooter's Seven Days." *CWTI,* Feb. 1996, pp. 20–28.
Carmichael, Peter S. "Stuart's Ride Around McClellan." *Civil War,* June 1995, pp. 50–53.
Chamberlayne, John Hampden. "Address on the Character of General R. E. Lee." *SHSP* 3 (Jan. 1877): pp. 28–37.
Chambers, C. C. "Mississippians at Gaines Mill." *CV* 19 (Nov. 1911): pp. 510–11.
"Colonel Eugene Waggaman." *SHSP* 16 (Jan.-Dec. 1888): pp. 446–51.
Cooke, J. Churchill. "With Jackson Around Richmond." *CV* 39 (July 1931): p. 248.
Cooke, Philip St. George. "The Charge of Cooke's Cavalry at Gaines's Mill." *BL,* vol. 2, pp. 344–46.
Crocker, James F. "Colonel James Gregory Hodges." *SHSP* 37 (Jan.-Dec. 1909): pp. 184–97.
———. "My Personal Experiences in Taking Up Arms and in the Battle of Malvern Hill." *SHSP* 33 (Jan.-Dec. 1905): pp. 111–18.
Crozier, Granville H. "A Private with General Hood." *CV* 25 (Dec. 1917): pp. 556–58.
Davenport, Alfred. "One of the Seven Days." *NT,* July 26, 1894, pp. 1–2.
"Death of Col. Black at Gaines's Mill." *NT,* June 11, 1885, p. 3.
DeMotte, John B. "The Cause of a Silent Battle." *BL,* vol. 2, p. 365.
Doubleday, J. M. "Oak Grove." *NT,* Oct. 8, 1914, p. 7.
———. "The Seven Days' Battles." *NT,* Sept. 14, 1916, p. 7.
Dunning, Orlando. "Gaines's Mill." *NT,* Mar. 26, 1891, p. 4.
Ellis, F. P. "Wounded Boy's Night on a Battlefield." *CV* 17 (Sept. 1909): p. 456.
Evans, Thomas. "At Malvern Hill." *CWTI,* Dec. 1967, pp. 38–43.
———. "There is No Use Trying to Dodge Shot." *CWTI,* Aug. 1967, pp. 40–45.
Facer, Theo. "Did Not Run Away." *NT,* Feb. 21, 1901, p. 3.
Fagan, Peter. "Imagination's Work." *NT,* Aug. 2, 1894, p. 3.
"Flag of the 16th Mississippi Regiment." *CV* 26 (Feb. 1918): pp. 75–76.
Flowers, George W. "The Thirty-Eighth North Carolina Regiment." *SHSP* 25 (Jan.-Dec. 1897): pp. 245–63.
Franklin, William B. "Rear-Guard Fighting During the Change of Base." *BL,* vol. 2, pp. 366–82.
Frayser, Richard E. "Stuart's Raid in the Rear of the Army of the Potomac." *SHSP* 11 (Nov. 1883): pp. 505–17.
Frye, C. J. "Savage Station." *NT,* Mar. 6, 1913, p. 5.

Fulton, W. F. "Archer's Brigade at Cold Harbor." *CV* 31 (Aug. 1923): pp. 300–301.
Gallagher, Gary W. "The Fall of 'Prince John' Magruder." *Civil War*, Aug. 1989, pp. 8–15.
Galloway, G. Norton. "Battle of Gaines' Mill." *Philadelphia Weekly Times*, Feb. 21, 1885, p. 1.
Garnett, F. E. "The Retreat to Malvern." *Philadelphia Weekly Times*, June 23, 1883, p. 1.
Garnett, James M. "Personal Reminiscences of Seven Days' Battles Around Richmond." *SHSP* 30 (Jan.-Dec. 1902): pp. 147–51.
"The Gatling Gun." *NT*, Oct. 22, 1881, p. 1.
"General Joseph R. Anderson." *SHSP* 19 (Jan. 1891): pp. 416–17.
"General Thomas J. Jackson." *SHSP* 19 (Jan. 1891): pp. 298–318.
Gilmore, J. F. "With the 4th Mich." *NT*, July 7, 1910, p. 7.
Graham, H. C. "Battle of Gaines' Mill," *Philadelphia Weekly Times*, Dec. 8, 1883, p. 1.
Gray, John J. "An Artillerist's Yarn." *NT*, Aug. 16, 1900, p. 7.
Hale, G. W. B. "Recollections of Malvern Hill." *CV* 30 (Sept. 1922): pp. 332–33.
Hamby, William R. "Fourth Texas in Battle of Gaines's Mill." *CV* 14, pp. 183–85.
Hankins, Samuel. "Simple Story of a Soldier—V, VI." *CV* 21 (Jan. 1913): pp. 21–22.
Harrison, Mrs. Burton. "Richmond Scenes in '62." *BL*, vol. 2, pp. 439–48.
Henderson, Don E. "General Hood's Brigade." *SHSP* 29 (Jan.-Dec. 1901): pp. 297–310.
Herndon, John G. "Infantry and Cavalry Service." *CV* 30 (May 1922): pp. 172–74.
Hill, Daniel H. "Lee's Attacks North of the Chickahominy." *BL*, vol. 2, pp. 347–62.
———. "McClellan's Change of Base and Malvern Hill." *BL*, vol. 2, pp. 383–95.
Hogan, H. R. "Battle of Frazier's Farm—A Correction." *CV* 1 (Nov. 1893): pp. 333–34.
Hogan, N. B. "Thrilling War Experiences." *CV* 2 (Sept. 1894): p. 268.
"Horrors of the Battlefield." *CV* 15 (July 1907): pp. 305–307.
"How the Seven Days' Battle Around Richmond Began." *SHSP* 28 (Jan.-Dec. 1900): pp. 90–97.
Hoyt, James A. "Anderson's Brigade at Gaines's Mill." *CV* 7 (May 1899): pp. 223–27.
Hunter, T. J. "At Yorktown in 1862 and What Followed." *CV* 26 (Mar. 1918): pp. 112–15.
Imboden, John D. "Stonewall Jackson in the Shenandoah." *BL*, vol. 2, pp. 282–98.
Ingraham, Lyman R. "A Correction." *NT*, Nov. 26, 1881, p. 4.
"Jackson and Ewell." *SHSP* 20 (Jan.-Dec. 1892): pp. 26–33.
Jeffreys, Thomas D. "The 'Red Badge' Explained." *SHSP* 36 (Jan.-Dec. 1908): pp. 248–49.
Johnson, Bradley T. "Memoir of the First Maryland Regiment." *SHSP* 10 (Apr. 1882): pp. 145–53.
———. "Memoir of the First Maryland Regiment." *SHSP* 10 (May 1882), pp. 214–23.
Johnson, W. Gart. "Barksdale-Humphreys Mississippi Brigade." *CV* 1 (July 1893): pp. 206–207.
Jones, J. William. "The Career of General Jackson." *SHSP* 35 (Jan.-Dec. 1907): pp. 79–98.
———. "Reminiscences of the Army of Northern Virginia No. 6." *SHSP* 9 (July–Aug. 1881): pp. 362–69.
———. "Reminiscences of the Army of Northern Virginia No. 7." *SHSP* 9 (Sept. 1881): pp. 426–29.
———. "Reminiscences of the Army of Northern Virginia No. 8." *SHSP* 9 (Oct.–Dec. 1881): pp. 557–70.
———. "A Visit to Beauvoir." *SHSP* 14 (Jan.-Dec. 1886): pp. 447–54.
Kent, William C. "Sharpshooting with Berdan." *CWTI*, May 1976, pp. 4–9, 42–48.
Lamb, John. "Malvern Hill—July 1, 1862." *SHSP* 25 (Jan.-Dec. 1897): pp. 208–21.

Landugan, Rody. "At Savage Station." *NT,* Feb. 13, 1913, p. 7.
Law, E. M. "On the Confederate Right at Gaines's Mill." *BL,* vol. 2, pp. 363–65.
Leach, John W. T. "The Battle of Frazier's Farm." *SHSP* 21 (Jan.–Dec. 1893): pp. 160–65.
Ledbetter, M. T. "Mechanicsville and Gaines Mill." *CV* 1 (Aug. 1893): pp. 244–45.
———. "With Archer's Brigade." *SHSP* 29 (Jan.-Dec. 1901): pp. 349–54.
LeDuc, William G. "McClellan and Richmond." *NT,* July 30, 1914, p. 7.
Long, A. L. "Memoir of General John Bankhead Magruder." *SHSP* 12 (Mar. 1884): pp. 105–10.
Longstreet, James. "'The Seven Days,' Including Frayser's Farm." *BL,* vol. 2, pp. 396–405.
Luce, M. A. "A Brave Cook." *NT,* Mar. 25, 1915, p. 7.
"M, J. J." "Charge of Kemper's Brigade at Frazier's Farm." *SHSP* 18 (Jan.-Dec. 1890): pp. 391–93.
McCaleb, E. Howard. "Featherstone-Posey-Harris Mississippi Brigade." *SHSP* 32 (Jan.-Dec. 1904): pp. 329–37.
McClellan, H. B. Untitled address. *SHSP* 8 (Oct.-Dec. 1880): pp. 433–56.
McCrady, Edward. "Boy Heroes of Cold Harbor." *SHSP* 25 (Jan.-Dec. 1897): pp. 234–39.
McGuire, Hunter. "General T. J. ('Stonewall') Jackson, Confederate States Army." *SHSP* 25 (Jan.-Dec. 1897): pp. 91–112.
Mason, John B. "What Regiment?" *NT,* Sept. 3, 1885, p. 3.
Mattison, J. W. "Orr's South Carolina Rifles." *SHSP* 27 (Jan.-Dec. 1899): pp. 157–65.
Milano, Anthony J. "Letters from the Harvard Regiments." *Civil War,* June 1988, pp. 15–18, 20–27.
Miller, James Cooper. "Serving under McClellan on the Peninsula in '62." *CWTI,* June 1969, pp. 24–30.
Miller, Robert H. "Letters of Lieutenant Robert H. Miller to His Family, 1861–1862." Ed. Forrest P. Connor. *Virginia Magazine of History and Biography,* Jan. 1962, pp. 62–91.
Miller, William J. "The Battle of Oak Grove." *Civil War,* June 1995, pp. 55–56.
Moore, J. Staunton. "Malvern Hill." *SHSP* 35 (Jan.-Dec. 1907): pp. 121–24.
Mosby, John S. "The Ride Around General McClellan." *SHSP* 26 (Jan.-Dec. 1897): pp. 246–54.
Mundy, F. H. "The Thrilling Battle of Frazier's Farm." *CV* 2 (Mar. 1894): p. 87.
Murray, Robert K. and Warren W. Hassler Jr., "Gettysburg Farmer." *Civil War History* 3, no. 2 (June 1957): pp. 179–87.
Nabours, W. A. "Active Service of a Texas Command." *CV* 24 (Feb. 1916): pp. 69–72.
"On to Prison." *CWTI,* May-June 1990, pp. 28–31, 58–67.
Palfrey, Francis W. "The Battle of Malvern Hill." *PC,* pp. 193–215.
———. "The Period Which Elapsed Between the Fall of Yorktown and the Beginning of the Seven-Days Battles." *PC,* pp. 93–155.
———. "The Seven Days' Battles to Malvern Hill." *PC,* pp. 157–91.
Park, Robert E. "Sketch of the Twelfth Alabama Infantry." *SHSP* 33 (Jan.-Dec. 1905): pp. 193–296.
———. "Diary of Robert E. Park, Macon, Georgia, Late Captain Twelfth Alabama Regiment, Confederate States Army." *SHSP* 1 (May 1876): pp. 370–86.
Pindell, Richard. "The Most Dangerous Set of Men." *CWTI,* July-Aug. 1993, pp. 42–53.
Porter, Fitz John. "The Battle of Malvern Hill." *BL,* vol. 2, pp. 406–27.
———. "Hanover Court House and Gaines's Mill." *BL,* vol. 2, pp. 319–43.

"The Purcell Battery." *SHSP* 21 (Jan.-Dec. 1893): pp. 362–65.
Reed, M. "A Timely Sprint." *NT*, Dec. 9, 1897, p. 2.
———. "Too Busy to Run." *NT*, Apr. 4, 1901, p. 3.
Reese, James. "Private Soldier Life—Humorous Features." *CV* 16 (Apr. 1908): pp. 161–66.
Robert, Rev. P. G. "Justice to General Magruder." *SHSP* 5 (May 1878): pp. 249–50.
Roberts, R. Biddle. "The Battle of Charles City Cross Roads." *Philadelphia Weekly Press*, Mar. 3, 1886, p. 1.
Robins, W. T. "Stuart's Ride Around McClellan." *BL*, vol. 2, pp. 271–75.
Ropes, John C. "General McClellan's Plans for the Campaign of 1862, and the Alleged Interference of the Government with Them." *PC*, pp. 1–28.
Sanborn, Lucius. "Savage Station." *NT*, Oct. 12, 1905, p. 3.
Slater, J. S. "At Gaines's Mill." *NT*, Sept. 17, 1881, p. 3.
———. "The Fray at Gaines' Mill." *Philadelphia Weekly Times*, Jan. 26, 1884, p. 1.
———. "Malvern." *NT*, Sept. 10, 1881, p. 3.
———. "Scenes at Malvern Hill." *Philadelphia Weekly Times*, Dec. 11, 1880, p. 1.
Smith, Asa. "Asa Smith Leaves the War." Ed. Bruce Catton. *American Heritage*, Feb. 1971, pp. 54–59, 103–105.
Sneden, Robert Knox. "Pen and Sword at Savage's Station." *CWTI*, Oct. 2000, pp. 42–51.
Stewart, William H. "Colonel John Bowie Magruder." *SHSP* 27, pp. 205–10.
Stillwell, A.W. "Incidents of McClellan's Retreat." *NT*, Apr. 15, 1909, p. 7.
Suddath, James B. "From Sumter to the Wilderness: Letters of Sergeant James Butler Suddath, Co. E, 7th Regiment, S.C.V." Ed. Frank B. Williams Jr. *South Carolina Historical Magazine*, Apr. 1962, pp. 93–104.
Sydnor, Henry Clinton. "A Virginia Boy in the Sixties." *CV* 20 (Mar. 1912): pp. 105–107.
Taylor, Isaac L. "Campaigning with the First Minnesota." Ed. Hazel C. Wolf. *Minnesota History* 25 (June 1944): pp. 117–52.
Taylor, P. H. "Savage's Station." *NT*, Jan. 31, 1884, p. 7.
Terrell, J. G. "Gaines's Mill." *NT*, Aug. 8, 1895, p. 3.
Thurston, Edward N. "Memoir of Richard H. Anderson, C.S.A." *SHSP* 39 (Apr. 1914): pp. 146–52.
Tuffs, Richard W. "Malvern Hill." *NT*, Apr. 27, 1893, p. 4.
Wheat, Leo. "Memoir of Gen. C. R. Wheat, Commander of the 'Louisiana Tiger Battalion.'" *SHSP* 17 (Jan.-Dec. 1889): pp. 47–60.
Wieland, W. F. "Did Not Lose Them." *NT*, Dec. 20, 1894, p. 3.
Wiley, Bell I. "The Soldier's Life North and South." *Life*, Feb. 3, 1961, pp. 44–77.
Williams, J. H. "Wilcox's Brigade at Gaines' Mill." *CV* 8 (Oct. 1900): pp. 443–44.
Wood, H. E. "Black Eagle Company." *SHSP* 37 (Jan.–Dec. 1909): pp. 52–59.
Wray, William J. "Malvern Hill." *NT*, Apr. 17, 1890.
Wright, J. A. "Old Peninsular Days," *NT*, Mar. 22, 1900, p. 3.
———. "Rear Guard Fighting at Savage Station." *NT*, Nov. 7, 1912, p. 5.

Books

Adams, F. Colburn. *The Story of a Trooper.* New York: Dick and Fitzgerald, 1865.
Adams, John G. B. *Reminiscences of the 19th Massachusetts Regiment.* Boston: Wright and Potter, 1899.
Adams, Michael C. C. *Our Masters the Rebels.* Cambridge, Mass.: Harvard University Press, 1978.

Alexander, E. P. *Military Memoirs of a Confederate: A Critical Narrative.* New York: Charles Scribner's Sons, 1907.

——. *Fighting for the Confederacy.* Ed. Gary W. Gallagher. Chapel Hill: University of North Carolina Press, 1989.

Allan, William. *The Army of Northern Virginia in 1862.* Cambridge, Mass.: Riverside Press, 1892. Reprint, Dayton, Ohio: Morningside, 1984.

Ames, Nelson. *History of Battery G, First Regiment, New York Light Artillery.* Marshalltown, Iowa: Marshall Printing Co., 1900.

Andrews, J. Cutler. *The North Reports the Civil War.* Pittsburgh: University of Pittsburgh Press, 1955.

——. *The South Reports the Civil War.* Princeton, N.J.: Princeton University Press, 1970.

Andrews, W. H. *Footprints of a Regiment.* Atlanta: Longstreet Press, 1992.

Andrus, Michael J. *The Brooke, Fauquier, Loudoun and Alexandria Artillery.* Lynchburg, Va.: H. E. Howard, 1990.

The Annals of the War Written by Leading Participants North and South. Dayton, Ohio: Morningside Press, 1988.

Army of the Potomac. Pt. 1. Reprint of vol. 1 of the report of the Joint Committee on the Conduct of the War. Millwood, N.Y.: Kraus, 1977.

Austin, Aurelia. *Georgia Boys with "Stonewall" Jackson.* Athens: University of Georgia Press, 1967.

Bache, Richard Meade. *The Life of General George Gordon Meade, commander of the Army of the Potomac.* Philadelphia: Henry T. Coates, 1897.

Banes, Charles H. *History of the Philadelphia Brigade.* Philadelphia: J. B. Lippincott, 1876.

Baquet, Camille. *History of the First Brigade, New Jersey Volunteers from 1861 to 1865.* Trenton: State of New Jersey, 1910.

Barnard, J. G. *The Peninsular Campaign and its Antecedents, as Developed by the Report of Maj.-Gen. Geo. B. McClellan, and Other Published Documents.* New York: Van Nostrand, 1864.

Bates, David Homer. *Lincoln in the Telegraph Office.* New York: Century, 1907.

Battle, Jesse Sumner, and James Norman Adams. *Civil War Letters.* Cleveland: Halle Park Press, 1979.

Beale, R. L. T. *History of the Ninth Virginia Cavalry.* Richmond, Va.: B. F. Johnson, 1899.

Beall, John B. *In Barrack and Field.* Nashville: Smith and Lamar, 1906.

Bearss, Edwin C. "Jeb Stuart's Ride around McClellan." In *The Peninsula Campaign of 1862: Yorktown to the Seven Days.* Vol. 1. Ed. William J. Miller. Campbell, Calif.: Savas Woodbury, 1993.

Beringer, Richard E., Herman Hattaway, Archer Jones, and William N. Still Jr. *Why the South Lost the Civil War.* Athens: University of Georgia Press, 1986.

Bicknell, George W. *History of the Fifth Regiment Maine Volunteers.* Portland, Me.: Hall L. Davis, 1871.

Blackford, W. W. *War Years with Jeb Stuart.* New York: Charles Scribner's Sons, 1945.

Boggs, Elsie B. *The Hammers and Allied Families, with their Family Circles Centering in Pendleton County, West Virginia.* Harrisonburg, Va.: Joseph K. Ruebush, 1950.

Bohannon, Keith S. *The Giles, Allegheny and Jackson Artillery.* Lynchburg, Va.: H. E. Howard, 1990.

Booth, G. W. *Personal Reminiscences of a Maryland Soldier in the War Between the States.* Baltimore: Fleet, McGinley, 1898.

Borcke, Heros von. *Memoirs of the Confederate War for Independence.* 2 vols. Edinburgh,

Scotland: W. Blackwood and Sons, 1866. Reprint, Dayton, Ohio: Morningside, 1985.

Bowen, Roland E. *From Ball's Bluff to Gettysburg . . . And Beyond.* Ed. Gregory A. Coco. Gettysburg, Pa.: Thomas, 1994.

Bowers, John. *Stonewall Jackson: Portrait of a Soldier.* New York: Morrow, 1989.

Brainerd, Wesley. *Bridge Building in Wartime.* Ed. Ed Malles. Knoxville: University of Tennessee Press, 1997.

Brent, Joseph Lancaster. *Memoirs of the War Between the States.* N.p.: Privately printed, 1940.

Brewster, Charles H. *When This Cruel War Is Over.* Ed. David W. Blight. Amherst: University of Massachusetts Press, 1992.

Bridges, Hal. *Lee's Maverick General: Daniel Harvey Hill.* New York: McGraw-Hill, 1961.

Bright, Michael, and Adam Bright. *"Respects to All."* Ed. Aida C. Truxall. Pittsburgh: University of Pittsburgh Press, 1962.

Brown, Campbell. "Down the Peninsula with Richard Ewell." Ed. Terry Jones. In *Peninsula Campaign of 1862: Yorktown to the Seven Days.* Vol. 2. Ed. William J. Miller. Campbell, Calif.: Savas Woodbury, 1993.

Brown, Philip F. *Reminiscences of the War of 1861–1865.* Roanoke, Va.: Union, 1912.

Bruce, George A. *The Twentieth Regiment of Massachusetts Volunteer Infantry.* Boston: Houghton, Mifflin: 1906.

Butts, Francis B. "The Organization and First Campaign of Battery E, First Rhode Island Light Artillery." In *Personal Narratives of Events in the War of the Rebellion, Being Papers Read Before the Rhode Island Soldiers and Sailors Historical Society.* Vol. 8. Providence: Rhode Island Soldiers and Sailors Historical Society, 1894–99. Reprint, Wilmington, N.C.: Broadfoot, 1993.

Caldwell, J. F. J. *The History of a Brigade of South Carolinians First Known as "Gregg's" and Subsequently as "McGowan's Brigade."* Philadelphia: King and Baird, 1866. Reprint, Dayton, Ohio: Morningside Press, 1992.

Campbell, James Havelock. *McClellan: A Vindication of the Military Career of General George B. McClellan, A Lawyer's Brief.* New York: Neale, 1916.

Carpenter, Kinchen J. *War Diary of Kinchen Jahu Carpenter.* Rutherfordtown, N.C.: n.p., 1955.

Casdorph, Paul D. *Lee and Jackson: Confederate Chieftains.* New York: Paragon House, 1992.

———. *Prince John Magruder: His Life and Campaigns.* New York: John Wiley and Sons, 1996.

Case, Lynn M., and Warren F. Spencer. *The United States and France: Civil War Diplomacy.* Philadelphia: University of Pennsylvania Press, 1970.

Casler, John O. *Four Years in the Stonewall Brigade.* Girard, Kans.: Appeal, 1906.

Castleman, Alfred L. *The Army of the Potomac Behind the Scenes.* Milwaukee: Strickland, 1863.

Catton, Bruce. *Mr. Lincoln's Army.* Garden City, N.Y.: Doubleday, 1962.

Chamberlayne, John Hampden. *Ham Chamberlayne—Virginian: Letters and Papers of an Artillery Officer in the War for Southern Independence 1861–1865.* Richmond: Dietz, 1932.

Chambers, Lenoir. *Stonewall Jackson.* 2 vols. New York: Morrow, 1959.

Clark, Charles A. "Campaigning with the Sixth Maine." In *War Sketches and Incidents as Related by the Companions of the Iowa Commandery Military Order of the Loyal Legion of the United States.* Vol. 2. Des Moines: Iowa Commandery, MOLLUS, 1887. Reprint, Wilmington, N.C.: Broadfoot, 1993.

Coker, James L. *History of Company G, Ninth S.C. Regiment, Infantry, S.C. Army and of Company E, Sixth S.C. Regiment, Infantry, S.C. Army*. Charleston, S.C.: Walker, Evans and Cogswell, 1899.

Conyngham, D. P. *The Irish Brigade and Its Campaigns*. New York: Fordham University Press, 1994.

Cook, Joel. *The Siege of Richmond: A Narrative of the Military Operations of Major-General George B. McClellan During the Months of May and June, 1862*. Philadelphia: George W. Childs, 1862.

Cooke, John Esten. *The Life of Stonewall Jackson*. New York: C. B. Richardson, 1863. Reprint, Salem, N.H.: Ayer, 1989.

———. *Wearing of the Gray*. New York: E. B. Treat, 1867. Reprint, Bloomington: Indiana University Press, 1959.

Coward, Asbury. *The South Carolinians*. Ed. Natalie J. Bond and Osmun L. Coward. New York: Vantage Press, 1968.

Crook, D. P. *The North, the South, and the Powers: 1861–1865*. New York: John Wiley and Sons, 1974.

Cudworth, Warren H. *History of the First Regiment (Massachusetts Infantry)*. Boston: Walker, Fuller, 1866.

Cullen, Joseph P. *The Peninsula Campaign 1862: McClellan and Lee Struggle for Richmond*. New York: Bonanza, 1973.

Curtis, Newton M. *From Bull Run to Chancellorsville*. New York: G. P. Putnam's Sons, 1906.

Dabney, Robert L. *Life and Campaigns of Lieut.-Gen. Thomas J. Jackson*. New York: Blelock, 1866. Reprint, Harrisonburg, Va.: Sprinkle, 1983.

Davenport, Alfred. *Camp and Field Life of the Fifth New York Volunteer Infantry*. New York: Dick and Fitzgerald, 1879.

Davis, Burke. *They Called Him Stonewall: A Life of Lt. General T. J. Jackson, CSA*. New York: Rinehart, 1954.

Davis, Jefferson. *The Rise and Fall of the Confederate Government*. 2 vols. New York: D. Appleton, 1881.

Davis, Nicholas A. *Chaplain Davis and Hood's Texas Brigade*. Ed. Donald E. Everett. San Antonio: Principia Press of Trinity University, 1962.

Davis, William C. *Jefferson Davis: The Man and His Hour*. New York: HarperCollins, 1991.

Davis, William W. H. *History of the 104th Pennsylvania Regiment*. Philadelphia: James B. Rodgers, 1866.

Dawson, Francis W. *Reminiscences of Confederate Service*. Baton Rouge: Louisiana State University Press, 1980.

Day, W. A. *A True History of Company I, 49th Regiment, North Carolina Troops, in the Great Civil War Between North and South*. Newton, N.C.: Enterprise Job Office, 1893.

DeLeon, T. C. *Four Years in Rebel Capitals*. Mobile, Ala.: Gossip, 1890.

Dickert, D. Augustus. *History of Kershaw's Brigade*. Newberry, S.C.: E. H. Aull, 1899. Reprint, Wilmington, N.C.: Broadfoot, 1990.

Dickey, Luther S. *History of the 103d Regiment Pennsylvania Veteran Volunteer Infantry*. Chicago: L. S. Dickey, 1910.

Diket. *wha hae wi' [Pender] . . . bled*. New York: Vantage Press, 1979.

Dobbins, Austin C. *Grandfather's Journal*. Dayton, Ohio: Morningside Press, 1988.

Donald, David Herbert. *Lincoln*. New York: Simon and Schuster, 1995.

Donn, John W. "With the Army of the Potomac from the Defences of Washington to Harrison's Landing." In *War Papers being Papers Read Before the Commandery of the District of Columbia Military Order of the Loyal Legion of the United States*. Vol. 1. Washington, D.C.: Commandery of the District of Columbia, MOLLUS, 1887. Reprint: Wilmington, N.C. Broadfoot, 1993.

Douglas, Henry Kyd. *I Rode with Stonewall*. Chapel Hill: University of North Carolina Press, 1940. Reprint, St. Simons Island, Ga.: Mockingbird Books, 1961.

Dowdey, Clifford. *The Seven Days: The Emergence of Robert E. Lee*. Wilmington, N.C.: Broadfoot, 1988.

Dunaway, Rev. Wayland F. *Reminiscences of a Rebel*. New York: Neale, 1913.

Early, Jubal A. *War Memoirs: Autobiographical Sketch and Narrative of the War Between the States*. Philadelphia: J. B. Lippincott, 1912. Reprint, Bloomington: Indiana University Press, 1960.

Eckenrode, H. J., and Bryan Conrad. *George B. McClellan: The Man Who Saved the Union*. Chapel Hill: University of North Carolina Press, 1941.

———. *James Longstreet: Lee's War Horse*. Chapel Hill: University of North Carolina Press, 1936.

Edmondston, Catherine Ann Devereux. *"Journal of a Secesh Lady."* Ed. Beth G. Crabtree and James W. Patton. Raleigh, N.C.: Division of Archives and History, Department of Cultural Resources, 1979.

Eisenschiml, Otto. *The Celebrated Case of Fitz-John Porter*. Indianapolis: Bobbs-Merrill, 1950.

Ellis, Thomas T. *Leaves from the Diary of an Army Surgeon*. New York: John Bradburn, 1863.

Evans, Clement A., ed. *Confederate Military History*. 17 vols. Atlanta: Confederate, 1899. Reprint, Wilmington, N.C.: Broadfoot Publishing Company, 1987.

Farwell, Byron. *Stonewall: A Biography of General Thomas J. Jackson*. New York: W. W. Norton, 1992.

Favill, Josiah M. *The Diary of a Young Officer*. Chicago: R. R. Donnelley and Sons, 1909.

Fergurson, Ernest B. *Ashes of Glory: Richmond at War*. New York: Alfred A. Knopf, 1996.

Fishel, Edwin C. *The Secret War for the Union*. Boston: Houghton Mifflin, 1996.

Fitzpatrick, Marion Hill. *Letters to Amanda: The Civil War Letters of Marion Hill Fitzpatrick, Army of Northern Virginia*. Macon, Ga.: Mercer University Press, 1998.

Ford, Andrew E. *The Story of the Fifteenth Regiment Massachusetts Volunteer Infantry in the Civil War*. Clinton, Mass.: W. J. Coulter, 1898.

Fox, William F. *Regimental Losses in the American Civil War 1861–1865*. Albany, N.Y.: Albany, 1889. Reprint, Dayton, Ohio: Morningside, 1985.

Freeman, Douglas Southall. *R. E. Lee*. 4 vols. New York: Charles Scribner's Sons, 1934–35.

———. *Lee's Lieutenants: A Study in Command*. 3 vols. New York: Charles Scribner's Sons, 1942–44.

French, Samuel Livingston. *The Army of the Potomac from 1861 to 1863*. New York: Publishing Society of New York, 1906.

Fuller, Charles A. *Personal Recollections of the War of 1861*. Sherburne, N.Y.: News Printing House, 1906.

Fuller, J. F. C. *A Military History of the Western World: From the American Civil War to the End of World War II*. 3 vols. New York: Funk and Wagnalls, 1957.

Fuller, Richard F. *Chaplain Fuller*. Boston: Walker, Wise, 1863.

Fulton, William Frierson II. *The War Reminiscences of William Frierson Fulton II*. Gaithersburg, Md.: Butternut Press, 1986.

Gache, Pere Louis-Hippolyte, S.J. *A Frenchman, A Chaplain, A Rebel.* Trans. Cornelius M. Buckley, S.J. Chicago: Loyola University Press, 1981.

Gill, John. *Courier for Lee and Jackson.* Ed. Walbrook D. Swank. Shippensburg, Pa.: Burd Street Press, 1993.

Goode, John. *Recollections of a Lifetime.* New York: Neale, 1906.

Gordon, John B. *Reminiscences of the Civil War.* New York: Charles Scribner's Sons, 1903. Reprint, Baton Rouge: Louisiana State University Press, 1993.

Goree, Thomas J. *Longstreet's Aide.* Ed. Thomas W. Cutrer. Charlottesville: University Press of Virginia, 1995.

Goss, Warren Lee. *Recollections of a Private.* New York: Thomas Y. Crowell, 1890.

Graves, Henry Lea. *A Confederate Marine.* Ed. Richard Harwell. Tuscaloosa, Ala.: Confederate, 1963.

Greene, A. Wilson. *Whatever You Resolve to Be: Essays on Stonewall Jackson.* Baltimore: Butternut and Blue, 1992.

Grubb, E. Burd. *Notes of a Staff Officer of our First New Jersey Brigade on the Seven Day's Battle on the Peninsula in 1862.* Moorestown, N.J.: Moorestown, 1910.

Haden, B. J. *Reminiscences of J. E. B. Stuart's Cavalry.* Charlottesville, Va.: Progress, n.d.

Hagerman, Edward. *The American Civil War and the Origins of Modern Warfare.* Bloomington: Indiana University Press, 1988.

Hale, Laura V., and Stanley S. Phillips. *History of the Forty-Ninth Virginia Infantry C.S.A.* Lanham, Md.: S. S. Phillips, 1981.

Hall, H. Seymour. "Experience in the Peninsula and Antietam Campaigns." In *War Talks in Kansas.* Kansas City, Mo.: Franklin Hudson, 1906. Reprint, Wilmington, N.C.: Broadfoot, 1992.

Hamlin, Percy Gatling. *"Old Bald Head": The Portrait of a Soldier.* Gaithersburg, Md.: Ron R. Van Sickle, 1988.

Handerson, Henry E. *Yankee in Gray.* Cleveland: Press of Western Reserve University, 1962.

Hanifen, Michael. *History of Battery B, First New Jersey Artillery.* Ottawa, Ill.: Republican-Times, 1905.

Hanks, O. T. *History of Captain B. F. Benton's Company, Hood's Texas Brigade.* Austin, Tex.: W. M. Morrison, 1984.

Hard, Abner. *History of the Eighth Cavalry Regiment Illinois Volunteers.* Aurora, Ill.: n.p., 1868.

Harrer, William. *With Drum and Gun in '61.* Greenville, Pa.: Beaver, 1908.

Harris, J. S. *Historical Sketches of the Seventh Regiment North Carolina Troops.* Mooresville, N.C.: Mooresville, 1893.

Harrison, Mrs. Burton. *Recollections Grave and Gay.* New York: Charles Scribner's Sons, 1911.

Hassler, Warren W. Jr. *General George B. McClellan: Shield of the Union.* Baton Rouge: Louisiana State University Press, 1957.

——. *Commanders of the Army of the Potomac.* Baton Rouge: Louisiana State University Press, 1962.

Hassler, William W. *A. P. Hill: Lee's Forgotten General.* Chapel Hill: University of North Carolina Press, 1962.

——, ed. *The General to His Lady: The Civil War Letters of William Dorsey Pender to Fanny Pender.* Chapel Hill: University of North Carolina Press, 1962.

Hattaway, Herman, and Archer Jones. *How the North Won: A Military History of the Civil War.* Urbana: University of Illinois Press, 1983.

Haydon, Charles B. *For Country, Cause and Leader.* Ed. Stephen W. Sears. New York: Ticknor and Fields, 1993.

Haynes, Martin A. *History of the Second Regiment New Hampshire Volunteers.* Manchester, N.H.: Charles W. Livingston, 1865.

Hays, Gilbert A. *Under the Red Patch.* Pittsburgh: Sixty-third Pennsylvania Volunteers Regimental Association, 1906.

Henderson, G. F. R. *Stonewall Jackson and the American Civil War.* 2 vols. New York: Longmans, Green, 1898.

History of the First Regiment Minnesota Volunteer Infantry. Stillwater, Minn.: Easton and Masterman, 1916.

Holmes, Oliver W. Jr. *Touched with Fire.* Ed. Mark D. Howe. Cambridge, Mass.: Harvard University Press, 1946.

Hood, John B. *Advance and Retreat.* New Orleans: Hood Orphan Memorial Fund, 1880. Reprint, Bloomington: Indiana University Press, 1959.

Howard, McHenry. *Recollections of a Maryland Confederate Soldier and Staff Officer under Johnston, Jackson and Lee.* Baltimore: Williams and Wilkins, 1914.

Hoyt, James A. *The Palmetto Riflemen, Co. B, Fourth Regiment, S.C. Vols. Co. C, Palmetto Sharpshooters.* Greenville, S.C.: Hoyt and Keys, 1886.

Humphreys, Henry H. *Andrew Atkinson Humphreys: A Biography.* Philadelphia: John C. Winston, 1924.

Hunter, Alexander. *Johny Reb and Billy Yank.* New York: Neale, 1905.

Hurst, Marshall B. *History of the Fourteenth Regiment Alabama Volunteers.* Richmond, Va.: n.p., 1863.

Hyde, Thomas W. *Following the Greek Cross, or Memoirs of the Sixth Army Corps.* Boston: Houghton Mifflin, 1894.

Hyndman, William. *History of a Cavalry Company.* Philadelphia: James B. Rodgers, 1870.

Jackson, Edgar A., James F. Bryant, and Irvin C. Wills. *Three Rebels Write Home.* Franklin, Va.: News, 1955.

Jackson, Mary Anna. *Memoirs of Stonewall Jackson.* Louisville: Prentice Press, 1895.

Jenkins, Brian. *Britain and the War for the Union.* Montreal: McGill-Queen's University Press, 1980.

Joinville, Prince de. *The Army of the Potomac: Its Organization, Its Commander, and Its Campaign.* Trans. William H. Hurlbert. New York: Anson D. F. Randolph, 1862.

Jones, Archer. *Civil War Command and Strategy: The Process of Victory and Defeat.* New York: Free Press, 1992.

Jones, Howard. *Union in Peril: The Crisis over British Intervention in the Civil War.* Chapel Hill: University of North Carolina Press, 1992.

Jones, J. B. *A Rebel War Clerk's Diary.* 2 vols. Philadelphia: J. B. Lippincott, 1866.

Jones, Rev. J. William. *Life and Letters of Robert Edward Lee Soldier and Man.* New York: Neale, 1906. Reprint, Harrisonburg, Va.: Sprinkle, 1986.

Jones, Katherine M., ed. *Heroines of Dixie: Spring of High Hopes.* St. Simons Island, Ga.: Mockingbird Books, 1955.

Jones, Terry L. *Lee's Tigers: The Louisiana Infantry in the Army of Northern Virginia.* Baton Rouge: Louisiana State University Press, 1987.

Jordan, David M. *Winfield Scott Hancock: A Soldier's Life.* Bloomington: Indiana University Press, 1988.

Judd, David W. *The Story of the Thirty-third* N.Y.S. *Vols.* Rochester, N.Y.: Benton and Andrews, 1864.

Judson, A. M. *History of the Eighty-Third Regiment Pennsylvania Volunteers.* Erie, Pa.: B. F. H. Lynn, 1865.

Kearny, Thomas. *General Philip Kearny: Battle Soldier of Five Wars*. New York: G. P. Putnam's Sons, 1937.

Keyes, Erasmus D. *Fifty Years' Observation of Men and Events, Civil and Military*. New York: Charles Scribner's Sons, 1884.

LeDuc, William G. *Recollections of a Civil War Quartermaster*. St. Paul, Minn.: North Central, 1963.

Lee, Fitzhugh. *General Lee*. New York: D. Appleton, 1884. Reprint, Wilmington, N.C.: Broadfoot, 1989.

Lee, Robert E. *Lee's Dispatches*. Ed. Douglas Southall Freeman. New York: G. P. Putnam's Sons, 1957.

———. *The Wartime Papers of Robert E. Lee*. Ed. Clifford Dowdey and Louis H. Manarin. Boston: Little, Brown, 1961.

Lee, Robert E. Jr. *Recollections and Letters of Robert E. Lee*. New York: Doubleday, Page, 1905.

Lee, Susan P., ed. *Memoirs of William Nelson Pendleton, D.D.* Philadelphia: J. B. Lippincott, 1893. Reprint, Harrisonburg, Va.: Sprinkle, 1991.

Leech, Margaret. *Reveille in Washington, 1860–1865*. New York: Harper and Row, 1941.

Lewis, George. *The History of Battery E, First Regiment Rhode Island Light Artillery*. Providence, R.I.: Snow and Farnham, 1892.

Lincoln, Abraham. *The Collected Works of Abraham Lincoln*. Ed. Roy P. Basler. New Brunswick, N.J.: Rutgers University Press, 1953.

Livermore, Thomas L. *Numbers and Losses in the Civil War in America: 1861–65*. Boston: Houghton Mifflin, 1901. Reprint, Bloomington: Indiana University Press, 1957.

Loehr, Charles T. *War History of the Old First Virginia Infantry Regiment*. Richmond, Va.: William Ellis Jones, 1884.

Long, A. L. *Memoirs of Robert E. Lee*. New York: J. M. Stoddart, 1886. Reprint, Secaucus, N.J.: Blue and Gray Press, 1983.

Long, E. B., with Barbara Long. *The Civil War Day by Day: An Almanac 1861–1865*. Garden City, N.Y.: Doubleday, 1971.

Longstreet, James. *From Manassas to Appomattox*. Ed. James I. Robertson Jr. Philadelphia: J. B. Lippincott, 1896. Edited ed., Bloomington: Indiana University Press, 1960.

Lyons, W. F. *Brigadier-General Thomas Francis Meagher*. New York: D. and J. Sadlier, 1870.

Macartney, Clarence E. *Little Mac: The Life of George B. McClellan*. Philadelphia: Dorrance, 1940.

Macnamara, Daniel G. *The History of the Ninth Regiment Massachusetts Volunteer Infantry*. Boston: E. B. Stillings, 1899.

Markle, Donald E. *Spies and Spymasters of the Civil War*. New York: Hippocrene, 1994.

Marks, Rev. J. J. *The Peninsula Campaign in Virginia*. Philadelphia: J. B. Lippincott, 1864.

Marshall, Charles. *An Aide-de-Camp of Lee*. Ed. Sir Frederick Maurice. Boston: Little, Brown, 1927.

Martin, James M., E. C. Strouss, R. G. Madge, R. I. Campbell, and M. C. Zahniser. *History of the Fifty-Seventh Regiment, Pennsylvania Veteran Volunteer Infantry*. Meadville, Pa.: McCoy and Calvin, 1904.

Martin, Samuel J. *The Road to Glory: Confederate General Richard S. Ewell*. Indianapolis: Guild Press of Indiana, 1991.

Maurice, Sir Frederick. *Robert E. Lee the Soldier*. Boston: Houghton Mifflin, 1925.

McClellan, George B. *The Civil War Papers of George B. McClellan*. Ed. Stephen W. Sears. New York: Ticknor and Fields, 1989.

——. *McClellan's Own Story*. New York: Charles L. Webster, 1887.

McClellan, H. B. *I Rode with Jeb Stuart*. Bloomington: Indiana University Press, 1958.

McCormick, Robert R. *The War Without Grant*. New York: Bond Wheelwright, 1950.

McDaniel, Henry. *With Unabated Trust*. Ed. Anita B. Sams. Monroe, Ga.: Walton Press, 1977.

McDaniel, J. J. *Diary of Battles, Marches and Incidents of the Seventh S.C. Regiment*. N.p., n.d.

McMurray, Richard M. *Two Great Rebel Armies: An Essay in Confederate Military History*. Chapel Hill: University of North Carolina Press, 1989.

——. *John Bell Hood and the War for Southern Independence*. Lexington: University Press of Kentucky, 1982.

McPherson, James M. *Battle Cry of Freedom: The Civil War Era*. New York: Oxford University Press, 1988.

Meade, George. *The Life and Letters of George Gordon Meade*. New York: Charles Scribner's Sons, 1913.

Miller, William J., ed. *The Peninsula Campaign of 1862: Yorktown to the Seven Days*. 2 vols. Campbell, Calif.: Savas Woodbury, 1993, 1995.

——. "The Grand Campaign." In *Peninsula Campaign of 1862: Yorktown to the Seven Days*. Vol. 1. Ed. William J. Miller. Campbell, Calif.: Savas Woodbury, 1993.

Michie, Peter S. *General McClellan*. New York: D. Appleton, 1915.

Moore, Alison. *The Louisiana Tigers or the Two Louisiana Brigades of the Army of Northern Virginia, 1861–1865*. Baton Rouge: Louisiana State University Press, 1961.

Moore, Edward A. *The Story of a Cannoneer under Stonewall Jackson*. New York: Neale, 1907.

Murray, Alton J. *South Georgia Rebels*. St. Marys, Ga.: Alton J. Murray, 1976.

Myers, William Starr. *General George B. McClellan: A Study in Personality*. New York: D. Appleton-Century, 1934.

Naisawald, L. Van Loan. *Grape and Canister: The Story of the Field Artillery of the Army of the Potomac, 1861–1865*. Oxford: Oxford University Press, 1960.

Nevins, Allan. *The War for the Union: War Becomes Revolution, 1862–1863*. New York: Charles Scribner's Sons, 1960.

Newell, Joseph K. *"Ours." Annals of 10th Regiment, Massachusetts Volunteers, in the Rebellion*. Springfield, Mass.: C. A. Nichols, 1875.

Newton, Steven H. *The Battle of Seven Pines, May 31–June 1, 1862*. Lynchburg, Va.: H. E. Howard, Inc., 1993.

Nichols, Edward J. *Toward Gettysburg: A Biography of General John F. Reynolds*. State College: Pennsylvania State University Press, 1958.

Nisbet, James C. *Four Years on the Firing Line*. Chattanooga, Tenn.: Imperial Press, 1915.

Norton, Oliver W. *Army Letters, 1861–1865*. Chicago: O. L. Deming, 1903.

Oates, William C. *The War Between the Union and the Confederacy and its Lost Opportunities*. New York: Neale, 1905.

Official Records of the Union and Confederate Navies in the War of the Rebellion. 31 vols. Washington, D.C.: Government Printing Office, 1894–1927.

Osborn, Thomas W. *No Middle Ground*. Ed. Herb S. Crumb and Katherine Dhalle. Hamilton, N.Y.: Edmonston, 1993.

Osborne, William H. *The History of the Twenty-Ninth Regiment of Massachusetts Volunteer Infantry*. Boston: Albert J. Wright, 1877.

Owen, William M. *In Camp and Battle with the Washington Artillery of New Orleans.* Boston: Ticknor, 1885.

Owsley, Frank Lawrence. *King Cotton Diplomacy: Foreign Relations of the Confederate States of America.* 2nd ed. Chicago: University of Chicago Press, 1959.

Paludan, Phillip Shaw. *"A People's Contest": The Union and Civil War, 1861–1865.* New York: Harper and Row, 1988.

Parker, John L. *Henry Wilson's Regiment.* Boston: Regimental Association, 1887.

Patterson, Edmund D. *Yankee Rebel.* Ed. John G. Barrett. Chapel Hill: University of North Carolina Press, 1966.

Pennypacker, Isaac R. *General Meade.* New York: D. Appleton, 1901.

Perkins, Charles C. "The Civil War Diary of Private Charles C. Perkins." Ed. Richard J. Sommers. In *Peninsula Campaign of 1862: Yorktown to the Seven Days.* Vol. 1. Ed. William J. Miller. Campbell, Calif.: Savas Woodbury, 1993.

Pickett, George. *Soldier of the South: General Pickett's War Letters to His Wife.* Ed. Arthur Crow Inman. Boston: Houghton Mifflin, 1928.

Pickett, LaSalle C. *Pickett and His Men.* Philadelphia: J. B. Lippincott, 1913.

Pinkerton, Allan. *The Spy of the Rebellion.* New York: G. W. Carleton, 1884.

Pinto, Francis E. *History of the 32nd Regiment, New York Volunteers, In the Civil War, 1861 to 1863, And personal recollection during that period.* Brooklyn, N.Y.: n.p., 1895.

Poague, William Thomas. *Gunner With Stonewall.* Jackson, Tenn.: McCowat-Mercer Press, 1957.

Polley, J. B. *Hood's Texas Brigade: Its Marches, Its Battles, Its Achievements.* New York: Neale, 1910.

——. *A Soldier's Letters to Charming Nellie.* New York: Neale, 1908.

Potter, William W. *Reminiscences of Field-Hospital Service with the Army of the Potomac.* Buffalo, N.Y.: n.p., 1889.

Powell, William H. *The Fifth Army Corps (Army of the Potomac): A Record of Operations During the Civil War in the United States of America, 1861–1865.* London: G. P. Putnam's Sons, 1896. Reprint, Dayton, Ohio: Morningside Press, 1984.

Putnam, Sallie A. *Richmond During the War.* New York: G. W. Carleton, 1867.

Rable, George C. *The Confederate Republic: A Revolution Against Politics.* Chapel Hill: University of North Carolina Press, 1994.

Reed, Rowena. *Combined Operations in the Civil War.* Lincoln: University of Nebraska Press, 1978.

Rhoades, Jeffrey L. *Scapegoat General: The Story of Major General Benjamin Huger, C.S.A.* Hamden, Conn.: Archon Books, 1985.

Rhodes, Elisha Hunt. *All For the Union.* Ed. Robert H. Rhodes. Lincoln, R.I.: Andrew Mowbray, 1985.

Rhodes, James Ford. *History of the United States from the Compromise of 1850.* Ed. Allan Nevins. Chicago: Phoenix Books, 1966.

Rhodes, John H. *The History of Battery B. First Regiment Rhode Island Light Artillery in the War to Preserve the Union 1861–1865.* Providence, R.I.: Snow and Farnham, 1894.

Ripley, William Y. W. *Vermont Riflemen in the War for the Union, 1861 to 1865.* Rutland, Vt.: Tuttle, 1883.

Robertson, James I. Jr. *General A. P. Hill: The Story of a Confederate Warrior.* New York: Random House, 1987.

——. *Stonewall Jackson: The Man, The Soldier, The Legend.* New York: Macmillan, 1997.

Robertson, Robert S. *Diary of the War.* Ed. Charles N. and Rosemary Walker. Fort Wayne, Ind.: Fort Wayne Historical Society, 1965.

Roe, Alfred S. *The Tenth Regiment Massachusetts Volunteer Infantry.* Springfield, Mass.: Tenth Regiment Veteran Association, 1909.

Ruffin, Edmund. *The Diary of Edmund Ruffin.* 3 vols. Ed. William Kauffman Scarborough. Baton Rouge: Louisiana State University Press, 1972–89.

Sanger, Donald Bridgman. *James Longstreet.* Vol. 1, *Soldier.* Baton Rouge: Louisiana State University Press, 1952.

Sauers, Richard A. "The Pennsylvania Reserves: General George A. McCall's Division on the Peninsula." In *Peninsula Campaign of 1862: Yorktown to the Seven Days.* Vol. 1. Ed. William J. Miller. Campbell, Calif.: Savas Woodbury, 1993.

Schenck, Martin. *Up Came Hill: The Story of the Light Division and Its Leaders.* Harrisburg, Pa.: Stackpole, 1958.

Sears, Stephen W. *George B. McClellan: The Young Napoleon.* New York: Ticknor and Fields, 1988.

———. *To the Gates of Richmond: The Peninsula Campaign.* New York: Ticknor and Fields, 1992.

Sedgwick, John. *Correspondence of John Sedgwick, Major General.* N.p.: Privately printed, 1903.

Shoemaker, John J. *Shoemaker's Battery.* Memphis, Tenn.: S. C. Toof, 1908.

Silbey, Joel H. *A Respectable Minority: The Democratic Party in the Civil War Era, 1860–1868.* New York: W. W. Norton, 1977.

Simpson, Harold B. *Hood's Texas Brigade: Lee's Grenadier Guard.* Dallas: Alcor, 1983.

Slocum, Charles E. *The Life and Services of Major-General Henry Warner Slocum.* Toledo, Ohio: Slocum, 1913.

Smith, James E. *A Famous Battery and its Campaigns, 1861–'64.* Washington, D.C.: W. H. Lowdermilk, 1892.

Smith, William F. *Autobiography of Major General William F. Smith 1861–1864.* Ed. Herbert M. Schiller. Dayton, Ohio: Morningside, 1990.

Sorrel, G. Moxley. *Recollections of a Confederate Staff Officer.* New York: Neale, 1905. Reprint, Wilmington, N.C.: Broadfoot, 1987.

Southwick, Thomas P. *A Duryee Zouave.* Washington, D.C.: Acme, 1930.

Spencer, William H. "How I Felt in Battle and in Prison." In *War Papers Read before the Commandery of the State of Maine, Military Order of the Loyal Legion of the United States.* Vol. 2. Portland, Me.: Lefavor-Tower, 1902. Reprint, Wilmington, N.C.: Broadfoot, 1992.

Stanley, F. *E. V. Sumner, Major-General United States Army (1797–1863).* N.p.: Privately printed, 1968.

Starr, Stephen Z. *The Union Cavalry in the Civil War.* Baton Rouge: Louisiana State University Press, 1979.

Stevens, George T. *Three Years in the Sixth Corps.* Albany, N.Y.: S. R. Gray, 1866.

Stevenson, James. *History of the Excelsior or Sickles' Brigade.* Paterson, N.J.: Van Derhoven and Holms, 1863.

Stewart, Rev. A. M. *Camp, March and Battlefield.* Philadelphia: James B. Rodgers, 1865.

Stiles, Robert. *Four Years Under Marse Robert.* New York: Neale, 1903. Reprint, Dayton, Ohio: Morningside Press, 1988.

Stine, J. H. *History of the Army of the Potomac.* Washington, D.C.: Gibson Brothers, 1893.

Stovall, Pleasant A. *Robert Toombs: Statesman, Speaker, Soldier, Sage.* New York: Cassell, 1892.

Strong, George Templeton. *The Diary of George Templeton Strong.* 4 vols. Ed. Allan Nevins and Milton Halsey Thomas. New York: Macmillan, 1952.

Supplement to the Official Records of the Union and Confederate Armies. Wilmington, N.C.: Broadfoot, 2000.

Swanberg, W. A. *Sickles the Incredible.* New York: Scribner's, 1956.

Swinton, William. *Campaigns of the Army of the Potomac.* New York: Charles B. Richerdson, 1866. Reprint, Secaucus, N.J.: Blue and Grey Press, 1988.

Sypher, J. R. *History of the Pennsylvania Reserve Corps.* Lancaster, Pa.: Elias Barr, 1865.

Tap, Bruce. *Over Lincoln's Shoulder: The Committee on the Conduct of the War.* Lawrence: University Press of Kansas, 1998.

Taylor, Walter H. *Four Years with General Lee.* New York: D. Appleton, 1877. Reprint, Bloomington: Indiana University Press, 1962.

———. *General Lee: His Campaigns in Virginia, 1861–1865.* Brooklyn, N.Y.: Press of Braunworth, 1906. Reprint, Dayton, Ohio: Morningside, 1975.

Taylor, Richard. *Destruction and Reconstruction.* New York: D. Appleton, 1879. Reprint, New York: Longmans, Green, 1955.

Thomas, Emory M. *The Confederate Nation, 1861–1865.* New York: Harper and Row, 1979.

———. *Bold Dragoon: The Life of J. E. B. Stuart.* New York: Vintage Books, 1988.

Thomas, John P. *Career and Character of General Micah Jenkins, C.S.A.* Columbia, S.C.: State, 1908.

Toombs, Robert, et al. *The Correspondence of Robert Toombs, Alexander H. Stephens, and Howell Cobb.* Ed. Ulrich B. Phillips. New York: Da Capo Press, 1970.

Townsend, George A. *Campaigns of a Non-Combatant and His Romaunt Abroad During the War.* New York: Blelock, 1866.

Tribble, Byrd B. *Benjamin Cason Rawlings: First Virginia Volunteer for the South.* Baltimore: Butternut and Blue, 1995.

Trobriand, Regis de. *Four Years with the Army of the Potomac.* Trans. George K. Dauchy. Boston: Ticknor, 1889.

Underwood, George C. *History of the Twenty-Sixth Regiment of the North Carolina Troops in the Great War 1861–'65.* Goldsboro, N.C.: Nash Brothers, 1901.

Urban, John W. *My Experiences Mid Shot and Shell and in Rebel Den.* Lancaster, Pa.: John Urban, 1882.

Vanauken, Sheldon. *The Glittering Illusion: English Sympathy for the Southern Confederacy.* Columbia, S.C.: Southron Press, 1985.

Vandiver, Frank E. *Mighty Stonewall.* New York: McGraw-Hill, 1957.

Waitt, Ernest L. *History of the Nineteenth Regiment Massachusetts Volunteer Infantry.* Salem, Mass.: Salem Press, 1906.

Walker, Francis A. *History of the Second Army Corps in the Army of the Potomac.* New York: Charles Scribner's Sons, 1891.

Wall, Henry C. *Historical Sketch of the Pee Dee Guards.* Raleigh, N.C.: Edwards, Broughton, 1876.

Wallace, Lee A. Jr. *5th Virginia Infantry.* Lynchburg, Va.: H. E. Howard, 1988.

The War of the Rebellion: A Compilation of the Official Records of the Union and Confederate Armies. 128 vols. Washington, D.C.: Government Printing Office, 1880–1901.

Warfield, Edgar. *A Confederate Soldier's Memoirs.* Richmond, Va.: Masonic Home Press, 1936.

Warner, Ezra J. *Generals in Gray.* Baton Rouge: Louisiana State University Press, 1959.

———. *Generals in Blue.* Baton Rouge: Louisiana State University Press, 1964.

Wayland, John W. *Stonewall Jackson's Way.* Staunton, Va.: McClure, 1956.
Webb, Alexander S. *The Peninsula.* Campaigns of the Civil War. New York: Charles Scribner's Sons, 1881.
Weigley, Russell F. *A Great Civil War: A Military and Political History, 1861–1865.* Bloomington: Indiana University Press, 2000.
Wellman, Manly Wade. *Giant in Gray: A Biography of Wade Hampton of South Carolina.* New York: Charles Scribner's Sons, 1949.
Werstein, Irving. *Kearny the Magnificent: The Story of General Philip Kearny 1815–1862.* New York: John Day, 1962.
Wert, Jeffry D. *General James Longstreet: The Confederacy's Most Controversial Soldier—A Biography.* New York: Simon and Schuster, 1993.
Westbrook, Robert S. *History of the 49th Pennsylvania Volunteers.* Altoona, Pa.: Altoona Times, 1898.
White, William S. "A Diary of the War, or What I Saw of It." In *Contributions to a History of the Richmond Howitzer Battalion.* Pamphlet no. 2. Richmond, Va.: Carlton McCarthy, 1883.
Williams, Kenneth P. *Lincoln Finds a General.* 5 vols. Bloomington: Indiana University Press, 1949–59.
Williams, T. Harry. *Lincoln and the Radicals.* Madison: University of Wisconsin Press, 1941.
Winslow, Richard Elliott III. *General John Sedgwick: The Story of a Union Corps Commander.* Novato, Calif.: Presidio Press, 1982.
Wise, Jennings C. *The Long Arm of Lee.* Lynchburg, Va.: J. P. Bell, 1915.
Withers, Robert E. *Autobiography of an Octogenarian.* Roanoke, Va.: Stone, 1907.
Woodward, E. M. *History of the Third Pennsylvania Reserve.* Trenton, N.J.: MacCrellish and Quigley, 1883.
Woodworth, Steven E. *Davis and Lee at War.* Lawrence: University Press of Kansas, 1995.
Worsham, John H. *One of Jackson's Foot Cavalry.* New York: Neale, 1912.
Wyckoff, Mac. "Joseph B. Kershaw's South Carolina Brigade in the Battle of Savage Station." In *Peninsula Campaign of 1862: Yorktown to the Seven Days.* Vol. 2. Ed. William J. Miller. Campbell, Calif.: Savas Woodbury, 1993.

Index

Page numbers in italicsb refer to maps.

ABOUT THE AUTHOR

Brian K. Burton is Associate Professor of Management and Director of the MBA program at Western Washington University.